Table of Atomic Numbers and Element Symbols

The elements are listed in alphabetical order.

Element	Atomic Number	Symbol	Element	Atomic Number	Symbol	Element	Atomic Number	Symbol
Actinium	89	Ac	Iodine	53	I	Selenium	34	Se
Aluminum	13	Al	Iridium	77	Ir	Silicon	14	Si
Americium	95	Am	Iron	26	Fe	Silver	47	Ag
Antimony	51	Sb	Krypton	36	Kr	Sodium	11	Na
Argon	18	Ar	Lanthanum	57	La	Strontium	38	Sr
Arsenic	33	As	Lawrencium	103	Lr	Sulfur	16	S
Astatine	85	At	Lead	82	Pb	Tantalum	73	Ta
Barium	56	Ba	Lithium	3	Li	Technetium	43	Tc
Berkelium	97	Bk	Lutetium	71	Lu	Tellurium	52	Te
Beryllium	4	Be	Magnesium	12	Mg	Terbium	65	Tb
Bismuth	83	Bi	Manganese	25	Mn	Thallium	81	Tl
Bohrium	107	Bh	Meitnerium	109	Mt	Thorium	90	Th
Boron	5	B	Mendelevium	101	Md	Thulium	69	Tm
Bromine	35	Br	Mercury	80	Hg	Tin	50	Sn
Cadmium	48	Cd	Molybdenum	42	Mo	Titanium	22	Ti
Calcium	20	Ca	Neodymium	60	Nd	Tungsten	74	W
Californium	98	Cf	Neon	10	Ne	Ununbium	112	Uub
Carbon	6	C	Neptunium	93	Np	Ununnilium	110	Uun
Cerium	58	Ce	Nickel	28	Ni	Unununium	111	Uuu
Cesium	55	Cs	Niobium	41	Nb	Uranium	92	U
Chlorine	17	Cl	Nitrogen	7	N	Vanadium	23	V
Chromium	24	Cr	Nobelium	102	No	Xenon	54	Xe
Cobalt	27	Co	Osmium	76	Os	Ytterbium	70	Yb
Copper	29	Cu	Oxygen	8	O	Yttrium	39	Y
Curium	96	Cm	Palladium	46	Pd	Zinc	30	Zn
Dubnium	105	Db	Phosphorus	15	P	Zirconium	40	Zr
Dysprosium	66	Dy	Platinum	78	Pt			
Einsteinium	99	Es	Plutonium	94	Pu			
Erbium	68	Er	Polonium	84	Po			
Europium	63	Eu	Potassium	19	K			
Fermium	100	Fm	Praseodymium	59	Pr			
Fluorine	9	F	Promethium	61	Pm			
Francium	87	Fr	Protactinium	91	Pa			
Gadolinium	64	Gd	Radium	88	Ra			
Gallium	31	Ga	Radon	86	Rn			
Germanium	32	Ge	Rhenium	75	Re			
Gold	79	Au	Rhodium	45	Rh			
Hafnium	72	Hf	Rubidium	37	Rb			
Hassium	108	Hs	Ruthenium	44	Ru			
Helium	2	He	Rutherfordium	104	Rf			
Holmium	67	Ho	Samarium	62	Sm			
Hydrogen	1	H	Scandium	21	Sc			
Indium	49	In	Seaborgium	106	Sg			

Lena ~~Newman~~
Newman
P. ~~X~~ 3

Exploring Creation

with

Physical Science
2nd Edition

by Dr. Jay L. Wile

Exploring Creation with Physical Science, 2nd Edition

Published by
Apologia Educational Ministries, Inc.
1106 Meridian Plaza, Suite 220/340
Anderson, IN 46016
www.apologia.com

Manufactured in the United States of America
Eleventh Printing, January 2017

ISBN: 978-1-932012-77-4

Printed by LSC Communications

All Biblical quotations are from the New American Standard Bible (NASB) unless otherwise stated

Cover photos: [*agency: Dreamstime.com – glacier* © Michael Klenetsky]
[*agency: Istockphoto.com – cumulus clouds* © David Raboin, *aurora* © Roman Krochuk*],
sun and earth courtesy of NASA

Cover design by Kim Williams

INSTRUCTIONAL SUPPORT

Did you know that in addition to publishing award-winning curriculum Apologia also offers instructional support? We believe in helping students achieve their full potential, whatever their learning style. When you choose an Apologia curriculum, you are not just selecting a textbook. Every course has been designed with the student's needs in mind.

INDEPENDENT LEARNERS

Apologia textbooks and notebooks are written to the student in a conversational tone so that young people can easily navigate through the curriculum on their own. Apologia curriculum helps students methodically learn, self-check, and master difficult concepts before moving on.

AUDITORY LEARNERS

Sometimes students learn best when they can see and hear what they're studying. **Apologia Audio Books** are the complete text of the course read aloud. Students can follow along with the audio while reading or continue learning when they're away from home by listening in the car.

VISUAL LEARNERS

Sometimes subject matter is easier to comprehend when the topic is animated and presented by a knowledgeable instructor. **Apologia Video Instructional DVDs** enhance the student's education with more than 20 hours of instruction, including on-location video footage, PowerPoint lectures, animated diagrams of difficult concepts, and video presentations of all experiments.

SOCIAL LEARNERS

Some students learn best when they are able to interact with others in an online setting and ask questions of a live instructor. With **Apologia Online Academy**, students can interact in real time with both their classmates and a professional instructor in a structured virtual classroom. Also, we offer recordings of all our live classes on the Apologia Online Academy Video-On-Demand Channel.

At Apologia, we believe in homeschooling. We are here not only to support your endeavors, but also to help you and your student thrive! Find out more at apologia.com.

STUDENT NOTES
Exploring Creation With Physical Science, 2ⁿᵈ Edition

This course will take you on an amazing journey! It will begin with a detailed discussion of the world around you and what makes it work. It will then take you out into the universe so you can learn the majesty of God's Creation. Like anything worth doing, this course will be hard work, but in the end, you will find it interesting and (hopefully) enjoyable. From the inner-workings of atoms to the grandeur of galaxies, be prepared to be awed and amazed with what the Creator has made for **you!**

Pedagogy of the Text

This text contains 16 modules. Each module should take you about two weeks to complete, as long as you devote 30 to 45 minutes of every school day to studying physical science. At this pace, you will complete the course in 32 weeks. Since most people have school years that are longer than 32 weeks, there is some built-in "flex time." You should not rush through a module just to make sure you complete it in two weeks. Set that as a goal, but be flexible. Some of the modules might come harder to you than others. On those modules, take more time on the subject matter.

How will you know how much time per day to spend studying physical science? Well, start out working 30 minutes per day on the course. At the end of two weeks, see where you are. If you are done with the first module, you know 30 minutes per day is the right amount of time. If you aren't done with the module, you know you need to spend more time per day. Continue to change the amount of time per day until you find what it takes to cover a module in two weeks.

To help you guide your study, there are two sets of student exercises you should complete:

➢ The "On Your Own" questions should be answered as you read the text. The act of answering these questions will cement in your mind the concepts you are trying to learn. Answers to these questions appear at the end of the module. Once you have answered an "On Your Own" question, turn to the end of the module and check your work. If you did not get the correct answer, study the answer to learn why.

➢ You should answer the questions in the study guide at the end of the module *after* you have completed the module. This will allow you to review the important concepts from the module and help you prepare for the test.

Your teacher/parent has the answers to the study guides.

Any information you must memorize is centered in the text and put in boldface type. In addition, all definitions presented in the text must be memorized. Words that appear in boldface type (centered or not) in the text are important terms you should know. Some of the information in the course is presented in the form of tables or figures. Whether or not you will be given such information on the test depends on the information itself. If the study guide says you can use a particular figure or table, you will also be able to use that figure or table on the test. If a study guide question requires you to know the information in a table or figure and the study guide does not say you can use it, you will not be able to use it on the test.

<u>Learning Aids</u>

Extra material is available to aid you in your studies. For example, Apologia Educational Ministries, Inc. has produced a multimedia companion CD that accompanies this course. It contains videos of many things (such as erupting volcanoes) you have probably not seen before. These videos will help you better understand concepts in the course. In addition, it contains animated white board solutions of example problems such as the unit conversion problems you must solve in Module #1. There is also an audio explanation that is different from the explanation given in this book. Thus, if you are having trouble understanding how I worked a certain example problem, you might find more explanation on the multimedia CD. The following graphic in the book:

indicates there is a video or animation on the CD that relates to what you are reading.

Finally, the CD contains audio pronunciations of the technical words used in this book. Even though the book gives pronunciation guides for most of the technical words used, nothing beats actually hearing someone say the word! As you read through the book, you will see words that have pronunciation guides in parentheses. If you would like to hear one of those words pronounced, you will find it on the multimedia companion CD.

In addition to the multimedia companion CD, there is a special website for this course that you can visit. The website contains links to web-based materials related to the course. These links are arranged by module, so if you are having trouble with a particular subject in the course, you can go to the website and look at the links for that module. Most likely, you will find help there. In addition, there are answers to many of the frequently-asked questions regarding the material. For example, many people ask us for examples of how to properly record experiments in your laboratory notebook. Those examples can be found at the website. Finally, if you are enjoying a particular module in the course and would like to learn more about it, there are links to interesting websites that will allow you to learn more about the subject matter being discussed.

To visit the website, go to the following address:

http://www.apologia.com/bookextras

When you get to the address, you will be asked for a password. Type the following into the password box:

Physicalcreation

Be sure that you do not put spaces between any of the letters and that the first letter is capitalized. When you click on the button labeled "Log In," you will see a link that will send you to the course website. You must use Internet Explorer 5.1 or higher to view this website.

There are also several items at the end of the book you will find useful in your studies. There is a glossary that defines many of the terms used in the course and an index that will tell you where topics can be found in the course. In addition, there are three appendices in the course. Appendix A compiles some of the tables and figures that are found throughout the reading. For those of you living in the Southern Hemisphere, it also gives an alternate version of the discussion about the seasons presented in Module #7. Appendix B contains a summary of each module in the course. These summaries are presented as fill-in-the-blank exercises and practice problems. If you are having trouble studying for the tests, these summaries might help you. Your parent/teacher has the answers to the exercises in Appendix B. Appendix C contains a complete list of all the supplies you need to perform the experiments in this course.

Experiments

The experiments in this course are designed to be done as you are reading the text. I recommend you keep a notebook of these experiments. As you write about the experiment in the notebook, you will be forced to think through all the concepts explored in the experiment. This will help you cement them into your mind. I recommend you perform the experiments in the following way:

➤ When you get to an experiment, read through it in its entirety. This will allow you to gain a quick understanding of what you are to do.

➤ Once you have read the experiment, start a new page in your laboratory notebook. The first page should be used to write down all the data taken during the experiment. What do I mean by "data"? Any observations or measurements you make during the experiment are considered data. Thus, if you see a solution bubbling during an experiment, you need to either describe it or draw it. If you measure the length of something during the experiment, it is part of the experiment's data and should be written down. In addition, any data analysis you are asked to do as a part of the experiment should be done on this page.

➤ When you have finished the experiment and any necessary analysis, write a brief report in your notebook, right after the page where the data and calculations were written. The report should be a brief discussion of what was done and what was learned. You should not write a step-by-step procedure. Instead, write a brief summary that will allow someone who has never read the text to understand what you did and what you learned.

PLEASE OBSERVE COMMON SENSE SAFETY PRECAUTIONS! The experiments in this course are no more dangerous than most normal, household activity. Remember, however, that the vast majority of accidents do happen in the home. Chemicals used in the experiments should never be ingested; hot items and flames should be regarded with care; and all experiments should be performed while wearing eye protection such as safety glasses or goggles.

The experiments use household items, so there is no need to purchase a laboratory equipment set for the course. To give you the ability to prepare for the experiments, however, Appendix C lists the items you will need to perform the experiments in each module. Before you begin a module, then, look at Appendix C to make sure you have everything you need for that particular module.

Exploring Creation With Physical Science
Table of Contents

MODULE #1: The Basics

Introduction

In this course, you are going to learn a lot about the world around you and the universe it is in. We will study things as familiar as the air around you and others as mysterious as radioactivity and distant galaxies. We will learn about the structure of the earth as well as its place in the solar system and the universe. The study of these topics and many others like them are all a part of what we call **physical science**.

In order to make sure we are both starting on the "same page," I need to discuss some basic concepts with you. It is quite possible that you have learned some (or all) of this before, but it is necessary that we cover the basics before we try to do anything in depth. Thus, even if some of the topics I cover sound familiar, please read this module thoroughly so that you will not get lost in a later module. In fact, many of the subjects I will cover in later modules are probably familiar to you on one level or another. After all, most students your age know something about air, the construction of our planet, weather, and astronomy. Nevertheless, I can almost guarantee that you have not learned these subjects at the depth in which I will discuss them in this course. So, despite how much you might *think* you know about a given topic, please read the material I present to you carefully. I doubt that you will be disappointed.

If, on the other hand, all this is completely new to you, don't worry about it. As long as you read the material carefully, perform the experiments thoroughly, and really *think* about what you are learning, everything will be fine. Although this course might not be *easy* for you, there are very few things in life that are both easy *and* worthwhile. I promise that if you *work* at learning this course, you will gain a great deal of knowledge, a solid sense of accomplishment, and a grand appreciation for the wonder of God's creation!

Atoms and Molecules

In this course, I am going to illustrate as many concepts as possible with experiments. Hopefully, the "hands on" experience will help bring those concepts home better than any discussion could. In some cases, of course, this will not be possible, so we will have to make do with words and pictures. To start our discussion of atoms and molecules, I want you to perform the following experiment:

EXPERIMENT 1.1
Atoms and Molecules

Supplies:
- A small, clear glass (like a juice glass)
- Baking soda
- Tap water
- A 9-volt battery (the kind that goes in a radio, smoke detector, or toy. DO NOT use an electrical outlet, as that would be quite dangerous! A 1.5-volt flashlight battery will *not* work.)
- Two 9-inch pieces of insulated wire. The wire itself must be copper.
- Scissors
- Some tape (preferably electrical tape, but cellophane or masking tape will work.)
- A spoon for stirring
- Eye protection such as goggles or safety glasses

Introduction: Atoms and molecules make up almost everything that surrounds us. Individually, they are too small to see. However, you can distinguish between different kinds of atoms and different kinds of molecules by examining the substances they make up, as well as how those substances change. In this experiment, we will observe molecules breaking down while other molecules are built up. By observing these changes, you will learn about the difference between atoms and molecules.

Procedure:

1. Fill your small glass ¾ full of tap water.
2. Add a teaspoon of baking soda and stir vigorously.
3. Use your scissors to strip about a quarter inch of insulation off both ends of each wire. The best way to do this is to put the wire in your scissors and squeeze the scissors gently. You should feel an increase in resistance as the scissors begin to touch the wire. Squeeze the scissors until you feel that resistance and then back off. Continue squeezing and backing off as you slowly turn the wire round and round, as shown below:

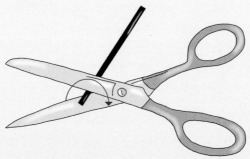

Be careful. You can cut yourself if you are not paying proper attention! You will eventually have a cut that goes through the insulation all the way around the wire. At that point, you can simply pull the insulation off. It will take some practice to get this right, but you *can* do it. Make sure there is at least ¼ inch of bare wire sticking out of both ends of the insulation.

4. Once you have stripped the insulation off both ends of each wire, connect the end of one wire to one of the two terminals on the battery. Do this by laying the wire over the terminal and then pressing it down. Secure it to the terminal with a piece of tape. It need not look pretty, but the bare wire needs to be solidly touching one terminal and not in contact with the other terminal.
5. Repeat step 4 with the other wire and the other battery terminal. Now you have two wires attached to the battery, one at each terminal. **Do not allow the bare ends of these wires to touch each other!**
6. Immerse the wires in the baking soda/water solution that is in the small glass so that the bare end of each wire is completely submerged. It doesn't really matter how much of the insulated portion of the wire is immersed; just make sure that the entire bare end of each wire is fully submerged. Once again, don't allow the ends to touch each other. In the end, your experiment should look something like this:

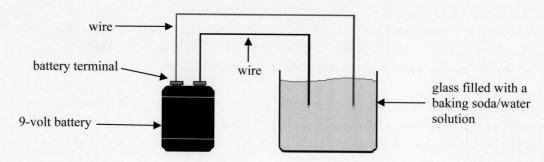

7. Look at the bare ends of the wires as they are submerged in the baking soda/water solution. What do you see? Well, if you set everything up right, you should see bubbles coming from both ends. If you don't see bubbles, most likely you do not have good contact between the wires and the battery terminals. Try pressing the ends of the wire hard against the terminals to which they are taped. If you then see bubbles coming from the submerged ends of the wire, then you know that electrical contact is your problem. If not, then your battery might be dead. Try another one.

8. Once you get things working, spend some time observing what's going on. Notice that bubbles are forming on *both* wires. That's an important point that should be written in your laboratory notebook.

9. Allow the experiment to run for about 10 minutes. After that time, pull the wires out of the solution and look at the bare ends. What do you see? Well, one of the wires should not look very different from when you started. It might be darker than it was, but that should be it. What about the end of the other wire? It should now be a different color. What color is it? Write that color down in your notebook.

10. If you let the experiment run for 10 minutes, it's very possible that your solution became slightly colored. Write in your notebook whether or not that happened and what color, if any, the solution became.

11. Looking at the wire that changed color, trace it back to the battery and determine the terminal (positive or negative) to which it is attached. Write that in your laboratory notebook as well.

12. **Clean up:** Disconnect the wires from the battery, dump the solution down the sink, run tap water to flush it down the drain, and wash the glass thoroughly. Put everything away.

Now, to understand what went on in the experiment, you need a little background information. Nearly everything you see around you is made up of tiny little units called **atoms.**

Atom – The smallest chemical unit of matter

Atoms are so small that you cannot see them. They are so small, in fact, that roughly 1,000,000,000,000,000,000 atoms are contained in the head of a pin. If we can't see them, how do we know they exist? Well, lots of experiments have been done that can only be explained if you *assume* that atoms exist; thus, there is a lot of *indirect* evidence that atoms exist. All this indirect evidence leads us to believe that atoms are, indeed, real.

When you stripped the insulation off the ends of each wire, you saw the familiar red-orange color of copper wire. Well, it turns out that copper is a type of atom. Thus, the copper that you observed in the wire was really just a bunch of copper atoms lumped together. You couldn't see the *individual* atoms, but when billions and billions and billions of them are put together, you can see the substance they make. When you have billions of billions of billions of copper atoms, you get the flexible, electricity-conducting, red-orange metal called copper.

We currently know that there are about 116 basic kinds of atoms in creation. This number increases as time goes on because every once in a while, scientists discover a new kind of atom. In a few years, then, the number of basic kinds of atoms in creation will probably be a little larger. That's why I say "about" 116 different kinds of atoms in creation.

If that were the end of the story, creation would be pretty boring. After all, if everything that you see were made up of atoms, and if there are only about 116 different kinds of atoms in creation, there are only 116 different substances in creation, right? Of course not! Although God used atoms as building blocks in creation, He designed those atoms to link together to form larger building blocks called **molecules**.

Molecule – Two or more atoms linked together to make a substance with unique properties

It turns out that the water you used in your experiment is made up of molecules. Although molecules are bigger than atoms, you still cannot really see them. Thus, the water you see is made up of billions and billions and billions of water molecules, just like the copper wire is made up of billions and billions and billions of atoms of copper. A water molecule is formed when an oxygen atom links together with two hydrogen atoms. When these atoms link together in a very specific way, the result is a water molecule. The difference between atoms and molecules is illustrated below.

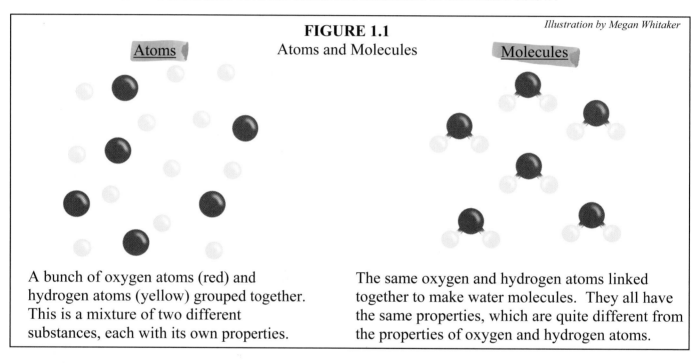

FIGURE 1.1
Atoms and Molecules

Illustration by Megan Whitaker

Atoms

Molecules

A bunch of oxygen atoms (red) and hydrogen atoms (yellow) grouped together. This is a mixture of two different substances, each with its own properties.

The same oxygen and hydrogen atoms linked together to make water molecules. They all have the same properties, which are quite different from the properties of oxygen and hydrogen atoms.

Now we are ready to really discuss the results of the experiment. When you filled the glass with water, you were filling it with billions and billions and billions of water molecules. When you placed the wires (which were connected to the battery) into the water, the electricity from the battery began flowing through the water. When this happened, the energy from the electricity flow actually broke some of the water molecules down into hydrogen and oxygen, which began bubbling out of the water, because hydrogen and oxygen are gases!

This tells us something about molecules. Each water molecule is made up of two hydrogen atoms and an oxygen atom linked together. When these atoms link together in that way, an odorless, colorless, tasteless liquid we call water is formed. When electricity is used to break the water molecules down, hydrogen and oxygen are formed. Hydrogen is an explosive gas, while oxygen is the gas we breathe to stay alive. Think about that. Oxygen and hydrogen are each gases with particular properties. When the atoms that make them up link together so that two hydrogen atoms are linked to one oxygen atom, however, these individual properties are lost, and a new substance (water) with new properties (odorless, colorless, tasteless liquid) is formed.

In one part of the experiment, then, you saw a molecule (water) breaking down into two gases made up of its two constituent atoms (hydrogen gas and oxygen gas). Well, when you pulled the wires out of the water after 10 minutes, you saw that the wire connected to the positive terminal of the battery had turned a bluish-green color. In this case, the copper atoms in the wire interacted with water molecules and baking soda molecules, aided by the energy contained in the electricity. The result was a bluish-green substance called copper hydroxycarbonate (hi drok' see car' buh nate). Copper hydroxycarbonate is formed when a copper atom links together with oxygen atoms, carbon atoms, and hydrogen atoms. In this experiment, the hydrogen and oxygen atoms came from both the water and the baking soda, the carbon atoms came from the baking soda alone, and the copper atoms came from the wire. In this case, then, you observed atoms (copper) linking up with other atoms (oxygen, carbon, and hydrogen) to make a molecule (copper hydroxycarbonate).

Interestingly enough, copper hydroxycarbonate is the same substance that you see on many statues, such as the Statue of Liberty. You see, if a structure made of copper (like the Statue of Liberty) is exposed to weather, a process similar to the one you observed turns the copper atoms in the statue into copper hydroxycarbonate. As a result, the structure turns bluish-green, just like one of the copper wires did in your experiment.

FIGURE 1.2
The Statue of Liberty and a Civil War Cannon

Photos © Daniel Slocum (left) and Geoffrey Kuchera (right) Agency: Dreamstime.com

The Statue of Liberty (left) turned bluish-green because hydrogen, oxygen, and carbon atoms from various substances in the air have combined with copper atoms to make copper hydroxycarbonate. This Civil War cannon (right) is made of bronze, which is a mixture of copper and tin. The copper in the mixture has also reacted to form copper hydroxycarbonate.

Chemical reactions like the ones you observed in your experiment are how we get all the incredible substances you see around you. Some substances (copper, aluminum, and some others) are made of billions and billions and billions of the same atom. These substances are often called **elements**. Other substances we see (water, salt, sugar, and many others) are made up of billions and billions and billions of molecules. They are often called **compounds**. Finally, many substances we see (wood, cereal, plastics, and many others) are actually **mixtures** of several different substances, each of which is made up of either atoms or molecules.

Okay, I am finally done discussing the experiment. Now that you know what the experiment shows, you can write a summary in your laboratory notebook. Write a brief description of what you did, followed by a discussion of what you learned. You will need to do each experiment in this way. Once you have done an experiment and written down any data and observations that come from the experiment, you need to read the discussion that relates to it. Once you have read the discussion, you can then write a summary explaining what you did and what you learned. This will help you get the most from your laboratory exercises.

Now that I am done presenting the concept of atoms and molecules, you need to answer the following "On Your Own" problems in order to make sure you understand what you have read. These kinds of problems will show up periodically, and you should answer them as soon as you come to them in the reading.

ON YOUR OWN

1.1 A molecule is broken down into its constituent atoms. Do these atoms have the same properties as the molecule?

1.2 When salt is dissolved in water, it actually breaks down into two different substances. Is salt composed of atoms or molecules?

Before you go on to the next section, I want to dispel a myth you might have heard. In many simplified science courses, students are told that scientists have actually seen atoms by using an instrument called a "scanning tunneling electron microscope." Indeed, students are shown figures such as the one below and are told that the conical shapes you see in the picture are atoms.

FIGURE 1.3
A Scanning Tunneling Electron Microscope Image of the Surface of a Nickel Foil

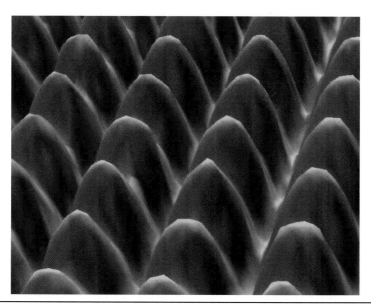

*Photo courtesy of the IBM
research division*

Is this what nickel atoms really look like? Are you really seeing a picture of atoms here? Well, although it looks good, it is not really a picture of atoms. You see, a scanning tunneling electron microscope does not allow you to *see* things the way a regular microscope does. Instead, it passes a charged probe across the surface of an object and measures slight changes in electricity flowing through the probe. It then sends that data to a computer, which uses a complicated set of mathematical equations from a theory called "quantum mechanics" to calculate what the surface of the object should look like. The computer then graphs the results of that calculation, adding colors to enhance the quality of the image. That's what is pictured in Figure 1.3.

So, what you are really seeing in Figure 1.3 is the result of a *calculation* that comes from a *theory* about how electricity flows under certain circumstances. Thus, *if* the theory is correct, and *if* the computer calculation is correct, *then* you are seeing *a representation* of atoms on the surface of the metal examined with the scanning tunneling electron microscope. Those are two big "ifs," however. Now I personally think that both the theory and the calculations are correct, so I think that what you see in Figure 1.3 (excluding the color, which has been artificially added) is probably a good representation of the surface of nickel foil. Never be fooled by someone who tells you that we have seen atoms, however. We have not. We have only seen the results of computer calculations that, if correct, simply give us a representation of atoms.

Measurement and Units

Let's suppose I'm making curtains for a friend's windows. I ask the person to measure his windows and give me their dimensions so I can make the curtains the right size. My friend tells me that his windows are 50 x 60, so that's how big I make the curtains. When I go over to his house, it turns out that my curtains are more than twice as big as his windows! My friend tells me that he's certain he measured the windows right, and I tell my friend that I'm certain I measured the curtains correctly. How can this be? The answer is quite simple. My friend measured the windows with a metric ruler. His measurements were in *centimeters*. I, on the other hand, used a yardstick and measured my curtains in *inches*. Our problem was not caused by one of us measuring incorrectly. Instead, our problem was the result of measuring with different **units.**

When we are making measurements, the units we use are just as important as the numbers that we get. If my friend had told me that his windows were 50 centimeters by 60 centimeters, there would have been no problem. I would have known exactly how big to make the curtains. Since he failed to do this, the numbers that he gave me (50 x 60) were essentially useless. Please note that a failure to indicate the units involved in measurements can lead to serious problems. For example, on July 23, 1983, the pilot of an Air Canada Boeing 767 passenger airplane had to make an emergency landing because his plane *ran out of fuel*. In the investigation that followed, it was determined that the fuel gauges on the aircraft were not functional, so the ground crew had measured the fuel level manually. However, the fuel gauges were metric, so those were the units with which the pilot worked. The ground crew, however, ended up using English units to report the amount of fuel. The number they reported was the correct *number*, but since the units were wrong, the airplane ran out of fuel. Thankfully, the pilot was skilled and was able to make the emergency landing with no casualties.

In the end, then, scientists never simply report numbers; they always include units with those numbers so that everyone knows exactly what those numbers mean. That will be the rule in this course. If you answer a question or a problem and do not list units with the numbers, your answer will be considered incorrect. In science, numbers mean nothing unless there are units attached to them.

Window illustration by
Megan Whitaker

FIGURE 1.4
Two Consequences of Not Using Units Properly

Airplane photo © Robert Cumming
Agency: dreamstime.com

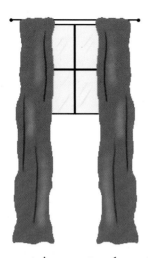

These curtains are too long for this window because the window was measured in centimeters, but the curtains were made assuming the measurements were in inches.

A Boeing 767 passenger aircraft like this one had to make an emergency landing because the pilot used metric units, while the ground crew that fueled the plane used English units. As a result, the airplane ran out of fuel during the flight.

Since scientists use units in all their measurements, it is convenient to define a standard set of units that will be used by everyone. This system of standard units is called the **metric system**.

The Metric System

There are many different things we need to measure when studying creation. First, we must determine how much matter exists in the object we want to study. We know that there is a lot more matter in a car than there is in a feather, since a car weighs significantly more than a feather. In order to study an object precisely, however, we need to know *exactly* how much matter is in the object. To accomplish this, we measure the object's **mass.** In the metric system, the unit for mass is the **gram**. If an object has a mass of 10 grams, we know that it has 10 times the matter that is in an object with a mass of 1 gram. To give you an idea of the size of a gram, the average mass of a Unites States dollar bill is about 1 gram. Based on this little fact, we can say that a gram is a rather small unit. Most of the things that we will measure will have masses of 10 to 10,000 grams. For example, when full, a twelve-ounce can of soda pop has a mass of about 400 grams.

Now that we know the metric unit for mass, we need to know a little bit more about the concept itself. Many people think that mass and weight are the same thing. This misconception arises because the more an object weighs, the more mass it has. Thus, people tend to think that mass and weight are equivalent. That's not true. Mass and weight are two different things. Mass measures how much matter exists in an object. Weight, on the other hand, measures how hard a planet's gravity pulls on that object.

For example, if I were to get on my bathroom scale and weigh myself, I would find that I weigh 205 pounds. However, if I were to take that scale to the top of Mount Everest and weigh myself, I would find that I only weighed 204 pounds there. Does that mean I'm thinner on top of Mount Everest than I am at home? Of course not. It means that on the top of Mount Everest, earth's gravity is not as strong as it is in my house. If I were to weigh myself on the moon, I would find that I only weighed 34 pounds. That's because the moon's gravity is weak. As a result, the moon cannot pull on me nearly as hard as the earth can.

On the other hand, if I were to measure my mass at home, I would find it to be 93,000 grams. If I were to measure my mass at the top of Mount Everest, it would still be 93,000 grams. Even on the moon, my mass would be 93,000 grams. That's the difference between mass and weight. Since weight is a measure of how hard gravity pulls, an object weighs different amounts depending on where that object is. Mass, on the other hand, is a measure of how much matter is in an object and does not depend on where that object is.

Unfortunately, there are many other unit systems in use today besides the metric system. In fact, the metric system is probably not the system with which you are most familiar. You are probably most familiar with the English system. The unit of pounds comes from the English system. Now, as I stated before, pounds are not a measure of mass; they are a measure of weight. The metric unit for weight is called the **Newton**. The English unit for mass is (believe it or not) called the **slug**. Although we will not use the slug often, it is important to understand what it means.

There is more to measure than just mass, however. We might also want to measure how big an object is. For this, we must use the metric system's unit for distance, which is the **meter**. If you stretch out your left arm as far as it will go, the distance from your right shoulder to the tip of the fingers on your left hand is about 1 meter. The English unit for distance is the **foot**. What about inches, yards, and miles? We'll talk about those a little later.

We also need to be able to measure how much space an object occupies. This measurement is commonly called "volume" and is measured in the metric system with the unit of **liter**. The main unit for measuring volume in the English system is the gallon. To give you an idea of the size of a liter, it takes just under 4 liters to make a gallon.

Finally, we have to be able to measure the passage of time. When studying creation, we will see that its contents have the ability to change.   The shape, size, and chemical properties of certain substances change over time, so it is important to be able to measure time so that we can determine how quickly the changes take place. In both the English and metric systems, time is measured in **seconds.** Once again, we'll talk about minutes, hours, and days a little later.

Since it is very important for you to be able to recognize which units correspond to which measurements, Table 1.1 summarizes what you have just read. The letters in parentheses are the commonly used abbreviations for the units listed.

TABLE 1.1
Physical Quantities and Their Base Units

Physical Quantity	Base Metric Unit	Base English Unit
Mass	gram (g)	slug (sl)
Distance	meter (m)	foot (ft)
Volume	liter (L)	gallon (gal)
Time	second (s)	second (s)

Manipulating Units

Now, let's suppose I asked you to measure the width of your home's kitchen using the English system. What unit would you use? Most likely you would express your measurement in feet. However, suppose instead I asked you to measure the length of a pencil. Would you still use the foot as your measurement unit? Probably not. Since you know the English system already, you would probably recognize that inches are also a unit for distance, and since a pencil is relatively small, you would use inches instead of feet. In the same way, if you were asked to measure the distance between two cities, you would probably express your measurement in terms of miles, not feet. This is why I used the term "Base English Unit" in Table 1.1. Even though the English system's normal unit for distance is the foot, there are alternative units for length if you are trying to measure very short or very long distances. The same holds true for all English units. Volume, for example, can be measured in cups, pints, quarts, or gallons.

This concept exists in the metric system as well. There are alternative units for measuring small things as well as alternative units for measuring big things. These alternative units are called "prefix units," and, as you will soon see, prefix units are much easier to use and understand than the alternative English units. The reason prefix units are easy to use and understand is that they always have the same relationship to the base unit, regardless of what physical quantity you are interested in measuring. You will see how this works in a minute.

In order to use a prefix unit in the metric system, you simply add a prefix to the base unit. For example, in the metric system, the prefix "centi" means one hundredth, or 0.01. So, if I wanted to measure the length of a pencil in the metric system, I would probably express my measurement with the centimeter unit. Since a centimeter is one hundredth of a meter, it can be used to measure relatively small things. On the other hand, the prefix "kilo" means 1,000. If I want to measure the distance between two cities, then, I would probably use the kilometer. Since each kilometer is 1,000 times longer than a meter, it can be used to measure long things.

Now, the beauty of the metric system is that these prefixes mean the same thing *regardless of the physical quantity you want to measure!* So if I were measuring something with a very large mass (such as a car), I would probably use the kilogram unit. One kilogram is the same as 1,000 grams. In the same way, if I were measuring something that had a large volume, I might use the kiloliter, which would be 1,000 liters.

Compare this incredibly logical system of units to the chaotic English system. If you want to measure something short, you use the inch unit, which is equal to one twelfth of a foot. On the other hand, if you want to measure something with small volume, you might use the quart unit, which is equal to one fourth of a gallon. In the English system, every alternative unit has a different relationship to the base unit, and you must remember all those crazy numbers. You have to remember that there are 12 inches in a foot, 3 feet in a yard, and 5,280 feet in a mile, while at the same time remembering that for volume there are 8 ounces in a cup, 2 cups in a pint, 2 pints in a quart, and 4 quarts in a gallon.

In the metric system, all you have to remember is what the prefix means. Since the "centi" prefix means one hundredth, you know that 1 centimeter is one hundredth of a meter, 1 centiliter is one hundredth of a liter, and 1 centigram is one hundredth of a gram. Since the "kilo" prefix means 1,000, you know that there are 1,000 meters in a kilometer, 1,000 grams in a kilogram, and 1,000 liters in a kiloliter. Doesn't that make a lot more sense than the English system?

Another advantage to the metric system is that there are many, many more prefix units than there are alternative units in the English system. Table 1.2 summarizes the most commonly used prefixes and their numerical meanings. The prefixes in boldface type are the ones we will use over and over again. You will be expected to have those three prefixes and their meanings memorized. Once again, the commonly used abbreviations for these prefixes are listed in parentheses.

TABLE 1.2
Common Prefixes Used in the Metric System

PREFIX	NUMERICAL MEANING
micro (μ)	0.000001
milli (m)	**0.001**
centi (c)	**0.01**
deci (d)	0.1
deca (D)	10
hecta (H)	100
kilo (k)	**1,000**
Mega (M)	1,000,000

Remember that each of these prefixes, when added to a base unit, makes an alternative unit for measurement. So, if you wanted to measure the length of something small, the only unit you could use in the English system would be the inch. However, if you used the metric system, you would have all sorts of options for which unit to use. If you wanted to measure the length of someone's foot, you could use the decimeter. Since the decimeter is one tenth of a meter, it measures things that are only slightly smaller than a meter. On the other hand, if you wanted to measure the length of a sewing needle, you could use the centimeter, because a sewing needle is significantly smaller than a meter. If you wanted to measure the length of an insect's antenna, you might use the millimeter, since it is one thousandth of a meter, which is a *really* small unit.

So you see that the metric system is more logical and versatile than the English system. That is, in part, why scientists use it as their main system of units. The other reason that scientists use the metric system is that most countries in the world use it. With the exception of the United States, almost every other country in the world uses the metric system as its standard system of units. Since scientists in the United States frequently work with scientists from other countries around the world, it is necessary that American scientists use and understand the metric system.

<u>Converting Between Units</u>

Now that you understand what prefix units are and how they are used in the metric system, you must become familiar with converting between units within the metric system. In other words, if you measure the length of an object in centimeters, you should also be able to convert your answer to any other distance unit. For example, if I measure the length of a pencil in centimeters, I should be able to convert that length to millimeters, decimeters, meters, etc. Accomplishing this task is relatively simple as long as you remember a trick you can use when multiplying fractions. Suppose I asked you to complete the following problem:

$$\frac{7}{64} \times \frac{64}{13} =$$

There are two ways to figure out the answer. The first way would be to multiply the numerators and the denominators together and, once you had accomplished that, simplify the fraction. If you did it that way, it would look something like this:

$$\frac{7}{64} \times \frac{64}{13} = \frac{448}{832} = \frac{7}{13}$$

You could get the answer much more quickly, however, if you remember that when multiplying fractions, common factors in the numerator and the denominator cancel each other out. Thus, the 64 in the numerator cancels with the 64 in the denominator, and the only factors left are the 7 in the numerator and the 13 in the denominator. In this way, you reach the final answer in one less step:

$$\frac{7}{\cancel{64}} \times \frac{\cancel{64}}{13} = \frac{7}{13}$$

We will use the same idea in converting between units. Suppose I measure the length of a pencil to be 15.1 centimeters, but the person who wants to know the length of the pencil would like me to tell him the answer in meters. How would I convert between centimeters and meters? First, I would need to know the relationship between centimeters and meters. According to Table 1.2, "centi" means 0.01. So, 1 centimeter is the same thing as 0.01 meter. In mathematical form, we would say:

1 centimeter = 0.01 meter

Now that we know how centimeters and meters relate to one another, we can convert from one to another. First, we write down the measurement we know:

15.1 centimeters

We then realize that any number can be expressed as a fraction by putting it over the number 1. So we can rewrite our measurement as:

$$\frac{15.1 \text{ centimeters}}{1}$$

Now we can take that measurement and convert it into meters by multiplying it with the relationship we determined above. We have to do it the right way, however, so that the units work out properly. Here's how we do it:

$$\frac{15.1 \ \cancel{\text{centimeters}}}{1} \times \frac{0.01 \text{ meters}}{1 \ \cancel{\text{centimeters}}} = 0.151 \text{ meters}$$

This tells us that 15.1 centimeters is the same as 0.151 meters. There are two reasons this conversion method, called the **factor-label method**, works. First, since 0.01 meters is the same as 1 centimeter, multiplying our measurement by 0.01 meters over 1 centimeter is the same as multiplying by 1. Since nothing changes when we multiply by 1, we haven't altered the value of our measurement at all. Second, by putting the 1 centimeter in the denominator of the second fraction, we allow the centimeters unit to cancel (just like the 64 canceled in the previous example). Once the centimeters unit has canceled, the only thing left is meters, so we know that our measurement is now in meters.

This is how we will do all our unit conversions. We will first find the relationship between the unit we have and the unit to which we want to convert. Then we will write the measurement we know in fraction form by putting it over 1. Next, we will use the relationship we found to make a fraction that, when multiplied by our measurement in fraction form, cancels out the unit we have and replaces it with the unit we want to have. You will see many examples of this method, so don't worry if you are a little confused right now.

It may seem odd to you that words can be treated exactly the same as numbers. Measurement units, however, have just that property. Whenever a measurement is used in any mathematical equation, the units for that measurement must be included in the equation. Those units are then treated the same way numbers are treated.

We will be using the factor-label method for many other types of problems as well, so it is very, very important for you to become an expert at using it. Thus, even if you can do these kinds of unit conversions in your head, *don't do them that way*. Instead, do them using the factor-label method so that you learn it. Also, since we will be using it so often, we should start abbreviating things so that they will be easier to write down. We will use the abbreviations for the base units listed in Table 1.1 along with the prefix abbreviations listed in Table 1.2. Thus, kilograms will be abbreviated "kg," while milliliters will be abbreviated "mL."

Since the factor-label method is so important in our studies of physical science, let's see how it works in another example:

EXAMPLE 1.1

A student measures the mass of a rock to be 14,351 grams. What is the rock's mass in kilograms?

First, we use the definition of "kilo" to determine the relationship between grams and kilograms:

$$1 \text{ kg} = 1,000 \text{ g}$$

Notice what we had to do. We put a "1" in front of the unit with the prefix (kg), and then for the base unit (g) we put in the definition of the prefix ("kilo" means 1,000). This is the way you should always write down these relationships. The "1" goes with the prefix unit, and then the base unit gets the number that corresponds to the definition of the prefix. Now that we have the proper relationship, we put our measurement in fraction form:

$$\frac{14,351 \text{ g}}{1}$$

Then we multiply our measurement by a fraction that contains the relationship we just determined, making sure to put the 1,000 g in the denominator so that the unit of grams cancels out:

$$\frac{14,351 \cancel{g}}{1} \times \frac{1 \text{ kg}}{1,000 \cancel{g}} = 14.351 \text{ kg}$$

Thus, 14,351 grams is the same as <u>14.351 kilograms</u>.

ON YOUR OWN

1.3 A student measures the mass of a book as 12,321 g. What is the book's mass in kg?

1.4 If a glass contains 0.121 L of milk, what is the volume of milk in mL?

1.5 In the National Basketball Association (NBA), the distance from the three-point line to the basket is 723.9 cm at the top of the arc. What is this distance in meters?

Converting Between Systems

As you may have guessed, the factor-label method can also be used to convert *between* systems of units as well as within systems of units. Thus, if a measurement is done in the English system, the factor-label method can be used to convert that measurement to the metric system, or vice versa. In order to be able to do this, however, you must learn the relationships between metric and English units. Although these relationships, summarized in Table 1.3, are important, we will not use them very often, so you needn't memorize them. If you need them on a test, they will be given to you.

TABLE 1.3
Relationships Between English and Metric Units

Measurement	English/Metric Relationship
Distance	1 inch = 2.54 cm
Mass	1 slug = 14.59 kg
Volume	1 gallon = 3.78 L

We can use this information in the factor-label method the same way we used the information in Table 1.2.

EXAMPLE 1.2

The length of a tabletop is measured to be 37.8 inches. How many cm is that?

To solve this problem, we first put the measurement in its fraction form:

$$\frac{37.8 \text{ in}}{1}$$

We then multiply this fraction by the conversion relationship given in Table 1.3 so that the inches unit cancels:

$$\frac{37.8 \text{ in}}{1} \times \frac{2.54 \text{ cm}}{1 \text{ in}} = 96.012 \text{ cm}$$

So, a measurement of 37.8 inches is equivalent to 96.012 cm.

Give yourself a little more practice with the factor-label method by solving the following "On Your Own" problems:

ON YOUR OWN

1.6 A piece of yarn is 3.00 inches long. How many centimeters long is it?

1.7 How many slugs are there in 12 kg?

1.8 If an object occupies 3.2 gallons of space, how many liters of space does it occupy?

The important thing to remember about the conversion system you just learned is that it can be used on *any* system of measurement, whether you are familiar with it or not. To see what I mean, perform the following experiment:

EXPERIMENT 1.2
Cubits and Fingers

Note: A sample set of calculations is available in the solutions and tests guide. It is with the solutions to the study guide.

Supplies
♦ A long piece of string
♦ Scissors
♦ A large tabletop (like the top of a kitchen table or a big desk)
♦ A person to help you
♦ Some cellophane tape
♦ A pencil
♦ Eye protection such as goggles or safety glasses

Introduction: In the Old Testament, a measurement unit for length called the **cubit** was used. You can find a reference to it in Genesis 6:15, for example, where God tells Noah the dimensions of the ark. Back then, a cubit was defined as the length from a man's elbow to the tip of his outstretched middle finger. There was also a smaller unit of length measurement called the finger. It was defined as the distance from the last knuckle on a man's index finger to the tip of his index finger. You should immediately see a drawback of this measuring system. Arm length and finger length changes from man to man. As a result, the cubit that one man used was different than the cubit another man used. The same can be said for the finger. Nowadays, we use precise definitions for our measuring units so that they are the same all over the world. No matter where you go, a meter is a meter. That's not the way it used to be! In this experiment, you will make your own measuring devices for the cubit and the finger, and then you will get some practice converting between these measurement units.

<u>Procedure</u>:

1. Hold your arm so that the elbow is bent but the rest of your arm stretches out horizontally. Open your palm so that your fingers stretch out in the same direction. Have your helper hold the end of the string at your elbow.

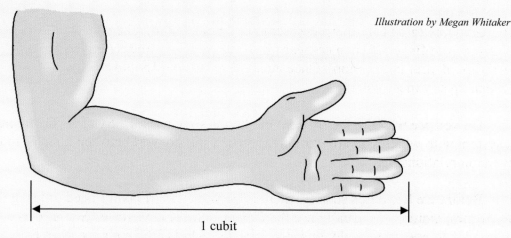

Illustration by Megan Whitaker

1 cubit

2. Have your helper stretch the string tightly from your elbow to the tip of your middle finger, and then have him or her cut it so that you have a length of string that runs from your elbow to the tip of your middle finger. This is your cubit.

3. Next, point your index finger straight out and have your helper stretch another piece of string so that it stretches from your last knuckle (the one nearest your fingernail) to the tip of your index finger. Have your helper cut the string so that it runs the length from your last knuckle to the tip of your index finger (not your fingernail). The string should be less than an inch long. This is your measurement for the "finger" unit.

4. Take the string that represents your cubit and tape it down to the tabletop so that it is stretched out to its full length.

5. Now, take the string that represents your finger and measure how many of those strings are in your cubit string. You can do this by simply starting at the beginning of your cubit string and stretching your finger string down next to it. Use your pencil to mark where the end of the finger string is on the cubit string. Now pick up the finger string and repeat the process, this time starting at the mark you made. Count the number of times you did this, and that will tell you how many fingers are in a cubit. Most likely, this will not be a whole number. Try to estimate the fraction of the finger string it took to reach the end of the cubit string on your last measurement. In other words, if it took 18 finger strings to reach the end of your cubit string, but the cubit string only covered $\frac{1}{3}$ of the 18th finger string, then it really took $17\frac{1}{3}$ (17.3) fingers to make a cubit.

6. Record the number of finger strings (including the decimal) it took to reach the end of your cubit string. Now you know the number of fingers in 1 cubit.

7. Unfasten your cubit string from the tabletop and measure the length of the tabletop in cubits. Do this the same way you measured the cubit before, laying the string end-to-end until you reach the end of the tabletop. Once again, if the end of the tabletop only covers a portion of the last cubit string in your measurement, try to estimate the fraction of a cubit that it covered. Record the length of the tabletop (including the decimal) in cubits.

8. Now repeat that measurement, this time using your finger string instead.

9. Do the same thing with the width of the tabletop, measuring it in both cubits and fingers.

10. Now, take your measurement for the length of the tabletop in cubits and convert it into fingers using the number of fingers in a cubit you determined in step 5. Compare your converted length in

fingers to the number of fingers you actually measured. If you did the conversion correctly, the answers should be similar. They won't be exactly the same because of inaccuracies in your measurements. Nevertheless, they should be close. If they aren't anywhere close to each other, you probably did the conversion wrong. Check the example solution for this experiment that appears in the Solutions and Tests Guide, so that you can find the mistake you made in your conversion.

11. Do the same thing for your measurement of table width; take your measured width in cubits and convert it to fingers. Then compare your answer to the measured length in fingers to check the validity of your conversion. Once again, the numbers should be close.

12. Clean up any mess you made.

Do you see why the factor-label method is so powerful? Even if you are not familiar with the unit system with which you are working, you can still convert between units as long as you have a conversion relationship.

Before we leave this section, there is one more metric unit I need to bring up. When scientists measure temperature, we usually use the **Celsius** temperature scale. Sometimes called the "centigrade" temperature scale, this temperature scale fits the metric system better than the Fahrenheit scale, with which you are probably more familiar. When we measure temperature on this scale, we list the unit as "degrees Celsius." This unit does not have prefixes or anything; degrees Celsius is the only way to use the unit. The reason we tend to use this temperature scale instead of the Fahrenheit one is because this scale is based on factors of 10. On this temperature scale, water freezes at 0.00 degrees Celsius and boils at 100.0 degrees Celsius. This seems to fit right in to the metric system, which is also based on powers of 10. So, when I talk about temperature in this course, I will usually use the Celsius scale.

Concentration

In the past few sections, we discussed the units used to measure mass, length, and volume. Although these are very important things to measure, there is one other quantity with which you must be very familiar: **concentration**.

Concentration – The quantity of a substance within a certain volume

To get an idea of what concentration means, perform the following experiment:

EXPERIMENT 1.3
Concentration

Supplies:
♦ Vinegar
♦ 6 Tums® tablets (You can use another antacid tablet, but it must have calcium carbonate as its active ingredient.)
♦ Water
♦ Measuring cups
♦ 3 large glasses (They each must be able to hold at least 2 cups of liquid.)
♦ A spoon
♦ Eye protection such as goggles or safety glasses

Introduction: Vinegar is a weak acid, a kind of substance you will learn a lot more about when you take chemistry. Tums are antacid tablets, designed to neutralize acid. Thus, when Tums are added to vinegar, a chemical reaction occurs. The Tums tablet disappears as it neutralizes the vinegar. While this happens, gas (carbon dioxide) bubbles off the tablet.

Procedure

1. Arrange your three glasses on a tabletop or countertop. Put 1 cup of vinegar in the first glass, ½ cup of vinegar in the second glass, and ¼ cup in the third.
2. Place a Tums tablet in each glass.
3. Observe what's going on in each glass. Note in your laboratory notebook any differences you see between what's going on in the glasses. If you don't see any differences, note that as well.
4. After you have finished observing the experiment, pour out the contents of each glass and rinse the glasses thoroughly.
5. Dry the glasses and set them back on the countertop or tabletop.
6. Put 1 cup of vinegar in the first glass, ½ cup of vinegar in the second glass, and ¼ cup of vinegar in the third glass.
7. Pour 1 cup of water in the first glass, 1½ cups of water in the second glass, and 1¾ cups of water in the third glass, so that each glass has a total of 2 cups of liquid in it.
8. Use the spoon to stir the contents of each glass thoroughly.
9. Now place a single Tums tablet in each glass.
10. Observe what's going on in each glass. Record in your lab notebook what you see. Note any differences between what's going on in the glasses.
11. **Clean up**: Pour the contents of each glass down the drain, and rinse each glass out. Put everything away.

What did you see when you observed the three glasses? Well, the first time, there really should have been little difference between what was happening in the three glasses. The antacid tablet in each of the three glasses should have bubbled and disappeared at roughly the same speed and in roughly the same fashion in each of the three glasses. The reason the tablet was bubbling and disappearing, of course, was that the chemical in the tablet was trying to neutralize the acid in the vinegar. The only difference between the glasses in the first part of the experiment was the total amount of vinegar present. Thus, it would take *less* of the tablet to neutralize the vinegar in the third glass than in the second or first glass. Nevertheless, while the acid in the vinegar was still present, the action in each of the glasses should have been essentially the same.

In the second part of the experiment, things were much different. In the first glass, you should have seen the Tums tablet bubbling and disappearing more slowly than what you saw in the first part of the experiment. In the second glass, the tablet should have been bubbling and disappearing at a much slower rate than that of the tablet in the first glass. If you could see the tablet in the third glass bubbling and disappearing at all, it should have been extremely slow.

Why the differences between the three glasses in this part of the experiment? Each of them had Tums and vinegar in them. Why did the tablet in the second glass disappear more slowly than the one in the first glass? Why did the tablet in the third glass disappear even more slowly or not at all? The answer: concentration. You see, each glass had vinegar in it, but the second glass had half as much vinegar as the first glass. In the first part of the experiment, there was half as much vinegar in the second glass, but there was also half as much volume. Thus, the concentration (how much exists in a *given volume*) of vinegar in the second glass was the same as it was in the first glass. In the second part of the experiment, however, there was half as much vinegar *in the same amount of volume* as the first glass. Since there was half as much vinegar in the same volume, the concentration of vinegar was half as much. As a result, the neutralization of acid by the Tums went much more slowly.

In the third glass, the concentration of vinegar was so small that the Tums tablet seemed to not disappear at all. So, this experiment shows us that the way chemicals behave depends on their concentration. When the concentration of vinegar is large, the neutralization of the acid in vinegar by a Tums tablet proceeds rather quickly. When the concentration of vinegar is low, however, that same process proceeds slowly or not at all. This is perhaps the single most important thing that you can learn about chemicals. At certain concentrations, chemicals behave in one way. At other concentrations, those same chemicals can behave in a different way.

 The multimedia CD has a video demonstrating how concentration can affect a chemical's behavior.

Consider, for example, vitamins. Certain vitamins are often called "fat soluble vitamins." These vitamins (A, D, E, and K) get stored in your body's fat reserves if your body has more than it needs. As time goes on, those vitamins build up. If they get too concentrated, they can actually become *toxic* to the human body! Think about that for a moment. Vitamins, which are very good for you, can become toxic to you if they reach high concentrations. It is possible, in fact, to get very sick or even die as a result of taking *too many* vitamins!

Now don't get paranoid about this! If you take one or two times the recommended daily allowance of vitamins A, D, E, and K, they will probably not reach toxic concentrations in your body. Only if you take several times the recommended daily allowance of these vitamins do you risk a buildup to toxic concentrations. The point, however, should not be lost. The behavior of chemicals depends on their concentration. Certain chemicals are good for you at one concentration and toxic for you at another. In the same way, chemicals we call poisons are not necessarily bad for you at low enough concentrations!

This discussion has relevance to many issues in modern society. Consider, for example, the cigarette smoking debate raging in the United States. For years, scientists have been able to directly link cigarette smoking to cancer. Scientific study after scientific study shows that smoking cigarettes dramatically increases your risk of getting lung cancer.

As the link between cigarette smoking and lung cancer became very clear, people began wondering about the effect of breathing someone else's smoke. After all, consider the person who does not smoke but has a friend who does. This person spends a great deal of time with his friend, and any time his friend smokes, he ends up inhaling the smoke as well. Scientists have called this phenomenon "second-hand smoke." Can the person who is continually inhaling second-hand smoke be at risk for contracting lung cancer? Well, many studies have been done to answer this question, and the answer is surprising. The studies indicate that *if* inhaling second-hand smoke increases a person's likelihood of getting cancer, the increased risk is very, very small. In fact, even in experiments where non-smokers who *lived with* smokers were studied, the increased risk for cancer caused by second-hand smoke was extremely small.

How can this be? If smoking significantly increases your risk of contracting lung cancer, why can't we see a similar link between second-hand smoke and lung cancer? The answer once again is concentration. When a smoker inhales cigarette smoke, the toxins in the smoke are very concentrated. When the smoke leaves either the cigarette or the smoker's mouth, it quickly spreads out into the surrounding air. This reduces the toxin concentrations significantly, in turn reducing the damage to anyone who inhales the smoke second-hand. As a result, second-hand smoke does not increase your risk of getting lung cancer much, if at all.

Of course, this is in no way an excuse for smokers who want to smoke around non-smokers. Even if a person's increased risk of lung cancer due to second-hand smoke is tiny (if it exists at all), it is simply unpleasant for non-smokers to breathe in smoke coming from a cigarette. Also, it is possible that second-hand smoke increases your risk of other illnesses. Thus, you should never feel bad about asking a smoker to put out his or her cigarette. In fact, you are doing the smoker a favor, since science has conclusively shown a direct link between smoking and lung cancer!

The information contained in the last four paragraphs might have surprised you. If you follow politics in the United States at all, you might have heard people claim that second-hand smoke causes cancer. Unfortunately, it seems that people can claim almost anything these days and rarely get challenged by the major media outlets if those claims happen to support a particular political agenda. It turns out that there have been *many* studies done on second-hand smoke, and the data simply say that there is little to no increased risk of contracting lung cancer, even for someone who inhales second-hand smoke on a regular basis. If you are interested in looking into this controversy a little more, you might look at the course website, which is described in the "Student Notes" section at the beginning of this book. There are links to several resources that discuss the science of second-hand smoke.

ON YOUR OWN

1.9 Muriatic acid is sold in hardware stores for use in cleaning. Pool owners, for example, use it to clean hard water stains and algae stains from their pools. Its active ingredient is hydrochloric acid. The Works® is a toilet bowl cleaner with hydrochloric acid as its active ingredient. There are approximately 350 grams of hydrochloric acid in a liter of muriatic acid, and there are approximately 30 grams of hydrochloric acid in a liter of The Works. Why is muriatic acid a more powerful cleaner than The Works?

1.10 Sodium (so' dee uhm) is a necessary part of a healthy diet. If a person does not ingest enough sodium every day, that person will get sick and perhaps die. Nevertheless, some people try to limit their sodium intake by eating a low-salt diet. How can it be good to limit your sodium intake, even though sodium is a necessary part of body chemistry?

Now that you are done with the first module of this course, solve the study guide so that you will be reminded of the important concepts and skills in this module. Then you can take the test. The study guide is a very good indicator of what information you will be responsible for on the test. Please note that if a question on the study guide provides you with certain information (like the conversion factors between metric and English units), that information will be provided on the test. However, if a study guide question requires information that it does not give you (such as the meaning of the abbreviation mL), you will be required to memorize that information for the test.

ANSWERS TO THE "ON YOUR OWN" PROBLEMS

1.1 <u>The atoms do not have the same properties as the molecule</u>. When atoms join to make a molecule, their individual properties disappear and the molecule takes on its own, unique properties. When the molecule is broken down into its atoms, the atoms regain their individual properties.

1.2 <u>Salt is composed of molecules</u>. Since atoms are the smallest chemical units of matter in creation, if salt can be broken into smaller parts, it must be made of atoms linked together. Thus, it is made of molecules. Now you might think that since molecules are made by linking atoms together, you could also say that salt is made of atoms. However, that is not really correct. The atoms that link together to form salt molecules have their own, unique properties, but those properties completely disappear when the atoms join to form salt molecules. Thus, it is not the *atoms* that give the salt its properties; the *molecules* do.

1.3 We need to do this conversion the way the example showed us. First, we find the relationship. Since we want to convert from grams to kg, we need to remember that since "kilo" means "1,000," one kilogram is the same thing as 1,000 grams. Remember, the "1" goes with the unit that has the prefix, and the base unit gets the "1,000," since that's what "kilo" means.

$$1 \text{ kg} = 1,000 \text{ g}$$

Next, we put the number in fractional form:

$$\frac{12,321 \text{ g}}{1}$$

Now our conversion relationship tells us that 1 kg = 1,000 g. Since we want to end up with kg in the end, we must multiply the measurement by a fraction that has grams on the bottom (to cancel the gram unit that is there) and kg on the top (so that kg is what's left). Remember, the numbers next to the units in the relationship above go with the units. Thus, since "g" goes on the bottom of the fraction, so does "1,000." Since "kg" goes on the top, so does "1."

$$\frac{12,321 \text{ g}}{1} \times \frac{1 \text{ kg}}{1,000 \text{ g}} = 12.321 \text{ kg}$$

Thus, 12,321 g is the same as <u>12.321 kg</u>.

1.4 We solve this the same way we solved problem 1.3. First, we find the conversion relationship. Since we want to convert from liters to mL, we need to remember that "milli" means "0.001." So, we write down our relationship, keeping the "1" with mL (since it is the unit with the prefix) and putting the definition of "milliliter" (0.001) with the base unit:

$$1 \text{ mL} = 0.001 \text{ L}$$

Then we put the number in fractional form:

$$\frac{0.121 \text{ L}}{1}$$

Our conversion relationship tells us that 1 mL = 0.001 L. Since we want to end up with mL, we must multiply the measurement by a fraction that has L on the bottom (to cancel the L unit that is there) and mL on the top (so that mL is the unit with which we are left):

$$\frac{0.121 \, \cancel{L}}{1} \times \frac{1 \, \text{mL}}{0.001 \, \cancel{L}} = 121 \, \text{mL}$$

Thus, 0.121 L is the same as <u>121 mL</u>.

1.5 Since we want to convert from centimeters to meters, we need to remember that "centi" means "0.01." So the "1" goes with the centimeter unit, and the "0.01" goes with the base unit. Thus, our conversion relationship is:

$$1 \, \text{cm} = 0.01 \, \text{m}$$

Next, we write the measurement as a fraction:

$$\frac{723.9 \ \text{cm}}{1}$$

Since we want to end up with meters in the end, we must multiply the measurement by a fraction that has centimeters on the bottom (to cancel the cm unit that is there) and meters on the top (so that m is the unit we are left with):

$$\frac{723.9 \ \cancel{\text{cm}}}{1} \times \frac{0.01 \, \text{m}}{1 \ \cancel{\text{cm}}} = 7.239 \, \text{m}$$

The three-point line is <u>7.239 m</u> from the basket.

1.6 We use the same procedure we used in the previous three problems. Thus, I am going to reduce the length of the explanation.

$$\frac{3.00 \ \cancel{\text{in}}}{1} \times \frac{2.54 \, \text{cm}}{1 \ \cancel{\text{in}}} = 7.62 \, \text{cm}$$

The yarn is <u>7.62 cm</u> long.

1.7
$$\frac{12 \ \cancel{\text{kg}}}{1} \times \frac{1 \, \text{slug}}{14.59 \ \cancel{\text{kg}}} = 0.82 \, \text{slugs}$$

There are <u>0.82 slugs</u> in 12 kg. Note that I rounded the answer. The real answer was "0.822481151," but there are simply too many digits in that number. When you take chemistry, you will learn about significant figures, a concept that tells you where to round numbers off. For right now, don't worry about it. If you rounded at a different spot than I did, that's fine.

1.8
$$\frac{3.2 \text{ gal}}{1} \times \frac{3.78 \text{ L}}{1 \text{ gal}} = 12 \text{ L}$$

The object has a volume of <u>12 L</u>. Once again, don't worry if you rounded your answer at a different place from where I rounded my answer.

1.9 <u>Muriatic acid is the more powerful cleaner because the active ingredient is more concentrated</u>. In the same amount of volume, muriatic acid has more than 10 times as much active ingredient. Since the active ingredient is more concentrated, it will clean better.

1.10 <u>Sodium is necessary for the body at a certain concentration. If you eat too much sodium, you raise the concentration too much</u>. In the same way, if you eat too little sodium, you lower its concentration too much. Either way, your body suffers. Thus, you need to keep the sodium concentration in your body at the right level. Too little sodium intake will reduce the sodium concentration to critical levels, while too much sodium intake will raise it to toxic levels.

STUDY GUIDE FOR MODULE #1

1. Write out the definitions for the following terms:

a. Atom
b. Molecule
c. Concentration

2. Fifty grams of a carbon disulfide can be broken down into 42.1 grams of sulfur and 7.9 grams of carbon. Is carbon disulfide made up of atoms or molecules?

3. If you put iron near a magnet, the iron will be attracted to the magnet. Rust is made up of molecules that contain iron atoms and oxygen atoms. Rust is not attracted to a magnet. If rust contains iron atoms, and iron is attracted to a magnet, why isn't rust attracted to a magnet?

4. A statue is made out of copper and displayed outside. After many years, what color will the statue be?

5. Have scientists actually seen atoms?

6. Give the numerical meaning for the prefixes "centi," "milli," and "kilo."

7. If you wanted to measure an object's mass, what metric unit would you use? What English unit would you use?

8. If you wanted to measure an object's volume, what metric unit would you use? What English unit would you use?

9. If you wanted to measure an object's length, what metric unit would you use? What English unit would you use?

10. How many centimeters are in 1.3 meters?

11. If a person has a mass of 75 kg, what is his or her mass in grams?

12. How many liters of milk are in 0.500 gallons of milk? (1 gal = 3.78 L)

13. A meterstick is 100.0 centimeters long. How long is it in inches? (1 in = 2.54 cm)

14. Ozone is a poisonous gas that can build up in the air in dense cities. Thus, there are many environmental initiatives to lower the amount of ozone in the air we breathe. One way you can make ozone, however, is by baking bread. The nice smell you associate with baking bread is actually due, in part, to ozone. If ozone is poisonous, why is baking bread not considered a dangerous activity?

MODULE #2: Air

Introduction

In this course, we will spend a great deal of time learning about the physical environment that surrounds you. Where better to start than air itself? After all, air completely surrounds you. Even though you cannot see it, you know it's there. You feel it move when there is a breeze, and you breathe it in and out continuously. Since it is such an important part of our everyday experience, it deserves some special attention.

Now you have probably learned a few things about air already. Nevertheless, I am sure you have not studied air in the detail with which I will present it. Do not "turn off," therefore, just because a few of the subjects discussed below sound familiar. There is a *lot* to the subject of air, and even though we will study this fascinating mixture of gases in some detail, we will still only scratch the surface of all the things that can be learned about the air that surrounds you.

The Air and Humidity

In order to begin our study of air, I want to look at its composition. Before I can do that, however, I need to tell you about a very important concept in the study of air: **humidity** (hyoo mid' ih tee).

Humidity - The moisture content of air

No matter where you are on the planet, the air that you breathe probably contains some moisture in the form of water vapor. This moisture affects you quite a bit. You see, your body has an ingenious means of cooling off when it is hot. God has designed you to sweat when you are too warm. When you sweat, water is released onto your skin. This water, once exposed to the air, tends to evaporate. Well, the process of evaporation requires energy, which is supplied by the heat on your skin. As a result, when your sweat evaporates, it takes energy (in the form of heat) away from your skin. Since the evaporation of sweat takes heat away from your skin, the net effect is that *your skin cools down!*

Isn't that marvelous? Your body has been designed with its own cooling system! When you get hot, your body releases sweat that evaporates from your skin. In the evaporation process, heat is removed from your skin, cooling it down. You know what's even more amazing? This cooling system in your body is *self-regulating*! You don't sweat when you are cool or comfortable; you only sweat when you need cooling off. Think about that for a moment. It took human science nearly 3,000 years to come up with a thermostat-regulated cooling system. Nevertheless, the human body has had one since it was made! This is just one of the many incredible design features we see in nature. It is a stirring testimony to the fact that we are "fearfully and wonderfully made" (Psalm 139:14). To see this effect, perform the following experiment:

EXPERIMENT 2.1
Evaporation and Temperature

Supplies:
- A small glass, like a juice glass
- Two cotton balls
- Tap water
- Eye protection such as goggles or safety glasses

♦   A bulb thermometer (It must be able to read room temperature and slightly higher, and it must have a bulb at the end.)
♦   A small piece of plastic such as a Ziploc® bag or a square cut from a trash bag.

Introduction: Everyone knows that water left in the presence of air evaporates. Well, it turns out that the process of evaporation actually takes energy. Thus, when water evaporates, it cools the surface it is touching. You will see this effect in this experiment.

Procedure:

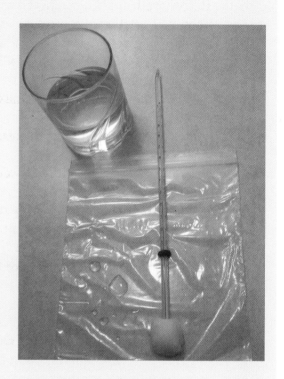

1. Fill your small glass ¼ full of lukewarm tap water. You should just open the tap and fill the glass right away. This will make the water as close to room temperature as possible.
2. Let it sit out for at least 15 minutes. This will ensure that the water attains room temperature.
3. While you are waiting, spread out the piece of plastic on the counter and lay the thermometer on the plastic. Make sure the thermometer bulb is touching the plastic.
4. Allow the thermometer to sit for a while and then read the temperature. Note that in your laboratory notebook.
5. After you have waited 15 minutes, soak the two cotton balls in the water.
6. Pull the cotton balls out, squeeze out the excess water, and use them to surround the bulb of the thermometer.
7. Wait 3 minutes and then read the temperature. Compare it to the previous temperature.
8. Clean up any mess you made and put everything away.

What happened in the experiment? Well, when the thermometer was sitting on the plastic, it was reading the temperature of the room. When you surrounded it with the wet cotton balls, it was still being exposed to room temperature, because the water was at room temperature. The thermometer read a lower temperature, however, because water was *evaporating* from the cotton balls. Since water was evaporating from the cotton balls, it was cooling them. Since the thermometer bulb was in contact with the cotton balls, it was cooled as well. Thus, the water was acting like your sweat and the cotton balls were acting like your skin. When the water (representing your sweat) evaporated, the cotton balls (representing your skin) were cooled.

What does all this have to do with humidity? Well, when there is a lot of moisture in the air already, your sweat does not evaporate as quickly as when there is only a little moisture in the air. Since the cooling effect of sweat is completely dependent on the sweat evaporating, the process of sweating does not cool you very quickly when the humidity (moisture content of the air) is high. When the humidity is low, however, your sweat evaporates quickly, cooling you off more quickly. Thus, for a given temperature, a high humidity will make you feel warmer than a low humidity. For this reason, many weather reports include a **heat index**, which is a combination of temperature and humidity. It tells you how hot you will feel as a result of humidity's effect on the sweating process.

This effect is further compounded by the fact that since your sweat does not evaporate quickly on a humid day, you tend to notice it more. On a warm day in which the humidity is low, you do not notice your sweat as much, because it evaporates away soon after it is released onto the skin. When it is humid, however, your sweat does not evaporate readily. It ends up pooling together in little droplets that run across your skin. This makes you even more aware of how hot it is, compounding the misery. This is why people often say, "It's not the heat; it's the humidity."

Before we leave this section on humidity, I need to introduce something we will discuss again later. When you listen to the weather report, you hear the humidity of the air reported in terms of percentage. You need to know what that means. You see, there are two ways of measuring humidity: **absolute humidity** and **relative humidity**. Absolute humidity is easy to understand.

Absolute humidity – The mass of water vapor contained in a certain volume of air

Absolute humidity, therefore, is a measure of the concentration of water vapor in the air.

Relative humidity is a little harder to understand. You see, you cannot put an infinite amount of water vapor in the air. Eventually, the air simply can't hold any more water vapor. As a result, there is a maximum absolute humidity that air can have. When air has that amount of water vapor in it, we say that the air is **saturated** with moisture. Now it turns out that the maximum absolute humidity changes depending on the temperature of the air. When air is warm, it can hold more moisture than when it is cold. Thus, in order to make the reporting of humidity a little easier to understand, weather reports list the humidity as a percentage of the maximum absolute humidity for whatever temperature it happens to be.

Relative humidity – The ratio of the mass of water vapor in the air at a given temperature to the maximum mass of water vapor the air could hold at that temperature, expressed as a percentage.

What does this definition mean? Suppose that on a given day, the air holds half as much moisture as it possibly could for that particular temperature. In that case, the relative humidity would be 50%. On the other hand, if the air contained three-quarters of the maximum amount of water for that temperature, the relative humidity would be 75%. If the air contained the maximum amount of water vapor it could hold at that temperature, the relative humidity would be 100%.

ON YOUR OWN

2.1 Suppose you left a glass of water outside on two different days. On the first day, it is warm and humid. On the second day, it is the same temperature, but the humidity is low. Each day, you measure how long it takes the water to completely evaporate from the glass. On which day will the time it takes the water to evaporate be the smallest?

2.2 Suppose you did the same experiment that was described in Problem 2.1 when the relative humidity was 100%. How quickly would the water evaporate from the glass?

The Composition of Air

Now that we have the concept of humidity out of the way, we can discuss the composition of air. Why did we need to discuss humidity first? Well, the first thing we need to do to really analyze the composition of air is to remove the water vapor in it. Since the humidity of the air changes from place to place as well as from time to time, there is no way to pin down how much water vapor is in the "average" sample of air. Thus, in order to discuss the composition of air, we will remove all water vapor from it. So the discussion in this section will focus on dry air, which has an absolute humidity of zero. The composition of dry air is shown in Figure 2.1.

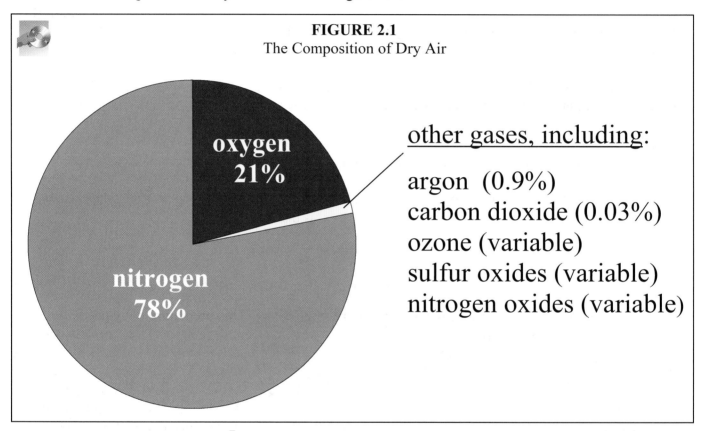

FIGURE 2.1
The Composition of Dry Air

other gases, including:

argon (0.9%)
carbon dioxide (0.03%)
ozone (variable)
sulfur oxides (variable)
nitrogen oxides (variable)

As shown in Figure 2.1, air is actually a mixture of gases. The major constituents of this mixture are nitrogen (which makes up 78% of the air we breathe), oxygen (which constitutes 21% of dry air), argon (0.9%), and carbon dioxide (0.03%). Hundreds of other gases make up the remaining 0.07%. The other gases listed in Figure 2.1 are the ones we will concentrate on in this module. Carbon dioxide is a gas that most living creatures release. Ozone is a gas, and its concentration in air varies with altitude. Both of these gases exist in small quantities but are absolutely critical for life to exist on this planet. We will see why in a moment. The other gases listed in Figure 2.1 are considered pollutants. We will discuss them in a moment as well. For a myriad of reasons, this mixture of gases is perfectly suited for the task of supporting life. If any of the constituent gases made up significantly more or less of the air than it currently does, earth would suddenly become a planet hostile to most living things!

Before we go into that, however, I need to point out something regarding concentration. In the previous module, I spent some time discussing concentration. I then used the concept again to explain humidity. One thing that I have not discussed, however, are the *units* we use to express concentration. There is a very good reason for this. It turns out that we use many different kinds of units to express concentration. In this figure, for example, we are using the unit of **percent**. If you think about it, percent can be used as a unit of concentration. After all, "percent" literally means "per hundred." In this case, then, of every 100 particles in the air, 78 are nitrogen, and 21 are oxygen. This tells us that the concentration of nitrogen in air is more than three times the concentration of oxygen. Thus, the first unit we will use to express concentration will be percent. Later on in this module, we will use another unit for concentration.

Now let's get back to studying the air we are breathing. In order to live, humans and most other forms of life must take in oxygen. This is because the chemical reactions that supply energy for our bodies are **combustion** reactions. Combustion is really just another word for burning. Oxygen is necessary for combustion; thus, most living organisms require a steady supply of it. We are, indeed, fortunate that 21% of the air we breathe is made up of oxygen. If there were significantly less oxygen in the air, we could not supply our bodies with the energy necessary to support their various functions, and we would suffocate.

You may not realize, however, that we are also very fortunate that there isn't significantly *more* oxygen in the air, either. You see, too much oxygen in the air would cause problems for many living creatures, including people. For example, when guinea pigs are allowed to breathe 100% oxygen for as little as 48 hours, they start experiencing significant lung damage. In people, breathing 100% oxygen has been shown to cause not only lung damage, but also blindness. Indeed, in some intensive care units, it would be beneficial for some of the patients' organs if they could breathe 100% oxygen. However, it has been shown that if the oxygen concentration is increased beyond 60%, severe lung damage takes place. Similar considerations must be made for premature babies, as discussed in the figure below.

Photo © Steve Lovegrove
Agency: dreamstime.com

FIGURE 2.2
A Premature Baby Receiving Elevated Concentrations of Oxygen

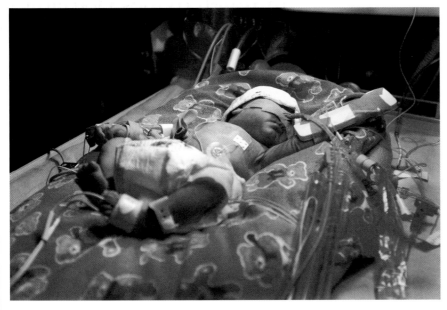

This premature baby needs to breathe elevated concentrations of oxygen, because he cannot efficiently extract oxygen from the air. However, prolonged exposure to high concentrations of oxygen can result in damage to his eyes. Indeed, this is why legendary singer Stevie Wonder is blind. As a result, the hospital staff must make sure he receives enough oxygen to keep him alive and prevent nerve damage, but at the same time, not so much oxygen that he is at risk of serious eye injury.

In addition, elevated oxygen content in the air would result in *significantly* greater risk of natural disaster by fire. For example, the probability that lightning will start a forest fire increases by 70% for every 1% rise in the oxygen concentration of the air. Thus, if oxygen made up 31% of the air we breathe instead of 21%, there would be *seven times more natural forest fires* than there are today! To see the profound effect that oxygen has on combustion, perform the following experiment:

EXPERIMENT 2.2
Oxygen and Fire

Supplies:

- A reasonably large glass or jar
- A candle (**DO NOT** use a lighter or any other gas or alcohol burner. You must use a candle in order to keep the experiment safe.)
- Matches
- 2 cups of hydrogen peroxide (sold at any drugstore)
- Baker's yeast
- A bottle (A plastic, 1-liter soda pop bottle, for example)
- A balloon
- A teaspoon
- Eye protection such as goggles or safety glasses

Introduction: Everyone knows that fire needs oxygen to burn. If you run out of oxygen, there is no fire. What happens, however, when there is more oxygen than usual?

Procedure:

1. Fill your bottle with about 2 cups of hydrogen peroxide. The exact amount is unimportant. Just make it around 2 cups.
2. Quickly add about a teaspoon of yeast to the hydrogen peroxide. Don't worry if you spill some getting it into the bottle. Speed is more important than neatness in this case.
3. Quickly open the balloon and cover the opening of the bottle with it. Be sure it is an airtight seal. The best way to ensure this is to pull as much of the neck of the balloon as possible down the lip of the bottle. If the seal is not airtight, try again.
4. Once you have an airtight seal, gently shake the bottle back and forth. As the yeast and the hydrogen peroxide mix, bubbles should begin to form. Those bubbles are oxygen gas being formed in a chemical reaction.
5. The oxygen gas should continue to form, inflating your balloon. Let this go on for a while.
6. While your balloon inflates, light the candle and then cover it by turning the jar upside down and placing it over the candle. **Be careful at this point. If the glass in the jar is weak, it could crack! Do not get your face close to the jar!** Note what happens in your laboratory notebook.
7. Uncover the candle and light it again, leaving it uncovered.
8. Next, go back to your balloon. It should be partially inflated now. It need not be anywhere near fully inflated. It just needs to have some oxygen in it.
9. Take the balloon off the bottle, being careful to not let too much oxygen escape.
10. Pinch (do not tie) the neck of the balloon so as to keep the oxygen from escaping.
11. Take your jar and cover the candle again, but this time tilt the jar so you can slip the neck of the balloon underneath the jar.
12. Once you have slipped the neck of the balloon under the jar, *slowly* let the oxygen out of the balloon and let it flow into the jar. **Once again, be careful! Do not let your face get too close to the jar, because the glass might crack from the heat! Also, DO NOT let the oxygen out quickly. Let it SLOWLY fill the jar. If you do it too quickly, the experiment could become dangerous!** Note what happens in your laboratory notebook.
13. Clean up your mess.

The multimedia CD has a video of an "extreme" version of the experiment you just did.

What happened in the experiment? Well, the first part is easy to understand. In fact, you've probably done that part of the experiment before. When you covered the burning candle with the jar, the flame got dimmer and dimmer until it went out. This is because it used up the oxygen in the air surrounding it, and because there was no source of oxygen to replenish what was used up, the candle burned out. What about the second part of the experiment, however? When you added oxygen from the balloon, the candle actually burned a lot brighter, didn't it? That's because the *speed* at which fire burns depends directly on the *concentration* of oxygen in the air surrounding it. In the second part of the experiment, you increased the concentration of oxygen in the air. That increased the speed at which the fire burned.

Let's suppose the candle flame represents a tiny fire started by a lightning bolt. Most fires like that die out before they have a chance to spread into real forest fires. With elevated oxygen concentrations, however, the tiny fires would burn much faster, greatly enhancing the chance of spreading into real forest fires! Increased oxygen concentration would also increase the ferocity of forest fires.

FIGURE 2.3
Fire

photo © Jessica Eden,
Agency: istockphoto.com

Fire is a chemical reaction between oxygen and the fire's fuel. In the case of this campfire, for example, there is a chemical reaction between oxygen and the molecules that make up the wood. This chemical reaction produces new molecules like carbon dioxide and water. In addition, energy is released. We see that energy in the form of light, and we feel it in the form of heat.

The more oxygen in the air, the more rapidly fires burn and the more likely they are to start given even a small spark or flame. This is why you see warning signs from time to time (like in a hospital) stating that oxygen gas is in use, and therefore smoking and open flames are not permitted.

So we see that although the air we breathe must contain oxygen, it cannot contain very much oxygen. The oxygen has to be "diluted" to exactly the right concentration for healthy lives and safe surroundings. It turns out that the gases used to dilute the oxygen in the air are very important as well. Nitrogen and argon, for example, make up the vast majority of the rest of the air we breathe. These gases are relatively inert. In other words, it is very difficult to get them to chemically react with anything else. Thus, when we breathe in nitrogen and argon, neither of them react with our bodies in any way. We simply breathe them in, and then we breathe them right back out again. It turns out there are lots of gases that *could* be used to dilute the air we breathe. Except for nitrogen, argon, and carbon dioxide, however, *most of the others are toxic to life at any reasonable concentration*! It's a very nice "coincidence" that the principal gases used to dilute the oxygen in the air we breathe are two of the very few gases that do not react with our bodies in any harmful way!

ON YOUR OWN

2.3 If a scientist were to measure the percentages of nitrogen and oxygen in a sample of air that was not dry, would they be greater than, less than, or essentially the same as the percentages shown in Figure 2.1?

2.4 At high altitudes, there is less air around you as compared to lower altitudes. Would a candle at high altitudes burn dimmer, brighter, or essentially the same as the same candle at low altitudes?

Carbon Dioxide in the Air

In addition to nitrogen, oxygen, and argon, there is a small amount of carbon dioxide in the air. This gas is necessary for life to exist on planet earth, but too much carbon dioxide is just as deadly as too little. Carbon dioxide performs two major functions for the maintenance of life on this planet. First, in addition to oxygen, plants need a steady supply of carbon dioxide in order to survive. Through a process called photosynthesis (which you will learn about in biology), plants convert the carbon dioxide they absorb from the air and the water they absorb from the ground into glucose, a sugar. This sugar is used by the plant to provide the energy necessary to sustain its life functions.

Photosynthesis not only produces glucose, but it also makes oxygen as a byproduct, which is then released into the air. This replenishes the oxygen supply, which is continually used by living organisms. Without carbon dioxide, plants would starve, and the oxygen content of the air we breathe would slowly decrease to zero.

In addition to providing the means by which plants can synthesize their own food, carbon dioxide also performs another vital function: It helps regulate the temperature of the earth. The earth's main source of energy is the sun. Every day, the sun bathes the earth with its light. The earth absorbs most of that light and uses it as a source of energy to grow plants, warm the surface of the planet, etc. Interestingly enough, the earth also radiates energy back into space in the form of infrared (in' fruh red) light. In fact, the earth radiates a lot of infrared light. If you aren't familiar with the term "infrared light," don't worry. You'll learn more about that in a later module.

The light the earth absorbs warms the planet. However, when the earth radiates infrared light, that process actually cools the earth. Thus, the earth gets warm when it absorbs light, but it cools down when it radiates light. We know that a significant amount of the light the earth absorbs gets radiated out again as infrared light. If that were the end of the story, earth would be a very, very cold place – far too frigid to support life.

The reason the earth is not an arctic wasteland is that carbon dioxide (and other gases such as water vapor, methane [meth' ayn], and ozone) tend to absorb the infrared light the earth radiates. This, in turn, heats up the atmosphere (at' muh sfeer), regulating the earth's temperature to near-perfect conditions for the maintenance of life. This process, known as the **greenhouse effect**, is illustrated in Figure 2.4.

<u>Greenhouse effect</u> – The process by which certain gases (principally water vapor, carbon dioxide, and methane) trap heat that radiates from earth

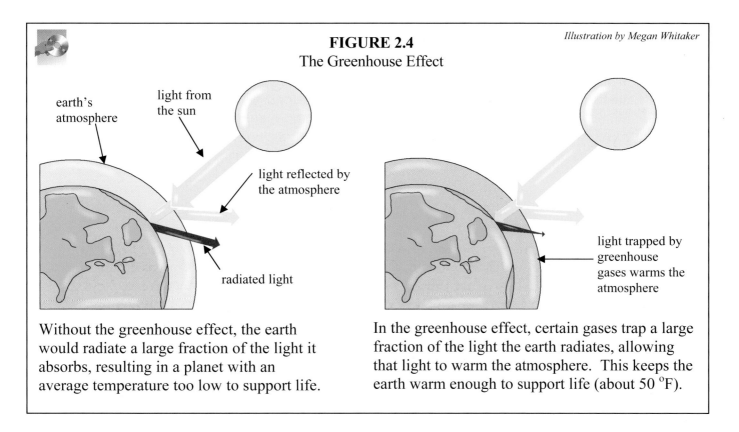

FIGURE 2.4
The Greenhouse Effect

Illustration by Megan Whitaker

earth's atmosphere

light from the sun

light reflected by the atmosphere

radiated light

light trapped by greenhouse gases warms the atmosphere

Without the greenhouse effect, the earth would radiate a large fraction of the light it absorbs, resulting in a planet with an average temperature too low to support life.

In the greenhouse effect, certain gases trap a large fraction of the light the earth radiates, allowing that light to warm the atmosphere. This keeps the earth warm enough to support life (about 50 $^\circ$F).

To see how carbon dioxide participates in the greenhouse effect, perform the following experiment:

EXPERIMENT 2.3
Carbon Dioxide and the Greenhouse Effect

<u>Supplies</u>:
♦ Thermometer (It can be the same thermometer used in Experiment 2.1. It needs to read from slightly lower than room temperature to slightly higher than room temperature.)
♦ A large, clear Ziploc® freezer bag (It needs to be large enough so that the thermometer can be "zipped" inside it.)
♦ Sunny windowsill (If it's not sunny today, just wait until it is.)
♦ Bottle (like the one used in Experiment 2.2)
♦ Vinegar
♦ Baking soda
♦ Teaspoon
♦ Eye protection such as goggles or safety glasses

Introduction: Carbon dioxide is what environmental scientists call a "greenhouse gas." This means it traps energy in the form of light. In the greenhouse effect, greenhouse gases trap energy being radiated out from the earth. In this experiment, you will observe carbon dioxide trapping energy coming in from the sun.

<u>Procedure:</u>

A. Running the experiment with air
1. Open the Ziploc bag.
2. You want to fill the bag with air. Do this by holding the bag wide open, with the open side facing down. Then raise the bag as high as you can and quickly lower it. This should fill the bag with air.
3. Put the thermometer in the bag and zip it closed. You should now have a Ziploc bag that is partially inflated with air and has a thermometer inside.
4. Place the bag on a sunny windowsill. Arrange the bag so you can look through it and read the thermometer.
5. Allow the bag and thermometer to sit for 15 minutes.
6. Read the temperature from the thermometer.

B. Running the experiment with carbon dioxide
1. Take the bag off the windowsill.
2. Open the bag and remove the thermometer.
3. Place the thermometer in a safe place while you prepare the next part of the experiment.
4. Fill the bottle about one-third of the way with vinegar.
5. Measure out one teaspoon of baking soda and add it to the vinegar. The contents of the bottle will begin to bubble. Those bubbles tell you that a gas is being formed. The gas is carbon dioxide. Wait for 2-3 minutes. This will allow the carbon dioxide to push the air out of the bottle.
6. Repeat step #5. By doing that step twice, you are ensuring that there is only carbon dioxide in the bottle above the vinegar and baking soda.
7. Measure out another teaspoon of baking soda, but this time, keep it in the spoon.
8. Open the Ziploc bag and press it flat to remove any air in it. Keep it handy.
9. Add the baking soda to the vinegar and then quickly hold the Ziploc bag over the opening of the bottle. Don't worry about making sure all of the baking soda lands in the bottle. In this step, speed is important. Immediately close the bag around the bottle opening so that the carbon dioxide coming from the bottle goes into the bag. Allow this to continue until the bubbling slows down significantly.
10. Although the bag will not be significantly inflated, it will contain a lot of carbon dioxide. Carefully lift the bag off the bottle and put the thermometer in the bag.
11. Quickly zip the bag closed. You should now have a bag with carbon dioxide and a thermometer in it.
12. Go to the windowsill and place the bag in the same position that you did in part A of the experiment.
13. Allow it to sit for 15 minutes.
14. After the 15 minutes, read the temperature.
15. Clean up any mess you made and put everything away.

What happened in the experiment? Well, the two temperatures you measured should be different. The temperature you got in part B should be higher than the one you got in part A. Why? Carbon dioxide absorbed energy from infrared light. This is what causes the greenhouse effect. In your experiment, because carbon dioxide absorbed the energy from infrared light, the bag got hotter when it contained more carbon dioxide.

Since carbon dioxide contributes to the greenhouse effect, if the carbon dioxide concentration (and the concentrations of the other greenhouse gases) were significantly lower, earth would be colder. In addition, plants would not be able to manufacture enough food via photosynthesis. If the concentration of carbon dioxide (and the other greenhouse gases) in the air were much greater, the greenhouse effect would warm the earth up too much, causing problems with the ecological balance. This is what some environmentalists have termed **global warming**. Now despite the fact that you usually hear the terms "global warming" and "greenhouse effect" side by side, please realize that they are two completely different things. The greenhouse effect is a very beneficial physical process for us. Indeed, without it, life could not exist! Global warming, however, is the result of too much greenhouse effect. In other words, while the greenhouse effect is a good thing, global warming is too much of a good thing!

We are going to study global warming in the next section, but before we do that, I need to tell you a little bit about *where* this carbon dioxide comes from. Carbon dioxide is one of the products of fire. When you burn something, carbon dioxide is usually one of the substances made as a result of the burning process. Remember from the previous section that the chemical reactions that supply us (and many of the creatures in creation) with energy are essentially combustion (burning) reactions. As a result, many creatures in creation produce carbon dioxide continuously, because the chemical reactions that supply living organisms with energy run continuously.

Now most of you know this already. You have already learned that we inhale oxygen and exhale carbon dioxide. If you examine Figure 2.5, however, you might be a little surprised about what *else* we exhale.

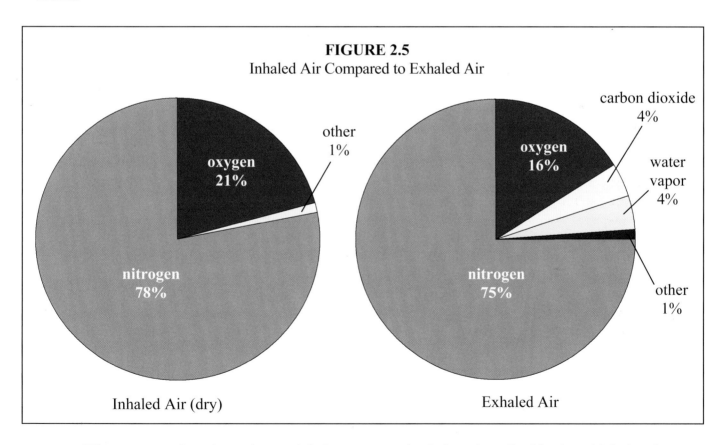

FIGURE 2.5
Inhaled Air Compared to Exhaled Air

Inhaled Air (dry)

Exhaled Air

When most students learn that we inhale oxygen and exhale carbon dioxide, they think that those are the only substances involved. Clearly this is not the case. As we learned previously, the *majority* of the air we inhale is nitrogen. Less than ¼ of what we inhale is oxygen. Notice that when we exhale, the majority of what we exhale is also nitrogen. This should make sense. Remember, nitrogen really doesn't interact with our bodies in any way. We breathe it in and then breathe it right back out. Since it is the majority of what we breathe in, it should also be the majority of what we breathe out.

Notice that we actually exhale a lot of oxygen as well. That's because under normal circumstances, our bodies do not use all of the oxygen they take in. As a result, there is still a lot of oxygen in a breath of exhaled air. In fact, there is more oxygen in exhaled air than carbon dioxide! Notice also that carbon dioxide and water vapor are of equal concentrations in exhaled air. This is because water is also a product of most combustion reactions. Since exhaled carbon dioxide comes from combustion reactions taking place in our bodies, it makes sense that water will be produced as well.

Thus, we have discussed two ways that carbon dioxide gets into the air around us: fires and living organisms. Both of these sources have combustion reactions at their root, so they both produce carbon dioxide (and water vapor). When you take biology, you will learn about the "carbon cycle," which is a more detailed means of tracking where carbon dioxide comes from and where it goes. At that point, you will learn about some other processes that put carbon dioxide into the air. For now, just realize that two of them are fire and the normal life processes of many creatures in creation.

ON YOUR OWN

2.5 We know that if the carbon dioxide concentration were too low, plants would starve. Conversely, experiments indicate that many plants actually flourish when the concentration of carbon dioxide in their vicinity increases. How can this fact help explain why some experiments indicate that houseplants tend to grow better when their caretakers talk to them?

2.6 We know that our bodies do not use the nitrogen we inhale. Nevertheless, in Figure 2.5, notice that the percentage of nitrogen in exhaled air is *lower* than the percentage of nitrogen in inhaled air. If our bodies do not use nitrogen in any way, why does the percentage decrease?

Global Warming

In the previous section, I mentioned that if the concentration of carbon dioxide and other greenhouse gases were to increase too much, the earth would get too warm. This phenomenon is called **global warming**. As you are probably aware, there are those who are worried that this very thing is happening today. Why? Well, as civilization has become more industrialized, people have been burning a lot more fuel than they used to. Before the Industrial Revolution, we burned wood and coal to heat our homes and businesses, but that was about it. As a result of the Industrial Revolution, however, we are burning coal, wood, natural gas, and gasoline in huge quantities to generate electrical power, run manufacturing machinery, power automobiles, etc. As a result, we have been putting a lot more carbon dioxide into the air than we used to.

At the same time, the population of the earth is greater than it has ever been. Did you know that the population of the earth is now over 6 *billion*? All those people exhale a lot of carbon dioxide and use many products produced by industry! So the Industrial Revolution, combined with the population of the earth, has resulted in a lot of extra carbon dioxide being pumped into the air. As a result, the concentration of carbon dioxide in the air has increased over time, as you will see in the figure below.

This is where worries about global warming come from. We know that carbon dioxide is a participant in the greenhouse effect, which warms the planet. We also know that the amount of carbon dioxide in the air has been rising steadily over the last 80 years or so. Well, increased carbon dioxide means an increased greenhouse effect, which will result in global warming, right? Not exactly.

Although the fear that too much carbon dioxide in the air could lead to global warming is based on sound scientific reasoning, reality is just a bit more complex than that. To illustrate what I mean, take a look at the data presented in Figure 2.6. These graphs show both the amount of carbon dioxide in the air and the change in the average temperature of the earth as a function of the year in which those measurements were taken.

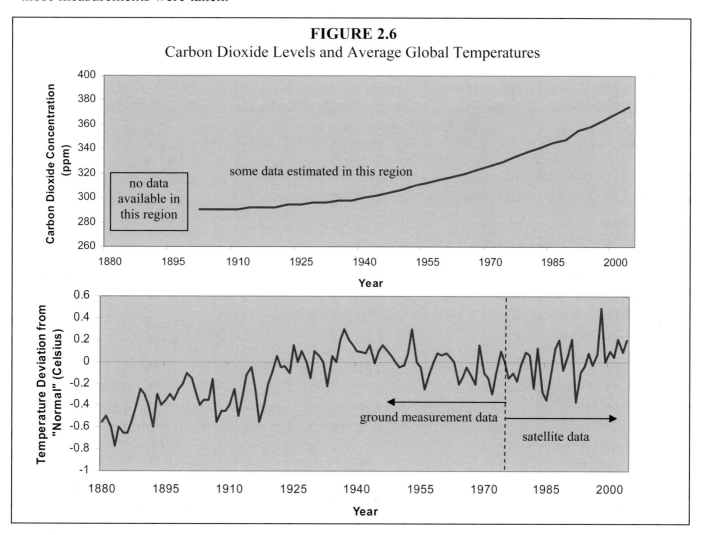

FIGURE 2.6
Carbon Dioxide Levels and Average Global Temperatures

Before we figure out what the data tell us, let's make sure you understand the graphs themselves. In the top half of the figure, the concentration of carbon dioxide in the atmosphere (we'll discuss the unit in a moment) is graphed versus the year in which the measurement was taken. These data are from the Mauna Loa observatory in Hawaii, and they make up the largest set of data regarding carbon dioxide concentration in the atmosphere. Notice that the data do not start until 1900, and we do not have a complete data set until the late 1950s. Thus, some of the data between 1900 and the late 1950s are estimated.

In the bottom half of the figure, the *change in global temperature* is plotted versus the year in which the change was measured. This means that the line representing zero in the graph is the "normal" average global temperature (about 50° F). Data that lie below that line represent years in which the average global temperature was lower than normal, and data that lie above that line represent years in which the average global temperature was warmer than normal. The data from 1880 to 1978 are from temperature measurements taken on the ground (K. H. Bergman: *International Journal of Environmental Studies*, Vol. 20, 1983, p. 93). Although these data are illustrative, they are not the most accurate data, as nearly 70% of the earth is covered by water. Thus, these data ignore the vast majority of the earth. The data from 1979 to the present are taken by NASA satellites (http://www.ghcc.msfc.nasa.gov/MSU/msusci.html, accessed January 12, 2005). These data are ideal, as the satellites measure the temperature of the *entire* earth.

Now what do all these data tell us? Well, the top graph tells us that there has been a steady increase in carbon dioxide levels in the air since about 1920. If you look at the bottom graph, however, you do not see a corresponding increase in the temperature of the earth. Instead, from about 1880 to 1920, the average global temperature increased in a very shaky pattern by about 0.5 degrees Celsius (0.9 degrees Fahrenheit). After that, however, the temperature change varies up and down quite a bit, but continues to hover around zero. In other words, over the time that the amount of carbon dioxide in the air increased steadily, the temperature of the earth, on average, did not change significantly.

Does this mean that the amount of carbon dioxide in the air does not affect the temperature of the earth? No. We know that the greenhouse effect is real, or we wouldn't be here. These data tell us that reality is more complex than theory. Remember, in order to see a change in the greenhouse effect, there must be a *significant* change in the amount of carbon dioxide in the air. Unfortunately, scientists do not know what a significant change would be. If the amount of carbon dioxide in the air doubled, would that be significant? From the standpoint of the greenhouse effect, we really do not know. What we know for sure, however, is that the sum total of all carbon dioxide produced by human activity is approximately 3% of the carbon dioxide produced by the natural processes that emit carbon dioxide into the air. One could argue, then, that this amount of added carbon dioxide is simply not significant compared to all the other processes that add carbon dioxide to the air.

Also, the way in which carbon dioxide is added to the air is very important in the greenhouse effect. When people burn fuels, carbon dioxide is not the only gas released. Many other gases are released as well. Some of these gases tend to reflect light rather than absorb it. This actually *reduces* the amount of energy absorbed by the earth, causing a net cooling effect. It could be that any increase in the greenhouse effect due to human-produced carbon dioxide is offset by the cooling caused by the other chemicals associated with human activity.

Although there are many things we do not know about the greenhouse effect, right now the reliable data indicate that the earth is not warming, at least not in any significant way. In addition, we know that the earth has been much warmer in the past. A team from Harvard University reviewed over 240 scientific studies on global temperatures in the past, and their research indicates that the earth was significantly warmer between the ninth and fourteenth centuries than it is today. As a result, it is awfully hard to believe that modern burning of fuels is leading to any kind of global warming, as people did not burn nearly as much fuel in the Middle Ages as they do now!

If the data seem to indicate that global warming is not happening, and if scientists agree that it has been much warmer in the past than it is now, why does the media seem to say that global warming is happening? There are a few possible reasons. First, most of the people who talk about the earth's ecosystems really do not understand them very well. Thus, they tend to use their own personal experiences and attempt to relate those experiences to the earth as a whole.

For example, many people who talk about global warming discuss the fact that in their area of the world, the winters have been unusually warm over the past few years. Thus, they say, global warming must be happening. This, of course, neglects the fact that the entire world is often quite different from one person's little corner of it. While one area of the world might be experiencing unusually warm winters, another part of the world might be experiencing unusually cool summers. As a result, the *global* temperature does not change very much, despite what might be happening in one region of it.

This can also be applied to other issues as well. For example, it is common to hear that certain large ice sheets that have been the same size for a long, long time are now starting to melt. This is then used to conclude that the earth as a whole is getting warmer. However, this is not sound scientific reasoning. The fact that an ice sheet is melting is only evidence that *the part of the world that holds the ice sheet* is warming up. For example, a large ice sheet in the Antarctic Peninsula, the Larsen B ice shelf, has experienced a remarkable decline in size over the past few years. Some say that this is evidence for global warming. The problem is that the west Antarctic ice sheet has been *thickening* over the past few years. Thus, while the Antarctic Peninsula is getting warmer, the western part of the Antarctic is getting cooler. It turns out that temperature measurements of Antarctica indicate that overall, Antarctica has actually been cooling since the 1960s. Does that mean that global cooling is happening? Of course not! It just means that when you talk about global warming, you must consider the entire earth, not just one part of it.

Another problem is that people who have a political agenda to push can often distort the facts in order to make their point more persuasive. For example, it is not unusual for people to say that the earth has experienced measurable warming over the past 100 years and that it is due to the carbon dioxide produced by people. While the first part of that statement is most certainly true, these people simply neglect to tell their audience that most (if not all) of this warming occurred in the early 1900s, *before* human beings were burning much fuel. Thus, the earth did warm up a bit in the past 100 years, but it was not because of rising carbon dioxide levels. That did not happen until after the warming ended.

Finally, if you dig hard enough, you can find *some* evidence that the earth is warming up as a whole. For example, land-based temperature measurements do show a slight warming trend, even over the past 20 years. The problem with these data, as I mentioned before, is that they ignore 70% of the earth's surface, because they ignore what is happening over the oceans. When the entire globe is measured by satellites, no significant warming trend is seen. Thus, to believe that global warming is occurring, you are forced to rely on the *least reliable* data and ignore the *most reliable* data. That is not good scientific practice.

In the end, then, if you want to make reliable statements about how the earth's temperature is changing, you need to look at global indicators. The best global indicator is the satellite temperature data, and they indicate no global warming. In addition, radiosonde balloons (balloons that carry disposable weather-measuring equipment into the air) have been used to measure global temperatures since 1979. These balloon measurements also indicate no significant warming trend over the entire earth. Thus, the two most reliable data sources indicate that there has been no significant warming trend since 1979. The best scientific conclusion to make, then, is that global warming is not happening, at least not in any significant way.

Before we leave this section on global warming, I want to make one more point. Often, the impact of scientific data presented in a graph depends on the *way in which the graph is presented*. For example, look at the following graph:

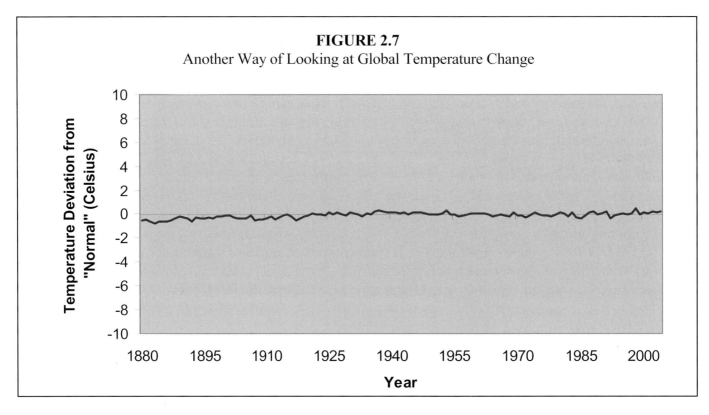

FIGURE 2.7
Another Way of Looking at Global Temperature Change

Believe it or not, this is the *same data* presented in the lower portion of Figure 2.6. What happened to all of the huge ups and downs? What happened to the increase in temperature from 1880 to 1920? Well, it's all still there, but look at the y-axis (vertical scale of numbers) on the graph and compare that to the y-axis on the graph in the lower portion of Figure 2.6. Do you see the difference? In Figure 2.6, the entire range of the y-axis was a total of 1.6 degrees Celsius (from -1.0 $^{\circ}$C to +0.6 $^{\circ}$C is a range of 1.6 $^{\circ}$C). That's a *tiny* range. If the temperature changed 1.6 degrees Celsius, you wouldn't even notice it! Since the graph plots such a tiny range of temperatures, even minuscule changes will be seen. In Figure 2.7, the same data is plotted on a graph with a y-axis spanning 20 degrees Celsius (from -10 $^{\circ}$C to +10 $^{\circ}$C).

The point to this discussion is simple. Whenever you see a graph, look at the scales (both the horizontal x-axis and the vertical y-axis). That way you will know the *range* over which the data is presented. In order to really learn what the data means, you must do this. In this case, by looking at the y-axis in the lower portion of Figure 2.6, you see that the temperature changes are tiny. That helps put the data in perspective.

ON YOUR OWN

2.7 One popular thing to do in American politics is to note that many of the past few years have been some of the warmest ever recorded. This is then used to support the idea that global warming is happening. What is wrong with this kind of argument?

Parts Per Million

Now that I have discussed the idea of global warming in some detail, I want to go back and discuss the unit that was used to measure the concentration of carbon dioxide in the atmosphere for Figure 2.6. Notice that the graph lists the units for the concentration of carbon dioxide as "ppm." What in the world is ppm? It is an abbreviation for **parts per million**.

Parts per million – The number of molecules (or atoms) of a substance in a mixture for every 1 million
molecules (or atoms) in that mixture

In other words, suppose I had a mixture of argon gas and water vapor. Argon is made up of individual atoms, while water is (of course) made of molecules. Now suppose further that I gathered up enough of the mixture so that the total number of water molecules plus argon atoms was exactly 1,000,000. If, out of those 1,000,000 argon atoms and water molecules, 3,123 were argon atoms and the rest were water molecules, the concentration of argon would be 3,123 parts per million.

Now realize, of course, that ppm can be converted so that it is expressed as percent. After all, percent just tells us how many parts exist per hundred. In other words, if I say that the concentration of nitrogen in air is 78%, it means that for every 100 constituents of air, 78 of them will be nitrogen. Thus, 78% just means 78 parts per hundred. How, then, can we relate ppm to percent? Well, to get 1,000,000 parts of a mixture, you just take 100 parts 10,000 times. This tells us the following:

$$1\% = 10,000 \text{ ppm}$$

If you don't understand the reasoning behind this conversion relationship, don't worry. All you have to do is memorize it, and then you can use it.

For example, think for a moment about the concentrations of carbon dioxide listed in Figure 2.6. For 1900, the graph indicates that the concentration of carbon dioxide in the air was 290 ppm. In percent, that would be:

$$\frac{290 \text{ ppm}}{1} \times \frac{1\%}{10,000 \text{ ppm}} = 0.0290\%$$

Notice what I did in order to convert ppm to percent. I simply used the conversion relationship I listed above in the factor-label method. It allowed me to determine that 290 ppm is a really small percentage. This is why ppm is often used instead of percent. In many people's minds, the unit ppm is easier to visualize when concentrations are small. Thus, small concentrations are often listed in terms of ppm.

To make sure you understand the relationship between ppm and percentage, please study the following example:

EXAMPLE 2.1

The concentration of carbon dioxide in the air today is approximately 380 ppm. What is this concentration in percent?

Remember, we know the relationship between ppm and percent. We can therefore just use the factor-label method to figure out the answer.

$$\frac{380 \; \cancel{ppm}}{1} \times \frac{1\%}{10,000 \; \cancel{ppm}} = 0.0380\%$$

The concentration of carbon dioxide in the air today is 0.0380%.

The concentration of oxygen in the air is 21%. What is that concentration in ppm?

Once again, now that we know the relationship, we can convert using the factor-label method.

$$\frac{21 \; \cancel{\%}}{1} \times \frac{10,000 \; ppm}{1 \; \cancel{\%}} = 210,000 \; ppm$$

The concentration of oxygen in the air is 210,000 ppm.

ON YOUR OWN

2.8 The concentration of argon in the air is about 0.9%. What is this in ppm?

2.9 Convert 11 ppm into percent.

<u>Ozone</u>

Oxygen and carbon dioxide are not the only gases that play a critical role in supporting life on earth. Life could not exist at all if it weren't for another gas called **ozone**. As I've mentioned already, the sun provides the earth with almost all the energy necessary to support life. Thus, the light that comes from the sun is a necessary ingredient for the maintenance of life on earth. Some of the light that comes from the sun, however, is harmful to living organisms. This light is called **ultraviolet** (uhl' truh vye' uh lit) **light**, and it is not visible to the human eye.

Ultraviolet light is energetic enough to damage or kill living tissue. If an organism is exposed to too much ultraviolet light, its cells will die at a very high rate. If the cells are killed by the ultraviolet light faster than the organism can replace them, the organism will die. If the exposure is not too great, the organism might be able to survive, but its increased rate of cellular production might result in various forms of illness, including cancer. Thus, in order to support life, the earth must somehow filter out the dangerous ultraviolet light while still allowing other kinds of light from the sun (like visible and infrared light) to reach its surface.

If you think about it for a minute, filtering light is not an easy task. For example, almost everyone has a filter they place in their furnace. The purpose of this filter is to remove dust from the air in their house. The way it works is rather simple. The filter is composed of a mesh that has many tiny holes. If dust particles in the air are too large to get through the holes in the mesh, they are stopped by the filter. If they are smaller than the holes in the mesh of the filter, they pass through the filter and remain in the air. Thus, a filter is good for getting rid of things larger than the holes in the mesh, but it does nothing to stop the things smaller than the holes in the mesh. Now think about this: Light has neither size nor mass. It is pure energy. How in the world is the earth able to filter out something that has neither size nor mass?

Ozone, a molecule composed of three oxygen atoms, makes up this amazing filter. It turns out that ozone is a molecule that breaks down in the presence of the ultraviolet light most damaging to living tissue. This ultraviolet light has just enough energy to break apart one of the bonds that holds the oxygen atoms together. The bond, in order to break, must absorb the ultraviolet light. In other words, when ultraviolet light encounters an ozone molecule, it uses its energy to destroy the ozone molecule instead of harming living tissue. One truly incredible thing about this wonderful filter is that ozone cannot be broken down by visible or infrared light. As a result, they pass right by ozone without interacting with it. So the most damaging ultraviolet light is stopped by ozone, but the kind of light earth needs (visible and infrared light) is allowed to hit the surface of the earth where it is needed by plants and animals! Now please understand that not *all* of the ultraviolet light from the sun is stopped by this filter. Some does end up getting through. As a result, if your skin is exposed to the sun for too long without adequate protection, the ultraviolet light that makes it through the ozone filter can cause a sunburn.

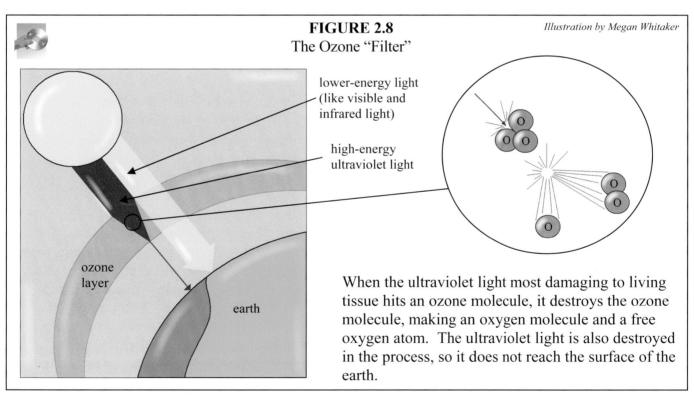

FIGURE 2.8
The Ozone "Filter"

Illustration by Megan Whitaker

lower-energy light (like visible and infrared light)

high-energy ultraviolet light

ozone layer

earth

When the ultraviolet light most damaging to living tissue hits an ozone molecule, it destroys the ozone molecule, making an oxygen molecule and a free oxygen atom. The ultraviolet light is also destroyed in the process, so it does not reach the surface of the earth.

That's not the end of the story, however. Because each ozone molecule is destroyed when it absorbs ultraviolet light, there must be some way of replenishing earth's supply of ozone so that the filtering system will stay intact. This is accomplished through a system of chemical reactions called the "Chapman cycle." Although the Chapman cycle is too complicated for the purposes of this discussion, suffice it to say that ozone is constantly being produced from the earth's supply of oxygen. Thus, not only is there an elegant filtering system that protects us from the sun's harmful rays, but the earth also has a system that ensures the constant renewal of the filter.

The most amazing aspect of the ozone filter hasn't even been presented yet! Although ozone is necessary for life as we know it, ozone is also poisonous to living organisms. If living organisms breathe in ozone at too high a concentration for too long, they suffer illness or even die. So, we must have ozone to protect us from the sun's ultraviolet rays, but we should not breathe it in, because it is toxic. Seems like a contradiction, doesn't it? Well, it would be, except the *Designer* of our planet is a little smarter than you and I. Earth's atmosphere contains plenty of ozone, but most of it exists in a layer ("the ozone layer") 20 to 30 kilometers (12.4 to 18.6 miles) above sea level, where no living organism breathes!

Have you heard about the "hole" that exists in the ozone layer? A large amount of time and money has been spent worrying about this problem. Well, now that you know what ozone in the ozone layer does for us, you might understand why everyone is so worried about it. In the next module, we will look at this ozone "hole" very carefully.

ON YOUR OWN

2.10 One evolutionary theory of how life originated on the planet requires that, at one point, there was no oxygen in the atmosphere. This theory, of course, assumes that the first life form did not breathe oxygen. Since there are organisms today that can exist without breathing oxygen, this is not as fantastic as it may first sound. Based on what you learned in this section, however, what serious objection can you raise against the theory that life originated on an earth with no oxygen in its air?

Before we go on, I want you to think about what you have learned for a moment. Earth just *happens* to have all the gases necessary for life, it just *happens* to have all the right quantities of those gases, and they just *happen* to be in the right place. If nearly any gas other than nitrogen or argon diluted the atmosphere, life could not exist. If too much or too little oxygen were in the air, life could not exist. Similarly, if too much or too little carbon dioxide were in the air, life on earth would not be possible. In addition, not only does life depend on ozone, but it also depends on ozone being far away from the life it is protecting! In addition to all of this, the gases in the air are all replenished when used, keeping their concentrations relatively constant over time!

Now think about one other thing. The air that surrounds the earth is just *one aspect* of the physical environment that makes life possible. There are thousands of aspects of the earth that make it a haven for life. If any one of these aspects were wrong, earth would suddenly be hostile to life. Do you see how wonderfully God's creation proclaims His majesty? The incredible design that exists in the world around us is powerful evidence that this world did not come about by chance. Accidents do not produce the intricacy we see in the air around us. Only intelligent design does! Truly, anyone who understands the science of air must exercise an *enormous* amount of faith to believe that all this occurred by chance!

Air Pollution

Now I can't discuss the air we breathe without discussing air pollution. Air pollution has been a major concern for many, many years, so it is important for us to spend some time studying it. Of course, the pollutants in the air are all part of that extra 1% I labeled as "other gases" in Figure 2.1. In that figure, I list sulfur oxides and nitrogen oxides as a part of these "other gases." The term "sulfur oxides" actually refers to two different gas molecules made when sulfur is burned. In the same way, the term "nitrogen oxides" refers to two different gas molecules that result when nitrogen is burned. Both of these groups of gases are toxic, so they are considered pollutants.

In today's air, sulfur oxides, nitrogen oxides, ozone, and carbon monoxide (muh nok' side) are important pollutants. Sulfur oxides and nitrogen oxides are gases that harm the lungs. Carbon monoxide is a gas that decreases the amount of oxygen that can be delivered to a person's tissues, so it is also a pollutant. Ozone that exists where people can breathe can also cause lung disorders and is therefore considered a pollutant. Finally, airborne lead is a pollutant we were very worried about in the past, but nowadays is virtually nonexistent in the air around us.

It is important to learn a little bit about the major pollutants in the air, so I will discuss each of them briefly. Before I do this, however, I need to stress an important point. Although human activity has increased the concentrations of each of these pollutants, they were already a part of the air long before human activity began increasing their concentrations. This is because *all* these pollutants have natural sources as well as human-made sources. Thus, as I discuss each pollutant, I will point out the human-made sources that create these pollutants, but I will also discuss the natural sources that create these pollutants regardless of human activity. As the discussion progresses, you will see why it is important to realize that there are natural sources for *all* these pollutants.

Let's start our discussion of pollutants with **sulfur oxides**. As I said before, the term "sulfur oxides" refers to two different gases. These gases, sulfur dioxide and sulfur trioxide, are formed when sulfur burns. So, you might think we can easily get rid of these pollutants if we just stop burning sulfur, right? Well, in principle, that's right. In practice, however, it's a lot tougher to keep from burning sulfur. You see, sulfur is a contaminant in all fuels we burn (coal, oil, wood, natural gas, etc.). I will focus my discussion on coal, as it is a major source of sulfur oxides and a major fuel burned all over the world. We burn coal mostly to generate electricity and heat for industry and homes. Well, when we burn the coal, we cannot help but burn the sulfur in the coal as well.

Now it turns out there are methods available to reduce the amount of sulfur contamination in coal. We can use a certain process to, in essence, "clean" much of the sulfur contamination out of coal before we burn it. This strongly reduces the sulfur oxides produced when the coal is burned. This, of course, increases the cost of burning the coal, but it does reduce the amount of pollutants the coal produces when it is burned.

Even though such cleaning processes *reduce* the amount of sulfur in coal, they do not eliminate it. As a result, even very "clean" coal will still produce sulfur oxides when burned. Therefore most coal-burning plants have installed devices in their smokestacks that help clean the sulfur oxides out of the mixture of gases that result from burning coal. These devices, commonly called **scrubbers**, use limestone, which tends to absorb sulfur oxides. In most scrubbers, limestone is mixed with water and sprayed into the gases produced when coal burns. The limestone absorbs a lot (but not all) of the sulfur oxides, forming a wet paste that can be disposed. Scrubbers, then, significantly reduce the amount of sulfur oxides emitted by the smokestacks of coal-burning plants.

Although burning fuels such as coal is the principal *human-made* source of sulfur oxides in the air, there are natural sources as well. One important natural source of sulfur oxides pollution is volcanic activity. When volcanoes erupt, they emit an *enormous* amount of sulfur oxides. For example, in October

2004, Mount Saint Helens (in Washington state) began erupting. This was not the *explosive* eruption Washington experienced in 1980, but the volcano did start emitting steam, ash, and eventually, lava. Over the course of the next few months, the volcano emitted 50 to 250 *tons* of sulfur dioxide *every day*. During that same timeframe, the combined industries of the entire state of Washington emitted only 120 tons of sulfur dioxide each day. During its eruption process, then, Mount Saint Helens was Washington's largest polluter! Other natural sources of sulfur oxides include the oceans, biological decay, and natural forest fires. Scientists estimate that natural sources emit about 80 to 290 million tons of sulfur oxides each year, while human industry emits about 70 to 100 million tons each year.

Nitrogen oxides, like sulfur oxides, are formed when nitrogen burns. Once again, no one purposely burns nitrogen. Nevertheless, nitrogen does get burned as the result of other processes. Automobile, airplane, and lawn mower engines, as well as power plants, burn fuel at very high temperatures. Since this happens in air, there is a lot of nitrogen surrounding these high-temperature systems. Although it is hard to burn nitrogen, the heat causes a tiny fraction of the nitrogen in the air to burn. This results in nitrogen oxides. Thus, engines and power plants are major human-made sources of nitrogen oxides.

As is the case with sulfur oxides, there are also natural sources that emit nitrogen oxides. The heat of volcanoes also produces nitrogen oxides, as does the heat of lightning bolts. In addition, biological decay and the oceans emit nitrogen oxides into the atmosphere. Scientists estimate that these natural sources emit about 20 to 90 million tons of nitrogen oxides into the air each year, while human-made sources are responsible for about 24 million tons of nitrogen oxides being put into the air each year.

Another important pollutant in the air today is **ozone**. Now remember, ozone is critically important to the survival of life on earth. In order to block the ultraviolet light coming from the sun, ozone *must* be in the air. At the same time, however, ozone is a poison. Thus, we *want* a lot of ozone to be in the air; we just don't want to *breathe* it. Thus, we would like to keep the ozone in the ozone layer (where no one is breathing), but we want to *reduce or eliminate* the ozone that exists near the earth's surface. So, ozone is a good thing when it is in the ozone layer, but it is a pollutant when it is near the ground where people are breathing. This is why environmental scientists often use the term **ground-level ozone**. Ground-level ozone is a pollutant, because we can breathe it.

Human activities such as driving, mowing lawns, and even baking bread tend to produce ozone. Basically, any activity that involves heat and air will produce some ozone, because ozone results from the interaction of chemicals in the air aided by energy. Thus, anywhere there is air and the energy necessary to make these interactions occur, there will be ozone. Sunlight also enhances these interactions, so more ground-level ozone is produced in the summer as compared to winter.

Now I want to ask you a question. Stop and answer this question in your mind before you go on. Is the concentration of pollutants in the air today greater than, similar to, or less than the concentration of those pollutants 30 years ago? What do you think? Well, the answer might surprise you. It turns out that *every major pollutant in the air has a lower concentration today than it had 30 years ago!* In fact, there are some pollutants that were a problem 30 years ago but have been basically eliminated today.

Consider, for example, **airborne lead**. Although lead is a solid, small amounts of it can become airborne. Well, as automobiles became popular, engineers realized that adding lead to gasoline improved an automobile's performance. As a result, gasoline companies started adding lead to the gasoline. As time went on, scientists finally realized that some of that lead made it into the air. This was a serious problem, as lead can be toxic in high enough concentrations. In small children, it can affect brain development, impeding intellectual development and causing learning difficulties. In older people, it can cause high blood pressure and kidney problems.

Because of this threat, the U.S. government mandated that automobile manufacturers had to make cars and trucks that ran only on unleaded fuel. As a result of this mandate, all new cars made in the United States after 1976 run only on unleaded gasoline. As time went on, fewer and fewer cars were burning leaded gasoline, and, as a result, airborne lead concentrations plummeted. Today, nearly every car and truck burns unleaded gasoline, and the result is that airborne lead is almost nonexistent in the air around us.

The fact that today's air is cleaner than it was 25 years ago is demonstrated not only by the virtual elimination of airborne lead, but also by the fact that the major measurable pollutants are less concentrated in the air today than in 1975. Consider the data presented in Figure 2.9.   In the top part of the figure, there is a table that lists each pollutant's concentration in both 1975 and 2002.   In the lower part of the figure, the decrease in air pollution is illustrated by showing the current air pollution (red bars) concentrations as a percentage of the levels that existed in 1975.

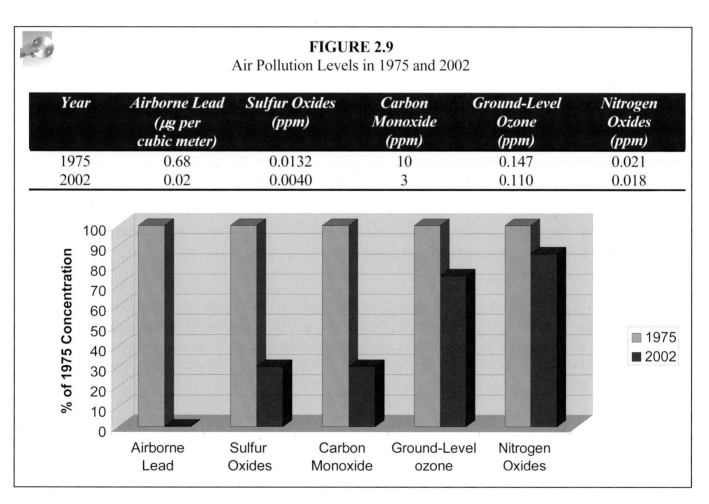

FIGURE 2.9
Air Pollution Levels in 1975 and 2002

Year	Airborne Lead (µg per cubic meter)	Sulfur Oxides (ppm)	Carbon Monoxide (ppm)	Ground-Level Ozone (ppm)	Nitrogen Oxides (ppm)
1975	0.68	0.0132	10	0.147	0.021
2002	0.02	0.0040	3	0.110	0.018

Notice that no matter what pollutant we consider, the concentration is lower today than in 1975. From the table, for example, you can see that sulfur oxides have fallen in concentration from 0.0132 ppm in 1975 to 0.0040 ppm in 2002. The graph illustrates this change in terms of percent. Looking at today's sulfur oxides level, for example, you can see that it is about 30% of what it was in 1975!

What was responsible for these dramatic changes? Well, when scientists began studying air pollution in detail, pollutant levels like those shown in the 1975 part of Figure 2.9 rightly caused the U.S. government great concern about the health and safety of the American people. As a result, the government began instituting regulations aimed at reducing pollutant levels. Consider, for example, the pollutant **carbon monoxide**. This gas is a toxic byproduct of incomplete combustion. Remember, combustion is fire, and when fire burns, it needs oxygen. When there is plenty of oxygen, fire produces carbon dioxide, along with other things such as water vapor. When the amount of oxygen available to fire is scarce, the fire begins producing carbon monoxide instead of carbon dioxide. Whenever fire produces carbon monoxide instead of carbon dioxide, we say that the fire is experiencing **incomplete combustion**. Unlike carbon dioxide, carbon monoxide can be deadly, even at concentrations as low as a few hundred parts per million.

At one time, automobiles were a huge source of carbon monoxide pollution. Automobiles require so much energy that they burn gasoline at a very fast rate. The gasoline is burned so quickly that there is just not enough time to supply it with plenty of oxygen. As a result, incomplete combustion occurs and carbon monoxide is produced. In 1975, however, the **catalytic** (kat' uh lit' ik) **converter** was introduced. This device converts most of the carbon monoxide produced by automobiles into carbon dioxide. Because it reduced the carbon monoxide emissions of automobiles so much, the government quickly mandated that all automobiles must have one. As a result of this mandate, the concentration of carbon monoxide in the air began to decline rapidly, so that today, it is only at 30% of its 1975 concentration.

Now although car exhaust does not produce much carbon monoxide today, it still does produce some. As a result, it is never safe to be in enclosed areas while an automobile is running. Under those conditions, even the small amount of carbon monoxide produced by the automobile will get more and more concentrated until it becomes deadly.

Other regulations have been passed over the years that have reduced air pollution levels. For example, remember the scrubbers I mentioned earlier? They cost industry money, but they have been mandated by the U.S. government, so most industries use them. This is one of the main reasons the concentration of sulfur oxides has plummeted since 1975.

These and other regulations produced many changes. First, they dramatically reduced the concentration of pollutants in the air (as clearly shown in Figure 2.9). Second, they made electricity, manufactured items, and automobiles more expensive. After all, scrubbers on smokestacks cost money. Catalytic converters and engines that use unleaded gasoline efficiently are expensive. As a result, the cost of many things increased significantly over the same period.

Finally, there were some unintended consequences as well. For example, in order to reduce the amount of gasoline burned by people as they drove their cars, the U.S. government began issuing "corporate average fuel economy standards." These standards, often referred to as **CAFE**, regulate the average number of miles an automobile can travel on a single gallon of gasoline. This required the automobile manufacturers to produce automobiles that burned gas more efficiently, which caused less gasoline to be burned, which of course led to less pollution per automobile. Over the years, the government has raised the CAFE standards, further reducing the amount of gasoline an individual car burns.

Now all of that sounds really good, doesn't it? When each car burns less gasoline, not only does it cost less to run, it also pollutes the air less. Unfortunately, however, the results are not all good. One way that automobile manufactures meet the CAFE standards is to make their automobiles lighter, and that makes them less safe. As a result, increasing CAFE standards have also increased the number of traffic fatalities in the United States.

So, the positive effect of the regulations that reduced air pollution was that they did, in fact, lower pollutant levels. The negative effects were higher prices and more traffic fatalities. Were these negative effects worth the positive effects? I think so. The pollutant levels measured in 1975 were significant. If they continued to grow, widespread health problems could have resulted. True, some people died as a result of the regulations, but most analysts agree that the increase in traffic fatalities was still less consequential than the deaths that would have resulted from unchecked pollution.

These days, there is still a constant debate as to whether or not we need even more government regulations to reduce pollutant concentrations even further. On the surface, those who want more regulations seem to have a good argument. After all, who can argue with cleaner air? If government regulations resulted in cleaner air from 1975 to 2002, won't more government regulations result in even cleaner air? Isn't that desirable?

Cleaner air is certainly desirable. However, you have to consider two very important questions. First, you must ask yourself how much benefit we will get as a result of cleaner air. Second, you have to ask yourself how much cost will accompany that benefit. For example, we can further reduce the carbon monoxide levels produced by automobiles by having the government raise the CAFE standards. This will most likely result in more traffic fatalities. Is the benefit worth the cost? That's what must be decided.

This kind of reasoning is often called a **cost/benefit** analysis. When the benefit achieved by a certain action is worth the cost involved, then the action should be taken. If the benefit is not worth the cost, however, the action should not be taken. The problem with applying a cost/benefit analysis to air pollution regulations, however, is that there are many things we do not know.

For example, we do not know what pollutant levels are "safe" for people! About the only way to do this is to experiment with people. For example, we could take a bunch of people and put them in a sealed environment and then start varying the concentrations of pollutants to which they are exposed. If we could do enough studies like that over a long, long period of time, we could determine what concentrations of pollutants are considered "safe." Such experiments, of course, are both immoral and illegal, so they cannot be done.

Even though experiments like that cannot be done on people, scientists have tried to get some idea of what is "safe" by doing other kinds of experiments. Some scientists do those kinds of experiments on animals. They expose animals to different concentrations of pollutants over different lengths of time and see how the animals tolerate the pollutants. Since humans and animals are different, however, such experiments can only give us an idea of what pollutant concentrations are "safe." Other scientists try to study people exposed to certain concentrations of pollutants because of the work they choose to do or the place they live. The scientists then try to understand whether or not those people get sicker than those not exposed to such concentrations of pollutants. Those studies have their own drawbacks, however. As a result, we really do not know for sure how much air pollution is considered "safe," and cannot, therefore, determine how much of a benefit would be derived from a reduction in air pollution.

Also, we know that there are natural sources for all these pollutants. What is very hard to determine, however, is what the concentration of these pollutants would be as a result of *only* those natural sources. Thus, it is hard to figure out what the "natural" concentrations of these pollutants should be. The concentration of sulfur oxides, for example, is 30% of what they were in 1975. How close are we to the "natural" concentration of sulfur oxides? It is difficult to say. For all we know, we could already be quite close.

Applying a cost/benefit analysis to air pollution regulations is also difficult from the cost side. Although we can have a pretty good idea of how much *money* any new air pollution requirement will cost, many of the other costs are totally unexpected. For example, when the government began issuing CAFE standards, no one had considered the effect those regulations would have on automobile safety. Thus, the tragic loss of life associated with these regulations was a *complete surprise*.

The point of this discussion is twofold. First, you must understand that the air you are breathing now is cleaner than it was 30 years ago. Thus, air pollution is certainly *less* of a problem today than it used to be. Second, you can't simply say that cleaner air is desirable. Instead, you have to do cost/benefit analyses to determine whether or not cleaner air is worth the cost. The problem is, these cost/benefit analyses are rather difficult. Therefore, you must be very careful when you approach the subject of air pollution regulations. Past experience has clearly shown that *some* of these regulations are good. It has also shown, however, that for *some* air pollution regulations, the small benefits have not been worth the cost.

Any reasonable discussion of air pollution regulations, therefore, must include a cost/benefit analysis. The next time you hear or read a news story about new air pollution regulations, see if it includes a cost/benefit analysis.

ON YOUR OWN

2.11 Suppose you could institute regulations that would be targeted at one specific air pollutant. Based on the data in Figure 2.9, which air pollutant would be best to target from a cost/benefit point of view?

ANSWERS TO THE "ON YOUR OWN" PROBLEMS

2.1 <u>The water will take the least time to evaporate on the second day</u>. Remember, when humidity is high, there is already a lot of water vapor in the air. Thus, water does not evaporate very quickly. On low humidity days, however, there is little water vapor in the air, so water evaporates quickly.

2.2 <u>You will not see any evaporation from the glass of water</u>. When the relative humidity is 100%, no more water can go into the air, so no net evaporation can occur! Now it turns out that water *will* evaporate from the glass, but water will also condense back into the glass from the air. The rate at which the water evaporates will equal the rate at which it condenses, however, so no *net* evaporation will occur.

2.3 <u>The percentages of nitrogen and oxygen would be less</u>. Think about this one. If there is water in the air, then the total amount of molecules in the air is greater. Well, the percentage of a substance is equal to the amount of that substance divided by the total amount in the mixture times 100. If you just add water vapor to the mixture of gases, you have not increased the amount of nitrogen, for example. Thus, the amount of nitrogen stays the same. However, the total amount of molecules in the mixture increases, because you added water molecules. As a result, when you calculate the percentage, you take the same number for the amount of nitrogen, but you divide by a larger number (for the amount of molecules in the mixture). As a result, the *percentage* of nitrogen goes down.

2.4 <u>The candle would burn dimmer</u>. If there is less air around you, there is also less oxygen around you. With less oxygen, the fire will burn more slowly, making the candle dimmer.

2.5 <u>Plants may grow better when their caretakers talk to them because when someone talks to a plant, he exhales some carbon dioxide on it</u>. This increases the concentration of carbon dioxide in the plant's vicinity, which might make some plants grow better.

2.6 You use the same reasoning here that you used in question 2.3. <u>Since exhaled air has more molecules in it (water vapor and carbon dioxide, for example), the percentage of nitrogen decreases not because the amount of nitrogen decreases, but because the total amount in the mixture increases</u>. Once again, the *amount* of nitrogen is the same in both inhaled and exhaled air. However, since there are more molecules in exhaled air, when you calculate the percentage of nitrogen in exhaled air, you take the same number and divide it by a larger number. This makes a smaller percentage.

2.7 There are at least two problems with this argument. Don't worry if you didn't get both of them. First, <u>studies indicate that average global temperatures in the Middle Ages were warmer than they are now</u>. Thus, even though the *recorded temperatures* are greater now than they have been before, we know it is not warmer now than in earth's past. If the warmer temperatures of the Middle Ages were not due to global warming, how can the current warm period that is actually cooler than the Middle Ages be a result of global warming? The second problem is even more important. <u>Global warming is a long-term effect, and you must therefore use long-term trends in the data to support it</u>. Notice from the lower portion of Figure 2.6 that in the late 1930s and the early 1950s, the temperatures were the warmest ever on record up to that point. However, the next 30 years experienced a long-term cooling trend. As a result, the "hot" years were offset by a number of "cool" years, so there was no long-term temperature change. As a result, the fact that we are experiencing a few years of extra warmth (notice the data from the late 1990s on) means nothing when it comes to global warming. If history is any indication, the earth will experience a cooling trend that will offset these slightly warmer temperatures.

2.8 Remember, we know the relationship between percent and ppm, so we can convert using the factor-label method.

$$\frac{0.9\ \%}{1} \times \frac{10{,}000\ \text{ppm}}{1\%} = 9{,}000\ \text{ppm}$$

The concentration of argon in the air is 9,000 ppm.

2.9 Since we know the relationship between ppm and percent, we can just use the factor-label method to figure out the answer.

$$\frac{11\ \text{ppm}}{1} \times \frac{1\%}{10{,}000\ \text{ppm}} = 0.0011\%$$

A concentration of 11 ppm is equal to 0.0011%.

2.10 No oxygen means no ozone. With no ozone layer, no life form would be able to exist on the surface of the earth. Remember, the earth replenishes its ozone supply from its oxygen supply. With no oxygen, there would be no ozone.

2.11 Nitrogen oxides would be the best pollutant to target, because the concentration of nitrogen oxides is still rather high. Thus, we could probably derive a lot of benefit from reducing nitrogen oxides.   It turns out this is rather hard to do, however, because nitrogen oxides are produced whenever there is a lot of heat and air, and most industries, automobiles, etc., need a lot of heat.

STUDY GUIDE FOR MODULE #2

1. Define the following terms:

a. Humidity
b. Absolute humidity
c. Relative humidity
d. Greenhouse effect
e. Parts per million

2. The temperature is the same at 1 P.M. on two consecutive days. For a person who is outside working, however, the second day feels cooler than the first day. On which day was the relative humidity higher?

3. A child decides to keep his goldfish outside in a small bowl. He has to add water every day to keep the bowl full. On two consecutive days, the temperatures are very similar, but on the first day the relative humidity is 90%, while on the second day it is 60%. On which day will the child add more water to the goldfish bowl?

4. If you put a glass of water outside when the relative humidity is 100%, how quickly will the water evaporate?

5. Why does sweating cool people down?

6. What is the percentage of nitrogen in dry air? What about oxygen?

7. What would be the consequence of removing all the carbon dioxide in earth's air supply?

8. What would be the consequence of removing all the ozone in earth's air supply?

9. What would be the consequence of a sudden increase in the concentration of oxygen in the earth's air supply?

10. Suppose astronomers found another solar system in which there was a sun just like our sun. Suppose further that a planet in this new solar system was just as far from its sun as is earth from our sun. Since the vast majority of energy that planets get comes from their suns, is it reasonable to assume that the new planet would have roughly the same average temperature as that of earth? Why or why not?

11. What makes up the majority of the air we exhale?

12. Do we exhale more carbon dioxide or more oxygen?

13. Do the data indicate any significant global warming?

14. The current concentration of ground-level ozone in the air is about 0.110 ppm. What is that in percent?

15. Suppose you had a sample of air in which the concentration of nitrogen oxides is 0.023%. What would the concentration of nitrogen oxides be if you expressed it in ppm?

16. Is the air cleaner today, or was it cleaner 30 years ago?

17. What is a cost/benefit analysis?

18. What does a catalytic converter do in a car?

19. What does a scrubber do in a smokestack?

20. In the United States, many regulations are aimed at decreasing the amount of ground-level ozone in the air, because ground-level ozone is considered a pollutant. At the same time, many regulations are aimed at increasing the amount of ozone in the ozone layer. Despite the fact that ozone in the ozone layer is the same as ground-level ozone, ozone in the ozone layer is not considered a pollutant. Instead, it is considered an essential substance. Why?

MODULE #3: The Atmosphere

Introduction

In the previous module, I told you about the wonderful mixture of gases we call air. In this module, I will continue that discussion, but I want to discuss air in its larger context. Instead of discussing the makeup, properties, and contaminants in the air itself, I will now talk about earth's air supply as a whole. When looked at in this way, we call earth's air supply the **atmosphere**.

> Atmosphere – The mass of air surrounding a planet

Since earth is a planet (of course), the mass of air surrounding earth is called "earth's atmosphere."

Atmospheric Pressure

The first thing to realize about the atmosphere is that it presses down on the earth and all its inhabitants. Remember, air has mass, and that mass is above us. If you put a heavy weight on your shoulders, it presses down on you, doesn't it? Well, the atmosphere can be thought of as a heavy weight, pressing down on us and everything else it contacts. Now, of course, not all the atmosphere's weight is pressing down on any one thing. After all, the weight of the atmosphere is distributed across the entire planet. Nevertheless, if you were to weigh a column of air measuring 1 inch by 1 inch from sea level to the top of earth's atmosphere, you would find that it weighs 14.7 pounds. What does that mean? It means that at sea level, the atmosphere exerts an average of 14.7 pounds of weight on every square inch it touches!

Think about that for a moment. At sea level, every square inch of the earth is being pressed down with an average weight of 14.7 pounds. What does that mean? Well, suppose you were standing at sea level. Depending on your build, each of your shoulders is about 3 inches wide by 4 inches long. This gives each shoulder an area (length times width) of 12 square inches. This means that on each of your shoulders, the atmosphere is pressing down with a weight of 12 x 14.7, or about *176 pounds!* This pressure, called **atmospheric pressure**, is exerted on all things that come into contact with earth's atmosphere.

> Atmospheric pressure - The pressure exerted by the atmosphere on all objects within it

Now please note that the weights I am talking about here are averages. Depending on weather conditions, the atmospheric pressure can be higher or lower than 14.7 pounds per square inch. However, at sea level, that is the *average* amount of atmospheric pressure.

Now wait a minute, you might think. It certainly doesn't *feel* like I have 176 pounds pressing down on each of my shoulders! It doesn't *feel* that way because there is equal pressure pushing on you from all sides, including from within! How does that help? Well, suppose I tied two ropes to a rock and asked two equally strong people to pull on the ropes in opposite directions. Would the rock move? Of course not! The two people pulling in opposite directions would cancel each other out. In the same way, the pressure pushing on you in one direction is canceled by pressure pushing on you in the opposite direction. The net effect is that you do not *feel* any pressure. Nevertheless, the pressure is there. To see that it is there, perform the following experiment.

EXPERIMENT 3.1
Atmospheric Pressure

Supplies:

- Stove
- Frying pan
- Two empty, 12-ounce aluminum cans (like soda pop cans)
- Two bowls
- Water
- Ice cubes
- Tongs
- Eye protection such as goggles or safety glasses

Introduction: This experiment will demonstrate the fact that the atmosphere actually does exert pressure on everything it touches.

Procedure:

1. Put a small amount of water in each aluminum can. You should use only enough to cover the bottom of the can with a small amount of water. The more water you use, the longer the experiment will take, and the less dramatic the effect.
2. Place the two aluminum cans in the frying pan so that they stand up.
3. Put the frying pan on the stove and turn the heat up to "high." This will heat up the water in the cans.
4. While you are waiting for the water in the cans to heat up, fill each bowl half full of water.
5. Place a few ice cubes in each bowl so that the water becomes ice cold.

6. Wait for steam to start rising out the opening of each can. That will tell you the water inside is boiling vigorously.
7. Once a steady stream of steam is coming out of each can, use the tongs to grab one can and place it upright in one of the bowls of water.
8. Note what happens.
9. Use the tongs to grab the other can and place it *upside down* in the bowl of water.
10. Note what happens.
11. Clean up your mess.

What happened in your experiment? Well, when you put the first can in the water upright, nothing exciting should have happened. The can obviously cooled off, and the water got warmer, but there should have been no noticeable change. However, when you put the second can in the water upside down, the can should have crumpled noticeably. Depending on how much water you put in the can, how long you let it boil, and how cold the water in the bowl was, it might have crumpled only a little, or it might have really been crushed.

What explains the results of the experiment? Well, remember that the air around you is exerting pressure on everything it touches, including the cans. The cans do not crumple from this pressure, however, because there is air *inside* the cans as well. The air outside each can pushes *in* on the can, and the air inside the can pushes *out* on the can. The pressure from the air outside is counteracted by the pressure from the air inside. As a result, the can does not crumple. This is, in fact, why you don't feel air pressure pushing in on you. The air inside your body is pushing *out* on you, and the air outside your body is pushing *in* on you. Thus, the air pressure inside your body counteracts the air pressure outside your body.

In the experiment, we changed this situation a bit. The results, however, depended on *how* we changed the situation. You see, as the water boiled, the steam rising from the boiling water pushed the air out of each can. Thus, once a steady stream of steam came billowing out of the cans, each can was mostly full of steam and had only a little air inside. The steam exerted pressure, however, so the cans did not crumple, because the pressure of the steam pushing out on the cans still counteracted the atmospheric pressure pushing in on the cans.

When you placed the first can upright in the water, the steam rapidly turned back into liquid, but as it did so, air was able to rush into the can through the opening in the top. Thus, steam was replaced by air, which means that the pressure being exerted in the can by the steam was replaced with pressure being exerted by the air that came inside the can. As a result, the pressure pushing out from the inside of the can did not change much. This meant that the air pressure pushing in on the can from the outside was still counteracted by pressure pushing out from the inside of the can, so the can did not crumple.

When you placed the second can upside down into the second bowl, the steam once again rapidly condensed into liquid. Unlike what happened with the first can, however, air could not rush in to replace the steam, because the opening of the can was under water. As a result, there was little air pressure inside the can. This meant that there wasn't much pressure counteracting the pressure being exerted on the can by the air outside. Since there was nothing to push against the air pressing in on the can, the pressure exerted by the air outside the can crushed it. Figure 3.1 illustrates this effect.

FIGURE 3.1

Air Pressure in the Cans Used In Experiment 3.1

Illustration by Megan Whitaker

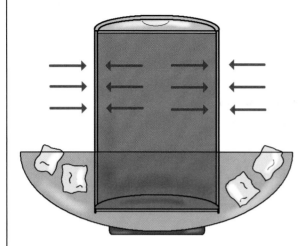
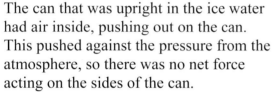
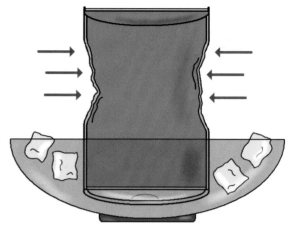

The can that was upright in the ice water had air inside, pushing out on the can. This pushed against the pressure from the atmosphere, so there was no net force acting on the sides of the can.

The can that was upside down in the ice water had very little air inside. As a result, there was little to push against the pressure from the atmosphere, so the atmosphere crumpled the can.

If you were very observant while you were cleaning up your mess, you might have noticed something. When you pulled the crumpled can out of the water, you might have seen water rushing out of the can. That's because the can partly filled with water as it crumpled. Why? Once again, it's because of air pressure. As the steam condensed, there was very little pressure inside the can. However, the atmosphere was exerting pressure on everything, including the water in the bowl. Since there was pressure on the water in the bowl, water was pushed into the can, where there was very little pressure.

Now think about that situation for a moment. Imagine if you had used something strong enough to stand up to atmospheric pressure. After all, an aluminum can is pretty flimsy. You can crush one with your bare hands, can't you? Suppose you used something stronger that could hold up to the atmospheric pressure without crumpling – perhaps a tube made out of thick glass. What would happen then?

Think about it. The pressure of the atmosphere pushes down on the surface of the water. If there is no pressure in the thick glass tube, water will be pushed into the tube. However, as the water level rises in the tube, the *weight* of the water starts pushing down. The higher the water level in the tube, the heavier the weight of the water. Eventually, the system would reach a point where the weight of the water in the tube equals the force with which the atmosphere is pressing on the surface of the water. At that point, what would happen? The water would stop rising. Think about it. The atmosphere pressed down on the surface of the water, which pushed water *up* the tube. However, once the weight of the water began pushing *down* with the same force, the force exerted by the atmosphere would be counteracted, and there would be no net force pushing the water up the tube. This is illustrated in Figure 3.2.

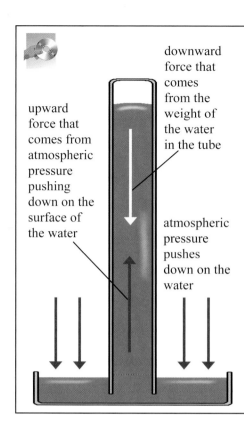

upward force that comes from atmospheric pressure pushing down on the surface of the water

downward force that comes from the weight of the water in the tube

atmospheric pressure pushes down on the water

FIGURE 3.2
A Barometer

Illustration by Megan Whitaker

In this drawing, a tube with no air inside is inverted over a pool of water. Since the atmosphere is pressing down on the pool, and since there is no air exerting pressure inside the tube, water is forced up the tube. However, as the water rises, its weight starts pushing down. This fights the force being exerted by the atmosphere, which is pushing water up the tube. As the amount of water in the tube increases, the weight increases. This increases the force pushing down against atmospheric pressure. At some point, the water in the tube gets high enough so that the weight pushing down is equal to the force with which atmospheric pressure is pushing up. At that point, the water stops rising in the tube.

This is the principle behind a barometer, an instrument used to measure atmospheric pressure. Rather than water, however, most barometers use mercury, because a given volume of mercury weighs significantly more than the same volume of water.

Now think a bit more about this situation. What would happen if the amount of pressure exerted by the atmosphere increased? If that happened, there would be more force pushing down on the surface of the water, which would mean there would be more force pushing water up the tube. As a result, water would rise in the tube until there was enough extra weight to counteract the extra force exerted by the atmosphere. On the other hand, if the pressure exerted by the atmosphere were to decrease, there would be less force pushing down on the surface of the water, which means there would be less force pushing water up the tube. As a result, the water level in the tube would lower.

What do we have here, then? We have an instrument that is sensitive to atmospheric pressure. The more pressure exerted by the atmosphere, the higher the water level in the tube. Such an instrument is called a **barometer** (buh rahm' uh ter).

Barometer - An instrument used to measure atmospheric pressure

Since atmospheric pressure changes due to changing weather patterns, this is a useful instrument for tracking and predicting the weather.

Now most barometers do not use water. This is because water-based barometers must be tall. Remember, the water level will stop rising when the force exerted by the weight of the water is equal to the force being exerted by the atmosphere. Well, average atmospheric pressure at sea level exerts 14.7 pounds for every square inch. A square-inch column of water would have to be just over 33¾ *feet* (10.3 meters) tall to exert that amount of force. Thus, a water-based barometer would have to use a tube that is more than 33 feet tall. That would be rather hard to work with!

Typically, a barometer uses mercury as its liquid. This very dense liquid is toxic, but it rises only 76 cm (29.9 inches) in a barometer exposed to average atmospheric pressure. As a result, a barometer that uses mercury is easier to work with than one that uses water.

At this point, I need to mention the units used to measure atmospheric pressure. It turns out that there are many, many units we use for this purpose. When I originally mentioned atmospheric pressure, I gave its "average" value at sea level as 14.7 pounds per square inch. In many applications, the measurement of atmospheric pressure is made based on how much weight it exerts over a certain area. Thus, 14.7 pounds per square inch means that on every square inch the atmosphere touches, it exerts 14.7 pounds. This number changes based both on altitude and weather conditions, but 14.7 pounds per square inch is a good average at sea level.

Now when you look at a weather report, atmospheric pressure will sometimes be listed as "barometric pressure." In such reports, it is usually not given in pounds per square inch. It is usually reported in terms of inches. What they are reporting, then, is how high the mercury in the tube of the barometer is. If the height of mercury in the tube is less than 29.9 inches, atmospheric pressure is lower than average; if it is higher than 29.9 inches, atmospheric pressure is higher than average. Of course, since this method of reporting on atmospheric pressure simply involves measuring the height of mercury in the tube, we could also report it in metric units. Usually, the metric measurement is listed as millimeters of mercury, abbreviated as **mmHg** (Hg is the symbol chemists use for mercury). In those units, average atmospheric pressure is 760 mmHg.

Since we often worry about the atmospheric pressure only in terms of whether it is above or below the average sea-level atmospheric pressure, there is yet another unit we can use. This unit, called the **atmosphere** (abbreviated "atm") is very easy to compare to the average sea-level atmospheric pressure. When the atmospheric pressure is 1.0 atm, it is at its average sea-level value of 14.7 pounds per square inch. If the pressure is less than 1.0 atm, you know that the atmospheric pressure is less than its average sea-level value. For example, an atmospheric pressure of 0.9 atm indicates that the atmospheric pressure is only 90% of its average sea-level value. In the same way, a value of 1.1 atm indicates that atmospheric pressure is 110% of the average sea-level value.

ON YOUR OWN

3.1 In general, should atmospheric pressure increase or decrease as altitude increases?

3.2 The atmospheric pressure is 1.1 atm. Which of the following values for atmospheric pressure would you see in the weather report: 29.9 inches, 32.9 inches, or 28.1 inches?

The Layers of Earth's Atmosphere

One thing you have to realize about earth's atmosphere is that the mixture of gases we discussed in the previous module applies only to a certain region of the atmosphere. You see, the atmosphere can be divided into two general layers called the **homosphere** (hoh' muh sfear) and the **heterosphere** (het' uh ruh sfear).

Homosphere – The lower layer of earth's atmosphere, which exists from ground level to roughly 80 kilometers (50 miles) above sea level

Heterosphere – The upper layer of earth's atmosphere, which exists higher than roughly 80 kilometers (50 miles) above sea level

The air we breathe, of course, comes from the homosphere. Thus, the mixture of gases we discussed in Module #2 is the composition of the air in the homosphere. In fact, that's where the term "homosphere" comes from. You see, the air in the homosphere is uniform in its composition. The prefix "homo" means "same"; thus, the homosphere contains air that has the same composition, regardless of where you are in the homosphere.

Now please realize that when I say "composition," I am talking about the percentages of each gas in the mixture. Thus, all air in the homosphere is 78% nitrogen, 21% oxygen, and 1% many other gases. The *amount* of air in the homosphere does change, however. The higher you go in the homosphere, the less air there is. In other words, the higher the altitude, the "thinner" the air. Regardless of *how much* air exists at a given altitude in the homosphere, however, it is always 78% nitrogen, 21% oxygen, and 1% other gases.

What about the heterosphere? Well, the prefix "hetero" means "different," so you can bet that the air in the heterosphere is not uniform. In fact, the composition of the air in the heterosphere actually depends on altitude. There is little nitrogen or argon in the heterosphere. In general, the lower portion of the heterosphere (altitudes of 80 kilometers to 965 kilometers) is predominantly made up of oxygen. At higher altitudes (965 kilometers to 2,415 kilometers), the heterosphere is dominated by helium, and the highest portion of the heterosphere (2,415 kilometers and above) is dominated by hydrogen.

Now remember, the *total amount* of air decreases with increasing altitude. By the time you reach the heterosphere, the air is *very* thin. Thus, there is not much air in the heterosphere, but what little exists is predominantly oxygen at altitudes of roughly 80 km to 965 km, predominantly helium from roughly 965 km to 2,415 km, and predominantly hydrogen above roughly 2,415 km.

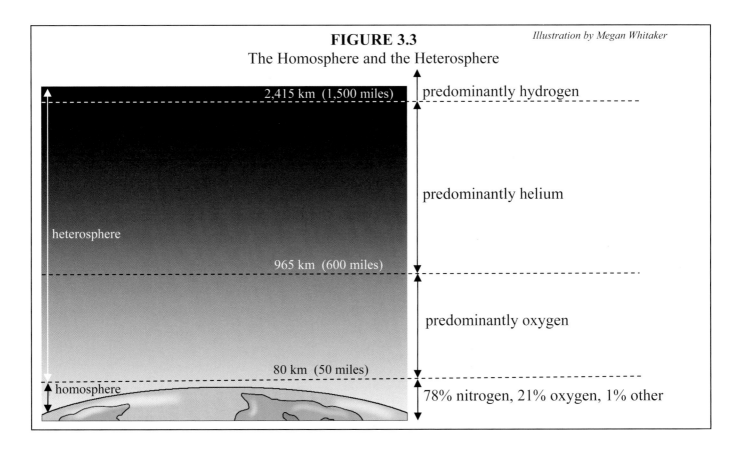

FIGURE 3.3
Illustration by Megan Whitaker
The Homosphere and the Heterosphere

2,415 km (1,500 miles) — predominantly hydrogen

predominantly helium

heterosphere

965 km (600 miles)

predominantly oxygen

80 km (50 miles)

homosphere — 78% nitrogen, 21% oxygen, 1% other

ON YOUR OWN

3.3 In chemistry, mixtures are classified as being either *heterogeneous* or *homogeneous*. Based on what you learned about the difference between the heterosphere and homosphere, classify milk as a heterogeneous or homogeneous mixture. What about Italian salad dressing?

3.4 If an airplane travels at altitudes of over 4 kilometers, it is required to have a special oxygen supply for the pilot. As you just learned, however, that altitude is well within the homosphere, where the air is 21% oxygen. Why, then, does the pilot need a special oxygen supply at this altitude?

<u>The Homosphere</u>

Although the composition of air is essentially the same no matter where you are in the homosphere, many other characteristics of the homosphere change with altitude. As a result, we can further divide the homosphere into three regions: the **troposphere** (troh' puh sfear), the **stratosphere** (stra' tuh sfear), and the **mesosphere** (meez' uh sfear).

<u>Troposphere</u> – The region of the atmosphere that extends from ground level to roughly 11 kilometers (7 miles) above sea level

<u>Stratosphere</u> – The region of the atmosphere that spans altitudes of roughly 11 kilometers to 48 kilometers (30 miles)

<u>Mesosphere</u> – The region of the atmosphere that spans altitudes of roughly 48 kilometers to 80 kilometers (50 miles)

The boundaries between these regions and the other regions of the atmosphere are given their own names. The **tropopause** (troh' puh pawz) is the boundary between the troposphere and the stratosphere, while the **stratopause** (strat' uh pawz) separates the stratosphere and the mesosphere, and the **mesopause** (meez' uh pawz) delineates the mesosphere from the heterosphere.

What are the differences between these layers? Well, there are actually many differences, so we will discuss each of these regions individually. However, I can tell you one general difference that exists between these layers. The amount of air in these regions decreases significantly as the altitude increases. In other words, the air is thinner in the stratosphere than in the troposphere, and the air in the mesosphere is even thinner. Even *within* a region of the homosphere, the air thins considerably with increasing altitude.

Now remember that the atmosphere exerts pressure because of the amount of air weighing down on an object. Since the amount of air in the atmosphere decreases with increasing altitude, the pressure the air exerts decreases as well. As a result, air pressure decreases with increasing altitude.

The troposphere, often called earth's "weather layer," is the region of the atmosphere that contains almost all the weather phenomena such as clouds, rain, snow, storms, lightning, hail, and the like. Because of the fact that the amount of air decreases significantly with increasing altitude, the vast majority of earth's air supply exists in this region. In fact, about ¾ of all earth's air supply exists within the troposphere. Even within the troposphere itself, the amount of air varies significantly with altitude. For example, the peak of Mount Everest is 8.9 kilometers (5.5 miles) above sea level. At that altitude (which is still in the troposphere), the amount of air is only about a third of what exists at sea level. Because of this fact, mountain climbers who climb Mount Everest (and other mountains) must bring their own oxygen supply.

Even at more common altitudes, you can notice that the amount of air decreases with increasing altitude. For example, athletes who are used to playing their sport at low altitudes find it much more difficult to play the same sport in cities like Denver, Colorado, where the elevation is approximately 1 mile above sea level. This is because the amount of air at that altitude is 90% of the amount at sea level, so the athletes must breathe harder to get the amount of oxygen to which they are accustomed.

The troposphere is also characterized by a steady drop in temperature as altitude increases. In general, for every kilometer you increase in altitude, the temperature decreases by about 6.4 degrees Celsius. Since the term "gradient" refers to a gradual change, this effect is often called the **temperature gradient** of the troposphere. This temperature gradient is responsible for snow existing on the upper parts of a mountain even in the summertime. By the time you reach altitudes of about 5 kilometers, the temperature is easily 30 degrees Celsius lower than the temperature at sea level. Since summer temperatures are usually in the range of 25-30 degrees Celsius, and since water freezes at 0 degrees Celsius, you can see that even on a summer day, the temperature at altitudes of 5 km stays well below the freezing point of water. By the time you reach the tropopause, the air is so thin and cold that an unprotected person would quickly lose consciousness and die.

FIGURE 3.4
Mount McKinley

Photo by Kathleen J. Wile

Despite the fact that this photograph was taken in the summer (note the green grass in the foreground), the mountain in the background is still covered with snow and ice because of the altitude.

The stratosphere, which is directly above the tropopause, has completely different characteristics from the troposphere. Virtually no weather phenomena exist there. The very highest clouds might reach the very lowest layers of the stratosphere, but that's about it. In addition, there is virtually no water vapor in this region of the atmosphere (or any higher regions, for that matter).

What you do find in the lower portions of the stratosphere (as well as the upper portions of the troposphere) are strong, steady winds that make up **jet streams**.

<u>Jet streams</u> – Narrow bands of high-speed winds that circle the earth, blowing from west to east

Winds in the jet streams can blow at speeds of up to 400 kilometers per hour (250 miles per hour)! Since these winds blow at the top of or above the clouds, they do affect the weather significantly. They tend to steer storms and affect which parts of the earth experience high atmospheric pressure or low atmospheric pressure.

One interesting characteristic of the stratosphere is that, unlike the troposphere, temperature actually *increases* with increasing altitude. In other words, once you reach the stratosphere, it actually starts getting warmer the higher you go. Thus, the stratosphere has a temperature gradient (steady change in temperature), but its temperature gradient is precisely *opposite* that of the troposphere! Although the temperatures vary with the season, the lower part of the stratosphere is usually somewhere around -65 degrees Celsius (-85 degrees Fahrenheit) and the temperature increases steadily to about 3 degrees Celsius (37 degrees Fahrenheit) by the time you reach the stratopause.

Above the stratopause (in the mesosphere), the air is very thin. Nevertheless, it is thick enough to protect earth from space rocks. When you see meteors (some people call them "falling stars"), you are seeing rocks from space entering the mesosphere and burning up due to their interactions with the air. In addition, the temperature gradient in the mesosphere is reversed as compared to what it was in the stratosphere. In other words, the temperature *decreases* with increasing altitude. By the time you reach the mesopause, the temperature is nearly -100 degrees Celsius (-150 degrees Fahrenheit).

You might be wondering why the temperature gradient reverses in the stratosphere and then again in the mesosphere. Remember, the temperature decreases with increasing altitude in the troposphere, increases with increasing altitude in the stratosphere, and then decreases with increasing altitude in the mesosphere. Well, it turns out that there is a good reason for this, and we will discuss it soon.

Interestingly enough, different types of airplanes tend to fly in different regions of the homosphere. You see, when you travel through the air, it resists your motion. This is often called **air resistance**, and the faster you travel, the more important air resistance becomes. Because the air is thinner the higher you go, airplanes burn less fuel flying through the air at high altitudes. In addition, airplane engines run more efficiently when the surrounding air is at a lower temperature, so the higher the plane is in the troposphere, the more efficiently its engines run. At the same time, however, airplanes burn a *lot* of fuel as they climb, because they are fighting earth's gravitational pull. In the end, most commercial airplanes fly at altitudes of 8 km to 13 km. At those altitudes, the fuel burned in order to reach the altitude is less than the fuel saved because of the thinner air at that altitude. Thus, most commercial (and private) airplanes fly in the troposphere. Since the amount of air resistance an object experiences depends on its speed, however, very fast airplanes (like supersonic jets) must fly in extremely thin air in order to travel most efficiently. Thus, they often fly in the stratosphere.

Most of what I have discussed is summarized in Figure 3.5. On the left side of the figure, the approximate altitudes of the atmospheric layers are shown. On the right side, sample temperatures are given. Notice how the temperature decreases with increasing altitude in the troposphere, then increases with increasing altitude in the stratosphere, and then decreases again with increasing altitude in the mesosphere. Notice also in the figure that the ozone layer is in the stratosphere. I will discuss more about that later on in this module.

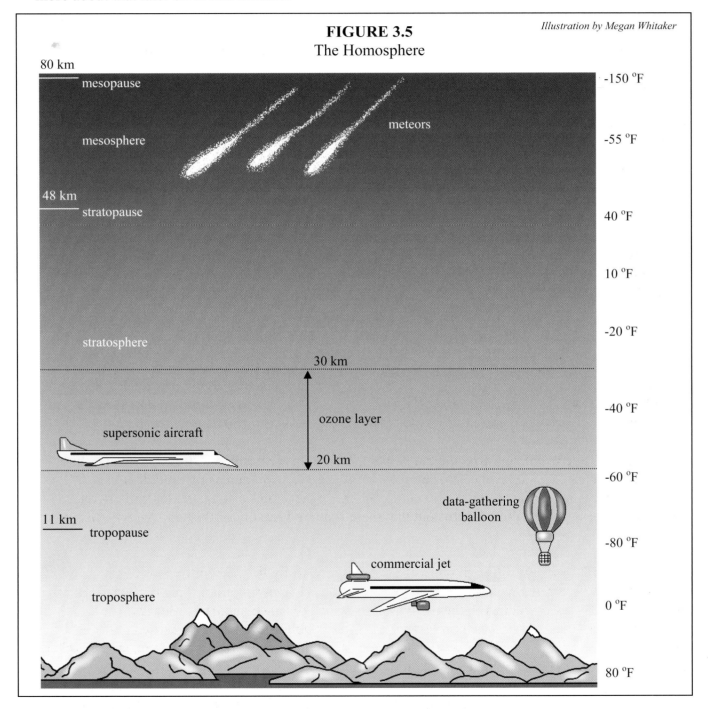

FIGURE 3.5
The Homosphere

Illustration by Megan Whitaker

80 km

mesopause — -150 °F

mesosphere   meteors — -55 °F

48 km

stratopause — 40 °F

— 10 °F

— -20 °F

stratosphere

30 km

ozone layer — -40 °F

supersonic aircraft

20 km

— -60 °F

data-gathering balloon

11 km — -80 °F

tropopause

commercial jet

troposphere

— 0 °F

80 °F

ON YOUR OWN

3.5 A supersonic jet travels in the stratosphere. If such a plane were flying over a region experiencing thunderstorms, how would the supersonic jet be affected?

3.6 Water freezes at 32 degrees Fahrenheit. Suppose you were able to watch a sealed vial of water travel up through the homosphere. It would freeze once it got 5 to 7 kilometers high. Would the frozen water ever melt as the vial traveled farther up? If so, where would this happen?

What Is Temperature?

Now that you know a little bit about the atmosphere, you need to know why the temperature gradient exists and why it reverses twice in the homosphere. In order to understand that, however, you really need to know what temperature measures. Most people think that temperature measures heat. They think this because as temperature gets higher, we feel hotter. Although that is certainly true, it does not follow that temperature measures heat. To understand what temperature really measures, perform the following experiment.

EXPERIMENT 3.2
Seeing the Effect of Changing Temperature

Supplies:

♦ Ice
♦ Water
♦ Plastic bottle (The best volume would be 1 quart or 1 liter, but any size will work.)
♦ Balloon
♦ Bowl
♦ Eye protection such as goggles or safety glasses

Introduction: In this experiment, you will see what happens to air when its temperature increases. This will help you understand what temperature really measures.

Procedure:

1. Fill the bowl about ¾ full of water and ice. There should be enough ice so there will still be ice left in 5 minutes.
2. Take the lid off the bottle. Hold the bottle in the ice water for about 5 minutes, so that the bottle gets cold. Try to keep as much of the bottle as possible in contact with the water. You probably can accomplish this best by tilting the bottle so that it lies in the bowl. DO NOT allow any water to get in the bottle, despite the fact that there is no lid on it.
3. Stand the bottle up in the bowl so that at least part of it is still in contact with the ice water.
4. Place the balloon on the opening of the bottle so that the neck of the balloon forms an airtight seal around the top of the bottle. The seal between the bottle and the balloon must be airtight, or this experiment will not work.
5. Take the bottle out of the bowl and set it on the counter.
6. Empty the bowl of its ice water and let hot water from the tap run until it gets as hot as possible.
7. Once the water is as hot as it can get, fill the bowl ¾ full with the hot water.
8. Stand the bottle in the bowl so that it is in contact with the hot water for a few minutes. What happens? Draw a "before and after" picture in your lab notebook.
9. Clean up your mess and put everything away.

What does this experiment show? Well, many science books use this kind of experiment to show that things tend to expand as the temperature increases. While this is certainly true, it also demonstrates what temperature really measures. You see, by sealing the bottle with the balloon when it was cold, you trapped a lot of cold air in the bottle. As the air's temperature was increased by the hot water, the air expanded, inflating the balloon. To understand temperature, you need to understand *why* the air expanded.

Since you cannot see the atoms and molecules in the air, it may be hard to believe this, but the molecules in the air are actually moving around at very high speeds. Why do they move around like that? They do so because they have a lot of energy. Believe it or not, all substances you see have molecules that are constantly moving. In liquids, the molecules move around more slowly than those in the air, but they still move around. In solid substances, the molecules cannot move around, but they do vibrate back and forth. Now of course, you do not see this motion because you cannot see the molecules involved. Nevertheless, the motion is still there.

Now what are you doing when you heat something up? You are *adding energy* to it. So when you placed the bottle in the hot water, the energy in the hot water started flowing into the bottle. Believe it or not, that's actually what **heat** is.

Heat – Energy that is transferred as a consequence of temperature differences

So heat is really energy that flows from one object to another. As energy flowed from the hot water to the bottle, two things happened. The bottle's temperature increased, and the water's temperature decreased.

What happened to that energy? Well, as it flowed into the bottle, it was picked up by the molecules that made up the bottle as well as the molecules that made up the air in the bottle. What happened when these molecules absorbed this energy? They began to move faster. Since the bottle is a solid object, the molecules that made up the bottle began vibrating faster. The molecules that made up the air in the bottle, however, started moving around faster.

Now what happened as a result of the molecules in the air moving faster? Well, think about an individual molecule in the air that is inside the bottle. As the molecule moves, it eventually reaches the wall of the bottle or the balloon. At that point, the molecule cannot move *through* the bottle's wall or the balloon, so it must bounce off the bottle's wall or the balloon and change direction. So, on a molecular level, there are billions and billions of molecules bouncing off the walls of the bottle and off the balloon. Now, as these molecules get more and more energy, they start traveling faster and faster. As a result, when they hit the bottle's wall or the balloon, they start hitting harder and harder. They also start hitting more and more frequently, because they move from place to place more quickly.

Think about this for a minute. If the molecules start hitting the bottle's wall and the balloon harder and faster, what will happen? Whatever the molecules strike will start to bulge outward, because of the increased violence of the collisions. Well, the balloon can bulge out much more easily than can the walls of the bottle, so the balloon begins to bulge. Thus, it looks like the balloon is inflating, when in fact, it is simply bulging out as the result of more violent and more frequent collisions by the molecules in the air.

So the molecules that make up a substance are constantly moving. As you add energy to those molecules, they start moving around faster and faster. This is actually why a solid substance will melt as you heat it, and if you continue to heat the liquid, it will eventually become a gas. Remember, the molecules that make up a solid can only vibrate back and forth. As you heat up the substance, you add energy to the molecules, and they begin to vibrate faster and faster as well as farther and farther back and forth. The more you heat the solid, the more violent the vibrations become. Eventually, the vibrations become so violent that the molecules break free of the forces that were keeping them from moving around. As a result, the molecules begin to move around, and the substance becomes a liquid! If you keep heating up the liquid, the molecules starting moving faster and faster as well as getting farther and farther apart. Eventually, the molecules move so quickly and are so far apart that they form a gas!

Thus, changes from solid to liquid to gas (and changes the other way as well) are due to changes in the energy of motion of the molecules involved. In addition, this is why things tend to expand when they are heated. The farther and faster a substance's molecules move, the more volume they will occupy.

 The multimedia CD has an animation that illustrates this discussion of heat.

How does all this apply to temperature? Well, when I put a thermometer in a substance, the molecules of that substance begin striking the thermometer. At the same time, the molecules that make up the thermometer are moving as well. Thus, collisions will be occurring between the molecules in the thermometer and the molecules of the substance that the thermometer is in. If the molecules of the substance are moving faster than those of the thermometer, energy will be transferred from the molecules of the substance to those of the thermometer. As a result, the liquid in the thermometer heats up and expands. This causes the column of liquid to rise, and we see a high temperature.

If, on the other hand, the molecules of the thermometer are moving faster than those of the substance, energy will go from the thermometer to the substance. As a result, the thermometer cools down, and the liquid in the thermometer contracts. This causes the liquid column to shrink, and we read a low temperature. Thus, a thermometer really measures *the average speed at which the molecules of a substance are moving.* Since the speed of the molecules is directly related to their energy, we say that a thermometer measures the energy of the molecules in a substance. That's what temperature is!

<u>Temperature</u> – A measure of the energy of random motion in a substance's molecules

So, in the end, temperature does not measure heat (energy that is transferred); instead, it measures the motional energy of the molecules in a substance.

If you think about it, this explains why you get hot when the temperature is high and get cold when the temperature is low. When the temperature is high, the molecules in the air colliding with your skin have much more energy than the molecules in your skin. As a result, energy is transferred from the air to you. This makes you hotter. When the temperature is low, the molecules in your skin have more energy than the molecules in the air colliding with your skin. As a result, energy is transferred from you to the air, and you end up getting colder.

ON YOUR OWN

3.7 Two cold bricks are put in contact with one another. The first one has a temperature of -1.00 degrees Celsius, and the other has a temperature of -10.00 degrees Celsius. Is there any heat in this two-block system?

3.8 A thermometer reads 25.00 degrees Celsius. Suppose you put that thermometer into a liquid, and the thermometer reading increases to 80.17 degrees Celsius. A bright observer notes that the temperature of the substance was actually a tad higher than 80.17 degrees Celsius the instant the thermometer was placed in it. Is the observer correct? Why or why not?

The Temperature Gradient in the Homosphere

Now that you know what temperature really measures, you can finally learn why there is a temperature gradient in the homosphere. Remember, the amount of air in the atmosphere decreases with increasing altitude. Now one reason the atmosphere is warm is the greenhouse effect, as discussed in Module #2. As you increase altitude, the amount of greenhouse gases decreases, so there are fewer molecules absorbing energy. As a result, the energy content of the troposphere *decreases* with increasing altitude. Since the energy content of the troposphere decreases with increasing altitude, and since temperature is really a measure of the energy in the molecules of a substance, the temperature decreases with increasing altitude.

Wait a minute, though. When you reach the stratosphere, the temperature gradient changes. Instead of decreasing with increasing altitude, the temperature begins increasing with increasing altitude in the stratosphere. Why is that? Does the amount of air increase in the stratosphere? No, not at all. The amount of air in the stratosphere still decreases with increasing altitude. Something else is responsible for the change in the temperature gradient. That something else is the ozone layer. Even though the *total* amount of air decreases with increasing altitude, the ozone layer introduces an increase in the amount of one particular gas: ozone.

Remember, ozone protects us from the ultraviolet rays of the sun by absorbing them before they reach the planet's surface. Well, when it absorbs ultraviolet rays, the ozone absorbs the ultraviolet rays' energy as well. Thus, even though the total amount of air decreases with increasing altitude, the amount of a certain greenhouse gas (ozone) increases in the stratosphere. As a result, the energy of the gases in the stratosphere is higher than the energy of the gases at the top of the troposphere, because the ozone in the stratosphere is absorbing more energy from the sun. As a result, temperature increases with increasing altitude in the stratosphere. Once you reach the stratopause, however, the amount of ozone falls away again, and the temperature begins to decrease with increasing altitude, as it does in the troposphere.

The "Hole" in the Ozone Layer

I am sure you have heard about the ozone "hole." The National Aeronautics and Space Administration (NASA) has been monitoring ozone levels over Antarctica for several years, and they have conclusively demonstrated that there is a "hole" in the ozone layer. Since you know what ozone in the ozone layer does for us, you understand why people are worried about this. Figure 3.6 is an example of a NASA graph that shows the ozone "hole."

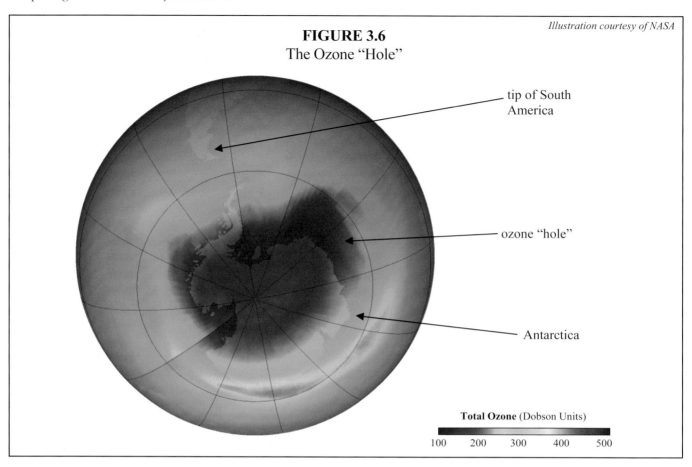

FIGURE 3.6
The Ozone "Hole"

Illustration courtesy of NASA

tip of South America

ozone "hole"

Antarctica

Total Ozone (Dobson Units)
100   200   300   400   500

This figure shows the concentration of ozone in the ozone layer over the Southern Hemisphere of the earth on October 8, 1993. The color bar on the right of the figure is a legend indicating the ozone level represented by the colors you see in the graph. Ozone concentration is measured in a unit called the "Dobson unit," named after the scientist who developed the first technique used to measure ozone concentration in the ozone layer.

Notice that blue area in the middle of the graph. Centered over Antarctica, it represents an area of low ozone concentration. Thus, it is not really a hole. It is an area of lower-than-normal ozone concentration in the ozone layer. In a series of very clever experiments, scientists eventually connected this lower-than-normal ozone concentration to chlorine in the stratosphere. They found that under certain conditions, chlorine atoms can break ozone down into oxygen, and they found such chlorine atoms in the ozone layer above Antarctica.

Well, once scientists connected the ozone "hole" to chlorine, the next question was, "What is the *source* of the chlorine?" It turns out that there are many sources that will put chlorine in the stratosphere, but one of the most important sources is a class of substances called **chlorofluorocarbons** (klor' oh flor' oh kar' buhns), or **CFCs**. These substances are human-made, and they turn out to be incredibly useful. The CFC known as Freon®, for example, can be used in refrigeration and air conditioning. Other CFCs are used in surgical sterilizers, and others are used as firefighting agents. In all their applications, these chemicals are *significantly* more efficient than what was used before CFCs were invented.

Not only are CFCs incredibly useful, they are also completely non-toxic. CFCs are so chemically inert that they do not react with our bodies or the bodies of animals. In fact, these chemicals do not interact significantly with any living organism. Since CFCs are so incredibly useful and at the same time non-toxic, they became very widely used only a few years after they were invented.

Since scientists linked the ozone "hole" to chlorine, and since they determined that a significant amount of this chlorine came from CFCs, many people immediately called for the elimination of CFCs. As a result, many world leaders signed a treaty called the Montreal Protocol on Substances That Deplete the Ozone Layer, which called for the elimination of CFC production and consumption. Depending on the CFC and the specific circumstances of a given country, this was to take effect between 1996 and 2010. Former U.S. president George H. W. Bush actually required the U.S. to move ahead of that schedule, and CFC production in the U.S. was halted by the end of 1995, except for small amounts needed for specific health and safety equipment.

Now that CFC production is eliminated in the U.S. and will soon be eliminated in other countries, lives will be saved, right? After all, if CFCs are destroying the ozone in the ozone layer, the elimination of CFCs will save lives, right? Believe it or not, the elimination of CFCs will, most likely, result in a *significantly larger loss of human life* than what would have happened if CFCs were not eliminated. How can I say that? Remember the cost/benefit analysis we discussed in Module #2? If you do such an analysis on the elimination of CFCs, you will see that the costs far outweigh the benefit!

Let's start with the benefits of CFC elimination. When CFCs are eliminated, the ozone "hole" will decrease, and lives will be saved, right? Not exactly. Remember, the ozone "hole" is caused by chlorine atoms under certain conditions. The important part of that phrase is "under certain conditions." You see, the ozone "hole" was actually discovered by Dobson (the scientist after whom the ozone concentration unit is named) back in 1956. At that time, Dobson noted that from August through November, the amount of ozone in the ozone layer over Antarctica was significantly lower than the amount during most of the rest of the year. This "hole" then filled up again by November, bringing the ozone layer back to full strength.

First of all, it is important to realize that back when Dobson first discovered the ozone "hole," CFCs were not being widely used. Thus, the ozone "hole" itself cannot be traced completely back to CFCs. It seems to be, in part, a natural phenomenon. It is also important to note, however, that over the years, the "hole" has gotten deeper and deeper. In other words, the concentration of ozone in the ozone layer over Antarctica during the months of August to November is significantly lower today than it was when Dobson first discovered the "ozone hole." Obviously, then, something has been happening to make the ozone "hole" worse than it used to be.

At the same time, however, *the concentration of ozone in the ozone layer over Antarctica during the rest of the year has not changed.* In other words, even though the ozone "hole" is deeper than it used to be, it is only deeper for a few months out of the year. Once November passes, the ozone concentration returns to essentially the same level it has been since ozone levels have been measured. How can this be? Well, remember the phrase "under certain conditions"? That's the key. In early August of every year, a weather phenomenon known as the **polar vortex** occurs. In the polar vortex, winds blowing around the South Pole prevent warmer air from entering the South Pole region, and the result is constant low temperatures, as low as -90 degrees Celsius (-130 degrees Fahrenheit), and a steady rush of wind blowing upwards.

Under the conditions of the polar vortex, water droplets freeze into tiny ice particles, and the winds push them up into the stratosphere. If these tiny ice particles happen to have trapped any molecules that have chlorine atoms in them, and if those chlorine-containing molecules survive the trip up to the stratosphere, certain chemical reactions occur on the surface of the tiny ice particles. These chemical reactions remove the chlorine from the chlorine-containing molecules, and the result is chlorine that can destroy ozone. By late November, however, the polar vortex is gone, and with it the conditions that produce ozone-destroying chlorine in the stratosphere.

In the end, then, the ozone "hole" is a seasonal phenomenon that happens only a few months out of the year. Also, *the ozone "hole" is centered over Antarctica*, because that's the only place in the world where a strong polar vortex exists. A weak polar vortex exists in the North Pole, but its effects are very small. Now think about it. How many people are living in Antarctica? Not many! Thus, the CFC ban will reduce the depth of the ozone hole (it won't eliminate the ozone hole because it was there *before* CFCs were really popular) for a few months out of the year over a region of the world where few people actually live. As a result, the ban on CFCs won't save many (if any) lives. In fact, although scientists expect that ozone depletion could result in higher rates of some diseases (like skin cancer), they have been unable to demonstrate any direct link between the ozone "hole" and these diseases. So it is not clear that the elimination of CFCs will even *improve* anyone's life!

What about the costs of the CFC ban? As I mentioned before, CFCs are the most efficient refrigerants, surgical sterilizers, and firefighting agents in the world. The CFC ban has caused these processes to become less efficient. As a result, *people will probably die.* Fires will most likely last longer before they are put out, resulting in loss of property and death. Surgical procedures will be less sterile, probably causing more infection, which will cause sickness and death. Finally, refrigerators will be less efficient, resulting in food poisoning and perhaps even starvation. Even one of the big supporters of the CFC ban (Robert Watson) has admitted that "probably more people would die from food poisoning as a consequence of inadequate refrigeration than would die from depleting ozone" (*Environmental Overkill*, Dixie Lee Ray, Regnery Gateway, 1993, p. 45).

So what does our cost/benefit analysis tell us? The ban on CFCs will result in essentially no lives saved because of less seasonal ozone destruction, but it will almost certainly result in a significant loss of human life! Why in the world, then, did the Montreal Protocol get signed? Why have we already banned CFC production? Mostly, it is because the people who make the laws are rather ignorant about real science. Unless you hear the whole story, it is very easy to be misinformed. If you ask any of the legislators who support a CFC ban, you will find that most of them do not know the details of the "ozone hole." As a result, they can be easily misinformed by those who are pushing some other agenda.

Please realize, however, that misinformation exists on both sides of the issue. Those who are against a CFC ban often quote the statistic that only 0.1% of all the chlorine-containing molecules released into the atmosphere come from human-made sources. This statistic is true, but it is utterly irrelevant in the ozone "hole" debate. You see, the vast majority of chlorine-containing molecules cannot survive the trip up the polar vortex, because most chlorine-containing molecules are so chemically reactive that they tend to react with other substances in the atmosphere long before they reach the ozone layer. Because CFCs are relatively inert, they tend to survive the trip. As a result, human sources are responsible for about 81% of the chlorine *in the ozone layer*. Since the chlorine in the ozone layer is what is important in terms of ozone-destruction, 81% is the important statistic, not 0.1%.

As a sidelight, the reason that CFCs became so popular was that they are efficient at certain tasks, and at the same time, they are non-toxic. The reason CFCs are non-toxic is because they are relatively inert. Well, what makes it possible for CFCs to survive the long trip up to the ozone layer in the polar vortex? *The fact that they are relatively inert.* We see, then, an example of an unintended consequence. CFCs were hailed as wonder chemicals because they were useful *and* non-toxic. The same property that makes them non-toxic, however, also makes them able to get up to the stratosphere to destroy ozone.

In the end, then, the ozone "hole" situation is a great example of how poorly educated our world leaders are in the sciences. Anyone with a rudimentary knowledge of science and an ability to do literature research could have easily found out the same facts I am telling you. However, because many leaders are ignorant about these matters, legislation that will most likely result in a tragic loss of life has been enacted.

Before you leave this section, I want to dispel a very popular myth that is promoted by radical environmentalists. It is common for certain extremists to link ozone depletion to global warming. Hopefully, you now see that this is absurd. Remember, the stratosphere is warmer than the tropopause *because ozone is a greenhouse gas*. If anything, then, ozone depletion will *cool the earth*, not warm it. Remember however, that the ozone "hole" effect is so short-lived that there is little overall effect. Nevertheless, *if* there were an effect, it would be opposite of what many environmental extremists claim!

ON YOUR OWN

3.9 Those who are against the CFC ban point out that CFCs are four to eight times heavier than the nitrogen and oxygen in the air. As a result, they say, there is no way that CFCs can float up to the ozone layer. Why are they wrong?

3.10 Those who are for the CFC ban claim that skin cancer rates have increased in Australia as a result of the "ozone hole." Although skin cancer rates have increased in Australia (and around the world), why is it hard to believe that the increase is a result of the ozone hole?

The Heterosphere

I have spent the majority of this module on the homosphere, because it is the region of the atmosphere that affects us most. However, I do need to spend some time discussing the heterosphere. The heterosphere consists of two layers, the **thermosphere** (thurm' uh sfear) and the **exosphere** (ecks' uh sfear).

Thermosphere – The region of the atmosphere between altitudes of roughly 80 kilometers and 460 kilometers

Exosphere – The region of the atmosphere above an altitude of roughly 460 kilometers

Now it is important to realize that, for all practical purposes, these two layers of the atmosphere can be considered "outer space." The first man went in outer space in 1961, but he never left the thermosphere. In fact, many space shuttle missions these days occur in the thermosphere.

An interesting effect occurs in the thermosphere. The number of molecules in the air is so small there that a thermometer would read incredibly low temperatures, because there would be very few collisions between the thermometer and the molecules in the thermosphere. Nevertheless, the average energy of the few molecules in the thermosphere is very high. Thus, if you define temperature as the average energy of each molecule in the thermosphere, the temperature of the thermosphere is very high. If, on the other hand, you define temperature as what a thermometer measures, the thermosphere has a very low temperature. This interesting effect is the source of the name "thermosphere."

The exosphere is composed of those atoms and molecules actually in orbit around the planet. Sometimes, the atoms and molecules in the exosphere escape their orbits and go into interplanetary space. This tends to blur the distinction between the exosphere and interplanetary space. As a result, it is really hard to say where the exosphere ends and interplanetary space begins.

Between the upper portions of the mesosphere and the lower portions of the thermosphere, there is a region called the **ionosphere** (eye on' oh sfear).

Ionosphere – The region of the atmosphere between the altitudes of roughly 65 kilometers and 330 kilometers, where the gases are ionized

Now, of course, this definition does you no good if you don't understand what the word "ionized" means. You will learn more about this in an upcoming module, but for right now, you need to know that atoms are composed of protons (which have positive electrical charge), electrons (which have negative electrical charge), and neutrons (which have no electrical charge). Atoms always have the same number of electrons and protons. As a result, they have the same amount of negative charge as positive charge. This means that overall, atoms have no net electrical charge.

In the ionosphere, various types of radiation from the sun collide with the atoms there and rip some of the electrons away from them. This causes the atoms to have an imbalance between positive and negative charges. With an imbalance of positive and negative charges, the atoms in the ionosphere become electrically charged. When an atom becomes electrically charged, it is no longer an atom. Instead, it is an **ion**. When an atom turns into an ion, we say that it has been **ionized**.

The ionosphere is actually a very useful portion of earth's atmosphere, because radio transmitters can use it to increase their range. Radio signals travel in straight lines. Thus, most radio signals (AM and FM radio, for example) can only be received by radios that are relatively close (within a few hundred miles) of the transmitter. Certain radio signals, however, can actually bounce off the ionosphere. As a result, these radio signals can be transmitted a great distance. Shortwave radios emit signals with the ideal properties for bouncing off of the ionosphere, so shortwave radios can really broadcast around the world.

Have you ever heard of the Northern Lights or the Southern Lights? Scientists call these phenomena **auroras** (uh ror' uhz). In the Northern Hemisphere they are called the **Aurora Borealis** (baw ree al' is), and in the Southern Hemisphere they are called the **Aurora Australis** (aw stray' lis). If you have never seen them, they appear in the night sky as glowing regions of brilliant colors that tend to move over the sky in interesting ways. The auroras are the result of high-energy collisions between ionized particles in the ionosphere. The collisions involve a lot of energy, and some of that energy is converted to light, which makes up the auroras. These collisions occur in the ionosphere above the North and South Poles, so they are usually visible in places far to the north (such as Canada and Alaska) or to the south (such as Australia and New Zealand). However, depending on the energy involved, they can sometimes be visible in regions farther away from the poles.

FIGURE 3.7
Aurora Borealis

Photo © Roman Krochuk
Agency: istockphoto.com

ON YOUR OWN

3.11 Sometimes, disturbances in the sun's magnetic field can cause disturbances in the ionosphere. Suppose you were listening to an AM radio at the time of such a disturbance. Would you notice? What if you were listening to a shortwave radio transmission from another continent?

In order to help you review, Figure 3.8 summarizes much of what I have discussed throughout this module.

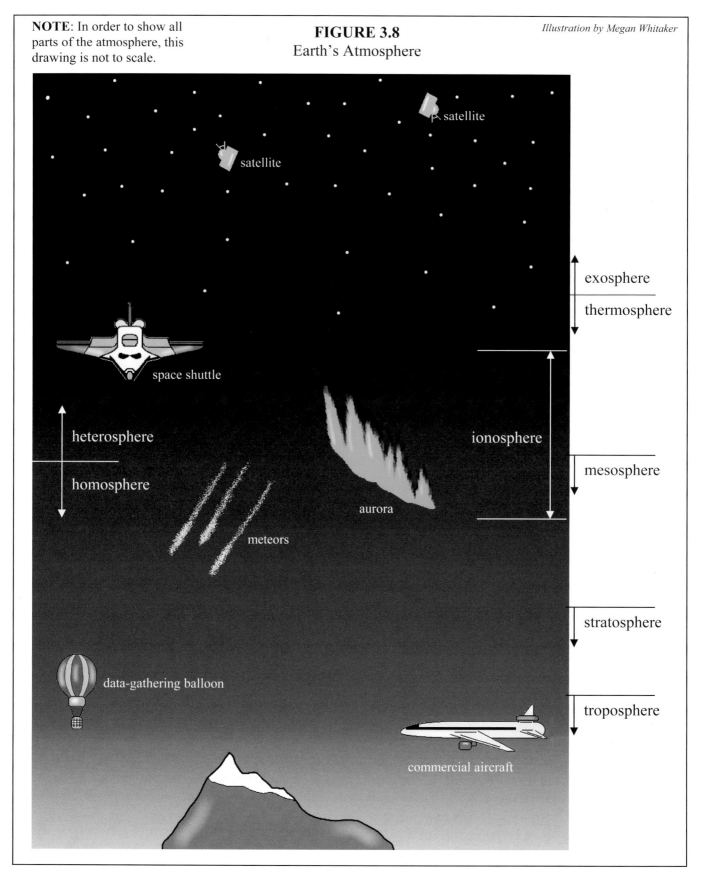

Illustration by Megan Whitaker

NOTE: In order to show all parts of the atmosphere, this drawing is not to scale.

FIGURE 3.8
Earth's Atmosphere

satellite

satellite

exosphere

thermosphere

space shuttle

heterosphere

ionosphere

mesosphere

homosphere

aurora

meteors

stratosphere

data-gathering balloon

troposphere

commercial aircraft

ANSWERS TO THE "ON YOUR OWN" PROBLEMS

3.1 <u>In general, atmospheric pressure decreases with increasing altitude</u>. Think of atmospheric pressure as the weight of air pressing down on what it touches. As you increase altitude, there is less air above you. As a result, there is less weight pressing down on you.

3.2 <u>The atmospheric pressure will be reported as 32.9 inches</u>. Remember, an atmospheric pressure of 1.0 atm means that atmospheric pressure is at its average sea-level value, which is the same as 29.9 inches of mercury. Since the atmospheric pressure is 1.1 atm, we know that it must be higher than its average sea-level value. The only number given that is greater than 29.9 inches of mercury is 32.9 inches of mercury.

3.3 <u>Milk is a homogeneous mixture, while Italian salad dressing is a heterogeneous mixture</u>. Think about it. The homosphere gets its name from the fact that the air composition is the same throughout. Milk has the same composition no matter what part of the container it comes from. Thus, it must be a homogeneous mixture. Italian salad dressing, however, has all these herbs and spices that tend to sink to the bottom. Thus, Italian salad dressing taken from the top of the bottle will be less spicy than that taken from the bottom of the bottle. Thus, Italian salad dressing does not have the same composition throughout the bottle and is therefore a heterogeneous mixture.

3.4 <u>Even though the air is 21% oxygen, there is *a lot* less air at that altitude</u>. Remember, there is less and less air the higher you go. Since there is less and less air, there is less and less oxygen as well. In other words, 21% of a small amount of air is a small amount of oxygen, which means you might not get the oxygen you need at that altitude.

3.5 <u>The supersonic jet will not be significantly affected</u>. Remember, the earth's weather occurs mostly in the troposphere. Since the stratosphere is above the troposphere, the supersonic jet will not be affected much by the weather.

3.6 <u>The water will melt near the stratopause</u>. Because of the change in the temperature gradient in the stratosphere, the vial will get warmer when it reaches the stratosphere. Near the top of the stratosphere, the temperature does creep above water's freezing point. At that point, the ice will melt.

3.7 <u>There will be heat in this system, because energy will be transferred from the warmer brick to the colder brick</u>. Despite the fact that both bricks are cold, one is warmer than the other. Thus, energy will flow from the warmer brick to the colder brick. Since heat is energy that is being transferred, heat is present!

3.8 <u>The observer is correct. When the thermometer was put into the substance, some energy got transferred from the substance to the thermometer. That's what caused the liquid in the thermometer to rise. Since energy went into the thermometer's liquid, it left the substance. This resulted in some small amount of cooling</u>. In other words, since the thermometer took a little energy from the substance, it cooled the substance slightly. Thus, the substance was slightly warmer the instant the thermometer was placed in it, and then it cooled as a result of transferring energy to the thermometer.

3.9 <u>Under normal conditions, CFCs cannot rise to the ozone layer. In the polar vortex, however, the steady rush of wind pushes them up to the ozone layer with ease</u>.

3.10 <u>The ozone "hole" is centered over Antarctica, and it exists for only a short time</u>. Although the edges of the ozone hole sometimes reach to Australia, it is hard to understand how the very edges of the hole can have a measurable effect on the population, especially since it exists for only a few months out of the year. In addition, since skin cancer rates are increasing around the world, there are obviously other reasons for skin cancer increases, because the ozone "hole" can only affect people who live near Antarctica.

3.11 <u>You will not really notice the disturbance while listening to the AM radio, but you will notice it while listening to the shortwave radio</u>. Remember, short-wave radios bounce their signals off the ionosphere. A disturbance in the ionosphere will affect the shortwave radio's signal.

STUDY GUIDE FOR MODULE #3

1. Define the following terms:

a. Atmosphere
b. Atmospheric pressure
c. Barometer
d. Homosphere
e. Heterosphere

f. Troposphere
g. Stratosphere
h. Mesosphere
i. Jet streams
j. Heat

k. Temperature
l. Thermosphere
m. Exosphere
n. Ionosphere

2. Suppose the earth's atmosphere contained twice the number of molecules it does today. Would atmospheric pressure be greater than, equal to, or less than it is now?

3. Two students make two different barometers. Although they are placed side by side so that they are both exposed to exactly the same atmospheric pressure, the column of liquid in the first student's barometer is significantly lower than the column of water in the second student's barometer. Assuming both students made their barometers correctly, what explains the difference?

4. The average, sea-level value for atmospheric pressure is 14.7 pounds per square inch, which is the same as 29.9 inches of mercury. If the atmospheric pressure is 0.85 atms, which of the following values would correspond to atmospheric pressure as reported in a weather report?

31.1 inches of mercury, 29.9 inches of mercury, 25.4 inches of mercury

5. Two vials contain air samples taken at different altitudes. The first is composed of 21% oxygen, 78% nitrogen, and 1% other. The second is 95% helium, 4% hydrogen, and 1% other. Which came from the homosphere?

6. You are reading the data coming from a data-gathering balloon as it rises in the atmosphere. You have no idea what altitude it is at, but the balloon is sending a signal from its thermometer, telling you the temperature of its surroundings. How will you know when the balloon enters the stratosphere? How will you know when it enters the mesosphere?

7. Name the three regions of the homosphere, from lowest to highest.

8. Although the temperature gradient changes from region to region in the homosphere, there is one gradient that stays the same. It continues to decrease as you increase in altitude, no matter where you are in the homosphere. To what gradient am I referring?

9. A plane is experiencing a *lot* of problems because of a storm in the area. Is the plane flying in the troposphere or the stratosphere?

10. A scientist has two vials of ammonia gas. She tells you that in the first vial, the gas molecules are traveling with an average speed of 1,000 miles per hour. In the second vial, they are traveling with an average speed of 1,300 miles per hour. Which vial contains the gas with the higher temperature?

11. As you are outside on a cold winter night, you begin to shiver from the cold. Your companion says that you are shivering from the heat. Is your companion correct? Why or why not?

12. Suppose there were a layer of carbon dioxide gas in the mesosphere. What would happen to the temperature gradient in that region?

13. Why will the ban on CFCs most likely not save or improve people's lives?

14. Why will the ban on CFCs most likely result in a tragic loss of human life?

15. Even though human civilization is responsible for less than 1% of all chlorine in the atmosphere, it is responsible for 80% of all ozone-destroying chlorine. Why?

16. What makes it possible for CFCs to travel up to the ozone layer and begin destroying ozone?

17. Where is the ionosphere, and what makes it useful to us?

Cartoon by Speartoons

MODULE #4: The Wonder of Water

Introduction

Have you ever spent a long, hot day working out in the sun? What makes that kind of work bearable? Tall glasses of ice-cold water! I'm sure at one time or another you've taken a big drink of water and finished with a refreshed "Ahhh!" A drink of water is probably the best all-around thirst-quencher and refresher known to man. As I am sure you already know, we can live for as many as two weeks without food, but if we were to go even a few days without water, we would surely die. Indeed, without water, life as we know it simply cannot exist.

In addition to its necessity for life, water has many other properties that make it a truly remarkable substance. In this module, we will study this wondrous substance in some detail. Do you find it surprising that I can spend a whole module talking about nothing but water? You shouldn't. Water has many interesting properties that make it worth a detailed study. In fact, when you are done with this module, you will still not know anywhere near all there is to know about water! That should give you some idea of just how much there is to this interesting molecule.

The Composition of Water

As you already know, water is a molecule. It contains hydrogen atoms and oxygen atoms linked together. In Experiment 1.1, you broke water molecules down into hydrogen and oxygen using the energy from electricity. Such a process is called **electrolysis** (ee leck trawl' uh sis).

Electrolysis – The use of electricity to break a molecule down into smaller units

If you do such an experiment in a controlled way, you can actually learn something very detailed about water. To see what I mean, perform the following experiment:

EXPERIMENT 4.1
The Chemical Composition of Water

Supplies:

- Water
- 9-volt battery (A new one works best.)
- Two test tubes (You can purchase these at a hobby store. If you cannot get them, skip the experiment or use the tubes that florists put on the stems of cut flowers.)
- Juice glass (It must be deep enough so that when it is nearly full of water, the battery can stand vertically in the glass and still be fully submerged in the water.)
- Epsom salts (You can get these at any drugstore or large supermarket.)
- Tablespoon
- Eye protection such as goggles or safety glasses

Introduction: In Module #1, you observed the electrolysis of water by attaching wires to a battery and placing those wires in a solution of water and baking soda. In this experiment, you will use a slightly different method of water electrolysis to collect information about the chemical composition of water.

Procedure:

1. Fill the glass with water.
2. Add 3 tablespoons of Epsom salts and stir so that they dissolve. Don't worry if there are some undissolved Epsom salts at the bottom of the glass.
3. Stand the battery vertically at the bottom of the glass. You should immediately see bubbles forming on each terminal. On the positive terminal of the battery, the bubbles are from oxygen gas. On the negative terminal, the bubbles are from hydrogen gas.
4. Allow the battery to sit like this for 10 minutes. The reason you must do this is that there is air trapped in the battery, and the air escapes in the form of large bubbles. If you watch your battery for a few moments and see some large bubbles coming from the center of the terminals or from the edges of the battery, those are air bubbles that will mess up the results of the experiment.
5. After 10 minutes, take your test tubes and fill them completely with the solution in the glass. The best way to do this is to fully immerse the test tubes, tilting them to let all the air out. In the end, there should be no air bubbles in the tubes. If you cannot fill the test tubes from the glass, make another mixture of water and Epsom salts in a bowl and fill the test tubes from the bowl.
6. Take the two tubes and, while keeping their openings fully immersed in the solution, hold them upside down. You should still see no air bubbles in the tubes. The solution will not pour out as long as you keep the tops of the tubes submerged in the solution at all times.
7. As simultaneously as possible, place one tube over each terminal of the battery, once again making sure that the openings of the tubes are always submerged in the solution. Your experiment should look something like this:

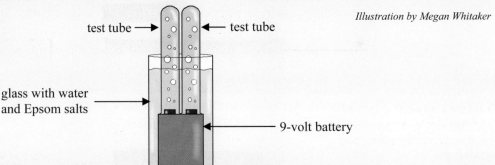

Illustration by Megan Whitaker

test tube →   ← test tube

glass with water
and Epsom salts →

9-volt battery

8. With a little effort, you can make the test tubes balance on the battery so that you do not have to hold them there. If you have trouble doing that, you can tape the test tubes together and then lay two knives across the glass, sandwiching the test tubes between the knives.
9. Once you have gotten the test tubes to stand on the battery on their own, watch what's happening. The gases forming at each terminal travel up the test tube until they reach the top. At that point, they fill the top of the test tube, pushing away the water that was there. As time goes on, then, the gases produced at the terminals will be collected at the top of the test tubes.
10. Let the experiment sit for a while. Go back periodically and check, and you will see that the water level in the test tubes is decreasing. This is happening because as the gases are produced, they exert pressure on the water in the tubes. This pushes down on the water in the tubes, forcing water out of the tubes and into the glass.
11. The solution will probably turn a nasty color after a while, because substances in the battery will eventually leak into the solution. That's okay, though. It looks ugly, but it does not affect the results of the experiment. **Be sure not to get any of the solution in your mouth! The chemicals coming from the battery can be toxic at high concentrations.**
12. When one of the test tubes is filled halfway with gas, draw what the experiment looks like in your laboratory notebook. Be sure to note which terminal is the positive one and which is the negative

one. If it is not marked on the battery, the larger terminal is negative, and the smaller terminal is positive.

13. **Clean up:** Throw the battery away, pour the contents of the glass into the sink, rinse the glass thoroughly, and flush all the liquid down the drain with plenty of water. Put everything away.

What can we learn from this experiment? Well, look at the amount of gas in each test tube. If your experiment worked correctly, there should be a lot more gas in the test tube that is over the negative terminal of the battery. Remember what I said was forming over the negative terminal of the battery? Hydrogen gas formed there, while oxygen gas formed on the other terminal. Since all of the hydrogen and oxygen gas comes from breaking down water, what can we conclude about the relative number of hydrogen atoms and oxygen atoms in a water molecule? Well, we can say that there must be more hydrogen atoms in a water molecule than oxygen atoms. In the end, then, this simple experiment gives us insight into the chemical composition of water.

In fact, if your experiment worked perfectly (which it probably did not), you should have collected *twice as much hydrogen as oxygen,* as shown below.

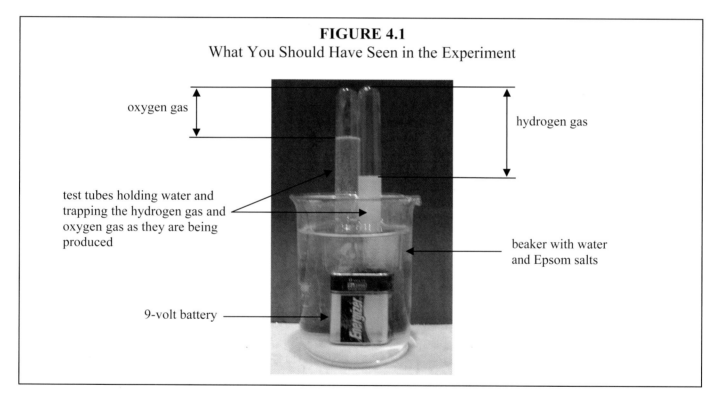

FIGURE 4.1
What You Should Have Seen in the Experiment

oxygen gas

hydrogen gas

test tubes holding water and trapping the hydrogen gas and oxygen gas as they are being produced

beaker with water and Epsom salts

9-volt battery

In the next section, we will discuss this result further. Before we do that, however, I need to make a point. Your experiment probably did not result in twice as much hydrogen as oxygen. Why? Because of **experimental error.** You see, every experiment has some errors in it. Hopefully, there aren't too many errors, and hopefully those few errors are small. However, sometimes the errors in an experiment are large. For example, remember when I said that air trapped in the battery escapes the battery in large bubbles? Suppose there was still air trapped in the battery despite the fact that you let it sit in the solution for 10 minutes before you started collecting the gases. If some of that air escaped into one of your test tubes, you could not tell the difference between it and the gas that was supposed to collect in the test tube. That would throw off the results of the experiment. Suppose, for example, those bubbles got into the test tube that also had oxygen in it. That would make it look like there was more oxygen than what was made by electrolysis.

Another source of error in this experiment comes from the behavior of the oxygen being made at the positive terminal. Oxygen can do things other than bubbling up to the top of the test tube. It can chemically react with other substances, such as the metal that makes up the terminal of the battery. It can also dissolve in the water. Of course, if that happens, it will not be collected at the top of the test tube, and that will make it look like there was less oxygen than what was made by electrolysis.

Part of being a good scientist is having the ability to recognize all sources of experimental error. Sometimes, the biggest source of experimental error is the experimenter himself! In other experiments, the procedure of the experiment may just lend itself to too many errors, and the results simply cannot be trusted. How do we know, then, when to trust the results of an experiment and when not to trust them? Part of the answer is that a good scientist can recognize which experiments are rife with experimental errors and which are not. The good scientist then trusts only the results of those experiments not full of experimental errors. The other part of the answer is what we in the scientific community call **peer review**. When a scientist performs an experiment that seems to lead to a new, interesting conclusion, other scientists in the field look closely at the experimental procedure and try to find sources of error. Sometimes, they actually perform the experiment again, trying to make sure the original experimenter didn't cause errors in the experiment. When an experimental result passes peer review, it is considered reasonably trustworthy.

An example of how peer review finds experimental errors can be seen in the phenomenon of **cold fusion**. In March 1989, Drs. Martin Fleischmann and Stanley Pons shocked the world with the announcement that they had seen cold fusion in one of their experiments. Briefly put, nuclear fusion is a clean, efficient, almost limitless source of energy. In fact, it is the process that gives the sun its energy. Compared to nuclear *fission*, which is what happens in today's nuclear power plants, nuclear *fusion* is a scientist's dream! Unlike in nuclear fission, there is no harmful waste produced, no possibility of meltdown, and no worry of running out of the raw materials needed. There is only one problem. Until 1989, the only way to get nuclear fusion going was to use expensive, high-energy reactors in a very inefficient way (this is typically called **hot fusion**). The practical upshot is that right now, nuclear fusion is simply too expensive and inefficient to be used as a power source for today's world.

The announcement made by Drs. Fleischmann and Pons seemed to change all of that. They claimed to have achieved nuclear fusion under very cheap, low-energy conditions. Compared to "hot fusion," it used so little energy that it was called "cold fusion." Well, the implications were mind-boggling. If they were right, the world had a cheap, limitless, and completely safe form of energy. Think what that would mean!

Unfortunately, Drs. Fleischmann and Pons did not submit their experiments to peer review before making their announcement. When other scientists began to examine their work, they found it riddled with experimental errors. They could not do the experiments and produce the same results that Drs. Fleischmann and Pons claimed. In the end, the vast majority of scientists who examined and tried to perform the experiments agreed that the results were from experimental error, not cold fusion. Had Drs. Fleischmann and Pons just submitted their experiments to peer review *before* announcing their results, they would have been saved a lot of embarrassment, and the world would not have had its hopes raised just to have them dashed by reality!

ON YOUR OWN

4.1 Suppose you want a precise measurement of rainfall in your area, so you set a rain gauge outside. After it rains, you measure the level of water in the gauge and record the result. You then empty the rain gauge and wait for the next rain. There are at least two sources of possible experimental error with this procedure. One will lead to a measurement that is too low and the other will lead to a measurement that is too high. What are these sources of error?

Chemical Formulas

Let's go back and think about the results of Experiment 4.1 for a moment. You collected more hydrogen gas than oxygen gas, which indicates there are more hydrogen atoms than oxygen atoms in a water molecule. In fact, if there were no experimental error in the experiment, it should have resulted in twice as much hydrogen gas as oxygen gas. What do you think that tells us? It tells us there are twice as many hydrogen atoms in a water molecule as there are oxygen atoms. Now I'm sure you know that the chemical symbol for water is H_2O. That's probably the first chemical symbol you learned. Well, our experiment demonstrates what that symbol means. The letter "H" stands for hydrogen, while the letter "O" stands for oxygen. The subscript of "2" after the "H" tells us that there are two hydrogen atoms in a water molecule. The fact that there is no subscript after the "O" tells us that there is one oxygen atom in a water molecule. Thus, the chemical symbol "H_2O" means "two hydrogen atoms and one oxygen atom linked together to make a molecule."

A chemical symbol like H_2O is called a **chemical formula**, because it provides a formula by which you can understand the chemical makeup of any substance. For example, natural gas stoves, water heaters, and furnaces burn a gas called methane, which has a chemical formula of CH_4. As we already know, the chemical symbol for hydrogen is "H." The chemical symbol for carbon is "C." Thus, this chemical formula tells us that a molecule of methane contains one carbon atom (there is no subscript after carbon's symbol) and four hydrogen atoms (there is a subscript of "4" after hydrogen's symbol). These atoms, when linked together in those numbers, make a molecule of methane.

Notice what I needed to know to interpret a chemical formula. First, I needed to know the chemical symbols for each atom. Second, I needed to realize that if there is no subscript after a chemical symbol, there is only one of those atoms in the molecule. If there is a subscript, it tells me how many of those atoms exist in the molecule. So, in order to really be able to use chemical formulas, we will need to memorize all the symbols for all of the atoms out there, right? Of course not! In this course, I will tell you the chemical symbol for any atom you need to know. Eventually, you will become used to associating the commonly used atoms with their symbols.

You need to remember, however, that not all atomic symbols are composed of just one letter. Some atoms have two letters in their symbol. The atomic symbol for neon, a gas that emits a pleasant, red-orange glow when excited by electricity, is "Ne." Notice that even though there are two letters in this symbol, only one of them is capitalized. That is a general rule. All atomic symbols have only one capital letter. If there is a second letter in the symbol, it is always a lower-case letter. Also, you must realize that chemical symbols are not always as easily recognized as "C" for carbon and "Ne" for neon. The symbol for an iron atom, for example, is "Fe." Where does that come from? Well, the Latin name for iron is **ferrum**. So sometimes we use two letters in an atom's symbol, and sometimes we use one. Also, sometimes we base the symbol for an atom on its English name, and sometimes we base it on its

Latin name. Given all that, make sure you understand the concept of chemical formulas by solving the "On Your Own" problems that follow.

ON YOUR OWN

4.2 The chemical formula for baking soda is $NaHCO_3$. How many atoms make up one molecule of baking soda?

4.3 Vinegar's active ingredient is acetic (uh see' tik) acid, $C_2H_4O_2$. How many of each atom (see the discussion above if you forget what the symbols mean) are present in a molecule of acetic acid?

4.4 The sugar in green, leafy vegetables is called glucose. A molecule of glucose contains six carbon atoms, 12 hydrogen atoms, and six oxygen atoms. What is the chemical formula of glucose?

Water's Polarity

Now that you know the chemical formula of water, it is time to investigate some of its very interesting properties. Perform the following experiment to learn one of those properties.

EXPERIMENT 4.2
Water's Polarity

Supplies:

- Glass of water
- Vegetable oil
- A Styrofoam® or paper cup
- A comb
- A pen
- Eye protection such as goggles or safety glasses

Introduction: In this experiment, you will see how water reacts to static electrical charge and compare it to how vegetable oil reacts under the same conditions. This will illustrate one of water's interesting properties.

Procedure:

1. Use the pen to punch a small hole in the bottom of the cup. The smaller the hole, the better.
2. While holding it over the sink, pour some water into the cup from the glass. Water should start running out of the hole in the bottom of the cup. Make sure that the water is pouring out of the hole in a steady stream, not dripping. If it is dripping, make your hole just a little bigger.
3. Once the water is pouring out of the cup in a steady stream, pick up the comb with your other hand and vigorously comb your hair. This is meant to make the comb develop an electrical charge. If your hair is wet or oily, this may not work too well.

4. Once you have combed your hair for a few seconds, bring the comb (teeth first) near the stream of water. You should let the comb get very close to, but not actually touch, the water stream. What happens? Write this down in your laboratory notebook.

5. Repeat this same experiment using vegetable oil instead of water. You may have to make the hole a little bigger this time, because vegetable oil doesn't flow as easily as water does. Once you do the experiment, however, you should observe a major difference between the way oil behaves and the way water behaves when they are both exposed to an electrically charged comb.

6. Clean up your mess and put everything away.

What did you see in the experiment? You should have seen the stream of water bending toward the comb. Why did that happen? To learn the answer to that question, I first have to show you a **model** of what a water molecule looks like:

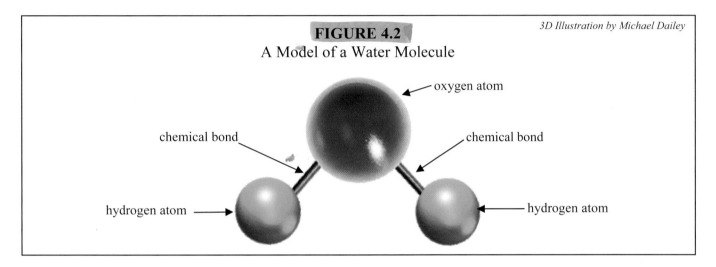

FIGURE 4.2
A Model of a Water Molecule

3D Illustration by Michael Dailey

oxygen atom

chemical bond   chemical bond

hydrogen atom   hydrogen atom

We call this diagram a "model" because we have never actually seen a water molecule. Since we can't see a water molecule, we need to use a picture like this to model what it looks like. Now, of course, we cannot prove this model is correct. There is a lot of evidence that indicates that this is probably a good model of the real thing, but there is just no way of knowing for sure.

Notice that, indeed, there are two hydrogen atoms in the water molecule as well as one oxygen atom, just like Experiment 4.1 indicated. Also, notice that the blue sphere representing the oxygen atom is larger than the green spheres that represent the hydrogen atoms. Once again, there is a lot of evidence that indicates oxygen atoms are, indeed, bigger than hydrogen atoms. The colors, of course, are arbitrary. They are just used to distinguish between oxygen atoms and hydrogen atoms. Finally, notice the bars between the oxygen atom and hydrogen atoms. They represent the **chemical bonds** that link the hydrogen atoms to the oxygen atom. Those chemical bonds are the reason for water's behavior in Experiment 4.2.

Remember from Module #3 that atoms are composed of protons, neutrons, and electrons. Well, protons have positive electrical charge, electrons have negative electrical charge, and neutrons have no electrical charge. As you will learn in detail when you take chemistry, chemical bonds like the ones in water result when atoms within a molecule *share* their electrons. Thus, the "sticks" in Figure 4.2

represent electrons shared between the oxygen atom and each hydrogen atom. This sharing of electrons keeps the atoms close together and is largely responsible for the properties of the molecule.

In the case of water, there is actually a tug-of-war going on between the electrons supposedly being "shared" by the atoms. Much like two little children who continually fight over a toy that they are supposedly "sharing," the oxygen atom and each hydrogen atom fight over the electrons they are supposedly sharing. Continuing this analogy, suppose one of the children is stronger than the other. In the absence of proper adult supervision, the stronger child will end up with the toy more often than the weaker child, right? Well, it turns out that oxygen is stronger at pulling on electrons than is hydrogen, so the oxygen atom will end up with the electrons more often than will the hydrogen.

What's the big deal? Sure, oxygen isn't "playing fair," but why worry about that? Well, remember that electrons are negatively charged. Since the oxygen gets the electrons more often than the hydrogens, it possesses more than its "fair share" of electrons. Since it possesses more than its "fair share" of electrons, it develops a very slight negative electrical charge. In the same way, since the hydrogen atoms get less than their "fair share" of electrons, they have less negative charge than they should. With less negative charge than they should have, they end up having a slight positive charge. In our model, we could illustrate this as follows:

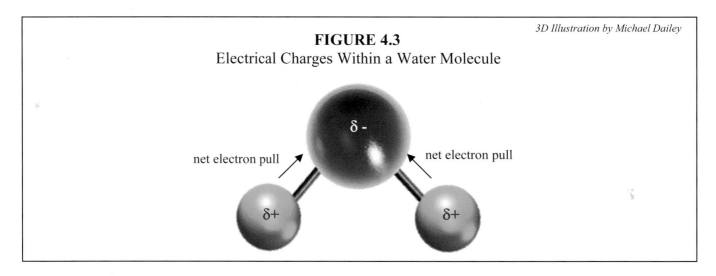

FIGURE 4.3
Electrical Charges Within a Water Molecule

3D Illustration by Michael Dailey

net electron pull

net electron pull

The symbol "δ" is the lower-case Greek letter "delta," and it is used to signify the fact that the electrical charges in the water molecule are very small. When you have opposite charges within the same structure, the phenomenon is called **polarity** (poh lair' ih tee). As a result, we call water a **polar molecule.**

Polar molecule – A molecule that has slight positive and negative charges due to an imbalance in the way electrons are shared

How does this explain the results of Experiment 4.2? Well, when you combed your hair vigorously, the comb picked up stray electrons in your hair and, as a result, became negatively charged. As you should already know, positive charges are attracted to negative charges and vice-versa. The negative charge on the comb attracted the small positive charges on the hydrogen atoms in the water molecules. Thus, the water molecules all turned around so that their hydrogen atoms pointed toward the comb, as shown in Figure 4.4.

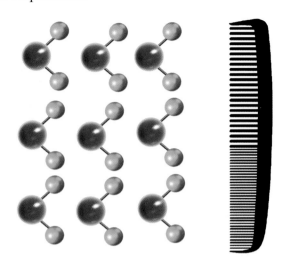

FIGURE 4.4
Water Molecules in the Experiment

Water molecules illustrated by Michael Dailey
Comb illustration from www.clipart.com

Before the comb was brought near the water stream, the water molecules were oriented in different directions.

The negative charge on the comb attracted the slight positive charges on the hydrogen atoms, causing the water molecules to reorient so that their hydrogen atoms pointed toward the comb.

Once the water molecules were aligned, the mutual attraction between the small positive charges on the hydrogen atoms and the negative charge on the comb was strong enough to *bend the water stream toward the comb.*

Now, when you did the same experiment with vegetable oil instead of water, did you see the same thing? You shouldn't have. The stream of vegetable oil should not have bent at all. Vegetable oil is *not* made of polar molecules. As you will learn in chemistry, electrons are shared equally between the atoms in certain kinds of molecules. These molecules, like the ones that make up vegetable oil, are called **nonpolar molecules**, because they have no polarity. As a result, they are not affected by electrical charges. Thus, the vegetable oil should not have reacted to the charge on the comb. You might have seen a little sputtering from the stream of oil. This is caused by small bits of water or alcohol contaminating the oil. This may not have happened to you, meaning your vegetable oil had no such contamination.

Before we leave this section, I need to make an important point about electrical charges in matter. *All substances have electrical charges in them,* because all substances are made of atoms, which have positive charges (protons) and negative charges (electrons). Individual atoms, however, have equal numbers of protons and electrons, so the positive charges cancel out the negative charges. Thus, we can say that an individual atom has no "net electrical charge." This means there are positive charges and negative charges all over the place, but they cancel each other out, leaving no overall charge. When atoms form molecules, there will be no net electrical charge as long as all electrons are shared equally. Once again, there are charges all over the molecule, but they cancel each other out, leaving no net charge. When electrons are shared unequally, however, they are concentrated around an atom. At that point, there are more negative charges around the atom than positive charges, and there is a net negative charge on that atom.

ON YOUR OWN

4.5 Suppose you had a positively charged object to hold next to the stream of water in Experiment 4.2. Would the stream bend the same way as it did with the comb, or would it bend the opposite way? Why?

4.6 Hydrochloric acid, HCl, is a powerful acid often used in cleaning. While "H" stands for hydrogen, "Cl" stands for chlorine. Chlorine atoms can pull on electrons much more strongly than can hydrogen atoms. Is HCl polar? If so, where is the small negative charge: on the chlorine atom or the hydrogen atom?

4.7 Chlorine gas, Cl_2, is a molecule composed of two chlorine atoms bonded together with a chemical bond. Is this molecule polar? Why or why not?

Water as a Solvent

The polarity of water is actually responsible for a great many of its properties, not the least of which is water's ability to dissolve many substances. You've experienced this property of water all your life. You've probably made a soft drink by mixing a powder in water. In many of the experiments you've done so far in this course, you've dissolved substances in water. When you dissolve a substance in a liquid, we say you have made a **solution**. When making a solution, you use a **solvent** to dissolve a **solute**.

Solvent – A liquid substance capable of dissolving other substances

Solute – A substance that is dissolved in a solvent

When you dissolve salt in water, for example, water is the solvent, salt is the solute, and saltwater is the solution.

Now while you usually think of solutes as solids, it is important to note that liquids and gases can be solutes as well. The fizz in soda pop, for example, comes from dissolved carbon dioxide. The sweet taste comes from liquid syrup also dissolved in the solution. In the end, then, soda pop is a solution in which water is the solvent and several solutes exist, including carbon dioxide gas and liquid syrup.

Water is sometimes called the "near-universal solvent," because it seems that water can dissolve nearly anything. In fact, that's not the case. As you will learn in the following experiment, water does not dissolve everything!

EXPERIMENT 4.3
Solvents and Solutes

Supplies:

♦ Five glasses
♦ Two stirring spoons
♦ Paper towel

♦ A measuring spoon that measures ½ teaspoon
♦ Sugar
♦ Table salt
♦ Canola oil (or some kind of cooking oil other than olive oil)
♦ Olive oil
♦ Eye protection such as goggles or safety glasses

Introduction: Although water dissolves many things, it does not dissolve everything. Demonstrate that for yourself with the following experiment:

Procedure

1. Fill four of the five glasses ¾ full with warm water.
2. Measure out ½ teaspoon of sugar and mix it with the water. Write in your laboratory notebook whether or not the sugar dissolved. If the sugar disappears after vigorous stirring with one of the stirring spoons, then it dissolved. If you can still see it, it did not dissolve.
3. Using the same stirring spoon, try to dissolve ½ teaspoon of canola oil in the water in the second glass. Record whether or not it worked.
4. Wipe the measuring spoon you are using with a paper towel to get rid of the oil.
5. Try to dissolve ½ teaspoon of table salt in the water in the third glass. Record whether or not it worked.
6. Try to dissolve ½ teaspoon of olive oil in the water in the fourth glass. Record whether or not it worked.
7. Pour a little canola oil into the fifth glass.
8. Try to dissolve some of the olive oil in the canola oil. Record whether or not it worked.
9. Clean up your mess.

So, does water dissolve everything? Of course not. In the experiment, water should have dissolved sugar and table salt, but not canola oil or olive oil. The results of the experiment shouldn't have surprised you. Although you were probably able to guess most of the results from the experiment, you probably don't know the explanation behind those results. Now you can learn that explanation. As you demonstrated in the previous experiment, water is made up of polar molecules. Polar molecules, as you learned, have small, net electrical charges. Well, those electrical charges would like to find other electrical charges with which to interact. It turns out there are two different categories of substances that contain electrical charges. You already learned that polar molecules have small, net electrical charges, so they represent one category. There is, however, another category of substances that have electrical charges in them: **ionic compounds**.

Remember our discussion of ions from Module #3? Atoms have equal numbers of electrons (negative charges) and protons (positive charges). As a result, atoms have no net electrical charge. When an atom loses or gains electrons (you'll learn how that happens in chemistry), it has an imbalance of charges. If the atom gains extra electrons, it has more negative charges than positive charges. As a result, it ends up with an overall negative charge. If the atom loses electrons, it has more protons than electrons and becomes positively charged. Either way, when that happens, we say the atom has become an ion.

Ionic compounds are made up of ions. For example, table salt is made up of sodium ions and chloride ions. The sodium ion results when a sodium atom loses an electron. As a result, sodium ions are positive. The chloride ion results when a chlorine atom gains an electron. Chloride ions, therefore, have a negative charge. The positive charge of the sodium ion is attracted to the negative charge of the chloride ion, and the result is that the ions come together to make sodium chloride, or table salt. When an ionic compound like salt is put in water, the following situation develops:

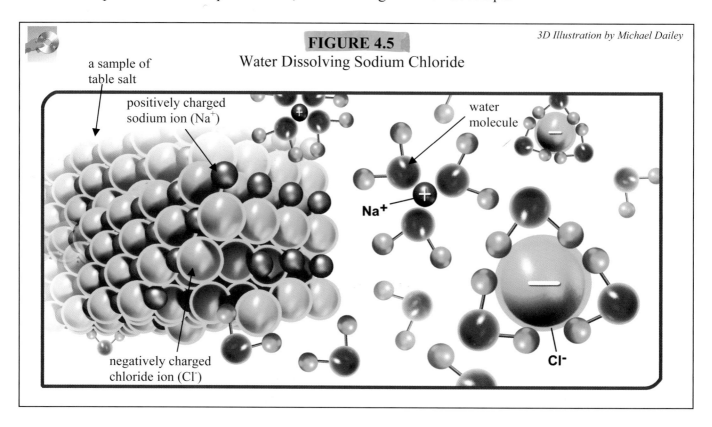

FIGURE 4.5
Water Dissolving Sodium Chloride

3D Illustration by Michael Dailey

a sample of table salt

positively charged sodium ion (Na$^+$)

water molecule

Na$^+$

negatively charged chloride ion (Cl$^-$)

Cl$^-$

    Notice what's happening in this figure. The positive sodium ions and the negative chloride ions are closely packed, because their opposite electrical charges attract one another. Water molecules, however, are attracted to the ions, so they move in close to the ions. The electrical charges in the water molecules attract the electrical charges of the ions, pulling the ions away from each other. Eventually, each ion in the solute molecule is pulled so far from the other ions that the substance is no longer visible in the solution. It is still there, but its ions are so far removed from each other that they exist on their own. Since the ions are too small to see, the substance seems to disappear.

    Notice how the water molecules are oriented in the figure. For the positively charged sodium ions, the water molecules orient themselves so that the small negative charge on the oxygen atom is close to the positive sodium ion. For the negatively charged chloride ion, however, the water molecules orient themselves so that the hydrogens, which have a small positive charge, are as close as possible to the negative chloride ion. As time goes on, more water molecules will come in and pull more ions away from each other, eventually dissolving the table salt completely.

    Although it is harder to picture, essentially the same thing happens when water dissolves a substance made of polar molecules. The electrical charges in the water molecules are attracted to the electrical charges in the solute molecules. The result is that the water molecules pull the solute molecules away from each other, dissolving the solute.

So, water tends to dissolve substances made up of either polar molecules or ions. If a molecule is nonpolar, however, water will not be attracted to it, since a nonpolar molecule has no net electrical charges in it. Olive oil and canola oil, for example, are made of nonpolar molecules. As a result, water will not dissolve them. In the end, then, water dissolves substances made of polar molecules or ions, and it will not dissolve substances made of nonpolar molecules. The reason that water seems to dissolve almost everything is that the vast majority of compounds in creation are either polar or ionic. Thus, water dissolves a great many substances, but not everything.

Before we leave this section, I need to discuss the result you should have gotten in step 8 of the experiment. In that step, you should have found that you could dissolve olive oil in canola oil. Why? Well, the reason water cannot dissolve olive oil is that water is attracted to molecules with net electrical charges. Olive oil is made of nonpolar molecules that do not have net electrical charges. Thus, water is not attracted to the molecules that make up the olive oil. However, since any nonpolar substance lacks electrical charges, the molecules that make up olive oil are attracted to other *nonpolar* substances. Since canola oil is also nonpolar, it can dissolve the nonpolar molecules in the olive oil. As a general rule, then, while substances made of ions and polar molecules can dissolve each other, nonpolar substances can only dissolve other nonpolar substances.

ON YOUR OWN

4.8 Water does not dissolve gasoline. Is gasoline most likely made up of ionic, polar, or nonpolar molecules?

4.9 Suppose you did Experiment 4.3 with gasoline instead of water. (Don't actually do it; the fumes are dangerous!) Would table salt dissolve in gasoline? What about canola oil?

Hydrogen Bonding in Water

Did you think that we were done studying the polar nature of water molecules? If so, you were sadly mistaken! It turns out that the polar nature of water leads to another interesting property: **hydrogen bonding**. In order to really understand hydrogen bonding, we need to think about a group of water molecules together. Remember, each water molecule has a small negative charge around its oxygen atom and a small positive charge around its hydrogen atoms. Now, if we have a whole lot of water molecules sitting around together, what do you think will happen? Well, since the positive charge on one molecule is attracted to any other negative charge, the water molecules will tend to align themselves so that the positive charge on the hydrogens of one molecule will be as close as possible to the negative charge on the oxygen of another molecule.

When this happens, the hydrogen atoms on one water molecule get very close to the oxygen atom on another water molecule. Now remember, the hydrogen atoms have less than their "fair share" of electrons, while the oxygen atom has more than its fair share. As a result, the hydrogen atoms on one water molecule try to make up for their lack of electrons by sharing some of the *extra* electron charge found on the oxygen atom of the *other* water molecule. This is something like a chemical bond. Remember, you already learned that a chemical bond is made up of shared electrons. Since the oxygen has only a small excess of electrons, there is not a lot to share. Nevertheless, some sharing goes on, and as a result, a weak bond is established between the hydrogens on one water molecule and the oxygen on another. This weak bond is called a **hydrogen bond** and is illustrated in Figure 4.6.

FIGURE 4.6
Hydrogen Bonding

Water molecules illustrated by Michael Dailey

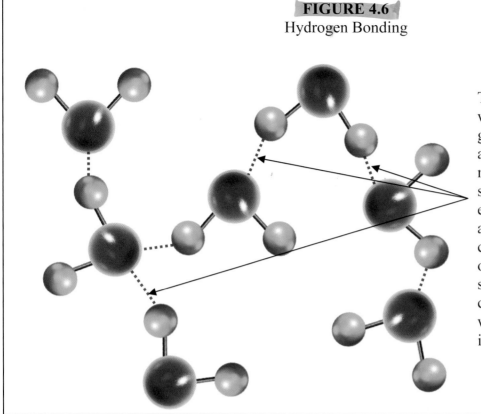

The hydrogen atoms on one water molecule that have gotten close to the oxygen atom in another water molecule actually end up sharing in the excess of electrons found on the oxygen atom. This is much like a chemical bond, but the amount of electron sharing is much smaller than a normal chemical bond. Thus, this is a weaker kind of "bond," and it is called a **hydrogen bond.**

Notice what hydrogen bonds do. They link *molecules* together. Chemical bonds link *atoms* together to form molecules. Hydrogen bonds, on the other hand, bring individual molecules close together, linking them. Thus, while a chemical bond forms between *atoms,* a hydrogen bond forms between *molecules.* Also, since hydrogen bonds are weak, they can be easily broken. For example, if you boil water, you are adding enough energy to the water to pull the water molecules far apart, breaking the hydrogen bonds. Despite the fact that the hydrogen bonds break, the chemical bonds that hold the two hydrogen atoms to the oxygen atom do not break. Water vapor is still H_2O, so the chemical bonds still hold. The molecules are so far apart, however, that the hydrogen bonds are eliminated.

So, what's the big deal? Why is hydrogen bonding so special? Well, there are a couple of reasons. First, because water molecules want to hydrogen bond to each other, and because they need to get close to one another to do that, water molecules tend to stick much closer together than do other molecules. For example, consider the following molecules: H_2S, H_2Se, and H_2Te. Those chemical formulas look a lot like H_2O, don't they? In fact, the only real difference is that the other molecules have a different atom in place of the oxygen atom. From a chemistry point of view, those three molecules are very similar to water. In fact, they are the chemicals most like water in all of creation. Guess what, though? All three of those molecules are *gases at room temperature*!

Why is water a liquid at room temperature, when other chemicals similar to water are gases? The answer is *hydrogen bonding.* Remember from Module #3 that the major difference between a liquid and a gas is how far apart the substance's molecules are and how quickly they move around. Well, hydrogen bonding keeps the water molecules close together and limits their movement somewhat. As a result, water is a liquid at room temperature when other chemically similar substances are gases. We are, in fact, very "lucky" this is the case. Water is one of the basic needs of life. All biochemists agree that if water were not liquid at room temperature, life as we know it could not exist! Despite the fact that *all chemically similar molecules* are gases at room temperature, water is a liquid, as it must be to sustain life. The chemical explanation for this is hydrogen bonding, but the real explanation, of course, is the Creator. He designed the world and its physical laws, and hydrogen bonding was a special provision He made in order to make life possible!

Hydrogen bonding actually gives water another interesting property. To learn about that property, perform the following experiment:

EXPERIMENT 4.4
Comparing Solid Water to Solid Butter

Supplies:

♦ Stick of butter or margarine (It must be fresh from the refrigerator so that it is solid.)
♦ Two small glasses
♦ Water
♦ Ice cube
♦ Stove
♦ Saucepan
♦ Knife (A serrated one works best. You will use it to cut the butter.)
♦ Spoon
♦ Eye protection such as goggles or safety glasses

Introduction: You should have already learned that when most things are heated, they expand, and when they are cooled, they contract. This is not always the case with water.

Procedure:

1. Look at the tablespoon markings on the wrapper that covers the stick of butter. Using those markings as a guide, cut ½ tablespoon off the end of the stick with the knife so that you have a small square of butter.
2. Unwrap both the piece you cut off and the rest of the stick.
3. Put the ½ tablespoon of butter you cut off the end back in the refrigerator until it is needed in step 8.
4. Put the rest of the stick of butter into the saucepan.
5. Heat the butter in the saucepan over low heat until it is completely melted. Stir it with the spoon to keep it from boiling.
6. When the butter is completely melted, carefully pour it into the small glass. You now have a glass of liquid butter.
7. Fill the other glass with water.
8. Go to the refrigerator and get the ½ tablespoon of butter you put there, and also get an ice cube from the freezer.
9. Drop the ice cube in the water.
10. Drop the ½ tablespoon of butter in the liquid butter.
11. Note in your laboratory notebook what happened to the ice cube and what happened to the solid square of butter.
12. Clean up your mess.

What was the difference in behavior between the ice cube and the square of butter? When you dropped the ice cube into the water, it should have floated. When you dropped the square of butter in the liquid butter, it should have sunk. Why the difference? Well, for the vast majority of substances in creation, the molecules get closer when the substance turns solid and farther apart as the substance turns into a liquid. Butter is an example of such a substance. Thus, the molecules that made up the solid butter were closer together than the molecules that made up the liquid butter. As a result, the solid butter pushed its way through the liquid butter and sank.

For water, however, precisely the opposite is true. When water is a solid, its molecules must stay in a rigid, geometric arrangement. That rigid arrangement requires the molecules to be a certain distance apart. When water is a liquid, however, its molecules are free to move around. As a result, hydrogen bonding can pull them closer together. As a result, *water molecules are closer together when water is a liquid compared to when water is a solid.* Because of this, the ice cube could not push its way through the water molecules, and the ice cube stayed afloat.

So, unlike most substances in creation, when water is a solid its molecules are actually farther apart than when it is a liquid. As a result, solid water (ice) floats in liquid water. Once again, we are quite "lucky" this is the case. After all, what happens to lakes in the winter? They freeze, don't they? Does all the water in the lake freeze? Of course not. If that were the case, all living things in that lake would die. Instead, as the water freezes, it *floats to the top of the lake* because of this property. As a layer of ice builds up on top of the lake, it insulates the water below, and at some point, no more water will freeze! Because of this, the living organisms in the lake survive the winter. Think about all the food we get from lakes or from other creatures that depend on the living organisms in a lake. If water didn't have this property, lakes in many regions of the world could not support life, and most likely we would not be able to survive! This is more striking evidence for the awesomeness of our Creator!

FIGURE 4.7
An Iceberg

Photo by Kathleen J. Wile

An iceberg can float because the molecules in ice are farther apart than they are in liquid water.

ON YOUR OWN

4.10 Water has a very high boiling point (the temperature at which it boils) compared to most other substances that are liquid at room temperature. Use hydrogen bonding to explain why this is the case.

4.11 Butane is a gas at room temperature, but it is stored under pressure as a liquid in a butane lighter. The chemical formula is C_4H_{10}. Isopropyl alcohol (commonly called rubbing alcohol) is another liquid you might have around the house. Its chemical formula is C_3H_8O. One of these liquids participates in hydrogen bonding. Which one?

Water's Cohesion

The polarity of water molecules, combined with hydrogen bonding, tends to keep water molecules close together when water is a liquid. Once they are close, they tend to want to stay close. Although the water molecules will move around, as all molecules do in liquid form, they still stay close together as they move. This phenomenon is often called **cohesion** (coh he' shun).

Cohesion – The phenomenon that occurs when individual molecules are so strongly attracted to each other that they tend to stay together, even when exposed to tension

What does this definition mean? Perform the following experiment to find out.

EXPERIMENT 4.5
Water's Cohesion

Supplies:

♦ Water
♦ Bowl
♦ Metal paper clip (Use a standard-sized paper clip. A big one will probably not work.)
♦ Toilet paper
♦ Dish soap
♦ Scissors
♦ Vegetable oil (optional)
♦ Eye protection such as goggles or safety glasses

Introduction: Water molecules are attracted to one another by hydrogen bonds as well as the electrical charges that are the result of polarity. Because they are attracted to one another, they do not like to be pulled apart, as this experiment will demonstrate.

Procedure:

1. Fill the bowl with water.
2. Tear off one square of toilet paper.
3. Cut a rectangle out of that square of toilet paper. It should be about 2 inches longer and 2 inches wider than the paper clip.
4. Set the paper clip on top of the rectangle of toilet paper, in the middle.

5. Carefully lift the rectangle of toilet paper by the corners so that the paper clip does not fall off.
6. Gently lay the toilet paper rectangle on the surface of the water. Watch what happens for a while.
7. Once the toilet paper gets completely soaked, it should fall to the bottom of the bowl. However, the paper clip should continue floating. If that didn't happen for you, try again with a new piece of toilet paper. If you can't get the paper clip to float, you might want to try the experiment with a different metal paper clip or distilled water, which can be found in any major supermarket.
8. Once the paper clip is floating freely, add a few drops of dish soap to the water, away from the paper clip.
9. Wait for a few moments and see what happens.
10. **Optional**: Try to repeat steps 1-7 using vegetable oil instead of water. It will take longer for the toilet paper to sink, and the paper clip should not float.
11. Clean up your mess.

What happened in the experiment? The paper clip floated on the water. Despite the fact that the metal paper clip is heavy enough to sink in the water, it did not. Why not? The answer is water's cohesion. You see, the water molecules are close together. In order for the paper clip to sink, it needs to push them out of the way. The water molecules fight that push, however, because they are attracted to one another due to hydrogen bonding and their own polarity. The paper clip, then, was exerting pressure on the water molecules. The water molecules, however, did not want to move apart, so they fought that pressure. That's cohesion. If you did the optional part of the experiment, you found that the paper clip would not float in vegetable oil. That's because vegetable oil does not have the cohesion that water has.

What happened when you added the dish soap? Well, most likely, the paper clip was shoved directly opposite of where you placed the dish soap, and then it probably sank suddenly. Why? Well, the active ingredient in dish soap (sodium stearate) is composed of long molecules. One end of each molecule is strongly attracted to water. When you added the dish soap, those long molecules got in between the water molecules and forced them apart. Once they got so far apart that they could not hydrogen bond to one another effectively, they lost their cohesion, and the paper clip was able to sink.

The phenomenon demonstrated in the experiment is called **surface tension**. Although that is an adequate term for the effect in the experiment, it is a rather specific term. It refers to the effect of cohesion at the surface of a liquid. The best way to think about this is to realize that cohesion *causes* surface tension. Because of cohesion, the surface of a liquid can resist tension. Water has one of the greatest tendencies towards cohesion, so it also has one of the largest surface tensions in all of creation. Even though water has a large surface tension, you have to realize that compared to most of what you and I are familiar with, that surface tension is still pretty small. After all, to get the experiment to work, you had to be very careful how you laid the paper clip in the water. If you had tried to put it on the water's surface with your hands, it would have sunk. So don't think that the surface tension of water is so great that it can keep most things from sinking. Nevertheless, the surface tension is real, as was demonstrated in the experiment.

Water's cohesion is a very important property for plants. As you will learn in biology, water travels up from the roots of a plant to its leaves in small tubes called **xylem** (zye' lum). Amazingly, there is no "pump" that causes the water to do this. You and I have blood running through our arteries and veins because our hearts pump the blood so that it can travel throughout our bodies. However, plants do not need any kind of pump to transport water. Water can travel from the roots all the way to the top of the tallest tree without any system that pushes it upward. How can this happen? You will learn more about this amazing process, called "cohesion-tension transport," in biology. As its name implies, however, water's cohesion is what makes it possible. Without its cohesion, water could not travel upward in plants, and only the very smallest of plants (like mosses) could exist. Once again, this is great testimony to the creative genius of God.

Water's cohesion is important for certain insects as well. The water striders (often incorrectly called "water spiders") pictured below are able to walk on water because of its surface tension.

FIGURE 4.8
Water Striders

Photo © Shaun Lowe
Agency: istockphoto.com

Notice how the surface of the water actually bends where the water striders' legs touch it. That shows you the water strider's weight is pushing down on the surface of the water. Nevertheless, water's surface tension is enough to keep the insects from sinking.

Now it is very important to note that while the attraction between water molecules is strong, sometimes the attraction between water molecules and *other* molecules is stronger. Perform the following experiment to see what I mean.

EXPERIMENT 4.6
The Forces Between Molecules

Supplies:

♦ A smooth glass surface (The underside of a drinking glass works well.)
♦ Wax (A candle will work.)
♦ Sink
♦ Eye protection such as goggles or safety glasses

Introduction: Water molecules are attracted to one another, but they can also be attracted to other molecules. This experiment explores the relative strengths of these attractions.

Procedure:

1. Rub the wax on half of the glass surface. You should be able to see the wax rub off the candle (or other source of wax) and onto the glass. Make sure that half of the surface is completely covered in wax.
2. Hold the glass surface horizontal, and put it under the sink's tap.
3. Turn on the tap so that water flows over the entire glass surface.
4. Turn off the tap, and while the glass surface is still horizontal, notice the difference between the water on the waxed portion of the glass surface and the water on the unwaxed portion.
5. Draw a picture of what you see in your lab notebook.
6. Clean up your mess.

What did you see in the experiment? If all went well, you should have noticed that the water on the waxed portion of the glass surface "beaded" into droplets, but the water on the unwaxed portion did not. How can this be explained? Well, when water is sitting on a surface, it can be attracted either by other water molecules *or* by the molecules that make up the surface upon which it sits. In your experiment, half the water ended up on a surface of wax, while the other half ended up on a surface of glass.

The results of the experiment tell us something about how water molecules are attracted to glass, wax, and other water molecules. Since the water on the wax formed droplets, you know that water molecules were attracted to one another, making them "clump up" into droplets. This tells you that water molecules are more attracted to each other than they are attracted to the molecules in wax. Indeed, if you spray water on a freshly waxed automobile, you will see the same effect for the same reason. On the other hand, since the water "spread out" over the glass, the glass must have attracted water molecules to itself. This tells you that water molecules are more attracted to the molecules in glass than they are to each other. In the end, then, even though water does have a lot of cohesion, a stronger force can reduce that cohesion.

Hard Water and Soft Water

Have you ever heard of "hard" water? You might have hard water coming out of your faucets. What is hard water? Well, water that comes into our homes was, at one time or another, in a lake, stream, or underground reservoir. For most people, that water goes through some sort of treatment process before it comes into their home. In the treatment process, the water is filtered to get rid of foreign particles, and then chlorine is usually added to kill the microscopic organisms that thrive in the water. Most water treatment plants also add fluoride to the water for good dental hygiene.

Many people think that hard water is a result of the treatment process I just described. This is not the case. In fact, if you get your water from a freshwater well with no treatment process at all, you are just as likely to have hard water as is someone who gets their water from a water treatment plant. Hard water is a result of the *source from which the water is taken*. Some areas of the world (especially the midwestern United States) have rocks (like limestone) that are rich in certain metal ions like calcium ions. These metal ions are part of ionic compounds that make up the rock.

What does water do to ionic compounds? It dissolves them. Water from regions of the world that are rich in limestone and other metal-containing rocks tends to have lots of metal ions dissolved in it. That's what hard water is.

Hard water - Water that has certain dissolved ions in it – predominately calcium and magnesium ions

Just like salt dissolved in water makes water taste bad, calcium ions dissolved in water also affect the taste of water. Some people who are used to the taste actually think it makes the water taste better, but many people think it makes the water taste worse. In addition, the metal ions in hard water react with soap to make a scum. This reduces the ability of soap to clean things. Finally, hard water tends to build up scales on pipes and fixtures. These scales are the result of ionic compounds that become undissolved when the water changes temperature. These scales build up in sinks, bathtubs, and toilets to make the stains referred to as "hard water stains." Although the ionic compounds in hard water pose no health risks, most people simply would rather not have them in the water due to the concerns I just mentioned.

As a result, many people get rid of hard water by "softening" it with a water softener. In a water softener, a chemical process called "ion exchange" removes ions like calcium and magnesium (mag nee' see uhm) from the water. In this process, however, the calcium and magnesium ions must be replaced with something else, usually sodium ions. If you have a water softener, or if you know someone who does, you probably know that in order for the water softener to work, salt must be added to it. Recall that salt is made up of sodium ions and chloride ions. In a water softener, the sodium ions from the salt are exchanged with the calcium and magnesium ions in the water.

This water-softening process works very well because our taste buds react differently to sodium ions than they do to calcium and magnesium ions. As a result, the "funny" taste of hard water is removed. Also, sodium ions do not form the ionic compounds that result in scales left behind on pipes and fixtures. Finally, sodium ions do not react with soap to make scum, so soap lathers better in soft water, and you feel cleaner when bathing or showering in soft water.

Although soft water is more pleasant than hard water, it can pose a minor health risk for some people. Sodium ions can cause heart troubles in certain people. The amount of sodium ions you get by drinking soft water is relatively small compared to the amount of sodium ions you get from your food. Nevertheless, people who are on strict low-sodium diets should either not soften their water or use more expensive, sodium-free water-softener salts, like potassium chloride.

ON YOUR OWN

4.12 Calcium and magnesium ions are both the result of atoms that lose electrons. Thus, they are positively charged ions. Suppose you actually could remove calcium and magnesium ions from water without replacing them with other positive ions. If you slowly started removing *only* calcium and magnesium ions from the water, you would find that as time went on, removal of the ions would become more and more difficult. Eventually, it would be *nearly impossible* to remove any more calcium or magnesium ions in the water, even though there might still be many ions left. Why?

ANSWERS TO THE "ON YOUR OWN" PROBLEMS

4.1 There will be a length of time between when it stops raining and when you measure the amount of water in the gauge. During that time, water will evaporate, causing your result to be too low. The second source of error occurs when you dump the water out. Unless you dry the gauge thoroughly, there will be water droplets left in the gauge. If the next rain falls before these water droplets have a chance to evaporate, your next measurement will be too large. There could be more errors as well. These are just the two major errors that come to mind.

4.2 The Na is one atom since the second letter is lowercase. The other letters each represent an atom since they are all capitals. There are no subscripts after the Na, H, or C, so there is only one each of them. There is a subscript of 3 after the O, indicating 3 oxygen atoms. This makes a total of 6 atoms.

4.3 The C stands for carbon and there is a subscript of 2, indicating 2 carbon atoms. The H is for hydrogen, and there is a subscript of 4 after the H, making 4 hydrogen atoms. Finally, the O represents oxygen and there is a subscript of 2, indicating 2 oxygen atoms.

4.4 Carbon is represented by C, the symbol for hydrogen is H, and oxygen is represented by O. You put subscripts after each to indicate the number. Thus, the chemical formula is $C_6H_{12}O_6$.

4.5 The stream will bend the same way it did before: toward the comb. If you thought it should bend the other way because of the opposite charge, think about it for a moment. The water molecules are originally all jumbled around, pointing different directions. The reason the stream bends is that in the presence of a charged object, the water molecules reorient themselves so that the opposite charge is facing the object. Thus, the water stream will always be attracted to the charged object, because the water molecules can point whichever way they want. They will always point so that the small charge on the molecule opposite the charge on the object is pointed toward the object.

4.6 HCl is polar. The chlorine will have the small negative charge. After all, if the chlorine can pull on the electrons with more strength, it will "win the battle" and get the electrons.

4.7 Chlorine gas is not polar, because the only two atoms in the molecule are the same. Thus, they pull on electrons with equal strength. Since they pull with equal strength, neither one of them will win more than its fair share of electrons.

4.8 Gasoline is made up of nonpolar molecules. If water cannot dissolve a substance, it is likely that the substance is nonpolar.

4.9 Table salt would not dissolve, but canola oil would. After all, nonpolar substances dissolve other nonpolar substances. Since table salt is ionic, it will not dissolve in a nonpolar substance. Since canola oil is nonpolar, it will dissolve in a nonpolar substance.

4.10 Water has a high boiling point because the hydrogen bonds hold the molecules together. In order to turn into a gas, the water molecules need to get far apart from one another. When you heat something, you are giving it energy. Because the hydrogen bonds hold the molecules together, it takes a lot of energy (thus a high boiling temperature) to pull them apart.

4.11 <u>Isopropyl alcohol participates in hydrogen bonding</u>. Remember, hydrogen bonding in water takes place between the hydrogen and oxygen atoms. There are plenty of hydrogen atoms in butane, but no oxygen atoms. The other way you can tell is that butane is a gas at room temperature, thus the molecules are not held together tightly. Isopropyl alcohol is a liquid at room temperature, indicating that its molecules are held more tightly together. Between the two, then, the alcohol is the more likely one to have hydrogen bonds.

4.12 Think about this one. Calcium and magnesium ions are positive. A sample of tap water, however, has no net electrical charge. Why? Well, for every positive ion in the tap water, there is a negative ion somewhere to cancel it out. If you removed only the positive ions, the negative ions that balance them out would still be there. As a result, <u>as time went on, the tap water itself would become more and more negatively charged. Negative charges *attract* positive charges. Thus, with each positive ion you removed, the tap water would become more negative, and that would more strongly attract the remaining positive ions. At some point, the negative charge of the tap water would be so great that it would attract the remaining positive ions so strongly that it would take enormous amounts of energy to pull the positive ions away</u>. This is why you cannot simply remove the calcium and magnesium ions from hard water. The water itself would quickly become negatively charged. Thus, rather than *removing* the calcium and magnesium ions, water softeners *replace* them with other positive ions. That keeps the tap water neutral overall.

STUDY GUIDE FOR MODULE #4

1. Define the following terms:

a. Electrolysis
b. Polar molecule
c. Solvent

d. Solute
e. Cohesion
f. Hard water

2. Suppose you did an electrolysis experiment like Experiment 4.1 on hydrogen peroxide, which has a chemical formula of H_2O_2. If it worked properly, which of the following results would you expect: (a) same as with water, (b) equal amounts of hydrogen and oxygen, or (c) twice as much oxygen as hydrogen?

3. Suppose you performed Experiment 4.1 with a test tube that had a crack in it. Gas could slowly leak out that crack, but not nearly as quickly as it was being made in the experiment. Suppose further that the crack was in the test tube that held hydrogen gas. Which chemical formula might result from such a botched experiment: HO or H_4O?

4. Epsom salts, which you used in Experiment 4.1, has the chemical formula $MgSO_4$. If Mg is the symbol for magnesium, S stands for sulfur, and O represents oxygen, how many of each atom exists in a molecule of Epsom salts?

5. Calcium carbonate is an ionic substance commonly called "chalk." If this molecule has one calcium atom (Ca), one carbon atom (C), and three oxygen atoms (O), what is its chemical formula?

6. One of the most common household cleaners is ammonia, which has a chemical formula of NH_3. How many atoms are in a molecule of ammonia?

7. A certain molecule is composed of atoms that all pull on electrons with the same strength. Will this molecule be polar?

8. Baking soda dissolves in water. Will it dissolve in vegetable oil, which is a nonpolar substance?

9. Carbon tetrachloride will not dissolve in water. Is it most likely made of ionic molecules, polar molecules, or nonpolar molecules?

10. Suppose you were able to count the molecules in a substance. Which would have more molecules, 1 liter of liquid water or 1 liter of ice?

11. If the substance in question #10 were virtually any other substance, what would the answer be?

12. What is responsible for water being a liquid at room temperature as well as for water's cohesion?

13. What causes surface tension?

14. Why is water harder in certain regions of the world than in others?

Introduction

Have you ever wondered what it would be like to travel in outer space? I confess that I dreamed of being an astronaut when I was young. Well, if I ever were to travel in outer space, I expect that one of the most breathtaking sights I would see would be one of my first: a look back at our planet. Astronauts have said that there are simply no words to describe that sight, and although no picture can do it justice, many have been taken. Figure 5.1 is one such picture.

FIGURE 5.1

Photo courtesy of NASA

The Earth As Viewed From Outer Space

Isn't God's creation marvelous? As you should be able to tell from its shape, the brown area in the picture is the continent of Africa, and you can also see the Arabian Peninsula. The white stuff is, of course, cloud cover (and the continent of Antarctica at the bottom). What color really dominates, however? The blue. In fact, blue dominates the picture so much that astronomers and astrophysicists call earth "the blue planet." What causes the blue color? The *water*. The earth is predominately water. In fact, about 71% of the surface of the earth is covered with water in the form of oceans, lakes, ponds, rivers, creeks, and streams. But that's not the end of the story! Some of the water on our planet isn't visible from above because it is underground. Even the white parts of Figure 5.1 are really water, because clouds are mostly made up of water. Finally, earth has many icebergs and glaciers, which are made up of water in its solid phase. In short, our planet is "overflowing" with water.

Collectively, all of these water sources are called the **hydrosphere** (hi' droh sfear), and they are essential for life's existence.

Hydrosphere – The sum of all water on a planet

As I said in the introduction to the previous module, people can live for two weeks or more with no food, but without water, we would die in about three days. That's why statesman and scientist Benjamin Franklin said, "When the well's dry, we know the worth of water."

As you know, water exists as liquid (what we usually call "water"), gas (which we often call "water vapor"), and solid (known as "ice"). Did you know that of all the planets in our solar system, earth is the *only one* that has a large quantity of water in its liquid form? It's one of the main reasons life cannot exist on any of the other planets but does exist here on earth. Liquid water, a necessity for life, can only be found in abundance on one planet: earth. Does that mean there isn't water on the other planets? No. It means that on the other planets, nearly all the water is either a gas or a solid, not a liquid. Why is earth so special? There are many reasons.

First of all, water is only a liquid in a certain temperature range (above 0 degrees Celsius [32 degrees Fahrenheit] and below 100 degrees Celsius [212 degrees Fahrenheit]). Thus, in order for a planet to have liquid water, there must be regions within that temperature range. Well, the vast majority of the earth is in that temperature range, so the vast majority of the water on the earth is liquid! What controls the temperature of a planet? There are two important factors: the distance from the sun and the atmosphere. As you have already learned, the greenhouse effect caused by earth's unique atmosphere keeps the average temperature of the earth at around 50 degrees Fahrenheit. As you have already seen, if the mixture of gases in the atmosphere were to change, the temperature would go up or down, potentially out of the range necessary for water to exist as a liquid. In addition, scientists have estimated that if earth were only a few percent closer to the sun than it is now, it would be so warm that the vast majority of its water would exist as a gas. Similarly, if the earth were just a few percent farther away from the sun, most of its water would exist as ice. Thus, earth has *just the right mixture of gases in its atmosphere*, and it is *just the right distance from the sun* to ensure that the vast majority of its water is liquid. No other planet we know of is like this!

Do you see what I'm trying to say? In the previous module, you learned that unlike the molecules most chemically similar to it, water is a liquid at room temperature. Now you have learned that earth's temperature is unique because of its atmosphere and its distance from the sun. That's an awful lot of coincidences, don't you think? If earth were just a little closer to or farther from the sun, water would not be a liquid on earth, and as a result, life could not exist. If the earth's atmosphere were slightly different in composition, we would have the same result. If water didn't participate in hydrogen bonding, it would not be liquid at the earth's temperature. In the end, it seems that water, earth, and life were all *designed* for each other, doesn't it? That should not surprise any scientist who believes in a supreme Designer, but it should certainly astound any scientist who does not!

The Parts of the Hydrosphere and the Hydrologic Cycle

Since the hydrosphere is actually the sum total of all water (gas, liquid, and solid) that exists on the planet, it is important to take a look at all the sources of water on the earth. The vast majority (97.25%) of earth's water is found in the oceans. Since the oceans contain saltwater, most of earth's water supply isn't even drinkable! Only 2.75% of earth's water supply is freshwater and therefore at least potentially drinkable. Where is the majority of earth's supply of freshwater? Most people think it is contained in the lakes, ponds, rivers, streams, and creeks on the planet, but they are wrong! It turns out that almost three-quarters of the freshwater on earth exists in the glaciers and icebergs of the planet. A large fraction of the remaining freshwater is underground. Scientists call this water **groundwater**. In the end, less than 0.01% of the earth's freshwater supply is in the lakes, ponds, rivers, streams, and creeks of the planet. This water, called **surface freshwater**, is what we typically think of when we think of earth's freshwater supply. However, it represents only a tiny, tiny fraction of the freshwater the earth really holds, and even a tinier fraction of all of earth's water. Table 5.1 summarizes the sources of water on the planet.

TABLE 5.1

Water Source	Type of Water	Percent of Hydrosphere
Oceans	saltwater	97.250%
Glaciers and Icebergs	freshwater	2.050%
Groundwater	freshwater	0.685%
Surface Water (not oceans)	mostly freshwater	0.009%
Soil Moisture	freshwater	0.005%
Atmospheric Moisture	freshwater	0.001%

Although you need not memorize this table, there are a few facts I would like you to remember:

1. **The vast majority of earth's water supply is contained in the oceans as saltwater.**
2. **The vast majority of earth's *freshwater* supply is stored in icebergs and glaciers.**
3. **The largest source of *liquid freshwater* is groundwater.**

If you remember these facts, there is no need to memorize the table.

I am going to discuss each water source in the table individually as I go through this module. Before I do that, however, I want to show you that these sources are *not isolated from each other*. Even though we can list them as different water sources and account for how much water is in each of them, they do interact with one another, which makes for some very interesting science.

The interaction between these sources of water is described by the **hydrologic** (hi droh loj' ik) **cycle**.

Hydrologic cycle – The process by which water is continuously exchanged between earth's various water sources

The hydrologic cycle is best illustrated by a figure, which is shown on the next page.

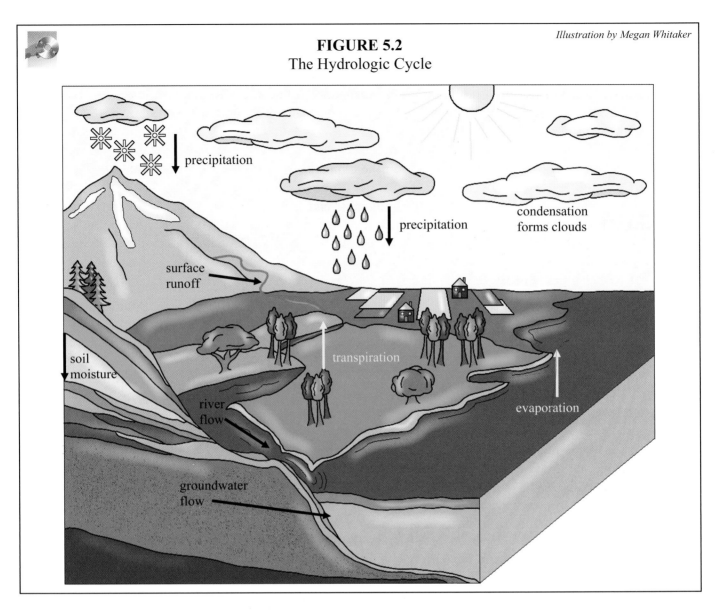

FIGURE 5.2
The Hydrologic Cycle

Illustration by Megan Whitaker

There are many ways of viewing and discussing the hydrologic cycle, but for the purposes of this course, Figure 5.2 covers the major concepts. Water gets into the atmosphere predominantly by **evaporation** and **transpiration**. Although you probably know what evaporation is, you might not be familiar with the other term:

Transpiration – Evaporation of water from plants

As a part of a plant's natural life processes, water vapor evaporates from its leaves. We call that process transpiration. If you think about it, evaporation takes water out of the oceans, lakes, rivers, and streams, while transpiration takes water from the soil. After all, plants absorb water from the soil, so any water they emit must have originally come from there. Thus, transpiration depletes **soil moisture**. Soil moisture can also be depleted when it soaks down into the groundwater sources and feeds into lakes, rivers, and streams by the process of **groundwater flow**.

When evaporation and transpiration take place, water vapor goes into the atmosphere. It then forms clouds by a process we call **condensation**.

Condensation – The process by which a gas turns into a liquid

I will discuss cloud formation in more detail a bit later, but for now, just realize it occurs when gaseous water (water vapor) turns into a liquid that stays suspended in the air. Eventually, the oceans, lakes, rivers, streams, and soil moisture all get replenished when the water in the clouds falls out of the atmosphere as **precipitation**.

Precipitation – Water falling from the atmosphere as rain, snow, sleet, or hail

Some of the precipitation falls directly into the oceans, lakes, rivers, and streams, and some of it falls onto land. That water can replenish the soil moisture, or it can run along the surface of the land into an ocean, lake, river, or stream as **surface runoff**.

Now don't get bogged down in the details so much that you miss the big picture here. It is important to know all the processes in the hydrologic cycle, but it is also important to step back and look at the cycle as a whole. Look at what's happening. Water that started in the ocean can evaporate and form clouds. When those clouds finally cause precipitation, that water might very well fall into a lake, river, or stream. It also might become surface runoff or groundwater which eventually feeds a river, lake, or stream. As a result, water that starts out in the ocean can very easily be transferred to one of the freshwater sources in the hydrosphere. In the same way, a freshwater river might dump into the ocean, allowing freshwater to be transferred to the ocean via **river flow**. Alternatively, water that evaporates from a freshwater source might eventually precipitate in an ocean, once again transferring water from a freshwater source to an ocean, which is a saltwater source. The point is that the hydrologic cycle constantly exchanges water between all the sources in the hydrosphere. Think about that. Because of the hydrologic cycle, the next drink you take might contain water that was once in the ocean!

If you think it odd that water can be transferred from the ocean to a freshwater source, perform the following experiment.

EXPERIMENT 5.1
Evaporation, Condensation, and Precipitation

Supplies:

♦ Water
♦ Salt
♦ Ice
♦ Tablespoon
♦ Small saucepan
♦ Saucepan lid or frying pan lid larger than the saucepan used
♦ Large bowl (It should not be plastic, as it will get hot.)
♦ Potholders
♦ Zippered plastic sandwich bag
♦ Stove
♦ Eye protection such as goggles or safety glasses

Introduction: In the hydrologic cycle, water can be transferred from a saltwater source (the ocean) to a freshwater source through the process of evaporation, condensation, and precipitation. This experiment will show you how that works.

Procedure:

1. Fill the saucepan about ¾ full of water.
2. Add three tablespoons of salt to the water and stir to make as much salt dissolve as possible. Do not be concerned if you can't get it all to dissolve.
3. Taste the saltwater you have made. Please note that you should **NEVER** get into the habit of tasting things in an experiment unless someone who knows a lot more chemistry than you do (like me) says to do so. In this case, I know that you are not at risk of poisoning yourself by tasting the saltwater you have just made. However, there may be times when you make something in an experiment that *you* think will not hurt you, but is, in fact, quite toxic. So **DO NOT TASTE THINGS IN AN EXPERIMENT UNLESS A PERSON OF AUTHORITY TELLS YOU TO DO SO!**
4. Tastes bad, doesn't it? Now set the pan of saltwater on the stove and start heating it up. Your goal is to have vigorously boiling water, so turn up the heat!
5. While you are waiting for the saltwater to boil, take the zippered sandwich bag and fill it full of ice. Zipper it shut so that no water from the ice can leak out.
6. Once the saltwater has started boiling vigorously, place the bowl next to the saucepan. The bowl should not be on a hot burner. You do not want to heat the bowl. You just want it close to the boiling water.
7. Now use the potholder to hold the saucepan lid and put the zippered sandwich bag full of ice on top of the lid. You may have to use a finger or two from the hand holding the lid to make sure that the bag of ice stays on top of the saucepan lid.
8. Hold the lid so that one end (the one with the most ice on it) is over the saucepan and the other end is over the bowl. Tilt the lid so that it tilts toward the bowl. In the end, your setup should look something like this:

Illustration by Megan Whitaker

9. Hold the lid there for a little while and watch what happens on the underside of the lid. **BE CAREFUL! EVERYTHING HERE IS HOT!** Notice that water droplets are forming on the underside of the lid over the saucepan, and they slowly drip down the lid towards the bowl.
10. If your arm gets tired, you can set the lid down so that part of it rests on the saucepan and the rest sits on the bowl. Make sure that the bowl is lower than the saucepan so that the lid still tilts towards the bowl.

11. Eventually, you will see water dripping off the pan lid and into the bowl. Wait until there is enough water in the bowl to be able to take a drink. Once that happens, turn off the burner and wait a moment.
12. **Using potholders**, take the lid away and put it in the sink. Pour the half-melted ice out of the bag and throw the bag away (or recycle it). **Still using potholders**, take the bowl away from the stove and set it on the counter. Empty the saucepan and put it in the sink as well.
13. Allow the bowl to cool down completely, and then taste the water in the bowl. Once again, you can only do this because I am telling you to!
14. What does the water taste like?
15. Clean up your mess.

What happened in the experiment? Well, the water in the saucepan was supposed to represent ocean water. When you tasted it, it tasted salty. If you allowed the pan of saltwater to sit out long enough, eventually the water would all evaporate away. It would take a while for that to happen, however, so in the experiment, we accelerated things by heating the pan until the water started boiling. Thus, boiling the saltwater was just a way to speed up the rate at which the water would evaporate from the pan. When the steam (water vapor) hit the pan lid, the coolness of the ice caused the water to turn from vapor back into liquid. This process is condensation, and it is basically the same thing that happens to form a cloud. Thus, the cool pan lid was supposed to represent the clouds formed when ocean water evaporates into the atmosphere. Eventually, so many drops of water formed that they trickled down the pan lid into the bowl. This, of course, represents precipitation. In the end, when you tasted the water in the bowl, there was no salt taste at all. The bowl, therefore, represents a freshwater source.

The point of the experiment was to show you that even though water might start out as part of a saltwater source, through the process of evaporation, condensation, and precipitation, it can very easily be transferred to a freshwater source. How can this happen? Water evaporates but salt does not. So in a mixture of saltwater, when the water evaporates, the salt stays behind. This keeps the salt in the ocean but allows the water from the ocean to be exchanged with the many other water sources in the hydrosphere.

The experiment you performed is actually a very standard technique in chemistry. It is called **distillation** (dis tuh lay' shun).

Distillation – Evaporation and condensation of a mixture to separate out the mixture's individual components

When a chemist does a distillation, he or she typically has a mixture of two or more substances that need to be separated. When the mixture is boiled, the substances tend to evaporate one at a time, allowing the chemist to separate them. In the distillation you performed, you could have allowed all the water to boil away and condense into the bowl. In the end, you would have had freshwater in the bowl and nothing but salt in the saucepan; thus, the saltwater mixture would have been separated into its components: salt and water.

Now that you have an easier time believing that water can, indeed, be exchanged between all the water sources in the hydrosphere, I want to introduce one more concept. Since water is continually being exchanged between the water sources of the hydrosphere, a given molecule of water can only stay in a given water source for a certain amount of time. For example, if a water molecule is in a river that eventually flows into the ocean, the water molecule will be in the river until it either evaporates away or follows the flow of the river and ends up in the ocean. Either way, the water molecule will eventually be transferred from the river to another water source in the hydrosphere.

This tells us that a given molecule of water will only stay in a given water source for a certain length of time. Scientists call that time the **residence time** of the water source.

Residence time – The average time a given particle will stay in a given system

When discussing water molecules, the residence time is the time a given water molecule spends in a given part of the hydrosphere.

Now the residence time of a water molecule depends on the source in which it resides. For example, the oceans hold a *lot* of water, and there is really only one way a molecule of water in the ocean can be transferred to another water source in the hydrosphere. It must evaporate from the ocean. As a result, the residence time for a molecule of water in the ocean is rather long. Most calculations of residence time indicate that the average water molecule spends as many as 4,000 years in the ocean before being transferred to another water source. Water in rivers, however, tends to be transferred to other water sources rather quickly. After all, there isn't nearly as much water in a river as compared to an ocean. Also, rivers tend to flow and dump their water somewhere. As a result, the average residence time for water in a typical river is about two weeks. In order to get some idea of residence times throughout the hydrosphere, look at Table 5.2.

TABLE 5.2
Residence Times for Different Water Sources

Water Source	Residence Time		Water Source	Residence Time
Ocean	4,000 years		Atmosphere	10 days
Glaciers and Icebergs	1,000 years		Lakes	10 years
Groundwater	2 weeks - 1,000 years		Rivers	2 weeks
Soil moisture	2 weeks - 1 year		Swamps	1 - 10 years

Now the first thing you have to realize when looking at Table 5.2 is that the numbers are only approximations. After all, there is no direct way to measure residence time. These numbers are based on calculations that make a lot of assumptions and use current theories of how the processes in the hydrologic cycle work. Only if the assumptions and theories used in the calculation are good will these numbers be accurate. If not, then you cannot rely on them. Nevertheless, the numbers at least illustrate what I am trying to say. The nature of the water source determines the length of the residence time.

The next thing you need to realize is that these numbers are averages. The residence time in a small lake will be much shorter than the residence time in a large lake. Averaged over all lake sizes, however, the typical residence time for water in a lake is 10 years. Finally, you need to realize that I don't want you to memorize this table. Instead, I want you to look at the numbers and understand *why* the residence times are so different. Water in the atmosphere, for example, has a short residence time. Why? Well, the water in the atmosphere is constantly forming clouds and precipitating. Thus, a drop of water doesn't spend much time there. In the same way, the residence time for a drop of water in a river is shorter than the residence time for a drop of water in a lake because rivers flow, transporting their contents to other sources in the hydrosphere. A lake does not flow, so it takes longer for water to move from a lake to some other source. That's the kind of thinking I want you to develop in reference to residence times.

ON YOUR OWN

5.1 Suppose you are given a sample of water taken from somewhere in earth's hydrosphere.

   a. Would it most likely be saltwater or freshwater?
   b. If it is freshwater, where did it most likely come from?
   c. If the person who collected the sample tells you it is freshwater that originally came from a liquid source, where did it most likely come from?

5.2 Water that was originally in a plant ends up in a cloud. What two processes of the hydrologic cycle caused it to be transferred in that way?

5.3 Rain that hits the land can travel as a liquid into a lake, river, stream, or ocean in two different ways. What are they?

5.4 Suppose a scientist studies two groundwater sources. The first is an underground river that flows quickly into a large lake. The second is a large basin of underground water that moves at a much slower rate towards a small pond. Which groundwater source has the longest residence time?

Before I end this section on the hydrologic cycle, I would like to point out that the Bible discussed the hydrologic cycle long before scientists did. In Job 36:27, 28, we read, "For He draws up the drops of water, they distill rain from the mist, which the clouds pour down, they drip upon man abundantly." This, of course, describes evaporation, condensation, and precipitation, which are all important processes in the hydrologic cycle. The river-flow process of the hydrologic cycle is also mentioned in the Bible. In Ecclesiastes 1:7 we read, "All the rivers flow into the sea, yet the sea is not full. To the place where the rivers flow, there they flow again."

Does it surprise you that the Bible described a scientific process long before it was understood by scientists? It shouldn't. After all, who is responsible for the Bible? The Creator of the universe, of course! God knows all the secrets of how the universe works. It only makes sense, then, that some of those secrets will be revealed when He speaks to His creation. The hydrologic cycle is just one of many scientific truths revealed in the Bible.

The Ocean

Since the ocean is the most important source of water in earth's hydrosphere, it seems only natural to look at it first. The ocean is mostly made up of salt and water. It is important to realize that scientists use the term **salt** differently from how most people use it. When you and I speak of "salt," we are referring to a specific substance: table salt. Scientists call this substance **sodium** (so' dee uhm) **chloride** (klor' eyed). When scientists speak of "salt," however, they are actually talking about a *large class* of substances, of which sodium chloride is a member. There are many other substances that fall within the classification of "salt," however. Have you ever heard of someone soaking their feet in a mixture of Epsom salt and water? Epsom salt is another member of the "salt" class; its specific name is magnesium sulfate.

Using the term "salt" in the scientific way, the ocean is about 96.5% water and 3.5% salt. However, a large fraction of the salt that is in ocean water is, in fact, table salt (sodium chloride). As a result, we can be a bit more specific about the makeup of ocean water, as shown in Figure 5.3.

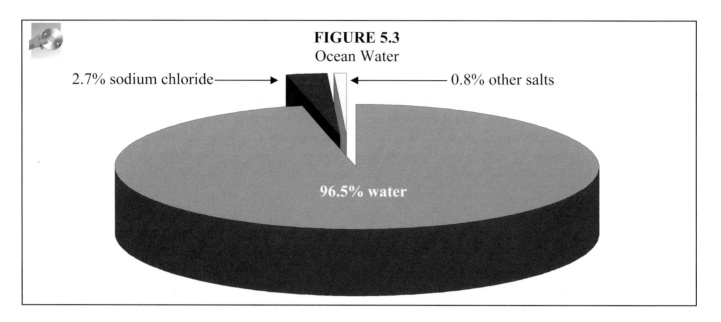

FIGURE 5.3
Ocean Water

2.7% sodium chloride ⟶ ◀— 0.8% other salts

96.5% water

As you can see, then, sodium chloride makes up more than ¾ of the dissolved salt in the ocean. Nevertheless, other salts do exist in ocean water.

This discussion brings me to the term **salinity** (suh lin' uh tee).

Salinity – A measure of the mass of dissolved salt in a given mass of water

In this definition, I am using the term "salt" in its broad sense, as I will throughout the rest of this module. In chemistry, you will learn how to tell whether or not a substance is a salt. For right now, however, you can think of most solids that dissolve in water as salts. Thus, salinity can be thought of as a measure of how much solid matter is dissolved in water.

The salinity of ocean water is about 35 grams per 1,000 grams, or 35 g per kg. What does that mean? It means that in every kilogram (1,000 grams) of ocean water, there are 35 grams of dissolved salt. As Figure 5.3 illustrates, the majority of the salinity comes from one substance, sodium chloride, but you can't forget the other salts that account for the rest of the salinity. Of course, the salinity of the water varies from place to place in the ocean. In places where freshwater rivers are dumping into the ocean, the freshwater dilutes the saltwater, so the salinity is lower in those regions. In other regions, the salinity is higher due to a variety of conditions. In the end, then, the figure of 35 grams per kilogram is really just the *average* salinity of ocean water.

With all the talk about the salinity of ocean water, you might wonder why ocean water is salty while freshwater is not. Well, the answer to that lies in the hydrologic cycle. Remember that water can get into the ocean via surface runoff, river flow, and groundwater flow. As this water travels, it tends to dissolve the salts contained in the rocks or soils over which it passes. As a result, salts are constantly being added to the ocean. Some of these salts get used by organisms in the ocean, so they don't build up there. For example, calcium is dumped into the ocean, but a lot of it is used by shellfish to make their shells. As a result, even though calcium gets dumped into the ocean, there isn't a lot of calcium in ocean water.

Now wait a minute, you might be thinking. Lakes, rivers, and streams receive water from surface runoff and groundwater flow. Why aren't they salty? Also, if rivers carry water that has dissolved salts in it, why aren't rivers salty? Well, first of all, there is salt in every lake, river, and stream in the hydrosphere. The water is still considered freshwater because, as you learned in Module #1, the *concentration* of a chemical is as important as its presence. In most lakes, rivers, and streams, the salt concentration is so low that it is not really noticeable. In some lakes, however, the salt concentration is high. You will learn about that in an upcoming section of this module. For right now, the proper way to ask the question is, "Why is the salt concentration so high in the ocean and so low in freshwater sources?"

The answer to that question lies in the way in which the ocean participates in the hydrologic cycle. The ocean's principal way of putting water into the hydrologic cycle is through evaporation. Since, as Experiment 5.1 showed you, salt gets left behind when that happens, the salt in the ocean stays in the ocean. This concentrates the salt in the ocean, making ocean water salty. Most lakes, rivers, and streams not only put water into the hydrologic cycle via evaporation, but they also tend to exchange water directly with other sources. For example, lakes tend to feed rivers, which tend to dump water into the ocean. The net result is that the salts in most lakes, rivers, and streams never have a chance to concentrate, because they tend to leave whenever water leaves by any mode except evaporation. Thus, since the ocean keeps getting salts and tends not to lose them, the result is salty water. Lakes, rivers, and streams get salts as well, but they tend to get rid of them through the hydrologic cycle. The result is water with such a low salinity that it is considered freshwater.

The amount of salt in the oceans actually provides an argument for the fact that the earth is not nearly as old as what some scientists would like you to believe. You see, we have studied the hydrologic cycle enough to know how much salt gets put into the ocean every year. In addition, we have a pretty good idea of how much salt is removed from the ocean every year. In the end, then, we can actually "add up" the amount of salt going into the ocean and "add up" how much is being removed. As you might expect, this inventory leads us to the conclusion that more salt is going into the oceans than what is being removed. In the end, then, the oceans are getting saltier and saltier. Suppose we assume that the oceans originally had *absolutely no salt in them*, and that *all* of the salt in them today came from the hydrologic cycle. Well, based on the inventory that scientists have done, you can actually determine how long it would take for freshwater oceans to become as salty as they are now. It turns out that the data indicate it would take, at the very most, 62 million years to go from freshwater oceans to oceans with the salinity we see today.

What does this tell us about the age of the earth? Well, first of all, it makes it awfully hard to believe that the earth is billions of years old as some scientists want you to believe. After all, if it really were billions of years old, then why aren't the oceans *a lot* saltier than they are now? No one who believes that the earth is billions of years old has any convincing answer to this question. Secondly, the times that one calculates this way are, in fact, only upper limits to the real age of the earth. God certainly created the oceans with salt in them, since the organisms in the ocean are designed to live with salt. Thus, the assumption that the oceans were, at one time, completely freshwater is pretty silly. Any salt that the ocean initially had would lower the time it would take to reach the salinity we see now. Also, careful analysis of the hydrologic cycle tells us that the rate of salt being dumped into the ocean most likely decreases as time goes on. As a result, the rate of salinity increase we measure now is probably *lower* than what it was a few thousand years ago. Finally, the worldwide Flood most likely added a *lot* of salt to the ocean. Thus, the salinity of the oceans really tells us that the earth is *significantly* younger than a few million years old.

ON YOUR OWN

5.5 Suppose you analyzed the salinity of three samples of ocean water. One was taken from deep in the ocean, one was taken from near the surface, and one was taken from a place near where a large river emptied into the ocean. If the salinities of samples 1, 2, and 3 were 37 grams per kilogram, 25 grams per kilogram, and 35 grams per kilogram, respectively, which sample was taken near the river?

5.6 If a lake were completely isolated from all rivers and streams so that the only way it could get rid of water was by evaporation, would it most likely be a freshwater or saltwater source?

Glaciers and Icebergs

As I mentioned previously, glaciers and icebergs hold the vast majority of the hydrosphere's freshwater. It is therefore important to spend some time studying these vast reserves of drinkable water. Begin your study by performing the following experiment:

EXPERIMENT 5.2
Ice and Salt

Supplies:
- Ice cube
- Table salt
- Measuring cup
- Water
- Plastic bowl that holds more than 2 cups of water
- Freezer
- Teaspoon
- Small plate
- Strainer
- Small glass or cup
- Eye protection such as goggles or safety glasses

Introduction: Saltwater freezes at a lower temperature than does freshwater. You will see that fact demonstrated in this experiment. Additionally, this experiment will shatter a myth that seems to be quite popular among science students.

Procedure:

1. Fill your plastic bowl with 2 cups of water and then add 2 teaspoons of salt. Stir to dissolve as much of the salt as possible.
2. Keeping in mind that you should **NEVER** do this unless I explicitly tell you, taste the saltwater.

3. Place the bowl of saltwater in the freezer. While you are there, get an ice cube. Close the freezer.
4. Put the ice cube on the small plate and put a small pile of salt on one spot near the middle of the top of the ice cube. Do not cover the whole ice cube with the salt. Instead, make a small pile on top of the ice cube near the middle.
5. Watch the ice cube for a few minutes. It will be rather dull at first, but as time goes on, you should see something interesting happening. Make a drawing of what you see.
6. Go back to the freezer and take a look at the saltwater you put there. Continue to check on it periodically while you do other things (like more studying). Wait until about half the saltwater has frozen. Do not wait so long that it all freezes.
7. Once the contents of the bowl are about half ice and half saltwater, remove the bowl and pour the entire solution into the strainer, allowing the ice to separate from the saltwater. Rinse the ice in the strainer with *cold* water to remove any saltwater that might be clinging to it. You will re-melt a lot of ice in the process, but enough should survive so that you can take a drink.
8. Pour the remaining ice into a small glass and allow the ice to melt. Once it has melted, taste the water that results. What does it taste like?
9. Clean up your mess.

What happened in the experiment? Well, let's start with the obvious part first. When you placed salt on the ice cube, you should have seen the part of the ice cube under the pile of salt melt faster than the rest of the cube, so that the salt "burrowed" a hole in the ice cube. The main reason this happened (as you probably already guessed) is that saltwater freezes at a lower temperature than does pure water.

When the salt touched the ice cube, the ions in the salt attracted water molecules to them. Remember, the polarity of water means that water is attracted to ions. This caused some water molecules in the ice to move away from the other molecules in the ice, forming a saltwater solution. Once this happened, the solution stayed liquid, because the ice cube was not cold enough to keep saltwater frozen. This technique, of course, is used to help melt snow and ice on roads and sidewalks. When salt (either sodium chloride or calcium chloride) is spread on snow and ice, the snow and ice melt due to the fact that the salt pulls water into a saltwater solution, and since the saltwater freezes at a lower temperature than does pure water, it stays liquid even though the temperature is below the freezing point of water.

Now what about the second part of the experiment? Did the result surprise you? When students taste the melted ice in step 8 of the experiment, they usually expect the water to taste like freshwater. After all, they reason, if saltwater freezes at a lower temperature than does freshwater, then as a solution of saltwater freezes, the salt should be removed, leaving only freshwater. Sounds reasonable, doesn't it? The problem with this explanation is that it neglects what you learned back in Module #3.

When I talked about solids, liquids, and gases, I said that the major difference between them had to do with the motion of their constituent molecules or atoms. In a solid, the molecules or atoms are only allowed to vibrate back and forth, whereas in a liquid they can move around with a fair amount of freedom. In order for a liquid to freeze, then, enough energy must be removed to slow the motion of all the constituent molecules. In the case of saltwater, this means that the water molecules *and the dissolved salt* must be slowed down. As a result, the salt and the water are slowed down at the same time.

Even though they are slowed down at the same time, water and salt do not freeze as saltwater. They separate out as they freeze, typically making solid water that surrounds highly concentrated packets of saltwater called **brine**. Thus, a cube of frozen saltwater contains solid water surrounding little pockets of very concentrated saltwater. When the cube melts, the salt remixes with the freshwater, making saltwater again.

Why did I go through all of this? Well, I need to dispel a common myth among students these days. Many students seem to think that icebergs are the result of ocean water freezing. This is simply *not true*. Icebergs are composed of freshwater. They *do not* form as a result of ocean water freezing! After all, in your experiment, the mixture of salt and water was somewhat close to the salinity of seawater. Nevertheless, when you allowed part of the saltwater to freeze, the frozen portion still contained salt! The same thing happens when seawater freezes. In certain polar regions, the water in the ocean does freeze to form **sea ice**, but sea ice is not composed of freshwater. It is a mixture of solid water and brine. Now because some of that brine can be forced back into the sea, the amount of salt in sea ice is not as high as it is in seawater. Nevertheless, it is there. The salinity of sea ice ranges from 1 to 10 grams of salt per kilogram of ice.

Where, then, do icebergs come from? Believe it or not, they come from *glaciers*. Every iceberg starts as a glacier, so that's where I have to start in order to tell you about icebergs. As you already learned, the temperature of the troposphere decreases with increasing altitude. As a result, the upper portions of many mountains contain snow year round. Each winter, new snow falls, adding to the snow that is already there. The old snow underneath the new snow gets packed down into what is called **firn**.

<u>Firn</u> – A dense, icy pack of old snow

After a while, the whole mass of ice and snow gets so heavy that it starts to slowly slide down the mountain and move across the land, as shown in Figure 5.4.

FIGURE 5.4
The Malaspina Glacier in Alaska

Photo courtesy of NASA

glacier's
motion

The speed at which glaciers move is rather slow, usually less than 1 meter per day (less than 3 feet per day). Glaciers have been recorded moving more rapidly, however. In 1999, the Columbia Glacier in Alaska was observed moving at a rate of 35 meters (115 feet) per day.

As a glacier moves, it tends to sculpt the earth over which it is traveling, plowing earth and rocks out of the way, often making valleys where there were none before. As the glacier travels down the mountain, it will often reach an altitude where the snow and ice begin to melt faster than new snowfall can replenish it. At that point, the glacier starts to melt, feeding many freshwater sources in the hydrosphere. Glaciers in the polar regions of the earth, however, never reach that point, and they continue to flow into the sea, forming huge sheets of ice. Almost the entire Antarctic continent, which occupies an area of more than 13 million square kilometers (5 million square miles), is covered by ice that comes from glaciers. The glaciers have pushed some of this ice out into the sea, forming large floating sheets of ice (remember, ice floats on water) called **ice shelves**. One such ice shelf is called the *Ross Ice Shelf*, and it covers a portion of the Antarctic Ocean about the size of Texas.

When the edge of a glacier advances into the ocean, the ice weakens at some points, and large chunks of ice break off the glacier, floating away in the water. This process, called **calving**, is what makes **icebergs**.

FIGURE 5.5
A Glacier Calving

Photo © Michael Klenetsky Agency: dreamstime.com

The piece of ice falling off this glacier will begin floating in the water, at which point it will be an iceberg. Notice the dirt layered in the glacier. It was picked up as the glacier scraped across the land over which it moved.

As you probably know, the vast majority (about 90%) of an iceberg exists below the surface of the water, so what we can see of an iceberg is really only about 10% of the total. This is easy to understand if you look at an ice cube floating in a glass of water. We know that ice floats in water, but since the mass of ice is only slightly less than the mass of an equal volume of water, only a small portion of the ice cube can actually float above the surface of the water. The same is true for an iceberg. This is what makes them dangerous to ships. As a ship travels, it might see the tip of an iceberg and steer clear of it. However, since 90% of the iceberg is under water, it is very possible that even though the ship steers clear of the portion of the iceberg that can be seen, the bottom of the boat can still collide with the other 90% of the iceberg that is under water!

In the end, then, an iceberg is really a portion of a glacier that has broken off and floats in the ocean. Ice shelves are simply the ends of glaciers that float in the ocean. A glacier is the result of heavy snowfall in the mountains that does not melt away during the summer. So the largest sources of freshwater on the planet (icebergs and glaciers) are really the result of precipitation. After all, without snowfall in the mountains, none of what I just described would ever happen!

ON YOUR OWN

5.7 A sailor brings you a chunk of ice that he thinks came from an iceberg. Based on the description of what he saw, however, you think that it might have been a large chunk of sea ice. How could you tell whether the ice is from an iceberg or from sea ice?

Groundwater and Soil Moisture

Next to glaciers and icebergs, the largest source of freshwater is the groundwater that flows beneath us. Much like glaciers, the story of groundwater and soil moisture begins with precipitation, and it is best discussed using a figure.

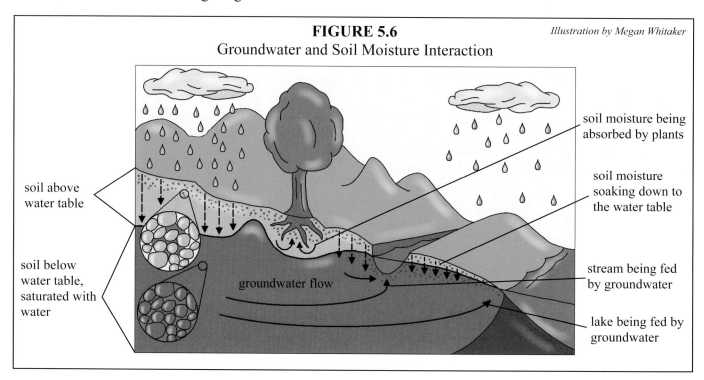

FIGURE 5.6
Groundwater and Soil Moisture Interaction

Illustration by Megan Whitaker

soil above water table

soil below water table, saturated with water

groundwater flow

soil moisture being absorbed by plants

soil moisture soaking down to the water table

stream being fed by groundwater

lake being fed by groundwater

When it rains on land, some of the water runs over the surface of the land and feeds another water source as surface runoff. Some of it, however, is absorbed by the soil. Some of that absorbed water is used by plants and gets put back into the atmosphere through transpiration, but some of it soaks into the soil and continues to travel deeper into the earth, becoming part of various groundwater sources.

As you can see from the figure, there is a region of soil that is completely saturated with water. This means there is no way that any more water can be put in the soil. This water is considered **groundwater**, and it flows towards bodies of water such as lakes, rivers, and oceans in order to feed them with new water. Above that region, the soil is not saturated, so it can hold more water. The water in this region is considered **soil moisture**. Some of the soil moisture goes into plants and is then ejected into the atmosphere through **transpiration**. Some of it can filter all the way down into the saturated soil to become part of the groundwater. The line that exists between the saturated and unsaturated soil is called the **water table**.

Water table – The line between the water-saturated soil and the soil that is not saturated with water

The depth of the water table changes based on how much water is available. After all, when water is scarce, soil that used to be saturated with water will eventually not be saturated any longer. Thus, if you wanted to find soil that was saturated with water, you would have to go deeper into the ground. The depth of the water table, therefore, *increases* under those conditions.

When soil moisture flows down through the soil, we say it **percolates**.

Percolation – The process by which water moves downward in the soil, toward the water table

If the water percolates deep enough, it will go past the water table. Since the water below the water table is saturated, however, that kind of percolation occurs only when some of the groundwater has flowed out of the region. At that point, there is some room for new groundwater, and soil moisture percolates through to resaturate the soil.

As I stated before, groundwater is our largest source of liquid freshwater. In fact, a large fraction of the water used in the United States comes from its groundwater supply. Typically, we access this groundwater by digging wells. Most groundwater flows quickly, at rates of up to 50 feet per day. Some groundwater moves slowly, however. Rates as slow as 1 foot every 10 days have been observed for certain groundwater sources. Many rivers continue to flow even when it does not rain for many days. This is because groundwater is feeding them.

ON YOUR OWN

5.8 You are studying a sample of soil and want to know if it came from above or below the water table. What could you do to determine this?

5.9 In a certain region, the depth of the water table is measured. If there is a lot less rain than usual over the summer, what will happen to the depth of the water table?

Surface Water

In addition to icebergs, glaciers, and groundwater, the lakes, rivers, ponds, and streams of the hydrosphere are sources of freshwater. It is very important to note, however, that *not all* lakes and ponds are sources of freshwater. In fact, some lakes have a larger salinity than the oceans! How is that possible? Well, remember why the oceans have salt in them. Salts get dissolved in the surface runoff, river water, and groundwater that feed the oceans, so salt is continually being dumped into the oceans. The only way that any significant amount of water leaves the oceans is by evaporation, which leaves the salt behind. Thus, lots of salt goes into the oceans and very little leaves them. As a result, the oceans are salty.

If a lake has a similar situation, the result would be pretty much the same. In fact, there are many lakes like this around the world. Most likely you have heard about the **Great Salt Lake** in northern Utah. This lake is about 75 miles long and 30 miles wide, with a maximum depth of 30 to 35 feet. It has three major rivers that feed into it, and it gets a lot of its water from surface runoff. All these sources carry small concentrations of dissolved salts. Unlike most lakes, however, the Great Salt Lake has no rivers or streams that flow from it. As a result, the only way it can get rid of water is through evaporation. This concentrates the salts in the lake, giving it a high salinity. No fish live in the Great Salt Lake, but scientists have found other forms of water life, such as microorganisms and brine shrimp.

Another salty lake you have probably heard about is the **Dead Sea**. Unlike what its name implies, the Dead Sea is not an ocean. It is a lake about 47 miles long and 10 miles wide, and it stands between Israel and Jordan. It actually has the lowest elevation of any body of water in the world, and as a result, it gets water from many sources. Like the Great Salt Lake, however, water only leaves this lake by evaporation, so the salts brought into the Dead Sea tend to stay there. The influx of water (mainly by the Jordan River) is large, but because evaporation occurs so quickly in the arid climate, the Dead Sea gets rid of water just as quickly as it comes in. This rapid filling and evaporation just increases the concentration of salts in the lake so that its average salinity is nearly 300 grams per kilogram! This number varies a lot by depth, but it makes clear the fact that the Dead Sea is *significantly* more salty than the oceans. This salinity makes it impossible for any life (except a few species of microscopic organisms) to exist there.

Atmospheric Moisture

The last water source I want to discuss is that which resides in the atmosphere. Once water enters the atmosphere through evaporation or transpiration, it can reside there in one of two forms. It can either exist as water vapor, making the **humidity** you learned about in Module #2, or it can condense to form clouds. To learn a little bit about how clouds form, perform the following experiment:

EXPERIMENT 5.3
Cloud Formation

Supplies:

♦ A clear, plastic 2-liter bottle (the kind that soda pop comes in) with the lid
♦ Water
♦ A match
♦ Eye protection such as goggles or safety glasses

Introduction: Cloud formation involves the condensation of water vapor. This experiment will show how water vapor in the atmosphere condenses to form clouds.

Procedure:

1. Clean the plastic bottle and remove any labels or wrapping so that you can see through the entire bottle.
2. Fill the bottle about one-eighth of the way with warm water.
3. Put the lid on the bottle tightly.
4. Squeeze the bottle with both hands. Hold it like that for a moment and then release the pressure, still holding on to the bottle. Do you see anything happening? Probably not.
5. Open the bottle. If necessary, re-shape it so that it is back to its original shape.
6. Light a match and allow it to burn for a moment.
7. Drop the match into the bottle. It will extinguish (of course) when it hits the water.
8. Put the lid on the bottle tightly and repeat step 4. Did you see something this time? Make a "before" and "after" drawing in your lab notebook.
9. Repeat step (4) several times. Record your observations.
10. Clean up your mess.

What happened in the experiment? Essentially, you formed a cloud. As you already know, when water vapor turns into liquid, we say that it has condensed. Typically, water vapor condenses as it gets cooler. If you leave a glass of ice water out on the counter, for example, water droplets will form on the outside of the glass. This is because water vapor in the air contacts the cold surface of the glass and condenses into liquid. In the same way, atmospheric water vapor condenses to form clouds.

The main way this happens was demonstrated in the experiment. When you squeezed the bottle, you put the air under pressure, containing it in a smaller volume. When you released the pressure, the air inside expanded back to its original size. Now think about the energy required to do this. While the air was in the bottle under pressure, it was moving about randomly, as you learned back in Module #3. This motion is responsible for the temperature of the air. When you released the pressure, the air had to expand outward.

Now think about that from a temperature point of view for a moment. In Module #3, you learned that a substance has a certain temperature because its atoms or molecules are moving about in a random manner. The atoms and molecules of solids vibrate back and forth, while those of liquids and gases actually move about in a random fashion. When these atoms or molecules strike a thermometer, they either transfer energy to the thermometer or take it away from the thermometer, depending on whether the thermometer's molecules are moving faster or slower than the substance's molecules. Well, suppose I had a certain number of gas molecules, and I suddenly let those gas molecules expand to fill up a much larger volume. What would happen to the temperature of the gas?

If you think about it, the collisions between the gas molecules and a thermometer would decrease in frequency. After all, if the same number of gas molecules fills a much bigger space, it would take a lot longer for each molecule to reach and collide with the thermometer. This would reduce the amount of energy that the molecules could give to the thermometer, and as a result, the thermometer would read a *lower* temperature. Thus, when a gas expands (and everything else stays the same), the gas cools. We call this **adiabatic** (aye dye' uh ba' tik) **cooling**.

<u>Adiabatic cooling</u> – The cooling of a gas that happens when the gas expands with no way of getting more energy

When you released the pressure on the bottle, the air inside expanded. This caused adiabatic cooling, which caused some of the water vapor in the bottle to condense. This made the cloud you saw in the bottle.

The vast majority of clouds you see are formed via adiabatic cooling. In the first part of your experiment, you probably did not see a cloud form, because even though the air cooled, there was nothing for the water vapor to condense on. That's why I had you use the match in the second part of the experiment. The match put small particles of smoke into the bottle. The water then could condense onto those smoke particles, forming a cloud. Most clouds in creation form around small particles in the atmosphere, like the smoke particles left by the match in your experiment. We call these particles **cloud condensation nuclei** (new' klee eye), because they form the "center" of water condensation.

<u>Cloud condensation nuclei</u> – Small airborne particles upon which water vapor condenses to form clouds

Cloud condensation nuclei come from sources such as volcanoes, fires, and dust blown up by the wind. Human industrial activity also contributes to the amount of cloud condensation nuclei in the atmosphere.

I will be talking a lot more about clouds in an upcoming module on weather, so I only want to say a couple more things about them in this module. First of all, the clouds you see in the sky often have ice in them as well. After all, they are far enough up in the troposphere that the temperature is cold enough for the water in the clouds to freeze. The ice crystals formed are so small, however, that they still stay suspended in the air. Second, when you see **fog**, what you are really seeing is a cloud that has formed on the ground. Fog usually forms when the humidity is very high and the temperature on the ground cools quickly. This causes a large amount of condensation in the air near the ground, forming a cloud.

A very thick fog is usually the result of a fog forming in dirty air. Such air is filled with a lot more cloud condensation nuclei and can result in very thick fog. Thus, when fog happens in air that has a lot of suspended particles in it (smoky air, for example), the fog is usually quite thick. London, especially since the Industrial Revolution, is famous for such thick, often foul-smelling fogs. This mixture of smoke and fog used to be called **smog**, but nowadays that term is usually reserved for the brownish haze you see hanging around a city due to large amounts of industrial and automobile pollution. To be completely correct, a thick fog brought on by smoke or other particles in the air is still called smog. The brownish haze from large amounts of industrial and automobile pollution, however, is more properly called **photochemical smog**.

Before I finish this topic, I need to make sure you do not confuse a couple of effects. We all know that as you heat things, they expand. In Experiment 3.2, for example, you partially inflated a balloon by heating the air in a bottle. So, when you heat up air, it expands. Wait a minute, however. I just told you that when air expands, it *cools*. Isn't that a contradiction? No, it is not. The thing you have to think about is *energy*. When I heat up a substance, I am giving it energy. As a result, it can expand without cooling. After all, if I heat up a gas, its molecules move more quickly. Thus, even when it expands, it will still be warm, because despite the fact that the molecules have more room to move, they move more quickly. Thus, they still hit the thermometer with a reasonably large frequency. Also, since they are moving faster, they transfer more energy to the thermometer with each collision. Thus, *because I give the substance energy*, it expands without cooling.

In the adiabatic cooling I talked about in this section, energy is not being given to the gas. Thus, it expands, but its molecules do not move any more quickly. They therefore hit the thermometer with less frequency and no extra violence. This results in a lower temperature. In the end, then, a gas will expand without cooling when it is heated because the process of heating gives it extra energy. Adiabatic cooling, however, happens when a gas is expanded *without* adding any extra energy to it. That's the distinction you must keep in mind if you want to understand why air expands when it is heated but also cools when it *adiabatically* expands.

ON YOUR OWN

5.10 Suppose you have a balloon whose volume you can change. You inflate it to a volume of 1 liter and measure the temperature of the gas inside. You then very quickly compress the balloon so that its volume is only 0.5 liters. What happens to the temperature of the gas inside?

Before I leave this section, I want to make a practical point. The correct answer to the "On Your Own" question is that the gas temperature would be higher. After all, if a gas cools when it expands, it must warm when it contracts, provided no energy is removed from it. That's why the cloud disappeared in step 9 of Experiment 5.3 each time you squeezed the bottle. The gas warmed when it was compressed, evaporating the water in the cloud. The fact that a gas cools on expansion and heats on compression is part of the principle behind a refrigerator. A refrigerator uses a substance that is a gas at room temperature. A compressor in the refrigerator compresses the gas, heating it up. It compresses the gas so much, in fact, that a large portion of the gas condenses into a liquid.

How does compressing a gas so that it heats up cause a refrigerator to get cold? Well, once compressed, the gas is released into a low-pressure portion of the system. As a result, the gas begins to expand. This, of course, causes adiabatic cooling, which cools down the contents of the refrigerator. In addition, the gas that had condensed evaporates, and as you learned in Module #2 (Experiment 2.1), that further cools the system. This process must be repeated over and over again, and the gas heats up each time it is compressed and cools down each time it is allowed to expand.

Obviously, then, in order to keep the inside of the refrigerator cold, the pipes that carry the expanded gas are on the inside of the refrigerator, and the pipes that carry the compressed gas and liquid are on the outside. In addition, there is insulation between the hot pipes and the cold pipes. So a refrigerator works by simply allowing a gas to expand, and the resulting adiabatic cooling (combined with evaporation) then cools the interior of the refrigerator. On the other side of an insulator, that same gas is compressed again so that the cycle can start over, and the resulting heat is dissipated into the room that contains the refrigerator. In a way, then, a refrigerator "pumps" heat out of the refrigerator and simply dumps it into the room. Since the volume of the room is usually huge compared to that of the refrigerator, you never really notice the heat. If you put a refrigerator in a small room, however, you will notice the heat it generates! This same principle governs air conditioning as well, but the heat from the gas compression in air conditioners is usually released outside.

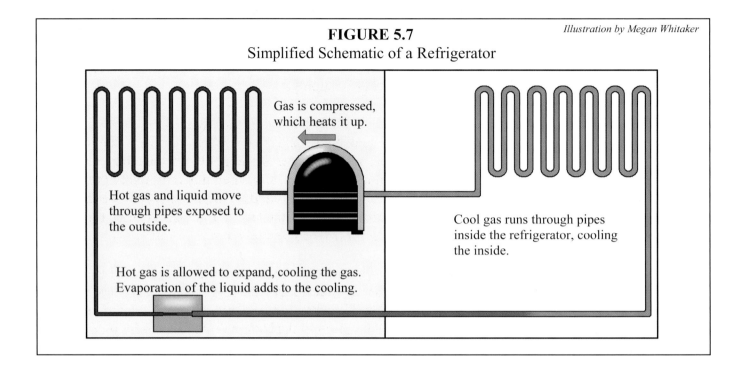

FIGURE 5.7
Simplified Schematic of a Refrigerator

Illustration by Megan Whitaker

Gas is compressed, which heats it up.

Hot gas and liquid move through pipes exposed to the outside.

Cool gas runs through pipes inside the refrigerator, cooling the inside.

Hot gas is allowed to expand, cooling the gas. Evaporation of the liquid adds to the cooling.

Water Pollution

Since this module is devoted to the hydrosphere, I cannot end it without mentioning one of the real environmental problems that exists today: **water pollution**. As you have hopefully learned in this course already, some of the environmental "crises" that supposedly exist today are blown way out of proportion. Many of them are mostly media hype with little science attached. Such is the case with global warming and, to a lesser extent, ozone depletion. Water pollution, however, is a real problem, and one that gets precious little media attention.

Industries dumping waste into rivers along with medical waste being thrown into the ocean are often what we think of when we think of water pollution. Although these problems are real and do exist, the more damaging water pollution today is happening to our groundwater supply. Pesticides, fertilizers, gasoline, and common industrial chemicals seep into the soil moisture and end up in the groundwater. From there, they feed all the other water sources in creation.

The reason groundwater pollution is so damaging is a result of two facts. First, it is very hard to control. After all, in most industrialized nations, there are laws about what can be dumped into rivers, oceans, and lakes. These laws are easily enforced because water in a river outside an industrial plant can be tested to see if the plant is dumping pollutants into it. The groundwater is a bit more difficult to test, however. Also, because of the nature of groundwater flow, pollutants that an industry allows to seep into the soil may show up in a lake far away! How will we know which industry to blame? The other reason groundwater pollution is so damaging is a result of the fact that about 50% of the population in the United States gets its drinking water from groundwater sources. Thus, groundwater pollution directly affects human health.

Of course, industry isn't the only culprit when it comes to water pollution. Pesticides and certain fertilizers that are fine on land can be devastating to a lake or river. If a farmer overuses such chemicals, they make their way into the groundwater and thus the drinking water supply as well. Also, underground storage vessels, such as those at gasoline stations, can leak. When they leak, gasoline filters into the groundwater and makes its way into our lakes and rivers, as well as our drinking water. Finally, when the wrong kind of trash is put in a landfill or dump, toxic chemicals can seep from them into the soil, eventually percolating into the groundwater supply.

Other types of water pollution exist as well. In many non-industrialized nations, human waste has so contaminated water sources that it is deadly to even drink from the lakes and rivers that once provided water for the population. In industrialized nations, water is often pulled from a lake or river to cool hot machinery. This cooling water gets hot in the process, and when it is returned to the water source, it changes the temperature of the water. This affects what kinds of organisms can live there, and if the temperature change is too severe, the entire balance of the lake's organisms can be thrown off. This kind of pollution, often called **thermal pollution**, can severely affect a local ecosystem.

Needless to say, water pollution is a very big problem today and should be addressed in several ways. Now I don't mean to imply that nothing is being done about water pollution. There has been legislation enacted over the years that has resulted in cleaner water. For example, the Environmental Protection Agency has found that the percentage of children in the United States served by public water systems that had dangerous levels of pollutants fell from 20% in 1993 to 8% in 1999. Thus, the quality of the water supply in the United States (and most industrialized nations) is improving. Unfortunately, however, the public rarely hears about this real environmental problem. Instead, they tend to hear media hype about things like global warming.

Cartoon by Speartoons

ANSWERS TO THE "ON YOUR OWN" QUESTIONS

5.1 a. It would most likely be <u>saltwater</u>. After all, more than 97% of the earth's water is ocean water, so the most likely source for water is the ocean.

b. If it is freshwater, it most likely came from <u>an iceberg or glacier</u>, since that's the largest source of freshwater on the planet.

c. If the person tells you it is from a liquid source, it is most likely <u>groundwater</u>, because groundwater is the largest source of *liquid* freshwater.

5.2 <u>Transpiration and condensation</u> put the water into the cloud. Since it was in a plant, the only way to get it into the atmosphere is by transpiration. At that point, however, it is water vapor, not in a cloud. To be in a cloud, the water vapor must condense.

5.3 Rain on the land can get into another water source via <u>surface runoff or groundwater flow</u>. If the rain never really gets absorbed by the soil, it becomes surface runoff. If it gets absorbed by the soil and enters into the groundwater, it will get to another water source by groundwater flow.

5.4 Residence time measures how long a single molecule of water stays in a water source. The slower the water source exchanges water with other sources, the longer the residence time. Thus, the <u>slow-moving groundwater source will have the longest residence time</u> because groundwater must flow into another source. If it flows slowly, it will take a long time to transfer water.

5.5 <u>Sample 2 was taken from the place near the river</u>. The other two salinities are at or above the average salinity of the oceans. Sample 2's salinity, however, is significantly lower. This means it must be near a place where freshwater dilutes the salt concentration.

5.6 <u>It would be a saltwater source</u>. If evaporation is the only way the lake loses water, it can never get rid of any salt that it gets. So salts keep building up, making the lake a saltwater lake.

5.7 <u>Melt the ice and taste the water. If it is salty, it came from sea ice. If it is not salty, it came from an iceberg</u>.

5.8 <u>Add some additional water to the soil. If the soil absorbs the water, it came from above the water table. If the soil cannot absorb the water, it came from below the water table</u>. Remember, soil below the water table is saturated. If the soil absorbs water, it is not saturated and therefore is not from below the water table.

5.9 <u>The depth of the water table will increase</u>. The water table separates saturated soil from unsaturated soil. With little rain, groundwater flow will deplete the saturated soil faster than percolation will replace it, and soil that used to be saturated will become unsaturated. That means the water table will be deeper than before.

5.10 <u>The temperature will increase</u>. Since air cools when it expands, it will warm when it is compressed, unless energy is removed in the process.

STUDY GUIDE FOR MODULE #5

1. Define the following terms:

a. Hydrosphere
b. Hydrologic cycle
c. Transpiration
d. Condensation
e. Precipitation
f. Distillation
g. Residence time

h. Salinity
i. Firn
j. Water table
k. Percolation
l. Adiabatic cooling
m. Cloud condensation nuclei

2. What kind of water makes up the majority of earth's water supply?

3. What is the largest source of freshwater on the planet?

4. What is the largest source of *liquid* freshwater on the planet?

5. In the hydrologic cycle, name the ways water can enter the atmosphere.

6. When a raindrop hits the ground, name three ways it can eventually end up in a river.

7. What process in the hydrologic cycle puts soil moisture into the atmosphere?

8. In which body of water would the residence time be shorter: a quickly moving river or a lake that has no river outlets?

9. What must a lake have in order for it to be a freshwater lake?

10. Why is the salinity of the ocean evidence that the earth is not billions of years old?

11. If you tasted melted sea ice, would it taste like freshwater or saltwater?

12. Where do icebergs come from?

13. Where do glaciers come from?

14. What is the term for the process by which a portion of a glacier breaks off and falls into the water?

15. The captain of a ship sees an iceberg and steers clear of it. Why is the captain still worried about a collision?

16. Suppose you studied two areas of land close to one another. In the first, there are a lot of trees. In the second, there are almost no trees at all. Other than that, the two areas seem identical. They have the same kind of grass and experience the same weather. Which one has the deeper water table?

17. If no energy is added to air, what happens to the temperature when the air expands?

18. Will fog be thicker in a smoky area or an area free of smoke?

19. What kind of cooling is responsible for most cloud formation?

20. A bright student notes that with a few modifications, a refrigerator can become a "hot box," keeping things warm instead of cold. Explain.

21. What kind of water pollution is the hardest to track back to its source?

MODULE #6: Earth and the Lithosphere

Introduction

In physical science, the earth is typically viewed as being made up of five sections. We have already talked about the first two: the atmosphere and the hydrosphere. In this module, we will cover the other three sections (illustrated in Figure 6.1): the **crust**, the **mantle**, and the **core**.

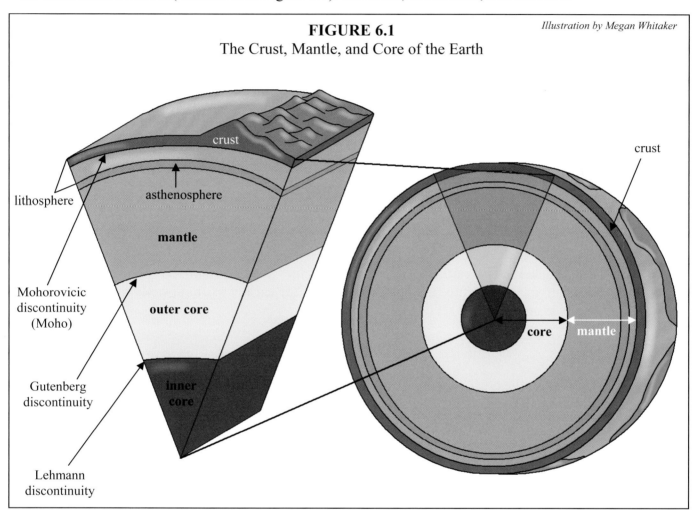

FIGURE 6.1
Illustration by Megan Whitaker
The Crust, Mantle, and Core of the Earth

As you can see from the figure, the crust is the top portion of the earth. Underneath the crust we find the mantle. Underneath the mantle is the core, which is split into two regions: the **inner core** and the **outer core**.

In this module, I will spend the majority of time discussing the crust, because scientists understand that section of the earth better than the others. There is a very good reason for this. We have never directly observed any part of the mantle or the core. You see, no drill has come anywhere close to penetrating even the topmost part of the earth's mantle. As a result, all information we have been able to learn about the mantle and the core comes from *indirect* observation.

What do I mean by indirect observation? Well, in science, we often want to learn about things we cannot see. For example, we want to know everything we can about atoms. Nevertheless, we cannot see them. The way we learn about atoms, then, is to do experiments that "disturb" them in some way and then watch what happens as they react. For example, when a glass tube is filled with neon gas and electricity is passed through it, the tube will glow with an orange-yellow light. We call this a "neon light." The reason the tube glows is that the neon atoms in the tube are disturbed by the electricity. In response, they emit the orange-yellow light. It turns out that the color of light changes if you put different kinds of gas in the tube.

Well, that fact tells us something about atoms. It tells us that they are disturbed by electricity and that each atom reacts to this disturbance differently. Scientists developed several theories to try and learn more from this little fact, and in the end, a scientist named Niels Bohr came up with a theory that could actually predict the various colors of light emitted by a hydrogen atom when it is disturbed by electricity. This theory, called the "Bohr Model," was accepted as a good theory, because it could explain some indirect observations of atoms. You will learn about the Bohr Model in a future module, so I don't want to go into it here. The point I want to make is that even though we cannot see atoms, we have a good idea of what they look like because of indirect observation. The same can be said of the earth. We cannot directly observe any part of the earth except the crust. However, because of indirect observation and some theories that have tried to explain these observations, we have a good idea of what all sections of the earth look like.

What kind of indirect observation can be made of the earth? Well, just like when scientists study atoms, an indirect observation of the earth's interior involves "disturbing" the earth and watching how it reacts. We can disturb the earth ourselves with explosives, or we can wait for times when the earth gets disturbed by earthquakes and other such events. If we observe how the earth reacts to these disturbances, we can learn about the parts of the earth we cannot study directly. I will discuss this further in an upcoming section of this module.

The Crust

As I said before, the crust is the only section of the earth we really know well because it is the only section of the earth we can actually observe directly.

<u>Earth's crust</u> – Earth's outermost layer of rock

The thickness of the crust varies depending on where you are. The majority of it ranges in thickness from about 90 km (55 miles) to about 20 km (12 miles). The crust can get fairly thin (less than 5 km thick), but only beneath the deepest parts of the ocean. There are thicker parts as well. Now you know why we have not observed any section of the earth other than the crust. The deepest that any drill has ever penetrated the crust is under 15 kilometers, and that was on land. Even the drilling that has taken place in the deep ocean has not penetrated through the crust and into the mantle. The main ingredient in the crust is a substance known as silica. You have probably had some experience with silica, because it is also the principal component of sand and glass.

The crust of the earth often contains **soil** and **sediment** as well as rock. If soil is present, it is the top layer, and underneath that, there is often a layer of sediment.

<u>Sediment</u> – Small, solid fragments of rock and other materials that are carried and deposited by wind, water, or ice. Examples would be sand, mud, or gravel.

Sometimes, chemical reactions turn sediment back into rock, which is (not surprisingly) called **sedimentary** (sed i men' tuh ree) **rock**.

Sedimentary rock – Rock formed when chemical reactions cement sediments together, hardening them

The rock that composes the earth's crust is a mixture of sedimentary rock, **igneous** (ig' nee us) **rock**, and **metamorphic** (met uh mor' fik) **rock**.

Igneous rock – Rock that forms from molten rock

Where does igneous rock come from? Like anything else, if rocks get hot enough under the right conditions, they will melt, forming liquid rock. There is an enormous amount of this hot, liquid rock underneath the earth's crust. Technically, it is called **magma**. When magma cools, the result is igneous rock. One way this magma can cool is when it is emitted by a volcano. As the liquid rock flows out of a volcano, it is called **lava**, and as it cools in the air, it solidifies into igneous rock.

Both sedimentary and igneous rock can be altered by heat and pressure to form metamorphic rock.

Metamorphic rock – Igneous or sedimentary rock that has been changed into a new kind of rock as a result of great pressure and temperature

You are probably familiar with rock known as marble. It is a metamorphic rock often used in sculptures and homes.

ON YOUR OWN

6.1 Consider the three types of rock mentioned in this section. Which one would be more likely to be found deep in the crust?

The Mantle

Directly under the earth's crust, we find the earth's mantle. As I mentioned before, we have never made direct observations of the earth's mantle, but we have learned a great deal about it by indirect observation. To see what I mean, perform the following experiment.

EXPERIMENT 6.1
How Sound Travels Through Different Substances

Supplies:

♦ Two metal spoons
♦ About 3 feet of string (Nylon kite string is ideal, but any reasonably strong string will work. Thread and yarn do not work well.)
♦ Large sink with a plug
♦ Water
♦ Eye protection such as goggles or safety glasses

Introduction: Study of the mantle and core makes use of the fact that waves travel differently in different substances. In this experiment, you will make use of sound waves in order to experience this effect.

Procedure:

1. Plug the sink's drain and fill the sink with water.
2. While you are waiting for the sink to fill, take about 3 feet of string and tie the two spoons to the center of it. Tie them individually right next to each other so that when you hold the string by both ends and let the spoons dangle, they bang against each other to make a dull ringing sound.
3. Once the sink is reasonably full, turn off the water.
4. Hold the string by both ends and bounce it up and down, allowing the spoons to jingle, to get an idea of what they sound like when they bang into each other. Write a description of the sound in your notebook.
5. Now stick each end of the string into your ears, and hold them there with your fingers. In order for the experiment to work, the ends of the string must be pushed into your ear and held there tightly with your fingers, so that you can only hear sounds that travel through the string.
6. Lean forward so that the spoons dangle in front of you. Both sides of the string should be held taut by the weight of the spoons. If not, adjust the way you are leaning or the way you are holding the string in your ears in order to make sure that both sides of the string are taut.
7. With one of your free fingers, flick one side of the string near your ear so that the spoons jangle together. What kind of sound do you hear? Write a description of that in your notebook, comparing it to the sound you heard in step 4.
8. Take the ends of the string out of your ears and dangle the spoons so that they are under water in the sink.
9. Bounce the string up and down again to get an idea of what they sound like banging together under water. Once again, write a description of the sound.
10. Once you have an idea of what they sound like, tilt your head and lay it sideways in the water, so that one of your ears is completely under water. Now repeat step 9, listening to how the spoons sound when your ear is under water with them. Write a comparison between this sound and the one you heard in step 9.
11. Finally, pull your head out of the water and repeat steps 5 through 7, this time keeping the spoons under water when you flick the string to make them jingle. Compare the sound you hear to the sounds you heard in step 9 and step 10. What are the differences? Write them down.
12. Drain the sink and put away everything.

What did you hear? In the first part of the experiment (before you put the spoons under water), the spoons should have sounded much different when you had the string in your ears. This is because sound travels as a wave. I haven't really talked about waves yet, and I really don't want to go into detail about them until a much later module. In brief, a wave is like a vibration that passes through a substance. When sound travels through air, the air vibrates back and forth, eventually hitting a series of vibration sensors in your ear. The vibration sensors send signals to the brain, and the brain interprets those signals. That's how you hear.

For the purpose of this experiment, all you have to understand is that sound travels as a vibration in the substance through which it is moving. Before you put the ends of the string in your ears, you heard the sound vibrations as they traveled through air. When you put the ends of the string in your ears, however, you heard the vibrations that traveled through the string. Which was louder? The spoons should have sounded much louder when you listened to the sound traveling through the string. That should make sense. After all, if sound really does travel as a vibration, the easier the material is to vibrate, the better the sound should travel, right? Well, the string is much easier to make vibrate than is the air. Thus, the sound travels better in the string.

Now think about the second part of the experiment. In the second part, you listened to the spoons bang together under water. First, you listened with your ears in air. Next, you put your ears in the water, and finally, you listened through the string. They sounded different in each case, right? That's because the substances through which the vibrations traveled were different in each case. In the end, then, the experiment should definitely show you that vibrations travel differently depending on the substance through which they travel.

Scientists make use of this fact in order to study the portions of the earth they cannot observe directly. When earthquakes occur, they emit vibrations called **seismic** (size' mik) **waves**. These seismic waves travel through the earth, eventually reaching the surface. If enough vibration detectors, called **seismographs** (size' muh grafs), are used to analyze the vibrations at different points of the earth, scientists can determine the speed at which the seismic waves traveled, how much energy they lost as they traveled, and how their courses changed in different parts of the earth. All these things are affected by the type of substance through which the waves traveled.

The first scientist to really make use of this fact in relation to the interior of the earth was a Croatian scientist named Andrija Mohorovicic (moh' huh roh' vuh chich). By careful study of seismic waves as recorded by seismographs in several different locations, he came to the conclusion that the earth was not the same throughout its interior. He postulated that many miles beneath the surface, there was a border beyond which the composition of the earth was much different from that of the earth's crust. That border became known as the **Mohorovicic discontinuity**, or **Moho** (moh' ho) for short. We now know that Moho marks the boundary between the earth's crust and the beginning of the earth's mantle.

As time went on and the study of seismic waves became more detailed, scientists began proposing models of the earth's mantle. They would make calculations of how seismic waves (and waves that resulted from human-made explosives) should travel through the earth's mantle (and core) if it really was composed the way the theory said, and then they would compare studies of those waves to the calculations. As scientists learned more, the models were refined, and eventually, the calculations based on the models were in excellent agreement with the data. Thus, even though we have never directly seen the mantle, we think we know its composition and its general properties simply because we have analyzed how certain waves travel through it.

Now before I actually tell you what the mantle is thought to be like, I want to make a couple of points. The majority of real science going on in this day and age involves trying to understand things we cannot really see: atoms, the earth's interior, the details of distant galaxies, the origin of life, etc. Since we cannot observe these things directly, we are forced to perform indirect observations. We then come up with a theory that "guesses" at the nature of what we are studying and predicts what the results of certain experiments should be. If the experiments agree with the theory's predictions, we consider the theory to be a good one. If not, we refine the theory or come up with another one until the predictions of the theory match the experimental results.

The second point I want to make is very important. Although indirect observations are used all the time in science, the conclusions to which they lead *may be completely wrong*. After all, it might be pure coincidence that a theory correctly predicts the results of an experiment. There might be a completely different explanation for the results. Alternatively, the experiments that confirm the theory's predictions might be fatally flawed in some way that no one has considered. We have no way of knowing for sure without direct observation. The history of science is littered with theories we now know are wrong, even though they had a lot of experimental confirmation at one time. Thus, it is important to understand that a lot of scientific knowledge today most likely will be shown to be wrong later on. Nevertheless, until direct observation is possible, indirect observation at least tells us *something*, so it is worth trying to understand what we can.

So what do the indirect observations of the earth's mantle tell us? Well, they tell us that the rock of the mantle is mostly silica (like the rocks in earth's crust), but the properties of that rock are incredibly different from the rocks with which you are familiar. First, the matter in the mantle is more densely packed than that of the crust. As one travels deeper into the core, matter becomes even more tightly packed. At the same time, the temperature of the rock in the mantle increases the deeper you go. At the Moho, the temperature is about 1,000 °F (500 °C), while the lower portion of the mantle gets as hot as 7,000 °F (4,000 °C). That's some *hot* rock! As you might expect, the pressure that the rock is under increases with increasing depth as well. After all, the more rock that's above, the more weight that's pressing down on it. By the time you reach the bottom of the mantle, the pressure is about 1.4 *million* times that of atmospheric pressure!

The fact that pressure and temperature increase as you travel deeper into the mantle leads to some very interesting effects. First, the upper part of the mantle is composed of solid rock. This and the crust above it (see Figure 6.1) are called earth's **lithosphere** (lith' uh sfear). Below the lithosphere, there is a small portion of the mantle called the **asthenosphere** (as then' uh sfear). At the pressure and temperature found in the asthenosphere, rock is not completely solid. It behaves more like very thick syrup, flowing around in the mantle. When subjected to an abrupt force, however, the "syrup" hardens into a firm solid. After the force passes, the rock returns to its syrupy, flowing state. Scientists call this **plastic rock**.

Plastic rock – Rock that behaves like something between a liquid and a solid

Most theories that describe earth's mantle have this plastic rock moving about in huge currents in the asthenosphere. To get an idea of how plastic rock behaves, perform the following experiment:

EXPERIMENT 6.2
A Simulation of Plastic Rock

Supplies:

- A shallow pan (a pie pan, for example)
- Cornstarch
- Measuring cups
- Water
- Spoon for stirring
- Eye protection such as goggles or safety glasses

Introduction: Plastic rock flows like a thick liquid and then solidifies when subjected to an abrupt force. In this experiment, you will produce a mixture that simulates such behavior.

Procedure:

1. Put one cup of cornstarch into the pan.
2. Add $\frac{2}{3}$ cup of water.
3. Stir the water and cornstarch together. You should find it very hard to stir at first, but as you continue to stir, you should get to the point where you have an evenly mixed, white liquid in the pan.
4. Add ½ cup of cornstarch to the mixture.
5. Stir the newly added cornstarch into the mixture. Now you should start seeing an interesting behavior. As you stir, the mixture should solidify, making it hard to stir. However, when you stop stirring and let the mixture sit, it should liquefy again. If you don't see that behavior, your mixture is not correct. If the mixture stays liquid, you have too much water. To fix this, add cornstarch a little at a time until you get the desired behavior. If the mixture never turns to liquid, you have too much cornstarch. Add water a little at a time until you get the desired behavior.
6. Explore this interesting behavior for a while.
7. Pick up some of the mixture with your hand. As you pick it up, it should become solid.
8. Squeeze the solid into a ball, then relax your hand and watch what happens to the ball.
9. Repeat this a few times.
10. To clean up everything, you will need to use hot water from the tap. As you add hot water to the pan, the mixture will become a liquid and pour down the drain. Make sure to leave the hot water running for a while after the mixture has been cleaned up, as you need to flush it down the drain.

The behavior of the mixture in your experiment is similar to the behavior of plastic rock. When subjected to an abrupt force (like your hand closing around it), the mixture solidified. However, when left alone, the mixture behaved more like a thick liquid, slowly flowing under the influence of gravity. Plastic rock has similar properties. It will solidify if subjected to an abrupt force, but otherwise, it will flow like a thick liquid.

If you are wondering why the cornstarch and water mixture has such an odd behavior, believe it or not, we aren't completely sure. There are at least two different explanations for the effect, but they both rely on the fact that cornstarch is made up of long molecules. When you mix these long molecules with water, they don't really dissolve. The molecules just get water in between them.

One explanation says that this water lubricates the molecules as they rub up against each other, which allows them to flow like a liquid. However, when you push or squeeze on the mixture, the water gets squeezed out from between the starch molecules, which makes it much harder for them to move. Thus, the mixture cannot flow anymore and becomes more like a solid. A second explanation is that these long molecules can flow easily when allowed to do so slowly. However, when you push on them, they tangle up with one another, which makes it much harder for them to move, once again making the mixture behave more like a solid. Regardless of which explanation is correct, the mixture provides a good illustration of the behavior of plastic rock.

ON YOUR OWN

6.2 Suppose you had a long, steel rod, and you stood at one end of it while a friend stood at the other end. Consider the following experiment: Your friend hit his end of the rod with a hammer, and you listen for the sound. You then press an ear against the rod, and your friend hits it with the hammer again. In which case would the sound be louder? **NOTE:** Please don't try this at home!

6.3 Suppose you were able to remove a sample of the plastic rock from the asthenosphere and take it into a laboratory. Would it behave differently than a rock sample you took from earth's crust? Why or why not?

The Earth's Core

In 1914, a German geologist, Beno Gutenberg (goo' ten burg), analyzed seismic waves and concluded that there is another drastic change in the makeup of the earth significantly below the Moho. The boundary marking that change is now known as the **Gutenberg discontinuity** and signals the beginning of the earth's core. The core is, indeed, remarkably different from the mantle. First, it is composed mostly of iron, not silica. There is a small amount of nickel in the core, along with at least one other element. Second, below the Gutenberg discontinuity, the core is actually *liquid,* not solid. It is a liquid because, at the depth of the Gutenberg discontinuity, the temperature is hot enough to melt iron and the other constituents of the outer core.

Interestingly enough, in 1936, Danish scientist Inge Lehmann's (lay' mahn) work with seismic waves led her to the realization that the core actually has an inner region that is *solid*. This leads us to separate the core into two sections: the **inner core** and the **outer core**. The boundary between these two regions is, not surprisingly, called the **Lehmann discontinuity**. The outer core lies just below the Gutenberg discontinuity and is mostly molten iron. The inner core lies below the Lehmann discontinuity and is mostly solid iron. The exact distance from the surface of the earth to the Lehmann discontinuity was not well known until 1960. At that time, underground nuclear tests were performed, and the resulting seismic waves were so well-suited to indirect observation of the earth that many interesting facts about the earth's core and mantle were learned. The precise position of the Lehmann discontinuity was one of those facts.

"Now wait a minute," you should be saying, "how can the outer core be hot enough to be molten and yet the inner core still be a solid? Is the inner core that much cooler than the outer core?" No. Actually, the inner core is *hotter* than the outer core. How, then, can the inner core be a solid? Well, remember from Module #4 that in almost all substances (except water), the molecules and atoms are close together when the substance is a solid, and they are farther apart when it is a liquid. The reason substances melt is that as you heat them up, you are giving them more energy. This allows the atoms or molecules that make up the substance to travel farther apart from one another, turning the solid into a liquid. That effect can be counteracted by pressure. Think about it: With a lot of pressure pushing against a substance, its atoms or molecules will actually be pushed close together.

In the outer core, the temperature is high enough that the iron atoms in the core are given plenty of energy to stay far enough apart from one another to remain liquid. Even though the iron is under high pressure, the pressure is not strong enough to counteract the effect of high temperature. Deeper in the core, however, the pressure increases due to all of the rock pressing down from above. In the inner core, the force of that pressure is great enough to counteract the effect of high temperature, and the atoms actually get pushed closer together again, causing the inner core to be solid! This effect is known as **pressure freezing**. In the end, then, the physical pressure caused by the great mass of rock above the inner core is high enough that the atoms making up the inner core stay close together, keeping the inner core solid, despite its high temperature.

Probably the most interesting (and at the same time controversial) aspects of the earth's core is the magnetic field that it generates. Most of you probably already know that the earth has a magnetic field. In some ways, the earth acts like a big magnet, as illustrated in the following figure.

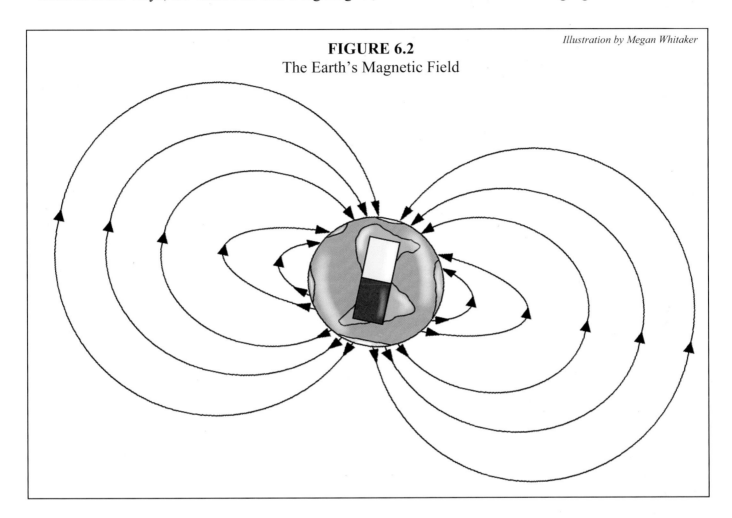

FIGURE 6.2
The Earth's Magnetic Field

Illustration by Megan Whitaker

The lines in the figure are called **magnetic field lines**, and you will learn a lot more about them when you take a detailed physics course. For the purposes of this course, you just need to realize that these lines map out how the earth's magnetic field interacts with other magnets. For example, we know that a compass always points to the north. This is because the earth's magnetic field exerts a force on the magnet in the compass, turning that magnet toward the north, no matter where you are on the planet.

Now it is important to note that even though the earth *behaves* as if there is a big magnet like the one drawn in the figure, that's not the reason the earth has a magnetic field. Earth doesn't have some huge bar magnet inside of it. Why does the earth have a magnetic field, then? Well, the short answer to that question is, "We don't completely know." The long answer, however, is a little more interesting.

Almost all scientists agree that the magnetic field is caused by something that goes on in the earth's core. To get an idea of what that "something" is, perform the following experiment:

EXPERIMENT 6.3
Making an Electromagnet

<u>Supplies:</u>

♦ A 1.5-volt battery (Any size cell [AA, A, C, or D] will do; just make sure it is nothing other than one of those. A battery of higher voltage could be dangerous.)
♦ Tape (Electrical tape works best, but cellophane tape will do.)
♦ Large iron nail (at least 3 inches long)
♦ Metal paper clip
♦ 2 feet of insulated wire (24-gauge wire works best. It should not be thicker than 18-gauge.)
♦ Eye protection such as goggles or safety glasses

Introduction: Some materials are naturally magnetic and generate their own magnetic field. It is possible, however, to create a magnetic field with electricity. This experiment shows you how it is done.

<u>Procedure:</u>

1. Lay the paper clip out on a table or desk.
2. Touch the nail to the paper clip and then pull it away. Did the paper clip stick to the nail as if the nail were a magnet? No, of course not. The nail is not a magnet.
3. If the insulated wire is not stripped so that bare conductor is exposed at each end, strip the wire like you did in Experiment 1.1.
4. Wrap the wire around the nail as many times as you can. The tighter you can wrap the wire around the nail, and the more turns of wire you have, the better. In the end, your nail should look something like this:

Illustration from the MasterClips collection

5. Use the tape to attach the bare conductor on one end of the wire to one terminal of the battery, and then the other bare conductor to the other end of the battery. That way, electricity will flow through the wire. The wire will get hot, because the flow of electricity results in energy. You can wear gloves if the heat gets too uncomfortable.
6. With the electricity still flowing, touch the nail to the paper clip. What happens this time?
7. Disconnect the wires from the battery and put everything away.

    In the experiment, you took a non-magnetic substance (the nail) and made it into a magnet by forcing electricity to flow around it. The motion of the electricity caused the nail to become a magnet. That is basically the same way that scientists think the earth gets its magnetic field. Most scientists think that the core has enormous electrical current running through it. That electrical current is what most scientists think is responsible for the earth's magnetic field. Just as the electrical current in your experiment caused the nail to become a magnet, the electrical current in the earth's core is thought to make the earth a big magnet.

If most scientists agree that electrical current in the earth's core is responsible for the earth's magnetic field, where is the controversy? I said that the earth's magnetic field is one of the most controversial things about the earth's core. What is controversial about it? Well, if electrical current in the earth's core is responsible for the earth's magnetic field, it is only natural to ask, "Where does that electrical current come from?" *That's* where the controversy lies.

There are basically two theories that try to explain where this electrical current in the earth's core originates. The first theory, called the **dynamo theory**, is believed by the majority of scientists today. This theory says that the motion of fluid in the outer core of the earth is caused by temperature differences in the outer core as well as the rotation of the earth. This motion causes the motion of electrical charges in the core, which creates electrical current. Just like electricity running through the wire in Experiment 6.3 caused the nail to be magnetic, the electrical current in the core causes the earth to be magnetic.

The second theory, which is believed by a minority of scientists, is called the **rapid-decay theory**. This theory states the electrical current of the earth is a consequence of how it was created. If one makes a few assumptions about how the earth was created, it is possible to actually calculate how much electrical current would be generated as a result. That electrical current would then begin to slow down over time, because electrical flow is resisted by all matter through which it flows. That is why the wire in the experiment got hot. The wire resisted the flow of electricity, and a lot of heat was generated as a result of that resistance. In the end, then, just as the flow of electricity is resisted by the wire in which it moves, the flow of the electrical current in the earth's core would be resisted as well. This would cause the current to slow down, eventually stopping.

Do you see the difference between the two theories? The dynamo theory says that temperature differences in the outer core and the rotation of the earth work together to keep the electrical current in the core going. The rapid-decay theory says that the earth's inner core is actually slowing down the flow of electricity that was started as a consequence of how the earth was created. Well, since the majority of scientists believe the dynamo theory, it must be the correct one, right? Not necessarily. Science is not done by majority rule; it is done by experiment. We cannot directly observe the core of the earth to see whether it is helping the electrical current or slowing it down, but we can observe it indirectly.

How do we observe the inner core indirectly? We determined its size and composition by examining the way it responded to seismic waves. Another way to examine it indirectly is to make careful measurements of the magnetic field it produces. Now remember how we try to determine the validity of a scientific theory when we are making indirect observations. We use the theory to make predictions, and then we compare those predictions to data we collect. In the end, the theory most consistent with the data is the one we should believe.

The first thing we can observe about the magnetic field is that its strength is decaying. Over the past 170 years, scientists have been making careful measurements of the strength of earth's magnetic field, and these measurements tell us that over time, the earth's magnetic field is getting weaker. Which theory best explains this fact? Well, they both do, but the rapid-decay theory does a slightly better job. The rapid-decay theory predicts a rather steady decay in the earth's magnetic field, and that's what has been observed over the last 170 years. The dynamo theory predicts a *changing* magnetic field, because temperature differences in the earth's outer core change, which will cause a change in the flow of fluid. It could be that during the past 170 years, the changing fluid flow has been such that the magnetic field of the earth is decreasing. However, the dynamo theory predicts that eventually, the fluid flow will change such that the magnetic field of the earth will increase again. Thus, both theories predict changes in the earth's magnetic field, but the changes they predict are different. The rapid-decay theory predicts a general decrease in the earth's magnetic field, while the dynamo theory predicts a *fluctuating* magnetic field, with the field sometimes getting weaker and sometimes getting stronger. In the end, then, both theories are consistent with the data, but the rapid-decay theory explains the data more directly, as it directly predicts a decaying magnetic field. If the dynamo theory is correct, we "just happen" to be living during one of the times when the earth's magnetic field is decreasing.

The next thing we can observe about the magnetic field is that throughout the history of the earth, it has *reversed* a few times. What this means is that during certain times in earth's past, there is evidence to indicate that the field actually pointed in the *opposite* direction. How do we know this? Well, there are certain materials in the crust that are naturally magnetic. These materials tend to point in the direction of the magnetic field, like a compass. In certain rock layers of the crust, however, the natural magnets imbedded in the rock are pointed in the *opposite* direction. This would indicate that when those rock layers formed, the earth's magnetic field was actually pointed in the opposite direction, as compared to the direction in which it is pointed today.

Which theory explains this fact? Well, they both do. Once again, however, one theory has the edge. This time, it is the dynamo theory. The dynamo theory predicts such reversals, because it predicts that the fluid motion in the outer core will, every now and again, reverse. This will cause the magnetic field to reverse. The rapid-decay theory allows for magnetic field reversals, too, but only in the event of cataclysmic volcanic and geological activity. If such activity happened in the past, the rapid-decay theory allows for several magnetic reversals as well. However, since the dynamo theory *predicts* such behavior, and the rapid-decay theory only *allows* for such behavior *if* certain things happened in the past, the dynamo theory is a better explanation of the fact that the earth's magnetic field has reversed in the past.

Now even though the dynamo theory is better at directly explaining the fact that earth's magnetic field has reversed in the past, a *detail* of these reversals is a serious problem for the dynamo theory. The dynamo theory predicts that all changes in the magnetic field will occur slowly, because it takes time for the temperature differences in the core to cause the fluid flow to change. As a result, the dynamo theory predicts that reversals in the earth's magnetic field should happen slowly. Many dynamo theory calculations, for example, indicate that 2,000 years is a minimum time frame for a magnetic field reversal. However, since 1989, scientists have found evidence that at least some reversals happened over a period of 15 *days* or less! While this time scale is a problem for the dynamo theory, it fits well in the rapid-decay theory, since that theory assumes such reversals are the result of cataclysmic volcanic and geological activity, which would cause rapid changes.

The final thing we can observe is the magnetic fields of other planets. After all, any theory that explains the earth's magnetic field should be able to explain the magnetic fields of the other planets that have them, right? It should also be able to explain why certain planets do not have magnetic fields. Which theory best fits the data in this case? *Only the rapid-decay theory*. The rapid-decay theory has correctly calculated the magnetic field of every planet that has one. By contrast, the dynamo theory cannot even correctly predict which planets have a magnetic field and which planets do not.

The dynamo theory, for example, predicts a magnetic field on the planet Mars, while the rapid-decay theory says there was a magnetic field there in the past, but there should not be one now. The data indicate that Mars currently has no planetary magnetic field. Conversely, the dynamo theory predicts no magnetic field on Mercury, while the rapid-decay theory predicts that Mercury should have a magnetic field. It turns out that Mercury does have a magnetic field. Even more convincing, years before the Voyager spacecraft measured the magnetic fields of Uranus and Neptune, scientists used both the rapid-decay theory and the dynamo theory to make predictions of the strength of both planets' magnetic fields. The rapid-decay theory correctly predicted the results of Voyager's measurements, while the dynamo theory was off by a factor of 100,000!

In the realm of science, a theory that attempts to explain a phenomenon we cannot observe directly must be consistent with any measurements we make. In the case of a planet's magnetic field, only the rapid-decay theory is consistent with all measured data. Why, then, do the majority of scientists believe in the dynamo theory? Well, it turns out that the rapid-decay theory has two consequences that the majority of scientists don't want to believe. First, in order to be consistent with the idea of magnetic field reversals, the rapid-decay theory must rely on a global, cataclysmic event. Most scientists don't believe that such an event ever occurred. Scientists that believe in the worldwide flood during Noah's time, however, know that such an event did happen. Rapid-decay theorists say that an event such as the Flood explains these magnetic field reversals in the context of their theory.

The other consequence makes even more scientists uneasy. The timescale of the rapid-decay theory is on the order of a few thousand years. In fact, according to the way the rapid-decay theory is constructed, the earth must have been formed less than 10,000 years ago. This makes many geologists uneasy, because they want to believe that the earth is much older than that! Thus, since the rapid-decay theory assumes that a worldwide, cataclysmic event such as Noah's flood occurred sometime in earth's past, and since the rapid-decay theory concludes that the earth must be less than 10,000 years old, most scientists reject it. They reject it *despite the fact that it is the only theory consistent with all of the data collected!*

Christians who believe that the entire book of Genesis should be taken as literal history, of course, have no problem with assuming that Noah's flood really happened and that the earth is less than 10,000 years old. Thus, it is easy for them to accept the consequences of the rapid-decay theory. As a result, most of the scientists who believe the rapid-decay theory are Christians who have a very strict, literal view of Genesis. If you want to learn more about the rapid-decay theory, go to the course website I told you about in the "Student Notes" section of this book.

This brings me to one of the most important points you will ever learn when it comes to science: **There is no such thing as an unbiased scientist**. People seem to have the view that scientists are unbiased observers who look at the facts and draw conclusions based only on those facts. Although this is the ideal scientist, such a scientist does not exist. A scientist's preconceived notions will strongly affect the way he or she does science! The two theories that try to explain the earth's magnetic field provide a great illustration of this point. Scientists whose preconceived notions rule out Noah's Flood and a young earth refuse to believe the most scientifically valid theory for the earth's magnetic field. Instead, they rely on a theory that is contrary to the data. They go against the dictates of science solely because of bias caused by preconceptions. Scientists who have different preconceptions are free to choose the more scientifically valid theory. This is not to say that rapid-decay theorists are unbiased. They have their preconceptions as well. In this particular case, however, their preconceptions aid in following the dictates of science.

Before I leave this section, I want to point out that life on earth would not be possible without earth's magnetic field. You see, there are certain high-energy electrically charged particles that are emitted from the sun and travel toward our planet. These particles are called **cosmic rays**. If they were allowed to strike the earth, they would kill all life on the planet. Fortunately for us, however, the earth's magnetic field deflects the vast majority of these particles, keeping them from hitting the planet. As a result, life can flourish. If the earth's magnetic field were too small, it would not deflect enough of these cosmic rays. If it were too strong, it would deflect the cosmic rays, but it would cause deadly magnetic storms that would make life impossible! Thus, the earth has a magnetic field at *just the right strength to support life*. This is just one more piece of evidence that the earth was *designed* for life and did not occur by chance!

ON YOUR OWN

6.4 Would water be subject to pressure freezing? Why or why not?

6.5 Regardless of whether the dynamo theory, the rapid-decay theory, or some as yet unknown theory is correct in explaining the earth's magnetic field, we are reasonably certain that substances in the core of the earth are in motion. Why?

Plate Tectonics

It is now time to discuss a theory related to earth's lithosphere. It is called **plate tectonics** (tek tahn' iks). This theory relies on the idea that the earth's lithosphere is fractured and broken. It is thought to be comprised of several "plates" that all move about on the plastic rock of the asthenosphere (see Figure 6.1). The lithosphere's major plates are illustrated in Figure 6.3.

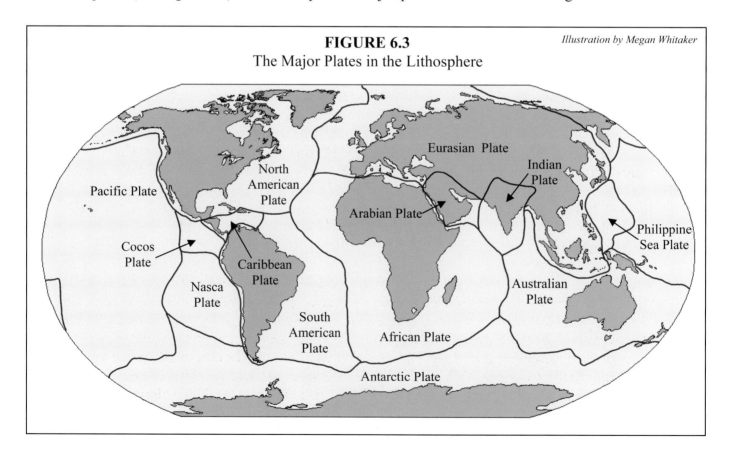

FIGURE 6.3   *Illustration by Megan Whitaker*
The Major Plates in the Lithosphere

According to plate tectonics, these plates are like islands of rock that "float" on the asthenosphere (remember, that's the section of the mantle made of plastic rock). The plates supposedly move independently of one another, and tend to push up against each other. This results in some rather interesting geological effects. Before I tell you about these effects, I want you to try an experiment in which you will simulate plate tectonics yourself. Hopefully, you will see the effects I will then discuss.

EXPERIMENT 6.4
A Model of Plate Tectonics

Supplies:

♦ A hard-boiled egg (You might want a second in case you mess up the first time.)
♦ A dull knife, like a butter knife
♦ A marker or something else that will make a mark on the egg shell
♦ Eye protection such as goggles or safety glasses

Introduction: A hard-boiled egg can be used to model the idea of plate tectonics. The shell represents the crust of the earth, while the rubbery egg white represents the plastic rock of the mantle. If you cut out a "plate" on the egg and move it around, you will get an idea of what plate tectonics is all about.

1. Use the marker to draw a circle somewhere on the shell of the hard-boiled egg. The circle should be about three times the diameter of the end of your thumb.
2. Use the dull knife to cut the circle out of the egg shell. Do this by simply pushing the knife through the shell along the circle's edge. If the knife penetrates the egg white, that's fine. Just make sure the circle is completely cut away from the rest of the shell. Portions of the egg shell will crack. That's okay, too.
3. Once you have cut the circle out of the shell, do not remove the circle. Instead, place your thumb on the circle and use your thumb to move the circle around. Push it back and forth, allowing it to collide with the rest of the shell.
4. The circle of egg shell represents a plate of the earth's crust, while the egg white represents the plastic rock of the mantle. As you move the egg shell circle back and forth, you are simulating a plate moving back and forth on the mantle. When the circle of egg shell collides with the rest of the egg shell, you are simulating that plate running into another plate. Draw pictures of the different things that happen when the circle of egg shell interacts with the rest of the shell.
5. Once these collisions have broken enough of the shell so that the circle has a lot of room to move, slide the circle along the edge of the rest of the shell. In other words, don't push the circle so that it hits the rest of the shell head-on. Instead, move the circle along the edge of the rest of the shell. Note how the circle moves.
6. Clean up your mess.

What kind of interactions did you find between the circle and the rest of the egg shell? Most of the time, you probably saw that both shells cracked and buckled when they ran into each other. You might have even noticed that as the shells cracked, bits of shells piled up to form a "mountain" of egg shell. When two plates of the earth collide, they can buckle and form mountains, just as the egg shells did. You might have seen other interactions as well. For example, did the circle end up sliding under the rest of the egg shell or vice versa? That can happen between plates of the earth as well. When one plate actually slides under another one, a trench can be formed. When you slid the circle along the edge of the rest of the shell in step 5, what did you see? The circle should have been hard to move because it was scraping against the rest of the shell. This can happen with plates of the earth as well.

The different types of interactions that can occur between the earth's plates are illustrated in the figure below. Because large rock masses moving against each other like this can be rather violent, all of these interactions can lead to earthquakes.

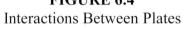

FIGURE 6.4
Interactions Between Plates

Illustrations by Megan Whitaker

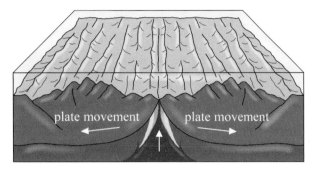

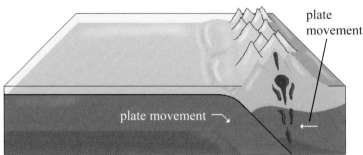

Plate Separation: When plates move away from each other, magma leaks up from the mantle, creating new crust. This typically occurs in the middle of the ocean floor.

Plate Subduction: When plates collide, one can slide under the other, generally forming a trench with mountains on one side. When this happens, crust is destroyed as it melts into the mantle. This typically occurs along the edge of a continent. The Cascade Mountains mark such an interaction.

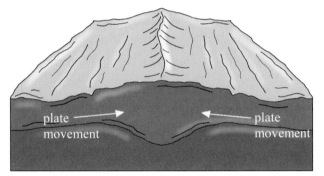

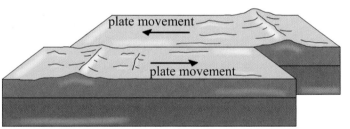

Plate Collision: When plates collide and neither slides under the other, they buckle, forming mountains. Crust is not made or destroyed. It just buckles. The Himalaya Mountains mark such an interaction.

Plate Sliding: When plates slide (or shear) against each other, their edges scrape against each other. Crust is neither made nor destroyed, but this motion can result in severe earthquakes. This is what is happening at the San Andreas Fault in California.

Plate tectonics, then, says that the continents (and all things in the lithosphere) are moving around on "islands" of rock. When these islands interact with each other, earthquakes can occur, mountains can form, or deep trenches can form. Why would anyone believe such an outlandish theory? Because there is a lot of evidence to back it up! Many of our observations of earthquakes, mountains, and volcanoes seem to support the theory. We have also found deep trenches at the bottom of the oceans, the characteristics of which are well described by the theory that the plates in that region of the earth are moving away from each other. In the end, then, most geologists do believe that the plate tectonics theory is correct and that the lithosphere is, indeed, composed of many independently moving plates.

There is an interesting possibility regarding earth's past that becomes apparent if you believe that the continents are not really fixed but can move about. If you look at the continents, they seem to fit together like a jigsaw puzzle. This has led some scientists to speculate that years ago, all the continents were connected in a giant supercontinent, which has been called **Pangaea** (pan gee' uh). Since plate tectonics says that the continents can move on their plates, it is possible, then, that the continents moved apart from each other, destroying Pangaea, and taking the positions we see them in today. This hypothetical scenario is illustrated in Figure 6.5.

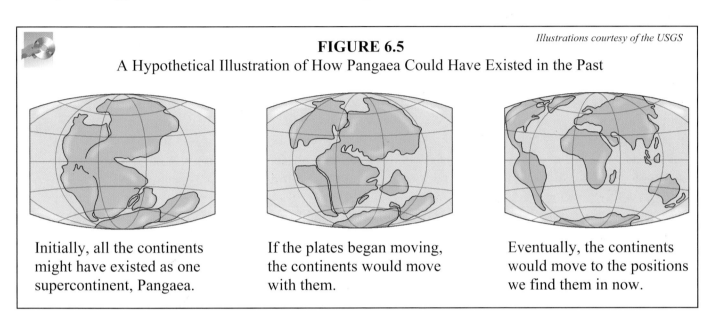

FIGURE 6.5

Illustrations courtesy of the USGS

A Hypothetical Illustration of How Pangaea Could Have Existed in the Past

Initially, all the continents might have existed as one supercontinent, Pangaea.

If the plates began moving, the continents would move with them.

Eventually, the continents would move to the positions we find them in now.

Now this is all just conjecture, of course. First of all, we aren't even sure that plate tectonics is really true. There is a lot of evidence that tends to support it, but many theories that had evidence in their favor were later proven wrong. Furthermore, even if plate tectonics is true, it doesn't mean that Pangaea ever existed. It is possible that the plates are quite limited in their movement. Thus, the continents might not be able to move very far at all. Clearly, then, the whole process in Figure 6.5 might never have happened. Plate tectonics does make it possible, however. Also, there is certain evidence to support the idea. For example, in the figure shown above, South America and Africa rest against one another in Pangaea, with the eastern side of South America touching the western side of Africa. Well, it turns out that if you look at both continents, you find large sections of rock that are the same, and these sections "match up" when you put the two continents together the way they are assumed to have existed in Pangaea.

Let me point out something really important here. Most geologists who believe in plate tectonics believe that the plates move very slowly. Thus, if Pangaea really did exist, they think it must have existed hundreds of millions of years ago. That's the only way the plates would have time to drift as far as they have. Since this is the prevailing thought behind plate tectonics, many scientists who are convinced that the world is young refuse to consider plate tectonics as a valid theory. These scientists, typically those who believe that the entire book of Genesis is literal history, assume that plate tectonics requires the earth to be billions of years old. As a result, they will not even consider it as a theory. This is another example of unscientific bias, but in this case, it is on the part of the scientists who take Genesis to be literal history. If you really look at the evidence, there is simply too much data in support of plate tectonics to dismiss it outright. The theory has a *lot* of scientific merit. Thus, we cannot reject it out of hand and still remain good scientists.

We can, however, quarrel with the geologists about the time scale. It is true that plates seem to move very slowly *right now*. There is no reason to believe, however, that the plates *always* moved slowly. In fact, if a global cataclysm (like Noah's flood) happened, the plates would have probably reacted by moving very quickly. In the end, then, the whole concept of plate tectonics, even the existence of Pangaea, is not contrary to a literal interpretation of Genesis. It is quite possible that Pangaea did exist and the worldwide flood was the cause of its breakup. Under such cataclysmic conditions, the continents could have easily moved to their present locations in a very short time. In fact, there is a very successful theory called "catastrophic plate tectonics" that uses the Flood as a mechanism for the breakup of Pangaea. If you want to learn more about this theory, look at the course website I told you about in the "Student Notes" section of this book. There you will find links to detailed discussions of catastrophic plate tectonics.

The last thing I need to mention about plate tectonics is that this theory is not a full explanation of the geological features of the earth. There are some data that seem to speak against plate tectonics, but they are a bit too complex to discuss in this course. If you are interested in a more in-depth discussion of plate tectonics, the course website I mentioned above has a link to a debate between two scientists, one who believes that plate tectonics is generally correct and one who does not.

ON YOUR OWN

6.6 Would plate tectonics work if the mantle were made out of normal, solid rock?

6.7 Look at Figure 6.3. Assuming plate tectonics is true, where would you expect the majority of the earthquakes in the United States to occur?

Earthquakes

Since I've already talked about how earthquakes can be used to indirectly observe the interior of the earth, it only seems natural to spend some time talking about how earthquakes occur and what the results of earthquakes are. Let's start with a definition:

Earthquake – Vibration of the earth that results either from volcanic activity or rock masses
                suddenly moving along a fault

That's quite a definition. What does it mean? The "vibration of the earth's surface" part is pretty self-explanatory, as is the "volcanic activity" part. But what does the rest of the definition mean? Well, scientists know that portions of the earth's surface move relative to each other. We already discussed plate tectonics, which theorizes that the entire crust of the earth is composed of islands of rock that move relative to each other. Even *within a plate*, however, there can be great masses of rocks that move relative to one another. The boundary between two separate rock masses is called a **fault**.

Fault – The boundary between two sections of rock that can move relative to one another

Wherever a fault exists, there is the possibility of an earthquake.

You see, the rock on one side of a fault does not move smoothly relative to the rock on the other side, because the fault is rough and jagged. As a result, the masses of rock tend to get hung up on each other. This resists any motion between the two masses of rock. If forces acting on the rocks are pushing them in different directions, however, the rocks can actually "bend" in response. This bending occurs very slowly, so it is not really noticeable. At some point, however, the forces become too great, and the moving rock finally breaks free of the jagged fault edges. When this happens, the two masses of rock "unbend," returning to their original shapes. This results in vibrations, which we observe as an earthquake.

It is hard to prove that the scenario I described is really what causes an earthquake, but there is a lot of indirect evidence indicating that it does. As a result, the whole idea I just described to you is a theory we call the **elastic rebound theory**. Figure 6.6 is an illustration of this theory.

FIGURE 6.6
The Elastic Rebound Theory

Illustration by Megan Whitaker

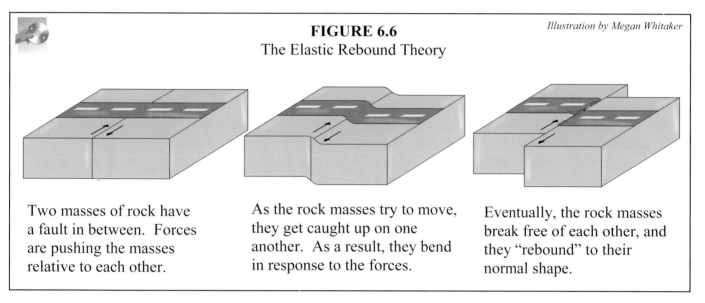

Two masses of rock have a fault in between. Forces are pushing the masses relative to each other.

As the rock masses try to move, they get caught up on one another. As a result, they bend in response to the forces.

Eventually, the rock masses break free of each other, and they "rebound" to their normal shape.

Hopefully, you can now see how this theory gets its name. The term "elastic" comes from the fact that the rock masses act a bit like rubber bands, deforming as a result of stress and then "rebounding" back into place.

One of the places that scientists can actually observe this activity is in California. Along an 800-mile stretch on the western side of California, there is a well-known fault called the "San Andreas Fault." This fault is most likely a portion of the border between the North American plate and the Pacific plate (see Figure 6.3). Along this fault, the western edge of California is moving at a rate of about 5 cm (2 inches) per year. The movement is halting, however, because the rocks keep getting caught on the fault. As a result, the motion stops, the rocks bend, and eventually the rocks release, rebounding back into place. Each time this happens, an earthquake occurs. Sometimes the earthquake is mild and can only be detected by the most sensitive equipment. At other times, the vibrations are severe, causing massive damage.

Now it is important to realize that even though I discussed a fault that exists between two plates, that's not the only kind of fault that exists. There are many small faults located within a plate that can result in severe earthquakes. When these earthquakes happen, many interesting geological events can occur. For example, suppose one rock mass along a fault is stationary and the other is moving upward. When the elastic rebound occurs, the moving rock mass will thrust upward, while the stationary rock mass will rebound back into place. What will result? A cliff! Right along the fault there will be a cliff, because the moving rock mass moves higher than the stationary rock mass. If the moving rock mass continues to move, the cliff might get so high that a mountain forms!

An earthquake tends to begin somewhere below the surface of the earth along a fault or around volcanic activity. The place at which the earthquake begins is called the **focus** of the earthquake.

Focus – The point where an earthquake begins

Since we live on the surface of the earth, however, the actual point at which the earthquake begins is not all that interesting. Instead, we would like to know where the vibrations first hit the surface of the earth. This will occur at the earthquake's **epicenter**, which is the point on the surface of the earth directly above the earthquake's focus.

Epicenter – The point on the surface of the earth directly above an earthquake's focus

The effects of an earthquake are most severe at its epicenter.

The study of earthquakes, called **seismology** (size mol' uh gee), has developed quite a bit over the past few decades. Seismologists have delicate instruments called seismographs that can measure vibrations that are too small for us to notice. This has led to a scale that classifies earthquakes based on their strength. The **Richter** (rik' ter) **scale** was developed by a seismologist named Charles Richter. It measures the strength of an earthquake based on the nature of the seismic waves it produces. The Richter scale runs from 0 to 10. Each step along this scale is an increase of approximately 32 in the energy of an earthquake. This means that an earthquake measuring 2 on the Richter scale releases roughly 32 times more energy than an earthquake that measures 1 on the Richter scale. In the same way, an earthquake that measures 3 on the Richter scale releases approximately 1,024 (32 x 32) times more energy than an earthquake that measures 1.

Typically, earthquakes that measure 5.5 or more on the Richter scale are powerful enough to damage buildings and roads. If the earthquake measures much less than 3 on the Richter scale, it can hardly be noticed by us without the aid of seismographs. Most seismologists consider any earthquake over 7 to be a major earthquake. The San Francisco earthquake that struck on October 17, 1989, for example, caused enormous damage, even to some structures that were considered "earthquake safe." This earthquake measured 7.1 on the Richter scale. The most powerful recorded earthquake occurred in Chile in 1960 and measured 9.3 on the Richter scale. Since this is a little over 2 units higher than that of the San Francisco earthquake, it was a little over 1,024 times more energetic!

We usually think of an earthquake causing damage because it shakes buildings, roads, and the like. However, sometimes an earthquake's damage is indirect. On December 26 of 2004, for example, an earthquake that measured 9.1 on the Richter scale occurred. Its epicenter was *under the ocean* off the coast of Sumatra, Indonesia. The vibrations it caused triggered a series of huge tsunamis (soo nah' meez – ocean waves caused by violent activity) that flooded and destroyed coastal communities throughout South and Southeast Asia. More than 200,000 people died or were missing as a result of this earthquake. It is considered one of the most deadly earthquakes in history. However, the Bible says that the most devastating earthquake is yet to come (Revelation 16:18).

Since earthquakes often occur along faults, areas with a lot of geological faults will have a lot of earthquakes. If you think about it, the biggest faults will always occur along the boundaries between plates of the earth. Thus, if plate tectonics is correct, the majority of earthquakes should occur along the boundaries shown in Figure 6.3. In fact, that's exactly what we see today. The majority of earthquakes have epicenters directly above the boundary between certain plates of the earth. This is one of the many pieces of evidence indicating that the theory of plate tectonics has merit. I must stress again, however, that earthquakes will occur at places other than the boundaries between plates, because there are other faults that exist on the planet, and earthquakes are also caused by volcanic activity. Nevertheless, places like western California will be prone to earthquakes because they rest on the boundaries between plates in the earth's crust.

ON YOUR OWN

6.8 Suppose you could measure the energy of an earthquake at its focus. How would it compare to the energy of the earthquake at its epicenter?

6.9 A seismologist is studying a region near a fault. She measures two earthquakes. One measures 2 on the Richter scale and the next measures 5. How many times more energy does the second earthquake release as compared to the first?

<u>Mountains and Volcanoes</u>

One of the more prominent features of earth's crust is its mountains. How do mountains form? There are actually several different ways. One of them I have already mentioned briefly. If a fault exists in which one rock mass is moving up and the other is stationary or moving down, the upward-moving mass of rock will form a mountain that rises up from the stationary or downward-moving rock, as illustrated in Figure 6.7. This kind of mountain is called a **fault-block mountain**.

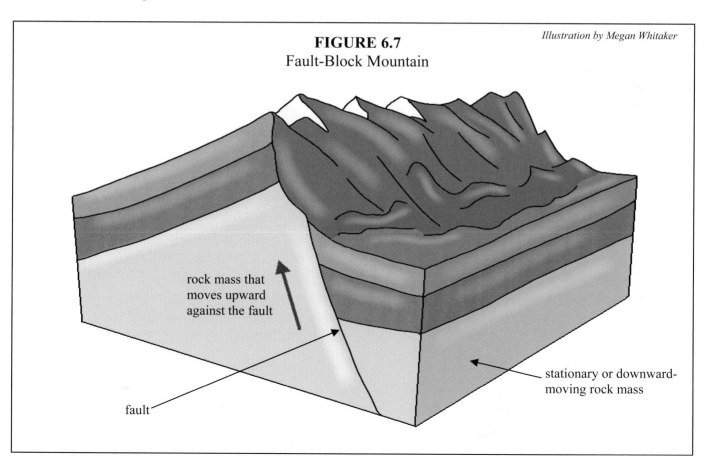

FIGURE 6.7
Fault-Block Mountain

Illustration by Megan Whitaker

rock mass that moves upward against the fault

stationary or downward-moving rock mass

fault

The Sierra Nevada mountains in California and Nevada and the Grand Teton mountain range in Wyoming are examples of such mountains.

When two moving rock masses push against each other with extreme force, the crust can bend in an up-and-down, rolling pattern. This forms mountains we call **folded mountains**. This process is illustrated in Figure 6.8.

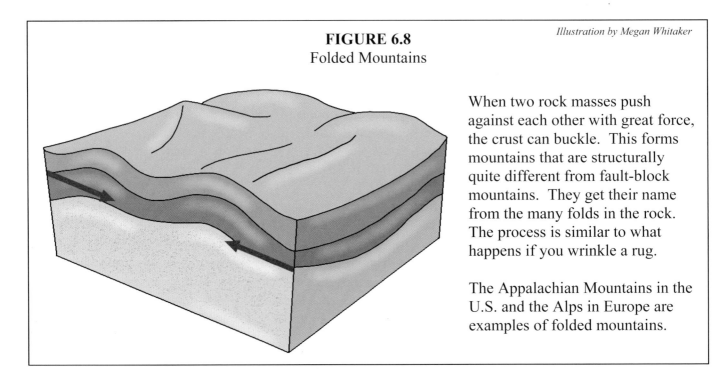

FIGURE 6.8
Folded Mountains

Illustration by Megan Whitaker

When two rock masses push against each other with great force, the crust can buckle. This forms mountains that are structurally quite different from fault-block mountains. They get their name from the many folds in the rock. The process is similar to what happens if you wrinkle a rug.

The Appalachian Mountains in the U.S. and the Alps in Europe are examples of folded mountains.

Another type of mountain can be formed as the result of magma moving from the mantle and into the earth's crust. Remember, the rock from the mantle is hot enough to melt, but the extreme pressure of the mantle keeps the rock in its plastic form. However, suppose a crack formed in the earth's crust. Magma from the mantle would rise into that crack. If the crack actually reached all the way to the earth's surface, the magma would pour out as lava. As the lava accumulates, a mountain would be formed. Not surprisingly, this kind of mountain is called a **volcanic mountain**, which most people call a **volcano**. Mount St. Helens in southwestern Washington is a volcanic mountain, as is Mount Pinatubo in the Philippines.

In general, volcanoes are classified as being **active, dormant**, or **extinct**. Active volcanoes have erupted (lava has come out of them) recently. Mt. St. Helens and Mt. Pinatubo are both active volcanoes. Dormant volcanoes have not erupted in a long time, but could possibly erupt in the future. Mauna Kea, Hawaii's largest volcano, is dormant. Extinct volcanoes are those that scientists think will never erupt again. Mt. Kilimanjaro in Tanzania is an extinct volcano. Of course, since we don't know everything about volcanoes and the processes that govern them, it is possible that some volcanoes that scientists think are extinct are really just dormant.

Volcanoes are scientifically interesting for a number of reasons. First of all, the magma released comes from the mantle, so it allows us to learn more about the nature of the interior of the earth. Secondly, scientists are just now beginning to realize how much a volcanic eruption can affect the landscape of the volcano's surroundings. Detailed studies from the 1980 eruption of Mount St. Helens, for example, seem to indicate that a *lot* of the geological features of the earth might have been formed rapidly as the result of volcanic eruptions and the catastrophes they cause. For example, scientists found a canyon that formed *overnight* as the result of a flood that accompanied the Mount St. Helens eruption!

Sometimes, there is not a vent through which magma can escape to the surface of the earth. However, the magma can still apply a large amount of force, pushing the crust upward. When this happens, the overlying rock still forms a mountain, but the magma is never released. Thus, there is no lava, and a volcano does not form. Because the rock is pushed upward, however, a mountain that often looks similar to a volcanic mountain is formed. Typically, this kind of mountain, called a **domed mountain**, is rounder and more sloping than a volcanic mountain, which usually has a rather conical shape. The Zuni Mountains in New Mexico are domed mountains. The differences between a volcanic mountain and a domed mountain can be seen in Figure 6.9.

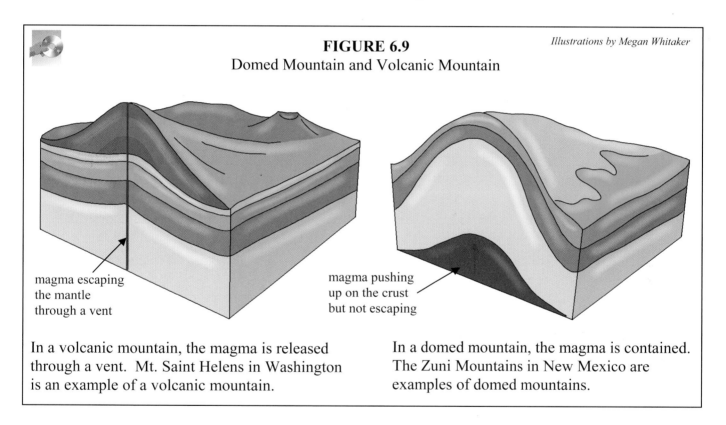

FIGURE 6.9
Domed Mountain and Volcanic Mountain

Illustrations by Megan Whitaker

magma escaping the mantle through a vent

magma pushing up on the crust but not escaping

In a volcanic mountain, the magma is released through a vent. Mt. Saint Helens in Washington is an example of a volcanic mountain.

In a domed mountain, the magma is contained. The Zuni Mountains in New Mexico are examples of domed mountains.

In the next two modules, I want to try and bring the concepts from this module and the past four together. In Modules 2 and 3 you studied air and the atmosphere. In Modules 4 and 5 you studied water and the hydrosphere. In this module, you studied earth and the lithosphere. In the next two modules, I will put all that together in the study of weather. Until then, study what you have learned in this module so you will be ready for what lies ahead.

ON YOUR OWN

6.10 Which kinds of mountains are formed as the result of rock masses moving against each other?

ANSWERS TO THE "ON YOUR OWN" PROBLEMS

6.1 <u>Metamorphic rock</u> is more likely to be found deep in the crust. Remember, metamorphic rock forms because of great pressure. The deeper the rock is in the crust, the more weight presses down on it, so the more pressure it experiences. There are other ways to get a high pressure situation, however, so metamorphic rock does not *have* to be deep in the crust.

6.2 <u>The sound would be louder when you put your ear to the rod</u>. Experiment 6.1 showed that sound travels better through a solid (the string) than through air. Since steel is solid, sound will travel better through it.

6.3 <u>It would not behave differently than any other rock</u>. Remember, the plastic nature of the rock in the mantle is due to the extreme heat and pressure found there. <u>As soon as you remove the rock from the mantle and take it to the lab, that heat and pressure are gone</u>. It will then behave just like any other rock.

6.4 <u>No, it would not</u>. Water is one of the few substances in creation that has its molecules closer when it is a liquid compared to when it is a solid. Thus, if I press water molecules closer together they become more liquid. In fact, if you exert pressure on ice it will melt, because you are pushing the molecules closer together, like they are in liquid water. Please note that at *extreme* pressures, water can become a solid, but that solid is not what you and I would call "ice."

6.5 <u>The earth has a magnetic field that must be caused by the motion of electricity</u>. Thus, something in the core must be moving, or there would be no electrical flow and thus no magnetic field.

6.6 <u>No, it would not work</u>. If the mantle were normal, solid rock, the plates would not be able to move. The plastic nature of the mantle's rock (a bit like the interior of the hard-boiled egg you used in the experiment) makes it possible for the plates to move.

6.7 <u>The majority of earthquakes should occur in California, Oregon, Washington, and Alaska</u>. Those are the places in the U.S. that rest on a plate. Since earthquakes can be caused by plates moving against each other, a lot of earthquakes should occur in these states, which lie along a boundary between plates. Since most U.S. earthquakes do, indeed, occur in these states, this is another piece of evidence in favor of plate tectonics.

6.8 <u>It would be larger</u>. Just like other vibrations, the farther the vibrations from an earthquake travel, the less energy they have. The focus is where the vibrations start, so they will have the most energy there.

6.9 Since the Richter scale says that every unit corresponds to a 32-times increase in energy, an earthquake that measures 3 will release 32 times more energy than the one that measures 2. An earthquake that measures 4 will release 32 x 32 = 1,024 times more energy than the one that measures 2. Finally, the one that measures 5 will release 32 x 32 x 32 = <u>32,768 times more energy</u> than the one that measured 2.

6.10 <u>Fault-block mountains</u> and <u>folded mountains</u> are the result of the motion of rock masses against each other. Domed mountains and volcanic mountains are formed as the result of magma pushing up from the mantle.

STUDY GUIDE FOR MODULE #6

1. Define the following terms:

a. Earth's crust
b. Sediment
c. Sedimentary rock
d. Igneous rock

e. Metamorphic rock
f. Plastic rock
g. Earthquake
h. Fault

i. Focus
j. Epicenter

2. Scientists often separate the earth into five distinct sections. Name those sections.

3. Of the five sections listed in problem 2, which can we observe directly?

4. What two regions of the earth does the Moho discontinuity separate? What about the Gutenberg discontinuity? What about the Lehmann discontinuity?

5. What is the difference between the ways that igneous rock and sedimentary rock form?

6. Of the three types of rock discussed in this module, which type starts out a different type of rock?

7. What is unique about the rock in the asthenosphere?

8. What is the main thing scientists observe in order to learn about the makeup of the earth's interior?

9. Which is solid: the inner core or the outer core? Why is it solid when the other is liquid?

10. Where is the magnetic field of the earth generated?

11. What causes the magnetic field of the earth?

12. Give a brief description of the two main theories that attempt to explain the earth's magnetic field.

13. What makes the rapid-decay theory more scientifically valid than the dynamo theory?

14. Why is a catastrophe like the worldwide flood in Noah's time an essential part of earth's history if the rapid-decay theory is true?

15. What two reasons make otherwise good scientists ignore the more scientifically valid rapid-decay theory?

16. Why would life cease to exist without the earth's magnetic field?

17. What are the "plates" in plate tectonics?

18. What can happen when plates collide with one another?

19. What is Pangaea?

20. Why do otherwise good scientists ignore the plate tectonics theory despite the evidence that exists for it?

21. What causes earthquakes?

22. Briefly describe the elastic rebound theory of earthquakes.

23. A seismologist detects an earthquake that measures 4 on the Richter scale. Later, he detects one that measures 8. How many times more energy does the second earthquake release as compared to the first?

24. Name the four kinds of mountains. What is required for the formation of each?

MODULE #7: Factors That Affect Earth's Weather

Introduction

What's the weather going to be like tomorrow? How many times have you asked yourself that question? People want to know what the weather is going to be so they can plan their activities, determine what to wear, or even decide what mood they will be in. Gorgeous weather can make an otherwise dull day pleasurable or make a good day even better. Bad weather can put us in a foul mood, make us cancel our plans, or, in some cases, cause great amounts of damage to both property and life. People have always searched for a deeper understanding of the weather. You will start your search in this module.

Before I start my discussion of weather, however, it is important to define a couple of terms. Many people use the words **weather** and **climate** interchangeably, but they are two completely different things. The term "weather" refers to the condition of the earth's atmosphere (mostly the troposphere) at any particular time. The current temperature, humidity, precipitation, and wind speed are all part of today's weather. Climate, on the other hand, is a steady condition that prevails day in and day out in a particular region of creation. For example, Southern California is known for its warm, sunny climate. That's because the *general* atmospheric conditions are warm and sunny. Despite what the song says, however, it *really does* rain in Southern California. Whether it is raining or sunny on a particular day is a question of that day's *weather*, whereas the general expectation to experience warm and sunny days when you travel to Southern California is a question of climate. The Scripps Institute of Oceanography in San Diego puts it this way: "Climate is what you expect, but weather is what you get." Keep that distinction in your mind.

Factors That Influence Weather

A region's weather is influenced by many, many factors. Principal among these factors are **thermal energy, uneven distribution of thermal energy**, and **water vapor in the atmosphere**. I have already talked a bit about thermal energy. Earth's thermal energy comes from the sun. You have already learned how the makeup of the atmosphere affects this energy. In this module, you will learn about other factors that affect the thermal energy that the earth receives. Once the thermal energy hits the earth, it is distributed across the planet through an incredibly complex set of interconnected systems. I will talk a little about that.   Finally, the water vapor in the atmosphere exists either as humidity, or it condenses into clouds. I have talked a bit about each of those subjects, but you will learn more about them here. I will start with a detailed discussion of clouds, because you need to know a bit more about clouds before you perform an important experiment.

Clouds

When water vapor condenses out of the atmosphere onto cloud condensation nuclei, the result is a cloud. You have already had some experience with clouds, having formed one in a plastic bottle during Experiment 5.3. In this module and the next, I hope to give you a good understanding of how clouds affect the weather. I need to start by telling you about the different kinds of clouds that can form.

Meteorologists (people who study weather) separate clouds into four basic groups: **cumulus** (kyoom' yoo lus), **stratus** (stra' tus), **cirrus** (seer' us), and **lenticular** (len tik' yoo ler). These basic cloud types are shown in the figure below.

FIGURE 7.1

The Four Basic Cloud Types

Photos by Kathleen J. Wile

7.1a – Cumulus

7.1b – Cirrus

7.1c – Stratus

7.1d – Lenticular

You generally find each type of cloud at a characteristic altitude. There are exceptions to this rule, however. As a result, a prefix of "alto" might be added to one of those four group names if a cloud is found at a higher altitude than what is typical for other members of its group. For example, altocumulus clouds are cumulus clouds that are found higher in the atmosphere than the majority of cumulus clouds. Finally, a prefix of "nimbo" or a suffix of "nimbus" will be added if the cloud is dark. Dark clouds are often the ones that bring precipitation. For example, dark cumulus clouds are called cumulonimbus clouds and are a common type of rain cloud.

Cumulus clouds (Figure 7.1a) are named from the Latin word "cumulus," which means "a pile." Their name describes them well. They are fluffy clouds that look like piles of cotton in the sky. They form just as the cloud in your bottle (Experiment 5.3) formed. As air rises, it fans out in all directions, increasing the volume in which it is occupied. This is one means of adiabatic expansion, which causes the same cooling effect and condensation you observed in your experiment. Unusually large, upward-moving wind currents can produce huge, towering **cumulonimbus clouds** that most people call "thunderclouds." Cumulonimbus clouds are usually dark at the bottom and whiter at the top. Some of them are so tall that they stretch from a few thousand feet above the ground all the way to the top of the troposphere!

Speaking of the top of the troposphere, that's where you can find **cirrus clouds** (Figure 7.1b). The name for these clouds is derived from a Latin word that means "wisp" or "curl." Since the air is so cold at the top of the troposphere, these clouds are made completely of tiny ice crystals. This gives the clouds their feathery appearance. In addition, the winds at the top of the troposphere tend to spread these clouds out, making them look thin and flowing. If you think it's odd that ice can stay suspended in the air, remember that for the same volume, ice is actually lighter than water (remember Experiment 4.4). If water droplets can stay suspended in the air, ice crystals of the same size can as well!

At the other extreme, **stratus clouds** (Figure 7.1c) typically form low in the sky. They are formed when a mass of warm air is lifted slowly upward. I will explain how this happens in a later section of this module. For right now, you just need to know that as the warm air is being lifted, the vapor in it will condense and form clouds when it reaches the higher, cooler air. This forms a flat layer of clouds relatively close to the ground. Indeed, the name "stratus" comes from the Latin word for "layer." Because there can be a lot of water in warm air, stratus clouds can easily turn into dark, rain-producing **nimbostratus clouds**. Like cumulonimbus clouds, nimbostratus clouds get darker and darker until they start precipitating.

The last family of clouds, **lenticular clouds** (Figure 7.1d), are generally formed in mountainous regions. In these areas, there can be pockets of low pressure in the sky. When air encounters these low-pressure regions, it expands. As you know from Experiment 5.3, this causes the air to cool. If the air cools enough, it will condense to form clouds. The name "lenticular" actually means lens-shaped, because these clouds usually form an oval.

As is the case in virtually all of creation, these four broad groups, along with the "alto" and "nimbus" prefixes and suffixes, are just not enough to classify every cloud you might see. You can often go out and see clouds that seem to be crosses between two of the groups I mentioned here. **Cirrocumulus clouds**, for example, have the feathery appearance of cirrus clouds because they are made of ice crystals, but they are not blown apart by the wind. Instead, they form thin puffs that look like a cross between cirrus clouds and cumulus clouds. In the same way, some stratus clouds do not end up forming in a flat layer, but instead form puffs that look very similar to cumulus clouds. Because they form so low in the sky, however, they are clearly formed in the same way that stratus clouds are formed, so they are called **stratocumulus clouds**. Finally, some clouds have the feathery appearance of cirrus clouds, but they form flat layers like that of stratus clouds. They are too high to be formed in the way that stratus clouds are formed, however, so they are called **cirrostratus clouds**.

The kinds of clouds that exist in the sky can tell you a lot about the weather fronts moving through an area. You will learn about that in a later section of this module. For right now, study Figure 7.2 so you can get familiar with the way clouds are named and classified.

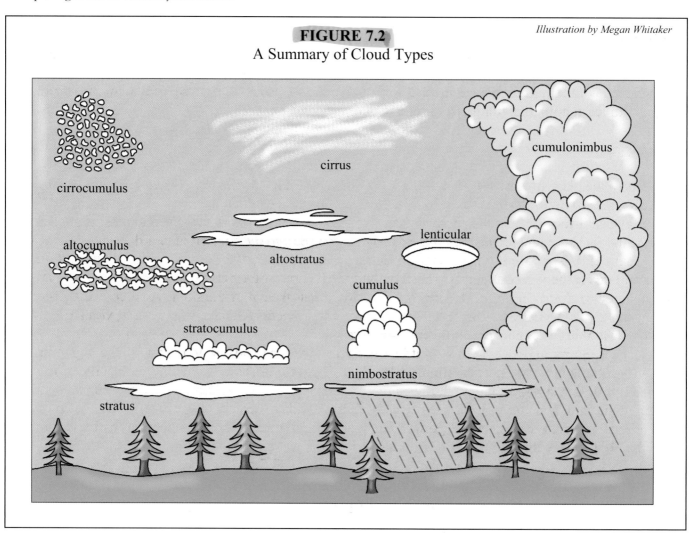

FIGURE 7.2
A Summary of Cloud Types

Illustration by Megan Whitaker

ON YOUR OWN

7.1 Is it possible to have altocirrus clouds? Why or why not?

7.2 If a group of cumulus clouds were higher than typical cumulus clouds but were also dark, what would they be called?

EXPERIMENT 7.1
A Long-Term Weather Experiment

Supplies:

♦ Daily local weather information source that contains:
   1. High and low temperatures for yesterday
   2. High and low atmospheric (sometimes called "barometric") pressure for yesterday.
   3. Amount of precipitation for yesterday
   If you have a hard time finding this information, check the course website I described in the "Student Notes" at the beginning of the book. You will find links to websites that contain it.

Introduction: This is a long-term experiment. Over the course of this module and the next, you will get an in-depth look at weather and what causes it. The purpose of this experiment is to help you correlate the information you learn with some observations you make. In addition, you will get some experience with long-term data gathering and interpretation. Stick with this experiment. It is important for you to learn how to do long-term projects like this one.

Procedure:

1. Find a weather information source that contains all the data mentioned in the supplies list above.
2. Choose two times during the day (one in the morning and one in the early evening) that are convenient for you to make an observation of the types of clouds in the sky. Go outside at each of those two times and identify the type of clouds you see and the amount of cloud cover. For example, if the entire sky is covered in clouds, it is "cloudy." If there are a lot of clouds but they don't cover the whole sky, it is "mostly cloudy." If somewhere between ¼ and ½ of the sky is covered in clouds, it is "mostly sunny." Finally, if less than ¼ of the sky is covered in clouds, it is "sunny." If the cloud cover is so thick that you can't determine the type of clouds, you are most likely looking at stratus or nimbostratus clouds.
3. Make a record in your notebook that lists each day, the high and low temperature, the high and low atmospheric pressure, precipitation, and early and late cloud observations. Remember to put the data with the appropriate day. For example, you will be getting yesterday's temperatures, precipitation, and atmospheric pressures. Put those with yesterday's date. Your cloud cover observations, however, should go with today's date. In the end, then, the beginning of your table should look like this:

Date	High Temp	Low Temp	High Pressure	Low Pressure	Precip	Early cloud cover	Late cloud cover
11/01/06	55 °F	38 °F	30.1 in	29.8 in	0.10 in	N/A	N/A
11/02/06						Cumulonimbus and cumulus, mostly cloudy	Stratus and cirrus, mostly sunny

Notice how the first day has no cloud cover observations. This is because 11/2/06 was the first day I started the experiment. Thus, I got all of the other data for yesterday and filled it in on yesterday's date (11/1/06), but my cloud cover observations were for today, so they went in today's date. On 11/3/06, I would fill in all of the data for 11/2/06 from my weather information source, and then I would start a new line for 11/3/06 and put my cloud cover observations in there.

4. Continue recording these facts throughout the rest of this module and the next. That's almost four weeks worth of data. Do not give up on this! What you learn from this experience will be well worth it. In Module #8, I will discuss how you should interpret the results of your experiment.

Earth's Thermal Energy

Thermal energy is another big factor that affects earth's weather. As I mentioned in the introduction, earth's thermal energy comes from the sun in the form of light. Now remember from Module #2 that light comes in many different forms (infrared, ultraviolet, visible, etc.). The light we see is really just a tiny fraction of the light that comes from the sun. In order to be more precise, scientists refer to the light that comes to earth as **insolation** (in so lay' shun), which is an abbreviation for "incoming solar radiation." Although you might have heard the term "radiation" in the context of radioactivity, it is important to realize that the term "radiation" is actually a general term scientists use for light and certain other forms of energy you will learn about in later modules.

Now it turns out that the earth has been placed *perfectly* in space to absorb *just the right* amount of insolation from the sun. The amount of insolation earth gets from the sun is affected primarily by two factors: earth's **distance from the sun** and earth's **axial** (ax' ee uhl) **tilt**. As you have already learned from Module #5, the earth has been placed at *exactly the right distance from the sun*. If earth's average distance from the sun were different by just a few percent, life as we know it could not exist. Why do I say "average" distance from the sun? I say this because the earth does not orbit the sun in a perfect circle. Instead, the earth's path as it travels around the sun is a slight oval, which mathematicians call an **ellipse** (ee lips').

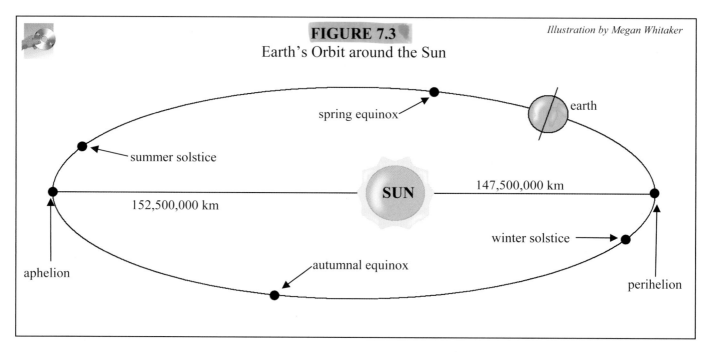

FIGURE 7.3
Earth's Orbit around the Sun

Illustration by Megan Whitaker

spring equinox

earth

summer solstice

147,500,000 km

152,500,000 km

SUN

winter solstice

aphelion

autumnal equinox

perihelion

Now please understand that the oval shape of earth's orbit is exaggerated in the figure for the purpose of illustration. Earth's actual orbit is a lot more circular than the oval shown in the drawing.

Notice from the figure that earth does not hang in space completely vertically. Instead, earth is "tilted" in space by about 23.5 degrees on average. This is what scientists call earth's axial tilt, and together with the elliptical nature of earth's orbit, it is responsible for earth's seasons and the timing of how they change. Also, please note that some of this terminology is reversed between the hemispheres, so if you live in the Southern Hemisphere (Australia, New Zealand, or South Africa, for example), you should check Appendix A after reading this section. There you will find a few details (such as a different form of Figure 7.3) that modify this discussion to make it more relevant for you.

How does this work? When the earth is at its **aphelion** (uh fee' lee uhn), it is the farthest it will ever be from the sun. At that point, the earth receives about 3% less than its average amount of insolation. When it is at its **perihelion** (pair uh he' lee uhn), the earth is closest to the sun, and it gets about 3% more insolation than it does on average.

Aphelion – The point at which the earth is farthest from the sun

Perihelion – The point at which the earth is closest to the sun

This means that it is summer when the earth is near its perihelion and winter when it is near its aphelion, right? Surprisingly, the answer is *no*. The earth's axial tilt is actually the reason for the seasons we experience. The aphelion and perihelion act only to slightly modify the effect of earth's axial tilt.

Because the earth is tilted, insolation hits it in different ways depending on which **hemisphere** you are looking at. Remember, the earth can be split into equal halves (hemispheres) above and below the equator. The Northern Hemisphere contains all regions north of the equator, and the Southern Hemisphere contains all regions south of the equator. Notice how those hemispheres are oriented relative to the sun at aphelion and perihelion.

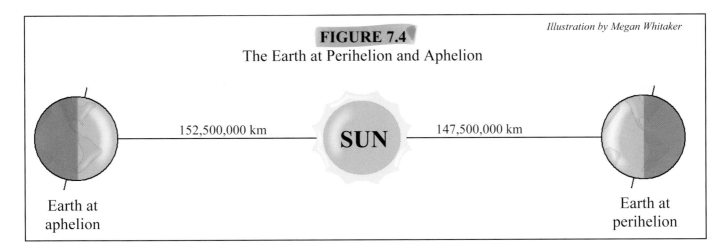

FIGURE 7.4
The Earth at Perihelion and Aphelion

Illustration by Megan Whitaker

152,500,000 km   **SUN**   147,500,000 km

Earth at aphelion

Earth at perihelion

When the earth is at perihelion, the Southern Hemisphere tilts toward the sun, and the Northern Hemisphere points away from the sun. Because of this, the sun's light shines more directly on the Southern Hemisphere than it does on the Northern Hemisphere. As a result, the sun's light warms the Southern Hemisphere more effectively, which results in summer for the *Southern Hemisphere.* At the same time, however, the sun's light is not heating the Northern Hemisphere nearly as effectively because it shines less directly on the Northern Hemisphere. This makes it winter in the *Northern Hemisphere.*

Thus, even though the earth receives more insolation at perihelion, only the Southern Hemisphere experiences summer during that time. Conversely, at aphelion, the Northern Hemisphere points toward the sun. Even though the earth receives the least insolation at that point, it is summer in the Northern Hemisphere, because that's when the sun's light shines most directly on the Northern Hemisphere, heating it up the best. Of course, the Southern Hemisphere is pointed away from the sun at that time, so when it is summer in the Northern Hemisphere, it is winter in the Southern Hemisphere.

You see, then, that earth's axial tilt is responsible not only for the seasons that we have, but also for the fact that the seasons are reversed between the hemispheres. There is more to this discussion, however. While the earth is orbiting around the sun, it is also spinning on its axis, turning day into night and night into day. When a region of the earth is pointed toward the sun, it receives light, and it is therefore daytime. When it is pointed away from the sun, it receives no light from the sun, and it is nighttime. During the day, then, it is typically warmer because insolation is hitting that region of the planet. During the night it is typically cooler, because that region of the planet is getting little or no insolation.

Our practical experience tells us that the days get longer in the summer and shorter in the winter. As you might expect, this is due to the way the earth orbits the sun and due to its axial tilt. Because the earth is tilted, it usually exposes more of one hemisphere to the sun than the other.   As a result, the days are longer in the hemisphere that points more directly to the sun, and they are shorter in the hemisphere that points away from the sun. June 21 or 22 (depending on the year) is called the **summer solstice** (see Figure 7.3). This is the time when the earth's path around the sun has forced the Northern Hemisphere to start pointing directly at the sun. At that point, every part of the Northern Hemisphere sees the sun for more than 12 hours and every part of the Southern Hemisphere sees the sun for less than 12 hours. On December 21 or 22 (depending on the year), the **winter solstice** (see Figure 7.3) occurs. At this time, the Southern Hemisphere becomes pointed directly at the sun. As a result, the situation is exactly reversed, and every part of the Northern Hemisphere has daylight for less than 12 hours while every part of the Southern Hemisphere has daylight for more than 12 hours.

There are two points in earth's orbit around the sun where, because of the position of the earth relative to the sun, the axial tilt is no longer relevant. It is still there, of course, but the way the earth is positioned relative to the sun cancels its effect. At that point, neither hemisphere is tilted toward the sun, and both hemispheres have a day length of 12 hours and a night length of 12 hours. These are called the **spring equinox** (ee kwuh' nahks) and the **autumnal** (aw tum' nuhl) **equinox**. They occur (see Figure 7.3) on March 20 or 21 and September 22 or 23, respectively. From the summer solstice to the winter solstice, then, the length of the day decreases in the Northern Hemisphere and increases in the Southern Hemisphere. The autumnal equinox marks the halfway point between those two events. In the same way, from the winter solstice to the summer solstice, the length of the day increases in the Northern Hemisphere and decreases in the Southern Hemisphere, with the spring equinox marking that halfway point.

All four of these particular events in earth's orbit have been celebrated as holidays by different pagan religions, because the pagans did not understand how all these things worked together according to God's plan. For example, pagan sun worshipers in the Northern Hemisphere used to celebrate December 25 as the "birthday of the sun." Despite the fact that the days in the Northern Hemisphere start getting longer after the winter solstice, the pagans didn't actually notice it happening until December 25, a few days later. Since they noticed the day length decreasing every day before the winter solstice and noticed them increasing again on December 25, they actually thought that the sun was "reborn" on that day. They celebrated the sun's supposed new birth as a religious holiday. When Christians came to witness to these people, they changed that holiday into the "birthday of the *Son*," to try and make Christianity a little more directly relevant to their culture. That's why we celebrate Christ's birth (Christmas) on December 25 even though early church literature indicates that Christ was most likely born in early April.

Now that you know earth's axial tilt is the main cause of the seasons, it is important to understand the effect that earth's elliptical orbit has on the seasons. First, it determines *when* the seasons change. If earth's orbit were different in shape, the timing of the spring and autumnal equinoxes as well as the summer and winter solstices would be different.

Second, as mentioned before, earth's elliptical orbit does affect the amount of insolation the earth receives. Earth gets more insolation at perihelion and less at aphelion. Now if you think about it, you might come to the conclusion that the Southern Hemisphere's summers are hotter (on average) than the Northern Hemisphere's summers. After all, the Southern Hemisphere experiences summer when earth gets the largest amount of insolation, and the Northern Hemisphere experiences summer when it gets the least amount of insolation. It should stand to reason, then, that summers in the Southern Hemisphere are hotter, right? Well, not exactly.

Such reasoning would be correct if *everything else* about the two hemispheres were the same. However, there is more land in the Northern Hemisphere than in the Southern Hemisphere. It turns out that land heats up much more easily than does water. Thus, the fact that the Northern Hemisphere has more land means it heats up more easily than does the Southern Hemisphere. As a result, even though earth gets the least amount of insolation during the Northern Hemisphere's summer, the Northern Hemisphere's summer is, on average, warmer than the Southern Hemisphere's summer. This, of course, just tells you that earth's axial tilt and its elliptical orbit are not the only things that influence the temperature.

Another big factor that influences the temperature is **cloud cover**. Clouds reflect insolation, keeping it from hitting the earth. On an extremely cloudy day, the amount of insolation that hits the earth can be reduced significantly. This, of course, will lower the temperature. As you will learn in this and the next module, there are many other factors that influence temperature as well.

ON YOUR OWN

7.3 Suppose the earth were tilted opposite of the way it is now. Would the Northern Hemisphere experience summer at the earth's aphelion or perihelion?

7.4 Between what dates is the length of the day less than 12 hours in the Southern Hemisphere and at the same time decreasing from day to day?

7.5 Suppose the earth's orbit around the sun were circular rather than elliptical. If that were true, the earth would always be the same distance from the sun. Under these conditions, would there still be seasons?

Latitude and Longitude

Before I discuss the uneven thermal energy distribution of the earth, I need to get some terminology squared away. In order to make referring to different regions of the earth a little easier, geographers have divided the earth with two groups of imaginary lines called **lines of longitude** and **lines of latitude**.

Lines of longitude – Imaginary lines that run north and south across the earth

Lines of latitude – Imaginary lines that run east and west across the earth

These lines are illustrated in Figure 7.5.

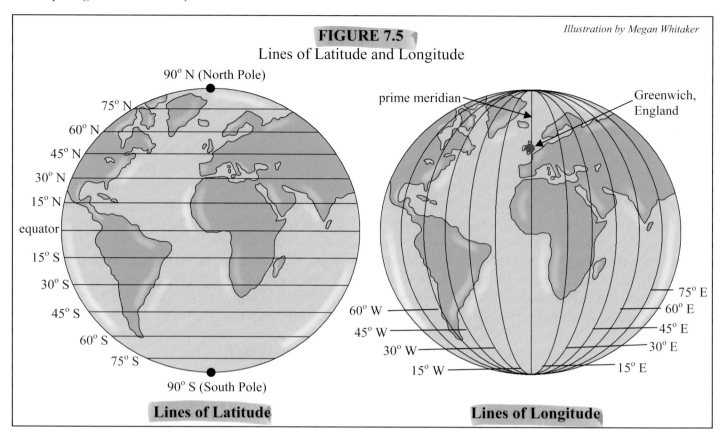

FIGURE 7.5
Lines of Latitude and Longitude

Illustration by Megan Whitaker

Lines of Latitude

Lines of Longitude

Notice that the lines of latitude are labeled in angles referenced from the **equator**, which is the imaginary line that runs directly between the Northern and Southern Hemispheres of the earth. The latitude lines, then, essentially tell you how far north or south you are from the equator. Thus, it is an easy system for referencing your north/south position on the globe. If you are at a latitude of 60° N, for example, you know that you are quite a bit north of the equator. A position of 15° N, on the other hand, tells you that you are still north of the equator, but not by much.

In the same way, the lines of longitude are a convenient way to determine your east/west position on the earth. The reference line of longitude is an imaginary line, called the **prime meridian,** that runs through Greenwich (gren' itch), England. Any longitude line east of Greenwich is labeled as an eastern line and any line west of Greenwich is labeled as a western line. Thus, if you are at 15° E, you know that you are close to but still east of Greenwich, England. If you are at 60° E, however, you are far east of Greenwich, England.

I will use latitude references in my discussion of uneven thermal energy distribution, so you need to be familiar with this terminology before you proceed into the next section.

Uneven Thermal Energy Distribution

One of the more complex factors that influences earth's weather is the uneven distribution of thermal energy that comes from the sun. As you have already learned, earth's axial tilt causes the sunlight to shine differently on different parts of the earth. The more directly the sun's light shines on the earth, the better it heats the planet. Well, the sun's light shines most directly on the equator. That's why it is always warm at the equator. Above and below the equator, the sun's light shines on the earth at an angle, reducing its effectiveness at heating. The farther up or down from the equator, the more pronounced this effect is. At the North or South Pole, the sun's light is shining at such a large angle that its heating effect is very poor. That's why it is always cold at the poles.

If you think about this on a global scale, then, there is a tremendous temperature difference between the earth's equator and its poles. What happens as a result of this temperature difference? Wind! You see, when air gets hot, it expands. This causes a given mass of air to take up more volume. Because of this fact, a given volume of hot air is lighter than a given volume of cold air. As a result, **hot air rises**. As the hot air rises, there is a deficit of air left behind, creating a region of low pressure, referred to (reasonably enough) as a **low**. Conversely, **cold air sinks**. As the cold air sinks, it creates a buildup of air, resulting in a high pressure region called (you guessed it) a **high**.

Now what will air tend to do if there is a buildup at one location and a deficit at another? It will tend to move from the buildup to the deficit, in order to even out the amount of air everywhere. When air moves, we call it wind. Thus, temperature differences result in wind, and the wind blows near the surface of the earth from the cold region (the high) to the warm region (the low).

This situation is reversed at higher elevations. After all, as the hot air rises, it "piles up" at the higher elevations, causing an excess of air at higher elevations. In the same way, as the cold air sinks, it leaves behind a deficit of air at the higher elevations. Thus, at higher elevations, the wind will travel in the opposite direction (from the warm region to the cold region).

Remember why I started this whole discussion. The equator is much warmer than the poles. As a result, warm air rises at the equator, creating a low there. At the same time, cold air at the poles sinks, creating a high there. Thus, at the surface of the earth, winds tend to blow from the poles (the high) to the equator (the low). In the upper atmosphere, however, the situation is reversed, and winds blow from the equator to the poles.

Simple enough, right? Well, it would be if I stopped there. Unfortunately, there are three factors that complicate the situation immensely: **changing air temperature**, the **Coriolis** (kor ee oh' lus) **effect**, and **local winds**. The first of these effects is the easiest one to understand. Remember, near the surface of the earth, there is a high at the poles. Thus, cold air will move from the poles toward the equator. Well, consider the cold air traveling near the surface of the earth from the North Pole toward the equator. As it makes its way there, it encounters warmer temperatures. As a result, the air warms up. What happens to warm air? It *rises*. Thus, as the air travels near the surface of the earth from the North Pole to the equator, it warms up, and as a result, it rises. By the time the air makes it to a latitude of about 60° N (see Figure 7.5), it becomes so warm that it rises into the upper troposphere. What does that do? It causes a high at the upper altitudes, which forces the air to begin *moving back toward the pole!* In the end, this sets up a loop of winds that travel continuously from the pole to a latitude of about 60° N and back again.

If we now turn our attention to the equator, we will see the exact opposite effect. As the warm air rises, it starts traveling toward the poles. At a latitude of about 30° N, however, it cools down enough to sink and begin traveling back toward the equator. Thus, from the equator, there is also a loop of winds that travel to a latitude of about 30° N, sink, and then turn around and come back again. In the middle of these two loops of wind there is a third loop that occurs as a reaction to these two loops. The result of all this mess is shown in Figure 7.6.

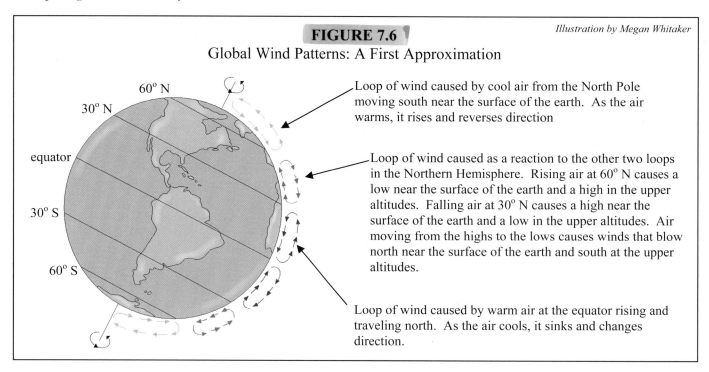

FIGURE 7.6
Global Wind Patterns: A First Approximation

Illustration by Megan Whitaker

60° N

30° N

equator

30° S

60° S

Loop of wind caused by cool air from the North Pole moving south near the surface of the earth. As the air warms, it rises and reverses direction

Loop of wind caused as a reaction to the other two loops in the Northern Hemisphere. Rising air at 60° N causes a low near the surface of the earth and a high in the upper altitudes. Falling air at 30° N causes a high near the surface of the earth and a low in the upper altitudes. Air moving from the highs to the lows causes winds that blow north near the surface of the earth and south at the upper altitudes.

Loop of wind caused by warm air at the equator rising and traveling north. As the air cools, it sinks and changes direction.

Now please note that even though I have discussed winds only in the Northern Hemisphere, three similar loops of wind (shown in the figure) exist in the Southern Hemisphere, caused by the same effects. Also, notice that I titled the figure a "first approximation." That's because I still haven't dealt with the next factor: the Coriolis effect.

Remember that the whole time air is moving, the planet is also spinning. This tends to distort the wind directions a bit. To understand why this happens, you first have to realize that each latitude north and south of the equator rotates at a different speed. Although this statement may surprise you at first, it should make sense after studying Figure 7.7.

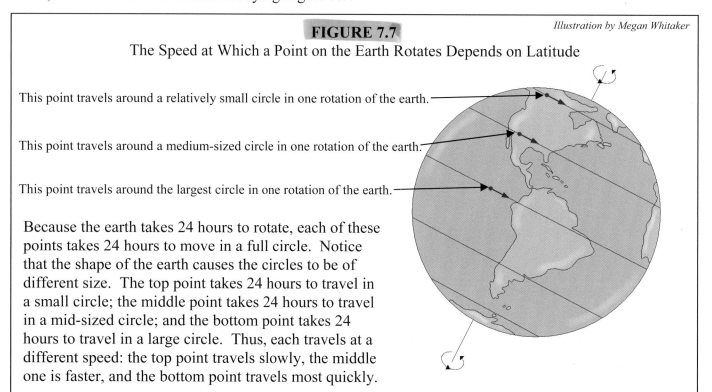

FIGURE 7.7
The Speed at Which a Point on the Earth Rotates Depends on Latitude

Illustration by Megan Whitaker

This point travels around a relatively small circle in one rotation of the earth.

This point travels around a medium-sized circle in one rotation of the earth.

This point travels around the largest circle in one rotation of the earth.

Because the earth takes 24 hours to rotate, each of these points takes 24 hours to move in a full circle. Notice that the shape of the earth causes the circles to be of different size. The top point takes 24 hours to travel in a small circle; the middle point takes 24 hours to travel in a mid-sized circle; and the bottom point takes 24 hours to travel in a large circle. Thus, each travels at a different speed: the top point travels slowly, the middle one is faster, and the bottom point travels most quickly.

So you see that because the circumference of the earth is different at different latitudes, the speed at which a point rotates on that latitude of the earth is different from that of points on other latitudes. How does this relate to wind? Well, consider a mass of air sinking near the North Pole. Because it starts there, it is rotating around the earth at the speed of everything else near the North Pole. As Figure 7.7 indicates, things near the poles rotate around the earth slowly. As the air starts to move toward the equator, however, the ground below starts moving faster, because things closer to the equator rotate around the earth faster than things closer to the poles. Thus, the ground beneath this air mass starts "outrunning" the air above it. This makes the wind bend away from the rotational motion of the earth. I am sure this is a bit confusing, so I will explain it again with a figure.

FIGURE 7.8
The Coriolis Effect

Illustration by Megan Whitaker

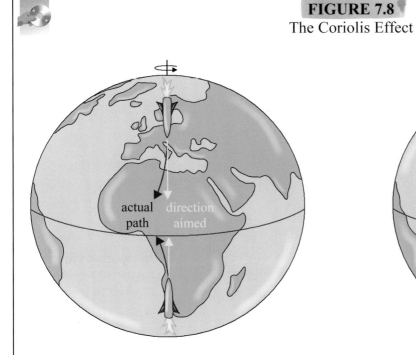

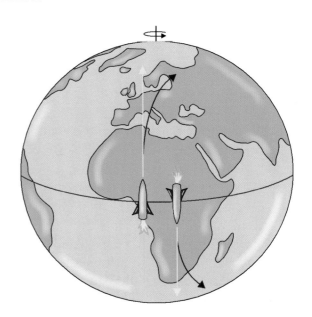

A missile fired toward the equator from the poles will rotate with the earth more slowly than the ground over which it passes. This will cause the missile to "lose ground," and it will bend to the west, opposite the rotation of the earth.

A missile fired toward the poles from the equator will rotate with the earth more quickly than the ground over which it passes. This will cause the missile to "gain ground," and it will bend to the east, with the rotation of the earth.

As the figure indicates, when something travels above the earth, its path will bend depending on where it originated and where it is going. If it originated near the poles and heads towards the equator, it will rotate with the earth more slowly than the ground over which it passes. This will make its path bend to the west when viewed from the ground. Objects traveling from near the equator toward the poles will bend to the east as they "outrun" the ground over which they travel. This is called the Coriolis effect, and it alters the paths of the winds as well as currents in the sea.

Coriolis effect – The way in which the rotation of the earth bends the path of winds, sea currents, and objects that fly through different latitudes

When you add the Coriolis effect to the effect of changing air temperature discussed above, you get the global wind patterns illustrated in Figure 7.9.

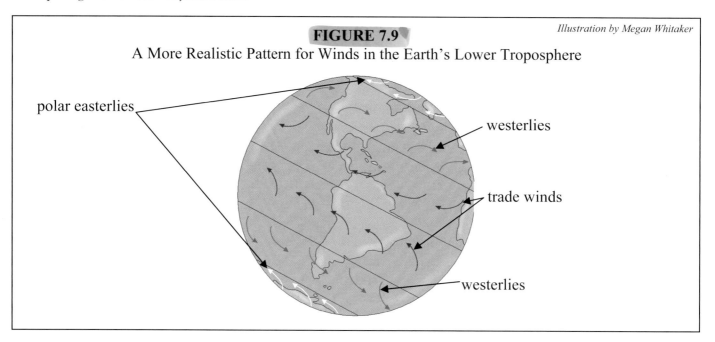

Illustration by Megan Whitaker

FIGURE 7.9
A More Realistic Pattern for Winds in the Earth's Lower Troposphere

polar easterlies

westerlies

trade winds

westerlies

Now please realize that these wind currents are only those found in the lower troposphere. Thus, I am concentrating on the winds that blow near the ground (or the surface of the water), which are the winds we experience. The wind currents in the upper troposphere are even more complicated. Thankfully, I will not discuss them in this course!

Look at Figure 7.9 for a moment and try to understand *why* the air currents are bent in the way they are bent. Begin by looking at the air currents near the North Pole (called **polar easterlies**). As Figure 7.7 indicates, things near the poles rotate rather slowly around the earth, because in the space of a day, they travel a shorter distance around than things closer to the equator. As a result, the winds that start out at the North Pole are rotating at a slow speed. As they travel south, they pass over land that is traveling faster. Figure 7.8 gives you the direction of earth's rotation, so the land will "outrun" the wind in that direction. This makes the wind look like it bends in the opposite direction. Thus, the winds near the poles bend opposite the direction of the earth's rotation. Between the latitudes of 30° N and 60° N, however, the winds travel from south to north. Thus, they start out rotating quickly and end up passing over land that is rotating more slowly. As a result, they "outrun" the land. This makes them look like they bend in the direction of the earth's rotation. In the end, then, winds traveling towards the equator get "outrun" by the land they are passing over and end up bending opposite the direction of the earth's rotation. Winds that travel towards the poles "outrun" the earth they are passing over, so they bend in the direction of the earth's rotation.

Now please realize that Figure 7.9 shows the *general* wind patterns that exist on the planet. At any given time, however, there is no reason to believe that you can predict the way the wind is blowing by looking at Figure 7.9. Why? Well, remember that temperature differences are the driving forces for these winds and that the temperature of a region is affected by several factors. For example, if the cloud cover over a region of the equator is high, that portion of the equator will not receive as much insolation as another portion of the equator. This will make the cloudy region of the equator cooler, and the global winds in that area of the planet will be weakened. At the same time, another region near the equator might not be at all cloudy, causing a temperature difference between different regions along the equator. This will set up a different wind pattern, interfering with the global wind patterns. In addition to all this, local winds can dominate the global wind patterns completely, or they can just interfere a bit. In the end, then, Figure 7.9 shows us a general rule for global wind circulation, but the real picture is significantly more complex!

Since local winds can affect the global wind patterns in Figure 7.9, it is important to know how local winds develop. Just like the global winds, they start as a result of a temperature difference. Consider, for example, a region of the earth near a large lake (or the ocean). During the day, the sun's light warms the area. Water, however, does not warm up as quickly as soil and sediment. As a result, the **land gets warmer than the sea when the sun's light shines on them both equally**. This temperature difference causes a low to form over the land as the warm air rises. At the same time, a high forms over the lake as the cool air sinks. This results in a **sea breeze**, shown in Figure 7.10a. At night, the **land cools faster than the water**. This eventually causes the opposite temperature difference, and the breeze blows the other way as a **land breeze** shown in Figure 7.10b.

FIGURE 7.10   *Illustration by Megan Whitaker*
Sea Breeze (a) and Land Breeze (b)

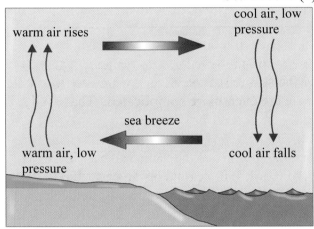

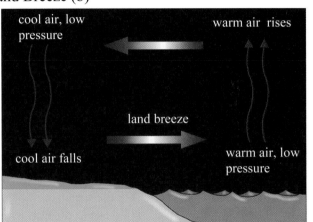

a. Because land heats up faster than water during the day, the land is warmer than the water. This temperature difference causes a surface breeze that blows from the water to the land.

b. Because land cools faster than water during the night, the land is cooler than the water. This temperature difference causes a breeze opposite the one that happens during the day.

Wherever regions of the earth have areas that warm up and cool down faster than other areas, local temperature differences will occur. This will result in local winds that will interfere with the global winds shown in Figure 7.9. How does all of this affect the weather? I want to start to answer that question in the next section.

ON YOUR OWN

7.6 On a day at the beach, you notice that the sand is so hot that it is hard to walk on it with bare feet. At the same time, however, the ocean is quite cool. When you left your hotel, you noticed no breeze at all, but when you got to the beach, you noticed a reasonably strong breeze. Is the wind blowing from the ocean to the shore or vice versa?

7.7 Suppose you want to fire a missile from Southern California to a point in northern Canada that is due north of your location in California. Ignoring the effects of wind and weather, would you aim the missile due north, northwest, or northeast?

7.8 The global patterns of wind circulation in Figure 7.9 indicate that in Mexico the winds should be blowing basically east to west. Does this mean that in Mexico the wind will never blow from west to east?

Air Masses

When the factors I discussed in the previous section cause a stillness in the wind in a particular region of the earth, the air tends to pick up the region's temperature, humidity, and pressure. When this happens, we call the result an **air mass**.

Air mass – A large body of air with relatively uniform pressure, temperature, and humidity

Because an air mass is relatively uniform throughout, it tends to stay together, moving as a unit.

When an air mass moves into a region, it brings with it the weather characteristic of the region in which it was formed. Wherever the air mass stays, the weather in that region of the earth is similar from day to day, until the air mass moves away and another takes its place. By tracing the movements of air masses across the earth's surface, **meteorologists** (scientists who study weather) can predict the kind of weather a region will have by predicting what air mass will be moving over the region.

There are three basic types of air masses: **arctic, polar,** and **tropical.** As their names imply, arctic air masses are very cold, polar air masses are cold (but not as cold as arctic air masses), and tropical air masses are warm. Polar and tropical air masses can further be divided into **maritime** (formed over the ocean) or **continental** (formed over a continent). **Maritime tropical** (abbreviated as **mT**) air masses, for example, are warm air masses that form over the ocean. These air masses tend to have high humidity, so we typically say they are warm and moist. Likewise, **maritime polar (mP)** air masses are cold and moist. Since continental air masses form over continents, they are considerably less humid than their maritime counterparts. Thus, **continental tropical (cT)** air masses are warm and dry, while **continental polar (cP)** air masses are cold and dry. Arctic air masses are low in humidity, so we say they are very cold and dry.

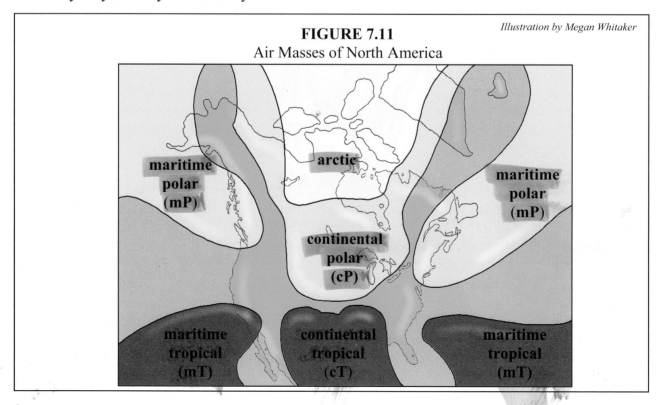

FIGURE 7.11

Illustration by Megan Whitaker

Air Masses of North America

As air masses move, they can encounter other air masses. As I mentioned before, air masses stay together as a unit because of their uniform characteristics. Thus, when one air mass encounters another, it does not mix with the other air mass. Instead, it collides with the other air mass and "fights" to "take over" the region. When two air masses collide like that, it is called a **weather front**.

Weather front – A boundary between two air masses

There are four basic types of weather fronts: **cold fronts, warm fronts, stationary fronts,** and **occluded fronts.**

In a **cold front**, a cold air mass moves in on a region of warmer air. Since cold air tends to sink, the cold air mass wedges under the warm air mass and lifts it up off the ground, pushing it up and away. This situation is illustrated in Figure 7.12.

Illustration by Megan Whitaker

FIGURE 7.12
A Cold Front

cumulonimbus cloud forming

cold air mass moving into a region

warm air mass being lifted up

Since the cold air mass comes in under the warm front, it lifts up the warm air as it advances. As this happens, moisture in the warm air condenses into clouds. If the warm air is really moist and thick, severe weather clouds can form. Since the warm air gets lifted up, the clouds tend to pile up. Usually, cumulus clouds form first, and as the warm air continues to rise, altocumulus clouds can form. If the warm air is particularly moist, cumulonimbus clouds can form. In fact, if the cold front moves in fast enough, you can often see the curved shape of the cold front in the edge of the clouds that form.

Cold fronts are generally the cause of the most severe weather systems. The violent upheaval of a warm air mass, especially a warm air mass that is high in humidity, can result in the rapid formation of thunderclouds with little warning. A storm can come just as quickly. As you might expect, the temperature drops as a cold front moves in. This generally signals better weather, however, as the sky generally clears once the cold air mass has taken the warmer air mass's place.

A **warm front**, on the other hand, results when a warm air mass moves into a region occupied by colder air. Since warm air tends to rise, a warm front usually moves *over* a cold front. This flattens the cold air below and forms an upwardly sloping front that can stretch for several hundred miles, as illustrated in Figure 7.13.

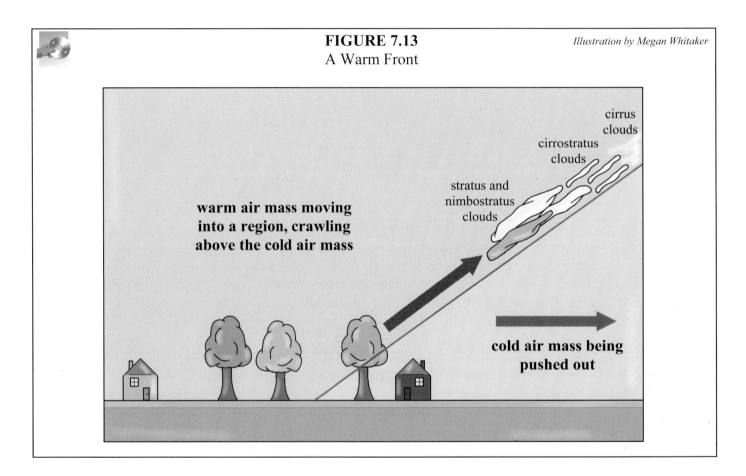

FIGURE 7.13
A Warm Front

Illustration by Megan Whitaker

cirrus clouds

cirrostratus clouds

stratus and nimbostratus clouds

warm air mass moving into a region, crawling above the cold air mass

cold air mass being pushed out

This kind of weather front is usually less violent than a cold front, so the resulting weather is usually less severe. The end result is still warm air rising, so clouds do form as the warm air cools. In a warm front, this usually starts out with cirrus clouds, followed by cirrostratus clouds. Then altostratus and stratus clouds are formed, and finally, nimbostratus clouds appear. The rain that results from this kind of front is typically less heavy than that formed by cold fronts, but it often lasts quite a bit longer.

When two air masses collide and neither moves, the result is a **stationary front**. A stationary front looks much like a warm front, but winds typically blow along a stationary front in opposite directions up and down the front rather than against the front. Also, since neither mass makes headway in a stationary front, the weather tends to stick around longer than that produced by a warm front. Stationary fronts often turn into warm fronts or cold fronts when one of the air masses actually begins to make some progress.

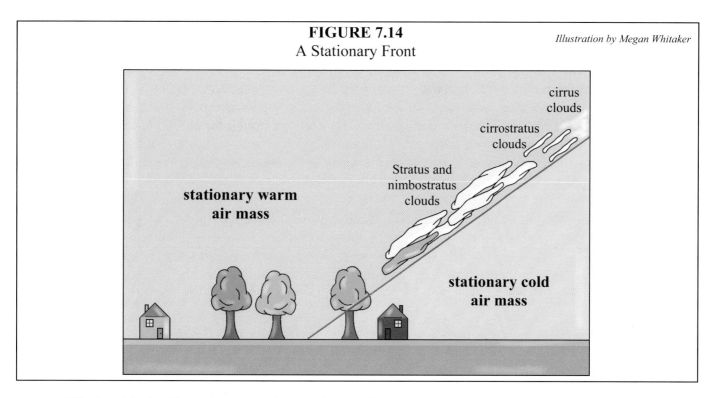

FIGURE 7.14
A Stationary Front

Illustration by Megan Whitaker

cirrus clouds

cirrostratus clouds

Stratus and nimbostratus clouds

stationary warm air mass

stationary cold air mass

The last kind of front I want to discuss is called an **occluded** (uh clew' did) **front**. It arises when two air masses traveling in the same direction collide. How can two air masses traveling in the same direction collide? Well, it turns out that **cold air masses travel faster than warm air masses**. So it is possible for cold air masses to overtake and collide with warm air masses. When that happens, an occluded front forms.

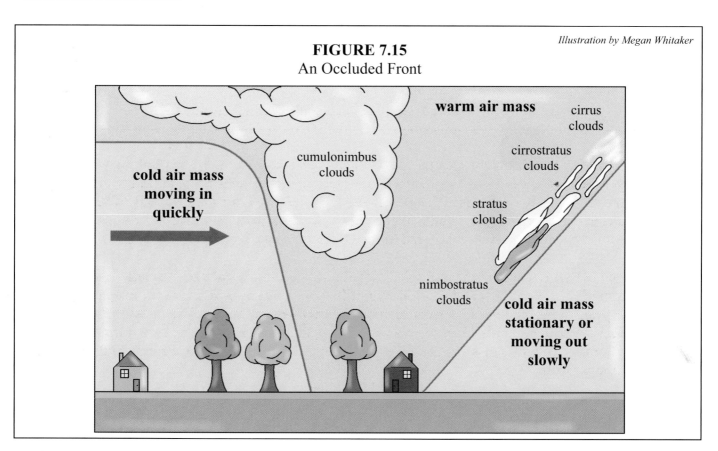

Illustration by Megan Whitaker

FIGURE 7.15
An Occluded Front

warm air mass   cirrus clouds

cirrostratus clouds

cumulonimbus clouds

cold air mass moving in quickly

stratus clouds

nimbostratus clouds

cold air mass stationary or moving out slowly

Usually, an occluded front forms when a warm front is traveling over a cold air mass. If another fast-moving cold air mass comes in from behind, it can collide with the warm front, lifting the warm air mass up and away.

Because an occluded front starts out as a warm front and ends up much like a cold front, the weather produced is a combination of that produced by each type of front. First, the clouds that herald a warm front form. They are then followed by the cumulus and cumulonimbus clouds of a cold front. As you might expect, the weather starts out as the slow, light rain of a warm front, and then the severe weather typical of a cold front moves in behind it.

Hopefully this module has given you a glimpse at the incredibly complex nature of earth's weather. Now that you know the basics of the factors that influence weather, you can move on to the next module, which will cover weather and how we try to predict it. As you might expect from the complexities you have already learned, our attempts at weather prediction are often not very good!

ON YOUR OWN

7.9 Suppose you were to observe a long, light rain. After the rain is over and the sky is clear, would you expect warmer temperatures or colder temperatures?

7.10 Why can't an occluded front start out with the weather typical of a cold front and then end with the weather typical of a warm front?

Even though this module has come to an end, do not stop performing Experiment 7.1! I will be discussing the results toward the end of the next module, and you will need a *lot* of data in order to really learn from the experiment. Therefore, you need to keep recording the data.

ANSWERS TO THE "ON YOUR OWN" PROBLEMS

7.1. <u>Altocirrus clouds cannot exist because cirrus clouds are the clouds at the highest altitudes</u>. Since the prefix "alto" means "higher than usual," it just doesn't apply to these kinds of clouds.

7.2. Dark clouds have the "nimbus" suffix or the "nimbo" prefix, and higher-than-expected clouds have the "alto" prefix. Thus, they would be called <u>altocumulonimbus clouds</u>. Although altonimbocumulus is technically right, nimbus is generally used as a suffix with cumulus clouds.

7.3. If earth were tilted opposite of what it is now, the Northern Hemisphere would be pointed toward the sun during perihelion. Since summer occurs when the hemisphere receives the most direct sunlight, <u>summer in the Northern Hemisphere would occur at perihelion</u>.

7.4. Since the names of the solstices and equinoxes are different between the hemispheres, I will give you the answer using both sets of terminology.

Using Northern Hemisphere terminology: The days decrease in length in the Southern Hemisphere from the winter solstice to the summer solstice. At the spring equinox, the days in both hemispheres are 12 hours long. This tells us that from the winter solstice to the spring equinox, the length of the day in the Southern Hemisphere is more than 12 hours. After all, the length of the day must decrease from the winter solstice to the summer solstice. Since the spring equinox is in between the two, the length of the day in the Southern Hemisphere is decreasing up until the spring equinox. If the day length must be 12 hours at the spring equinox, and it had to be decreasing up to that point, it must have been longer than 12 hours to begin with. After the spring equinox, though, the day length keeps decreasing, so it becomes less than 12 hours. Thus, from the spring equinox to the summer solstice, the day length decreases and at the same time is less than 12 hours. This means the date range is <u>March 20 or 21 to June 21 or 22</u>.

Using Southern Hemisphere terminology: The days decrease in length in the Southern Hemisphere from the summer solstice to the winter solstice. At the autumnal equinox, the days in both hemispheres are 12 hours long. This tells us that from the summer solstice to the autumnal equinox, the length of the day in the Southern Hemisphere is more than 12 hours. After all, the length of the day must decrease from the summer solstice to the winter solstice. Since the autumnal equinox is in between the two, the length of the day in the Southern Hemisphere is decreasing up until the autumnal equinox. If the day length must be 12 hours at the autumnal equinox, and it had to be decreasing up to that point, it must have been longer than 12 hours to begin with. After the autumnal equinox, though, the day length keeps decreasing, so it becomes less than 12 hours. Thus, from the autumnal equinox to the winter solstice, the day length decreases and at the same time is less than 12 hours. This means the date range is <u>March 20 or 21 to June 21 or 22</u>.

7.5. <u>Yes, there would still be seasons</u>. Remember, the most important factor in the seasons is the earth's axial tilt. That determines when a hemisphere is pointed at the sun or away from the sun, which determines winter and summer. If the earth's orbit were perfectly circular, the dates for the season changes would be different, however.

7.6. <u>The wind is blowing from the ocean to the shore</u>. Since you notice no breeze at the hotel, the breeze at the beach is a local wind. Near the surface of the earth, wind blows from cold (the high) to warm (the low), so the wind must be blowing from the ocean to the shore.

7.7. Since we are not considering wind at all, the only thing we have to worry about is the Coriolis effect. Like the winds, the missile will be rotating with the earth when it is fired. As the speed at which the ground rotates changes, this will bend the missile's path. Since the missile starts in Southern California, it is near the equator. This means it starts out rotating quickly. As it travels north, it passes over land that is rotating more slowly. Thus, the missile's path is bent in the direction of the earth's rotation. Based on the rotation of the earth in Figure 7.7, then, if you aimed the missile due north, it would end up hitting east of the target. Thus, you must aim the missile northwest. This will correct for the Coriolis effect.

7.8. No. Those are the *global* wind patterns, but local wind patterns can interfere with and even change those winds. The most likely wind you will experience in Mexico blows from east to west, but that changes based on local weather conditions.

7.9. Long, light rains are typical of warm fronts. This means that warmer air is moving in on a colder air mass. Once the warm air is done moving in, the weather clears, and there should be warmer temperatures.

7.10. Occluded fronts occur because a cold front catches up to and collides with the warm air of a warm front. This happens because cold air masses travel more quickly than warm air masses. To get the kind of weather discussed in this question, you would have to start out with a cold front and have a warm air mass catch up to it. This should not happen because warm air travels more slowly than cold air, so a warm front will not catch up to a cold front.

STUDY GUIDE FOR MODULE #7

1. Define the following terms:

   a. Aphelion
   b. Perihelion
   c. Lines of longitude
   d. Lines of latitude
   e. Coriolis effect
   f. Air mass
   g. Weather front

2. What is the difference between weather and climate?

3. What are the three main factors that affect earth's weather?

4. Be sure that you can identify each of the cloud types in Figure 7.1.

5. If stratus clouds are dark, what are they called?

6. If you find lenticular clouds higher than normal, what are they called?

7. What does "insolation" stand for?

8. In the Northern Hemisphere, is the length of the days greater than or less than 12 hours between June 21 and September 22? Are the day lengths increasing or decreasing during that time?

9. In the Southern Hemisphere, between what dates are the day lengths less than 12 hours but increasing?

10. Is the Northern Hemisphere's summer during aphelion or perihelion?

11. What causes wind?

12. Why isn't there a constant stream of wind blowing from the poles to the equator?

13. What causes the wind patterns to bend in different regions of the globe?

14. Suppose you are in Alaska and would like to fire a missile to hit a target at the equator, due south of your location. Ignoring the effects of wind and air resistance, in which direction should you aim the missile?

15. At nighttime, high elevations usually cool faster than low elevations. Thus, at night, the land on a mountain is usually cooler than the land in the valley next to the mountain. Will the local wind produced by this effect blow from the mountain into the valley or from the valley up to the mountain?

16. Is the humidity high or low in a continental polar air mass? Is this air mass warm or cold?

17. Is the humidity high or low in a maritime tropical air mass? Is this air mass warm or cold?

18. Over a period of a couple of days, the clouds slowly build and then a gentle, long rain ensues that lasts about 20 hours. What kind of front causes this weather?

19. Over a period of a few days, you notice cirrus clouds forming, followed by stratus and nimbostratus clouds. In just a few hours, however, dark cumulonimbus clouds form, heralding a thunderstorm. What kind of front caused this?

20. In less than a day, dark cumulonimbus clouds form and unleash a thunderstorm that lasts only a few hours. After the thunderstorm is over and the sky clears, do you expect cooler or warmer temperatures as compared to the temperature before the clouds began forming?

MODULE #8: Weather and Its Prediction

Introduction

In this module, I want to discuss weather and how to predict it. Now you have already learned a lot about weather. You know what causes the seasons, what causes wind, the major types of clouds, the major types of weather fronts, the different types of air masses, and the general patterns of wind in creation. I will now build on that knowledge so that you have a better understanding of both weather and its prediction.

Precipitation

As you learned in Module #5, water vapor enters the atmosphere as a result of evaporation. In fact, over 400 trillion tons of water evaporate from the lakes, rivers, and oceans of earth each year. That's a lot of water! Eventually, all that water falls back to earth, mostly in the form of **precipitation**. Precipitation can be **rain, sleet, snow, drizzle**, or **hail**. Besides precipitation, water can leave the atmosphere and return to the earth in the form of **dew** or **frost**.

By far, the most common form of precipitation is **rain**. We all know that rain comes from clouds, but do you actually know *how* this happens? I doubt that you do. Meteorologists have two theories that they think do a pretty good job of describing how clouds produce rain. These theories do not compete with each other. Instead, they describe how rain forms in two different situations.

The first theory, called the **Bergeron** (bur' jur on) **process**, deals with how rain is formed in cold clouds. Cold clouds are clouds with temperatures that remain below freezing. Thus, these clouds are composed mostly of ice crystals. As more water condenses out of the atmosphere, the ice crystals grow larger. Eventually, the ice crystals grow too large to remain suspended in the air, and they begin to fall through the cloud. As they fall, they typically pick up more ice, growing even heavier. Eventually, these ice crystals become so big that they fragment. This results in several ice crystals falling through the cloud, each growing bigger and eventually fragmenting as well. This process goes on and on until there are billions of ice crystals falling from the cloud.

As these ice crystals fall out of the cloud and descend to the lower portions of the troposphere, they encounter the warmer air of the lower troposphere. If the temperature of the air is above freezing, the ice crystals begin to melt, forming rain. If not, they remain the tiny ice crystals that we call snow. This theory has a lot of evidence in its favor. In mountainous regions, for example, snow can be observed falling on a mountain while rain is falling in the valley below, despite the fact that all the precipitation is coming from just *one* cloud.

Not all rain is formed in the Bergeron process, however. In warm clouds, meteorologists think that rain forms according to the **collision-coalescence** (koh uh les' ents) **process**. In this theory, each cloud contains many water droplets that have condensed on cloud-condensation nuclei. As air currents in the cloud move these droplets around, they collide with other water droplets. Sometimes the droplets stick together, forming a bigger water droplet. Eventually, a water droplet gets big enough to start dropping through the cloud. This, of course, can lead to more collisions and more growth. Often, updrafts of air blow the water droplet back into the cloud, allowing it to grow even bigger. Eventually, billions of raindrops are formed in the process, and the result is rain.

Another less prevalent form of precipitation is **drizzle**. Drizzle usually forms in stratus clouds. It consists of tiny droplets of water. In fact, the size of the water droplets is all that sets drizzle apart from rain. Raindrops typically have a diameter of about 2 mm, while drizzle drops have diameters of less the 0.5 mm. Because they are so small, drizzle drops do not fall very quickly. They tend to drift downwards, staying close together and evenly spaced. This makes drizzle seem more like a fog that is slowly moving downward.

If raindrops fall through a layer of cold air, they can freeze, forming **sleet**. Because raindrops are large (as these things go), when they freeze they form solid ice pellets. These ice pellets hit the ground and either pile up or melt, depending on the temperature. Now please realize that sleet is much different than **freezing rain**. In freezing rain, the raindrops fall through a layer of air that is just at or slightly below the freezing point of rain. When this happens, the raindrops do not freeze until they hit something solid. As soon as they do, however, they freeze almost instantaneously. Freezing rain is *much* more dangerous than sleet because freezing rain causes a smooth glaze of ice to form over all solid surfaces. This makes roads very hazardous. Also, power lines can be destroyed due to the extra weight of the ice that forms on them.

Hail is similar to sleet but a lot more destructive. It starts out as a raindrop or an ice crystal blown back into the cloud by an upward gust of wind. If blown high enough, the raindrop will freeze, or the ice crystal will pick up more ice and get larger. Either way, the end result is a larger-than-normal ice crystal. Depending on the wind conditions, the ice crystal might be blown back up into the clouds several times. On each successive trip back up, the ice crystal grows bigger. Eventually, it gets so big that the upward gusts of wind are no longer strong enough to push it back up into the clouds, and it falls to the earth as a hailstone.

Hail usually forms in the strong thunderstorms of summer and spring. Remember, most thunderstorms result from a cold front that is lifting a warm air mass. This produces the strong upward gusts of wind necessary for hailstones to form. The stronger the winds, the larger the hailstone produced. The largest hailstone on record in the U.S. fell in Aurora, Nebraska, on June 22, 2003. It had a diameter of 7 inches and a circumference of 19 inches!

FIGURE 8.1

Photos courtesy of the NOAA

The Largest Hailstone to Fall in the U.S.

The last form of precipitation I want to discuss is, by far, the most beautiful. I am talking, of course, about **snow**. Snow starts out as cold-cloud precipitation. As the ice crystals fall from the clouds, they absorb more water, freezing and growing into bigger ice crystals. This process is responsible for the intricate design of snowflakes. Both the design and the size of the snowflake depend on the temperature. When the temperature is close to the freezing point of water, snowflakes can get quite large. Surprisingly enough, when the temperature is well below freezing, the snowflakes formed are small and powdery.

You may have heard that no two snowflakes are alike. That's not really true, but it's a close approximation. The formation of a snowflake involves several random processes that happen over and over again. Since there are several of these processes, and since they each occur several times, there is a *huge* number of possible shapes and patterns for a snowflake formed under a given set of circumstances. Because there is such a huge number of possible shapes, sizes, and patterns for a snowflake, the probability of two snowflakes coming out exactly the same is very small. Nevertheless, the odds do not preclude two identical snowflakes forming from time to time!

Although not considered forms of precipitation, **dew** and **frost** are two other means by which water can leave the atmosphere and make it back to the earth. Dew forms when air near the surface of the earth gets cool. As this happens, the water vapor in the air will tend to condense into liquid. The problem, however, is that water vapor will not condense unless it can do so *onto* something. That's why clouds need cloud-condensation nuclei in order to form. Near the surface of the earth, water will condense onto plants and soil, forming water droplets. These water droplets are called dew. The temperature at which dew forms, called the **dew point**, depends on the pressure and humidity of the air. The higher the pressure and humidity, the higher the dew point.

During autumn or winter, the air near the surface of the earth may get colder than the freezing point of water. When this happens, water vapor skips the liquid stage and immediately freezes on any surface with which it can come into contact, covering the surface with frost. Like dew, however, frost can only form on a surface. The temperature at which this occurs is called the **frost point**. The low temperatures that cause frost can be deadly for certain plants, so gardeners often cover their plants during cold nights in an attempt to keep the cold air away from them.

ON YOUR OWN

8.1 If a thunderstorm is not accompanied by strong, upward gusts of wind, will the thunderstorm produce hail?

8.2 How can you tell the difference between sleet and freezing rain?

Thunderstorms

Now that you know how rain forms, I want to spend some time looking at the more severe weather in creation. I will start out with something with which you are rather familiar: thunderstorms. Thunderstorms are localized weather phenomena that involve thunder (of course), lightning, heavy winds, driving rains, and sometimes hail. Although you might not think it at first, they are very common. Meteorologists estimate that thousands of thunderstorms occur on the earth *every day*!

All thunderstorms start in the same way. They begin with a strong **updraft** of air.

Updraft – A current of rising air

Usually, this updraft is caused by a cold front moving in on a warm front. As you learned in the previous module, the cold air mass tends to get under the warm air mass and lift it up, making an updraft. Updrafts can occur in other ways, however. For example, storms can be frequent in some mountainous regions because air must rise to pass over the mountains. This can result in a storm-producing updraft.

When a strong updraft occurs, the current of air rises, causing it to cool. As you already know, when air cools, water vapor tends to condense out of the air and form clouds. What you may not know, however, is that when water condenses, it actually releases energy. This might be hard to believe at first, but look at it this way. In Module #2, you did an experiment to show that when water evaporates, it absorbs energy, cooling whatever surface it evaporated from. Now think about it. Water condensing is essentially the opposite of water evaporating, isn't it? Well, if evaporating water tends to *absorb* energy and *cool* the surface off which it evaporated, condensation should *release* energy and *warm* the surface on which it occurs. In a cloud, the surface is on the cloud-condensation nuclei. So condensation tends to heat up the cloud-condensation nuclei. This makes the updraft even stronger! As the updraft pulls more and more warm, moist air into the atmosphere, a rapidly growing cumulus cloud begins to form. This is the **cumulus stage** of the thunderstorm.

The cumulus stage does not last very long. In less than 20 minutes or so, the updraft has pushed so much moist air high into the troposphere that a tall, cumulonimbus cloud has formed. These cumulonimbus clouds can get so tall that they actually reach the top of the troposphere and begin to flatten out because of the high winds blowing there. This typically gives the cumulonimbus cloud the shape of an anvil.

FIGURE 8.2
The "Anvil" Shape of Cumulonimbus Clouds

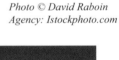
Photo © David Raboin
Agency: Istockphoto.com

Eventually, the water droplets and/or ice crystals in the cloud become too large for the updraft to support. At that point, one of the processes I discussed in the previous section takes over, and it begins to rain. This marks the **mature stage** of the thunderstorm, which consists of heavy rain, thunder, lightning, strong winds, and sometimes hail.

As the rain falls during the mature stage of a thunderstorm, it causes winds that blow downward, hitting the land and spreading out in strong gusts of wind. These downward rushes of air are called, reasonably enough, **downdrafts**. These downdrafts can be quite severe if concentrated in a small enough area. Winds of up to 170 miles an hour can be caused by local downdrafts in a thunderstorm. Sometimes they are as destructive as a tornado!

As time goes on (typically less than 30 minutes), the downdrafts caused by the rain overpower the updrafts that started the storm, and the entire area is full of only downdrafts. This marks the final stage of the thunderstorm, the **dissipation** (dis uh pay' shun) **stage**. During this stage, the rain gets lighter and lighter, and the downdrafts get less and less powerful. Eventually, the storm runs its course and the rain stops. Figure 8.3 illustrates the stages I just described.

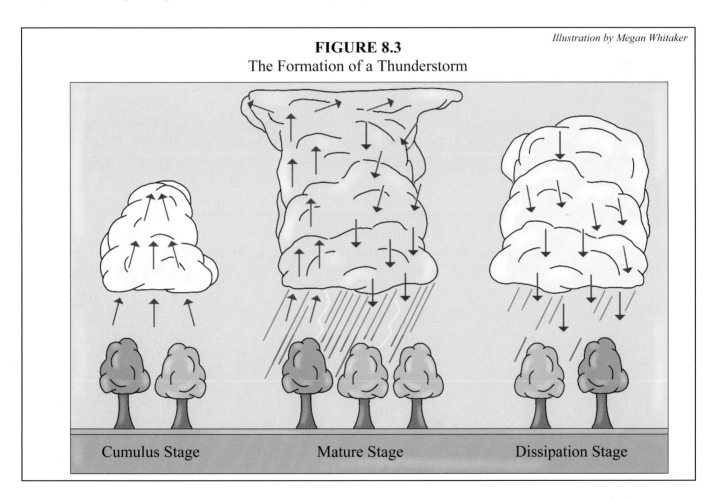

FIGURE 8.3
The Formation of a Thunderstorm

Illustration by Megan Whitaker

Cumulus Stage   Mature Stage   Dissipation Stage

What I just described to you is called a **thunderstorm cell**. In a thunderstorm cell, there is one updraft system and one resulting thundercloud. Most thunderstorms consist of several such cells. Thus, although a single thunderstorm cell usually lasts for much less than an hour, a thunderstorm composed of several cells can last a *lot* longer. Figure 8.4, for example, is an aerial shot of a thunderstorm system that consists of several cells.

FIGURE 8.4
Multiple Thunderstorm Cells in One Thunderstorm System

Photo © David Raboin
Agency: Istockphoto.com

Thunderstorms, of course, are best known for their **thunder** and **lightning**. These two effects always accompany one another. I am sure you have wondered where thunder and lightning come from. Perform the following experiment to find out. Remember, you should still be doing Experiment 7.1. Don't stop doing it just because there is another experiment to do!

EXPERIMENT 8.1
Making Your Own Lightning

Supplies:

♦ Balloon
♦ Dark room
♦ Eye protection such as goggles or safety glasses

Introduction: Thunder and lightning are produced as a result of electrical imbalances between a cloud and the ground. In this experiment, the balloon will represent the cloud, and your hand will represent the ground.

Procedure:

1. Blow up the balloon and tie it off.
2. Go into a dark room and allow your eyes to get accustomed to the lack of light.

3. Hold the balloon with one hand and rub it back and forth against your hair. This will cause the balloon (and your hair) to become electrically charged.
4. Now form a fist with the other hand and put it 6 to12 inches from your face at eye level. Hold your fist so that your knuckles point straight up.
5. Slowly use your other hand to pass the balloon over your fist, and look at your fist carefully. You should not be able to see your fist because of the darkness. Just look where you know your fist is. The balloon should pass by close to your knuckles, but *do not allow the balloon to touch them.* You may have to do this several times, but you will eventually see an effect. If you try several times and see nothing, the humidity might be too high. Try the experiment on a drier day.
6. Note in your laboratory notebook what your fist felt like as the balloon passed over it and what you eventually saw and heard.
7. Do the experiment again, this time holding your hand flat instead of in a fist. Hold it palm-up at eye level and see if you can duplicate the effect you saw. You probably will not be able to see anything, but your hand should feel roughly the same as your fist did in the first part of the experiment.

In your experiment, you should have seen a bluish-purple spark leap from the balloon to your hand. Believe it or not, that was a small lightning bolt. Obviously it did not have the power of the lightning that accompanies a thunderstorm, but it was produced in a similar way. The snap that you heard when the spark formed was actually thunder; it just didn't have the power of the thunder in a storm.

How did the lightning form in your experiment? Well, when you rubbed the balloon against your hair, the balloon picked up some negative electrical charges from your hair. Remember from Module #4 that all matter (including your hair, the balloon, and your fist) contains positive and negative electrical charges. When the balloon picked up some of the negative charges in your hair, it became negatively charged. Since your hair lost those electrical charges, it became positively charged. This explains why your hair tends to stand up when you rub a balloon in it. Your positively charged hair is attracted to the negatively charged balloon, and it stands up to get closer to the balloon.

Once you got the balloon to be negatively charged, you passed it near your fist, which has just as many positive charges as negative charges in it. When the negatively charged balloon came close to your fist, the positive charges in your fist were attracted to it. Thus, they moved in your fist to be as close to the negatively charged balloon as possible. When they reached your skin, however, they had to stop because electrical charges do not move well in air. Because of this, air is called an **insulator**.

Insulator – A substance that does not conduct electricity very well

Since the positive charges could not pass through the air, they built up on the surface of your skin and on the hairs of your skin. The strange feeling you felt as the balloon passed over your hand was that electrical charge buildup.

Eventually, the electrical charge buildup became so strong that the air was forced to allow some of the positive charges to move toward the balloon. Even though the electrical charges began to move in the air, they had a hard time traveling through it because air is an insulator. Thus, they lost a lot of energy. That energy was transformed mostly into light. The light, obviously, was the spark that you saw. The rest of the energy heated the surrounding air. The heat was rather substantial, and it happened very quickly. As a result, the hot air began to rush outward, forming waves of air. In

Module #6, what did you learn about sound? It moves as a wave through air and other substances. Thus, the motion of the hot air actually forms sound waves. Those sound waves created the crackle you heard.

Most likely, you didn't see the lightning in step #7 of the experiment. Why not? Well, remember that in order for the charges to travel from your hand to the balloon, they need to build up enough to overcome the insulating properties of the air. When you had a fist formed, the positive charges moved as close as they could to the balloon, so they built up in your knuckles, because your knuckles were closer to the balloon than was the rest of your fist. Since this concentrated the positive charge, the charge was able to overcome air's insulating properties, making the spark. When you had your hand flat, the charge did not concentrate anywhere. Instead, it spread out along your hand. Thus, you probably felt the electrical buildup over a larger area, but you never saw a spark because it was not concentrated enough at any one spot to overcome air's insulating properties.

Lightning forms in almost an identical way as did the spark in your experiment. Take a look at Figure 8.5:

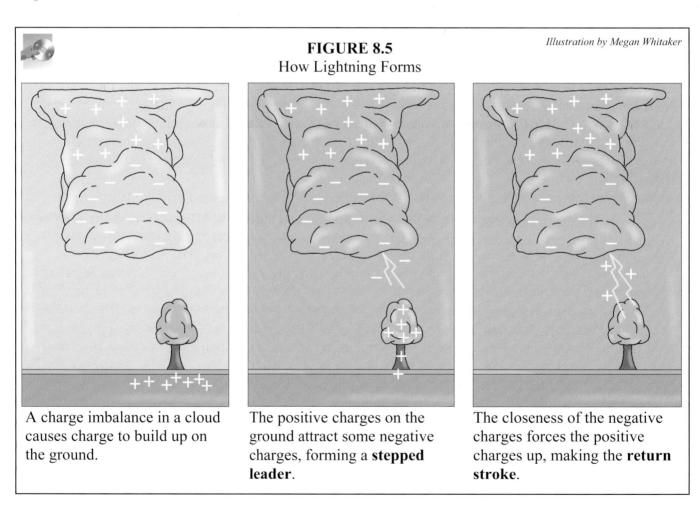

FIGURE 8.5
How Lightning Forms

Illustration by Megan Whitaker

A charge imbalance in a cloud causes charge to build up on the ground.

The positive charges on the ground attract some negative charges, forming a **stepped leader**.

The closeness of the negative charges forces the positive charges up, making the **return stroke**.

In a large cumulonimbus cloud, the heavy ice crystals near the top of the cloud eventually are too heavy to be supported by the updraft that formed the cloud in the first place. The ice crystals therefore begin to fall through the cloud, starting the Bergeron process you learned about in the first section of this module. Since a thunderstorm cloud is so large, the ice crystal makes several collisions with water droplets and other ice crystals on the way down. When those collisions are glancing collisions rather than head-on collisions, electrical charges can be transferred, much like what happened when the balloon rubbed up against your hair in the experiment.

This transfer of charge that occurs in glancing collisions results in an imbalance of electricity within the cloud. The bottom of the cloud starts building up negative charge (like the surface of the balloon in the experiment), and the top of the cloud starts building up positive electrical charge (like your hair in the experiment). The negative charges at the bottom of the cloud attract the positive charges in the ground (like the positive charges in your hand were attracted to the balloon). This causes a buildup of positive electrical charge on the ground. This positive electrical charge causes some of the negative charge in the cloud to move in a jerky, stepwise fashion toward the earth. This jerky movement of negative charges toward the earth is called a **stepped leader**.

Since the negative charges are moving through air, they lose a lot of energy due to the insulating properties of the air. Thus, a stepped leader is often accompanied by a dim spark. As the negative charges get closer to the ground, however, the positive charges build up more force, eventually overcoming the insulating properties of air and rushing up to meet the negative charges that are moving down. This **return stroke**, as it is called, is responsible for most of the light and sound of a lightning strike.

Notice where the lightning bolt strikes in the figure. It strikes the tree. Just like the spark in the experiment tended to hit a knuckle because it was closest to the balloon, lightning tends to hit things that are tall. That's because the positive charges concentrate on those things, trying to get as close to the negatively charged cloud as possible. That's why it's dangerous to stand under trees during a thunderstorm. The trees may shield you from rain, but they tend to attract lightning bolts!

Just as the spark in the experiment caused a snapping sound, the return stroke in lightning causes the booming sound we call thunder. This is caused by the intense heating that results when the charges push their way through the air. The charges lose so much energy fighting their way through air that a single lightning bolt can heat the surrounding air to temperatures in excess of 50,000 $^{\circ}$F! This superheated air quickly rushes outwards in waves, forming sound waves that our ears detect as thunder.

The lightning I just described to you is called **cloud-to-ground** lightning. Although this is what we usually think of when we hear the word "lightning," it is not the most common type of lightning that occurs in thunderstorms. The typical lightning that accompanies thunderstorms is called **cloud-to-cloud** lightning and is commonly referred to as "sheet lightning." This kind of lightning is caused by the same process, but the electrical building and charge transfer occurs between two clouds, not between the ground and a cloud. This kind of lightning lights up the sky in big sheets instead of striking the ground in a bolt. Since the air is still heated as a result of the charges moving, however, there is still thunder.

ON YOUR OWN

8.3 If a thunderstorm produces hail, in which stage of the thunderstorm would it come?

8.4 A thunderstorm begins, raining heavy sheets of rain for more than an hour before the rain begins to lighten. Was this thunderstorm composed of one cell or many cells?

8.5 Survivors of lightning strikes say that just before the lightning hit, their hair stood up. Why does this happen?

<u>Tornadoes and Hurricanes</u>

Although the winds and lightning in a thunderstorm can do a lot of damage, there are no weather phenomena more devastating than tornadoes and hurricanes. I want to start my discussion with tornadoes.

FIGURE 8.6
A Tornado

Photo © Clint Spencer
Agency: Istockphoto.com

Although tornadoes have been studied extensively, the details of how they form are still a mystery to us. There are many theories that attempt to explain the formation of a tornado, and they all have strengths and weaknesses. As a result, I will not try to explain them to you. Even though the details of their formation are not well known, there are certain things we know for sure. First of all, tornadoes start as the result of updrafts that form thunderstorms. In the first stage of their development, known as the **whirl stage**, the updraft of air forming a cumulonimbus cloud begins being hit by winds blowing in a different direction at higher altitudes. The origin of these winds is one of the mysteries related to tornado development. These winds cause air to begin rotating horizontally. Combined with the updraft, this causes a funnel of air to form, with air whirling both around and up. This is often called a **vortex**.

The funnel of air then touches the ground, starting the **organizing stage** of the tornado. Once the funnel touches the ground, it forms a solid base, and the upward, whirling motion of the vortex sucks debris up into the funnel. This darkens the tornado, marking the fact that it has reached the **mature stage**. It is in this stage that the tornado is most destructive. Eventually, the forces that hold the vortex together begin to dissipate, and the tornado begins to get smaller. This is called its **shrinking stage**. Finally, the tornado weakens to the point that it is no longer visible, and it slowly dies out in its final stage, the **decaying stage**. Because a tornado starts as a result of the updrafts that form a thunderstorm, you always see thunderstorm-like conditions before a tornado, and a tornado "hangs" from a cumulonimbus cloud.

Tornadoes can form anywhere, but the conditions that make tornado formation ideal seem to exist in the Mississippi Valley and Eastern Great Plains of the United States. These areas make up "Tornado Alley," so called because tornadoes form more frequently there than anywhere else. Wind speeds within a tornado are often over 100 miles per hour, but rarely exceed 250 miles per hour. Compared to hurricanes, tornadoes are relatively small. They are typically 400 to 500 feet in diameter at their base and might travel 4 to 5 miles before they enter their decaying stage.

When tornadoes form over the water, the result is called a **waterspout**. For reasons still relatively difficult to understand, waterspouts are not nearly as strong as tornadoes. If a waterspout is strong, it is usually the result of a tornado that formed over land and then moved into the water. Even though waterspouts are typically weaker than tornadoes, they are a great danger to boats!

An even weaker version of a tornado is called a **dust devil**. It forms as the result of an updraft, but the updraft is not the powerful kind you find in a cumulonimbus cloud. Instead, a dust devil will typically form in the afternoon when the ground has reached its maximum temperature. Under the proper conditions, this will heat the air directly above the ground relatively quickly. Since the warm air rises, an updraft occurs. Horizontal winds might form the updraft into a weak vortex, which picks up some debris and dust from the ground. Dust devils rarely exceed 15 feet in diameter and usually do not last longer than a minute or so. They are quite weak. Although some have been powerful enough to knock down animals and small children, they are generally considered harmless.

Left photo © David Brimm
Agency: Dreamstime.com

FIGURE 8.7
A Waterspout (Left) and a Dust Devil (Right)

Right photo © Gerald Legere
Agency: Shutterpoint.com

Now let's move on to hurricanes, which are significantly more destructive than tornadoes. The wind speeds in a hurricane (75 to 200 mph) are somewhat lower than those of a tornado (85 to 250 mph), but the size of a hurricane is immense! Hurricanes usually have diameters of a few hundred miles! Although commonly called hurricanes, these destructive giants are properly called **tropical cyclones**, because they always start in the tropics.

FIGURE 8.8

Photo courtesy of NASA

Hurricane Charley Over Florida (August 2004)

eye

A hurricane begins as a thunderstorm over a tropical sea. If the sea is warm enough, there will be a lot of moisture in the air. As the updraft begins to form thunderclouds, the rate of condensation into the cloud will be very high because of the warm, moist air being lifted up. This causes a pocket of low pressure in the cloud. As winds blow along this low-pressure pocket, they begin to rotate due to the Coriolis effect. This causes a vortex of whirling winds to form, which meteorologists call a **tropical disturbance**. The warm, moist air of the tropical sea continues to feed the vortex, increasing the strength of the wind.

If the rotating winds reach a sustained speed of 23 miles per hour, the tropical disturbance is "upgraded" to a **tropical depression**. As the warm sea continues to feed the tropical depression, its winds might increase in strength. If they reach a sustained speed of 39 miles per hour, the depression is "upgraded" again to a **tropical storm**. Finally, if the winds reach 74 miles per hour, it becomes a full-fledged hurricane and is called by meteorologists a **tropical cyclone**. Once a storm system has become a tropical cyclone, there are five categories that tell how strong a hurricane it is. Reasonably enough, they are simply called category 1 through category 5. The category of a hurricane depends on its wind speeds. Category 1 hurricanes have wind speeds of 74 to 95 miles per hour, while category 5 hurricanes have wind speeds in excess of 155 miles per hour. As the category of a hurricane increases, so does its destructive power. Hurricane Charley, pictured in Figure 8.8, was a Category 4 hurricane. Hurricane Katrina, which devastated New Orleans and the surrounding areas in August 2005, was a category 5 hurricane before it hit land.

As you can see in Figure 8.8, the most pronounced feature of a hurricane is its **eye**. This is an area of low pressure that originally formed the vortex that led to the hurricane. Typically 10 miles or so in diameter, the eye of a hurricane is a calm area, with calm winds and often a sunny sky! At the edge of the eye, however, things are not nearly as pleasant. Meteorologists call this the **eye wall**, and it is a cylinder of whirling clouds and rain that can be several miles high. As the clouds and rain rise up through the eye wall, they exit at the top and are thrown into a spiral that spins counterclockwise in the Northern Hemisphere and clockwise in the Southern Hemisphere.

Why do hurricanes spin in opposite directions in opposite hemispheres? Well, remember the Coriolis effect discussed in Module #7? In the Northern Hemisphere, air that is north of the eye will travel toward the eye, because the eye is an area of low pressure. That air is moving more slowly than the sea it must travel over to get to the eye. Thus, the air will be bent west as the sea "outruns" it. Air south of the eye will be traveling more quickly than the sea it passes as it heads towards the eye, so it will be bent east as it "outruns" the sea below. Well, if winds north of the eye bend west and winds south of the eye bend east, the result is counterclockwise rotation. In the Southern Hemisphere, the opposite occurs. Winds south of the eye are bent west because the sea they pass over "outruns" them, and winds north of the eye are bent east because they "outrun" the sea they pass over. This results in clockwise rotation. So the hurricanes rotate differently in the Northern Hemisphere and the Southern Hemisphere because the wind is bent differently in each hemisphere by the Coriolis effect.

Have you ever heard that when toilets are flushed they swirl the opposite way in the Northern Hemisphere as compared to the Southern Hemisphere because of the Coriolis effect? Although this sounds reasonable based on what you have learned about hurricanes, it is actually a myth. Although the Coriolis effect can bend winds on a large scale, its effect diminishes as the scale gets smaller. Remember, the Coriolis effect is based on the idea that the speed of objects rotating with the earth is different for different latitudes. For the Coriolis effect to be important, then, it must occur over an area large enough that those speed differences are noticeable. Since a hurricane is several hundred miles across, it spans enough latitudes for that to happen. A toilet, however, is simply not big enough for the Coriolis effect to matter significantly. As a result, the way the water in a toilet swirls when it flushes or the way the water drains in a sink is due almost entirely to the way in which the basin is filled, the irregularities in the shape of the basin, and the way in which the water was disturbed prior to draining. The tiny Coriolis effect present in a basin is typically not large enough to counter those other effects.

Surrounding the eye wall are **rain bands**. These are lines of thunderstorm cells that rotate around the eye, spiraling slowly inward as they go. Winds in the rain bands peak near the eye and become less severe as the rain band is farther from the center. A hurricane moves as a whole in the direction of the prevailing winds. As the hurricane leaves the tropics, it weakens because it loses its supply of warm, moist air. If it reaches land, it dissipates into several thunderstorm systems.

Now if you think about it, a hurricane really needs two things in order to form. It needs a warm ocean to continually feed it warm, moist air, and it needs to be formed in a place where the Coriolis effect is most pronounced. Where can both of these conditions be found? Well, the earth rotates most quickly at the equator, which is also the warmest spot on the earth. This is why hurricanes always form in the tropics, usually between 10° and 20° north or south of the equator.

Although the winds of a hurricane can cause severe damage, most of the devastation of a hurricane comes in the form of floods. The low pressure of the eye causes the ocean beneath the hurricane to bulge upward. In addition, the winds in a hurricane tend to push water along in the direction of its motion, causing huge waves. The waves, combined with the bulge, cause the ocean to rise many feet higher than it otherwise would. This front, called a **storm surge**, can devastate low-lying shoreline communities. The largest storm surge ever recorded was produced by a hurricane in 1899 and was 43 feet high. The storm surge of Hurricane Katrina was 30 feet high.

ON YOUR OWN

8.6 The early warning stage of a tornado is called a "funnel cloud." This is a cone-shaped extension of a cloud that is pointed toward the ground. When a small funnel cloud that is still high off the ground is spotted, which stage is the tornado in?

8.7 Suppose you are unfortunate enough to be caught in a hurricane. The winds are blowing, the rain is coming down, and water is everywhere. Suddenly, it is sunny and calm. Is the hurricane over?

Weather Maps and Weather Prediction

The heart of predicting the weather is taking measurements of the factors that influence weather. Temperature, atmospheric pressure, wind direction and speed, humidity, amount of precipitation, cloud cover, cloud type, and conditions in the upper atmosphere all play a role in determining the weather. By measuring and recording these phenomena, we can put together a picture of the weather that will allow us to predict what will happen in the near term. Of course, since there are still a lot of things we really don't understand about the weather, these predictions are shaky at best!

In the experiment you are still conducting (Experiment 7.1), you have been recording the temperature, pressure, cloud cover, cloud type, and amount of precipitation for several days in a row. In the next section of this module, you will look at all that data and try to see trends that will help you understand how the data you collected allow someone to predict the weather in the near future. Meteorologists, of course, have a lot of other data at their disposal to help them in trying to understand and predict weather.

Radar (which stands for "**ra**dio **d**etection **and r**anging"), for example, provides meteorologists with a lot of data regarding cloud cover and the types of clouds currently forming in the atmosphere. In a radar unit, a transmitter emits radio waves at a rate of several hundred per second. As those waves encounter objects, they bounce off the objects and head back toward the radar unit. A receiver in the radar unit then records when the bounced signals return. The time it takes for the radio waves to travel to an object and then bounce back indicates how far away the object is. In addition, differences between the outgoing and returning waves provide information about the makeup of the object. Weather radar, for example, can determine whether a cloud is made up of ice crystals (a cold cloud) or water droplets (a warm cloud). If the radar unit is slowly turned in a circle so that it sends out waves in all directions, it can provide a good view of the surrounding area.

Doppler radar is a well-known tool in both weather and law enforcement. This radar uses the **Doppler effect**, which you will learn about in a later module. The Doppler effect says that by analyzing a specific kind of difference (the wavelength) between the outgoing and returning waves, the speed of the object being observed can actually be determined. Traffic police use Doppler radar to determine the speed of automobiles, while meteorologists use it to measure the speed of winds and air masses.

Meteorology probably made its greatest step forward when satellites were deployed for weather-related measurements. The first successful weather satellite, TIROS I, was launched in 1960. Today, many weather satellites circle the globe, taking constant measurements of the kinds of data I mentioned above. They give us an accurate, global picture of the weather fronts and patterns that exist on a day-to-day basis.

As a brief sidelight, weather satellites have given us the best evidence yet that global warming is *not* happening. Weather satellites take data continuously all over the world. Thus, when satellite data are used to measure the average temperature of the earth, a *very* accurate number – the most accurate possible – is determined. Courtesy of NASA, here are the average global temperature changes since 1979 based on satellite data. The line at zero indicates the ideal global temperature. Any data above that line indicates a time that was warmer than the ideal temperature, and anything below that line indicates a time that was cooler than the ideal temperature.

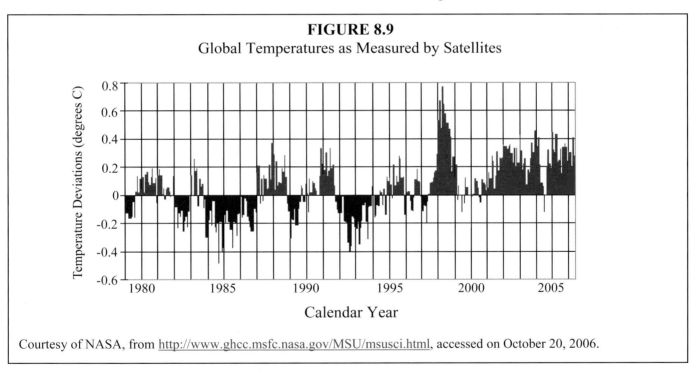

FIGURE 8.9
Global Temperatures as Measured by Satellites

Courtesy of NASA, from http://www.ghcc.msfc.nasa.gov/MSU/msusci.html, accessed on October 20, 2006.

Notice first that the y-axis plots a range of 1.4 degrees (-0.6 to 0.8), telling you that all variations are quite minor. Notice also that there are just as many colder temperatures as warmer temperatures. Indeed, up until 2001, there were more colder temperatures than warmer ones. Only in recent years have we experienced enough warmer temperatures in a row so as to even out the cooler temperatures experienced in the 1980s and 1990s. Once again, then, there is little if any global warming happening. Now this data is different from that shown in Figure 2.6, where I first discussed global warming. That's because the early data in Figure 2.6 come from land-based measurements, whereas only the later data come from satellites. The data discussed here are only the later data that come from satellites.

Since satellites can take measurements over the entire world, the network of weather satellites augments the data being taken on the ground. This data can all be compiled in something called a **weather map**. An example of a weather map is given below.

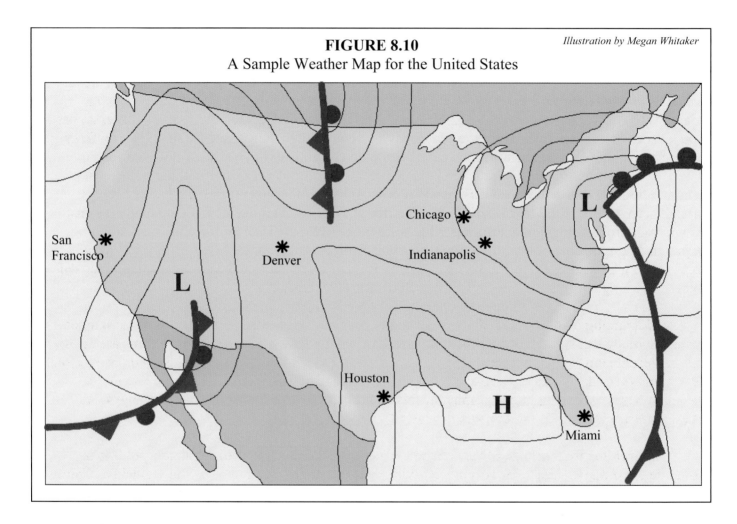

FIGURE 8.10
A Sample Weather Map for the United States

Illustration by Megan Whitaker

There are many different kinds of weather maps. Some have detailed information while others have less detailed, more general information. This weather map is one of the less detailed ones. Notice the thin black lines drawn all around the map. These lines are called **isobars**, and they represent regions of equal atmospheric pressure. If you travel along a single isobar, the atmospheric pressure does not change. Notice that between Houston and Miami the isobars form irregular ovals and at the center is a large "H." That "H" tells you the isobar surrounding it represents high pressure. As you move away from the "H," each isobar represents a lower pressure. Thus, the atmospheric pressure in Miami is *higher* than the atmospheric pressure in Houston, because Miami is between the first and second isobar away from the "H," while Houston is just past the second isobar. Thus, Houston is more isobars away from the "H" and therefore has lower atmospheric pressure. Chicago and Indianapolis, however, have similar atmospheric pressures because they are very near the same isobar.

Look at the "L" centered over the Northeast. This tells us that the isobar surrounding the "L" represents the lowest atmospheric pressure. Each isobar moving outward from that "L" represents areas with increasing atmospheric pressure. Thus, we can tell the general atmospheric pressure of a region by looking at such a map and reading the isobars. Why is atmospheric pressure important? Well, remember that winds blow from highs to lows. Thus, these regions of differing atmospheric pressure affect the winds you will experience.

Now look at the heavier, colored lines on the map. These lines represent the weather fronts in the region. The blue line with triangles represents a cold front. The triangles tell us the direction in which the cold front is traveling. The red line with the ovals represents a warm front, and the ovals tell us which direction the lines are moving. The purple line toward the north with ovals on one side and triangles on the other is a stationary front. Finally, the purple line in the west that has ovals and triangles on the same side represents an occluded front. If you look at the cold front off the east coast, you know that it is moving toward the east, away from the United States. Likewise, the warm front in the Northeast is moving northward.

The fronts on the map give us a great deal of information about the weather. After all, we already know the weather characteristic of each front. Thus, we can predict that the area to the east of Miami will probably experience storms because of the cold front. The Northeast will probably experience long, wet days due to the warm front. The northern United States and Canada will be experiencing similar weather due to the stationary front. Finally, the southwestern United States will experience long, wet days followed by storms due to the occluded front.

Depending on how detailed you want to get, there are many other different kinds of weather maps. Some weather maps plot **isotherms** instead of, or in addition to, isobars. Isotherms are lines that represent constant temperature. In addition, there are special maps that plot the wind speed, cloud cover, and other data related to weather. If you visit the course website I described to you in the "Student Notes" section at the beginning of this book, you will find links to websites that provide many different kinds of weather maps for you to investigate.

In weather forecasting, all the weather-related data that has been collected gets put into a computer, and mathematical models predict where weather fronts will move and how quickly. The people interpreting the results decide, based on the characteristics of the weather fronts, what kind of weather is likely. Since we know so little about weather, these forecasts are not able to predict the weather accurately. Instead, they predict the percentage chance of weather events. For example, a weather forecast might say that there is a 30% chance of rain tomorrow. This forecast means that most likely there will not be rain tomorrow. Nevertheless, it is *possible* for it to rain. Not very accurate, is it? Nevertheless, today's weather forecasting is significantly more accurate than it used to be!

ON YOUR OWN

8.8 Ground-based temperature measurements tend to be made near places where people live, whereas satellite temperature measurements cover essentially the whole earth. Would you expect the average temperature of the earth, as calculated by ground-based measurements, to be higher than or lower than that calculated by satellite measurements? As time moves on and cities get larger, would you expect the difference between satellite measurements and ground-based measurements to be the same or increase?

8.9 Based on Figure 8.10, would you expect to experience higher or lower atmospheric pressure if you left San Francisco and started heading east?

8.10 Based on Figure 8.10, where will the occluded front be in the next few days: Mexico or Denver?

<u>Interpreting the Results of Experiment 7.1 and Making Your Own Weather Predictions</u>

Now that you have been taking weather-related data for about three weeks, it is time to learn from it. First of all, look through the table of data you have collected and find the days that had precipitation. Get an idea of what constitutes a lot of precipitation over this time span and what constitutes a little. Next, use markers or colored pens or pencils to mark those days. If there was a lot of precipitation in a day, mark it with one color. If there was only a little, mark it with another color. If there was no precipitation, don't mark it at all.

Once you have finished doing that, find the first day that was marked and look at the cloud cover, temperature, and pressure in the few days leading up to the day of precipitation. Was there a progression of clouds typical of a warm front? Did the clouds rush in quickly, typical of a cold front? Was there precipitation several days in a row, perhaps indicating a stationary or occluded front? What about temperature? Was there a progression from warm to cold or vice versa, or did the temperature stay constant for a long time, indicative of a stationary front? What about atmospheric pressure? Was there a steady rise or fall?

Think about the data in terms of weather fronts. If a cold front moves in, for example, you expect reasonably quick, heavy rain or snow. After the rain or snow is finished, the temperature should be cooler than before. The atmospheric pressure should be lower during the storm, but it should rise again once the storm is done. So if you see a single day of precipitation preceded by warmer temperatures and followed by cooler temperatures, the weather was probably caused by a cold front.

On the other hand, a progression of clouds from cirrus to stratus before a day of precipitation most likely means a warm front. If the precipitation lasts only a day or two, this is more evidence of a warm front. Once the precipitation ends, warmer temperatures as compared to the day before the precipitation began give even more evidence of a warm front. If the precipitation lasted for two or more days and there was no appreciable change in temperature, the weather was probably caused by a stationary front. Finally, light precipitation followed by heavy precipitation can be indicative of an occluded front. A progression of temperatures from cold to warm back to cold would be more evidence for such a front.

Analyze each of the days with precipitation using these questions. Try to determine the weather front that caused the precipitation you experienced. Once you have done that, you should see some patterns emerging. Based on those patterns, it is time to do some weather predictions with the following experiment. I have purposely made this module short in order to give you time to do this because it is important for you to learn to apply knowledge. Thus, please do the experiment and check your results!

EXPERIMENT 8.2
Turning Experiment 7.1 into a Weather Prediction Tool

Supplies:

♦ The data table from Experiment 7.1
♦ The same source of weather data you used before
♦ A source that gives you the weather forecast for tomorrow

Introduction: It is time to take the knowledge you gained from Experiment 7.1 and try to use it to predict the weather. You will use the patterns you recognized in analyzing Experiment 7.1 to predict the weather for the next few days.

Procedure:

1. Add two other columns to your table. In the first column, make a general prediction about tomorrow's weather. Based on the weather data for yesterday and before, and based on the cloud cover you see today, try to determine if a weather front is moving in or not.
2. If there is no indication of a weather front, you can probably expect no change in the weather, and that's your prediction. If you do think that the data indicate a weather front, predict whether there will be precipitation, predict the cloud type and cover, and predict whether the temperature will be warmer or cooler.
3. In the second new column, write down the prediction made by the source that gives you a weather forecast. First, make sure you don't check that source until *after* you have made *your* prediction. Also, the source will probably give you a more detailed prediction than what you make. Thus, you need to "convert" its prediction to be more like yours. For example, your source will probably say something like "30% chance of rain." Assume that if the percentage chance of rain is 50% or below, the forecast is calling for no rain. If the chance is 50% or higher, the forecast is calling for rain. That way, the source's forecast will be more like yours. Also, the forecast will probably give you predicted highs and lows. Just use those to indicate whether or not the source is predicting cooler or warmer weather, which is what you will be predicting.
4. The next day, check your prediction to see how accurate it is. Make a mark to indicate whether you were right, partially right, or dead wrong.
5. Do the same for the prediction of the weather source you used.
6. Continue this for at least a week. See if you get any better as time goes on. Perhaps you will get some idea of how hard a meteorologist's job really is!
7. At the end of the experiment, you will probably find that even your weather source was at least partially wrong a few times!

ANSWERS TO THE ON "YOUR OWN" PROBLEMS

8.1 <u>Without strong, upward gusts of wind, there will be no hail.</u> In order for hail to form, it must be recycled through the cloud by strong, upward gusts of wind.

8.2 Sleet falls to the ground as ice, while freezing rain falls to the ground as water and then freezes. To tell the difference, <u>catch some in your hand. If it is frozen when it touches your hand, it is sleet; if it is liquid, it is freezing rain.</u> Another answer would be to look at the ground. Sleet piles up like tiny chunks of ice, while freezing rain makes a glassy glaze over everything.

8.3 <u>It would be in its mature stage.</u> Hail is the result of precipitation recycled by a strong updraft. Thus, there must be both precipitation and a strong updraft. Both of those conditions exist only in the mature stage of a thunderstorm.

8.4 <u>The thunderstorm was composed of many cells.</u> Strong, heavy sheets of rain are indicative of the mature stage of a thunderstorm, which lasts only 30 minutes or less. Thus, there must have been several cells to make the heavy rain go on so long.

8.5 <u>Their hair stood up because of the positive charges on the ground trying to rise to the negative charges in the sky. Some of them traveled up the person and into his or her hair.</u> Remember the effect you felt in the experiment. Imagine that effect all over your body; that's what a lightning strike victim feels an instant before the stroke.

8.6 <u>The tornado is most likely in its whirl stage.</u> The next stage (organization) does not occur until the funnel touches the ground. Now please note that as the funnel cloud extends down, the funnel of air that makes up the tornado will hit the ground before the visible funnel cloud hits the ground. That's because the vortex of air extends below the visible funnel cloud. Note, for example, how you can see that the waterspout in Figure 8.7 has reached the water, even though the visible funnel cloud has not. However, the funnel cloud has to be well developed before the funnel of air hits the ground, so a small funnel cloud indicates the whirl stage.

8.7 <u>The hurricane is probably not over.</u> You are currently in the eye of the hurricane. When the eye passes, you will be back into the thick of things.

8.8 <u>Ground-based temperature measurements are, on average, warmer than satellite measurements.</u> After all, people tend to live where it is warm or moderate, not where it is very cold. Thus, the measurements on the ground are biased toward warmer areas. As a result, the average temperature of the earth as calculated by ground-based measurements is higher than that calculated by satellites. <u>As cities get larger, this discrepancy increases,</u> because cities are built with materials (like concrete) that heat up easily during the day. Thus, the larger the city, the larger the area of artificially increased heat. This is one explanation for why ground-based measurements seem to indicate that the earth is getting warmer, but satellite measurements do not.

8.9 San Francisco is past the second isobar from a low-pressure minimum. As you travel east, you will get closer to the low-pressure minimum. <u>This means your atmospheric pressure will decrease as you travel east.</u>

8.10 <u>Mexico will get the occluded front.</u> The ovals and triangles are pointed toward Mexico.

STUDY GUIDE FOR MODULE #8

1. Define the following terms:

a. Updraft
b. Insulator

2. Both the Bergeron process and the collision-coalescence process explain precipitation, but they each begin with a different kind of cloud. With what kind of cloud does each theory begin?

3. Which of the two theories of precipitation governs the fall of rain from the top of a cumulonimbus cloud? What kind of rain cloud would be most likely described by the collision-coalescence process?

4. What is the difference between drizzle and rain?

5. What are the differences between sleet, hail, and freezing rain?

6. A meteorologist measures the dew point on two different mornings. The first morning is very humid and the atmospheric pressure is high. The second morning is not nearly as humid and the atmospheric pressure has fallen. On which day will the dew point be coldest?

7. Name the three stages of a thunderstorm cell in the order they occur. At each stage, indicate whether an updraft, downdraft or both are present. Also, indicate whether or not precipitation occurs.

8. If the heavy rain of a thunderstorm lasts for more than 30 minutes, what can you conclude about its makeup?

9. Lightning forms as a result of electrical charge imbalance. Where does that charge imbalance originate and why does it occur?

10. Which is responsible for most of the light and sound in a lightning bolt: the stepped leader or the return stroke?

11. Where does the thunder in a thunderstorm come from?

12. Why do lightning bolts tend to strike targets that are high?

13. What is the difference between sheet lightning and a lightning bolt?

14. What kind of cloud is necessary for tornado formation?

15. List the five stages of a tornado in order. At which stage is the tornado most destructive?

16. What are the four classifications that lead to a hurricane? What is used to determine which classification a storm fits in?

17. What are the conditions in the eye of a hurricane?

18. What causes a hurricane in the Southern Hemisphere to rotate in a different direction than a hurricane in the Northern Hemisphere?

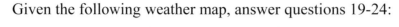

Given the following weather map, answer questions 19-24:

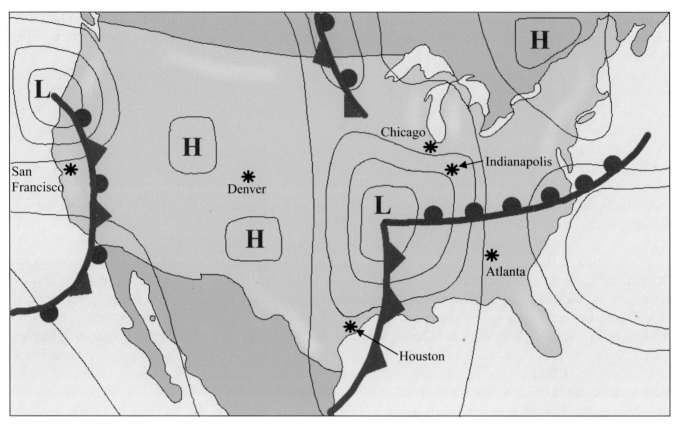

19. Is the atmospheric pressure in Houston higher, lower, or nearly equivalent to that of Chicago?

20. Is the atmospheric pressure in Houston higher, lower, or equivalent to that of Atlanta?

21. Is the occluded front nearer to San Francisco or Canada?

22. Will Atlanta or Indianapolis be in for some warmer weather soon?

23. At the time this map was drawn, what city drawn on the map might be experiencing thunderstorms?

24. What city probably experienced long rains followed by thunderstorms recently?

MODULE #9: An Introduction to the Physics of Motion

Introduction

Over the previous semester, I gave you a basic introduction to the earth's physical environment. You have (hopefully) learned about the atmosphere, hydrosphere, lithosphere, mantle, and core of the earth. You have also seen how those "regions" of the physical environment interact to form weather phenomena and other physical effects in our daily experience. Now it is time to take a *deeper* look into your physical environment. In this semester, I want to give you an introduction to the most fundamental of all sciences: physics.

What do I mean when I say "fundamental"? Well, physics lies at the root of all the other sciences. For example, in the previous semester, you learned about weather. The study of weather is a science unto itself. Called **meteorology**, this science analyzes weather fronts, winds, humidity, cloud cover, etc. in an attempt to better understand weather and the factors that cause it. The science of physics, however, describes how all things, including weather fronts, move. It describes how water evaporates to form humidity and then condenses again to form clouds. It also describes how the temperature imbalances that cause wind actually form. In the end, then, *every* science relies on the science of physics. As a result, we call physics the most fundamental of all the sciences.

Before I begin introducing the science of physics to you, there is one important thing you must realize. Even though I will spend a lot of this semester on physics, please understand that what you learn here is just a bare-bones introduction to this fascinating field. I cannot go into nearly enough detail because you do not have the mathematical skills necessary. Physics is an inherently mathematical science. You may not fully appreciate that fact as a result of taking this course, because I have had to weed out a great deal of the mathematics. In high school, however, you will (hopefully) spend a whole year on physics. At that point, you will develop a deeper appreciation for the mathematical nature of the science!

Mechanics – The Study of Motion, Forces, and Energy

If you look around, you will see many things in motion. Trees, plants, and sometimes bits of garbage blow around in the wind. Cars, planes, animals, insects, and people move about from place to place. In Module #3, you learned that even objects that appear stationary are, in fact, filled with motion, because their component molecules or atoms are moving. In short, the world around us is alive with motion.

In fact, St. Thomas Aquinas listed the presence of motion as one of his five arguments for the existence of God. He said that in all of our experience, humans have found that motion cannot occur without a mover. In other words, in order for something to move, there must be something else that moves it. When a rolling ball collides with a toy car, the car will move because the ball gives it motion. But, of course, the ball would not have been rolling to begin with if it had not been pushed or thrown. Thus, Aquinas says that our practical experience tells us that any observable motion should be traceable back to the original mover. When the universe began, then, something had to be there to start all the motion that we see today. Aquinas says that God is this "original mover."

While philosophers and scientists can mount several objections to St. Thomas Aquinas's argument, it nevertheless shows how important motion is in the universe. Thus, it is important for us to be able to study and understand motion. It is so important that an entire branch of science is devoted to the study of motion and related issues. The science of **mechanics** is the branch of physics that deals with analyzing and understanding objects in motion, the forces applied to those objects, and the energy that exists in them.

Photo © AVTG, Agency: Istockphoto.com

FIGURE 9.1
The Science of Mechanics Is Used To Study the Motion of These Cars

Now if you want to study the motion of an object, what's the first thing you need to know? You need to know its **position**. If the position of an object changes, we know that the object is in motion. That should seem like a rather obvious statement to you, but it really is not. Think about it: Suppose you placed a book on a picnic table and then stepped back 3 feet to observe it resting on the table. Is the book in motion? Your first answer might be "no," but that answer is only partially correct. Certainly as far as *you* are concerned, the book is not moving, because it's just sitting there on the table. What if a person on the moon were able to use a very powerful telescope to observe the book? Would he or she conclude that the book is in motion? Yes! You see, even though the book is resting on the table, it is rotating along with the rest of the earth. You don't notice that motion, however, because you are rotating right along with the book. Thus, *relative to you*, the book is not moving. The person on the moon, however, is not rotating with the earth. As a result, he thinks that both you and the book are moving because *relative to him*, your position is changing.

What does this tell you about position? **Position must always be given *relative* to something else**. That "something else" is usually called a **reference point**.

<u>Reference point</u> – A point against which position is measured

In the case of the book I was discussing, you could say that its position *relative to you* was 3 feet in front of you. In that case, you are the reference point. As time went on, that position did not change, so you concluded that the book was not moving. If the person on the moon were to mark the book's position relative to the moon, the book's position would constantly change, indicating that *relative to the moon*, the book was moving. In that case, the moon was the reference point. The observer on the moon could, however, use the same reference point you did. If the observer saw both you and the book, the observer could say that the book was 3 feet in front of you. If the observer continued to use you as the reference point, the observer would also conclude that the book was not moving, because its position *relative to you* remained the same.

This little discussion illustrates one of the most important concepts in all of physics:

All motion is relative.

In other words, motion depends on the reference point that is used. In the case of the book, if your position is used as the reference point, the book is not in motion. If the moon's position is used as the reference point, the book is in motion. Thus, the motion of any object depends on the reference point used to describe that object's position.

FIGURE 9.2
Motion Is Relative

Photo © Susi Bikle
Agency: Istockphoto.com

Are these four people moving? It depends. Relative to the mountain, their positions change, because the lift is taking them up the mountain. However, *relative to each other*, their positions do not change. Thus, they are in motion relative to the mountain, but not relative to each other.

ON YOUR OWN

9.1 Suppose you go to a department store that has two floors, and you stand still on an escalator (a moving stairway) that allows you to travel to the second floor. Perhaps because you are a shady-looking character, three security guards are watching you. The first one is on the escalator with you, also standing still. The second one is standing still on the first floor near the escalator but not on the escalator. The third is standing still on the other escalator that is moving down. Relative to which security guard(s) are you in motion? Relative to which security guard(s) are you not in motion?

Speed: How Quickly Motion Occurs

If an object is in motion, its position is changing. Over time, that will result in a certain distance over which the object travels. If I take the distance an object travels and divide by the time it takes to travel that distance, I end up getting the object's **speed**. I can write that mathematically as:

$$\text{speed} = \frac{\text{distance traveled}}{\text{time traveled}} \qquad (9.1)$$

Of course, you are already familiar with the concept of speed. After all, you know that the speed limit on most interstate highways in the United States is 65 miles per hour. This means that if a car is moving at the speed limit, it travels 65 miles for each hour it is on the road.

Notice, then, that speed needs to have units attached to it in order for us to really understand what it means. If I say that I want you to walk with a speed of 65, could you do it? Well, it all depends on the units, doesn't it? You certainly could walk with a speed of 65 feet per minute, right? In fact, you would have to walk really slowly to match that speed. No matter how fast you try to walk (or run), however, there is no way you could walk with a speed of 65 miles per hour! Thus, the units attached to speed are very important.

In physics, this is true of *all* quantities you measure or calculate. The units for the quantity are just as important as the quantity itself. For example, when I took high school physics, my teacher allowed us to do something I would *never* allow you to do. On the day before our first test, he said, "I will allow you to use a 3x5 card on the test. You can write anything you want on the card in order to help you with the test." Of course, he was far too easy on his students, but nevertheless, I was quite happy about it. I even raised my hand and said, "You mean we can use any 3x5 card we want?" He replied, "Yes." The next day, I brought a 3-foot by 5-foot poster to class. It had notes scribbled *all over it*! In the end, he had to let me use it on the test because he had not mentioned the units! Thus, units are very important when communicating physical quantities. Any answer you give will be counted wrong unless you give the proper units!

Going back to Equation (9.1), we can calculate an object's speed by dividing the distance it travels by the time it takes to travel that distance. Thus, we can use an equation to take two measured quantities (distance and time) and calculate another quantity (speed). However, distance and time have units associated with them. Distance might be measured in miles, meters, kilometers, etc. Time might be measured in seconds, minutes, hours, etc. Since the units are a part of the measurements, they must go in the equation as well! Study the following example problems to see how this is done.

EXAMPLE 9.1

A car travels 78 miles down the highway. It takes the car 1.2 hours to travel that far. At what speed is the car traveling?

Speed can be calculated using Equation (9.1). All we need to know is the distance (78 miles) and the time (1.2 hours). I can put those into the equation and come up with an answer:

$$\text{speed} = \frac{78 \text{ miles}}{1.2 \text{ hours}} = 65 \frac{\text{miles}}{\text{hour}}$$

Notice what I did here. When I put the values for speed and time in the equation, I *kept their units with them.* This is very important:

When working with physical quantities in equations, keep the units with the numbers.

Once I put the numbers in there, look at what I did. Since "78 over 1.2" means "78 divided by 1.2," I divided 78 by 1.2 and got 65. Look at what I then did with the units. I left the units in the same way they appeared in the equation. That's how I got 65 miles/hour. When we have units in a fraction like that, we generally use the term "per" to represent the line in the fraction. That's why these units are called "miles per hour."

What is the speed of the car from the previous problem in meters per second? (1 mile = 1,609 meters, 1 hour = 3,600 seconds)

In this problem, we are told to report the answer in metric units rather than English units. How can we do that? Well, way back in Module #1, you learned how to convert from one unit to another. If we convert 78 miles to meters and 1 hour to seconds, we can then reuse Equation (9.1). First, let's convert from miles to meters:

$$\frac{78 \text{ \sout{miles}}}{1} \times \frac{1609 \text{ meters}}{1 \text{ \sout{mile}}} = 125,502 \text{ meters}$$

If you don't remember how to do this, go back and review Module #1. Now we need to convert the time from hours to seconds:

$$\frac{1.2 \text{ \sout{hours}}}{1} \times \frac{3,600 \text{ seconds}}{1 \text{ \sout{hour}}} = 4,320 \text{ seconds}$$

Now we can use *those* values in our speed equation:

$$\text{speed} = \frac{125,502 \text{ meters}}{4,320 \text{ seconds}} = 29.1 \frac{\text{meters}}{\text{second}}$$

If you do this calculation with a calculator (as you should), you will notice that the answer is 29.05138889. I rounded that to 29.1. When you take chemistry, you will learn about "significant figures," which will tell you where to round a number off. For this course, don't worry too much about where to round a number off. Your answers will be right even if you round off at a different place than I do. Now realize that 29.1 meters per second and 65 miles per hour *are both the same speed*. They simply express that speed in different units. This is why it is so important to put the units in any equation you use.

When a physical quantity involves units, you must carry the units along with the quantity in any equation you use. That will allow you to determine the proper units for your answer. Try these "On Your Own" problems to make sure you understand what I am talking about.

ON YOUR OWN

9.2 What is the speed of an aircraft that travels 115 miles in 30 minutes? Put your answer in units of miles per hour.

9.3 When measuring the speed of a snail, a good unit to use is millimeters per minute. A snail takes all day (12 hours) to travel 5 meters. What is its speed in millimeters per minute?

<u>Velocity: Speed and Direction</u>

In everyday conversation, you probably use the terms "velocity" and "speed" interchangeably. When you want to sound smart, you probably say "velocity," otherwise, you probably say "speed." In physics, however, there is a *big difference* between speed and velocity. Velocity contains more information than does speed. Speed tells you how quickly an object moves, while velocity tells you how quickly *and in what direction* the object is moving. This might not sound like a big difference, but it really is. If an airplane pilot who is trying to land a plane tells the control tower that the plane is moving at 122 miles per hour, that's not enough for the control tower to tell the airplane where to land. The pilot must tell the control tower at what speed *and what direction* the plane is traveling. When the pilot does that, he is telling the control tower the plane's *velocity*.

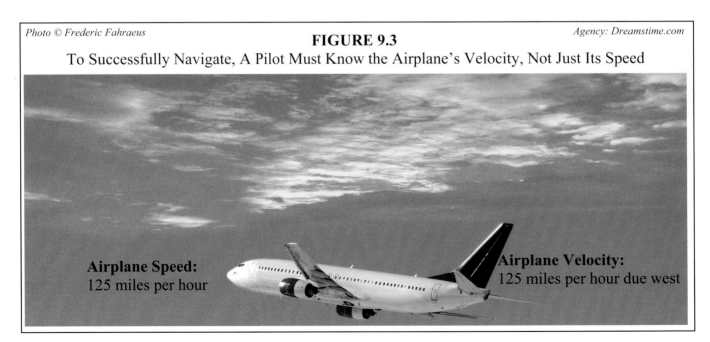

Photo © Frederic Fahraeus   **FIGURE 9.3**   *Agency: Dreamstime.com*
To Successfully Navigate, A Pilot Must Know the Airplane's Velocity, Not Just Its Speed

Airplane Speed:
125 miles per hour

Airplane Velocity:
125 miles per hour due west

When a physical quantity carries information concerning direction, we call it a **vector quantity**. When the physical quantity does not carry information concerning direction, we call it a **scalar quantity**.

Vector quantity – A physical measurement that contains directional information

Scalar quantity – A physical measurement that does not contain directional information

Using this terminology, speed is a scalar quantity, while velocity is a vector quantity. Why is the distinction between speed and velocity so important? Perform the following experiment to find out!

EXPERIMENT 9.1
The Importance of Direction

Supplies:

♦   At least four eggs
♦   Two pieces of reasonably strong cardboard (like the cardboard found on the back of writing tablets)
♦   Several books
♦   A pair of scissors
♦   A large tray or cooking sheet
♦   Newspapers or paper towels
♦   Kitchen table
♦   Eye protection such as goggles or safety glasses

Introduction: The difference between speed and velocity is very important in physics. This experiment demonstrates that fact.

Procedure:

1. This is a potentially messy experiment, so put some newspapers or paper towels on the table.
2. Make a pile of books about 8 inches high.
3. Take the cardboard and fold the long edges up to form "railings" on each side. Next, lay it so that it leans against the pile of books, making what looks like a slide going from the top of the books to the table.
4. About 1 inch from the top of the cardboard, cut through the railings as far as the fold.
5. Fold back the cardboard at the cuts, allowing the part that is above the cuts to lie flat on the top book.
6. Lay a book on top of the pile, so that it holds the cardboard in place. Your setup should look like this:

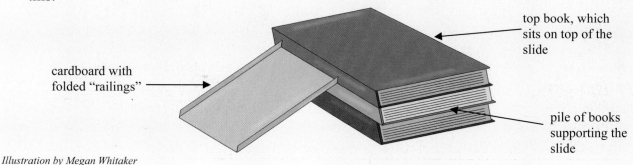

cardboard with folded "railings"

top book, which sits on top of the slide

pile of books supporting the slide

Illustration by Megan Whitaker

7. Put the tray on the table so that anything that rolls down the slide will roll onto the tray.
8. Hold two eggs together on top of the slide. Hold them so that one egg is behind the other. Release them together, allowing them to roll down the slide one behind the other. Use your other hand to stop them when they roll off the slide and onto the tray. Note whether the eggs have been damaged or not. If they were damaged, get new eggs. If not, you can reuse them.
9. Lay one egg on the table at the bottom of the slide. Allow the other egg to roll down the slide and hit the egg at the bottom of the slide. Note the damage caused, if any. Once again, reuse any undamaged eggs.
10. Build another slide like the one you just built. It needs to be close to the same height as the first slide.
11. Place the two slides so that they meet in the center of the tray that is on the table.
12. Place one egg at the top of one slide and the other at the top of the other slide.
13. Simultaneously let both eggs go, allowing them to roll down the slides and crash into each other. Note the damage to the eggs.
14. Clean everything up!

Besides making a mess, what did this experiment accomplish? Well, it demonstrated the importance of direction in velocity. In the first part of the experiment, the eggs traveled down the slide together. When they reached the bottom, they had essentially the same speed. Nevertheless, since they were traveling in the same direction, they did not damage each other. In the last part of the experiment, the eggs were still traveling at roughly the same speed when they got to the bottom of their respective slides, since the slides were of essentially the same height. Did this situation result in the same lack of damage to the eggs? Of course not! Since the eggs collided with each other, at least one of them was strongly damaged. In fact, at least one of them probably broke. Thus, the direction made all the difference. Even though the eggs had the same *speed* in the last part of the experiment, they had different *velocities*, and the result was devastating to the eggs.

Why did I have you do the middle part of the experiment? Why did I have you allow the eggs to collide when one was sitting still? Well, compare the damage done to the eggs in the middle part of the experiment to that done at the end of the experiment. In which case was more damage done? The last part of the experiment resulted in more damage. Why? Since the eggs were traveling at the same speed but in opposite directions, they were actually approaching each other much faster than if one egg was traveling at that speed and the other was just sitting still. As a result, more damage resulted from the collision.

Now I'm sure you could have predicted the results of this experiment before you did it, but I want a vivid picture in your mind. When two objects are in motion, their velocities can allow us to compare their motion and determine certain outcomes of the situation. Think about the experiment, for example. For the sake of argument, let's say that when an egg reached the bottom of the slide, it was rolling at a *speed* of 0.25 meters per second. When the eggs were rolling down the slide in the same direction, they would neither approach nor pull away from each other. They would stay in the same position relative to each other, right? How could we denote that? Well, we could subtract their speeds. Since each of them was traveling at 0.25 meters per second, the speed that they had relative to each other was 0.25 m/sec - 0.25 m/sec = 0. Since their relative speed was 0, that tells us that they were not moving relative to each other.

Carrying this idea a little further, suppose we concentrated on the second part of the experiment. In that part of the experiment, one egg came rolling down the slide, and when it got to the bottom, it was rolling at 0.25 meters per second. The other one was sitting still, however, so its speed was 0. The difference would be 0.25 m/sec - 0 m/sec, or 0.25 meters per second. In this case, then, the *relative speed* of the eggs was 0.25 meters per second. Since one egg was sitting still and the other egg was moving toward it, the distance between the eggs was decreasing. The *relative velocity* of the eggs, then, was 0.25 meters per second *toward each other*. Thus, the eggs collided, and at least some damage resulted.

What happened in the last part of the experiment? In that situation, the eggs had opposite velocities. One was traveling one way and the other was traveling in the opposite direction. Thus, they were approaching each other. If they approached one another with a speed of 0.25 meters per second each, what was their relative velocity? It was much greater than 0.25 meters per second, as evidenced by the greater amount of damage done in the last part of the experiment. It turns out that the *relative speed* in this case was 0.25 m/sec + 0.25 m/sec, or 0.50 meters per second. Once again, the eggs were moving toward each other, so the distance between them was decreasing. Their *relative velocity*, then, was 0.50 meters per second towards each other.

What did we learn from all this? Well, we learned that when objects are moving in the same direction, we can get their relative speed by subtracting their individual speeds. When objects travel in opposite directions, however, you must get their relative speed by adding their individual speeds together. This is an important fact to remember.

When objects travel in the same direction, their relative speed is the difference between their individual speeds. When they travel in opposite directions, their relative speed is the sum of their individual speeds.

Once you determine the relative speed, you can turn that into the velocity by adding whether they are approaching each other or traveling away from each other. See what I mean by studying the following example problems.

EXAMPLE 9.2

Two cars are traveling down a road. The first car is traveling north at 55 miles per hour, and the second is a few hundred yards behind, traveling north at 45 miles per hour. What is their relative velocity?

The first thing to notice is that we are given the velocities of each car, because we are told what speed *and* what direction each car travels. They are both traveling in the same direction (north), so we determine their relative speed by subtracting their individual speeds.

relative speed = 55 miles per hour - 45 miles per hour = 10 miles per hour

Notice that I subtracted the small number from the big one to ensure that I got a positive number. Notice also that I listed the units with each speed and then carried that unit to the answer. That's how you treat units when adding and subtracting numbers. You put them into the equation to remind you of what they are. When you are done, you use the same unit in the answer. It is against the rules of mathematics to add or subtract two numbers that have different units, so you will never have to choose one unit over another. All terms in addition or subtraction must have the same units.

Is 10 miles per hour our answer? Not quite. The problem asks for relative *velocity*. Thus, we need to include a direction. We must determine whether or not the cars are approaching one another or moving apart. Since the car that is behind is traveling slower than the car that is ahead, the car that is ahead will pull away. Thus, the relative velocity is <u>10 miles per hour away from each other</u>.

Two cars are traveling down a road. The first car is traveling north at 55 miles per hour, and the second is a few hundred yards south, traveling south at 45 miles per hour. What is their relative velocity?

This problem sounds a lot like the first one, but there is a difference. The cars are traveling in opposite directions. Thus, we calculate their relative speed by adding their individual speeds:

relative speed = 55 miles per hour + 45 miles per hour = 100 miles per hour

Notice that the car moving south is *already* south of the car moving north. Thus, these cars are moving away from each other. The relative velocity, then, is <u>100 miles per hour away from each other</u>.

Notice the difference between the two example problems above. In the first problem, the cars are moving in the same direction, but nevertheless, they are moving away from one another. The speed at which they are moving apart is rather slow, however. In the second problem, they are moving with the same individual speeds as they were in the first problem. Because they are moving in opposite directions, however, they are moving apart from each other *ten times faster* than in the first problem. Obviously, then, the difference between speed and velocity is of critical importance in analyzing motion.

ON YOUR OWN   *Illustrations from www.clipart.com*

9.4 Which of the following quantities could represent a velocity?

a. 123 km/sec   b. 34 m/min east   c. 24 miles/hour and slowing   d. 15 meters west

9.5 A plane is flying due east at 520 miles/hour. Another plane is 20 miles east of that plane, flying with a velocity of 650 miles/hour due west. What is their relative velocity?

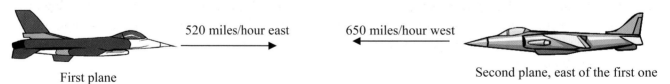

520 miles/hour east   650 miles/hour west

First plane   Second plane, east of the first one

<u>Acceleration: The Rate of Change in Velocity</u>

Suppose you were to throw a ball up into the air. What would happen to the ball? Would it go up forever, or would it eventually come back down? It will come back down, of course. If you were able to look at the position of the ball at certain time intervals, this is what you would see:

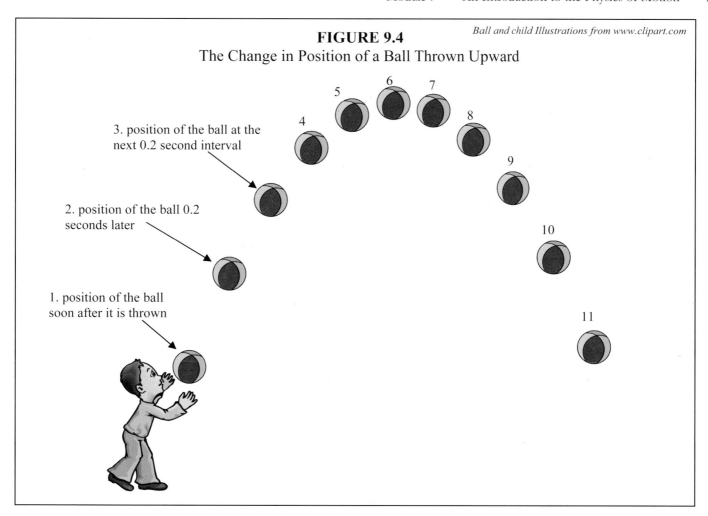

FIGURE 9.4

The Change in Position of a Ball Thrown Upward

Ball and child Illustrations from www.clipart.com

3. position of the ball at the next 0.2 second interval

2. position of the ball 0.2 seconds later

1. position of the ball soon after it is thrown

In this figure, I am not showing multiple balls. Each image of the ball in the figure is a drawing of the same ball. It was thrown up in the air by the child, and I am showing you its position every 0.2 seconds. Thus, the image of the ball closest to the child's hand represents where the ball would be shortly after he released it. The next image represents where the ball would be 0.2 seconds later. The next one is drawn at the position it would occupy 0.2 seconds after that, and so on. Each image of the ball in the figure, then, represents the position of the ball in 0.2 second intervals.

Now look closely at the figure. The distance between the first image of the ball and the second image of the ball is fairly large. The distance between the second and third image, however, is significantly smaller. The distance between the third and fourth images is even smaller, the distance between the fourth and fifth is smaller still, and the distance between the fifth and sixth image is the smallest. Starting at the next image, however, the distance between images begins to grow again. How can this be explained?

These images each represent the position of the ball 0.2 seconds after the previous image. Since the ball's position changed over each time interval, we know that it was traveling with a certain velocity. Over the first 0.2-second time interval, the ball traveled up and over a certain distance. Over the next 0.2-second time interval, the ball traveled up and over, but not nearly as far. What does that tell us about the difference in the velocities between the two time intervals? In the first time interval a larger distance was traveled than in the second time interval, despite the fact that each interval was 0.2 seconds. If the ball travels less distance in the second time interval, we know that the ball's velocity is lower in the second time interval than in the first. Using that same reasoning, all the way up to the sixth image of the ball, the ball's velocity *decreased*.

What happened after the sixth image of the ball? Well, by the eighth image, it is clear that the distance between the images of the ball begins to increase. This tells us that during that time, the ball's velocity *increased*. Thus, the ball started out with a certain velocity given to it by the child. That velocity decreased until it reached the very top of its path, and then the velocity started increasing again. What do we call this phenomenon? We call it **acceleration**.

<u>Acceleration</u> – The time rate of change of an object's velocity

When an object is in motion and its velocity changes, we say that the object has experienced acceleration. Although the word definition of acceleration is important, we can also express the definition of acceleration mathematically:

$$\text{acceleration} = \frac{\text{final velocity} - \text{initial velocity}}{\text{time}}$$

(9.2)

Thus, the acceleration of an object can be calculated if you take the difference in its velocities over a certain time interval and divide by the number of seconds in that time interval.

Let's think for a moment about the units that will go along with acceleration. Remember, as my former high school physics teacher learned, the units on a physical quantity are just as important as the quantity itself. If we want to learn about acceleration, then, we need to learn about its units. The units on velocity are a distance unit divided by a time unit. Thus, units like meters/second, miles/hour, and kilometers/minute are all valid velocity units. When I take a unit like that and divide by time, what do I get? Well, let's look at a quick example:

EXAMPLE 9.3

Suppose a ball is falling. A person with a radar gun measures its velocity to be 2.0 feet/second straight down. Just 0.30 seconds later, he measures the velocity again and finds that it is 11.6 feet/second straight down. What is the ball's acceleration?

To calculate acceleration, we use Equation (9.2). The initial velocity is 2.0 feet per second down and the final velocity is 11.6 feet per second down. As the problem indicates, the time interval is 0.30 seconds.

$$\text{acceleration} = \frac{\text{final velocity} - \text{initial velocity}}{\text{time}}$$

$$\text{acceleration} = \frac{11.6 \frac{\text{feet}}{\text{second}} - 2.0 \frac{\text{feet}}{\text{second}}}{0.30 \text{ seconds}} = \frac{9.6 \frac{\text{feet}}{\text{second}}}{0.30 \text{ seconds}} = 32 \frac{\text{feet}/\text{second}}{\text{second}}$$

What kind of unit is that? Well, we could say that it is "feet per second per second," but there is a better way to express it. Remember that a fraction merely represents a situation in which you divide the numerator by the denominator. Thus:

$$32 \, \frac{\frac{feet}{second}}{second} = 32 \, \frac{feet}{second} \div second$$

How do we divide by a fraction? We invert and multiply:

$$32 \, \frac{feet}{second} \div second = 32 \, \frac{feet}{second} \times \frac{1}{second} = 32 \, \frac{feet}{second^2}$$

The acceleration can therefore be expressed as 32 feet per second^2 downward.

The units on acceleration, then, are a distance unit divided by a time unit squared. Thus, units like feet/second^2, meters/second^2, miles/hour^2, and kilometers/minute^2 are all valid acceleration units.

Now that you know the units that accompany acceleration, you need to know a few more specifics. Acceleration is a vector quantity. This means it contains directional information. How do you attach directional information to acceleration? Well, in order to determine the direction of acceleration, you need to know the direction of the velocity, and you need to know whether velocity is increasing or decreasing. Remember, acceleration is the change in velocity, and velocity can change in one of three ways. If an object speeds up, the velocity obviously changes. If an object slows down, the velocity changes as well. Finally, if an object changes direction, the velocity changes. Remember, velocity is a vector quantity. Thus, direction is a part of velocity. Even if an object's speed does not change, if its direction changes, its velocity changes. In all three of these cases, then, there is an acceleration, because there is a change in the velocity.

We can determine the direction of the acceleration if we examine how the velocity is changing. For example, suppose a car is heading west and begins to increase its speed. The car is accelerating, but in what direction? Well, since the westward velocity is getting larger, the change in velocity results in *more* westward movement. Thus, the acceleration must have a direction of west. Suppose that car were to then begin to slow down. What's the direction of the acceleration then? Well, if the westward velocity decreases, that means the acceleration is going *against* the velocity. Thus, the acceleration's direction is east. If an object is speeding up, then, its acceleration is in the same direction as its velocity. If it is slowing down, its acceleration is in the opposite direction as its velocity. See how that works in the following example problems.

EXAMPLE 9.4

A rock is dropped from a bridge into a river. It starts out with zero initial velocity and it hits the river 2 seconds later, traveling with a velocity of 19.6 meters per second downward. What is the acceleration?

The rock starts off with an initial velocity of zero. Its final velocity is 19.6 meters per second, and the time is 2 seconds. We can now just plug those numbers into our equation:

$$\text{acceleration} = \frac{\text{final velocity} - \text{initial velocity}}{\text{time}}$$

$$\text{acceleration} = \frac{19.6 \frac{\text{meters}}{\text{second}} - 0 \frac{\text{meters}}{\text{second}}}{2 \text{ seconds}} = \frac{19.6 \frac{\text{meters}}{\text{second}}}{2 \text{ seconds}} = 9.8 \frac{\text{meters}}{\text{second}^2}$$

The rock sped up, because it started at zero and ended traveling 19.6 meters per second downward. Thus, the acceleration must be in the same direction as the velocity. Therefore, the acceleration is 9.8 meters per second^2 downward.

A bicyclist is traveling down a road at 18 feet per second to the east. The cyclist sees an obstacle in the road ahead, so he hits the brakes. In 1.8 seconds, the cyclist has come to a complete halt. What is the cyclist's acceleration?

To determine the acceleration, we need to know the initial velocity, the final velocity and the time. Well, before the brakes are slammed, the cyclist is traveling 18 feet per second east. That's the initial velocity. In 1.8 seconds (that's the time), the cyclist comes to a complete halt. What is the final velocity? If the cyclist is at a halt, the velocity is zero. Thus, the final velocity is zero. This makes the equation:

$$\text{acceleration} = \frac{\text{final velocity} - \text{initial velocity}}{\text{time}}$$

$$\text{acceleration} = \frac{0 \frac{\text{feet}}{\text{second}} - 18 \frac{\text{feet}}{\text{second}}}{1.8 \text{ seconds}} = \frac{-18 \frac{\text{feet}}{\text{second}}}{1.8 \text{ seconds}} = -10 \frac{\text{feet}}{\text{second}^2}$$

Now what does this mean? When we subtracted 18 from zero, we got -18. When we divided that number by 1.8, the negative sign stayed around. What does a negative acceleration mean? Well, it tells you about the direction of acceleration. The bicyclist slowed down. That means the acceleration is in the *opposite direction* as the velocity. That's what the negative means. It is reminding you that the cyclist slowed down, making the acceleration opposite of the velocity. Since the velocity's direction is east, you know the acceleration is 10 feet per second^2 to the west. Notice that I dropped the negative sign. Why? Well, the negative sign helped me determine the direction of the acceleration. Thus, I didn't really drop the negative, I just turned it into a direction. That's what you should do as well. If you come across a negative acceleration, you should use that negative to help you determine the direction, but only the direction should show up in your answer.

Before we move on, there is a point of terminology I want to make. Some people use the term "deceleration" to describe acceleration that slows the speed of an object. Although that is an accepted term in everyday English, it is not an acceptable term in physics. When we talk about acceleration that slows an object down, we do not say deceleration. Instead, we give the direction of the acceleration. When compared to the direction of the velocity, the acceleration's direction tells a physicist whether an object slows down or speeds up. In the end, then, when you read "acceleration," don't assume it means that an object is speeding up! Acceleration can either speed up or slow down an object, depending on its direction. In fact, an object's *speed* need not change at all in response to acceleration. Remember, if the object's direction changes, its velocity changes. Thus, an object might be accelerating even though its *speed* is not changing, because the object might be changing direction.

 The multimedia companion CD has a video that discusses determining the direction of acceleration during the operation of NASA's space shuttle.

When solving physics problems, there is one thing for which you must always be on your guard. I want to use the subject of acceleration to show you what that is. Study the next example problem carefully.

EXAMPLE 9.5

A sports car travels from 0 to 60 miles per hour north in 6.1 seconds. What is its acceleration?

At first glance this seems like an easy problem. We are given the initial velocity (0), the final velocity (60 miles per hour north), and the time (6.1 seconds). Thus, we just put those numbers into the equation, right?

$$acceleration = \frac{final\ velocity - initial\ velocity}{time}$$

$$acceleration = \frac{60\ \frac{miles}{hour} - 0\ \frac{miles}{hour}}{6.1\ seconds} = \frac{60\ \frac{miles}{hour}}{6.1\ seconds}$$

There is something terribly wrong with that equation. Can you see it? The numerator of the fraction has a unit of miles per hour. The denominator has the unit "seconds." ***That makes the math difficult!*** In order to do math on numbers with units, *make sure the units agree with one another*. You should not have feet and miles in the same equation; you shouldn't even have millimeters and centimeters in the same equation. Every unit for length should be the same, every unit for time should be the same, and so on. In this equation, we have hours and seconds (both units of time) in the same equation. We shouldn't have that. We must convert one of those two quantities. The 6.1 seconds is easiest to convert, so that's what we'll do. Since there are 3,600 seconds in an hour:

$$\frac{6.1\ \cancel{seconds}}{1} \times \frac{1\ hour}{3600\ \cancel{seconds}} = 0.00169\ hours$$

Now that we have all time units in agreement, we can finally use the acceleration equation properly:

$$acceleration = \frac{final\,velocity - initial\,velocity}{time}$$

$$\text{acceleration} = \frac{60\frac{\text{miles}}{\text{hour}} - 0\frac{\text{miles}}{\text{hour}}}{0.00169 \text{ hours}} = \frac{60\frac{\text{miles}}{\text{hour}}}{0.00169 \text{ hours}} = 35,503\frac{\text{miles}}{\text{hour}^2}$$

That's a big number! Since the car's speed increased, the acceleration and velocity have the same direction. The acceleration, then, is 35,503 miles/hour² north.

When looking at a physics problem, then, you need to figure out the equation you are going to use. If you are looking for velocity or speed, you use Equation (9.1). If you are solving for acceleration, you use Equation (9.2). Then you determine where the values you are given fit into the equation. Finally, you need to make sure that all the units agree with one another. If you end up with kilograms and grams in the same equation, for example, you cannot solve the equation until you have converted one of those mass units to the other. Make sure you can do this by solving the "On Your Own" problems below.

ON YOUR OWN

9.6 A child is sledding. He starts at the top of the hill with a velocity of zero, and 3 seconds later he is speeding down the hill at 12 meters per second. What is the child's acceleration?

9.7 Once that same child reaches the bottom of the hill, the sled coasts over a long, flat section of snow. If the child's velocity when the sled starts coasting is 12 meters per second east, and the child coasts for 6 seconds before coming to a halt, what is the child's acceleration?

9.8 A good runner can keep up a pace of 0.15 miles per minute for quite some time. If a runner starts from rest and settles into a velocity of 0.15 miles per minute south after 3 seconds of running, what is the runner's acceleration over that 3-second interval?

The Acceleration Due to Gravity

In your everyday experience, you know that in order to get something moving, you usually must push it. In the next module, you will learn why this is the case. Before you do, however, let me remind you that there is one situation in which you do not need to push something to get it moving. When you drop something, you need not push it. It starts moving all by itself. Why? Because of gravity. But what does gravity *do* in order to make a dropped object begin to move? It gives that object some acceleration. In the next module, you'll learn how gravity does that. In this module, however, I want you to learn a few consequences of that fact.

Whenever any object is falling toward the earth without anything inhibiting its fall, we say that the object is in **free fall**.

Free fall – The motion of an object when it is falling solely under the influence of gravity

In free fall, gravity accelerates an object. Without some force inhibiting the motion, the object will continue to speed up because it is under constant acceleration due to gravity. If you drop a rock from a tall cliff, then, it will continue to pick up speed until it hits the ground below. That's free fall.

You need to learn something about the acceleration that objects experience while they are in free fall. It is best illustrated by experiment.

EXPERIMENT 9.2
The Acceleration Due to Gravity Is Independent of the Object Falling

Supplies:

♦ A large (at least 21 cm by 27 cm), heavy book
♦ A small (about 3 cm by 3 cm) piece of paper
♦ Eye protection such as goggles or safety glasses

Introduction: One of the properties of free fall is that all objects experience the same acceleration regardless of their weight or physical makeup. That tends to go against your everyday experience. This experiment shows you that it is, indeed, true.

Procedure:

1. Hold the book in one hand and the paper in the other. Hold both of them out at arm's length, and make sure that they are at exactly the same height. Make sure that there are no obstructions beneath the two objects so that they can fall to the floor without running into something.
2. Now, release them both at precisely the same instant. Note what happens. Specifically, note which object (the book or the paper) hits the ground first. If they hit simultaneously, note that.
3. Next, repeat the experiment in a slightly different way. This time, place the piece of paper on top of the book and hold the book out at arm's length with both hands. Now release the book and paper. Note what happens this time.

What happened in this quick experiment? In the first part, the book hit the ground first. That is what you would expect from your everyday experience. After all, the book is heavier than the paper. Thus, it should fall faster than the paper, right? This leads most people to believe that gravity accelerates heavy things faster than it accelerates light things. After all, both the book and the paper were being accelerated by gravity as they fell. The book fell faster, so it must have experienced more acceleration, right?

If that's the case, how can we explain the second part of the experiment? In that situation, the piece of paper stayed on top of the book, falling just as fast as the book fell! Why did this happen? The paper was not stuck to the book; therefore, it did not *have* to stay on the book. If it were really experiencing a smaller acceleration due to gravity than the book, the book should have started traveling faster than the piece of paper, eventually pulling away from it. Instead, they both fell at the same rate. Why? They both fell at the same rate because they both experienced the same acceleration. Thus, the conclusion I just stated from the first part of the experiment is wrong. How, then, do we explain the first part of the experiment?

The explanation has to do with something we call **air resistance**. You see, when an object falls through the air, there are countless gas molecules (like nitrogen and oxygen) and atoms (like argon) in the object's way. In order to fall, the object must shove the gas molecules and atoms out of its way. Well, the molecules and atoms resist this movement, and thus the object must force its way through them. A heavy object is much better at doing this than a light object. Therefore, heavy objects fall faster than light objects not because their acceleration due to gravity is larger, but because they are not as strongly affected by air resistance as light objects are.

The fact that light objects are affected by air resistance more than heavy objects is illustrated by the first part of the experiment. When you held the book and paper in each hand and dropped them, they were both subjected to air resistance. Since the paper was much more affected by air resistance than the book, it fell more slowly, because it had a harder time shoving through the molecules and atoms in the air. When you placed the paper on top of the book in the second part of the experiment, however, the book shoved the molecules and atoms in the air out of the way. The paper, therefore, did not have to. As a result, it was not subject to much air resistance. Under those circumstances, then, the paper and the book fell with the same velocity, demonstrating the fact that gravity accelerates all objects equally.

What we learn from the experiment, then, is that when we neglect air resistance, all objects falling near the surface of the earth accelerate equally. I will discuss air resistance a bit more in the next module, but a detailed understanding of that difficult subject is beyond the scope of this course. Therefore, when dealing with objects falling near the surface of the earth, we will always neglect air resistance. For most relatively heavy objects, this is a reasonable thing to do, because air resistance does not affect heavy objects very much.

In fact, any object that is affected greatly by air resistance cannot experience free fall when dropped near the surface of the earth. After all, remember the definition of free fall. It tells us that in order to really experience free fall, an object must be falling *solely* under the influence of gravity. Air resistance is an influence other than gravity; thus, objects significantly affected by air resistance do not experience free fall when dropped near the surface of the earth. We will be neglecting air resistance, however. As far as we are concerned, then, when an object falls near the surface of the earth, we will say it is in free fall.

Well, now that we know all objects accelerate equally under the influence of gravity, we need to know *what* that acceleration is. Near the surface of the earth, the acceleration due to gravity is 9.8 meters per second^2. In English units, that turns out to be 32 feet per second^2. These are numbers that you must memorize.

The acceleration due to gravity for any object is 9.8 meters/second^2 in metric units and 32 feet/second^2 in English units.

Whenever you do problems involving free fall, you will use one of those values for acceleration. Which one will you use? Well, that depends on the problem. If the problem deals with metric units, you will use 9.8 meters per second squared. If the problem deals with English units, you will use 32 feet per second squared. You will see what I mean in a moment.

It turns out that because the acceleration an object experiences in free fall is constant, there is one neat thing we can do. If an object is dropped without being given any initial push, we can determine how far it falls given just the time it is in the air. In other words, if we time an object as it falls, we can use the acceleration due to gravity to determine the distance it fell. We can do this with the following equation:

$$\text{distance} = \frac{1}{2} \times (\text{acceleration}) \times (\text{time})^2 \qquad (9.3)$$

You will learn where this equation comes from if you take high school physics. For right now, just accept the equation and study the following example to see how it is used.

EXAMPLE 9.6

A young woman is standing on a bridge overlooking a river. If she drops a rock from the bridge, and it takes 1.2 seconds for it to hit the river, how many meters did the rock fall?

We are trying to determine the distance over which the rock fell. For that, we use Equation (9.3). We know the time (1.2 seconds) and we know that the acceleration is due to gravity alone. Do we use 9.8 meters per second^2 or 32 feet per second^2? Well, the problem asks for the answer in meters, so we had better use the acceleration that has meters in it:

$$\text{distance} = \frac{1}{2} \times (\text{acceleration}) \times (\text{time})^2$$

$$\text{distance} = \frac{1}{2} \times (9.8 \, \frac{\text{meters}}{\text{second}^2}) \times (1.2 \text{ seconds})^2 = \frac{1}{2} \cdot (9.8 \, \frac{\text{meters}}{\text{second}^2}) \times (1.2 \text{ seconds}) \times (1.2 \text{ seconds})$$

$$\text{distance} = \frac{1}{2} \times (9.8 \, \frac{\text{meters}}{\cancel{\text{second}^2}}) \times (1.44 \, \cancel{\text{seconds}^2}) = 7.056 \text{ meters}$$

Notice what happened here. When you square something, you take it times itself. Thus, (1.2 seconds)^2 is (1.2 seconds) x (1.2 seconds). What does that work out to? Well, 1.2 x 1.2 = 1.44, and seconds times seconds is seconds^2. When that was multiplied by acceleration, the second^2 unit canceled, leaving just the meters unit. Since distance is measured in meters, it is good that the equation worked out that way.

It turns out that this will always happen in physics and chemistry. When you use physical quantities in an equation, the units will always work out like they did here. That's the reason the units in an equation must agree with one another before you can solve the equation. If they do not, units that are supposed to cancel will not be able to, and the answer will be nonsense. This answer is not nonsense, however. <u>The rock fell 7.056 meters</u>.

If you think about it, this little fact of physics can be incredibly useful. Perform the following experiment to see what I mean.

EXPERIMENT 9.3
Measuring Height with a Stopwatch

Please note: Sample calculations for this experiment can be found in the Solutions and Tests Guide, after the solutions to the study guide.

<u>Supplies</u>:

♦ A stopwatch (must read hundredths of a second)
♦ A chair or small stepladder
♦ A ball or rock (something heavy so that air resistance won't be a factor)
♦ A tape measure (A meterstick or yardstick will work if you do not have a tape measure.)
♦ Eye protection such as goggles or safety glasses

Introduction: Sometimes it is hard to measure the height of something because you do not have a ruler long enough. In this experiment, you will see how to measure the height of something like that.

Procedure:

1. Stand on the chair or stepladder and hold your rock or ball so that it touches the ceiling of the room.
2. Hold the stopwatch in your other hand. Simultaneously drop the rock or ball and start your stopwatch. When the rock or ball hits the ground, stop the stopwatch.
3. Read the time from the stopwatch and write it down.
4. Perform steps (1-3) 10 times, each time writing down the result. Most likely, the result will differ from one time to the next. That's okay. *Please realize that this is not busywork.* There is a very important reason you must do this 10 times. I will explain that reason when you finish the experiment.
5. Once you have done the experiment ten times, average the results by adding them all together and dividing by 10. Unless you live in a *very* tall house, the result you get should be less than 1 second.
6. Use that time and Equation (9.3) to determine the distance over which the rock or ball fell. If the tape measure you have is marked off in feet, use 32 feet per second^2 for the acceleration. If it is marked off in meters, use 9.8 meters per second^2 as the acceleration.
7. Now measure the height of the ceiling with your tape measure or ruler.
8. Compare your two measurements. They should be within 15% of each other.

What did you learn in the experiment? Well, you should have learned that you do not need to have a ruler to measure the height of something. In your experiment, you used the time it took for a rock or ball to fall from the ceiling as a way to measure the height of the ceiling. When you checked your result with the measurement you got from a tape measure, you should have seen that the measurements agree to within a few percent.

Why didn't they agree exactly? Experimental error, which I discussed back in Module #4, is the reason that the measurements did not match exactly. First of all, there was experimental error when you measured the height of the ceiling with the tape measure. Why? Think about it. The tape measure had to be perfectly straight in order to read the true height of the ceiling. How could you be sure you were holding it perfectly straight? You couldn't. Thus, error was introduced. Also, I'm sure it was hard to determine exactly where to read the tape measure. Thus, another error was introduced there. My point is that the measurement you got from the ruler or measuring tape had some experimental error in it.

What about the measurement you got by dropping the rock? There was experimental error in that as well. After all, you tried as hard as you could to start the stopwatch and drop the rock or ball simultaneously, but there was no way to be sure that you did. You might have started the stopwatch an instant before you dropped the rock; you might have dropped the rock an instant before you started the stopwatch. There is almost no way to tell. Also, there was no way to tell that you stopped the stopwatch at the same instant that the rock or ball hit the ground.

In the end, then, there were errors in your measurement. That's the reason I had you do the experiment 10 times and average the result. If you look at your data, you will see that the times you measured varied quite a bit. They varied because of experimental error. By averaging 10 results, you lowered the effects of experimental error. After all, in some of the trials you probably started the stopwatch before you dropped the rock. In other trials, you probably started the stopwatch after you dropped the rock. By averaging your results together, you helped these errors cancel each other out.

Averaging out several trials of the same experiment is a common method scientists use to minimize the effects of experimental error. The process of averaging does not *eliminate* experimental error, but the more trials you do, the less effect the experimental error will have. Thus, if you did the experiment 50 times and averaged the results, it would have less experimental error than the error in the measurement you had.

So, in the experiment, you had two numbers, each of which had experimental error. Which was better? In this case, your measurement with the tape measure was probably better than your measurement from dropping the rock or ball. Why? Well, the experimental error was probably lower in the case of the tape measure. After all, when you dropped the rock, the time it took for the rock to fall was pretty small. In the end, the experimental error associated with starting and stopping the stopwatch was probably very important. At the same time, although there were problems using the tape measure, they were not that severe.

What if you wanted to measure the height of your house, however? At that point, the rock or ball would take a lot longer to fall. Thus, the experimental error associated with stopping and starting the stopwatch would be lower. At the same time, it would be much harder to use the tape measure. At that point, then, dropping a rock would most likely give you a more accurate measurement than would measuring the height with a tape measure.

In the end, when a scientist makes a measurement, she needs to consider the experimental error involved. One method might have the least amount of experimental error. In the case of your experiment, for example, the tape measure method of measuring height had the least experimental error, so that result is probably the correct one. In another case, another method might prove to have less experimental error. In the case of measuring the height of your house, for example, the rock-dropping method would probably give you the best answer. In the end, then, whenever a scientist does an experiment, he or she must be keenly aware of the potential experimental errors. If not, the experiment might very well be meaningless.

ON YOUR OWN

9.9 A ball is dropped from the roof of a house. If the ball takes 1.1 seconds to fall, how many feet tall is the house?

9.10 In order to measure the height of a skyscraper, a person stands on the roof and drops a ball. The instant that he drops the ball, he yells to an observer on the ground. The observer starts the stopwatch. When the observer sees the ball hit the ground, the observer stops the stopwatch. From the time elapsed, the observer calculates the height of the skyscraper. List all experimental errors associated with this experiment.

ANSWERS TO THE "ON YOUR OWN" QUESTIONS

9.1 <u>Relative to the security guard on the escalator, you are not in motion. Relative to the other two, you are in motion.</u> Since you and the guard on the escalator are standing still, the escalator determines your motion. You are, therefore, both moving at the same speed, and the distance between you is not changing. Thus, relative to each other, you are not moving. The distance between you and each of the other guards is changing, so relative to those two, you are in motion.

9.2 In this problem, we are given the distance (115 miles) and the time (30 minutes), and we are asked to calculate the speed. Thus, we can use Equation (9.1). The problem, however, asks for the answer in miles per hour. To do that, we have to convert time to hours:

$$\frac{30 \text{ minutes}}{1} \times \frac{1 \text{ hour}}{60 \text{ minutes}} = 0.5 \text{ hours}$$

Now we can use Equation (9.1):

$$\text{speed} = \frac{\text{distance}}{\text{time}} = \frac{115 \text{ miles}}{0.5 \text{ hours}} = 230 \underline{\frac{\text{miles}}{\text{hour}}}$$

9.3 This is another use of Equation (9.1) with the distance equal to 5 meters and the time equal to 12 hours. The problem asks for the answer in millimeters per minute, however. Thus, we need to convert meters to millimeters and hours to minutes:

$$\frac{12 \text{ hours}}{1} \times \frac{60 \text{ minutes}}{1 \text{ hour}} = 720 \text{ minutes}$$

$$\frac{5 \text{ meters}}{1} \times \frac{1 \text{ millimeter}}{0.001 \text{ meters}} = 5,000 \text{ millimeters}$$

Now that we have our measurements in the proper units for this problem, we can go ahead and use the equation:

$$\text{speed} = \frac{\text{distance}}{\text{time}} = \frac{5,000 \text{ millimeters}}{720 \text{ minutes}} = 6.94 \underline{\frac{\text{millimeters}}{\text{minute}}}$$

9.4 Velocity is speed with direction. So, in order for a number to represent velocity, it needs a speed unit (a distance unit divided by a time unit) and a direction. Answer (d) does not have a speed unit. Answers (a-c) all have speed units, but only answer (b) also has a direction. Thus, the only velocity is <u>answer (b)</u>.

9.5 The planes are flying in opposite directions, which is clear from the picture. Thus, we get their relative speed by adding their individual speeds:

$$\text{relative speed} = 520 \text{ miles/hour} + 650 \text{ miles/hour} = 1,170 \text{ miles per hour}$$

The picture shows that they are approaching one another. Thus, their relative velocity is <u>1,170 miles per hour toward each other</u>.

9.6 The initial velocity is zero, and the final velocity is 12 meters/second down the hill. The time is 3 seconds. All units agree, so we can directly use the equation:

$$acceleration = \frac{final\,velocity - initial\,velocity}{time}$$

$$acceleration = \frac{12\,\dfrac{meters}{second} - 0\,\dfrac{meters}{second}}{3\,seconds} = \frac{12\,\dfrac{meters}{second}}{3\,seconds} = 4\,\frac{meters}{second^2}$$

The sled's velocity increased, so the acceleration has the same direction as the velocity. Thus, the acceleration is 4 meters per second^2 down the hill.

9.7 The final velocity is now zero and the initial velocity is 12 meters per second east. It takes 6 seconds for the sled to come to a halt. All units agree with each other, so we can use the equation:

$$acceleration = \frac{final\,velocity - initial\,velocity}{time}$$

$$acceleration = \frac{0\,\dfrac{meters}{second} - 12\,\dfrac{meters}{second}}{6\,seconds} = \frac{-12\,\dfrac{meters}{second}}{6\,seconds} = -2\,\frac{meters}{second^2}$$

The negative sign tells us that the acceleration is in the opposite direction as the velocity. This makes sense, since the sled slowed down. Since the negative sign just tells us about direction, we drop it from the answer, replacing it with the actual direction. The acceleration, then, is 2 meters/second^2 west.

9.8 The initial velocity is zero because the runner started from rest. The final velocity is 0.15 miles per minute south. The time is 3 seconds. Wait a minute: The time units don't agree. In velocity, we have the minute unit, but in time we have seconds. Let's fix this by converting seconds to minutes:

$$\frac{3\,\cancel{seconds}}{1} \times \frac{1\,minute}{60\,\cancel{seconds}} = 0.05\,minutes$$

Now that the units agree, we can use the equation:

$$acceleration = \frac{final\,velocity - initial\,velocity}{time}$$

$$acceleration = \frac{0.15\,\dfrac{miles}{minute} - 0\,\dfrac{miles}{minute}}{0.05\,minutes} = \frac{0.15\,\dfrac{miles}{minute}}{0.05\,minutes} = 3\,\frac{miles}{minute^2}$$

Since the runner sped up, the acceleration and velocity are in the same direction. Thus, the acceleration is <u>3 miles per minute^2 south</u>.

9.9 The ball is in free fall. This means its acceleration is due to gravity alone. The problem asks for the height of the house in feet, so we need to use 32 feet per second^2. The time is 1.1 seconds, so this is a direct application of Equation (9.3):

$$\text{distance} = \frac{1}{2} \times (\text{acceleration}) \times (\text{time})^2$$

$$\text{distance} = \frac{1}{2} \times (32 \; \frac{\text{feet}}{\text{second}^2}) \times (1.1 \text{ seconds})^2 = \frac{1}{2} \times (32 \; \frac{\text{feet}}{\text{second}^2}) \times (1.1 \text{ seconds}) \times (1.1 \text{ seconds})$$

$$\text{distance} = \frac{1}{2} \times (32 \; \frac{\text{feet}}{\cancel{\text{second}^2}}) \times (1.21 \; \cancel{\text{second}^2}) = \underline{19.36 \text{ feet}}$$

9.10 There are many sources of error here. <u>First, the person who drops might not yell at the precise instant the ball is dropped. Second, the person with the stopwatch might not start the watch the instant he hears the yell. Third, the person might not stop the stopwatch at the instant the ball hits the ground.</u> You could also include the fact that it takes time for the sound to travel, so the stopwatch will always be started after the person yells.

STUDY GUIDE FOR MODULE #9

1. Define the following terms:

   a. Reference point
   b. Vector quantity
   c. Scalar quantity
   d. Acceleration
   e. Free fall

2. If an object's position does not change relative to a reference point, is it in motion relative to that reference point?

3. A glass of water sits on a counter. Is it in motion?

4. A child is floating in an inner tube on a still lake. His position does not change relative to a tree on the shore. He watches two girls jog along the shore of the lake. The girls are keeping perfect pace with each other. Neither is pulling ahead of nor falling behind the other.

   a. Relative to whom is the child in motion?
   b. Relative to whom is the first girl in motion?
   c. Relative to whom is the second girl not in motion?

5. What is the speed of a boat that travels 10 miles in 30 minutes? Please answer in miles per hour.

6. What is the speed of a jogger who jogs 6 kilometers in 45 minutes? Please answer in meters per second.

7. Label each quantity as a vector or scalar quantity. Also, identify it as speed, distance, velocity, acceleration, or none of these.

   a. 10 meters
   b. 1.2 meters/second^2 east
   c. 3.4 feet/hour and slowing

   d. 56 liters
   e. 2.2 miles/minute west
   f. 2.2 millimeters/year

8. A car and a truck are traveling north on a highway. The truck has a speed of 45 miles per hour and the car has a speed of 57 miles per hour. If the truck is ahead of the car, what is the relative velocity?

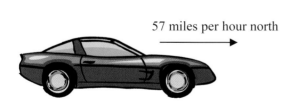

57 miles per hour north

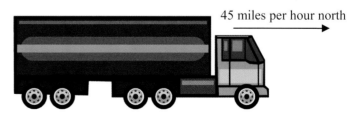

45 miles per hour north

Illustrations from www.clipart.com

9. If an object travels for 15 minutes with a constant velocity of 12 miles per hour west, what is the acceleration?

10. A sports car goes from a velocity of zero to a velocity of 12 meters per second east in 2 seconds. What is the car's acceleration?

11. A train takes a long time to stop. That's what makes trains so dangerous to people who cross the tracks when one is near. If a train is traveling at 30 miles per hour south and takes 12 minutes to come to a stop, what is the train's acceleration?

12. A very picky physicist states that it is impossible for any object to experience free fall near the earth's surface. Why is the physicist technically correct?

13. Even though the physicist in question #12 is technically correct, why do we go ahead and assume that heavy objects are in free fall when they fall near the surface of the earth?

14. A long, vertical glass tube contains a feather and a penny. All the air is pumped out, and the tube is inverted, causing the penny and the feather to fall. Which hits the bottom first, the feather or the penny?

15. What is the height of a building (in meters) if it takes a dropped rock 4.1 seconds to fall from its roof?

16. A hot-air balloonist drops a rock from his balloon. It takes 7 seconds for the rock to fall to the ground. What is the balloonist's altitude in feet?

17. A scientist decides to study the acceleration of an object moving in a straight line. He measures the distance the object travels in 30-second time intervals. The scientist notices that in each interval, the object travels a shorter distance than it did in the previous interval. Is the direction of the acceleration the same as or opposite of the velocity?

MODULE #10: Newton's Laws

Introduction

In the previous module, you learned a lot about analyzing motion. You now understand and can calculate both speed and velocity. You know about acceleration. You even know a little bit about free fall. This knowledge and those skills are very valuable in trying to understand the physical creation around you. However, in all of what you have learned so far, you have not understood *why* objects in motion behave the way they do. That's what I hope you will learn in this module.

The history of humankind's attempts to understand the physical nature of motion really begins with the ancient Greeks. In particular, the Greek philosopher **Aristotle** (384-322 BC) spent an enormous amount of time observing and thinking about the world around him. He wrote many works covering such diverse subjects as physics, biology, morals, and even politics! His teachings were influential during his lifetime, but they actually became more important during the Middle Ages, as they were used as the basis for Roman Catholic philosophy.

During and following the time of the Renaissance, however, scientists began to notice many discrepancies between the theories of Aristotle and their observations of the world around them. Aristotle's teachings had become so ingrained in the minds of the scientific (and religious) community, however, that most scientists were quite resistant to giving them up. It took many years of careful experiments by several scientists to turn the tide and dispose of Aristotle's mistakes. Three scientists are considered pivotal characters in this accomplishment: **Copernicus, Galileo,** and **Newton**. In this module, I will concentrate on Newton. In a later module, I will discuss Copernicus and Galileo in more detail.

Sir Isaac Newton

Sir Isaac Newton is an incredibly important figure in the history of science. His portrait and a brief biography are given in Figure 10.1.

FIGURE 10.1
Sir Isaac Newton

Image in the public domain

Sir Isaac Newton was born in England in 1642. From an early age, he was interested in learning about how the world worked, and he devoted his life to performing experiments designed to help him understand creation. He is credited with many, many discoveries. As we will see in this module, he discovered three laws of motion, but that's not all. He developed a theory describing gravity (which you will learn in detail when you take physics); he did the famous prism experiment that showed white light is composed of many colors; and in order to help his scientific investigations, Newton developed a new kind of mathematics we now call "calculus." Amazingly enough, these three accomplishments were completed in less than 18 months! He also built the first reflecting telescope. Newton was knighted for his accomplishments by Queen Anne in 1705, and he died in 1727.

Clearly, Sir Isaac Newton was a genius. Most science books discuss this fact, but they do not tell the whole story. In fact, Newton was a devoutly religious man who spent as much time studying the Bible as he did studying science. As *The Columbia History of the World* says, "...at the end of his days he spent more time studying and writing about the prophecies in the Book of Daniel than he did in charting the heavens" (J.A. Garraty and P. Gray, eds., [New York: Harper & Row, 1972], 709). Although not an orthodox Christian (he rejected the Trinity and the divinity of Christ), he held to many standard Christian beliefs. Here is a good quote that sums up Newton's theological views: "There is one God, the Father, ever living, omnipresent, omniscient, almighty, the maker of heaven and earth, and one mediator between God and man, the man Christ Jesus" (Sir Isaac Newton, *Theological Manuscripts*, Ed. H. McLachlan [Liverpool: Liverpool University Press, 1950], 56). As you can see, he clearly saw God as the almighty Creator, and he saw Christ as the mediator between man and God. At the same time, however, he did not see Christ as divine. Instead, he refers to Christ as a man throughout his theological works. This is part of what made his religious views unorthodox.

Isaac Newton believed that in studying science, he was actually learning about God. In fact, it was his strong belief in God that made him study science. After all, he reasoned, studying science was a way of learning about creation, and learning about creation was a way of learning about God. Of course, Newton also realized that studying creation cannot be the sole means of learning about God. That's why he spent so much time studying the Bible as well. Newton applied his strong mind to interpreting Scripture and wrote many commentaries on passages in the Bible. He was especially drawn to the book of Daniel, as the quote from *The Columbia History of the World* indicates. Clearly, Newton had a great sense of priorities. He recognized the importance of science, but he also realized that learning about God is even more important. Many scientists today could learn an important lesson from this brilliant man.

Newton's First Law of Motion

As I mentioned in the previous section, Newton laid down three laws of motion that are the basis of physics. His first law, often referred to as the **law of inertia**, says the following:

<u>Newton's First Law</u> – An object in motion (or at rest) will tend to stay in motion (or at rest) until it is acted upon by an outside force.

What does this law mean? Basically, it means that if an object is at rest, it will stay at rest until a force causes it to move. In the same way, an object in motion will continue in motion at its current velocity until a force causes its velocity to change.

Now that might seem to be a pretty obvious statement to you, but it flies directly in the face of Aristotle's teachings. You see, Aristotle taught that the natural state of an object is for the object to remain at rest. An object, therefore, would not move until it was forced to move. In addition, if an object was forced to move, it would stop soon after the force was removed, because it "preferred" to be at rest.

How did Aristotle come up with that idea? Well, it tends to make sense given our everyday experience. After all, if I put a rock on a sidewalk, it will just sit there. It will continue to sit there until I force it to move by kicking it. Once I kick it, however, the rock will not continue to move indefinitely, will it? Of course not! It will skitter across the sidewalk for a little while and then eventually come to rest. Based on observations such as this, Aristotle believed that all objects "desire" to be at rest. Thus, if they are at rest, they will stay at rest until forced to do otherwise. If they are not at rest, they will come to rest as soon as possible after all forces on the object are removed.

Now the first thing you need to see is the difference between this idea and Newton's First Law of Motion. Both Aristotle and Newton agree that an object at rest will stay at rest until acted on by an outside force. They disagree, however, when it comes to an object in motion. Aristotle says that an object in motion will come to rest as soon as possible after all forces on the object are removed. It will do that because it "wants" to be at rest. Newton's First Law says quite the opposite. It says that once an object starts moving, it will *continue to move at that same velocity indefinitely* until it is acted on by an outside force. Newton's Laws indicate that there is no preferred state for an object. Objects neither "want" to be at rest nor do they "want" to stay in motion. Instead, they stay in the state in which they are placed until acted on by an outside force.

Based on your everyday experience, which sounds more logical, Newton's First Law or Aristotle's idea? Aristotle's idea does, of course! After all, in our everyday experience, things that are in motion tend to slow down and stop unless continually pushed along by an outside force. Thus, everyday experience lends a lot of support to Aristotle's position. Because of this, it took quite a bit of experimenting on the part of Newton to convince others that his law was correct. Try some experiments of your own.

EXPERIMENT 10.1
Two Experiments Demonstrating Newton's First Law

Supplies:

♦ A coin
♦ A 3-inch by 5-inch index card (note that I listed the units)
♦ A small glass (like a juice glass)
♦ A raw egg
♦ A hard-boiled egg
♦ Eye protection such as goggles or safety glasses

Introduction: Newton's First Law of Motion goes against our everyday experience. Experiments such as these help you visualize that this law of motion is really true.

Procedure:

First Experiment:

1. Place the small glass on the table, right side up.
2. Place the index card on top of the glass so that it covers the opening. Center the index card so that the center of the card is over the center of the glass.
3. Place the coin on the center of the index card.
4. Flick the card quickly with your fingers so that it moves forward, uncovering the glass. What happens to the coin?
5. Set up the experiment again. This time, instead of flicking the card, grasp the card with your fingers and slowly pull it away from the glass. Keep the card level as you pull it away. What happens to the coin this time?

Second Experiment

1. Place the hard-boiled egg on the table.
2. Spin the egg and watch how it spins. You should not try to spin the egg on one of its ends. Instead, allow the egg to lie on the table on its side, and then spin it in that position.
3. Do the same thing with the raw egg. Note the difference in the way the eggs spin, if any.
4. Next, spin the hard-boiled egg, and once it is spinning, reach down and stop it. The instant after you stop it, let it go again. Note what happens.
5. Do the same thing with the raw egg. Note what happens in this case.
6. Clean up your mess.

Let's start with the second part of the experiment. You should have noticed a difference in the way the eggs spun. The raw egg has liquid inside, whereas the hard-boiled egg does not. That's why they spun differently. Now, what explains the results in steps 4 and 5? In step 4, once you stopped the hard-boiled egg, it should have stayed motionless after you let it go. In step 5, however, if you let the raw egg go immediately after you stopped it, the egg began spinning again. Why is there a difference? It stems from the same reason you initially saw a difference in the way the eggs spun.

The raw egg was filled with liquid. When you got the egg spinning, the liquid inside the egg spun as well. When you stopped the egg and instantly let it go again, the egg stopped spinning, but the liquid inside it did not. Thus, when you let go again, the spinning liquid forced the raw egg to start spinning again. The hard-boiled egg, of course, did not exhibit this effect, because there was no liquid in it. When you stopped the hard-boiled egg, everything stopped; thus, when you let go, there was no motion.

Think about how to interpret this using Newton's First Law of Motion. Initially, the raw egg had no motion. It therefore continued to stay at rest until it was acted on by the force of you spinning it. Once in motion, it stayed in motion until you stopped it abruptly with your hands. Although your hand applied enough force to stop the egg itself, it did not apply the force long enough to stop the liquid. Thus, when you let go, the liquid was still in motion. This motion applied a force to the egg, causing it to spin again.

What would have happened if you had stopped the raw egg and then held it for a few seconds? When you let go, would it have started spinning again? Of course not! If you held onto the egg long enough, you would have eventually stopped both the egg *and* the liquid inside. At that point, both the egg and the liquid inside would be at rest, and then they would remain at rest until acted on by an outside force.

The fact that holding onto the egg for a longer period would change the result of the experiment tells you something, doesn't it? It tells you that while the raw egg's motion was rather easy to stop, the motion of the liquid inside was not. In physics, we use the term **inertia** to describe how hard it is to change the velocity of an object.

<u>Inertia</u> – The tendency of an object to resist changes in its velocity

In discussing the second part of the experiment, a physicist would say that the moving liquid had a certain amount of inertia, and the force applied to the liquid when you stopped the egg momentarily was not enough to overcome its inertia. Thus, the liquid continued to spin.

Have you ever been riding down the road in a car when the driver suddenly slammed on the brakes? What happened? You were thrown forward in your seat until your safety belt pulled you back. Actually, you weren't "thrown" forward at all. What happened was Newton's First Law of Motion at work. While you were riding in the car, you were traveling down the road with a certain velocity. The car had the same velocity, so you and the car were moving together. When the driver hit the brakes, the car began to stop because the brakes applied a force to the car. You, however, continued to move with the same velocity you had before because the brakes did not apply a force to you. Thus, the car slowed a lot and you continued moving quickly, so you lurched forward in your seat. Once your seat belt applied a force on you, however, you slowed down too.

Thus, as you were riding in the car, you had a certain amount of inertia. When the car began to stop, your inertia kept you moving at the same velocity until your seat belt exerted a force that overcame your inertia. Once the force was able to overcome your inertia, you stopped along with the car. This is another example of how an object stays in motion until acted on by an outside force.

Now let's go back to the first part of the experiment. In the first part of the experiment, you should have seen the coin fall directly into the glass when you flicked the index card away. When you pulled the index card away slowly, the coin should have traveled with the index card. Thus, it did not fall into the glass. Think about how Aristotle would interpret the first result. Initially, the card and the coin were at rest. This, according the Aristotle, is the "natural" state of both objects. When you flicked the card, you applied a force to *the card* but not *the coin*. Thus, the force caused the card to move, even though it did not "want" to. Since there was no force applied to the coin, it stayed motionless because it "wanted" to stay motionless. Once the card moved out of the way, the coin was acted upon by the force of gravity, and it fell into the glass. Aristotle, then, could easily explain this part of the experiment.

What about the next result? You grasped the card and pulled on it slowly, and the coin and card traveled together. Believe it or not, Aristotle could not explain that result, at least not in a consistent way. After all, as far as Aristotle would be concerned, there was no real difference between the two scenarios. In both cases, you applied a force to the *card*, not the *coin*. Thus, the coin should have stayed in its "natural" state, and it should not have moved with the index card.

Unlike Aristotle, Newton could explain both results. In each case, Newton would say, there was a force that Aristotle did not consider: **friction**. We will learn about friction in detail in the next section of this module. For right now, just realize that friction is a force that results from surfaces rubbing against one another. To explain the second result you found, Newton would say that the coin would have stayed at rest except that the frictional force between the card and the coin acted on the coin, causing it to move with the card. Thus, *you* did not apply a force to the coin, but *friction* did. The result was that the coin moved with the card. In the first part of the experiment, that same frictional force existed, but it was not given time enough to get the coin moving because the card moved so quickly. The coin therefore did not move with the card, not because of a lack of force, but because the force could not act for a long enough time to get the coin to move.

Another way of saying all this is that the coin had a certain amount of inertia sitting at rest. In order to overcome this inertia and get the coin moving, a strong enough force would have to be applied over a long enough time interval. When you flicked the index card, friction was not allowed to work long enough to overcome the coin's inertia, so the coin did not move with the card. When you slowly pulled on the card, however, friction was allowed to work long enough to overcome the coin's inertia, and the coin moved with the card.

These kinds of experiments slowly convinced the scientific community that Aristotle was wrong. Physicists finally realized that the reason an object in motion eventually slows down and comes to rest has nothing to do with its "desired" state. Instead, it is because of friction. When you kick a rock that is lying on the sidewalk, it eventually skitters to a halt because there is friction between the rock and the sidewalk. The friction is an outside force that works against the motion, eventually bringing the rock's velocity to zero. If it were not for friction, the rock would continue to move indefinitely.

You can approximate this outcome by comparing how the rock behaves when there is ice on the sidewalk. If you were to kick the rock down the sidewalk on an icy day, the rock would move a lot farther before coming to a halt. Why? Because the friction between a rock and ice is much smaller than the friction between a rock and the sidewalk. Thus, when the sidewalk is icy, the frictional force is weak, and the rock will not stop for a long time.

In the end, then, if an object has a certain velocity and there is no friction working on it, the object will continue to move at that velocity *for as long as it exists*. Consider, for example, the Voyager 1 and Voyager 2 spacecraft launched from earth in 1977. They were sent to explore Jupiter and Saturn, but they ended up performing so well that they were able to study Uranus and Neptune as well. In fact, these robotic spacecraft were built so well that they are *still* flying through space today, sending information back to earth as they go. Their communication systems are powered by nuclear processes, but their engines have long since run out of fuel. Nevertheless, they are still traveling at a speed of 38,000 miles per hour. Why? Because their engines and the gravity of the planets they passed by accelerated them to high speeds, and since very little friction exists in space, they continue to travel at those high speeds, because no significant outside force is acting on them. In the end, then, objects will continue to move *as they have been moving* until acted on by an outside force. That's the heart of Newton's First Law of Motion.

Image courtesy of NASA

FIGURE 10.2
The Voyager Spacecraft

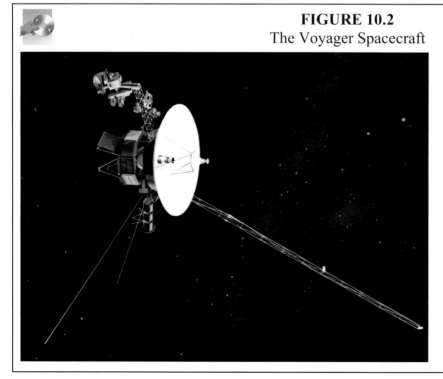

This is an artist's conception of a Voyager spacecraft (both Voyager 1 and 2 have the same design) as it flies through space. Currently, Voyager 1 is more than twice as far from the earth as is Pluto. This makes it the farthest human-made object from earth. Both Voyager spacecraft will eventually reach the heliopause (he' lee uh pawz), which is the edge of our solar system. If they pass the heliopause, they will finally be in interstellar space. The spacecraft have traveled such a great distance because of Newton's First Law.

Now, as I said before, all this might sound *really* simple to you, but it is not. To illustrate what I mean, perform the following experiment.

EXPERIMENT 10.2
An Experiment to See How Well You Understand Newton's First Law

<u>Supplies</u>:

♦ Aluminum pie pan
♦ A pair of scissors
♦ A marble or other small ball
♦ Eye protection such as goggles or safety glasses

Introduction: In this experiment, you will make a prediction about the outcome of an experiment. If you really understand Newton's First Law, you will correctly predict the result.

<u>Procedure</u>:

1. Use the scissors to cut a quarter of the pie pan away. Examine the diagram under step 2 to see what I mean.
2. In this experiment, you are going to roll the marble into the pie pan as shown below. The marble will roll around the pan, guided by the pan's walls. When it hits the edge where the quarter was cut out, it will begin to roll on its own.

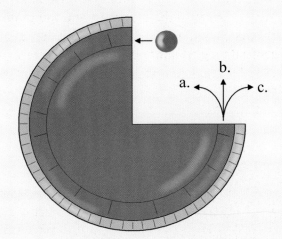

Illustration by Megan Whitaker

3. Before you actually do this, I want you to first predict the path on which the ball will roll once it begins to roll on its own. There are three possible choices. Write down your prediction (a, b, or c).
4. Now you should actually perform the experiment. Hold the pie pan in place with one of your hands so that it doesn't move.
5. Using your other hand, propel the marble straight into the pan so that it rolls around the side of the pan as shown above. Watch which way it ends up moving. Note whether you were right or wrong.
6. Put everything away and clean up any mess you made.

Why did the ball end up moving the way it did? Well, consider Newton's First Law of Motion. When you rolled the ball into the pie pan, you gave it a certain velocity. It would have continued to travel with that speed in that direction, but it ran into the wall of the pie pan. The wall exerted a force on the ball, causing it to change direction. As it began traveling in a new direction, the wall curved, exerting more force on it, causing it to continue to change direction. This continued to happen, causing the marble to travel in a circle. That all stopped the moment the wall ended. At that point, there was no more force acting on the ball. Thus, the ball continued moving without changing the velocity it had the moment it left the pie pan. Looking at the drawing in the experiment, you can see that the ball was traveling straight up right before the wall ended. Thus, once the wall ended, it would continue to travel straight up. As a result, path "b" is the correct answer.

Most students choose path "a." They think that the ball will continue to travel in a circle. Remember, however, that the ball travels in a circle because the wall of the pie pan exerts a force on it, causing it to change direction. You started rolling the ball straight. It would have continued to roll straight, but once it hit the wall of the pie pan, it was acted on by an outside force. As a result, it started moving in a circle. Once that force was removed, however, the ball no longer traveled in a circle, because the force causing it to travel in a circle was no longer acting on it. Thus, it continued moving straight, in the direction it was moving the instant before the force was removed. That's the essence of Newton's First Law of Motion.

ON YOUR OWN

10.1 A cowboy is riding his horse at a fast gallop. Suddenly, the horse plants his feet and stops. As a result, the cowboy falls off the horse. Will the cowboy fall forward, backward, to the left, or to the right?

10.2 A car is traveling down the road at 30 miles per hour. A truck, driven by a reckless driver, comes up from behind with a speed of 50 miles per hour. The truck slams into the back of the car. Will the car's passengers be flung forward or backward in their seats?

10.3 A bomber is dispatched to drop a bomb on a factory. The figure below illustrates three points at which the bomb could be dropped as the plane travels from left to right. Assuming the bomb has no propulsion system of its own, at which point should the bomb be dropped?

  a.

  b.

 c.

Illustrations from www.clipart.com

Before I leave this section, I want to use Newton's First Law of Motion to explain a phenomenon that is probably very familiar to you. Have you ever spun yourself around really fast and then suddenly stopped? How did you feel when you stopped? Dizzy! It turns out that this is a consequence of how your body maintains its balance along with Newton's First Law. In order to maintain balance, you have certain canals in your ears. These canals, called **semicircular canals**, are full of fluid that can slosh around inside them. When the fluid sloshes around, a sensory organ, the cupula (kup' yoo luh), moves back and forth, sending signals to your brain. These signals tell the brain what nerves it must activate to control whatever muscles are needed to keep your balance so that you don't just fall over.

Well, when you start spinning, the fluid starts spinning as well. That tells your brain you are spinning and allows it to control the muscles necessary to make sure that you don't fall down as you spin. When you stop suddenly, the fluid has so much inertia that it continues to move around for a while, until friction forces it to stop. While the fluid is moving, the cupula sends messages to your brain telling it that you are still moving. This confuses the brain, because the eyes and muscles are sending it signals that say you have stopped. Dizziness is the result. Once the fluid in your semicircular canals stops moving, however, the dizziness goes away.

<u>Friction</u>

Friction is the reason that Newton's First Law of Motion goes against your everyday experience. After all, when you roll a ball down a sidewalk, it does not continue to roll forever. Instead, it rolls for a while and then stops. Observations such as this forced Aristotle to conclude that all objects "want" to remain at rest and that an outside force must be used to cause and sustain motion. It took the brilliance of Newton to show that the force of friction was an "invisible" force that caused objects to slow down and eventually come to a halt. Without that frictional force, objects in motion would continue in motion indefinitely.

But what exactly is friction? We know it exists. We know it causes objects in motion to slow down and eventually come to a halt, but what *is* it? Perform the following experiment to give you some idea of what friction is.

EXPERIMENT 10.3
Friction

<u>Supplies</u>:

♦ An unfinished board at least 2 feet long
♦ A block eraser
♦ An ice cube
♦ A small block of wood
♦ A relatively flat rock
♦ Sandpaper
♦ Several books
♦ A ruler
♦ Eye protection such as goggles or safety glasses

Introduction: Friction is present any time one surface meets another surface. In this experiment, you will learn some of the details regarding friction.

<u>Procedure</u>:

1. Place the board on the ground.
2. Use your hand to note how rough or smooth its surface is.
3. Put the ice cube, block of wood, rock, and eraser all at one end of the board.

4. Begin the experiment by lifting the board on the same side that you placed all the objects. Leave the other side of the board on the ground, making the board tilt. Continue to tilt the board until the side you have lifted is high enough to stick a book under it. At that point, stick the book under that end of the board and allow the board to rest there, as illustrated below:

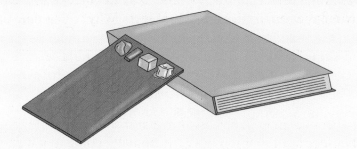

Illustration by Megan Whitaker

5. Note whether or not any of the items begins to slide down the board. If so, measure the height of the book, and note which items began to slide at this height.
6. Continue to increase the height of the stack one book at a time. Each time, check for objects beginning to slide. If an object begins to slide, note which object it was and the height of the books that caused it to slide. Do this until all objects have begun sliding down the board.
7. Next, use the sandpaper to sand down the board. In the end, you want the board to be noticeably smoother than when you started.
8. Repeat the experiment with the sanded side of the board facing up.
9. Clean everything up and put it all away.

What happened in the experiment? Well, if everything went well, you should have noticed that some objects slid down the board sooner than other objects. In addition, you should have seen that the height at which the objects slid down the board changed after the board had been sanded. Why? Well, as soon as you tilted the board, gravity began pulling down on the objects, trying to force them to slide down the board. They did not move initially because of friction. Despite the fact that gravity was pulling them down, friction was fighting gravity, holding them in place. The higher you tilted the board, the more gravity was able to pull on the objects in an attempt to force them to move down the board. When the force of gravity's pull down the incline became stronger than friction, the objects began to slide down the board.

Thus, by tilting the board and waiting for the objects to slide down, you were essentially measuring the strength of the frictional force between the board and each object. Objects that slid down the board when the board was tilted only a little had only a small frictional force holding them in place. Objects that did not slide down the board until it was tilted very high had a large frictional force holding them in place.

What do the results tell you? They should tell you that the strength of the frictional force between two objects depends on the physical characteristics of each object. Think about it. The ice cube, eraser, rock, and block of wood were all resting on the same board. However, they had different frictional forces holding them in place. Thus, the physical characteristics of each of those objects played a role in friction. Of course, the physical characteristics of the board played a role as well. This is demonstrated by the fact that once the board was sanded, the height at which the objects began to slide down changed.

What is friction, then? It is a force that exists whenever two surfaces are touching each other. Where does it come from? Well, the experiment gives you a clue. When you sanded the board, about the only thing you changed was the nature of the board's surface. That changed the frictional force between it and each object. In the same way, each object had a different frictional force with the board because each had a different kind of surface. Thus, the nature of an object's surface fundamentally affects the frictional force it will experience with another object. Why? Examine the figure below.

Illustration by Megan Whitaker

FIGURE 10.3
Why Friction Exists

Suppose a box is on the floor. From experience, we know that if someone were to give the box a quick shove, it might slide across the floor a little, but it would eventually come to a halt. Newton's First Law says that once the box is put in motion by the shove, it should stay in motion until acted on by an outside force. Since the box stops sliding, we know that there must be an outside force. I have already explained that the outside force that stops the box is friction. The question is, "Why does friction exist?" Well, let's picture the box sitting on the floor:

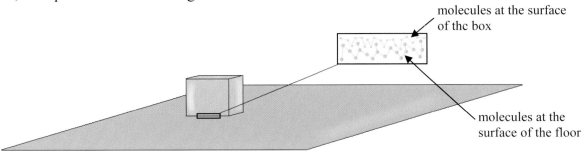

molecules at the surface of the box

molecules at the surface of the floor

From our point of view, the surface of the box and the surface of the floor are both pretty smooth. However, suppose we could magnify a portion of the box and the floor where the two surfaces contact one another. If it were possible to magnify that portion so much that we could see things on the atomic scale, we would see something like what is drawn in the inset picture above. You see, on the atomic scale, there are no really smooth surfaces. All surfaces have grooves and bumps in them. These grooves and bumps determine how close the molecules (or atoms) of one surface can get to the molecules (or atoms) of the other surface. This is important, as these molecules (or atoms) are attracted to one another, and the closer they can get to one another, the more they can attract each other. The more they attract each other, the more they will be able to resist motion, which means the more friction will exist between the surfaces.

You should now see more clearly why friction exists. It exists because on the atomic scale, there is no such thing as a smooth surface. A surface might feel smooth to the touch, but it really is not smooth. On the atomic scale, it is rough. The roughness affects how closely the molecules can get to one another, which affects how much they are attracted to each other. The more they are attracted to one another, the stronger the frictional force.

Now please note that the level of smoothness we can detect with our eyes or our hands does *not* affect friction nearly as much as the level of smoothness at the atomic scale, which is something we can't really detect without the aid of sophisticated equipment. Thus, even though we see the ice cube as being smoother than the rock in the experiment, it is not really possible for us to be sure that the ice cube will have more or less friction with the board than the rock. In the end, we have to look at the objects on the atomic scale to make such determinations.

The experiment, combined with the explanation in the figure, leads us to a definition of friction:

Friction – A force that opposes motion, resulting from the contact of two surfaces

Since the molecules and atoms of one surface are attracted to the molecules and atoms of the other surface, friction will always oppose motion in an attempt to keep the molecules or atoms as close as possible.

Now you can see why Aristotle was fooled in his attempts to understand motion. It is impossible to have motion without surfaces rubbing together. As a result, once motion begins, friction opposes the motion and eventually causes it to stop. Aristotle observed the fact that objects in motion eventually halted, and since he did not know about friction, he insisted that this was because objects "wanted" to stay at rest. Now that we know about friction, we know that Aristotle's idea was wrong and Newton's First Law of Motion is right.

You should have been bothered by something I just said. I said that motion was impossible without surfaces rubbing together. You should have immediately thought, "What about free fall?" After all, in free fall, the object that is falling isn't rubbing up against any other surface is it? Yes, it is! It is rubbing up against the molecules and atoms in the air! Thus, objects in free fall experience friction as well. We already talked about that kind of friction. We called it **air resistance**. Air resistance is the friction experienced by objects traveling through the air. Because a moving object must rub up against molecules and atoms in the air through which it travels, it experiences friction.

ON YOUR OWN

10.4 Look at the situation illustrated in Figure 10.3. Suppose you wanted to push the box across the floor. If the box was filled with something really heavy, would you have to overcome more or less friction compared to a situation in which the box was filled with something light?

10.5 Suppose you were to drop an object from the top of a building and measure its speed the instant before it hits the ground. Suppose further that you did the experiment twice: once on a clear, sunny day and once during a thick fog. Would there be any difference in the speed of the object? If so, on which day would the object be traveling faster?

Newton's Second Law of Motion

Newton's Second Law of Motion allows us to become more familiar with a term we have been using quite a bit: **force**. Although we all have some idea of what "force" means, a physicist has a very specific meaning when using the term "force." That specific meaning comes from Newton's Second Law of Motion.

<u>Newton's Second Law</u> – When an object is acted on by one or more outside forces, the total force is equal to the mass of the object times the resulting acceleration.

In other words, if you push on an object, the amount that it accelerates depends on two things: the mass of the object and the magnitude of the force with which you push. Newton's Second Law is more often expressed with an equation:

$$\text{total force} = (\text{mass}) \cdot (\text{acceleration}) \qquad (10.1)$$

Notice that the equation says "the total force is equal to the mass times the acceleration." This is identical to what the above definition says. Thus, the equation is equivalent to the definition.

What is force, then? Well, a force is essentially a push or a pull exerted on an object in an effort to change that object's velocity. Equation (10.1) tells us that we can calculate force by multiplying mass and acceleration. Let's think about the units that result when we make this multiplication. In physics, we typically work with relatively large things, so mass is usually measured in kilograms. Acceleration, as you recall, has a distance unit over a time unit squared. In metric units, that's usually meters/second^2. When we multiply these two quantities together, we get the unit $\frac{\text{kg} \cdot \text{m}}{\text{sec}^2}$.

This rather complicated unit is often referred to as the **Newton**, in honor of Sir Isaac Newton. This is fitting. Since Newton is one of the most important scientists in the history of physics, he deserves to have a unit that belongs in one of the most important equations in all of physics. This unit is something you'll have to remember:

The <u>Newton</u> is the standard unit of force and is defined as a $\boxed{\dfrac{\text{kg} \cdot \text{m}}{\text{sec}^2}}$

Now, of course, any unit that has a mass unit multiplied by a distance unit divided by a time unit squared would be considered a force unit. Thus, $\boxed{\dfrac{\text{g} \cdot \text{km}}{\text{min}^2}}$ would also be a valid force unit; we just don't use it that often. One force unit you might see occasionally is the "dyne." It is used when dealing with smaller forces, and is equivalent to a $\boxed{\dfrac{\text{g} \cdot \text{cm}}{\text{sec}^2}}$. To give you an idea of how much force is associated with these units, if you were to hold a gallon of water in your hand, it would pull your hand down with a force of about 40 Newtons. On the other hand, when a fly lands on your finger, it pushes your finger down with a force of approximately *1,000 dynes*. Thus, whereas one Newton is a pretty significant force, one dyne is a very, very tiny amount of force.

The only thing left to learn about force is that it is a vector quantity. If you think about this, it should make sense. After all, if you push an object, the direction in which it will begin to accelerate depends on the direction in which you push it. If you push left, the object will accelerate to the left. If you push right, the object will accelerate to the right. Thus, if acceleration is a vector quantity, force must be as well. In fact, any acceleration that occurs as a result of a force must be in the same direction as the force.

We now know about force. It is a vector quantity whose magnitude is usually measured in Newtons. When a force is applied to an object, that object will experience acceleration in the same direction as the applied force. The magnitude of the acceleration depends on both the magnitude of the force and the mass of the object. Massive objects take a lot of force to achieve even a little acceleration. Objects that have little mass need only a little force to achieve a large acceleration. Now that we know what force is, we can use Equation (10.1) in some problems.

EXAMPLE 10.1

A man's car (mass = 1,500 kilograms) has broken down, and he is pushing it to a gas station. Ignoring friction, with what total force (in Newtons) must the man push in order to make the car accelerate 0.03 meters per second squared to the east?

This problem gives the mass of the car and the acceleration. It asks us to calculate the total force. Thus, we use Equation (10.1) to solve the problem.

$$\text{total force} = (\text{mass}) \cdot (\text{acceleration})$$

$$\text{total force} = (1,500 \text{ kg}) \cdot \left(0.03 \ \frac{m}{\sec^2} \right) = 45 \ \frac{kg \cdot m}{\sec^2}$$

Since the final unit is the same as a Newton, we know that we used the correct units in the problem. Since the acceleration is always in the same direction as the force, we know that the man must push with a force of <u>45 Newtons to the east</u>.

If you think about the answer to that last problem, you should be a bit confused. The answer says that the man must push his car with a force of 45 Newtons to the east. Now remember, if you hold a gallon of water in your hand, the force you feel pulling the gallon of water down is 40 Newtons. That's not a lot of force. Thus, this problem tells us that pushing a car is only a bit harder than holding a gallon of water in our hands. That doesn't make much sense, does it?

Why doesn't the answer make any sense? There is a small phrase in the problem that answers this question. The problem says, "Ignoring friction…" That destroys the reality of the problem, doesn't it? After all, friction exists in *all* motion on earth. Thus, it exists in this problem as well. Ignoring friction causes the result of the problem to be rather unrealistic. To solve the problem realistically, then, we must take into account the effects of friction.

How do we do this? Well, to take the effects of friction into account, you need to look back at Newton's Second Law. It says that when multiple forces are applied to an object, the *total force* is equal to mass times acceleration. Thus, if multiple forces are being used, we must figure out what the *total force* is in order to determine the acceleration. Let's go back to the problem of a man pushing his car. Since the man is pushing, he is obviously applying a force. We all know that if he doesn't push hard enough, the car will not move. Why? Because there is friction resisting the motion. Thus, the car will not move until the man applies *more* force than friction can apply.

So what does that tell us? It tells us that when applying a force to an object, the only way we will learn about the acceleration of the object is to look at *all* the forces involved. Study Figure 10.4 to see what I mean.

FIGURE 10.4

Forces Can Be Added or Subtracted When Applied to the Same Object

Illustrations from www.clipart.com

total force = $F_m - F_f$

F_m

F_f

In this figure, the man is pushing his car with a force of F_m. Friction fights that motion with a force of F_f. Since the man's force is opposite that of friction, the total force is the difference between the two. Now let's change the situation a bit. Suppose the man has a (very well trained) dog helping him:

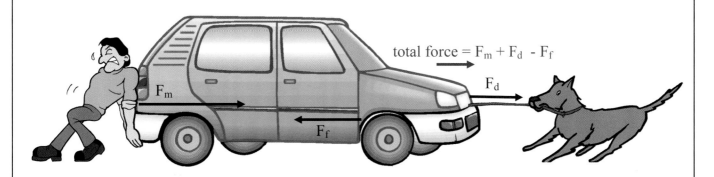

total force = $F_m + F_d - F_f$

F_m

F_d

F_f

Now there is a third force: the force applied by the dog (F_d). Since the dog is pulling the car in the same direction that the man is pushing, their forces add together. The force of friction opposes those forces, though, so it still subtracts.

In the end, then, friction simply subtracts from the force being applied in an attempt to move the car. If the man applies 300 Newtons of force to the car in an easterly direction, and the frictional force is 290 Newtons, the total force will be 10 Newtons to the east. If the dog helps the man by pulling with another 150 Newtons to the east, the total force will be 160 Newtons to the east. Make sure you understand this by studying the example problem.

EXAMPLE 10.2

Illustration copyright GifArt.com

F_w

F_f

In order to clear an area, a construction worker pushes on a large rock (mass = 300 kg) that is in the way. Once he gets the rock moving, it begins to accelerate at 0.12 meters/second^2 to the north. If the construction worker is able to apply 400 Newtons of force, what is the frictional force between the rock and the ground?

This is a problem involving force, mass, and acceleration. We will therefore have to use Equation (10.1). We know the mass of the rock and its acceleration, so we can figure out the total force being applied to the rock:

$$\text{total force} = (\text{mass}) \cdot (\text{acceleration})$$

$$\text{total force} = (300 \text{ kg}) \cdot (0.12 \ \frac{\text{meters}}{\text{second}^2})$$

$$\text{total force} = 36 \text{ Newtons}$$

So the *total* force acting on the rock is 36 Newtons. This total force is made up of the force applied by the construction worker (let's called it "F_w") and the frictional force (F_f) that opposes it (see the drawing on the previous page). Thus:

$$F_w - F_f = 36 \text{ Newtons}$$

We are told that the construction worker exerts a force of 400 Newtons, so this equation becomes:

$$400 \text{ Newtons} - F_f = 36 \text{ Newtons}$$

So what is F_f? Well, we have to ask ourselves, "What number, when subtracted from 400, leaves 36?" If you think about it, F_f must be 364 Newtons, because 400 Newtons – 364 Newtons = 36 Newtons. What is its direction? Well, the motion is north, and friction always opposes motion. Thus, the direction of the frictional force must be south. Therefore, the answer is <u>364 Newtons to the south</u>.

Notice the reasoning I used to solve this problem. Since I was given the mass and the acceleration, I knew that I could calculate the total force using Equation (10.1). I realized that this total force was made up of 2 components: the force applied to the rock by the construction worker *and* the force applied to the rock by friction. Since these two forces opposed each other, the total force was the construction worker's force *minus* the frictional force. Since the problem told me the construction worker's force, I just had to figure out what number, when subtracted from the construction worker's force, would equal the total force that I calculated from Equation (10.1).

Static and Kinetic Friction

Have you ever noticed that it is harder to get something moving than to keep it moving? For example, if you are trying to push a heavy box across the floor, it is very hard to get the box moving. You have to push really hard. As soon as the box starts moving, however, you suddenly do not have to push as hard, and the box will continue to slide. Why is that? Well, physicists usually split friction up into two classes: **kinetic** (kuh net' ik) **friction** and **static friction**.

<u>Kinetic friction</u> – Friction that opposes motion once the motion has already started

<u>Static friction</u> – Friction that opposes the initiation of motion

It turns out that static friction is generally greater than kinetic friction. Thus, before the box starts moving, you are fighting static friction. This is a large force, so you must, in turn, apply a large force so as to overcome it. Once the box gets moving, however, you are fighting kinetic friction, which is a smaller force.

In the end, then, when something is stationary relative to the surface upon which it sits, the frictional force (static friction) is large, and the object is hard to move. Once the object begins moving relative to the surface, the frictional force (kinetic friction) is smaller. Thus, it is easier to keep moving. Of course, the most important question is, "*Why* is static friction generally greater than kinetic friction?"

Actually, if you think about why friction exists, the explanation is really pretty simple. Consider Figure 10.3 again. Suppose the box was sitting still on a floor. In order to get it moving at all, you would have to apply enough force to overcome the force with which the molecules of the box and floor attract one another. Since the box has been sitting there, the bumps and grooves have "settled" a little, nestling the molecules close together. This makes the force with which the molecules attract one another large. Once the box gets going, however, the bumps and grooves really don't have a chance to settle into each other, because they move past each other before they have a chance to line up well. As a result, the molecules do not interact as strongly, and they can't attract each other with as strong a force as they did when the box was stationary. To see the practical effect of all this, study the following example.

EXAMPLE 10.3

Illustration copyright GifArt.com

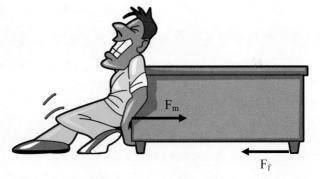

A man needs to push a desk (mass = 100 kg) across the floor. The static frictional force can resist motion with as much as 196 Newtons of force, while the kinetic frictional force is only 110 Newtons. How much force is necessary to get the desk moving? If the desk accelerates at 1.0 meters per second^2 to the west when the force is applied, how much force did the man use?

In order to get the desk moving, the man must apply more force than what static frictional force is capable of supplying. Thus, <u>the man must apply a little more than 196 Newtons of force to get the desk moving</u>.

The second part of the problem asks us to calculate the actual force applied by the man, given the acceleration. Since we know the desk's mass and acceleration, we can use Equation (10.1) to determine the total force acting on the desk:

$$\text{total force} = (\text{mass}) \cdot (\text{acceleration})$$

$$\text{total force} = (100 \text{ kg}) \cdot (1.0 \, \frac{\text{meters}}{\text{second}^2})$$

$$\text{total force} = 100 \text{ Newtons}$$

So the *total* force acting on the desk is 100 Newtons. This total force is made up of two components: the force the man applies (F_m) and friction (F_f). Since friction opposes motion, these two forces fight one another. Thus, the forces subtract:

$$F_m - F_f = 100 \text{ Newtons}$$

The problem tells us the frictional force. However, it gives us both the static and the kinetic frictional force. Which do we use here? Well, the desk is moving now, so we use the kinetic frictional force. Thus, we can put the kinetic frictional force into our equation:

$$F_m - 110 \text{ Newtons} = 100 \text{ Newtons}$$

To figure out F_m, then, we must think about what number will give us 100 Newtons after 110 Newtons is subtracted from it. Well, if $F_m = 210$ Newtons, we would have 210 Newtons – 110 Newtons, which equals 100 Newtons.

We know, then, that the man used a force that had a strength of 210 Newtons. What is its direction? Well, the desk is accelerating west, so that must be the direction of the man's force. In the end, then, the man applied a force of 210 Newtons to the west.

ON YOUR OWN

10.6 A box (mass = 15 kg) is given an initial shove and allowed to slide across the floor with no person pushing on it. If the box slides north and experiences an acceleration of 1.1 meters per second^2 to the *south*, what is the kinetic frictional force between the box and the floor?

10.7 Suppose someone wanted to keep the box in problem 10.6 moving at a constant velocity. What force must be applied in order to accomplish this feat?

10.8 A child wants to slide a block (mass = 10 kg) to the east. Static friction between the block and the floor is capable of resisting motion with a force of 30 Newtons west, while the kinetic frictional force is 20 Newtons west. What force must the child exert in order to get the block moving? If the block accelerates at 1.5 m/sec^2 east as a result of the child's force, what was the actual force used?

Newton's Third Law of Motion

Well, I've discussed two of Newton's laws of motion, so there is only one more to go. It can be stated as follows:

Newton's Third Law – For every action, there is an equal and opposite reaction.

You've probably heard that before. However, I need to make sure that you understand exactly what it means. Perform the following experiment to find out:

EXPERIMENT 10.4
Newton's Third Law

Supplies:

- A plastic, 2-liter bottle (like the kind soda pop comes in)
- A stopper that fits the bottle (It could be rubber or cork, but you cannot use the screw-on cap. It has to be something that plugs up the opening of the bottle but can be pushed out by a pressure buildup inside the bottle. Modeling clay can work as well. You could also try a large wad of gum, as long as the gum has dried out and has the texture of firm rubber.)
- A cup of vinegar
- Two teaspoons of baking soda
- Aluminum foil
- Four pencils
- Eye protection such as safety goggles or safety glasses

Introduction: Newton's Third Law of Motion states that for every action there is an equal and opposite reaction. You will observe this law at work and, as a result, understand its meaning. **You may want to do this experiment outside, because it is loud and messy!**

Procedure

1. Pour about a cup of vinegar into the 2-liter bottle.
2. Put the four pencils on the ground parallel to each other and about 2 inches apart. Lay the bottle on its side on top of the pencils. Do this carefully so that none of the vinegar spills out.
3. Take the aluminum foil and make a long, thin trough. The trough should be thin enough to fit inside the mouth of the bottle.
4. Once you have made the trough, fill it with two teaspoons of baking soda.
5. Gently push the trough into the bottle, so that it floats on top of the vinegar. Try to spill as little baking soda as possible.
6. **Be careful to stay on the side of the bottle. You should not be in front of or behind it!** Carefully use the stopper to plug up the mouth of the bottle.
7. **Staying to one side of the bottle**, roll the bottle to the side, allowing the baking soda to mix with the vinegar. For best results, make sure the bottle stays on the pencils.
8. Stand away to one side of the bottle. **BE SURE TO STAY TO ONE SIDE OF THE BOTTLE. DO NOT GET IN FRONT OF OR BEHIND IT!** Note what happens.

What happened in the experiment? When the baking soda mixed with the vinegar, a chemical reaction took place. The sodium bicarbonate in the baking soda reacted with the acetic acid in the vinegar. One of the products of that reaction is carbon dioxide, which is a gas. As the carbon dioxide gas formed, it filled up the bottle. Eventually, so much gas was formed that the bottle became pressurized. This exerted an enormous force on the stopper. Eventually, that force was great enough to push the stopper right out of the bottle. What happened as a result? The bottle started moving in the opposite direction.

What you saw was Newton's Third Law in action. The gas exerted a force (an action) on the stopper. In response, the stopper exerted a force (a reaction) on the gas. Newton's Third Law states that these two forces are equal in strength but opposite in direction. Thus, the gas pushed the stopper in one direction, and the stopper pushed the gas with the same strength, but in the other direction. As a result, the stopper flew off in one direction and the bottle (which contained the gas) flew off in the opposite direction.

The "action" in Newton's Third Law of Motion really refers to a force. Thus, Newton's Third Law says that every time a force is applied to an object, an equal but opposite force is applied by that object to something else. In your experiment, the gas applied a force to the stopper. In response, the stopper applied an equal but opposite force to the gas. Just to make sure you understand this principle, let me give you one more example in the form of a figure.

FIGURE 10.5

A Young Lady on a Trampoline

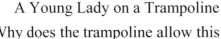
Image provided by Dreamstime.com

Why does the trampoline allow this young lady to travel upward against the pull of gravity? Well, when she jumps on the trampoline, she exerts a force on it. If you were watching that happen, you would see the trampoline's surface bend in response to the force. What does Newton's Third Law say will happen as a result? It says that the trampoline will exert an equal but opposite force on her. You know this happens, because once she hits the trampoline, she slows down, stops, and then starts moving up into the air. Thus, her velocity changes. According to Newton's First Law of Motion, that cannot happen unless a force acts on her. What force was that? It was the equal and opposite force demanded by Newton's Third Law. In other words, she exerted a force on the trampoline (causing the surface to bow), and the trampoline exerted a force right back on her (causing her to accelerate in a different direction). The force the trampoline exerted on her was equal in strength to the force she exerted on the trampoline.

It is very important to realize that the equal and opposite forces talked about in Newton's Third Law do not act on the *same* object. If that were the case, there would never be any acceleration. After all, if equal and opposite forces act on the same object, they cancel each other out, and the resulting force is zero. Instead, the equal and opposite forces discussed in Newton's Third Law affect *different* objects. In the experiment, the gas exerted a force on the stopper. The equal and opposite force was exerted not on the stopper, but on the gas. Thus, the forces acted on two completely different objects. As a result, both objects ended up moving. In the trampoline, the young lady exerted a force on the trampoline, causing it to bend. The trampoline then exerted an equal and opposite force on her, accelerating her upward. Once again, the two forces worked on two *different* things. One force worked on the trampoline, the other on the young lady. Both things moved, since the forces did not cancel, because they acted on different things.

Newton's Third Law of Motion explains a lot of things that happen to us. For example, have you ever fired a gun? When you fire a gun, it "kicks" back toward you. People who shoot guns for the first time are often surprised by this effect. In fact, there have been cases in which novices were injured because they fired a gun and were not expecting the "kick." What causes the gun's "kick?" Well, when you pull the trigger, you cause a chemical reaction to take place in the chamber. That reaction produces a lot of heat and gas. The gas is under pressure, so it exerts a force on the bullet, pushing the bullet out at an amazing speed. In response, the bullet pushes back against the gas in the gun. That's what causes the "kick."

Newton's Third Law of Motion also explains how rockets fly. When a rocket or missile is launched, its fuel begins burning. As the fuel burns, it produces hot gas in great volumes. The pressure caused by the gas being formed pushes the gas out of the rocket. In response, the gas being pushed out pushes back on the rocket, causing the rocket to move in the opposite direction. This force is often called the **thrust** of the rocket. Thus, a rocket flies because gases are constantly being shoved out of the nozzles at its bottom. The equal and opposite force required by Newton's Third Law pushes the rocket in the opposite direction.

FIGURE 10.6
Launching a Rocket

Photo courtesy of NASA

The gases push back on the rocket, causing it to launch.

The gases produced in the rocket's engines are pushed out of the rocket.

Make sure you really understand Newton's Third Law of Motion by answering the following "On Your Own" problems.

ON YOUR OWN

10.9 A tennis player hits a ball with her racket. The ball was traveling towards the player but, once she hits it with the racket, the ball begins traveling in the opposite direction. During the hit, the strings on the racket bow. What evidence do you have that the racket exerted a force on the ball? What applied the equal and opposite reaction as required by Newton's Third Law, and where was the force applied? What evidence do you have for this force?

10.10 An ice skater stands on the ice in his skates. He is holding a ball. Assuming that friction is so small it can be ignored, what will happen to the ice skater if he suddenly throws the ball hard to the west?

In this module, you learned about the laws that govern motion. Despite the fact that they were discovered long ago, they still guide physics as the main laws that govern how objects move! Notice that each law deals with force. Although we intuitively know what a force is, in the next module you will learn about where forces come from.

ANSWERS TO THE "ON YOUR OWN" PROBLEMS

10.1 <u>The cowboy will fall forward off the horse</u>. While the horse is galloping, the cowboy and the horse have the same velocity. When the horse suddenly stops, the only force that can stop the cowboy is the friction between him and the saddle. If the horse stops quickly enough, friction will not have time to do this. As a result, the cowboy will continue to travel at the velocity he had, which is much faster than the horse's velocity once the horse has stopped. Thus, the cowboy falls forward, right over the horse.

This actually happened to the famous actor Christopher Reeve. In 1995, he was in an equestrian (horse riding) competition and was making his horse jump over some fences. The horse was running toward one fence at a quick pace and, for no apparent reason, stopped dead in its tracks. Mr. Reeve fell forward off the horse and landed head-first on the fence. This caused a spinal cord injury that left him a quadriplegic. Mr. Reeve died on October 10, 2004.

10.2 Before the truck hits, the passengers in the car are traveling with the car at 30 miles per hour. When the truck comes up from behind and hits the car, it will push the car forward, accelerating the car. Thus, the car will begin traveling faster than 30 miles per hour. The passengers, however, are still traveling at 30 miles per hour, so they will be <u>flung backward</u> in their seats until the backs of their seats apply enough force to accelerate them to the same velocity as the car.

10.3 The bomb should be dropped from <u>point a</u>. Remember, the bomb has been traveling with the plane. Thus, it has the same velocity as the plane. When it is dropped, it will still have that velocity, because no outside force (other than air resistance, which we will ignore) pushes against it. Since it takes time for the bomb to fall, if the bomb were dropped at point b, it would pass by the factory, being carried on by its initial velocity. If the bomb is dropped at point a, however, the bomb will continue to approach the factory as it falls. If the bomber times it right, the bomb will hit the factory by the time it reaches the ground.

10.4 You would have to overcome <u>more friction</u> if the box was heavier. Think about it: If the box was heavier, it could push down harder on the floor, bringing its molecules closer to the molecules in the floor. This would increase the amount they are attracted to one another, which would increase the friction experienced.

Interestingly enough, the weight of each object was not a factor in Experiment 10.3. This is because gravity was being used to move the objects, and the force that gravity could apply in the experiment was affected by the weight of each object. In the end, the heavier the object, the greater the force being applied to the object by gravity. This exactly counteracted the fact that the heavier the object, the more friction it experienced. Thus, I *constructed* the experiment so that the weight of each object was not a factor. In general, however, the heavier the object, the more friction it will experience with a surface upon which it rests.

10.5 Remember from your study of weather that fog is the result of water condensing on cloud condensation nuclei close to the ground. This makes the air thicker. Thus, the air resistance would be greater on a foggy day than on a clear, sunny day. Since air resistance is larger, the final velocity will be smaller on the foggy day. So, <u>yes, there would be a difference, and the object would be traveling faster on the clear, sunny day</u>.

10.6 Since the box is not being pushed, the only force acting on it is friction. Thus, the acceleration is due completely to friction. Now remember, the word "acceleration" does not mean "speeding up." It means "a change in velocity." If you look at the problem, you will see that the direction of the velocity is north, and the acceleration is south. Thus, the acceleration is opposite to the velocity, which means the box is slowing down. That should make sense, since friction opposes motion.

We have the mass and the acceleration, so we can calculate the total force the box experiences:

$$\text{total force} = (\text{mass}) \cdot (\text{acceleration})$$

$$\text{total force} = (15 \text{ kg}) \cdot (1.1 \frac{\text{meters}}{\text{second}^2})$$

$$\text{total force} = 16.5 \text{ Newtons}$$

Since there is nothing pushing on the box, the total force is composed of only one thing: friction. Thus, this is the strength of the frictional force. Since the box is moving, we also know this is the kinetic frictional force, which is what the problem wanted. The problem tells us that the box is moving north, so the direction of the force is south, since friction opposes motion. This should make sense, as the acceleration is south. Thus, the kinetic frictional force is <u>16.5 Newtons south</u>.

10.7 The goal is to keep the box moving at a constant velocity. What does that tell us about acceleration? When the velocity is *constant*, there is *no change*. This means that acceleration (which is the *change in* velocity) must be zero. Thus, the box must have *zero* acceleration. How much total force leads to an acceleration of zero? We can answer that question with Equation (10.1):

$$\text{total force} = (\text{mass}) \cdot (\text{acceleration})$$

$$\text{total force} = (15 \text{ kg}) \cdot (0 \frac{\text{meters}}{\text{second}^2})$$

$$\text{total force} = 0 \text{ Newtons}$$

The total force on the box, then, must be zero. What is the total force? Since a force must be applied to the box, we will call it "F_a." Friction (F_f) opposes that force, so the total force is $F_a - F_f$. Thus, $F_a - F_f$ must equal zero. We know from the previous problem that friction is applying a force of 16.5 Newtons against the motion, so $F_f = 16.5$ Newtons. To get a total force of zero, then, the applied force must be 16.5 Newtons as well. In what direction will the force go? It must be in the same direction that the box is moving, which the previous problem said was north. Thus, <u>a force of 16.5 Newtons north must be applied</u>. This will counteract friction, allowing the box to move at a constant velocity.

10.8 To get the block moving, the child must overcome static friction, which is resisting motion. Since static friction can resist with a force of 30 Newtons west, the child <u>must exert a force of slightly more than 30 Newtons east</u>.

To answer the second part of the question, we need to determine the total force on the block. Since we know the mass and acceleration, we can calculate the total force with Equation (10.1):

$$\text{total force} = (\text{mass}) \cdot (\text{acceleration})$$

$$\text{total force} = (10\,\text{kg}) \cdot (1.5\,\frac{\text{meters}}{\text{second}^2})$$

$$\text{total force} = 15\,\text{Newtons}$$

Now remember, this is the *total* force to which the block is subjected. It is the result of *two* forces: the force the child uses (F_c) and the frictional force (F_f). Since friction opposes motion, the total force is the difference between the two:

$$F_c - F_f = 15\,\text{Newtons}$$

Since the block is moving, the frictional force will be the kinetic frictional force, which is given as 20 Newtons west. Thus, $F_f = 20$ Newtons.

$$F_c - 20\,\text{Newtons} = 15\,\text{Newtons}$$

To figure out the force the child uses, then, we need to figure out what number will leave 15 Newtons once 20 Newtons has been subtracted away. Well, if $F_c = 35$ Newtons, there will be 15 Newtons left after 20 Newtons have been subtracted. The child, therefore, is exerting a force with a strength of 35 Newtons. Its direction is east, since that's the direction the child wants the block to move. Thus, the force is 35 Newtons east.

10.9 We know that the racket exerted a force on the ball because the ball's velocity changed. The ball had to slow down, stop, and then start moving in a new direction. This is a change in velocity, which means there was acceleration, which means there was a force. The equal and opposite force demanded by Newton's Third Law of Motion was applied by the ball on the racket. We know that the ball exerted a force on the racket because the strings on the racket bowed.

10.10 If the ice skater throws the ball, he must exert a force on it. In compliance with Newton's Third Law of Motion, the ball will apply an equal and opposite force on the skater. Since there is no friction, that force will cause the skater to accelerate. Thus, the skater will begin to move in the opposite direction as compared to the ball. You do not normally get shoved backward when you throw a ball because the force does not overcome the friction between you and the ground. Thus, the ball does exert a force on you, but you don't notice it because friction resists the force.

STUDY GUIDE FOR MODULE #10

1. Define the following terms:

a. Inertia
b. Friction
c. Kinetic friction
d. Static friction

2. State Newton's three laws of motion.

3. In space, there is almost no air, so there is virtually no friction. If an astronaut throws a ball in space with an initial velocity of 3.0 meters per second to the west, what will the ball's velocity be in a year? Assume there are no nearby planets.

4. A boy is running north with a beanbag in his hands. He passes a tree and at the moment he is beside the tree, he drops the beanbag. Will the beanbag land next to the tree? If not, will it be north or south of the tree?

5. Suppose the situation in question #4 is now changed. The boy is running, but now his friend stands beside the tree with the beanbag. As the boy passes, he barely taps the beanbag, causing it to fall out of his friend's hands. Will the beanbag land next to the tree? If not, will it be north or south of the tree?

6. A busy shopper is driving down the road. Many boxes lie piled on the back seat of the car – evidence of shopping activity. Suddenly, the shopper must hit the brakes to avoid a collision. Will the boxes be slammed farther back into the back seat, or will they slam into the front seat where the driver can feel them?

7. When roads get wet, they can get slick. Obviously, then, the friction between a car's tires and the road decreases when the road is wet. Why?

8. In order to slide a refrigerator across the floor, a man must exert an enormous amount of force. Once it is moving, however, the man need not exert nearly as much force to keep it moving. Why?

9. A child is pushing her toy across the room with a constant velocity to the east. If the static friction between this toy and the floor is 15 Newtons, while the kinetic friction is 10 Newtons, what force is the child exerting?

10. A father is trying to teach his child to ice skate. As the child stands still, the father pushes him forward with an acceleration of 2.0 meters per second^2 north. If the child's mass is 20 kilograms, what is the force with which the father is pushing? (Since they are on ice, assume you can ignore friction.)

11. In order to get a 15-kilogram object moving to the west, a force of more than 25 Newtons must be exerted. Once it is moving, however, a force of only 20 Newtons accelerates the object at 0.1 meters per second^2 to the west. What is the force that static friction can exert on the object? What is the force of kinetic friction?

12. Static friction can exert a force of up to 700 Newtons on a 500-kilogram box of bricks. The kinetic frictional force is only 220 Newtons. How many Newtons of force must a worker exert to get the box moving? What force must the worker exert to accelerate the box at 0.1 meters per second^2 to the south?

13. In order to shove a rock out of the way, a gardener gets it moving by exerting just slightly more than 100 Newtons of force. To keep it moving at a constant velocity eastward, however, the gardener needs only to exert a 45-Newton force to the east. What are the static and kinetic frictional forces between the rock and the ground?

14. Two men are trying to push a 710-kg rock. The first exerts a force of 156 Newtons east and the second exerts a force of 220 Newtons east. The rock accelerates at 0.20 meters per second^2 to the east. What is the kinetic frictional force between the rock and the ground?

15. A child pushes against a large doghouse, trying to move it. The doghouse remains stubbornly unmoved. What exerts the equal and opposite force which Newton's Third Law of Motion says *must* happen in response to the child's push? What is that force exerted on?

16. In a baseball game, a player catches a fast-moving ball. The ball stops in the player's hand. What evidence tells you that the player exerted a force on the ball? What exerts the equal and opposite force required by Newton's Third Law? What evidence does the player have for this force?

17. A man leans up against a wall with a force of 20 Newtons to the east. What is the force exerted by the wall on the man?

Cartoon by Speartoons

MODULE #11: The Forces in Creation - Part 1

Introduction

In the previous module I talked a lot about force. Indeed, the concept of force is integral to the physics of motion. What is force, however? It's easy to say that when you push on something, you exert a force. That's true, but there are many other ways that force is exerted in creation. When you drop a ball, it accelerates downward. Since the ball accelerates, it must be experiencing a force – the force of gravity. But what is gravity? In this module, you will hopefully find out. Along the way, you will learn about the other forces that exist in creation.

The Four Fundamental Forces of Creation

Believe it or not, physicists think that there are only four different kinds of force in creation: the **gravitational force**, the **electromagnetic force**, the **weak force**, and the **strong force**. These forces are called "fundamental" forces, because all forces in creation can be traced back to one of them. I am going to discuss each of these forces in detail, but first I want to give you a brief overview of them all.

The gravitational force is the easiest one to recognize. When you drop a ball, it accelerates toward the earth because the gravitational force attracts the ball to the earth. The moon orbits the earth because the moon and the earth are attracted to one another by the gravitational force that exists between them. In fact, any two objects that have mass are attracted to one another via the gravitational force. Of the four forces in creation, this is the weakest. In addition, it is always an attractive force.

The electromagnetic force exists between particles with electrical charge. Unlike the gravitational force, the electromagnetic force can be either attractive or repulsive, depending on the charge of the objects involved. Two positively charged objects, for example, repel each other, as do two negatively charged objects. A positively charged object and a negatively charged object, however, attract one another.

The weak force governs certain radioactive processes in atoms. It is, by far, the hardest of the four forces to comprehend. Physicists have used a variety of mathematical models and experimental results to show that the electromagnetic force and the weak force are, in fact, different facets of the same force. Thus, scientists have actually combined the two names and called this force the **electroweak force**. In reality, then, there are only three fundamental forces in creation. In this course, however, we will discuss the electromagnetic force and the weak force separately, as the mathematics required to understand how they are the same is rather intense!

The strong force is responsible for holding the center of the atom (called the **nucleus**) together. In a later module, I will talk more about this force and the structure of the atom. For now, you just need to know that it is the strongest force in creation. Although this force is strong, its range is very, very small. Because its range is so small, it only applies to the particles found in an atom's nucleus.

The Gravitational Force

As I mentioned before, the gravitational force is the easiest of the three fundamental forces to recognize. This is mostly because we experience gravity every day. Although easy to recognize, the gravitational force is surprisingly hard to truly understand. Even today, scientists are not sure exactly what *causes* the gravitational force. We have two major theories that try to explain what gravity is, but we really do not know which (if either) is correct. There are even those who say that *both* theories are correct to some extent! Needless to say, we still have a *lot* to learn about this force!

Even though we still have a lot to learn about gravity, we have come a long way in understanding this perplexing force. At one time, scientists did not even know that the gravitational force that causes a ball to fall to the earth is the same as the force that holds the planets in orbit around the sun. It took the brilliance of Sir Isaac Newton (surprise!) to show that gravity is a universal force that applies to small things near the earth's surface as well as large things such as planets.

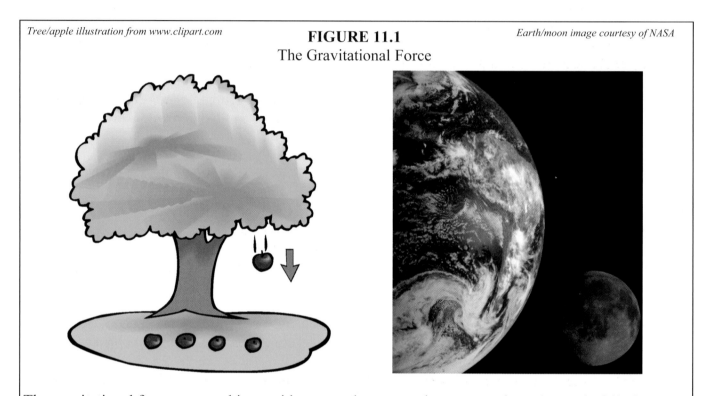

Tree/apple illustration from www.clipart.com   **FIGURE 11.1**   *Earth/moon image courtesy of NASA*
The Gravitational Force

The gravitational force causes objects with mass to be attracted to one another. An apple falls from a tree (left) because it is attracted to the earth. The moon stays in its orbit around the earth (right) because the gravitational force attracts it to the earth.

In fact, Newton developed an equation (which we call the **Universal Law of Gravitation**) that allows physicists to calculate the strength of the gravitational force between two objects. Although that particular equation is beyond the scope of this course, it leads to three general principles I want you to know:

1. **All objects with mass are attracted to one another by the gravitational force.**

2. **The gravitational force between two masses is directly proportional to the mass of each object.**

3. **The gravitational force between two masses is inversely proportional to the square of the distance between those two objects.**

What do these principles mean? Well, the first principle tells us that all matter is attracted to all other matter. If you look around the room you are in, every object you see is attracted to every other object that you see. In addition, they are all attracted to the earth. The earth is attracted to the sun, etc., etc. This is why we call Newton's law the "Universal" Law of Gravitation. It is called "universal" because it applies to anything in the universe that has mass.

The second principle tells us that the strength of the gravitational force between two objects increases as the mass of either object increases. Suppose I have two objects, and I measure the gravitational attraction that exists between them. Then, suppose I replace one of those objects with an object that is twice as massive. The new gravitational attraction I measure will be twice as large as the one I had previously measured. If I then replaced the other object with one that is twice as massive, the gravitational attraction would get twice as large again. Compared to my first measurement, then, this gravitational attraction would be four times as large. So whatever factor by which the mass of each object changes, the gravitational force changes by that same factor.

The final principle says that the gravitational force is *inversely proportional* to the *square* of the distance between the objects. The term "inversely proportional" means that when the distance is big, the force is small. Conversely, when the distance is small, the force is big. This effect is so strong, however, that the gravitational force between two objects changes as the *square* of the distance between the objects. In other words, suppose I took two objects and measured the gravitational force that exists between them. Then, suppose I pulled the objects away from each other so that the distance between them doubled. If I were to then measure the gravitational force between them, I would see that it decreased by a factor of 4 (which is 2 squared). Thus, when the distance between two objects increases by a given factor, the gravitational force decreases by the square of that factor. Alternatively, when the distance between two objects decreases by some factor, the gravitational force increases by the square of that factor.

Now let me make sure you understand what I mean when I say "factor." When a mathematician multiplies or divides something by a number, we can call that number a "factor." Thus, suppose I multiplied 8 by 5. I could say that the result (40) is a factor of five larger than the original number (8). If I took that same number (8) and divided by 4, the result would be 2. I could therefore say that 2 is a factor of 4 lower than 8. In the end, then, when I say "smaller by a factor of 4," I mean "divided by 4." When I say "larger by a factor of 5," I mean "multiplied by 5." Let me put all of this together for you in a couple of example problems.

EXAMPLE 11.1

The gravitational force between two objects separated by a distance of 3 centimeters is measured. The objects are then brought closer together so that the distance between them is only 1 centimeter. What is the gravitational attraction now compared to when it was first measured?

What is the difference between the two situations described in the example? Well, the distance decreased from 3 centimeters to 1 centimeter. Now remember, gravitational force is proportional to the *factor* by which the distance changes. In other words, it depends on what the distance is multiplied or divided by. So we first need to decide what I must multiply or divide the first distance by in order to get the second distance. In this case, then, the first distance was *divided by 3*. Thus, the distance *decreases* by a factor of 3. Since Newton says that the gravitational force is inversely proportional to the square of the distance between the masses, we know that the gravitational force is *increased* when the distance is decreased. The distance between the objects was divided by 3, and 3 squared is 9. Thus, the new gravitational force will be nine times larger than it was previously.

The gravitational force between two objects separated by a distance of 5 centimeters is measured. Both objects are then replaced. The first object is replaced with one that has half of its mass, and the second object is replaced by one that has eight times its mass. What is the gravitational attraction now compared to when it was first measured?

Newton says that the gravitational force between two objects is directly proportional to the mass of the objects. Thus, when the first object is replaced with one that has half its mass, the gravitational force is cut in half as well. When the second is replaced with an object that has eight times more mass, the gravitational force is increased by a factor of 8. In total, then, the gravitational force was first cut in half and then that value was multiplied by 8. This leads to a gravitational force that is four times larger than the original force (because ½ x 8 = 4).

Make sure you really understand this by doing some "On Your Own" problems.

ON YOUR OWN

11.1 The gravitational force between two objects (mass$_1$ = 10 kg, mass$_2$ = 6 kg) is measured when the objects are 10 centimeters apart. If the 10 kg mass is replaced with a 20 kg mass, and the 6 kg mass is replaced with a 3 kg mass, how does the new gravitational force compare to the first one that was measured?

11.2 The gravitational force between two objects (mass$_1$ = 1 kg, mass$_2$ = 2 kg) is measured when the objects are 10 centimeters apart. The objects are then replaced with two different ones (mass$_1$ = 4 kg, mass$_2$ = 1 kg), and the distance is decreased to 5 centimeters. How does the new gravitational attraction compare to the first one that was measured?

There are a couple of things you must keep in mind when you think about the gravitational force. Remember, it is the weakest of all forces. When you place two wooden blocks on the table, they are attracted to one another by the gravitational force. Why don't they just move toward each other? Well, the gravitational force is so weak that it cannot even overcome the friction that exists between the blocks and the table. As a result, the blocks stay stationary, not because they aren't attracted to one another, but because the attraction is so weak that it cannot overcome static friction. To give you some idea of how weak the gravitational attraction is, think about the weight of a fly that lands on your hand. The weight is so small that you don't really feel it. Well, that weight is more than *70,000 times larger* than the gravitational attraction of two 1-pound blocks placed 1 centimeter away from each other!

Now although the gravitational force between objects in our everyday experience is so weak that it can be neglected, when the mass of either object is huge, the gravitational force can become considerable. For example, when you drop a ball, the gravitational force that makes it fall comes from the attraction between the ball and the earth. The mass of the ball is rather small, but the mass of the earth is *really* large. Thus, the gravitational attraction between the ball and the earth is large because the mass of the earth is so large. The gravitational force is a weak force, but it can become substantial when one (or both) of the objects involved has a really large mass.

There is one more thing you need to realize about the gravitational force. Think about the situation in which you are dropping a ball. The ball falls because it is attracted to the earth by the gravitational force. Thus, the earth applies a gravitational force to the ball, pulling it toward the earth. What does Newton's Third Law of Motion say? It says that whenever a force is applied, an equal and opposite force must be applied in reaction. What is that equal and opposite force here? Well, if the *earth* applies a gravitational force on the *ball*, the *ball* must apply an equal but opposite force on the *earth*! Thus, the ball is attracted to the earth, but at the same time, the earth is attracted to the ball.

Wait a minute. Because the earth applies a force on the ball, the ball moves toward the earth (it falls). If the ball applies an equal but opposite force on the earth, what does the earth do? *It moves toward the ball*. In other words, when you drop a ball, it falls to the earth. Because of Newton's Third Law of Motion, however, at the same time, *the earth rises toward the ball*! That statement seems rather crazy, but it is true. When an object falls toward the earth, the earth also rises toward the object.

How can we make any sense of this? When we drop a ball, we don't feel the earth accelerating toward the ball. Why? Well, think of Newton's Second Law of Motion. It says that the force applied to an object equals the object's mass times the resulting acceleration. The force that the ball applies to the earth is *equal* to the force that the earth applies to the ball. Since the ball's mass is rather small, the acceleration that results from the force applied by the earth is rather large. When the ball applies that same force to the earth, however, the resulting acceleration is really tiny, because the earth's mass is so large. Thus, the only reason we don't notice the earth accelerating upward to meet the ball is because Newton's Second Law of Motion says that the same force will accelerate objects of small mass much more than objects of large mass. As a result, the acceleration of the earth is so tiny that it isn't noticeable, but the acceleration of the ball is quite noticeable.

The important point for you to understand from all this is that two objects exert *equal* gravitational forces on each other, as illustrated in the figure below.

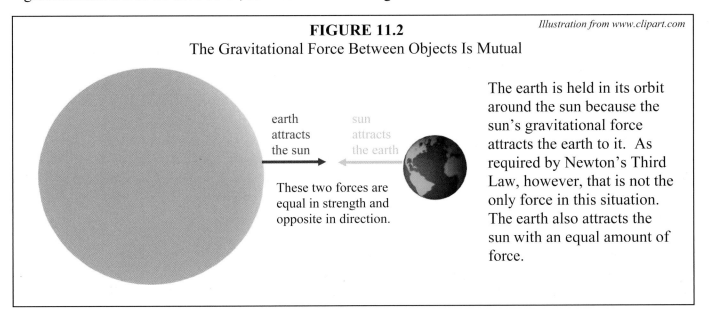

FIGURE 11.2
The Gravitational Force Between Objects Is Mutual

Illustration from www.clipart.com

earth attracts the sun

sun attracts the earth

These two forces are equal in strength and opposite in direction.

The earth is held in its orbit around the sun because the sun's gravitational force attracts the earth to it. As required by Newton's Third Law, however, that is not the only force in this situation. The earth also attracts the sun with an equal amount of force.

Force and Circular Motion

Now that you know a bit about the gravitational force itself, you need to see how the gravitational force acts throughout God's creation. You know, of course, that the gravitational force causes objects near the surface of the earth to fall. That is one way in which the gravitational force acts in creation. I have already covered that extensively in Module #9, where I concentrated on the motion of free fall. Another way that the gravitational force acts is to hold the planets and their moons in an orderly arrangement we call the **solar system**. I will concentrate on that in an upcoming section of this module.

Before you can learn about how the gravitational force works in our solar system, however, you must first learn about how objects move in circles. To learn about this important concept, perform the following experiment.

EXPERIMENT 11.1
Force and Circular Motion

Supplies:
- A mechanical pen
- A black marker
- Thin string or thread (preferably white)
- Five metal washers, all the same size
- Stopwatch
- Eye protection such as goggles or safety glasses
- Scissors

Introduction: Circular motion requires a special kind of force. In this experiment, you will learn a few things about that force and its properties.

Procedure:

1. Set up your experimental device by following these instructions:

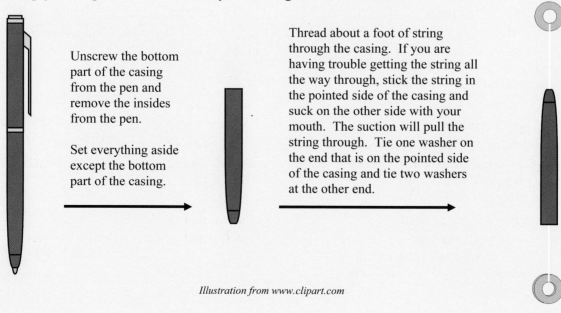

Unscrew the bottom part of the casing from the pen and remove the insides from the pen.

Set everything aside except the bottom part of the casing.

Thread about a foot of string through the casing. If you are having trouble getting the string all the way through, stick the string in the pointed side of the casing and suck on the other side with your mouth. The suction will pull the string through. Tie one washer on the end that is on the pointed side of the casing and tie two washers at the other end.

Illustration from www.clipart.com

2. Lay your device on the table and pull the string so that about 6 inches of string comes out the pointed side of the casing. Next, use your marker to make a strong black mark all around the string, right where it comes out the *other side* of the casing. The mark needs to be easy to see.

Illustration from www.clipart.com   make mark here   6 inches

3. Hold the device by grasping the pen. Make sure that the pointed end of the pen points up. Begin twirling the single washer on the end so that it moves in a circle.
4. Get used to how this thing operates. Notice that as you twirl the washer faster, the string pulls out the end, causing the circle that the washer sweeps out to become larger. If you slow the twirling down, the string goes the other way, making the circle smaller.
5. Adjust the rate you are twirling until the black mark you made is visible right at the bottom of the pen casing. This tells you that there are 6 inches of string extended from the pointed end of the casing. In other words, the radius of the circle swept out by the single washer is 6 inches.
6. Watch the washer as it moves in a circle. You are going to begin counting the number of full circles that the washer makes. This can be a little tricky, so get used to the motion of the washer, keeping the black mark just at the bottom of the casing.
7. When you are ready, start the stopwatch and time how long it takes for the washer to make 20 full circles. Do this five times and average the result.
8. Next, tie two more washers onto the end of the string that already has two washers on it. That way, there are now four washers on one end and one washer on the other.
9. Repeat steps (5-7), determining how long it takes the washer to make 20 full circles in this new configuration.
10. This step might be hard, but try to do it anyway. Try to twirl the washer so that the time it takes the washer to make 20 full circles is *equal* to what you got in step 7, when you had only two washers on the other end. In other words, you are trying to twirl the washer with the same speed you did in step 7. You don't have to do this perfectly; just try to get reasonably close.
11. Notice where the black mark is when the washer twirls with the same speed as it had in step 7.
12. Finally, while the washer is still twirling around, cut the four washers off the string with the scissors. **Make sure no one else is near when you do this. Also, make sure there are no breakables in the room!** Note what happens.
13. Clean up your mess.

What happened in the experiment? Well, let's start with the last part of the experiment. When you cut the washers from the end of the string, the washer that was twirling around suddenly went flying off straight. Why? Circular motion requires a special force, which physicists call **centripetal** (sen trip' uh tul) **force**.

<u>Centripetal force</u> – The force necessary to make an object move in a circle. It is directed perpendicular to the velocity of the object, which means it points toward the center of the circle.

In the experiment, the washers hanging on the end of the string were supplying centripetal force. Gravity was pulling them toward the earth, which, in turn, caused the washers to pull on the string. Thus, the washers were pulling on the string with a force equal to the force with which gravity was pulling on them. Of course, the string was attached to the lone washer on the other side of the pen, so the string was pulling on the lone washer. As the washer was twirling around, then, it was being pulled toward the pen (the center of the circle). Thus, the washer was experiencing a centripetal force. When you cut the two washers from the string, the lone washer that was traveling in a circle suddenly sped off, traveling in a straight line. It did so because the centripetal force causing it to turn in a circle was suddenly removed. Without the centripetal force, it no longer moved in a circle. Instead, it moved in a straight line, the direction of which was determined by the direction the washer was traveling at the instant you cut the string.

This should tell you something about circular motion. In accordance with Newton's First law, an object that is not acted on by outside forces will travel at a constant velocity. Since velocity includes direction, this means the object will travel in a straight line. The only way you can change that is to apply a force. If that force happens to be perpendicular to the velocity of the object, the object will begin to curve. If the force *continues* to be directed perpendicular to the velocity of the object, the object will move in a circle.

Now think about it. When a force is applied, acceleration must occur. Thus, an object moving in a circle is constantly accelerating. Does that mean an object can never travel in a circle at a constant speed? Of course not! When an object moves in a circle at a constant speed, there is still acceleration, because the object's *direction* keeps changing. Since the direction keeps changing, that means the velocity (which includes direction) keeps changing as well. Thus, the object is accelerating, even though its *speed* is not changing. Not surprisingly, this acceleration is called **centripetal acceleration**.

FIGURE 11.3
Centripetal Force Causes Circular Motion

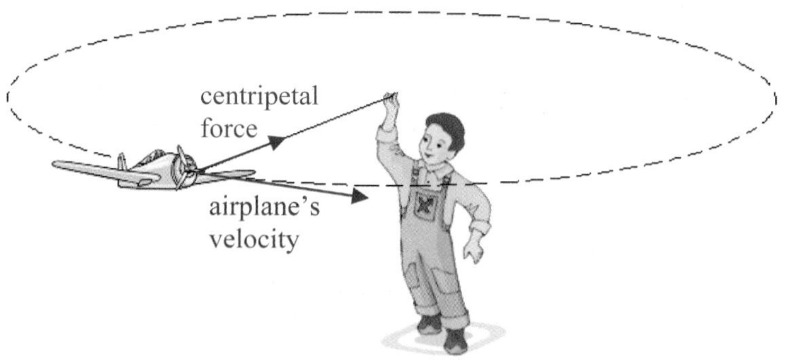

Illustration copyright GifArt.com

In the circular motion of this toy airplane, the airplane's velocity at any instant is directed straight ahead. However, the centripetal force provided by the string causes a centripetal acceleration, which changes the direction of the velocity. The airplane's velocity continues to change, causing it to travel in a circle. The center of the circle is defined by the direction of the centripetal force. If the string is cut, the centripetal force would vanish, and the plane would travel straight, in the direction of the blue arrow.

In the end, then, circular motion requires centripetal force, which is a force that stays perpendicular to the direction of the velocity. In order to stay perpendicular to the velocity, the force will always be directed toward the center of the circle.

Okay, now let's look at the other results you got from the experiment. What did you learn from steps 5-9? If things went well, you should have noted that it took *less* time for the washer to make 20 circles when there were four washers hanging on the other end of the string rather than just two. This indicates that the washer traveled *faster* when there was more weight on the string. More weight would be the same as more centripetal force. Thus, the larger the centripetal force, the faster an object can travel in a circle of a given size.

What happened in steps 10 and 11? In these steps, you weren't worried about the size of the circle. Instead you tried to keep the lone washer twirling at the same speed as when there were only two washers pulling on it. If you were able to do this, you should have noticed that the black mark had traveled well below the pen, indicating that the radius of the circle the lone washer swept out was *smaller* than it was when only two washers were hanging on the end. What does this mean? It means that at a given speed, the *larger* the centripetal force, the *smaller* the circle.

We can sum up what we learned in the experiment by stating three general principles regarding centripetal force:

1. **Circular motion requires centripetal force.**

2. **The larger the centripetal force, the faster an object travels in a circle of a given size.**

3. **At a given speed, the larger the centripetal force, the smaller the circle.**

So when an object is traveling in a circle, it is subject to a centripetal force. The size of the centripetal force can affect both the speed at which the object travels as well as the size of the circle in which it travels. If the size of the circle is not allowed to change, the larger the centripetal force, the faster the object will travel. However, if the speed is not allowed to change, the larger the centripetal force, the smaller the circle.

A Fictional Force

Before I discuss the gravitational force at work in our solar system, I want to take a minute to make sure you do not get the concept of *centripetal* force confused with the notion of "*centrifugal* (sen trif' you gul) force." It is important to distinguish between the two, because while centripetal force is a real force, *centrifugal force is not*! Although you might have heard about centrifugal force (indeed, it is even in the dictionary), *it is not a real force*.

The notion of centrifugal force is a result of poor physical analysis of certain situations. For example, think about traveling down the road in a car. Suppose there are some books on the car's dashboard. If the car turns a corner at a high rate of speed, what will happen to the books? They will begin to move across the dashboard, won't they? The books were stationary on the dashboard; then they suddenly started moving when the car made a turn. Thus, a person might conclude that the books must have experienced some sort of force in order for them to start moving like that. The person might call this a "centrifugal force."

It turns out that such an analysis is wrong. There is a force at play in this situation, but it is not a "centrifugal" force. The force is simply friction, and the motion of the books is a result of the fact that the frictional force is not very strong. Remember Newton's First Law: The books are traveling along with the car. Thus, they have the same velocity as the car. When the car makes a quick turn, the books will continue to travel with their *previous* velocity until acted on by a force. The friction between the books and the dashboard is the force that acts. It pushes the books, changing their velocity so that the books continue to travel with the car.

What happens, however, when the friction between the dashboard and the books is not strong enough to change the velocity of the books to match the new velocity of the car? The books will begin sliding along the dashboard in the general direction of the car's previous velocity. That's why the books move. They are not acted on by "centrifugal" force. They are simply obeying Newton's First Law, and friction is not powerful enough to give them the acceleration they need to travel with the car.

It is easy to get centrifugal force and centripetal force confused, since they both are associated with circular motion. For example, chemists and biologists often use a machine called a centrifuge (sen' trih fyooj), which is pictured below.

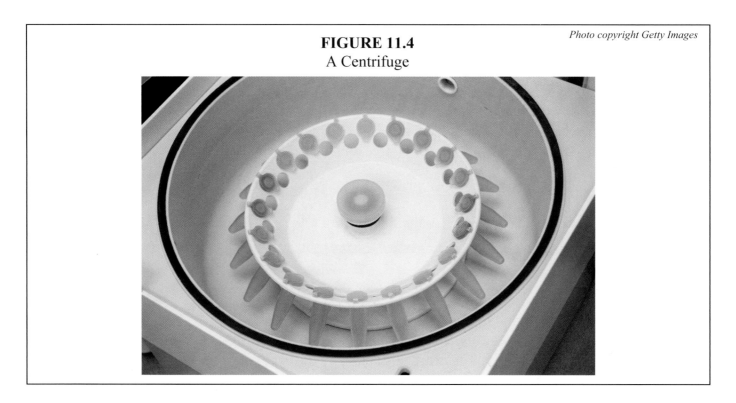

FIGURE 11.4
A Centrifuge

Photo copyright Getty Images

The plastic vials you see in the centrifuge are often filled with a liquid that has a solid suspended in it. When the centrifuge is turned on, the vials begin spinning around in a circle at high speed. When the spinning stops, the solid is separated from the liquid. Not only can a centrifuge separate solids from liquids, but it can also separate liquids of different densities. The cellular components of blood, for example, can be separated from blood plasma using a centrifuge.

Once again, however, a centrifuge does not separate solids from liquids and cellular components from blood plasma because of "centrifugal force." It does so simply because the components in the vials must obey Newton's First Law. As the vials spin in a circle, their contents initially continue to travel straight. This continues until a force is exerted to change their velocity. The only way this can happen is for the vials to exert a force on their contents, accelerating them so that they continue to travel in a circle. The more massive substances require more force to achieve the same acceleration, so they typically continue to move straight until they hit the edge of the vial. At that point, the vial can exert enough force to accelerate the substance so that it continues to follow the circular motion. Thus, even a centrifuge does not use "centrifugal force," as there is really no such thing!

ON YOUR OWN

11.3 Consider an object traveling in a circle as shown on the right. If the arrows indicate the direction of the circular motion, draw an arrow representing the direction of the object's velocity at the instant it is shown above.

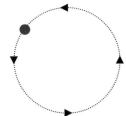

11.4 In the same drawing, draw another arrow indicating the centripetal force the object experiences.

The Gravitational Force at Work in Our Solar System

As I already discussed in Module #7, the earth orbits the sun in an oval orbit we call an "elliptical orbit." That orbit determines the length of a year and when the seasons change. The figure I showed for the orbit of the earth (Figure 7.3) exaggerated the oval nature of the orbit just to make the illustration easier to understand. In fact, the orbit of the earth around the sun is nearly circular. Why? Well, the earth is traveling with a speed of approximately 30,000 meters per second relative to the sun. To put that in terms more familiar to you, that is about the same as a speed of 70,000 miles per hour! The earth, therefore, is moving *fast* relative to the sun. The sun, however, attracts the earth with its gravitational force. That gravitational force pulls the earth toward the sun and is perpendicular to the earth's velocity. What does that mean? It supplies a *centripetal force* to the earth. This, of course, makes the earth travel in a circle. The circle is not perfect because there are other forces at play in the solar system. Nevertheless, those forces have only a minor effect, so earth's orbit is mostly circular. With the exception of Mercury, this is true for the other planets as well.

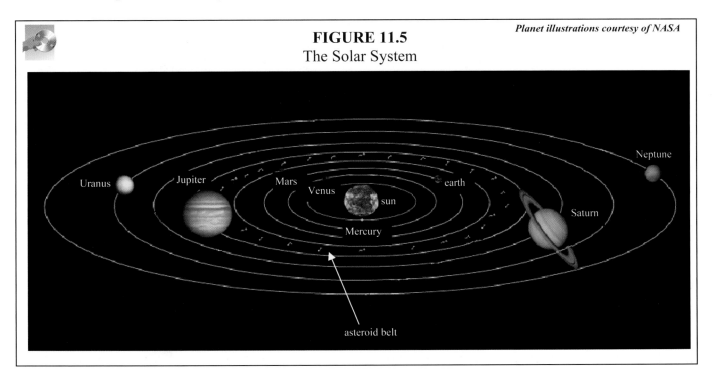

FIGURE 11.5
The Solar System

Planet illustrations courtesy of NASA

It is extremely difficult to provide an illustration of the solar system, mostly because the sizes and orbits of the planets vary so much. The diameter of Jupiter, for example, is 11 times that of earth and almost 30 times that of Mercury. At the same time, the distance from Neptune to the sun is 30 times that of the distance from the earth to the sun and almost 80 times that of the distance from Mercury to the sun. Thus, while the relative sizes of the planets in Figure 11.5 are fairly close to accurate, the relative distances from the sun are not. In addition, the size of the sun is not at all accurate in Figure 11.5, because its diameter is roughly 110 times that of the earth and 10 times that of Jupiter!

Given the shortcomings of any figure that tries to illustrate the solar system as a whole, you can at least see from Figure 11.5 that the sun sits at the center of the solar system. All planets orbit around the sun because of the gravitational attraction between each planet and the sun. The planets don't "fall into" the sun, because they all have velocities that are perpendicular to the sun's gravitational force. Thus, the gravitational force between each planet and the sun acts as a centripetal force that causes each planet to travel around the sun in a nearly circular orbit. The closest planet to the sun is Mercury, and continuing out from there, you find Venus, earth, and Mars. Between Mars and the next planet (Jupiter), you find the solar system's highest concentration of asteroids. As a result, this region of the solar system is often called the **asteroid belt**. Beyond Jupiter, you find Saturn, Uranus, and Neptune.

Although Figure 11.5 is nice because it shows you the solar system as a whole, the huge scale of the solar system makes it hard to see all the planets. Thus, Figure 11.6 shows you a different view. The relative sizes of the planets are not as accurate anymore, and although the sun is pictured larger than in was in Figure 11.5, it is still too small given the sizes of the planets. Of course, the relative distances between the planets and the sun are also not correct.

FIGURE 11.6
The Planets in the Solar System

Illustration © George Argyropoulos
Agency: Istockphoto.com

1. **Mercury** is the planet closest to the sun. Its average orbital radius is 58,000,000 km, and it takes 0.24 years to make one orbit around the sun.
2. **Venus** is the next planet out. Its average orbital radius is 108,000,000 km, and it takes 0.62 years to make one orbit around the sun.
3. **Earth** is the "third rock from the sun." Its average orbital radius is 150,000,000 km, and it takes one year to make a complete orbit.
4. **Mars** is next, with an average orbital radius of 228,000,000 km and an orbit time of 1.88 years.
5. **Jupiter** comes after the asteroid belt, with an average orbital radius of 780,000,000 km and an orbit time of 11.9 years.
6. **Saturn**, the next planet, has an average orbital radius of 1,400,000,000 km and an orbit time of 29.4 years.
7. **Uranus** has an average orbital radius of 2,900,000,000 km and takes 84 years to make one full orbit.
8. **Neptune** has an average orbital radius of 4,500,000,000 km and takes 164 years to make one full orbit.

Since the sizes of the planets and their distances from the sun are so large, it is hard to get mental images of them. To visualize the relative sizes of the planets, try this. Suppose that the earth was the size of a ping-pong ball. Mercury would be the size of a small marble; Venus would also be about the size of a ping-pong ball; Mars would be a big marble (the kind you use to shoot small marbles); Jupiter would be about the size of a beach ball; Saturn would be the size of a basketball; and Neptune and Uranus would each be softball-sized, with Neptune being just slightly smaller than Uranus. In this scenario, the sun would just barely fit in your bedroom.

To visualize the relative distances of the planets from the sun, imagine rolling out a roll of toilet paper. The toilet paper is divided into little squares. Suppose you rolled out enough toilet paper so that 90 little squares of it are lying on the floor, all stretched out. Assuming that the sun is at the end of the roll, Mercury would be at the perforation that marks the end of the first square; Venus would be at the second perforation; earth would be at the third; Mars would be at the fifth; Jupiter would be just beyond the 15th; Saturn would be at the 30th; Uranus would be just before the 60th; while Neptune would be near the 90th perforation.

Typically, the planets of the solar system are placed into one of two groups: the **inner planets** (Mercury, Venus, earth, and Mars) and the **outer planets** (Jupiter, Saturn, Uranus, and Neptune). The presence of the asteroid belt between Mars and Jupiter seems to make this distinction natural, but the real reason it is made is based on the composition of the planets. The inner planets are small and mostly composed of rock and iron. The outer planets, on the other hand, are much larger and consist mostly of gases such as helium and hydrogen.

Each planet exerts a gravitational force on every object in the solar system, and as a result, most planets have objects that orbit around them. The earth, for example, is orbited by the moon. Typically, when an object orbits around a planet, we call that object a **satellite** of the planet. Although the earth has only one notable satellite, most planets have more than one. Mars, for example, has two small satellites: Phobos (diameter of 21 km) and Deimos (diameter of 12 km). Jupiter has 60 known satellites. The four biggest were discovered by Galileo (a scientist we will discuss later) and are consequently called the **Galilean satellites**. They are Io, Europa, Callisto, and Ganymede. Please note that as our technology improves, we discover more moons around the outer planets. Thus, Jupiter may have more than 60 known satellites by the time you read this book.

Saturn, Uranus, Jupiter, and Neptune all have many satellites as well, but they also have another interesting feature: **planetary rings**. We usually think of Saturn when we think of rings, because Saturn's rings are so pronounced. There are actually more than 100,000 individual rings surrounding the planet. Each ring is composed of small bodies of rock, ice, and frozen gases. These bodies vary greatly in size from dust particles (0.0005 cm diameter) to boulders (10 m diameter), and they all orbit the planet. Although Saturn's rings are, by far, the most popularly known, Uranus has at least 13 rings encircling it. The first were discovered in 1977. Neptune has at least nine rings; the first set was discovered in 1989. Jupiter has a series of rings, the first of which was seen in 1979. These relatively recent dates of discovery explain why the presence of rings on these planets is not well known.

In addition to the planets in the solar system, asteroids are shown in Figure 11.5. Asteroids are small, rocky bodies that orbit the sun under the same gravitational influence that governs the orbits of the planets. Although there are asteroids all over the solar system, the primary concentration of asteroids exists in the asteroid belt, between Mars and Jupiter. Asteroids range in size; the largest known asteroid has a diameter of about 900 km, and the smallest is a tiny grain.

Let me ask you a question at this point. Of all the planets in the solar system, which receives the most insolation (energy from the sun)? Obviously Mercury does, because it is closest to the sun. Thus, you would expect Mercury to be the hottest planet in the solar system, right? Wrong! Mercury is warm (it can reach temperatures above 750 °F) during the day, but it is really cold (it can reach -300 °F) at night. Venus is, in fact, the warmest planet in the solar system, with a relatively constant temperature of about 860 °F.

If Venus is farther away from the sun than Mercury, why is it hotter? Well, Mercury has a very thin atmosphere, whereas Venus has a very thick atmosphere. Its atmosphere is nearly 100 times as thick as earth's atmosphere. In addition, Venus' atmosphere is almost entirely made up of *carbon dioxide*. Remember what carbon dioxide is? It's a greenhouse gas. Thus, even though Venus receives significantly less insolation than Mercury, its strong greenhouse effect traps nearly all the energy it receives. This regulates the temperature (Venus has the most steady temperature of all the inner planets) and makes it quite warm. All planets farther from the sun than Venus have temperatures that decrease as their distance from the sun increases.

Now if you think about it, there are *a lot* of gravitational forces at play in the solar system. The sun is the most massive object around, so its gravitational force is, by far, the strongest. Thus, the bulk of the properties of the solar system are governed by the gravitational attraction that exists between the sun and every other object in the vicinity. Nevertheless, each planet and asteroid also attracts every other planet and asteroid, because the gravitational force is an attractive force that is present between all objects that have mass.

All of these gravitational forces work together to produce certain effects. For example, even though the orbit of a planet is mostly influenced by its gravitational attraction to the sun, the other planets' gravitational forces can cause small variations in its motion. Physicists call these variations **perturbations** (pur tur bay' shunz), and they can be mapped by careful study. Such studies led to the discovery of Neptune. French scientist Urbain Jean Joseph Leverrier mapped the perturbations in Uranus' orbit and used them to calculate the position of a previously undiscovered planet. With the help of those calculations, German astronomer Johann Gottfried Galle found Neptune in 1846.

Perturbations that affect asteroids can cause even more dramatic effects. When an asteroid's orbit is perturbed enough, it can be thrown out of its standard orbit and toward a planet. Many asteroids are flung towards earth, for example. When they intersect earth's orbit, they are called **meteoroids** (mee' tee uh roydz). When they actually hit earth's atmosphere, they experience an enormous amount of friction (due to air resistance), which causes them to heat up to high temperatures. This causes them to become white-hot, making brilliant streaks of light in the sky. At that point, scientists call them **meteors** (and some people call them "shooting stars"). The intense heat usually breaks up the meteor, except for a few small pieces that fall to the ground and are called **meteorites**.

Although most meteors burn up when they interact with the earth's atmosphere, exceptionally large ones can survive, hitting the surface of the planet with great impact. Since the surface of earth is constantly eroding due to weather and wind, most evidence of such incidents is gone, except for a few very large craters. Other planets, however, bear the striking scars of meteor impacts, as shown in Figure 11.7.

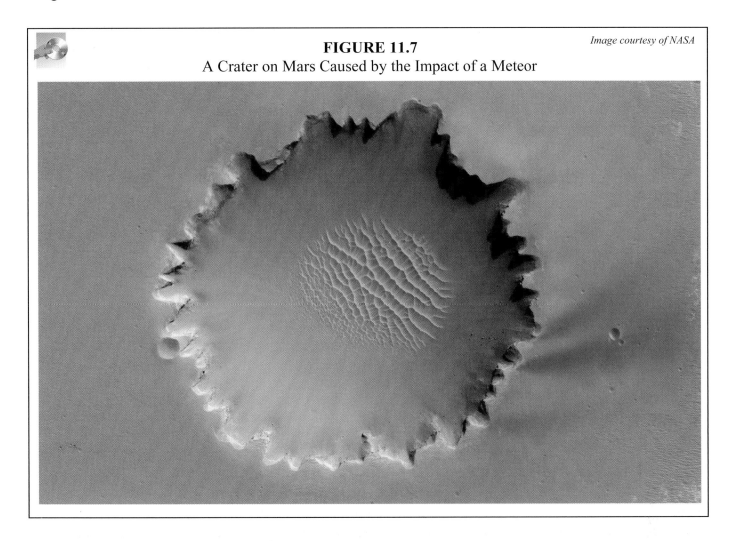

FIGURE 11.7
A Crater on Mars Caused by the Impact of a Meteor

Image courtesy of NASA

ON YOUR OWN

11.5 Which receives more insolation: Mars or Saturn?

11.6 Saturn, Uranus, and Neptune have at least three things in common. List them.

11.7 A scientist analyzes a rock found in a nearby field. She says that based on its characteristics, it must have come from an asteroid. What should the scientist call this rock?

<u>Comets</u>

In addition to planets and asteroids, gravity works on **comets** as well. Comets are called "dirty snowballs" by some physicists. They get that nickname because they are mostly composed of dust grains, chunks of dirt, and ice. The "ice" I refer to is not just frozen water, but also frozen carbon dioxide (which we call "dry ice"), frozen ammonia, and frozen methane (in its gaseous form we call methane "natural gas"). Comets are typically less than 300 km in diameter.

Comets orbit the sun in elliptical orbits that often take them very close to the sun and then send them far from the sun (see Figure 11.8). When they are far from the sun, comets are not detectable except by the most advanced telescopic devices. However, when its elliptical orbit takes a comet close to the sun, something amazing happens. Its proximity to the sun causes the "dirty snowball" to heat up. This causes the ice on the surface of the comet to turn directly into a gas, forming a "fuzzy" atmosphere around it. When a substance turns from solid to gas (without passing through the liquid phase), we say it has **sublimated**. At this point, the chunk of dust, dirt, and ice that makes up the solid part of the comet is called the **nucleus** of the comet, and the "fuzzy" atmosphere around the comet is called the **coma** (koh' muh).

Because the gases in the coma are heated by the comet's proximity to the sun, they begin to emit light, causing them to glow. The gases from the coma usually form a long, glowing **tail**. Figure 11.5 shows a picture (left) and the orbit (right) of comet Kohoutek (kuh' hoh tek), which was visible in the night sky during the last quarter of 1973 and the early quarter of 1974.

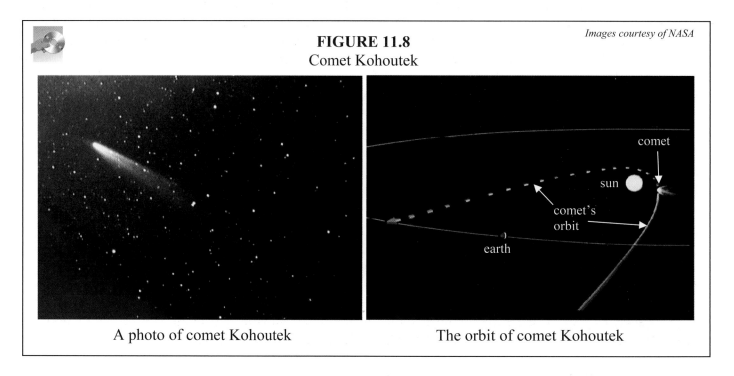

FIGURE 11.8
Comet Kohoutek

Images courtesy of NASA

A photo of comet Kohoutek   The orbit of comet Kohoutek

In the photograph, you can see the coma (the bright spot at the front of the comet) and the tail. Note from the illustration of its orbit how close the comet comes to the sun. The enormous amount of insolation it receives at that proximity to the sun is what makes the coma and causes it to glow. Note also that the comet's tail points away from the sun. This is typical of most comets. You see, there are certain particles that are constantly being emitted from the surface of the sun. These particles are pushed away from the sun, causing a "wind," which physicists call the **solar wind**. This wind blows the gases of the coma away from the nucleus of the comet, giving the comet its tail. Although some comets are bright enough to be seen with the naked eye, most are not.

When a comet is far from the sun, it has neither coma nor tail. It is simply a "dirty snowball." When its elliptical orbit takes it near the sun, however, the insolation from the sun forms the gaseous coma. The solar wind then pushes those gases away from the sun, forming the tail. Thus, when a comet is close to the sun, it is composed of a nucleus, a coma, and a tail. Once it passes away from the sun, the gases of the coma either blow away or freeze, and once again the comet is simply a "dirty snowball."

If you think about it, each time a comet makes its pass near the sun, it loses a significant amount of mass. After all, some of the ice that makes it up sublimes, and much of the dust and dirt blows off as well. Thus, with enough passes near the sun, a comet will simply disintegrate. Unlike planets, then, comets are transient objects in the solar system. Some could last for a long time because it takes them a long time to orbit around the sun. Nevertheless, they will only survive for a certain number of orbits.

The time it takes for a comet to orbit the sun (called the **period** of the comet) is used as a means of classification. The **short-period** comets are comets that take less than 200 years to make an orbit. Typically, a short-period comet's orbit doesn't take it much farther than Jupiter before it turns around and heads back to the sun. Encke's comet has the shortest known orbital time, which is 3.3 years. The **long-period** comets typically have orbits that extend to the planet Neptune or beyond, and they can take quite a while (more than 200 years) to orbit the sun. The famous Halley's comet has an orbital period of 76 years. If you were old enough to pay attention in 1997, you saw the Hale-Bopp comet, which has a calculated orbit time of more than 3,000 years. Finally, there are **very long-period** comets that have orbits that carry them so far out to the edges of the solar system that they take more than 5,000 years to make one orbit. Physicists have identified some comets that they postulate will never make more than one trip around the sun because their orbits are so large!

If comets are transient objects in the solar system, where do they come from? Well, that's an interesting question, and the answer is a bit tricky. Remember, comets are only bright when they pass by the sun. Once they are far from the sun, they lose their coma and tail, and become small, dark chunks of dirt, dust, and ice. That makes them *very* hard to detect. Thus, their origins remain a bit of a mystery.

In 1950, Dutch astronomer Jan Oort proposed a hypothesis that comets come from a big shell of icy bodies that surrounds the solar system well beyond Pluto. This shell is now called the "**Oort cloud**" by astronomers. Although many textbooks talk about the Oort cloud as a fact, it remains only a hypothesis to explain where certain comets come from. Since even our best telescopes could not hope to see such small, dark bodies so far away, the Oort cloud exists only hypothetically.

The hypothesis of the Oort cloud was given some credence in 1992, however, when a 150-mile wide body was discovered just beyond Neptune. In 1951, astronomer Gerard Kuiper had suggested that if the Oort cloud exists, a smaller band of comet material should exist just beyond Neptune. Astronomers decided that this 150-mile wide body must be a member of that band, so they named the band the **Kuiper** (kye' per) **belt**. The Hubble space telescope has since detected many objects that orbit the sun beyond the orbit of Neptune, confirming that the Kuiper belt is, indeed, real.

This evidence has convinced most astronomers that short-period comets originate from this Kuiper belt. They assume that gravitational perturbations of objects in the Kuiper belt send them hurtling toward the sun, turning them into comets. There are at least two problems with this idea, however. The first is that the objects detected in the Kuiper belt are typically much larger than comets. If the Kuiper belt is the source of short-period comets, why are these comets generally much smaller than the objects in the Kuiper belt? The second problem is that there don't seem to be enough objects in the Kuiper belt to account for the number of short-period comets we see today.

If science eventually confirms that short-period comets come from the Kuiper belt, it is probably not all that unlikely that long-period comets and very long-period comets come from a similar source. Thus, the Oort cloud hypothesis is at least consistent with what most physicists believe about the Kuiper belt. Unfortunately, confirmation of the Oort cloud may take quite some time. After all, it took a lot of effort and technology to determine that the Kuiper belt exists. It will, most likely, take an even longer time to be able to detect comet material that might be much, much farther away from us.

Why is it important to understand where comets come from? Well, as I mentioned before, comets don't last very long. As a result, if there is not a source from which they can be renewed, their very presence in the solar system tells us that the solar system is quite young, probably on the order of a few thousand years old. However, if there is a source of icy bodies that continually makes new comets, it is possible the solar system is very old. Thus, scientists who want to believe that the solar system is billions of years old must find sources that replenish the solar system's supply of comets. Scientists who want to believe the solar system is very young don't think such sources exist. Thus, whether or not the Kuiper belt is really a source of short-period comets and whether or not the Oort cloud exists both have implications concerning the age of the solar system.

ON YOUR OWN

11.8 The diagram below maps out two orbits around the sun. Which would most likely belong to a comet that would be relatively easy to see? Can the other orbit still be that of a comet?

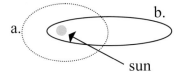

Hey, What About Pluto?

You might have been wondering why I didn't mention **Pluto** in my discussion of the planets in the solar system. The reason is simple: Pluto is no longer officially recognized as a planet. On August 24, 2006, the International Astronomical Union (the group of scientists that develops the standards for astronomy) decided to "demote" Pluto from its planetary status. It is now called a **dwarf planet**.

Why did they make the change? Well, as I mentioned before, recent discoveries have demonstrated that there are many bodies orbiting the sun beyond Neptune. While Pluto is one of the bigger ones, it seems to have most of the characteristics of these other bodies. As a result, some astronomers have argued for quite some time that Pluto isn't really a planet. Instead, it is just a very large Kuiper Belt Object (often abbreviated as KBO).

The debate between astronomers who thought that Pluto should not be considered a planet and those who did raged for some time within the astronomy community. However, those who wanted Pluto to keep its planetary status had one strong argument: Pluto was the largest body orbiting the sun beyond Neptune. Thus, it made sense to continue to call it a planet. However, that all changed with the discovery of another body orbiting the sun beyond Neptune that was *larger* than Pluto.

Now officially known as the dwarf planet **Eris** (ear' us), this body presented a real problem to the astronomy community. It had many characteristics in common with Pluto and was *larger* than Pluto. Thus, if Pluto is really a planet, Eris is a planet as well. As a result, the number of planets in the solar system would have to be officially changed from nine to ten. Also, there is no reason to think that Eris and Pluto are the only bodies of their size orbiting the sun beyond Neptune. As time goes on, most astronomers expect that more will be found. As a result, if Eris was added to the list of planets in the solar system, it would be possible for many more bodies to be added as time went on, making the list of planets longer and longer.

Members of the International Astronomical Union, therefore, recognized that *something* had to be done. Either the number of planets in the solar system would have to be increased (potentially by quite a lot as time went on), or the definition of a planet would have to change so that it would not include bodies like Pluto and Eris. Thus, the definition of a planet was put to a vote among members of the organization. The result of the vote indicated that a planet must meet the following criteria:

1. A planet must be in orbit around the sun.
2. A planet must be nearly round in shape.
3. A planet must have "cleared the neighborhood" around its orbit.

While the first two criteria are easy to understand, what does the third one mean? Well, the solar system is full of a lot of debris. Planets like the earth are massive enough that they attract the debris near them (in their "neighborhood"). As a result, the area around the orbit of a planet is very clean as compared to the parts of the solar system between the planetary orbits. Well, Pluto is so small compared to the planets that it does not have enough gravity to "clean up its neighborhood" very well. Thus, there is still a lot of debris in the vicinity of Pluto's orbit, and it therefore does not meet the third criterion.

Because of this new definition for a planet, the International Astronomical Union had to come up with a new classification for Pluto, Eris, and other bodies like it. Thus, they came up with the definition for a dwarf planet:

1. A dwarf planet must be in orbit around the sun.
2. A dwarf planet must be nearly round in shape.
3. A dwarf planet has not "cleared the neighborhood" around its orbit.
4. A dwarf planet is not a satellite.

Based on criterion #3, then, Pluto and Eris are dwarf planets. The fourth criterion just means that a dwarf planet cannot be orbiting around a planet. Thus, a dwarf planet cannot be a moon.

Based on this definition, there are currently three officially recognized dwarf planets: Pluto, Eris, and **Ceres** (sear' eez). While Pluto and Eris orbit the sun beyond Neptune, Ceres is actually much closer to the sun. It is in the asteroid belt. One thing you need to realize, however, is that there are many bodies in the solar system that could potentially meet the criteria for a dwarf planet. Thus, by the time you read this book, there may be more than three dwarf planets in the solar system.

What Causes the Gravitational Force?

Notice that so far you have learned a lot about gravity and its effects, but you still do not know what causes it. That's the situation physics was in until the last 90 years or so. Up until then, physicists could calculate gravitational forces, determine what would happen as a result of gravitational forces, and predict the future positions of the bodies in the solar system. Nevertheless, they had no idea what really *causes* the gravitational force.

That all changed in 1916 when Albert Einstein proposed his **General Theory of Relativity**. This theory is a broad theory that attempts to explain an entire way of looking at physics. The details are far, far beyond the scope of this course. Nevertheless, one of the byproducts of Einstein's General Theory of Relativity was an original explanation of what *causes* the gravitational force. The best way to explain what Einstein's theory says is to start with an experiment.

EXPERIMENT 11.2
The "Bent Space and Time" Theory of Gravity

Supplies:

- A soft seat cushion from a couch (A soft bed will work as well.)
- A bowling ball (A heavy rock will work as well.)
- A marble
- Eye protection such as goggles or safety glasses

Introduction: Einstein's General Theory of Relativity concludes that the gravitational "force" is not really a force at all. It is actually a result of the fact that mass bends space and time. This experiment will help illustrate such a strange concept.

Procedure:

1. Lay the seat cushion on the floor. If you are using a bed, just stand next to the bed.
2. Find a spot on the cushion that is away from the center and relatively flat. Lay the marble on that point so that it stays there without rolling.
3. Lay the bowling ball on the very center of the cushion. Note what happens to the marble.
4. Take the bowling ball off the cushion and smooth it out so that it is reasonably flat again.
5. Roll the marble (slowly) straight across the cushion, but not near the center. Note that it rolls reasonably straight.
6. Put the bowling ball back in the center of the cushion and roll the marble along the same path that you rolled it before, with the same slow speed. Note the path that the marble takes.
7. Put everything away.

Einstein's General Theory of Relativity states that space is not always the way it appears to us. Suppose, for example, you did not know that the world was round. Would you think it was? Probably not. After all, the earth looks pretty flat all around you. Thus, you would probably think that the earth was flat. We know that this is not the case, however. Despite what it looks like from our vantage point, we know that the earth is round. In the same way, Einstein postulated that although it does not appear to change at all, space actually bends in the presence of an object with mass.

In the first part of your experiment, the seat cushion represented space. With nothing on the seat cushion, it stayed relatively flat. However, when a massive object (the bowling ball) was placed there, the entire seat cushion bent. The bend was greatest in the middle and least around the edges, but nevertheless, the entire seat cushion bent. In response, the marble rolled toward the bowling ball. This is Einstein's picture of gravity. Space (the seat cushion) bends in the presence of mass (the bowling ball). As a result, all objects (the marble) accelerate toward the mass. This makes it look like a force is being applied to an object.

In the second part of your experiment, you watched the marble roll straight across the flat seat cushion. When the bowling ball was once again placed on the seat cushion, the marble did not roll straight. Instead, it rolled in a curved path. According to Einstein, this is why planets orbit the sun. In his theory, the planets are all actually moving in a straight line. Because space is so strongly bent by the mass of the sun, however, that straight line is deformed until it becomes a circle. Thus, as far as the planets are concerned, they are traveling in a straight line. Space itself, however, causes that straight line to become a circle. This would be very similar to what might happen to you if you could travel in a straight line on earth for about 25,000 miles. If you did that, you would think that you were traveling in a straight line. However, after about 25,000 miles (the circumference of the earth), you would end up back where you started. Thus, even though you thought you were traveling in a straight line, you were actually traveling in a circle.

I know this is a terribly complicated picture to put in your head. That's why I tried to illustrate it to you with an experiment. If you think of the marble as a planet, it rolled straight as long as space (the cushion) was flat. As soon as you bent space (the cushion) with a massive object (the bowling ball), however, the planet (the marble) then moved in a curved path. If the object deforms space enough, that curved path becomes a circle. It turns out that Einstein's view is even more complicated than that, however. You see, as far as Einstein is concerned, time is also a part of this situation. Thus, mass doesn't only bend space, it also bends time. That makes it even harder to understand. Nevertheless, if you think in terms of the following picture, it might help:

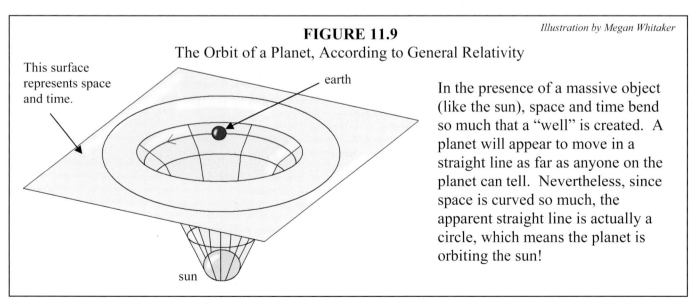

FIGURE 11.9

Illustration by Megan Whitaker

The Orbit of a Planet, According to General Relativity

This surface represents space and time.

earth

sun

In the presence of a massive object (like the sun), space and time bend so much that a "well" is created. A planet will appear to move in a straight line as far as anyone on the planet can tell. Nevertheless, since space is curved so much, the apparent straight line is actually a circle, which means the planet is orbiting the sun!

If Einstein is right, then, gravity is not really a force at all. It is, instead, a consequence of how mass bends space and time.

Is Einstein right? Well, we aren't really sure. The General Theory of Relativity has a lot of success in explaining things about space that could not be explained before. One of the first successes of Einstein's theory is its ability to fully explain the way Mercury orbits around the sun. Although the details of this observation are beyond the scope of this course, I can tell you that using all we knew about gravity before Einstein's theory, Mercury's orbit around the sun could only be predicted with an accuracy of about 92%. Using the equations of general relativity, however, Mercury's orbit is explained exactly.

Einstein's General Theory of Relativity also predicts that light will bend when it comes close to a massive object, like a star. After all, light must stay in the confines of space. Thus, if space bends, light should bend as well. Since Newton's Universal Law of Gravitation only predicts an attraction between masses, and since light has no mass, Newton would not predict an interaction between light and massive objects. Astronomers have observed that when light passes near a star, its path does bend. That's another piece of evidence supporting Einstein's theory. In addition, Einstein's theory predicts that time will move more quickly in the presence of weak gravity and more slowly in the presence of strong gravity. This effect has also been experimentally observed. Time on satellites, for example, has been shown to move faster than time on earth. This is because since satellites are farther from the earth, they experience less gravitational attraction than objects on the surface of the earth. Because of these evidences, Einstein's Theory of General Relativity is considered a reliable theory. Nevertheless, it has not been tested nearly enough to become a law. Thus, its explanation of gravity still remains a theory. It is a good theory, but it is still a theory.

There is another attempt to explain what causes the gravitational force. If anything, it is even more difficult to comprehend, but once again, let's try an experiment.

EXPERIMENT 11.3
The Graviton Theory of Gravity

Supplies:

- Two balls (Baseball-sized balls are best, but any will do.)
- Two people to help you
- A stopwatch or a watch with a second hand
- A large, open space
- Eye protection such as goggles or safety glasses

Introduction: Another theory regarding what causes gravitational force is the idea that massive objects exchange tiny particles called "gravitons." This experiment shows how the exchange of gravitons could create an attractive force.

Procedure:

1. Take one ball for yourself and hand the other to one of your helpers. The other helper needs to hold the stopwatch.
2. Stand about 1 foot away from the helper who has the ball.
3. Have the helper with the stopwatch start the stopwatch and at the same time yell "go." When he yells "go," throw the ball to your other helper, while she throws the ball to you. Then, right away, throw the balls back to one another so that you have the same ball you originally had. This all needs to happen in less than a second.

4. Every second, your helper with the stopwatch should yell "go" again, and you need to exchange balls with your other helper and then exchange them back again, all within a second. Do this ten times or so.

5. Now both you and your helper with the ball should each take a giant step backward, taking you farther apart from each other. Repeat the procedure, exchanging and re-exchanging balls every second for 10 times or so.

6. Repeat step (5) three or four times, continually stepping farther and farther away from your helper with the ball. If it gets too hard, you can stop.

7. Does the procedure become harder or easier as you move farther and farther away from each other?

8. Put everything away.

The other theory of gravity says that two massive objects tend to exchange tiny particles called **gravitons**. These gravitons must be exchanged within a very short time frame, so, just like in your experiment, the closer two massive objects are, the easier it is for them to exchange gravitons. Thus, in your experiment, you and your helper with the ball were representing massive objects. The balls were gravitons, and your helper with the stopwatch was making sure you exchanged balls within a certain time frame. As you and your helper got farther and farther apart from one another, it got harder and harder to exchange balls within the time interval, didn't it?

Now, if you and your helper were forced to do this continually, what would you do? You would move close to one another to make it easier, right? Well, if massive objects do exchange gravitons, and if they must be exchanged within a certain small time interval, massive objects would move closer to one another as well. That, then, could be what causes the attractive gravitational force. Massive objects might be attracted to one another because they exchange gravitons.

There is evidence for Einstein's General Theory of Relativity. Is there any evidence for the graviton theory? Well, not exactly. Gravitons have never been observed, and we have never witnessed massive objects exchanging particles. Thus, there is no direct evidence as of yet for this theory. Why would anyone believe it? Well, there are two basic reasons. First, there is a theory called "quantum mechanics" that has a lot of evidence to show that it is a good explanation of how atoms interact. Since quantum mechanics is so successful in explaining the behavior of atoms, many scientists think it must apply to all of creation. For this theory to be consistent with what we know about the gravitational force, however, gravity must be the result of the exchange of particles.

The other reason some scientists think that gravity is caused by the exchange of gravitons is that the *other* forces in nature (the electromagnetic force, the weak force, and the strong force) can all be explained by particle exchange. Thus, it is natural to think that the only other force in creation should be explained that way as well. Wait a minute: Did I just say that this strange theory of particle exchange explains the other forces in creation? I sure did! Believe it or not, negatively charged particles are attracted to positively charged particles because they exchange small particles of light (called "photons") with one another. I will tell you more about that in an upcoming module. In addition, the other two forces are explained by the exchange of particles. Thus, even though there is no direct evidence at this point that gravity is caused by the exchange of gravitons, it seems like a likely explanation, since the other forces in creation are explained in a similar way.

Indeed, all physicists agree that gravitons would be very, very hard to detect. Thus, even if they do exist, we should not be surprised that we haven't seen them yet. Of course, most physicists admit that Einstein's explanation is better right now, since it at least has some direct evidence supporting it. In fact, there are some who postulate that *both* theories are true. At the same time, of course, it is possible that *neither* theory is true. After all, the history of science is filled with theories that seemed to have a lot of evidence supporting them but were later found to be wrong.

ON YOUR OWN

11.9 If Einstein's General Theory of Relativity is true, how many forces are there in creation?

11.10 Suppose that a great physicist one day detected massive objects exchanging small particles with each other. That would not be conclusive evidence for the graviton theory. There is one other thing that must be shown to really provide conclusive evidence for the graviton theory. What is it?

A Brief History of Our View of the Solar System

In this module, you have learned a lot about gravity and how it works to make the solar system look like it does. Believe it or not, however, all this was known *before* human beings ventured into space. Even Einstein's Theory of General Relativity was produced long before spaceflight was developed. How in the world could scientists learn so much about the solar system without venturing out into it? That is a very interesting story, and it is one worth recounting.

The motions of the stars and moon in the night sky have always fascinated people. Since the beginning of recorded history, people have tried to understand them. Indeed, most calendars (even ancient ones) were based on the appearance of the moon in the sky. As time went on, people realized that if they could *predict* the motions of the stars, moon, and sun, keeping track of dates and times would be relatively easy.

The ancient Greeks were probably the first to develop a systematic view of the motion of the stars and the moon. Although many other cultures developed intricate calendars and the like, the ancient Greeks were the first to develop a systematic theory based on observations of the night sky. In the second century AD, the Greek astronomers Hipparchus and Ptolemy mapped the motion of 1,000 stars and thought of them as a "backdrop." They placed them on the surface of a rotating sphere, called the "celestial sphere," and then said that the earth was at the very center of the sphere. The moon and the planets, then, moved about in the sphere on circular orbits that were arranged within the sphere.

This was the start of what is called the **geocentric** view of our solar system. In a geocentric system, the earth is placed at the center of the solar system. Although there were several problems with this geocentric view of things, the ancient Greeks were able to use this system to predict the motion of the moon and other planets better than anyone else had ever done. Thus, although it was far from perfect, the success of the theory made it popular among scientists.

Many adjustments and commentaries were made on the geocentric theory, but it remained the general view of scientists until the sixteenth century A.D. By that time, too much data had been piled up that was inconsistent with the theory. Things began to change in 1543 when a Polish scientist named Nicolaus Copernicus published a book called *On the Revolution of Heavenly Bodies*. In that book, he declared the geocentric theory sorely lacking. Instead, he postulated that the solar system would be much more orderly if the sun was at its center and the planets orbited in circles around the sun. This was the beginning of what physicists call the **heliocentric** view of the solar system, where the earth was taken out of the center and replaced with the sun.

Copernicus was raised and educated in the Roman Catholic Church. At that time, the Roman Catholic Church adhered strictly to the geocentric view of the solar system. After all, since God created man, he must be the most important aspect of creation. Therefore, his dwelling place (the earth) must be at the center of everything. The Roman Catholic Church also pointed to various Scriptures, such as Joshua 10:12-13. In those verses, Joshua commanded the *sun* to stand still and, through the power of the Lord, it did. The Roman Catholic Church argued that Joshua would not have to command the sun to stand still if it were at rest in center of the solar system!

Copernicus' work was put on the Roman Catholic Church's list of banned books, but that didn't end interest in the heliocentric view. In 1609, Italian physicist Galileo Galilei made a crude telescope and pointed it skyward. He was able to use that telescope to notice the phases of Venus, which could only be explained with the heliocentric view. He also discovered the four largest moons of Jupiter. This lent more evidence for the heliocentric view because it showed that smaller bodies orbited larger bodies, and even back then it was known that the sun is larger than the earth.

When Galileo, a well-respected scientist, published a work showing all the evidence in favor of the Copernican system, the Roman Catholic Church put him on trial. They were firmly in support of the geocentric view, and they would not allow even a great scientist such as Galileo to say otherwise. Because Galileo was deeply committed to his church and did not want to be excommunicated, he publicly recanted his belief in the Copernican system. As a result, the Roman Catholic Church was lenient on him, and his punishment was house arrest for the remainder of his life. Even though he publicly recanted his belief in the heliocentric system, he continued to collect data that supported it.

At about the same time (1580-1597), a Danish astronomer named Tycho Brahe (brah) and his German assistant, Johannes Kepler, began compiling a huge amount of data on the motion of the planets. As a result of the data, Kepler devised a series of rules that the planets always followed. They became known as "Kepler's Laws." Even though these laws did nothing to explain *why* the planets moved as they did, they clearly indicated that the planets orbit the sun and that their motion is guided by an overriding principle. What that principle was, however, Kepler did not know.

Sir Isaac Newton was the one who figured that out. When he formulated his Universal Law of Gravitation, he showed that the heliocentric view was the best way in which to understand the solar system. By that time, so much evidence had been accumulated that the Roman Catholic Church had to back off its desire to cling to the geocentric theory, and the heliocentric theory quickly dominated the scientific community.

After Newton's time, astronomy really took off. The telescope became one of the most widely used instruments in physics. New stars were charted, the surfaces of planets were studied, and accurate predictions were made regarding the motion of the planets. After a while, physicists even developed a means of measuring the distance to a planet using a telescope. As technology increased, our ability to gather more data increased. Today, we can study the chemical composition of stars, comets, and other objects in space. We can do all that and more without even venturing into space!

Notice what happened in this story. From the second century AD to the sixteenth century AD (1,400 years), not much progress was made in the field of astronomy. That's because the scientists of the time were working with a flawed theory. No matter how much they tried, they could not get the geocentric view of the solar system to be consistent with the data. Nevertheless, they just kept trying. Rather than throwing out the bad theory and coming up with a new one, they tried to make the old one work.

Through the efforts of Copernicus, Galileo, Kepler, Brahe, and Newton, however, a new theory slowly took over. Once it really took hold, incredible advances were made in only a few centuries. This story should teach all scientists a valuable lesson: Don't cling to theories simply because they have been well-established in the scientific community. If you can't get the data to agree with the theory, find a better one! That's what will advance science.

In my opinion, scientists are doing the same thing today with the theory of evolution. Just like the geocentric theory, the theory of evolution has become well-established in the scientific community. As a result, it has a lot of support. Nevertheless, nearly all data that relate to the origin of life on the planet squarely contradict the theory of evolution. If scientists want to really advance the science of biology, they need to throw evolution away and work in a better theoretical framework. A creationist framework is much more in agreement with the data, so that's a good place to start!

Before I end this module, I do want to comment on the Scripture reference mentioned above (Joshua 10:12-13). Although the Roman Catholic Church interpreted that verse as evidence for the geocentric theory, it is not. The verses from the New American Standard Bible read as follows:

> Then Joshua spoke to the LORD in the day when the LORD delivered up the Amorites before the sons of Israel, and he said in the sight of Israel, "O sun, stand still at Gibeon, and O moon in the valley of Aijalon." So the sun stood still, and the moon stopped, until the nation avenged themselves of their enemies. Is it not written in the book of Jashar? And the sun stopped in the middle of the sky and did not hasten to go down for about a whole day.

Does this Scripture verse indicate that the sun moves around the earth? Of course not! It indicates that the sun moves *relative to Gibeon* (a city about 6 miles north of the center of Jerusalem) and the sky.

Remember, as you already learned, velocity is relative. If you stand still next to a tree, you are not moving relative to the tree, but you are moving relative to someone on the moon. Why? Because the moon is orbiting around the earth. In the same way, the sun does not move relative to the solar system as a whole, because it is fixed at the center. However, relative to the earth, it does move, because the earth is rotating (as well as orbiting around the sun). Thus, the sun moves *in the sky* because the earth rotates. Relative to the sky (and the surface of the earth), then, the sun *does move*.

In this set of verses, Joshua commands the sun to stand still *relative to a city*. In addition, it is reported that the sun stopped *relative to the sky*. Thus, the verses only tell us that the sun moves relative to Gibeon and relative to the sky. They do not in any way imply that the sun moves relative to the solar system. In the end, then, the verses are speaking like any modern-day physicist would speak. They define reference points (Gibeon and the sky) and then discuss the motion of the sun relative to those reference points.

ANSWERS TO THE "ON YOUR OWN" PROBLEMS

11.1 When the masses are changed, the distance between them is not changed. Thus, we don't have to worry about that. When the 10 kg mass is replaced by a 20 kg mass, the mass is multiplied by 2. This means the gravitational force will be multiplied by 2 as well. When the 6 kg mass is replaced with the 3 kg mass, the mass was divided by 2. That means the gravitational force will be divided by 2 as well. In the end, the gravitational force was multiplied by 2 and then divided by 2. The result, then, is that the gravitational force stayed the same.

11.2 When the 1 kg mass is replaced by the 4 kg mass, the mass is multiplied by 4. This means the gravitational force is multiplied by 4. When the 2 kg mass is replaced with the 1 kg mass, the mass is divided by 2, which means the gravitational force is divided by 2. Finally, when the masses are moved from 10 cm to 5 cm, the distance is divided by 2. This means that the gravitational force is multiplied by 2^2, or 4. Thus, the gravitational force is multiplied by 4, divided by 2, and multiplied by 4. In mathematical form, that's 4 x ½ x 4. This is an increase by a factor of 8.

11.3 The velocity of an object traveling in a circle is always straight ahead in the direction of motion. The centripetal force is what keeps it moving in a circle. Thus:

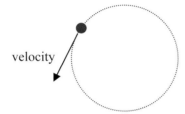

11.4 The centripetal force that keeps an object moving in a circle is always pointed toward the center of the circle:

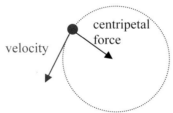

11.5 The insolation that a planet receives is dependent solely on its proximity to the sun. The closer to the sun, the more insolation a planet receives. Thus, Mars receives more insolation than does Saturn.

11.6 There are many things these planets have in common. They are all outer planets, they have similar compositions, they all have rings, they all have satellites, and they are all quite cold. Any three of these would work.

11.7 If the rock came from an asteroid, the asteroid must have first become a meteoroid and then burned up in the atmosphere to become a meteor. Finally, the remnants that fell to the ground are known as meteorites. Thus, she should call it a meteorite.

11.8 The most easily observed comet will be the one that gets bright. In order for a comet to get bright, it must come close to the sun. Thus, orbit (b) is the orbit of the most easily observed comet.

Orbit (a) can still be the orbit of a comet, however. A comet is a comet whether or not it ever develops a coma and tail. A comet is simply a "dirty snowball" in space.

11.9 If Einstein's Theory of General Relativity is true, the gravitational force is not really a force. Instead, it is just a consequence of what mass does to space and time. As a result, there would only be three fundamental forces. An answer of two is acceptable, if you think of the electroweak force as one force.

11.10 In order for the graviton theory to be true, the exchange of particles must be done within a certain time frame. If this is not the case, there is no impetus for the masses to move close together. Thus, it needs to be shown that the exchange of particles is restricted to a certain time frame.

Cartoon by Speartoons

STUDY GUIDE FOR MODULE #11

1. Name the four fundamental forces in creation. Which two forces are really different aspects of the same force?

2. Which is the weakest of the fundamental forces? Which is the strongest?

3. Name the three principles of Newton's Universal Law of Gravitation.

4. The gravitational force between two objects (mass$_1$ = 10 kg, mass$_2$ = 6 kg) is measured when the objects are 10 centimeters apart. If the 10 kg mass is replaced with a 20 kg mass and the 6 kg mass is replaced with a 12 kg mass, how does the new gravitational force compare to the first one that was measured?

5. The gravitational force between two objects (mass$_1$ = 10 kg, mass$_2$ = 6 kg) is measured when the objects are 10 centimeters apart. If the distance between them is increased to 40 centimeters, how does the new gravitational attraction compare to the first one that was measured?

6. The gravitational force between two objects (mass$_1$ = 1 kg, mass$_2$ = 2 kg) is measured when the objects are 12 centimeters apart. If the 1 kg mass is replaced with a 5 kg mass, the 2 kg mass is replaced with a 4 kg mass, and the distance between the objects is reduced to 4 centimeters, how does the new gravitational force compare to the first one that was measured?

7. If Venus orbits the sun because the sun exerts a gravitational force on it, what is the equal and opposite force required by Newton's Third Law of Motion?

8. What kind of force is necessary for circular motion? Give the definition of that force.

9. What are the three principles of circular motion?

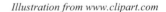
Illustration from www.clipart.com

10. In an Olympic event called the "hammer throw," an athlete twirls a massive ball on the end of a wire. Once he gets the ball twirling very quickly, the athlete releases the wire, allowing the ball to fly straight out into the field. The person who throws the ball the farthest this way is the winner.

a. As the athlete twirls the ball faster and faster, will the wire have to apply more, less, or the same amount of centripetal force?

b. Suppose the athlete starts by gripping the wire close to the ball so the ball sweeps out a small circle. Then, keeping the speed of the ball constant, he allows some of the wire to slip through his hands so the ball sweeps out a larger and larger circle. Will the wire exert more, less, or the same amount of force as the athlete makes his adjustment?

11. What is "centrifugal force?"

12. In the following diagram, the ball is traveling from "A" to "B" along the path drawn. Draw the velocity of the ball and the force it experiences if it is traveling at constant speed.

13. List the inner planets and the outer planets.

14. List the planets of the solar system from the closest to the sun to the farthest from the sun.

15. List the planets that have rings.

16. Where are most of the asteroids in the solar system?

17. What causes an asteroid to become a meteor?

18. What are the three parts of a comet? Which of those parts is always present in a comet?

19. During what part of a comet's orbit are all three parts present?

20. Are comets' orbits circular or elliptical?

21. Where do most physicists think short-period comets come from?

22. What causes gravity, according to Einstein's Theory of General Relativity?

23. What causes gravity, according to the graviton theory?

MODULE #12: The Forces in Creation - Part 2

Introduction

I want to continue my discussion of the four fundamental forces in creation by turning next to the **electromagnetic force**. I am sure you are at least somewhat familiar with this force. It is the force that makes electricity flow in an electrical circuit, holds electrons in an atom, and makes lightning. What you might be surprised to find out is that this very force also attracts the north pole of a magnet to the south pole of a magnet. This causes the compass needle to point north, refrigerator magnets to stick to the refrigerator, and electrical motors to turn.

At one time, physicists thought the force that governs electricity was completely different from the force that governs magnetism. After all, electricity and magnetism seem so different; how could they both be governed by the same force? It took the genius of a Scottish physicist named James Clerk Maxwell to demonstrate that both electricity and magnetism are, in fact, different facets of the same force. When Maxwell demonstrated this fact, enormous advances were made in the study of electrical and magnetic phenomena in physics. As a result, many people refer to Maxwell as the founder of modern physics. He is often ranked with Albert Einstein and Sir Isaac Newton as one of the three most important figures in the history of science. Because of his importance, a brief biography is in order.

James Clerk Maxwell

Born in a remote region of Scotland in 1831, Maxwell was home-educated until being accepted to Edinburgh University at the age of 16. The university offered him admission when a group of scientists there read a paper he had written about geometric curves when he was 14 years old. They were so impressed with it that they immediately accepted him as a student. When he came to the university, all the professors were amazed at his ability to design experiments that explained whatever interested him. He quickly outgrew the experimental facilities at Edinburgh University and transferred to Cambridge University in England to continue his studies.

Original photograph in the possession of Sir Henry Roscoe, courtesy AIP Emilio Segrè Visual Archives

After graduating from Cambridge, he took a teaching post at King's College and met **Michael Faraday**, the inventor of the electrical generator and the electrical transformer. Although great with experiments, Faraday lacked the mathematical insight of Maxwell. Together, they made a great team. Maxwell put Faraday's theories on a firm mathematical foundation, and as a result, real advances were made in the study of electricity and magnetism.

When he was 42, he published a book entitled *Treatise on Electricity and Magnetism*. In it, he used forty mathematical equations to show that electricity and magnetism were, indeed, governed by exactly the same force. As with most revolutionary works, it was not accepted right away. The later experiments of Heinrich Rudolph Hertz lent so much weight to Maxwell's work, however, that it eventually became the guiding force of electromagnetic study. With time, Maxwell's forty equations were reduced to only four, but they still bear the name "Maxwell's Equations." With two to four years of post-calculus mathematics, you can *begin* to understand Maxwell's Equations.

James Clerk Maxwell was known for many other things. He provided the mathematical foundation for the kinetic theory of gases, which allows chemists and physicists to explain the behavior of a gas under almost any set of conditions. That theory was later expanded to apply to all matter. It is now called the "kinetic theory of matter," and I touched on it in Module #3 when I explained the concept of temperature. In addition, Maxwell was the first to explain how we see in color, which led him to be able to make the first color photograph in 1861. Maxwell also developed several advances in the field of thermodynamics (thur' moh dye nam' iks), which you will learn about in chemistry.

Clearly, Maxwell is a genius of the caliber of Newton. Like Newton, he was also a devoted Christian, but he was more orthodox than was Newton. The fact that Maxwell was a devout Christian shouldn't surprise you. Many scientists and philosophers (Pierre Duhem and Stanley Jaki, for example) credit Christianity with the birth of the scientific method, so it is not surprising that most of the founders of modern science had a strong Christian faith. Maxwell's devotion to Christianity was demonstrated in the extemporaneous prayers he would say. One example is, "Teach us to study the works of Thy hands, that we may subdue the earth to our use and strengthen our reason for Thy service". [Dan Graves, *Scientists of Faith*, Kregel Resources: Grand Rapids, Michigan, p. 153, 1996].

As was the case with Newton, Maxwell studied science as a means of serving Christ. Indeed, when Maxwell founded the Cavendish Laboratory at Cambridge University, he wanted to remind all scientists who entered that they should perform their duties with reverence to the Lord. As a result, Maxwell insisted that the Scripture verse, "Great are the works of the Lord; they are pondered by all who delight in them" (Psalm 111:2) be carved in Latin on the great door that leads into the laboratory. Today more than ever, science needs people like James Clerk Maxwell!

The Electromagnetic Force

As I said before, everyone has some experience with the electromagnetic force. Nevertheless, to make sure we all "start on the same page," I want to go over the basics. The best way to start is by having you perform an experiment.

EXPERIMENT 12.1
Electrical Attraction and Repulsion

Supplies:

♦ Two balloons (Round balloons work best, but any kind will do.)
♦ Thread
♦ Cellophane tape
♦ Eye protection such as goggles or safety glasses

Introduction: This experiment teaches you when electrically charged objects attract one another and when they repel one another. It will also tell you something about the properties of the electromagnetic force.

Procedure:

1. Blow up the balloons and tie them off so they each stay inflated.
2. Tie some thread to one of the balloons and attach the other end of the thread to the ceiling with some tape so that the balloon hangs from the thread. Make the length of the thread so that the balloon hangs at about the same height as your chest.
3. Take the balloon that is hanging by the thread and rub it in your hair a little. This will cause the balloon to pick up some electrical charge. Now back away from the balloon and allow it to hang there.
4. Take the other balloon and rub it in your hair just a little.
5. Hold this balloon in both your hands and slowly bring it close to the balloon that is hanging from the thread. What happens?
6. Play with the situation a bit, trying to see what kind of motion you can induce in the hanging balloon.
7. Vigorously rub the balloon that is in your hands in your hair. Spend significantly more time doing it this time as compared to what you did in step 4.
8. Once again, bring the balloon in your hands close to the balloon that is hanging on the thread. Note what happens, and note how the motion of the hanging balloon compares to its motion in steps 5 and 6.
9. Put away the balloon that is in your hands.
10. Take a piece of tape that is at least 15 cm long and tape it to the top of a table. Leave a little part of it unfastened, so that you can remove it in a moment. Be sure to ask your parents which table you should use for this, as what you will do in the next step can damage the finish on some tables.
11. Quickly rip the tape off the table and grasp it at both ends. Hold the tape near the balloon, with the sticky side facing the balloon. What happens this time?
12. Once again, play with the situation a bit to see what kind of motion you can induce in the hanging balloon.
13. Clean up your mess.

Why did the hanging balloon behave the way it did in the experiment? Well, when you rub a balloon in your hair, it picks up some stray electrons in your hair. This causes the balloon to pick up an overall negative charge. Since you rubbed both the hanging balloon and the balloon in your hand in your hair, both of them developed a negative charge. When you brought one close to the other, they began to repel each other, because charges that have the same sign repel each other. The closer the balloons got together, the greater the repulsion. Also, when you rubbed the balloon in your hand more vigorously in your hair, it picked up more negative charge, which also increased the repulsion. This brings me to the first rule of electrical charge:

Like charges repel one another.

Two positively charged objects will repel each other, as will two negatively charged objects. The first object will exert a repulsive force on the second, and in compliance with Newton's Third Law, the second will exert an equal and opposite force on the first.

When you stuck the tape on the table and then ripped it off, you were actually causing the tape to lose negative charges. This is because the tape leaves electrons behind in the sticky residue left on the table. Since the tape lost negative charges, it became positively charged. When you held that up to the balloon, the balloon was attracted to it because negatively charged matter attracts positively charged matter. This brings me to the second rule of electrical charge:

Opposite charges attract one another.

When a negatively charged particle is in proximity to a positively charged particle, a mutual attractive force will develop. The first will exert a force on the second, and in compliance with Newton's Third Law, the second will exert an equal and opposite force on the first.

FIGURE 12.1
Opposite Charges Attract

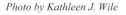 *Photo by Kathleen J. Wile*

The young lady in this photo rubbed the balloon in her hair and then held it above her head. Why did her hair "defy gravity" and rise up to stick to the balloon? The reason is the electromagnetic attraction between opposite charges.

When she rubbed the balloon in her hair, it picked up electrons from her hair. Since electrons are negatively charged, this made the balloon negatively charged. Because her hair lost electrons to the balloon, it became positively charged. As a result, her hair and the balloon are oppositely charged.

Since opposite electrical charges attract one another, her hair was attracted to the balloon. At the distance shown, the attraction between her hair and the balloon was stronger than the force of gravity pulling her hair down. As a result, her hair rose to the balloon.

The experiment you performed also demonstrated the way the force between electrically charged particles changes under different conditions. For example, the more vigorously you rubbed the balloon on your hair, the more charge it collected and, as a result, the stronger it repelled the other balloon. Thus, the larger the electrical charge, the stronger the force. Also, the closer you brought the balloons together, the stronger the repulsion became. That's because the force between electrical charges increases the closer the charges are to one another.

In fact, just as there were three principles regarding gravitational force, there are three principles regarding the force that exists between electrical charges. They are:

1. **All electrical charges attract or repel one another: Like charges repel, while opposite charges attract.**

2. **The force between charged objects is directly proportional to the amount of electrical charge on each object.**

3. **The force between charged objects is inversely proportional to the square of the distance between the two objects.**

Does this look familiar at all? It should. After all, if you replaced "electrical charge" with "mass" in #2 and #3, you would essentially have the last two principles of Newton's Universal Law of Gravitation! Indeed, the force between electrically charged particles behaves almost identically to the gravitational force. There are only two major differences. First, the force between electrical charges can be repulsive, while the gravitational force is always attractive. Second, the force between electrical charges is significantly stronger than the gravitational force.

The fact that the force between electrical charges behaves much like the gravitational force is another reason why physicists believe there is something to the graviton theory of gravity. After all, it would be an incredible coincidence if the gravitational force behaved just like the electromagnetic force unless they were both caused by essentially the same thing. Since the electromagnetic force is produced by the exchange of particles (see below), the gravitational force must also be produced by the exchange of particles. Otherwise, it would not behave so much like the electromagnetic force.

Scientists who are Christians, however, have no problem with the fact that there are many "coincidences" in creation. Since one Creator designed and put into place all the laws that govern the universe, it should not be surprising that they are similar. Thus, although there is some "tidiness" to believing in the graviton theory, its similarity to the electromagnetic force is no real reason to. If Einstein's Theory of General Relativity is right, there is no need to believe in the graviton theory. After all, God could have designed space and time so they curve just right in the presence of mass so that, as a result, the gravitational force and electromagnetic force behave essentially the same.

Since you have already dealt with example problems related to the gravitational force, I will not do any example problems on how to predict the change in the electromagnetic force when the charge or the distance between objects changes. Nevertheless, as "On Your Own" problem 12.2 demonstrates, you need to know how to do them. They are, however, exactly like the gravitation problems that you did, so if you have difficulty solving them, you might want to look back at Example 11.1.

ON YOUR OWN

12.1 For the diagrams below, use a blue arrow to point out the direction of the force exerted on the red ball by the blue ball. In addition, draw a red arrow to indicate the direction of the force exerted on blue ball by the red ball.

a.   b.

12.2 Two charged particles are placed 16 centimeters from each other and the resulting force is measured. The charge on object #1 is then halved and the charge on object #2 is divided by 4. The distance between the objects is also reduced to 4 centimeters. How does the new force compare to the old force?

Photons and the Electromagnetic Force

As I said in the previous module, the electromagnetic force is actually produced through the exchange of particles. Believe it or not, the particles exchanged are actually small bits of light, called **photons**.

Photon – A small "package" of light that acts like a particle

In the previous module, you learned how the exchange of particles can generate an attractive force. Opposite charges are attracted to each other through the exchange of photons, much like you were "attracted" to your helper in Experiment 11.3 through the exchange of balls. How does the exchange of particles lead to a repulsive force? That's a bit too hard to explain here. You will just have to believe that like charges repel one another because of the exchange of photons. If you go on to study physics in college, you will eventually learn enough physics and mathematics to see why. For now, you just have to trust me!

Part of the reason this is hard for you to believe is that you have no evidence to support it. After all, when you did the experiment, you didn't see the balloons glowing, did you? You didn't see light going between the tape and the balloon. How in the world, then, can I say that the force between electrically charged objects is governed by the exchange of photons? The answer to this question lies in a discussion of the nature of light. I don't want to have that discussion now, however, because I want to stay focused on the phenomena associated with electricity and magnetism. For now, then, I will just tell you that the vast majority of light in creation is invisible to you and me. As a result, it is rare for us to actually see the photons being exchanged by charged particles. Although it is rare, it nevertheless happens in certain situations. In fact, all the light you actually do see originates from exchange between two charged particles.

How can I say that? Well, let's start simple. When you ignite a candle, you see light coming from it, right? You see light because a chemical reaction has generated heat. That heat has moved around some electrons in the atoms of the candle and the surrounding air. When those electrons move in certain specific ways, they no longer need to exchange as many photons with the positively-charged particles to which they are attracted. Thus, there are "extra" photons left over. Some of those photons just happen to be the photons your eyes detect as the pleasant, yellow light of the flame. Thus, the light from the flame of a candle is really composed of photons that result from the interaction between the electrically charged particles that make up the atoms involved in the fire.

The lights that light your home also send out photons resulting from interactions between charged particles. Like a candle, a standard light bulb produces light by first producing heat. The heat comes from an electrical current that warms up the filament in the light bulb. This causes electrons in the filament to move around. When those electrons move in certain ways, they no longer need to exchange as many photons with their positively charged partners as they used to. As a result, the "extra" photons are ejected, and they hit your eyes as white light.

If you are still having problems believing that photons are exchanged between charged particles, there is one more thing you need to remember. The idea that the electromagnetic force is governed by the exchange of particles explains the three principles of the electromagnetic force between charged particles. The more charge a particle has, for example, the more photons it can exchange. This tells you why the electromagnetic force between charged particles is directly proportional to the charge of the particle.

The exchange of particles also explains why the electromagnetic force between charged objects is inversely proportional to the square of the distance between them. Suppose you wanted to throw a ball at a person but had a blindfold on and therefore could not see that person. If you just randomly threw the ball at the person, your chance of hitting him or her goes down as the distance between you and the person increases. After all, the farther away the person is, the harder it is to hit him or her, even when you *can* see. It turns out that when you randomly throw a ball at a person, your chance of hitting that person *is inversely proportional to the square of the distance between you*. Thus, the ability for charged particles to exchange photons also is inversely proportional to the square of the distance between them. As a result, the electromagnetic force is inversely proportional to the square of the distance between the charged particles.

In addition to such arguments, physicists can actually use mathematics to show that charged particles exchange photons. Thus, the idea that the electromagnetic force is governed by the exchange of photons is a rather solid idea in modern physics.

ON YOUR OWN

12.3 A black object is heated until it glows with a nice, orange-yellow glow. If the black object has no net electrical charge, where does the light come from?

How Objects Become Electrically Charged

In Module #3, I told you that atoms are electrically neutral, being composed of neutrons (that have no charge) and an equal number of protons (positively charged) and electrons (negatively charged). When an atom loses electrons, it ends up with a positive charge and is called a positive ion. When an atom picks up extra electrons, it ends up with a negative charge, making it a negative ion. How do atoms gain or lose electrons? Well, one way is through chemical reactions, but that is beyond the scope of this course. You will learn about it when you reach chemistry. There are, however, other ways that atoms can gain or lose electrons. I will cover them here. The best way to start is to do an experiment.

EXPERIMENT 12.2
Making and Using an Electroscope

Supplies:

♦ Tape
♦ A clear glass
♦ A plastic lid that fits over the glass. This lid can be larger than the mouth of the glass, but it cannot be smaller. The top of a margarine tub or something similar works quite well.

♦ A paper clip
♦ Two 5-cm x 1.5-cm strips of aluminum foil (the thinner the better)
♦ A balloon
♦ A pair of pliers
♦ Eye protection such as goggles or safety glasses

Introduction: In this experiment, you will build a device that detects the presence of electrical charge and learn two of the basic methods used to charge an object.

Procedure:

1. Using your hands and the pliers, straighten out and then bend the paper clip so that it ends up looking something like this:

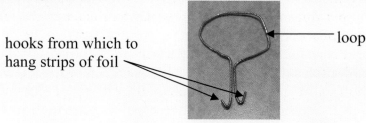

hooks from which to
hang strips of foil   loop

2. Cut a thin slot in the plastic lid. Slide the loop of the twisted paper clip into the slot, then twist it 90 degrees so that the slot holds the loop in place. The loop should stand perpendicular to the lid. You may need to use some tape to hold it in this position (see the photo below).
3. Poke a hole near one end of each strip of foil and hang the foil strips on the tiny hooks that are at the bottom of the twisted paper clip.
4. Place the lid on top of the glass, so that the foil strips hang on the inside of the glass. You have just made an **electroscope** (ih lek' truh skohp). It should look something like this:

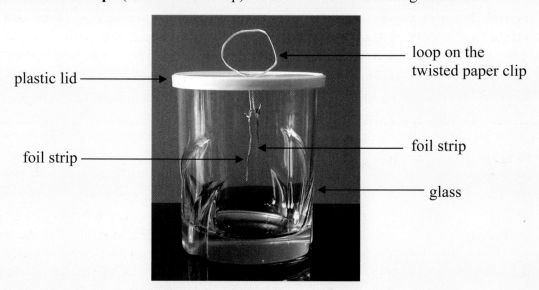

plastic lid   loop on the
                                                              twisted paper clip

foil strip   foil strip

                                                              glass

5. Well, now that you've made the electroscope, what good is it? An electroscope detects the presence of electric charge. To see this, inflate the balloon and tie it off so that it stays inflated.
6. Rub the balloon in your hair to charge it.
7. Slowly bring the balloon close to the loop of the twisted paper clip without actually touching it. The foil strips should start to move. If they do not, your balloon is probably not charged well. Rub it more vigorously in your hair, or rub it in someone else's hair.

8. Note how the foil strips move as you bring the balloon closer to the loop. Don't actually touch the loop with the balloon!

9. Pull the balloon away from the loop and note how the foil strips move. Do this a couple of times so that you can describe the motion of the foil strips well.

10. Bring the balloon near the loop one more time. This time, however, allow the balloon to touch the paper clip. Note what happens to the foil strips.

11. Pull the balloon away. This time, the behavior of the foil strips should be noticeably different from what it was in step 9.

12. I want you to do one more thing. This might be a little tricky. Touch the loop with your finger. You should notice that the foil strips respond to your touch. Note what they do.

13. Take your finger away from the loop.

14. Bring the balloon close to the loop, but do not touch it with the balloon. When you see the foil strips move significantly, hold the balloon where it is and touch the paper clip with a finger from your other hand. As soon as your finger touches the paper clip, the foil strips should move again. Keep your finger resting on the paper clip for a moment.

15. Pull your finger away so that it is no longer touching the paper clip.

16. Now pull the balloon away. The foil strips should move yet again, and behave similarly to what you saw in step 11. This doesn't always work the first time, so try it a few times until it eventually works.

17. Clean up your mess.

Now you need to know what happened in the experiment. The foil and the paper clip, like all forms of matter, have both positive and negative charges in them. The number of positive charges and negative charges, however, are equal; thus, the foil and paper clip have no overall charge. Because it picked up some electrons when you rubbed it in your hair, the balloon had more negative charges than positive ones, so it had an overall negative charge. When you brought it in close proximity to the paper clip, the negative charge of the balloon repelled the negatively charged electrons in the paper clip and the foil. Since they were repelled, they traveled away from the balloon, which caused the ends of the foil to be rich with electrons. At the same time, since electrons moved away from the atoms in the paper clip, those atoms lost electrons and therefore became positively charged. In the end, then, the foil strips developed an overall negative charge, and the paper clip developed an overall positive charge, as shown below.

Illustration by Megan Whitaker

FIGURE 12.2
What Happened in the First Part of Experiment 12.2

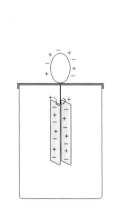 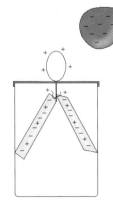

When brought in close proximity to the paper clip, the negative charge of the balloon repelled the negatively charged electrons in the paper clip and the foil. Since they were repelled, they traveled away from the balloon, which caused the ends of the foil to be rich with electrons. The excess of negative charges in the foil strips caused each strip to become negatively charged. This made the strips repel each other, and that's why they pulled apart from each other in the experiment.

If you did not touch the balloon to the paper clip, as soon as you pulled the balloon away, the foil strips should have relaxed back to their normal position. That's because once the negatively charged balloon moved away, the electrons that were crammed together in the foil were no longer repelled by anything. The paper clip had an overall positive charge, however, and this positive charge attracted electrons back to the paper clip. This made everything neutral again. When that happened, the foil strips hung down normally again.

What happened in the next part of the experiment? When you touched the balloon to the paper clip, the foil strips moved apart again and, after you removed the balloon, they stayed apart. This is because when you actually touched the balloon to the paper clip, some of the balloon's extra electrons were able to flow into the paper clip and into the foil strips. This gave the paper clip and foil strips a bunch of extra electrons. When you pulled the balloon away, those extra electrons stayed. This caused a permanent negative charge to develop on the foil strips. Since the foil strips stayed negatively charged, they still repelled each other. Thus, they stayed away from each other. You ended up getting rid of the charge by touching the paper clip with your finger. When you did that, the extra electrons flowed into your body. This got rid of the negative charge on the foil strips, and the strips relaxed.

When you charge something by touching an electrically charged object to it and allowing the charge to flow between the electrically charged object and the object that you are charging, physicists say that you are **charging by conduction**.

Charging by conduction – Charging an object by allowing it to come into contact with an object that already has an electrical charge

In other words, by allowing electrons to be conducted between the object you are charging and the object that already has charge, you are charging by conduction.

Although you might think that this is the only way to charge an object, it is not. In the last part of the experiment (illustrated in Figure 12.3 on the next page), you also ended up charging the foil strips. In that case, when the balloon was moved near the paper clip, the electrons in the paper clip and foil moved away from the balloon, concentrating negative charge in the foil strips, causing the strips to repel each other. When you touched your finger to the paper clip, however, the electrons could travel farther away from the balloon by traveling through your finger and into your body. Thus, you actually removed some of the electrons from the foil and paper clip. When you moved your finger and then the balloon away, the paper clip and foil were left with fewer electrons than they should have had, because some of those electrons stayed in your hand. This gave the foil strips and the paper clip an overall positive charge. Since the strips were both positively charged, they repelled each other, and they moved away from each other again.

When you performed the experiment in this way, you induced the negative charges to leave the foil by giving them an escape route: your hand. This caused the foil strips to become positively charged when you took your hand and the balloon away. This, as you might imagine, is called **charging by induction**.

Charging by induction – Charging an object without direct contact between the object and a charge

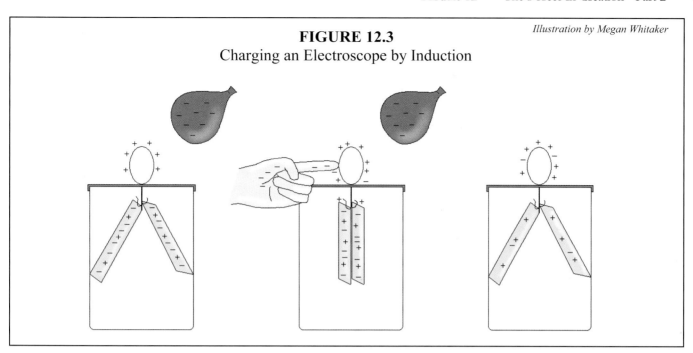

FIGURE 12.3
Charging an Electroscope by Induction

Illustration by Megan Whitaker

So what are the practical effects of charging by conduction and charging by induction? Think about what happened in the experiment. When you charged by conduction, you gave the foil strips some of the extra charge that was on the balloon. This caused the strips to become negatively charged, which was the same charge as the balloon. When you charged by induction, you forced negative charges out of the foil strips, causing the strips to become positively charged, which was opposite of the charge on the balloon. Thus, charging by induction gives the object a charge opposite of the charge you are using. When charging by conduction, the object you are charging gets the same charge as the charge you are using.

ON YOUR OWN

12.4 If you want to give an object a positive charge, but the only source of charge you have is negative, would you charge the object by conduction or induction?

<u>Electrical Circuits</u>

One of the most useful aspects of the force that exists between charged particles is that you can use it to make electrical circuits. In an electrical circuit, charges flow through a wire. The energy those charges have can be used by electrical devices, and the result is something useful. For example, when a light bulb is hooked up to an electrical circuit, the bulb glows. In order to understand how this works, you need to understand two things: how the charges begin moving in the first place, and how the energy of the moving charges is used by the light bulb. We'll start with the former concept and end with the latter.

In order to get electrical charges moving, you need something that uses the electromagnetic force. One device that does this is a battery. A battery stores electrical charge. The description of how a battery does this is a bit too difficult to explain here, but you will learn about it in chemistry. For right now, just realize that one side of the battery contains chemicals that want to lose electrons, while the other side contains chemicals that want to gain electrons. As a result, one side of the battery is a source of electrons, so it is considered negative. The other is the place where the electrons want to go, so it is considered positive. When the two sides of a battery are hooked together with a metal, electrons will flow through the metal from the negative side of the battery to the positive side.

As you no doubt already know, a battery is rated by its voltage. Most cylindrical batteries are rated at 1.5 volts, while the small, rectangular batteries with electrical posts at the top are typically 9 volts. But what does voltage mean? It tells you how hard the battery "pushes" electrons through an electrical circuit. The higher the voltage, the harder the battery "pushes" electrons through the metal.

Now remember why we want the electrons to travel from one end of the battery to the other. We want to use their energy. Thus, the more voltage the battery has, the more energy the electrons have, and the more we can do with them. If you think about it, however, the voltage of a battery is not the only factor that determines how much gets done in an electrical circuit. Not only does the energy of each electron influence what gets done, but so does the *number* of electrons that travel through the circuit. After all, when ten electrons travel through an electrical circuit, ten times more work will get done than when only one electron travels through the circuit. Thus, not only the voltage of the battery, but also the number of charged particles flowing through the circuit will determine what the circuit can do.

The number of electrons that flow through a circuit in a given amount of time can be determined by examining the **electrical current** in a circuit.

Electrical current – The amount of charge that travels past a fixed point in an electric circuit each
second

Electrical current is usually measured in Amperes, which are abbreviated as "amps" or "A." When you look at an electrical circuit, then, you need to know both the current (amps) and the voltage (volts) of the circuit. They each work together to tell you how much an electrical circuit can do.

For example, if you are playing with an electrical toy that works on a 9-volt battery and accidentally touch a bare wire while the toy is running, you might get shocked, but you won't be seriously hurt. That's because both the voltage and the current running through the toy's electrical circuit is low. On the other hand, if you were unfortunate enough to touch the bare wire of a fan that is plugged into a wall socket and running, you would almost certainly be seriously hurt, because the voltage and current running through that circuit are quite high.

It is important to realize that *only one* of these two quantities needs to be large for an electrical circuit to pack a good punch. The voltage in your car's battery is probably 12 volts. That's not much more than the 9-volt battery that runs an electrical toy. There are several hundred amps of current that flow through the ignition circuit when the car is being started, however. That's about a million times more current than what's flowing through the circuit of an electrical toy! Thus, even though the voltage of a car's electrical circuit is low, the current is high, and the circuit can therefore provide a lot of energy. As a result, touching an exposed battery cable in a car that is being started can be *very* dangerous!

This should make perfect sense. After all, the voltage simply tells you the energy of the electrons in the circuit. Thus, if the energy per electron is really large, just a few electrons can pack a lot of energy. As a result, a circuit with low current but high voltage can be harmful. In the same way, if the voltage is low, the circuit could still have a lot of energy just by having an enormous number of electrons flowing through it. In that case, voltage would be low, but current would be high. Such a combination is still harmful.

Now that you know about voltage and current, it is time to learn about electrical circuits. Suppose I take a metal wire and connect it to each side of a battery. The result might look something like the figure below.

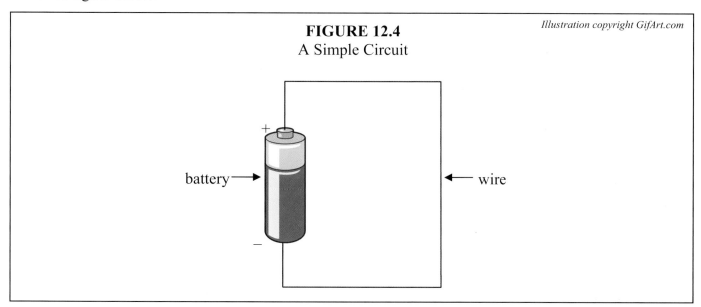

FIGURE 12.4
A Simple Circuit

Illustration copyright GifArt.com

This is a very basic electrical circuit. Electrons will flow through the wire from the negative side of the battery to the positive side. In order to reduce the time it takes to draw circuits, physicists have developed symbols to represent the major components of an electrical circuit. A battery is symbolized with two parallel lines, one longer than the other. The positive side of the battery is usually represented by the longer line. In the end, then, the simple circuit above can be drawn as follows:

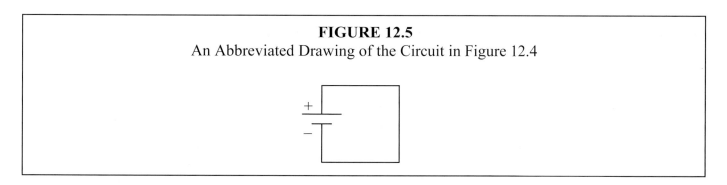

FIGURE 12.5
An Abbreviated Drawing of the Circuit in Figure 12.4

Since the longer line of the battery is supposed to represent the positive side, there is really no need to label the sides of the battery as I have in the drawing above. Thus, in all future circuit drawings, I will not. I just put them in this drawing to emphasize that the longer line represents the positive side of the battery, whereas the smaller line represents the negative side.

The first thing you need to be able to do when you look at a circuit like the one in Figure 12.5 is determine how the current flows. Unfortunately, Benjamin Franklin caused no end of confusion over this very point. Although he is best remembered for his political endeavors as one of the United States' Founding Fathers, Franklin was actually one of the most respected scientists in his time. His theories and experiments regarding electricity were known and admired the world over. Many of his ideas laid the groundwork for our modern theories of electricity.

You see, batteries were invented long before anyone really understood what electricity was. As a result, scientists tried to study batteries and the electricity they produced to better understand what electricity was. In Franklin's studies, he theorized that batteries had a positive and a negative side, and that electricity was composed of particles that flowed from one side of a battery to the other. These ideas were readily accepted and highly regarded by scientists around the world.

Now, although Franklin's concept of positive and negative sides of a battery helped revolutionize the way scientists studied electricity, it also caused a bit of confusion. You see, Franklin thought that the positive side of a battery had too many of these mysterious particles and the negative side had too few. Thus, he said that electricity must flow through a circuit from the positive side of the battery to the negative side. Since his ideas were highly regarded, this idea was accepted the world over. Scientists everywhere began drawing electrical circuits assuming that the electricity flowed from the positive side of the battery, through the circuit, and back to the negative side.

As is usually the case with technology, people began finding uses for electricity long before science figured out what electricity really was. Thus, engineers began designing electrical circuits, and they, too, drew the circuits assuming that electricity flowed from the positive side of the battery to the negative side. As time went on, however, science slowly showed the error of this assumption. The electron was discovered, and it was determined that electricity is actually the flow of electrons. Thus, in reality, electricity flows from the negative side of the battery (the source of electrons) to the positive side of the battery (where the electrons go).

This conclusion, however, contradicted thousands of circuit drawings that had been made over the years. Engineers had always drawn current as flowing from the positive side of the battery to the negative side. They didn't want to stop doing it just because science had shown that the reverse was true. As a result, people just kept on drawing electrical current as starting from the positive side of the battery and flowing to the negative side, even though they knew it was wrong.

Illustrating the current as flowing from positive to negative came to be known as **conventional current**, and it is still the way circuits are drawn today.

<u>Conventional current</u> – Current that flows from the positive side of the battery to the negative side.
                This is the way current is drawn in circuit diagrams, even though it is wrong.

The point to this long, drawn-out discussion is that Benjamin Franklin's inaccurate assumption regarding how current flows forces us to draw current in an electric circuit as flowing from the positive side of the battery to the negative side. Even though we know this is not what happens physically, we do it so as not to break with tradition. Thus, in our original circuit diagram, the current can be pictured as shown in Figure 12.6.

FIGURE 12.6
Conventional Current in an Electric Circuit

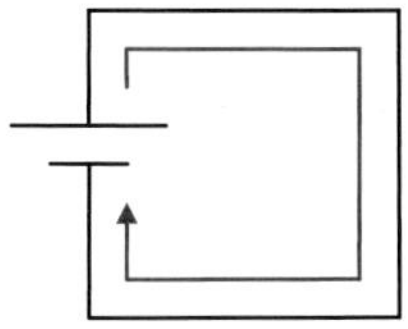

In this diagram, the red line shows the path of the current in the wire. Of course, even though the red line is not drawn right on top of the lines representing the wire, it is still understood that the current is actually flowing in the wire, not where the red line is drawn.

ON YOUR OWN

12.5 For the following circuit diagram, draw the current flow with a dashed line. Then draw the actual flow of electrons with a solid line.

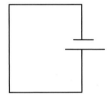

<u>Resistance</u>

Now that we know how to get electrons flowing through an electrical circuit, the next logical step is to figure out how we can use the energy in those electrons to do something useful. The best way to start is with a simple experiment.

EXPERIMENT 12.3
Current and Resistance

<u>Supplies</u>:

♦ A 1.5-volt battery (Any AA-, C-, or D-cell battery will work. Do not use any battery other than one of those, though, because a higher voltage can make the experiment dangerous.)
♦ Aluminum foil
♦ Scissors
♦ Eye protection such as goggles or safety glasses

Introduction: In order to get something useful out of an electrical circuit, we must use the energy of the electrons flowing through the circuit. In this experiment, you will learn one way this is accomplished.

<u>Procedure:</u>

1. Cut a small strip of aluminum foil about 1.3 times the length of the battery and only about 1 cm wide.
2. Lay the foil across the battery and, using your thumb and forefinger, pinch the foil so that it makes contact with both ends of the battery, as shown below:

Illustration copyright GifArt.com

3. Hold the foil there for a few moments. Note what you feel. Do not hold the foil for too long, as it can get painful!
4. Put everything away.

The heat you felt in the experiment comes from the electrons moving in the foil. As soon as you touched the aluminum foil to both ends of the battery, electrons flowed through the aluminum from the negative side of the battery to the positive side. The electrons accelerated under the electromagnetic force of the battery and, as a result, started moving quickly. Now, as electrons flowed through the aluminum, they began colliding with the electrons in some of the aluminum atoms. They also collided with impurities in the metal. These collisions produced heat, and you felt that heat in your fingers.

Before we go on, I need you to realize that you could touch the aluminum foil *only* because I knew that both the voltage *and* the current would be too low to cause you serious harm. **DO NOT DO THIS IN ANY OTHER SITUATION!!!!!!!** Since you do not know a lot about electricity, you will not know what is safe and what is not. Playing with electricity is deadly. Don't do *anything* with electricity unless someone experienced tells you to!!!!

So the heat you felt in the experiment was a result of the aluminum *resisting* the flow of electrons. Each metal resists electron flow differently, so we say that each metal has its own **resistance**.

<u>Resistance</u> – The ability of a material to impede the flow of charge

It turns out that the type of metal is not the only thing that determines resistance. The resistance of a wide piece of metal, for example, is lower than the resistance of a narrow piece made out of the same metal. This is because the electrons that move through the metal can "spread out" as they move through the metal, reducing congestion and thus the number of collisions. Also, as you might expect, the longer the metal, the larger the resistance. After all, the longer the metal, the more chance the electrons have to collide with things in the metal.

With the knowledge of current, electrical circuits, and resistance that you have under your belt, you can finally begin to understand how the simplest electrical devices work. For example, consider an electrical heater. This could be a space heater used to warm up a room, a coil on an electric stove, or even the wires on the inside of a toaster. When such a device is turned on, the heater begins to glow, emitting a large amount of heat. This works because the material used to make the heater has a certain amount of electrical resistance. Since there is resistance, there is heat and often light. The light causes the heater to glow, and the heat energy warms the room, cooks the food, or browns the bread.

FIGURE 12.7
A Stovetop Burner

Photo © Dana Heinemann, Agency: Dreamstime.com

As electrons flow through the coil on this burner, the resistance of the metal produces heat and light.

One way we get electrons to do something useful in an electrical circuit, then, is to use a metal's resistance to convert the energy of the electrons speeding through the circuit into heat and light. The type of metal used to do this will influence the effect you get. For example, most metals will resist the flow of electrons in such a way as to produce mostly heat and only a small amount of light. Those metals are used in heaters, stoves, and toasters. Other metals tend to produce more light than heat. Those metals are typically used in the filaments of light bulbs.

It is important that you really see what's going on in an electrical circuit. Most people think that electrical devices "use up" electrons. Thus, you plug your appliance in, and it "eats up" the electricity it pulls from the electrical socket. That's not what happens. The same number of electrons flow out of a toaster as the number that flowed into it. What the toaster does use up, however, is energy. As electrons flow through a circuit, the collisions they experience convert the energy produced by the electromagnetic force into heat.

ON YOUR OWN

12.6 When we work with most circuits, we assume that the resistance of the wire in the circuit is zero. Thus, the only resistance we consider is that of the device (or devices) in the circuit. Suppose a wire was made of aluminum. Would it have zero resistance? Hint: Think about the experiment you just did.

<u>Switches and Circuits</u>

With the tools you have learned so far, you can look at a simple circuit and determine in which direction the current flows. So let me ask you a question: In what direction does the current flow in this circuit?

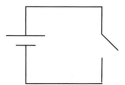

You should realize that I just asked you a trick question. No current flows in the circuit drawn above. Why? Remember, in order to have electricity, electrons must travel from one place to another. In the circuits we have discussed so far, they flow from one end of the battery to the other. The reason they do this is because there is metal linking the two sides of the battery.

In the circuit drawn above, the metal does not link the two sides of the battery, because there is a break in the wire. Thus, electrons cannot flow from one side of the battery to the other, because they cannot jump over the "gap" in the wire. As a result, there is no current in the circuit. Physicists call circuits such as the one drawn above **open circuits**.

<u>Open circuit</u> – A circuit that does not have a complete connection between the two sides of the power
             source. As a result, current does not flow.

Now suppose I took the diagonally pointing piece of wire in the figure above and pushed it down so that its end touched the end of the other wire. What would happen then? As soon as the two ends touched, there would be a complete connection between one end of the battery and the other. Thus, electrons would start to flow from one end of the battery to the other. Once that happened, of course, there would be current flowing through the circuit.

This is the way a switch works. When the switch is open, no current can flow, and the device you are using does not work. When you flip the switch, however, a connection is made, and electrons begin to flow. This allows the device you are powering to operate. This is illustrated in Figure 12.8, where a light is off and then turned on by a switch.

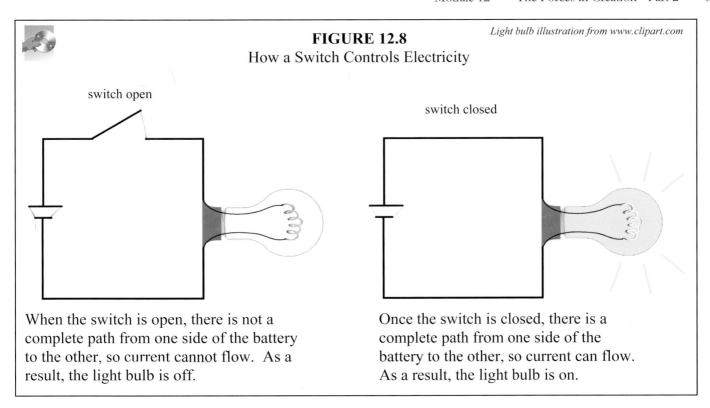

Light bulb illustration from www.clipart.com

FIGURE 12.8
How a Switch Controls Electricity

switch open

switch closed

When the switch is open, there is not a complete path from one side of the battery to the other, so current cannot flow. As a result, the light bulb is off.

Once the switch is closed, there is a complete path from one side of the battery to the other, so current can flow. As a result, the light bulb is on.

You should now see that when you flip a light switch, you are changing the circuit that powers the light. If the light is off, the circuit is open. By flipping the switch, you are actually connecting the two sides of the power source together so that current can flow. That turns on the light. If you flip the switch again, you are breaking that connection, and the current stops flowing, turning the light off. That's how a switch works.

Series and Parallel Circuits

The idea that a break in an electrical circuit can stop the current flow and thus stop the electrical device or devices in the circuit is quite useful most of the time. However, sometimes it's a real problem. Consider, for example the following circuit:

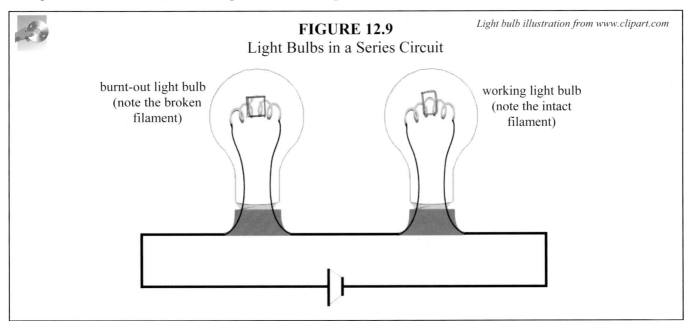

Light bulb illustration from www.clipart.com

FIGURE 12.9
Light Bulbs in a Series Circuit

burnt-out light bulb
(note the broken
filament)

working light bulb
(note the intact
filament)

In this circuit, despite the fact that one of the light bulbs is not broken, *neither* of them will light. Why? Well, a light bulb lights up because electrons flow through the filament of the bulb. The filament has a certain amount of resistance, which heats up the filament so much that it glows with a bright light. Now, the reason a light bulb burns out is that, eventually, the filament breaks due to wear and tear. When the filament breaks, the electrical connection from one side of the light bulb to the other is broken. Since the light bulb is a part of the circuit, this breaks the electrical connection of the entire circuit. Thus, a burnt-out light bulb is the same as an open switch! So, even though the second light bulb is fine, it will not light because electrons cannot flow through it.

When lights (or any electrical devices) are hooked up in this way, we say that they are hooked up in "series." All devices on such a circuit, called a **series circuit**, will cease to function when any one of the devices ceases to function. This, of course, is an undesirable situation. Fortunately, however, such a situation can be avoided. For example, consider the circuit shown below:

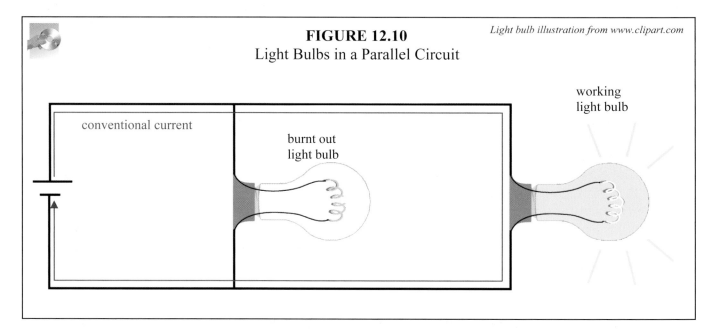

FIGURE 12.10
Light Bulbs in a Parallel Circuit

Light bulb illustration from www.clipart.com

working light bulb

conventional current

burnt out light bulb

In this case, the working light bulb still lights. Why? Well, look at the situation. Since the burnt-out light bulb is like an open switch, current cannot flow through it. But as you look at the drawing, you can see that electrons can still flow from one side of the battery to the other. They do not have to go through the burnt-out light bulb. They can take the longer route, through the working bulb, to get to the other end of the battery, as shown by the red line in the figure. This allows the intact light bulb to light up, even though the other bulb is burnt out. When devices are hooked up in this manner, we say that they are hooked up in "parallel." A **parallel circuit**, then, allows the devices to work independently of each other. If one stops working, the others can still work, because current can still flow through them.

ON YOUR OWN

12.7 When strings of Christmas tree lights were first produced, they were hard to use year after year, because once a single light bulb on the string burned out, none of the lights would light up. Nowadays, if one bulb on a string of lights burns out, the others stay lit. What is the difference between the way strings of Christmas tree lights used to be made and the way they are made now?

Magnetism

electrons are alligned

This module is supposed to be about the electromagnetic force, but I have spent the majority of it discussing electrical charge and electricity. What about magnetism? Well, as James Clerk Maxwell demonstrated, the force that is involved in magnetism is really the same as the force involved in electricity. Thus, a study of one is, in fact, a study of the other. Nevertheless, I need to discuss a few basics about magnets before you finish this module. First, I want you to remember an experiment you did a while ago.

In Module #6, I discussed the earth's magnetic field. In order to demonstrate what caused earth's magnetic field, I had you wind a wire around a nail and then run electricity through it. In the end, it made a magnet. The experiment demonstrated that the movement of charged particles (electrons, in this case) can create a magnetic force. Well, it turns out that *all magnetic force results from the movement of charged particles*! That might come as a bit of a surprise to you. After all, you know that there are such things as permanent magnets. These magnets have no electricity hooked up to them, but nevertheless, they are magnetic. How is their magnetic force generated by the movement of charged particles?

You first have to remember that all matter is composed of charged particles. All atoms contain positively charged protons and negatively charged electrons. As you will learn in the next module, the electrons in an atom are in constant motion. Thus, there is a continuous movement of electrons in all matter. Why isn't all matter magnetic, then? In your experiment, you created a magnetic force when electrons all flowed in one general direction. In order for a material to be magnetic, then, its atoms have to line up in a certain way so that the electrons in the material all have the same general motion. The atoms of most materials are not aligned in this way, so the electrons in the material have random motion. This causes the individual magnetic fields that result from that motion to cancel each other out. The result, then, is no magnetic behavior. However, certain materials under certain conditions can have their atoms arranged so that the electrons have the same general motion. When that happens, the result is a magnet.

Your refrigerator magnets, then, are simply made of a material whose atoms are arranged in a particular way. The motion of the electrons within those atoms mimics the flow of electrons in an electrical circuit. Thus, even your refrigerator magnets work because of electrical flow. That's what Maxwell's equations proved and experiments such as Experiment 6.3 demonstrate.

Under what conditions can a material align its atoms in order to make a magnet? Some materials simply cannot. The nature of their atoms makes such alignment impossible. Other materials, such as iron, however, can be made into a magnet at any time. If you re-do Experiment 6.3, but this time allow the electricity to flow for a long time, the nail will continue to be a magnet even after the electricity is turned off. You see, the magnetic field of the electrical current actually causes iron atoms to slowly align. If exposed to a strong enough magnetic field for long enough, iron will actually become a permanent magnet.

In the same way, most materials will not even respond to a magnet. For example, you can't stick your refrigerator magnets to one of the walls in your house, can you? Of course not. The reason is that the movement of electrons in the atoms of your house's walls are simply impossible to align. Thus, they can never simulate the concerted flow of electrons. As a result, they cannot participate in a magnetic interaction.

<u>Permanent Magnets</u>

Since you have some familiarity with permanent magnets, I want to spend a little time on them. If you've played with them at all, you'll recognize that there are two "sides" to a magnet. In physics, we call them the **north pole** and **south pole** of a magnet. In many ways, the poles in a magnet are much like charges. For example, if you point the north pole of a magnet toward the south pole of another magnet, the two poles will attract each other. If, however, you point the north pole of a magnet to the north pole of another one, they will repel each other. Thus, as I'm sure you're already aware, opposite poles attract one another, and like poles repel one another, just like charges.

Like magnetic poles repel one another, while opposite magnetic poles attract one another.

You can never find just one pole of a magnet hanging around. Whenever you have a magnet, you will always have a north pole and a south pole. Thus, magnets are called **dipoles**, because magnetic poles always come in pairs: one north and one south. Now I say this as a fact, but we are not 100% sure that it is. There are scientists out there looking for a magnetic pole isolated by itself. Scientists call this the search for a magnetic **monopole**. If such a thing were ever found, it would radically alter our understanding of magnetism, so that's why some scientists look for it. I am doubtful, however, that they will ever find one.

So, as far as we know, magnets always come with two poles. The image I will use to represent a magnet, then, is a long bar. The bar will be split down the middle. One half will be called the "south pole" of the magnet and the other will be the "north pole."

Although magnets come in all shapes and sizes, this will be my representation of a magnet. In general, we usually call this a "bar magnet."

You might think to yourself, "What if I take the magnet pictured above and split it right down the middle? Wouldn't I then have the north pole of the magnet in one hand and the south pole in the other? Couldn't I then take those poles and separate them far away from each other, thereby making two magnetic monopoles?" Well, that's a good idea, but interestingly enough, if you actually try to do that, it won't work!

As soon as you split a bar magnet, a very strange thing happens. Half of the north pole will turn into a south pole, and half of the south pole will turn into a north pole. As a result, instead of having two individual magnetic poles, you will have two magnets, *each of which has two poles!* Why does this happen? Remember that permanent magnets exist because their atoms are aligned so that the movement of their electrons mimics the concerted flow of electricity. When the material is cut and the pieces are pulled away from each other, the interactions between the atoms are altered. As a result, the alignment is altered as well. The alignment is altered so as to turn part of the north pole into a south pole and part of the south pole into a north pole. As a result, you can never split a magnet into two separate poles! Figure 12.11 illustrates this fact.

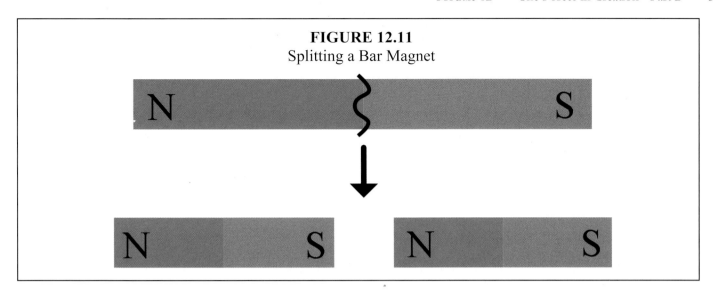

FIGURE 12.11
Splitting a Bar Magnet

Remember, the magnetic nature of a permanent magnet is caused by the alignment of the atoms in the material. It turns out that not all of the atoms in a material need to line up in order to make a magnet. In fact, only a small fraction of the atoms in a material need to line up to get some magnetic effect. As more atoms line up, you have more electrons simulating the flow of electricity, and the result is a stronger magnet. Thus, the strength of a magnet depends on what percentage of the atoms in the material are aligned. The larger the percentage, the stronger the pole of a magnet.

Do you want to guess how the magnetic force between poles varies with the strength of the poles? Not surprisingly, the magnetic force is directly proportional to the strength of each pole involved. Also not surprisingly, the strength of the magnetic force is inversely proportional to the square of the distance between the poles. This is expected, of course, because electricity and magnetism are really just different aspects of the same force. Thus, the force between the poles of a magnet behaves the same as the force between charges.

The force between the poles of a magnet is sometimes illustrated with **magnetic field lines**, which are shown in Figure 12.12.

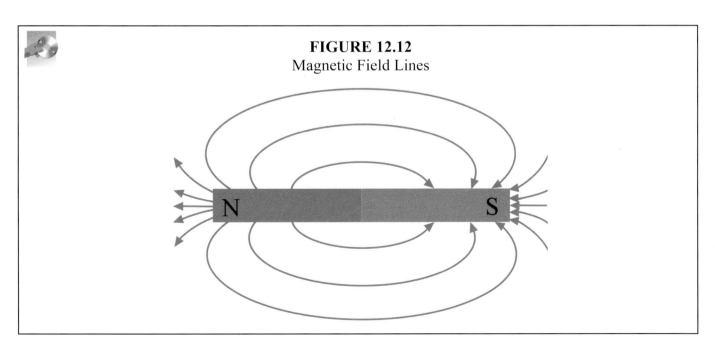

FIGURE 12.12
Magnetic Field Lines

These lines indicate the direction that the magnetic force pushes at any point near the magnet. If you cover a magnet with paper and then sprinkle iron filings on the paper, they will line up right along the lines drawn in the figure, because that's how the magnetic force pushes magnetic materials. Their significance is important, but the details are too complex to discuss here. If you take physics in high school, you will learn all about magnetic field lines then.

ON YOUR OWN

12.8 Suppose you have two wires lying side by side. In one wire, the current flows one way, and in the other wire, an equal amount of current flows the opposite way. Could you wrap those wires around a nail and make a magnet?

12.9 A scientist studies the relative strengths of two magnets that are both made of iron and have the same size, shape, and mass. The scientist places the north pole of magnet #1 a certain distance from the south pole of a third magnet, which he calls the "standard magnet." He measures the attractive force between magnet #1 and the standard magnet. He then replaces magnet #1 with magnet #2, making sure it is the same distance from the standard magnet. The attractive force he measures this time is four times stronger than the attractive force he measured previously. What is the difference between magnet #1 and magnet #2?

12.10 Just like magnetic field lines, scientists also use electrical field lines to illustrate the force that exists between electrical charges. From what you learned about magnets, draw the electrical field lines that exist between these two charges:

ANSWERS TO THE "ON YOUR OWN" PROBLEMS

12.1 Like charges repel one another. Thus, in part (a), each ball will exert a force pushing the other ball directly away. Opposite charges attract one another. Thus, in part (b), each ball will exert a force pulling the other directly toward itself.

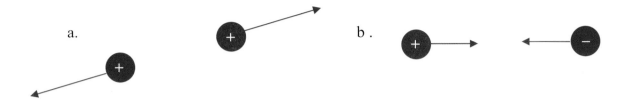

12.2 The electromagnetic force is directly proportional to the charge of each object. Thus, when one object's charge is halved, the electromagnetic force is halved. When the charge of the other object is divided by 4, the electromagnetic force is also divided by 4.

The electromagnetic force is inversely proportional to the square of the distance between the charges. In this problem, the distance changed from 16 to 4. That means it was divided by 4. When the distance *is divided by* 4, the force is *multiplied by* 4^2, which is 16.

Thus, the force was divided by 2, divided again by 4, and then multiplied by 16. When you divide by 2 and divide again by 4, it is the same as dividing by 8. If you divide by 8 and then multiply by 16, the net result will be that you have multiplied by 2. This means that the new force is <u>twice as strong as the old force</u>.

12.3 Light comes from the interaction of charged particles. Even though the black object has no *net* electrical charge, it is still composed of protons and electrons, which are each charged. Thus, <u>the light comes from the interactions between protons and electrons in the object</u>.

12.4 <u>You would charge by induction</u>. Induction gives you the charge opposite to what you are using.

12.5 We draw current flow from the positive to the negative, even though that is incorrect. The positive side of the battery is the longer edge of the battery symbol. Thus, conventional current (the red, dashed line) flows from the positive side to the negative side. Since electrons are negative, however, the actual flow (the blue, solid line) is from negative to positive:

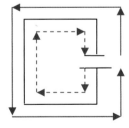

12.6 <u>The wire would *not* have zero resistance</u>. After all, in the experiment, you felt heat as the electrons traveled through the aluminum. The only way that heat could be produced is through resistance. Thus, the aluminum foil had resistance. In fact, *all wires (under normal conditions) have*

resistance. Nevertheless, we typically ignore the resistance of a wire in an electric circuit, because compared to the devices in the circuit, the resistance of the wire is very small.

12.7 Since modern Christmas tree lights can continue to work even after a few bulbs are burnt out, modern Christmas tree lights are wired in parallel. Since the old ones would cease to work when one burnt out, old Christmas tree lights were wired in series. This was a real problem, because if one light bulb burnt out, you would have to go through the string and replace each bulb one at a time to figure out which was the one that did not work.

12.8 You could not make a magnet that way. Think about it: The one wire will certainly cause a magnetic field, as will the other. However, since the currents are opposite of each other, the magnetic forces generated will be opposite as well. Thus, they will cancel each other out, resulting in no net magnetic force.

12.9 The difference is the number of atoms aligned in each magnet. Remember, the larger the number of aligned atoms, the stronger the magnet. Since the magnets are identical in size, shape, mass, and composition, magnet #2 must have more atoms aligned than magnet #1.

12.10 Remember, the electrical and magnetic forces are really different aspects of the same force. Thus, their properties are the same. Notice that the only real difference between this picture and Figure 12.10 is that we have a positive and negative charge instead of a north and south pole. Since magnetic and electric forces are really the same, however, the resulting field lines should be essentially the same.

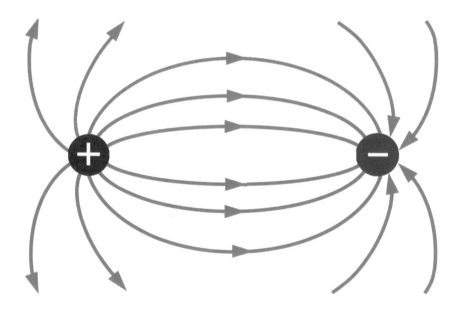

STUDY GUIDE FOR MODULE #12

1. Define the following terms:

a. Photon
b. Charging by conduction
c. Charging by induction
d. Electrical current
e. Conventional current
f. Resistance
g. Open circuit

2. For the following situations, use a solid arrow to draw the force exerted by the circle with the solid line. Use a dashed arrow to draw the force exerted by the circle with a dashed line.

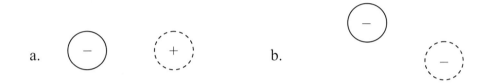

3. The force between the south pole of a magnet and the north pole of another magnet is measured. If the distance between the poles is increased by a factor of 3, how does the new force compare to the old one? Is the force attractive or repulsive?

4. Two charged particles are placed 10 centimeters from each other and the resulting force is measured. The charge on object #1 is then doubled and the charge on object #2 is left the same. Also, the distance between the objects is reduced to 5 centimeters. How does the new force compare to the old force?

5. What causes the electromagnetic force?

6. Given your answer to question #5, why don't charged particles glow?

7. If you were to use a positively charged rod to charge an object by induction, what charge will the object have?

8. If you were to use a positively charged rod to charge an object by conduction, what charge will the object have?

9. An electrical circuit uses a large voltage but a small current. Is the energy of each electron high or low? Are there many electrons flowing through the circuit, or are there few? Is the circuit dangerous?

10. Under what conditions is an electrical circuit reasonably safe?

11. Draw the conventional current flow in the following circuit:

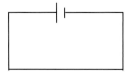

12. What is wrong with conventional current?

13. You have two wires. One is long and the other is short. Other than that, they are identical. Which has more resistance?

14. You have two wires. One is thin, and the other is very thick. When the same current is run through each wire, which will get hotter?

15. In which circuit will the light bulb glow?

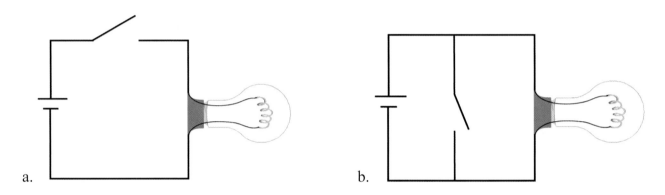

16. Three lights are in a circuit. When one burns out, they all go out. When the burnt-out one is replaced with a good light, the other two lights work again. Are the lights wired in a parallel circuit or a series circuit?

17. If it takes a flow of charged particles to make a magnet, where is the charged particle flow in a permanent magnet?

18. Is it possible to have a permanent magnet with only a north pole?

19. Is it possible to make a magnet from something that is not a magnet?

20. If a material does not respond to a magnet, what can you conclude about the atoms in that material?

MODULE #13: The Forces in Creation - Part 3

Introduction

In the two previous modules, you learned about the gravitational force and the electromagnetic force. Now it's time to learn about the "other" two forces in creation: the weak force and the strong nuclear force. I put "other" in quotes to emphasize that although we often think about the weak force as a separate force, scientists now know that the weak force is simply another manifestation of the electromagnetic force. Thus, many scientists call the electromagnetic force and the weak force together the "electroweak force." The processes governed by the weak force are so different from those governed by the electromagnetic force, however, that it is better for us to think of the weak force as an entirely different force.

You will notice that there are not any experiments in this module. Although this is unfortunate, it cannot be avoided. In this module, I will be discussing atoms and portions of atoms. As a result, everything I want to cover in this module is too small to see, even with the most powerful microscope. Thus, you can only do experiments concerning the concepts in this module if you have some very sophisticated equipment! Despite the lack of experiments, there are many interesting things in this module, so please read it carefully and try to understand it.

The Structure of the Atom

In Module #1 I talked a bit about atoms. I want to extend that discussion now, adding a little more detail about what an atom looks like. Now remember, we can't really see atoms. However, we can do experiments on them and see how they react. Based on the results of those experiments, we can develop theories about what an atom looks like. As long as the theories are in agreement with the experimental data, they can be assumed to be reasonably accurate. Thus, what we know about the structure of an atom comes from indirect observation, not direct observation. Nevertheless, the theories we have developed are consistent with so much of the data related to atoms that we assume they are pretty accurate.

The first thing these theories tell us is that the atom is made up of three smaller particles: **protons**, **neutrons**, and **electrons**. These three particles all have different properties. First of all, the electron is a tiny particle. It has a mass of approximately 0.000000000000000000000000000091 grams. Now that's small! It also has a negative electrical charge. In fact, as you have already learned, the motion of electrons through a wire is what we call "electricity." When you flip a light switch to turn on a light, for example, electrons travel through the wire to the light. The energy the electrons have in their motion is converted to light energy, and as a result, the light glows.

A proton's mass is approximately 0.00000000000000000000000017 grams. That's almost *2,000 times* more massive than an electron, but it's still pretty small! Like electrons, protons have electrical charge as well. Unlike electrons, however, protons are positively charged. Since we know that opposite charges attract one another, we can conclude that protons and electrons are attracted to one another. This will become important in a moment.

The last particle, the neutron, is slightly (0.14%) heavier than the proton. There are two other important differences between the proton and the neutron. First, the neutron has no electrical charge. It is considered electrically neutral, which is where it got the name "neutron." The other interesting difference between the proton and the neutron is that, by itself, the neutron is not a stable particle. A neutron that is not a part of an atom will eventually "fall apart" into a proton, an electron, and a smaller particle called an **antineutrino** (an' tee noo tree' noh). Once a neutron becomes part of an atom, however, it will generally stay a neutron for as long as it stays in the atom. There is a major exception to this general rule, and you will learn about that in an upcoming section of this module.

Protons, neutrons, and electrons have a very specific arrangement in the atom. What is that arrangement? Well, remember that we cannot *see* atoms. Thus, all of the information we understand about them comes from indirect observations. Thus, we cannot say exactly what an atom looks like. However, we can produce a **model** that allows us to "picture" the atom.

<u>Model</u> – A schematic description of a system that accounts for its known properties

Scientists use models quite a bit, because there are a lot of systems that we would like to understand but cannot see directly. A good model, as the definition tells you, will accurately reproduce the known properties of the system being modeled. If that is the case, the model is assumed to be a relatively accurate description of the system and therefore can be used to give us a "mental picture" of what the system might look like. The Bohr model, for example, was proposed by Niels Bohr in 1913. At that time, it was the first model of the atom that could account for the known properties of the atom. Figure 13.1 illustrates what the atom looks like in the Bohr model.

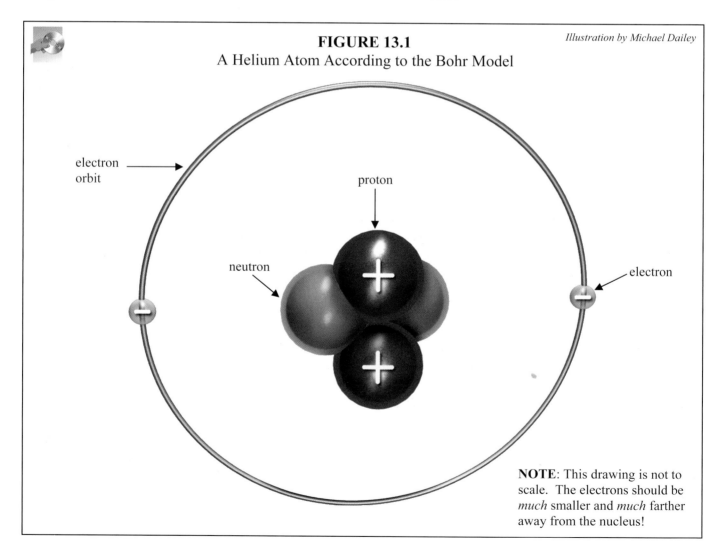

FIGURE 13.1

Illustration by Michael Dailey

A Helium Atom According to the Bohr Model

electron orbit

proton

neutron

electron

NOTE: This drawing is not to scale. The electrons should be *much* smaller and *much* farther away from the nucleus!

In the Bohr model, the neutrons and protons are packed together tightly in the center of the atom, which is called the **nucleus**.

<u>Nucleus</u> – The center of an atom, containing the protons and neutrons

The term "nucleus" is used in many different ways. In biology, for example, the nucleus of a cell is the part of the cell that contains most of the DNA. Thus, although I have defined "nucleus" here as the center of the atom, please realize that you will see that term again used in other ways.

The electrons are not in the nucleus. Instead, they orbit around the nucleus in circles, much like the planets orbit the sun. Why do the electrons orbit around the nucleus? They are moving with a specific velocity, but at the same time, they are attracted to the positive charges of the protons in the nucleus. Therefore, the electrical attraction between the protons and the electrons provides a centripetal force. This centripetal force changes the direction of electrons' velocity, producing circular motion. Thus, just as the gravitational attraction between the planets and the sun allows the planets to orbit the sun in circles, the electrical attraction between the electrons and protons allows the electrons to travel around the nucleus in a circle.

There are several things to note about this model of the atom. First and foremost, *we know that it is partially wrong*. Now wait a minute. Why would I show you something that scientists know is not completely correct? Well, the model we currently think is correct, the **quantum-mechanical model**, is horribly complex. When you take chemistry, you will learn a bit about that model, but even then, you will learn only the most basic aspects of the model. The quantum-mechanical model relies so heavily on mathematics that you need two years of post-calculus study to understand it. Needless to say, most people (even most scientists) never really learn the details of the quantum-mechanical model of the atom. Instead, most scientists learn this model for the atom, because even though we know it to be partially wrong, it still gives us a reasonably good picture of an atom.

So this model, while a good starting point, is not a 100% accurate view of the atom. What's wrong with it? The main problem with this model is the picture of how the electrons orbit the nucleus. After scientists worked with the Bohr model for a while, they realized that while the electrons do travel around the nucleus, they do not travel in fixed, circular orbits. Instead, their motion maps out interesting shapes we call "orbitals." When you take chemistry, you will learn about the many different orbitals in the quantum-mechanical model and some of their properties. For right now, however, we will stick with the Bohr model. Just keep in mind that the motion of the electrons in the atom is actually much more complex.

The next thing to note about the Bohr model is that I cannot draw it to scale. There are many reasons for this. Remember, the electrons are much, much smaller than the protons and neutrons. If I drew the electrons in the figure with the correct size relative to the protons and neutrons in the figure, they would be too small to see. Thus, in the figure, the electrons are drawn too large. Also, the electrons are, in reality, much farther away from the nucleus than what I can draw in the figure. If the protons and neutrons in the nucleus really were as large as what I have drawn in the figure, the electron orbit would have to be drawn about two miles away! If it is hard for you to visualize this, consider an analogy. Suppose the orbit that I drew in Figure 13.1 was represented by the outside walls of a circular, major-league baseball stadium. If that were the case, the nucleus of the atom would be represented by a marble placed at the center of the stadium.

Think about that for a moment. The nucleus is a tiny marble in the center of a major-league baseball stadium. The electrons orbit this "marble" out at the edges of the baseball stadium. What lies between the marble and the edge of the stadium? Nothing. Absolutely nothing. There is *nothing* between the nucleus and the electrons. What does this tell you about the atom? It tells you that the atom is made up mostly of empty space. Indeed, the atom is more than 99.99999% empty space! Since atoms make up all of matter, this tells us that *matter is mostly empty space.*

Now wait a minute. If you bang your fist against the top of a table, the tabletop certainly doesn't feel like empty space, does it? Your hand doesn't just pass right through it. Instead, the tabletop stops your hand, making it hurt. How can it do that if it is mostly empty space? Well, look at Figure 13.1 again. The tabletop and your hand are both made up of molecules, which, in turn, are made up of atoms. If you look at the figure, you can see that the positively charged portion of the atom (the nucleus) is "covered up" by the negatively charged electrons. Since the electrons orbit outside the nucleus, the electrons act like a negative "blanket," covering the nucleus.

Think of what happens as your hand gets nearer and nearer to the table. The atoms in your hand get closer to the atoms in the table. The negative "blanket" covering the atoms in your hand gets closer to the negative "blanket" that covers the atoms in the table. Since like charges repel each other, the atoms in the table repel the atoms in your hand. The closer your hand's atoms get to the table's atoms, the greater that repulsion becomes. Eventually, your hand's atoms will get so close to the tabletop's atoms that the repulsion will become great enough for the tabletop to stop your hand's motion. In the end, then, the fact that matter doesn't feel like empty space is a result of where the electrons are in an atom.

If all this isn't interesting enough, there are a few more fascinating facts you should know about the atom. Although Figure 13.1 makes the atom look like a pretty simple structure, it is actually quite complex. For example, consider the electrical charge that exists on the proton and the electron. The mutual attraction between the proton and the electron holds the electrons in orbit around the nucleus. Therefore, the opposite charges of the electron and proton are essential for atoms to exist. The overall electrical charge of an atom, however, is zero because an atom has equal numbers of protons and electrons. Thus, even though an atom has several positive charges in it, it has an equal number of negative charges, making the total charge on the atom equal to zero.

In order for this to work, the electron must have just as much negative charge as the proton has positive charge. In fact, calculations indicate that if the electron's negative charge were even *one billionth of one percent* different from the proton's positive charge, the resulting electrical imbalance in the atom would cause any sizable amount of matter to *instantaneously explode*! Now remember, the proton and electron are wildly different. The proton is almost 2,000 times more massive than the electron! Nevertheless, the proton has just as much positive charge as the electron has negative charge, to specifications better than 1 billionth of 1 percent!

Think about all of this for a minute. Suppose I designed something and asked a master machinist to build it for me. If I told him that the measurements had to be followed to within 1 billionth of 1 percent, the machinist would laugh at me. At *very best*, a machinist might be able to follow my specifications to within 1 tenth of 1 percent. Nevertheless, two of the components of the atom "fit together" with a precision of 1 billionth of 1 percent! Could something like that ever happen by chance? Of course not! When we see something that is so delicately balanced, we know that it is the result of *design*, not chance. When you see how perfectly the atom is put together, you know that it was built by the most incredible of engineers – God.

Now that you know something about the components of the atom and how they are arranged according to the Bohr model, it is time to learn a bit more about the nature of the atom according to this model. The atom illustrated in Figure 13.1 is a helium atom. When you buy a balloon that floats in the air, it is filled with trillions and trillions of such atoms. What makes the atom illustrated in the figure a helium atom? The number of protons it has makes it a helium atom. Any atom that has exactly two protons is a helium atom. Since the number of protons in an atom is fundamental in determining what kind of atom it is, there is a special term for the number of protons in an atom. It is called the **atomic number** of the atom.

Atomic number – The number of protons in an atom

If an atom has two protons, its atomic number is 2, and it is identified as a helium atom. If, however, an atom has six protons, its atomic number is 6, and it is identified as a carbon atom.

Blimp photo © Wayne Abraham
Agency: Dreamstime.com

FIGURE 13.2
Helium and Carbon

Coal photo © Greg Wireman
Agency: Dreamstime.com

A blimp floats in the air because it is filled with helium atoms, each of which has exactly two protons.

Coal is composed mostly of carbon atoms, each of which has exactly six protons.

In the end, then, the number of protons in an atom tells you what *kind* of atom it is, and since atoms must have equal numbers of protons and electrons, it also tells you how many electrons the atom has. What about the neutrons? How does the number of neutrons in an atom affect the nature of the atom? Well, the short answer to this question is, "Not much." Remember that the electrons in an atom act as a negatively charged "blanket" that covers the entire atom. As a result, when one atom gets close to another, each atom is strongly affected by the electrons in the other atom. If you think about it, then, the number of electrons in an atom will be the most important factor in determining how one atom behaves relative to another atom. Thus, the number of electrons in an atom determines the **vast majority** of an atom's properties. Since neutrons have no electrical charge, they do not affect how many electrons an atom has. As a result, the number of neutrons in an atom has only a small effect on the properties of that atom.

Of course, a *small* effect is not the same as *no* effect. First of all, the number of neutrons in an atom affects the atom's mass. After all, the more particles in the atom, the more mass it will have. Also, if an atom has too many or too few neutrons, it will be **radioactive**. What constitutes "too many" or "too few" neutrons? What is radioactivity? I want to put off these questions for right now, because I will answer them later on in this module when I discuss the weak force. For right now, just realize that the number of neutrons in an atom will only affect the atom's mass and whether or not the atom is radioactive.

Even though the number of neutrons in an atom affects the properties of the atom only slightly, it is still important to keep track of them. Thus, scientists have defined the **mass number** of an atom to be the sum of the protons and neutrons that exist in the nucleus of an atom.

Mass number – The sum of the numbers of neutrons and protons in the nucleus of an atom

The atom illustrated in Figure 13.1, for example, has two protons, two neutrons, and two electrons. The fact that it has two protons determines that it also has two electrons. It also tells us it is a helium atom. Since there are two neutrons in the nucleus as well, the mass number of the atom is four (2 neutrons + 2 protons). As a result, we call the atom "helium-4."

There are actually three different kinds of helium atoms in nature, and their Bohr models are shown in Figure 13.3.

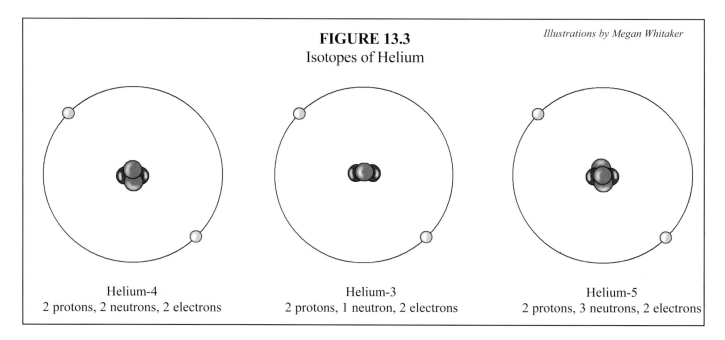

FIGURE 13.3
Isotopes of Helium

Illustrations by Megan Whitaker

| Helium-4 | Helium-3 | Helium-5 |
| 2 protons, 2 neutrons, 2 electrons | 2 protons, 1 neutron, 2 electrons | 2 protons, 3 neutrons, 2 electrons |

Notice that all three of the atoms illustrated in the figure have two protons and two electrons. Thus, they are all helium. Despite the fact that they all have the same number of protons and the same number of electrons, they have different numbers of neutrons. As a result, they all have different mass numbers. The atom with two protons and one neutron in its nucleus is helium-3, and the atom with two protons and three neutrons in its nucleus is helium-5.

When you buy a helium-filled balloon, it contains a mixture of helium-3 and helium-4. The vast majority of the atoms (more than 99.99%) are helium-4 atoms. However, a few (less than 0.01%) of them are helium-3. Since the only difference between these types of helium atoms is the number of neutrons in their nuclei (the plural of "nucleus"), they all have essentially the same properties. Nevertheless, they are different from one another. Helium-3 is less massive than helium-4. Scientists have a term for atoms like this. We call them **isotopes** (eye' suh tohps).

Isotopes – Atoms with the same number of protons but different numbers of neutrons

Thus, helium-3, helium-4, and helium-5 are called "isotopes of helium." It is possible to find all three of these isotopes of helium in nature. The most predominant isotope is helium-4, but the other isotopes are also present. In addition, helium-5 is radioactive. You will learn about radioactivity in an upcoming section of this module.

The subject of isotopes brings up a very important point. If the helium that fills up a balloon is really a mixture of different kinds of atoms, what do we call helium? We can't say that helium is an atom. We can say that helium-4 is an atom, and we can say that helium-3 is an atom. However, a sample of helium in a balloon contains *both* of those atoms. As a result, we must come up with another term to describe helium. Scientists say that helium is an **element**.

Element – A collection of atoms that all have the same number of protons

Carbon is another example of an element. There are three different isotopes of carbon: carbon-12, carbon-13, and carbon-14. A sample of carbon (like that which you find in coal) is a mixture of all of those isotopes. Thus, carbon is an element. This element contains three different isotopes: carbon-12, carbon-13, and carbon-14.

To make sure you really understand how an atom is put together, study the examples below and perform the "On Your Own" problems that follow.

EXAMPLE 13.1

All atoms that make up the element nitrogen have seven protons. If a particular nitrogen atom has eight neutrons, what is its name? How many electrons does it have?

Since we are talking about a nitrogen atom here, we know it has seven protons because all atoms that make up the element nitrogen have seven protons. Since all atoms have the same number of electrons and protons, this atom has seven electrons. With seven protons and eight neutrons in the nucleus, the mass number is 15 (7 + 8), so we call this atom nitrogen-15.

Which of the following atoms is an isotope of nitrogen-15? What is its name?

a. an atom with five protons, five electrons, and ten neutrons
b. an atom with eight protons, eight electrons, and seven neutrons
c. an atom with eight protons, eight electrons, and eight neutrons
d. an atom with seven protons, seven electrons, and seven neutrons

Two atoms are isotopes if they have the same number of protons but different numbers of neutrons. As we determined earlier, there are seven protons, seven electrons, and eight neutrons in nitrogen-15. Thus, any isotope of nitrogen-15 will also have to have seven protons. It must have something other than eight neutrons as well. Thus, the atom in choice (d) is an isotope of nitrogen-15. Its name is nitrogen-14, because its mass number is 7+7=14.

ON YOUR OWN

13.1 The element sodium is made up of all atoms with 11 protons. How many protons, electrons, and neutrons are in a sodium-23 atom?

13.2 All atoms with eight protons are oxygen atoms. If a particular oxygen atom has eight neutrons, what is its name and how many electrons does it have?

13.3 Of the following atoms, two are isotopes. Which ones are they?

a. An atom with 16 protons, 16 electrons, and 17 neutrons
b. An atom with 17 protons, 17 electrons, and 16 neutrons
c. An atom with 16 protons, 16 electrons, and 18 neutrons
d. An atom with 18 protons, 18 electrons, and 17 neutrons

The Periodic Table of the Elements

Since the number of electrons in an atom is responsible for determining the vast majority of an atom's properties, and since the number of electrons is the same as the number of protons, it is convenient to think about the atoms in creation in terms of what elements they belong to. Remember, an element is a collection of atoms that all have the same number of protons. This means that atoms that belong to the same element have essentially the same properties. As a result, it makes sense to group atoms together in terms of how many protons they have. Chemists have created a very organized way to do this. It is called the **Periodic Table of the Elements**, and it is shown on the next page, as well as on the inside of the front cover.

The Periodic Table of the Elements is often called the "periodic chart," and many chemists (including myself) just call it "the chart." In the chart, each box represents an element. The first box, for example, represents the simplest element in creation: hydrogen. Like helium, hydrogen is a gas that is lighter than air. Unlike helium, however, hydrogen is explosive when exposed to oxygen and a spark or flame. If you look at the first box, then, you will see that it has an "H" in it. This is the chemical symbol for hydrogen. The number above the "H" is the atomic number of hydrogen. Remember, the atomic number tells you how many protons an atom has. This tells us, then, that the element hydrogen is made up of all atoms that have only one proton.

It turns out that there are three isotopes of hydrogen. Hydrogen-1 has one proton, one electron, and no neutrons. This is considered the simplest atom in creation. Hydrogen-2 (sometimes called "deuterium") has one proton, one electron, and one neutron. Hydrogen-3 (sometimes called "tritium") is also an isotope of hydrogen. All these atoms have one proton, but they have different numbers of neutrons. Thus, we say that hydrogen has three isotopes: hydrogen-1, hydrogen-2, and hydrogen-3. Chemists tend to abbreviate things whenever possible. As a result, you can also refer to these isotopes as ^{1}H, ^{2}H, and ^{3}H. In this abbreviation scheme, we use the chemical symbol to tell us what element the atom belongs to, and we put the mass number as a superscript before the symbol.

THE PERIODIC TABLE OF ELEMENTS

1A	2A	3B	4B	5B	6B	7B	8B	8B	8B	1B	2B	3A	4A	5A	6A	7A	8A
1 **H** 1.01																	2 **He** 4.0
3 **Li** 6.94	4 **Be** 9.01											5 **B** 10.8	6 **C** 12.0	7 **N** 14.0	8 **O** 16.0	9 **F** 19.0	10 **Ne** 20.2
11 **Na** 23.0	12 **Mg** 24.3											13 **Al** 27.0	14 **Si** 28.1	15 **P** 31.0	16 **S** 32.1	17 **Cl** 35.5	18 **Ar** 39.9
19 **K** 39.1	20 **Ca** 40.1	21 **Sc** 45.0	22 **Ti** 47.9	23 **V** 50.9	24 **Cr** 52.0	25 **Mn** 54.9	26 **Fe** 55.8	27 **Co** 58.9	28 **Ni** 58.7	29 **Cu** 63.5	30 **Zn** 65.4	31 **Ga** 69.7	32 **Ge** 72.6	33 **As** 74.9	34 **Se** 79.0	35 **Br** 79.9	36 **Kr** 83.8
37 **Rb** 85.5	38 **Sr** 87.6	39 **Y** 88.9	40 **Zr** 91.2	41 **Nb** 92.9	42 **Mo** 95.9	43 **Tc** (98)	44 **Ru** 101.1	45 **Rh** 102.9	46 **Pd** 106.4	47 **Ag** 107.9	48 **Cd** 112.4	49 **In** 114.8	50 **Sn** 118.7	51 **Sb** 121.8	52 **Te** 127.6	53 **I** 126.9	54 **Xe** 131.3
55 **Cs** 132.9	56 **Ba** 137.3	57 **La** 138.9	72 **Hf** 178.5	73 **Ta** 180.9	74 **W** 183.9	75 **Re** 186.2	76 **Os** 190.2	77 **Ir** 192.2	78 **Pt** 195.1	79 **Au** 197.0	80 **Hg** 200.6	81 **Tl** 204.4	82 **Pb** 207.2	83 **Bi** 209.0	84 **Po** (209)	85 **At** (210)	86 **Rn** (222)
87 **Fr** (223)	88 **Ra** 226.0	89 **Ac** (227)	104 **Rf** (261)	105 **Db** (262)	106 **Sg** (266)	107 **Bh** (264)	108 **Hs** (269)	109 **Mt** (268)	110 **Ds** (281)	111 **Rg** (272)	112 **Uub** (285)	113 **Uut** (284)	114 **Uuq** (289)	115 **Uup** (288)	116 **Uuh** (292)		118 **Uuo** (222)

71 **Lu** 175.0

103 **Lr** (262)

58 **Ce** 140.1	59 **Pr** 140.9	60 **Nd** 144.2	61 **Pm** (145)	62 **Sm** 150.4	63 **Eu** 152.0	64 **Gd** 157.3	65 **Tb** 158.9	66 **Dy** 162.5	67 **Ho** 164.9	68 **Er** 167.3	69 **Tm** 168.9	70 **Yb** 173.0
90 **Th** 232.0	91 **Pa** 231.0	92 **U** 238.0	93 **Np** (237)	94 **Pu** (244)	95 **Am** (243)	96 **Cm** (247)	97 **Bk** (247)	98 **Cf** (251)	99 **Es** (252)	100 **Fm** (257)	101 **Md** (258)	102 **No** (259)

- Nonmetals
- Standard metals
- Transition metals
- Inner transition metals

If you look to the far right of the chart, you will see that the next box is labeled with "He" and has an atomic number of 2. This is the box that represents helium. As you already know, helium has two protons, and that's why its atomic number is 2. As you look at other boxes on the chart, you will see that they mostly contain either one-letter or two-letter chemical symbols. Additionally, if there is only one letter in the chemical symbol, it is capitalized. If there is more than one letter in the symbol, the first is capitalized, but the rest are not.

In general, the chemical symbol for an element consists of the first one or two letters of the element's name. Sulfur (atomic number 16), for example, is given the chemical symbol "S," while neon (atomic number 10) is represented by the symbol "Ne." That's not too bad. Although an element is usually given a chemical symbol that consists of the first one or two letters in its name, we do not always use the *English* name of the element. For example, iron (atomic number 26) is given the chemical symbol "Fe." Why? Well, the Latin name for iron is *ferrum*. Likewise, the element potassium (atomic number 19) is given the chemical symbol "K" from its Latin name *kalium*. Thus, the chemical symbol for an element is usually the first one or two letters from the English or Latin name of the element.

What about the number that appears underneath the chemical symbol for each element? That's the mass of the element. The units of this mass measurement are called "atomic mass units" or "amu," and they represent a very tiny amount of mass. You will learn more about that when you take chemistry. One thing you must understand about this mass is that *it is not the mass number of an atom*. It is an *average* mass for that element. Remember, an element is actually a collection of atoms, each of which is an isotope of that element. The element carbon (chemical symbol "C"), for example, is really a collection of ^{12}C, ^{13}C, and ^{14}C atoms. Each of these atoms has a different mass, because each has a different number of neutrons in its nucleus. Thus, the mass listed for carbon (12.0 amu) in the chart is actually an average of the masses of ^{12}C, ^{13}C, and ^{14}C. Once again, you will learn more about this when you take chemistry.

You might notice that a few of the masses listed in the Periodic Table of the Elements are in parentheses. This is because the mass for those elements can only be estimated. Some elements are unstable and, as a result, do not exist long enough for their mass to be accurately measured. For those elements, an approximate mass is listed in parentheses.

While we are discussing "unusual" things on the chart, notice the boxes that contain three letters instead of just one or two (atomic number 112, for example). Those boxes represent elements that have been recently discovered. Because their discovery is relatively recent, their official names have not been determined. As a result, they are given temporary names and symbols until they are officially named. To indicate that the name is temporary, the symbol has three letters. Please note that even though I say these elements have been "discovered," what I really mean is that they have been *made*. Scientists have used nuclear reactions to produce them.

Ignoring the individual boxes for a moment and looking at the chart as a whole, you will notice that the boxes are arranged in a very strange fashion. The boxes are not put in a square or rectangular grid. Instead, they are put in columns and rows that have different sizes. Some columns are taller than others, and some rows are shorter than others. In addition, there are two rows of boxes at the bottom of the chart that seem to have been pulled out of the middle. Why such a strange arrangement? Well, it turns out that this arrangement actually allows a chemist to look at the chart and quickly discern many of the properties of each element, just by finding where that element's box appears in the chart. Unfortunately, you need to study the chart in a lot more detail before you can do that! When you take chemistry, you will learn much more about what the chart actually tells us.

Even though you do not know a lot about the chart, you can already use it to learn a great deal about what an atom looks like according to the Bohr model. For example, by looking at the chart, a chemist can tell you that the Bohr model of a ^{12}C atom is as follows:

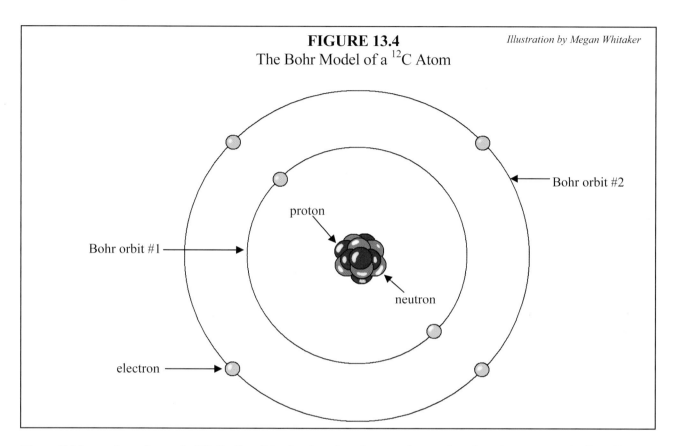

FIGURE 13.4

The Bohr Model of a ^{12}C Atom

Illustration by Megan Whitaker

Bohr orbit #2

proton

Bohr orbit #1

neutron

electron

How did I get that picture? Well, first I looked at the chart and saw that the element symbolized by "C" has an atomic number of 6. That told me there are six protons and six electrons in a ^{12}C atom. Since the mass number is 12, that tells me that there are also six neutrons, because the number of neutrons and protons must add up to the mass number. As a result, I put six protons and six neutrons in the nucleus. Then, I put the six electrons orbiting around the nucleus.

How did I know to use more than one orbit in the picture? Well, it turns out that you can't just stuff as many electrons as you want into a single orbit. After a while, the orbit gets "too full" of electrons. Thus, in the Bohr model of the atom, there are several orbits that the electrons can occupy. These orbits are referred to in many different ways. I like to refer to them as **Bohr orbits** and give them numbers. As illustrated in the figure, the orbit closest to the nucleus is the first Bohr orbit, and the next one is the second Bohr orbit. If this atom needed more orbits, there would be a third Bohr orbit, a fourth Bohr orbit, etc. Some chemists refer to these orbits as **energy levels** because the energy of the electrons increases the larger the orbit is. Finally, some chemists call them **electron shells** because each orbit of electrons is a "shell" that covers up the nucleus.

Because the orbits increase in size the further they are away from the nucleus, each subsequent Bohr orbit can hold more electrons than the one before it. The first few Bohr orbits and their electron capacities are listed in Table 13.1.

TABLE 13.1

Bohr Orbit	Electron Capacity
1	2
2	8
3	18
4	32
5	50

When you build up an atom, then, you put as many electrons as you can in the first orbit, then continue with the second orbit and continue to add more orbits until you have put in all the electrons that exist for that atom. The following example demonstrates how to do this.

EXAMPLE 13.2

Draw what the Bohr model says an aluminum-27 (^{27}Al) atom looks like.

The element Al has an atomic number of 13. That means there are 13 electrons and 13 protons. Since the mass number is 27, that tells us there are 14 neutrons. Thus, we put 13 protons and 14 neutrons in the nucleus. Since there are 13 electrons, we will use 2 electrons to fill up the first Bohr orbit, 8 to fill up the second, and we will still have 3 more to put in the third. Thus, the drawing would look something like this:

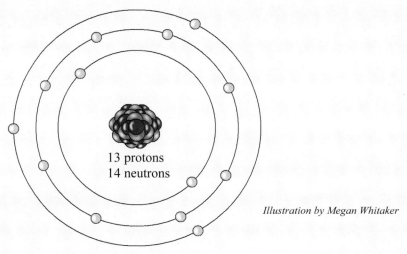

13 protons
14 neutrons

Illustration by Megan Whitaker

Make sure you understand this process by solving the "On Your Own" problems below. Please note that in solving *any* problem in this course (including the problems on the test), you should feel free to use the periodic chart.

ON YOUR OWN

13.4 Draw a picture of a ^{19}F atom, according to the Bohr model.

13.5 If you were to draw a picture of any isotope of cesium (Cs), what would be the largest Bohr orbit you would use and how many electrons would be in it?

Before you leave this section, I must once again point out that although the Bohr model gives us a good idea of what an atom looks like, we know that it is not entirely correct. Thus, the pictures of atoms that you draw based on the Bohr model are reasonable approximations of what an atom looks like, but they are *not* really correct. Currently, the quantum-mechanical model is what most chemists think gives an accurate representation of an atom. You will learn a little bit about that model when you take chemistry.

The Strong Force

Ever since you first saw Figure 13.1, something should have started to bother you. Over and over again, as I drew pictures of atoms, I continually clumped the protons and neutrons together in the nucleus of the atom. Remember, the nucleus is very small (a marble in a major-league baseball stadium); therefore, the protons and neutrons are crammed into a very tight space. This results in a bunch of protons *very* close to one another. That should bother you. After all, protons are positively charged. What happens when two objects with the same charge are put near each other? They *repel* each other! Remember, like charges repel, and opposite charges attract. The attraction between the protons and electrons keeps the electrons orbiting the nucleus. What about the repulsion between the protons, however? Why do they stay tightly packed within the nucleus when they repel one another?

This question puzzled scientists for quite a long time. Experiments done in the laboratory indicated that, just as you would predict, protons repel each other when put in close proximity to one another. Nevertheless, other experiments conclusively showed that as a part of an atom, protons exist tightly packed with one another in the nucleus. Thus, scientists suggested that there must be a short-range, attractive force called the **nuclear force** that attracts protons and neutrons to one another. They assumed that this force acted over such a short range that it was only important when protons were extremely close to one another, as is the case within the nucleus. Thus, under "normal" conditions, protons are so far apart from each other that the only force they experience is the electromagnetic force, which causes them to repel one another. When placed in a nucleus, however, the protons are so close to one another that the nuclear force has a chance to operate. Scientists assumed that the strong nuclear force is so strong that it overcame the repulsive electromagnetic force, holding the protons together in the nucleus.

It is important for you to realize that at the time, scientists had *no idea* what caused the nuclear force. Indeed, the nuclear force stayed shrouded in mystery for quite some time. Nevertheless, scientists concluded that the nuclear force *must* exist, or the nucleus would never hold together. They also concluded that the nuclear force *must* be attractive because it would have to overcome the repulsive electromagnetic force that exists between protons. Finally, they concluded that it *must* act over a very short range, or we would be able to see it work in situations other than a nucleus. Thus, although scientists had *no idea* what caused the nuclear force, observations of atoms allowed them to conclude a lot of things about the *nature* of this force.

Things began to change in 1935 when Hideki (hi dee' kee) Yukawa (you kah' wah) proposed that the nuclear force occurs as a result of the fact that protons and neutrons can exchange tiny particles with one another. In his initial theory, Yukawa called these tiny particles **pions** (pye' onz) and actually made a rough prediction of what their mass should be. In 1947, these pions were discovered by experiment, and their mass was, indeed, roughly what Yukawa predicted. Yukawa's explanation of the nuclear force revolutionized our understanding of the nucleus, and as a result, he was awarded the Nobel Prize for Physics in 1949.

Now remember from Module #12 that the electromagnetic force is understood to result from the exchange of photons between charged particles. Thus, the nuclear force is similar to the electromagnetic force in the sense that they are both governed by the exchange of particles. However, the particles are different, and that causes a difference in the nature of the two forces. First of all, photons can exist for a very long time. Pions, on the other hand, cannot. Pions are part of a vast class of particles that physicists call **short-lived particles**. As a result, although pions do exist, they only exist for a very short time. Therefore, when two protons exchange a pion, they must do so *very* quickly because the pion cannot exist for very long.

This probably sounds strange to you. Why are pions short-lived particles? Well, pions are made from protons and neutrons. Thus, if two protons decide to exchange a pion, one proton must "give up" a little bit of its energy to make the pion. That pion can then be given to another proton (or a neutron). The proton can then do the same thing, creating a pion from its energy and sending it to another proton or a neutron. Neutrons can do the same thing. Because pions can only live for a short time, however, the protons and neutrons must stay very close to one another in order to do this. Thus, the nuclear force can only operate over very small distances.

Once again, this might sound very strange, but many, many experiments back up this theory of the nuclear force. A nucleus is actually a very active place! Protons and neutrons are packed closely together, and they are constantly making, giving up, and receiving pions! The pions are exchanged among the protons and neutrons in the nucleus rapidly because they cannot exist for a very long time. Thus, you can picture the nucleus as a scene of wild activity, with all the constituents of the nucleus madly making and exchanging pions with one another.

The story of the nuclear force is a great example of how science works these days. Long before pions were discovered, scientists had figured out a great deal about the nuclear force. They had already concluded that it *must* exist, otherwise the nucleus would explode due to the repulsive electromagnetic force between protons. They had also concluded that it *must* be a force that operates over a very short range because it seems to exist only within the confines of the nucleus. When the pion was finally discovered, scientists then understood *why* the nuclear force exists and *why* it operates over a short range. It exists as a result of the exchange of pions, and it is a short-range force because the pions exist for but an instant. Thus, protons and/or neutrons can only exchange pions when they are extremely close to one another. In the end, then, scientists had used observations to determine that a mysterious force exists, developed a theory as to what might cause that force, and then went looking for experimental evidence to back up the theory. This is very typical of how scientific research is done today.

The title of this section is "The Strong Force," and that's the force I am supposed to be telling you about. Why, then, am I telling you about the nuclear force? Well, because the nuclear force is one manifestation of the strong force. The strong force is manifested in other ways, however. For example, experiments indicate that protons and neutrons are made of three smaller particles, called **quarks**. These quarks are also busy exchanging particles called **gluons** (gloo' onz), which hold them together so they can form protons and neutrons. This is yet another manifestation of the strong force. Thus, the strong force not only holds the nucleus together via the exchange of pions, but it also holds quarks together via the exchange of gluons, allowing the existence of protons and neutrons. As its name implies, the strong force is very strong. After all, at short enough distances, it is strong enough to overpower the mutual repulsion of protons. Of all the forces in creation, it is considered the strongest.

ON YOUR OWN

13.6 Suppose a new force is discovered, and scientists determine that it is governed by the exchange of a particle known as the "wileon." If the lifetime of a wileon is greater than that of a pion but shorter than that of a photon, what is the range of this new force relative to the range of the nuclear force and the electromagnetic force?

Radioactivity

I mentioned in the introduction that I want to talk about the weak force in this module. Once again, let me remind you that the weak force is really just another aspect of the electromagnetic force; therefore, many physicists say there are only three forces in creation: the gravitational force, the strong force, and the electroweak force. I don't really want to spend much time discussing the weak force because there is really no difference between it and the electromagnetic force. However, I do want to discuss the process that the weak force governs: **radioactivity**. In fact, the weak force governs only a portion of radioactive processes, but I want to use this opportunity to talk about radioactivity in general.

There is an enormous amount of misunderstanding when it comes to radioactivity, so I want to pay extra attention to this subject. Hopefully, I can dispel some of the myths most people believe about this complicated subject. Radioactivity is a result of atoms we call **radioactive isotopes**.

Radioactive isotope – An atom with a nucleus that is not stable

When an atom has a nucleus that is not stable, the nucleus must decay in order to become stable. This process is called **radioactive decay**, and it can take on several different forms.

One way an unstable nucleus can decay is through **beta decay**. In beta decay, a nucleus actually changes one of its neutrons into a proton. It does so by making the neutron emit an electron. If you think about it, this process makes some sense. After all, a neutron is electrically neutral. If a neutron were to somehow emit an electron, it would be getting rid of a negative charge. If it starts out neutral and "spits out" a negative charge, what would be left? A positive charge! Thus, when a neutron spits out an electron, the result is that the neutron turns into a proton!

Consider, for example, the uranium isotope ^{239}U. Based on the chart, you know that uranium has 92 protons and 92 electrons. The mass number indicates that there must therefore be 147 neutrons in the nucleus of a ^{239}U isotope. It turns out that the nucleus of this atom is unstable. It has too many neutrons. To fix this problem, a neutron changes into a proton by emitting an electron. What is the result of this process? If a neutron turns into a proton, the nucleus will no longer have 92 protons. Instead, as soon as the neutron turns into a proton, the result will be a nucleus with 93 protons. After all, there were 92 protons, and then a neutron changed into a proton. This means that, in the end, there will be 93 protons.

Once the nucleus of this atom has 93 protons, the atom is no longer an isotope of uranium. Instead, the chart tells us that all atoms with 93 protons are called neptunium (Np) atoms. Thus, when ^{239}U goes through beta decay, the result is that it turns into ^{239}Np. When beta decay occurs, the nucleus actually changes so that the atom is now a completely different element! In order to do this, a neutron in the nucleus emits an electron. In the terminology of nuclear physics, we call ^{239}U the

radioactive isotope and the ^{239}Np that results from the beta decay the **daughter product**. Since the electron produced comes from beta decay, we call it a **beta particle**. Nevertheless, it is just an electron. In other words, the radioactive isotope ^{239}U emits a beta particle so as to decay into the daughter product ^{239}Np.

There is another particle involved in beta decay. It is called an antineutrino, and I mentioned it earlier. The nature of this particle is beyond the scope of this course and is not necessary to understand beta decay at the level I want to cover it. Indeed, it took scientists quite some time to determine the particle even exists, since it is very hard to detect. If you are interested in learning more about the antineutrino, you can visit the course website I discussed in the "Student Notes" at the beginning of the course. There you will find links to information on this particle.

If all this is a bit confusing to you, don't worry. In a little while, I will give you a few examples that will hopefully clear everything up. For right now, however, I want to talk about other forms of radioactivity. The next form of radioactive decay is called **alpha decay**. Once again, this kind of radioactive decay starts with a radioactive isotope. Instead of emitting a beta particle in order to become stable, however, some radioactive isotopes emit an **alpha particle**. An alpha particle is a small nucleus that contains two protons and two neutrons. That should sound familiar to you. An alpha particle is actually the nucleus of a helium atom! Thus, when alpha decay occurs, a nucleus "spits out" two protons and two neutrons in the form of a helium nucleus.

Like beta decay, this process will turn the radioactive isotope into a completely different element. For example, an isotope of polonium, ^{214}Po, has such an unstable nucleus that it ejects two protons and two neutrons from the nucleus. The chart tells us that polonium has 84 protons. If it ejects two of them, the result is only 82 protons. Thus, the polonium turns into lead (Pb), which has an atomic number of 82. What's the mass number of this lead daughter product? Well, the nucleus spits out two protons and two neutrons. Since the mass number is the sum of the protons and neutrons in the nucleus, this tells us that the mass number decreases by 4. So the daughter product is ^{210}Pb. Figure 13.5 illustrates both beta decay and alpha decay so that you can better understand them.

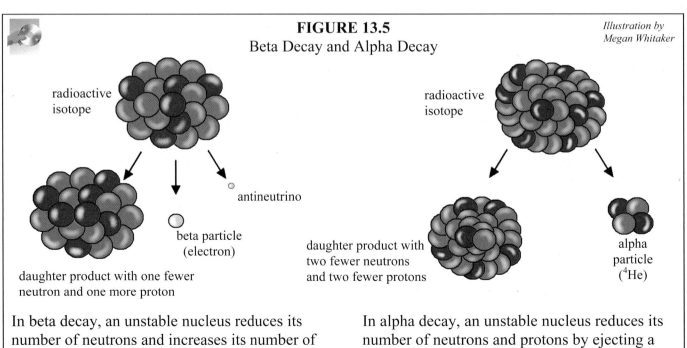

FIGURE 13.5
Beta Decay and Alpha Decay

Illustration by Megan Whitaker

radioactive isotope

antineutrino

beta particle (electron)

daughter product with one fewer neutron and one more proton

radioactive isotope

daughter product with two fewer neutrons and two fewer protons

alpha particle (^{4}He)

In beta decay, an unstable nucleus reduces its number of neutrons and increases its number of protons by ejecting an electron, or beta particle.

In alpha decay, an unstable nucleus reduces its number of neutrons and protons by ejecting a ^{4}He nucleus, or alpha particle.

The last form of radioactivity I want to discuss is **gamma decay**. In gamma decay, a radioactive isotope becomes stable by emitting a **gamma ray**. This is probably the easiest form of radioactive decay to understand because a gamma ray is actually just a high-energy photon. When a radioactive isotope goes through gamma decay, the isotope doesn't change its identity at all. For example, ^{229}Th is a radioactive isotope that goes through gamma decay. When this isotope decays, it starts out with 90 protons and 139 neutrons in its nucleus, and it ends up with the same number of protons and neutrons. The only thing that the gamma ray does is take energy away from the nucleus. Thus, gamma rays are emitted by radioactive isotopes that have too much energy in their nucleus. The gamma ray takes that energy away, but the radioactive isotope does not change in any other way.

As I said a moment ago, this might all be quite confusing to you. However, if you study the following examples, I think you will finally understand what I've been discussing here.

EXAMPLE 13.3

^{14}C is a radioactive isotope that goes through beta decay. What is the daughter product of this decay?

According to the chart, carbon (C) has an atomic number of 6. This tells us that a ^{14}C atom has six protons and eight neutrons in its nucleus. When a radioactive isotope undergoes beta decay, one of its neutrons turns into a proton. Thus, it will end up with one more proton and one less neutron. The daughter product (the nucleus that results from the beta decay), then, will have seven protons and seven neutrons. According to the chart, all atoms with seven protons are symbolized with an "N." The mass number of this nitrogen atom will be 7 + 7 = 14. The daughter product, then, is $\underline{^{14}N}$.

^{232}Th is a radioactive isotope that goes through alpha decay. What is the resulting daughter product?

According to the chart, thorium (Th) atoms have 90 protons. Thus, this particular atom has 90 protons and 142 neutrons in it. When it goes through alpha decay, it "spits out" two protons and two neutrons in the form of a helium-4 nucleus. The result will be only 88 protons and 140 neutrons in the daughter product. The chart tells us that Ra is the symbol for all atoms with 88 protons. The mass number of the resulting nucleus will be 88+140 = 228. Thus, the daughter product is $\underline{^{228}Ra}$.

If a ^{90}Y atom undergoes gamma decay, what nucleus will be produced?

Gamma decay simply takes energy away from the nucleus in the form of light. It does not change the identity of the nucleus. So the daughter product is still $\underline{^{90}Y}$.

ON YOUR OWN

13.7 What is the daughter product that results from the beta decay of ^{90}Sr?

13.8 What is the product of the alpha decay of ^{241}Am?

The Dangers of Radioactivity

Now that you know what radioactivity does (takes an atom with an unstable nucleus and either turns it into a different atom or takes energy away from the nucleus), you might be interested in knowing why everyone is so afraid of radioactivity. Well, part of the fear is based on ignorance, and part of the fear is based on fact. Radioactivity *can be* dangerous, but it is *not always* dangerous. That's a good thing, too, because we are *constantly* being exposed to radioactivity. You are exposed to gamma rays when you are outside in the sun. If you have a smoke detector in your house, you are exposed to alpha particles, because the main detection component of a smoke detector goes through alpha decay. In fact, you are exposed to beta particles and gamma rays each time you get close to someone, because people themselves are radioactive! It's a good thing, then, that radioactivity is not always dangerous.

The first thing you have to understand is why radioactivity can be dangerous. Radioactivity does not act like a poison. A poison is dangerous because it chemically reacts with your body, producing chemical processes that should not occur in your body. This upsets your body's chemistry, causing sickness or even death. Some poisons actually build up in your body. As you take them in small doses, they do not cause you any problems. However, as they continue to build up in your body, they eventually start causing chemical reactions that shouldn't happen in your body, and that's when you are in trouble.

Unlike poison, radioactivity is not dangerous because it directly upsets your body's chemistry. It also cannot build up in your body. Instead, radioactivity affects your body much like a tiny machine gun. You see, the danger in radiation comes from the particles emitted during the radioactive decay. Depending on the isotope involved, radioactive decay involves a nucleus "spitting out" something. In alpha decay, the nucleus spits out an alpha particle (composed of two protons and two neutrons). In beta decay, it spits out a beta particle (which is just an electron). In gamma decay, the nucleus spits out a high-energy photon. There is nothing chemically poisonous about these things. They are dangerous, however. They are dangerous because they have a lot of energy.

When produced as a result of radioactive decay, alpha particles, beta particles, and gamma rays have *a lot* of energy. As a result, they begin speeding away from the nucleus that emitted them. If you happen to be unfortunate enough to be in the way of the emitted particle, it might collide with one of the smallest constituents of your body: a cell. Every living organism is made up of tiny living units called cells. The vast majority of the time, when an alpha, beta, or gamma particle collides with a cell, it results in the cell's death. Every now and again, however, the cell will not die. If the particle hits the cell just right, it might mutate the cell's DNA rather than kill the cell.

Do you see why I say that radioactivity acts like a tiny machine gun? When you have a sample of radioactive material, each atom in that sample can "shoot" a "bullet" (an alpha particle, a beta particle, or a gamma ray). Since there are trillions and trillions of atoms in even a small sample of matter, that means a sample of radioactive isotopes can shoot off trillions and trillions of these "bullets." If you happen to be in the path of these "bullets," each one that hits you will most likely kill an individual cell. Thus, a radioactive sample is like a tiny machine gun that kills you one cell at a time. Every now and again, however, rather than killing a cell, the particle will cause a mutation in the cell's DNA.

Sounds dangerous, doesn't it? Well, it *can* be dangerous, but *not necessarily*. You see, your body *expects* cells to die. God therefore designed your body to reproduce cells. This helps you grow and mature, and it also replaces cells that die. Roughly 2 *million* blood cells die every *second* in a healthy adult's body. This is no problem, however, the body quickly replaces them. Thus, as long as cells do not die faster than they can be replaced by the body, there is no real problem.

When your cells are being destroyed by the little "bullets" being "shot" from a sample of radioactive isotopes, then, there is no problem as long as the "bullets" are not killing your cells faster than your body can replace them. If you are exposed to too much radiation too quickly, however, your cells will be killed faster than your body can replace them, leading to radiation burns, organ damage, and other nasty things.

What about the chance for mutating a cell's DNA? Isn't that bad? Well, yes, but once again, it depends on the amount of mutation going on. Everyone's body has a few mutant cells. Most of them simply die off or are killed by the immune system. The bad thing about mutation is that a mutant cell can result in cancer or some other sickness. This happens only rarely, however, so a few mutant cells in your body is not a bad thing. Everyone has them. The problem only occurs when you have too many mutant cells. Thus, as long as you are not exposed to too much radiation, the danger is minimal.

In the end, then, the important thing to remember about the danger of radioactivity is that it depends on the level of radioactivity to which you are exposed. A small amount of radioactivity is reasonably safe; a large amount is not. How much radioactivity exposure is too much? Well, scientists have examined that issue and have come up with certain limits to the amount of radiation exposure that a person should have. As a result, they limit the number of X-ray diagnoses (a source of gamma rays) a person can have in a year, and they limit the amount of exposure that people who work with radioactive isotopes can have.

Remember when I said that smoke detectors and people are radioactive? Indeed, you will be exposed to gamma rays just by going outside. The amount of radioactivity you are exposed to from these sources is hundreds of times lower than what scientists consider a dangerous level of radiation exposure. Thus, even though you are exposed to radioactivity from these sources, the cellular mutation and cellular death that result from them is so low that they are still quite safe.

Even if you are in a position in which you are exposed to large amounts of radioactivity, there are ways you can protect yourself. For example, it is possible to stop the little "bullets" before they ever reach your body. For example, alpha particles are extremely weak in terms of how much matter they can travel through. If you put a piece of paper between you and the radioactive source emitting the alpha particles, the vast majority of those alpha particles will stop in the paper. As a result, they will never hit you. Beta particles can travel through matter a bit better. It typically takes a thin sheet of metal to stop most of the beta particles coming from a radioactive isotope that emits them. Finally, gamma rays are the strongest type of radiation, requiring several inches of lead to stop them.

Thus, one way you can protect yourself is to block the radiation before it hits you. This method is called "shielding." The other way you can protect yourself from an intensely radioactive source is to simply move away from it. The farther you move away, the fewer "bullets" can hit you. Of course, in order to move away from a source of radiation, it must be localized, and you must know where it is. This is not always the case. Most people, however, will never be exposed to a large amount of radiation in their lifetime, so they will never be faced with such a situation.

ON YOUR OWN

13.9 People who regularly work with large samples of radioactive isotopes sometimes wear special suits lined with a thin layer of lead or other heavy material. What kinds of radiation are these people mostly protected against when wearing such a suit?

The Rate of Radioactive Decay

Many radioactive isotopes shoot only one "bullet," and then they are done. After all, the reason an isotope is radioactive in the first place is that its nucleus is unstable. Once it goes through whatever radioactive decay it goes through, the result is often a stable nucleus. Once the nucleus is stable, there is no more need for radioactive decay, so the isotope is no longer radioactive. For example, when ^{14}C beta decays into ^{14}N, the nitrogen atom is stable and, therefore, no longer radioactive. Thus, once a ^{14}C atom emits a single beta particle, it is no longer radioactive; therefore, it emits no more beta particles.

Although there are some radioactive isotopes that must emit several particles before becoming stable, many radioactive isotopes emit one particle and then stop. However, even a small sample of a radioactive isotope has trillions and trillions of atoms in it. Thus, even if each isotope emits only one "bullet," a small sample can emit trillions and trillions of "bullets." Nevertheless, at some point, nearly all the isotopes will have gone through the radioactive decay process. At that point, there will be essentially no radioactive isotopes left in the sample, and the result will be that the sample is no longer radioactive.

If I have a sample of a radioactive isotope, how long will it take before all the atoms in the sample have gone through the decay process, and the sample is no longer radioactive? Well, it depends on the isotope. For example, consider the case of ^{214}Po. I mentioned this radioactive isotope when I first discussed alpha decay. It emits an alpha particle and, as a result, turns into ^{210}Pb. If I have a sample of ^{214}Po, it will go through alpha decay so quickly that in about *one thousandth* of a second, nearly all of the ^{214}Po atoms will have emitted an alpha particle, and the result will be a sample of ^{210}Pb. Thus, ^{214}Po goes through radioactive decay rather quickly. On the other hand, ^{14}C beta decays into ^{14}N rather slowly. If I have a sample of ^{14}C, it will take more than 50,000 *years* for the vast majority of atoms to undergo beta decay. Thus, a sample of ^{14}C stays radioactive for a long, long time!

Is there any way to predict how long it will take for a radioactive isotope to decay into something that is no longer radioactive? Not really. However, the rate is easily measured. As a result, nuclear physicists have cataloged the rate of decay for thousands of radioactive isotopes. This rate is typically listed in terms of something called the **half-life** of the isotope.

Half-life – The time it takes for half of the original sample of a radioactive isotope to decay

For example, the half-life of ^{14}C is 5,700 years. This means that if I have 100 grams of ^{14}C, in 5,700 years, there will only be 50 grams of it left. The other half of the sample will have gone through beta decay and turned into ^{14}N. What would happen in the next 5,700 years? Would I have 0 grams left? No. In the next 5,700 years, half of the *remaining* ^{14}C would decay, leaving only 25 grams of ^{14}C.

Each time the half-life of a radioactive isotope passes, half of *what was there at the beginning* decays away. Thus, after one half-life, 100 grams of radioactive isotope will turn into 50 grams of radioactive isotope. After two half-lives, half of *that* will decay, leaving only 25 grams of radioactive isotope. After the next half-life, half of *that* will decay, and there will only be 12.5 grams of radioactive isotope left. In other words, the amount of radioactive isotope keeps getting divided by 2 after each half-life. Study the figure below and the example problem that follows to make sure you understand what I mean.

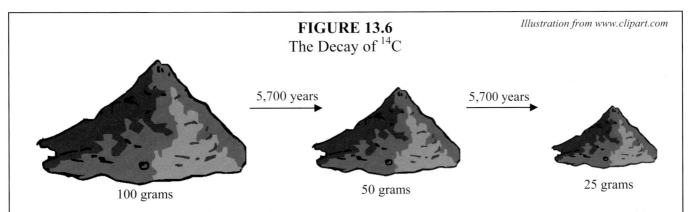

FIGURE 13.6

The Decay of ^{14}C

Illustration from www.clipart.com

5,700 years

5,700 years

100 grams

50 grams

25 grams

Half of a ^{14}C sample will decay into ^{14}N every 5,700 years. Thus, if you start with 100 grams of ^{14}C, only 50 grams of it will be left in 5,700 years. In 11,400 years (two half-lives), 25 grams will remain.

EXAMPLE 13.4

A radioactive isotope with a half-life of two hours is used in scientific research. If a scientist starts with 1,000 grams of the isotope, how many grams will be left in eight hours?

Since the half-life of the radioactive isotope is two hours, every two hours, the amount of radioactive isotope remaining will be cut in half. After two hours, then, the amount of isotope will decrease to 500 grams. After another two hours, the amount will decrease to 250 grams. In the next two hours, the amount will decrease to 125 grams, and in the next two hours, the amount will decrease to 62.5 grams. That completes the eight-hour time period. Thus, after eight hours, there will be 62.5 grams of the isotope left. This tells us that the rest of the sample (937.5 grams) went through the decay process in eight hours.

Something should be bothering you at this point. Earlier in this very section I mentioned that after a certain period of time, a radioactive sample will cease to be radioactive because nearly all its atoms will undergo the radioactive decay process and become stable. However, the previous discussion of half-life indicates that a radioactive sample never completely decays away. After all, if the amount of radioactive isotope is simply cut in half after every half-life, the amount will never drop to zero. Thus, a radioactive sample will never get rid of all its radioactivity.

While that is technically true, the fact is that from a practical standpoint, the amount of radioactive isotope in a sample drops off so quickly after a few half-lives that eventually there is very little radioactive isotope left. At that point, for all practical purposes, the amount of radioactive isotope can be assumed to be zero. Consider the example problem for a moment. The scientist started out with 1,000 grams of the isotope. After a mere 20 hours (10 half-lives), there would be only 0.9766 grams remaining! Thus, after only 10 half-lives, the amount of radioactive isotope decreases by more than a factor of one thousand! As a result, even though a sample of isotope never really goes away completely, at some point the amount of radioactive isotope left is so small that it can be ignored.

If we keep a radioactive sample around long enough, then, it will cease to be radioactive, for all practical purposes. Of course, each radioactive isotope has its own half-life. Some half-lives are short (like those of ^{214}Po), while others are quite long. As I already mentioned, the half-life of ^{14}C is 5,700 years! That's pretty long. It would take more than 50,000 years for most of a sample of ^{14}C to decay away. There are half-lives even longer than that, however. The half-life of ^{238}U is 4.5 *billion* years! Thus, even though a radioactive sample *eventually* loses its radioactivity, it can sometimes take a *very* long time for this to happen!

ON YOUR OWN

13.10 The half-life of ^{131}I is eight days. If you start with a 40-gram sample of ^{131}I, how much will be left in 24 days?

Radioactive Dating   C = Carbon

The fact that radioactive isotopes decay at a measurable rate allows scientists to use radioactive decay as a means of dating objects of unknown ages. This is known as **radioactive dating**. Although radioactive dating can be accurate under certain circumstances, it is important to note that it has some serious weaknesses as well. As a result, radioactive dating techniques must be viewed rather critically. Despite the fact that some scientists may try to convince you that radioactive dating is an accurate means of determining the age of an object, the scientific facts tell quite a different story.

The best way to examine the strengths and weaknesses of radioactive dating is to examine one of the radioactive dating methods in detail. Since ^{14}C dating is probably the best known radioactive dating technique, I will discuss that one. As I have already mentioned, ^{14}C decays by beta decay with a half-life of 5,700 years. It turns out that all living organisms contain a certain amount of ^{14}C, making all living organisms somewhat radioactive.

Interestingly enough, living organisms continually exchange ^{14}C with their surroundings. Human beings, for example, exhale carbon dioxide, some of which contains ^{14}C. In addition, human beings eat other organisms (plants and animals), that contain ^{14}C. Thus, organisms are continually exchanging ^{14}C with their environment. The practical result of all this exchange is that at any time when an organism is alive, it contains the same amount of ^{14}C as does the atmosphere around the organism.

This changes when the organism dies, however. At that point, the ^{14}C exchange ceases. Thus, the organism cannot replenish its supply of ^{14}C, and the amount of ^{14}C in the organism begins to decrease. Every 5,700 years, half the ^{14}C in the organism will decay away. In general, then, organisms that have been dead a long time tend to have less ^{14}C in them as compared to those that have been dead for only a short time.

Now if you think about it, this fact can be used to measure the length of time that an organism has been dead. After all, if we know how much ^{14}C was in an organism when it died, and if we measure the amount of ^{14}C in it now, the difference will be the amount of ^{14}C that has decayed away. Since we know how quickly ^{14}C decays, this can tell us how long the organism has been dead. Pretty simple, right?

Well, it *would* be simple, *if* we knew how much ^{14}C was in the organism when it died. The problem lies in figuring that out. After all, if the organism died before radioactive isotopes were being measured, there is no direct measurement of the amount of ^{14}C in the organism when it died. As a result, we must make an *assumption* about how much ^{14}C would have been measured if someone had measured it. As I have said before, there is nothing wrong with making assumptions in science. The trick is we have to know our assumptions are accurate.

In the case of ^{14}C dating, scientists assume that, on average, the amount of ^{14}C in the atmosphere has never really changed that much. They assume that the amount of ^{14}C in the atmosphere prior to the detonation of the first atomic bomb is essentially the same as it was 100 years ago, 1,000 years ago, etc. Atomic bombs increase the amount of ^{14}C in the atmosphere, which is why scientists use the pre-atomic-bomb era as their standard for the amount of ^{14}C in the environment.

Thus, when the age of a dead organism is being measured with ^{14}C dating, we assume that the amount of ^{14}C it had when it died was the same as the amount of ^{14}C that was in the atmosphere prior to the first atomic bomb explosion, which is something that was measured. That gives us a value for how much ^{14}C was initially in the dead organism. We can measure the amount of ^{14}C that is in the remains of the organism now, and the difference is assumed to be the result of radioactive decay. Since the rate of the decay is well known, we can then determine how long the organism has been dead.

Notice, however, that the age we get from this process is completely dependent on the assumption we made about how much ^{14}C was in the organism when it died. If that assumption is good, the age we calculate will be accurate. If that assumption is bad, the age we calculate will not be accurate. So the question becomes, "Is the assumption accurate?" In short, the answer is "No."

Through a process involving tree rings, there is a way we can measure the amount of ^{14}C in the atmosphere in years past. When a tree is cut down, the rings in the tree's trunk can be counted to determine how old each tree ring is. Each ring represents a year in the life of the tree. We know which ring corresponds to which year by simply counting the rings from the outside of the trunk to the inside. Well, it turns out that through a rather complicated process, we can actually measure the amount of ^{14}C in a tree ring and use it to determine how much ^{14}C was in the atmosphere during the year in which the tree ring was grown. As a result, scientists have determined the amount of ^{14}C in the atmosphere throughout a portion of the earth's past.

Scientists have studied the ^{14}C content in tree rings as much as 3,000 years old. From these measurements, they have determined the amount of ^{14}C in the atmosphere over the past 3,000 years. What they have seen is that the amount of ^{14}C has varied by as much as 70% over that time period. The variation is correlated to certain events that occur on the surface of the sun. As a result, *we know* that the amount of ^{14}C in the atmosphere has not stayed constant. Instead, it has varied greatly. Thus, *we know* that the initial assumption of ^{14}C dating is wrong. As a result, one must take most ^{14}C dates with a grain of salt. After all, we know that the assumption used in making those dates is wrong. Consequently, we cannot put too much trust in the results!

Notice that I said we must take "most" ^{14}C dates with a grain of salt. Why "most?" Why not all? It turns out that since we can determine the amount of ^{14}C in the atmosphere during the past using tree rings, we can actually use that data to help us make our initial assumption. As a result, the assumption becomes much more accurate. The problem is, however, that we don't have ^{14}C measurements for tree rings older than 3,000 years. That's because the vast majority of trees are younger than 3,000 years. Thus, we can only make an accurate assumption for organisms that have died within the past 3,000 years. As long as the organism died in that time range, we can use tree-ring data to help us make an accurate assumption of how much ^{14}C was in the organism when it died. For organisms that died longer than 3,000 years ago, we have no tree-ring data, so we have no way to make an accurate assumption. As a result, we cannot really believe the ^{14}C date.

In the end, then, the ^{14}C dating method can be believed for organisms that have been dead for 3,000 years or less. Thus, it is a great tool for archaeology. If an archaeologist finds a manuscript or a piece of cloth (both cloth and paper are made from dead plants), the archaeologist can use ^{14}C dating to determine its age. As long as the result is about 3,000 years or younger, the date can be believed. If the date turns out to be significantly older than 3,000 years, there is no reason to believe it.

So you should see that radioactive dating involves a pretty important assumption. If the assumption is good, the date obtained from radioactive dating is good. If the assumption is bad, the result obtained from radioactive dating will be bad. Now there are a lot of other radioactive dating techniques besides ^{14}C dating. Unfortunately, they all suffer from a similar malady. In every radioactive dating technique, we must make assumptions about how much of a certain substance was in the object originally. Such assumptions are quite hard to make accurately.

There is yet another assumption made in radioactive dating. We assume that the half-lives of radioactive isotopes have remained constant over time. Thus, no matter how old the object we are dating is, the half-lives of the radioactive isotopes in it have always been the same. While standard nuclear physics theories indicate this is a good assumption, there is some experimental evidence to suggest otherwise. The details of this experimental evidence are a bit beyond the scope of this course, but if you are interested in learning about it, go to the course website I described in the "Student Notes" at the beginning of this book.

Based on these facts, it's not surprising that radioactive dates are often found to be in conflict with each other or other dating techniques. In his book *Studies in Flood Geology*, John Woodmorappe has compiled more than 350 radioactive dates that conflict with one another or with other generally accepted dates. These erroneous dates demonstrate that the assumptions used in radioactive dating cannot be trusted.

Unfortunately, many in the scientific community are unwilling to admit to the inadequacies of radioactive dating because many scientists like the *results*. Because certain radioactive decay schemes have long, long half-lives, the dates that one calculates from these methods can be breathtakingly large. For example, there are rocks on the planet that radioactive dating techniques indicate are more than 4 *billion* years old. It turns out that many scientists *want* the earth to be that old because they believe in the hypothesis of evolution. This hypothesis *requires* a very old earth, and radioactive dating techniques provide dates that indicate earth is very old. As a result, they turn a blind eye to the inadequacies of radioactive dating because it gives them an answer they want! Hopefully, as time goes on, this unfortunate situation will change!

ANSWERS TO THE "ON YOUR OWN" PROBLEMS

13.1 Since all sodium atoms have 11 protons, this one has <u>11 protons</u>. This tells us that it also has <u>11 electrons</u>. Since the mass number is 23, we know that the sum of protons and neutrons in the nucleus must equal 23. The only way this can happen is if sodium-23 has <u>12 neutrons</u>.

13.2 Since all oxygen atoms have eight protons, this oxygen atom also has eight protons. This tells us that it has <u>eight electrons</u>. The name of an atom is its element name (oxygen) followed by the mass number. The mass number is the sum of protons and neutrons in the nucleus. Since there are eight protons and eight neutrons, the mass number is 16. This means the name is <u>oxygen-16</u>.

13.3 Isotopes have the same number of protons in their nuclei, but different numbers of neutrons. Only (a) and (c) have the same number of protons. They each have 16. In addition, they have different numbers of neutrons. The atom in (a) has 17 neutrons and the atom in (c) has 18 neutrons. Thus, since they have equal numbers of protons but different number of neutrons, <u>(a) and (c) are isotopes</u>.

13.4 The element symbolized by "F" (fluorine) has an atomic number of 9 according to the chart. This means all atoms symbolized by "F" have nine protons. This means they also have nine electrons. Since only two electrons fit in the first Bohr orbit, we will need to use the second Bohr orbit. That will hold an additional eight electrons, which is one more than we need. Since the mass number is 19, this tells us that the sum of protons and neutrons in the nucleus is 19. Thus, the atom must have 10 neutrons.

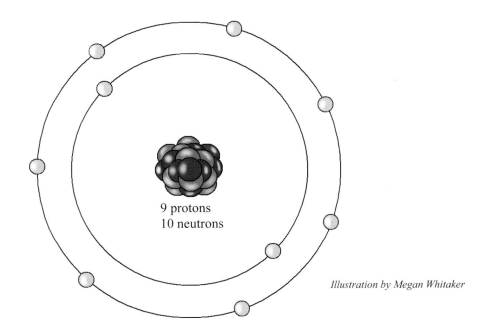

9 protons
10 neutrons

Illustration by Megan Whitaker

13.5 According to the chart, Cs has an atomic number of 55. This means there are 55 protons and 55 electrons in the atom. The first Bohr orbit will hold two. The next one will hold eight. That gives us space for 10 electrons so far. The third Bohr orbit holds 18. Now we have room for 28 electrons. There are still 27 to go, however. That's okay, though, because the fourth Bohr orbit holds 32. Thus, there is plenty of room for the extra 27 electrons. <u>The largest orbit will be the fourth Bohr orbit, and there will be 27 electrons in it</u>.

13.6 Since the wileon lives longer than the pion, the particles that exchange wileons can be farther apart than those that exchange pions. This means the force has a longer range than the strong nuclear force. Since the wileon does not live as long as a photon, however, the range is not as great as the electromagnetic force. Thus, <u>the range of this force is longer than that of the nuclear force but shorter than that of the electromagnetic force.</u>

13.7 According to the chart, the element Sr has an atomic number of 38. This means all Sr atoms have 38 protons. Since the mass number is 90, there must be 52 neutrons in the nucleus. In beta decay, a neutron turns into a proton. Thus, the daughter product will have one less neutron and one more proton than ^{90}Sr. This means it will have 39 protons and 51 neutrons. According to the chart, atoms with 39 protons are symbolized by "Y." The mass number is the sum of protons and neutrons, so it is still 90. Therefore, the daughter product is <u>^{90}Y</u>.

13.8 According to the chart, the element Am has 95 protons. Since the mass number is 241, this means there are 146 neutrons in the nucleus. In alpha decay, the nucleus loses two protons and two neutrons. So the daughter product will have only 93 protons and 144 neutrons. According to the chart, an element with 93 protons is symbolized by "Np." The mass number of this daughter product is 93 + 144 = 237. Thus, the daughter product is <u>^{237}Np</u>.

13.9 Since alpha particles can be stopped by a sheet of paper, a thin sheet of metal will definitely stop them. Also, it takes a thin sheet of metal to stop beta particles, so the protective suit will stop them as well. Gamma rays take several inches of lead to stop, however, so the suit provides little protection against them. Thus, the suit mostly protects against <u>alpha and beta particles</u>. Please note that for complete protection, the wearer of the suit must also use a respirator to avoid inhaling any radioactive isotopes that might be in the air.

13.10 After eight days have passed, the 40-gram sample will be cut in half, leaving only 20 grams. After another eight days, that 20-gram sample will be cut in half to 10 grams. After another eight days, that 10 gram sample will be cut in half to 5 grams. That's a total of 24 days. Thus, there will be <u>5 grams</u> left after 24 days.

STUDY GUIDE FOR MODULE #13

(Use the Periodic Chart to answer these questions. You will be able to use it on the test.)

1. Define the following terms:

a. Model
b. Nucleus
c. Atomic number
d. Mass number
e. Isotopes
f. Element
g. Radioactive isotope
h. Half-life

2. Order the three constituent parts of the atom in terms of their mass, from least massive to most massive.

3. What force keeps the protons and neutrons in the nucleus? What causes this force?

4. What force keeps the electrons orbiting around the nucleus?

5. What is an atom mostly made of?

6. An atom has an atomic number of 34. How many protons and electrons does it have? What is its symbol?

7. List the number of protons, electrons, and neutrons for each of the following atoms:

a. Neon-20 (neon's chemical symbol is "Ne")
b. ^{56}Fe
c. ^{139}La
d. ^{24}Mg

8. Two atoms are isotopes. The first has 18 protons and 20 neutrons. The second has 22 neutrons. How many protons does the second atom have?

9. Which of the following atoms are isotopes?

$$^{112}\text{Cd, } ^{112}\text{Sn, } ^{120}\text{Xe, } ^{124}\text{Sn, } ^{40}\text{Ar, } ^{120}\text{Sn}$$

10. Draw what the Bohr model says an ^{16}O atom would look like.

11. Draw what the Bohr model says a ^{25}Mg atom would look like.

12. What is the largest Bohr orbit in a uranium atom (the symbol for uranium is "U"), and how many electrons are in it?

13. Why is the strong nuclear force such a short-range force?

14. Determine the daughter products produced in the beta decay of the two radioactive isotopes shown below:

a. ^{98}Tc b. ^{125}I

15. Determine the daughter products produced in the alpha decay of the two radioactive isotopes shown below:

a. ^{212}Bi b. ^{224}Ra

16. A radioactive isotope goes through radioactive decay, but the isotope's number of protons and neutrons does not change. What kind of radioactive decay occurred?

17. The half-life of the radioactive decay of ^{226}Ra is 1,600 years. If a sample of ^{226}Ra originally had a mass of 10 grams, how many grams of ^{226}Ra would be left after 3,200 years?

18. The half-life of the man-made isotope ^{11}C is 20 minutes. If a scientist makes 1 gram of ^{11}C, how much will be left in one hour?

19. Why is radioactive dating unreliable in most situations?

20. List the three types of radioactive particles discussed in this module in the order of their ability to travel through matter. Start with the particle that cannot pass through much matter before stopping, and end with the one that can pass through the most matter before stopping.

MODULE #14: Waves and Sound

Introduction

Have you ever seen the ocean? I have. It's an amazing sight! Water stretches out as far as the eye can see, and waves crash against the shore on a regular basis. Consider the seashore pictured below:

FIGURE 14.1
Waves on a Seashore

Photo © David Hughes
Agency: Dreamstime.com

Look at the waves in the figure. There is a lot of energy in those waves. It turns out that a great deal of the energy in creation is in the form of waves, and that's what we are going to learn about in this module.

Although waves like those pictured in Figure 14.1 are the ones with which you are most familiar, the waves you see in the ocean or other large bodies of water are just one class of waves that exist in God's creation. In fact, water waves are not even the most prevalent kind of waves in creation. **Electromagnetic waves**, some of which we call "light," are much more common than water waves. Waves in the air, which we call sound, are also quite common. As you study this module, you will learn how sound can be described in terms of waves. In the next module, you will learn the same thing about light. Before you can learn that, however, you need to know a few things about waves in general.

Waves

Think for a moment about the waves you find on water. From a sideways view, such waves might look something like what you see in Figure 14.2.

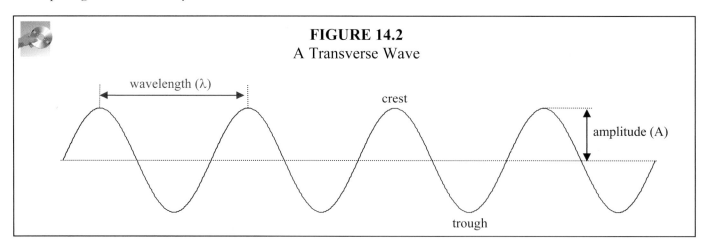

FIGURE 14.2
A Transverse Wave

In a wave, you have both **crests** (the highest points on the wave) and **troughs** (the lowest points on the wave). The distance between the crests (or the distance between the troughs) is called the **wavelength (λ)** of the wave, while the height of the wave is called the **amplitude (A)**. One characteristic of a wave that cannot really be drawn is **frequency**. The frequency of a wave indicates how many waves hit a certain point every second.

Suppose you were wading in the ocean at a beach. The amplitude of the waves would basically tell you how high the waves are. People riding surfboards would be happy if the waves had large amplitudes, because that would mean the waves would be high. People wanting a leisurely swim in the ocean would be happier with small-amplitude waves. The wavelength indicates how far apart the wave crests are. Frequency, on the other hand, indicates how many wave crests hit you each second if you simply stand there and do not move.

It should make sense to you that frequency and wavelength are related in some way. After all, if the wave crests are far apart, not very many of them will hit you in a second. If the wave crests are close together, several of them can hit you each second. Thus, when wavelength is large, frequency is small, and when wavelength is small, frequency is large. In other words, wavelength and frequency are *inversely proportional* to one another. When one gets large, the other becomes small.

I can be even more precise than that. Frequency and wavelength can be related to one another through the speed of the wave.

$$f = \frac{v}{\lambda}$$

(14.1)

In this equation, "f" represents the frequency of the wave, and "v" stands for the speed at which the wave passes a given point. Although the symbol used for speed in Equation (14.1) is "v," it does *not* stand for the velocity of the wave. Remember, velocity includes direction, and the frequency does not depend on the direction in which the wave is traveling. The funny-looking symbol, "λ," is the lower-case Greek letter "lambda," and it represents the wavelength.

First of all, we should examine the units of this equation. Speed is measured in m/sec, while wavelength, since it is a distance, is measured in meters. If I divide m/sec by m, what do I get? The m's cancel, leaving us with 1/sec. That's the unit for frequency. It is often called **Hertz** (abbreviated as "Hz"), in honor of the German physicist Heinrich Rudolf Hertz. Hertz discovered radio waves, which I will discuss in the next module.

In a moment, I'll use Equation (14.1) to analyze some waves, but first, I need to make a distinction between two different types of waves. The wave pictured in Figure 14.2 is called a **transverse wave**.

> Transverse wave – A wave with a direction of propagation that is perpendicular to its direction of oscillation

That's a mouthful, isn't it? Actually, this definition is rather simple once you get past the twenty-dollar words. The word "propagation" just means travel. For example, suppose you and a friend stretched a rope tightly between you. Then, suppose you flicked your end of the rope up and down really quickly. What would happen? A wave would travel from your end of the rope to your friend's end. That's the wave's direction of propagation. However, you can see the wave because the rope moves up and down as the wave passes. That's the **oscillation** (ah suh lay' shun) of the wave. So, the wave moves (propagates) horizontally (toward your friend), but it causes the rope to heave (oscillate) up and down. Thus, the direction of propagation is perpendicular to the direction of oscillation.

There is another type of wave, however. Some of the waves we see in creation are **longitudinal waves**.

> Longitudinal wave – A wave with a direction of propagation that is parallel to its direction of oscillation

The best way to think about a longitudinal wave is to get a Slinky® and stretch it out on an uncarpeted floor. Hold one end of the Slinky still and then start moving the other end back and forth. What will it look like? It will look something like Figure 14.3.

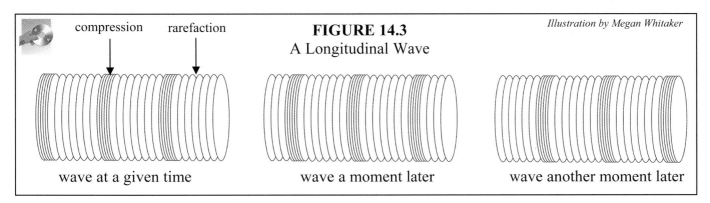

compression   rarefaction   **FIGURE 14.3**   *Illustration by Megan Whitaker*
A Longitudinal Wave

wave at a given time   wave a moment later   wave another moment later

Notice that portions of the Slinky are compressed together, while other portions are pulled apart. The compressed sections are called **compressions**, and they are similar to the crests of a transverse wave. The sections that are pulled apart are called **rarefactions** (rayr' uh fak' shunz), and they are similar to the troughs of a transverse wave. There are three drawings in the figure, and they each represent the wave at different times. Notice that as time moves on, the compressions move from left to right. That's also the direction of oscillation. Thus, both the direction of propagation and the direction of oscillation are horizontal. In other words, the directions of oscillation and propagation are parallel. That's what makes it a longitudinal wave.

Although transverse waves are what you and I think of when we think of waves, it is important to note that longitudinal waves are a part of creation as well. Sound, for example, is a longitudinal wave. Although transverse and longitudinal waves are fundamentally different from each other, Equation (14.1) applies equally to both. Since that is the case, let's use the equation to analyze a wave.

EXAMPLE 14.1

What is the frequency of a wave that travels at a speed of 3 meters per second and has a wavelength of 0.5 meters?

Remember, even though we use the symbol "v" in Equation (14.1), it means speed. Since we are given the speed and the wavelength, and since the units are consistent (both distance units are meters), we can just plug the numbers into the equation and get the answer:

$$f = \frac{v}{\lambda}$$

$$f = \frac{3 \frac{m}{sec}}{0.5 \, m} = 6 \frac{1}{sec}$$

Physicists typically like to write "Hz" instead of "1/sec," so the answer is 6 Hz. What does this answer mean? Well, it means that if you stand in the midst of this wave, six crests will hit you every second.

ON YOUR OWN

14.1 A longitudinal wave is suddenly stretched so that its wavelength is increased. If the speed of the wave does not change, what will happen to the wave's frequency?

14.2 Suppose you are wading on a beach that is experiencing waves that move with a speed of 0.5 meters per second and have a wavelength of 0.25 meters. If you stood still, how many waves would hit you every second?

Sound Waves

As I said in the introduction, sound is actually a longitudinal wave. It is important that you understand what I mean by that. For a moment, think about the waves you see in water. Why do you see those waves? You see them because water heaves up and down. The crests and troughs that result from such motion in the water produce visible waves. In physics terms, we say that water is the **medium** through which the waves in the ocean travel. We say this because water is the "stuff" that the wave causes to oscillate (move up and down).

Even though I specifically used water waves as an example, sound waves must also have a medium through which to travel. In other words, they must cause something to oscillate. What is the medium through which sound waves travel? Perform Experiment 14.1 to find out.

EXPERIMENT 14.1
The Medium Through Which Sound Waves Travel

Supplies:

♦ Plastic wrap
♦ Scissors

- ♦ Tape
- ♦ Candle (It needs to be either in a candleholder or able to stand up securely on its own.)
- ♦ Match
- ♦ Plastic 1-liter or 2-liter bottle (the kind soda pop comes in)
- ♦ Large pot
- ♦ Wooden spoon
- ♦ Large bowl
- ♦ Rice
- ♦ Eye protection such as goggles or safety glasses

Introduction: All waves must travel through some kind of medium. These two experiments demonstrate what the medium is for sound waves.

Procedure for Experiment #1:

1. Cut away the base of the plastic bottle so there is a big hole at the bottom.
2. Use the plastic wrap to cover the hole that was created when you cut away the bottle's base. You want to do this so that the plastic wrap stretches nice and tight, like you are making a drum. To do this, use the tape to secure the plastic wrap on one side of the bottle and then stretch the plastic wrap over the hole tightly. This will deform the bottle. That's okay. Once you have stretched the plastic, secure it on the other side. Continue to do this several times, using tape to hold the plastic wrap so that it is stretched tightly across the hole.
3. You should now have a makeshift drum on the bottom of the bottle. If you flick it with your finger, you should hear a dull thump.
4. Hold the bottle so that the opening from which you drink is pointed toward your ear. Flick the plastic wrap again and hear the sound as it comes through the bottle.
5. Light the candle.
6. Hold the bottle so that the opening from which you pour is pointed right at the flame. Try to hold the opening as close to the flame as you can without melting it or catching it on fire! See the illustration below:

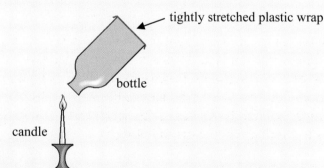

tightly stretched plastic wrap

bottle

candle

Illustration by Megan Whitaker

7. When the bottle opening is positioned properly, flick the plastic wrap at the other end so you hear the dull thump.
8. What happened to the candle flame?

Procedure for Experiment #2:

1. Stretch plastic wrap over the top (open end) of the large bowl, as if you were about to store some food in the bowl. As you did in the previous experiment, make sure the plastic wrap is stretched tightly across the bowl. Since most plastic wrap clings to dishes, you may not need tape in this case.

2. Spread some rice over the plastic wrap that is stretched across the top of the bowl.
3. Bring the large pot near the bowl, holding it so the top of the pot (the open end) points toward the bowl, as shown below:

Illustration by Megan Whitaker

4. Use the large spoon to start banging against the bottom of the pot.
5. Watch the rice. What happens?
6. Clean up your mess and put everything away.

What did you see in the two experiments? Hopefully, you "saw" sound. In the first experiment, the sound that traveled through the bottle once you flicked the plastic wrap actually blew out the candle. Why? The medium through which sound travels is air! Sound, therefore, causes air to oscillate when it travels. As a result, the sound that came out of the bottle caused the air to oscillate enough so that the candle's flame actually blew out. In the second experiment, the sound you made when you hit the pot with the spoon caused the air to oscillate. When that oscillating air hit the tightly stretched plastic wrap, it caused the plastic wrap to start vibrating. You saw the vibration because the rice grains on the plastic wrap began to bounce up and down.

The bowl in the second experiment is actually a pretty good illustration of the sound-sensing mechanism in your ears. Each of your ears has a thin layer of tissue, called the **tympanic** (tim pan' ik) **membrane**, that is tightly stretched across the ear canal. This structure is also called the "eardrum." When the sound waves enter your ear, they cause the tympanic membrane to start vibrating, much like the sound waves in the experiment caused the plastic wrap to vibrate. Those vibrations are then transmitted to your brain, and your brain interprets them as sound.

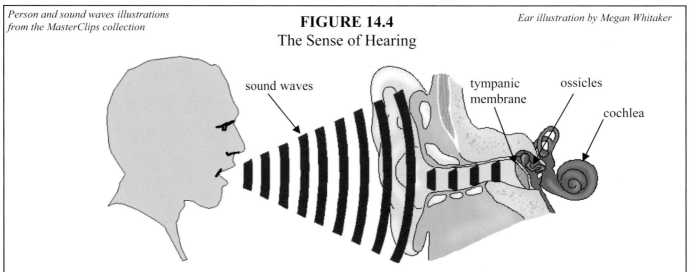

Person and sound waves illustrations from the MasterClips collection

FIGURE 14.4
The Sense of Hearing

Ear illustration by Megan Whitaker

sound waves

tympanic membrane

ossicles

cochlea

When sound waves reach the inner part of the ear, they cause the tympanic membrane to oscillate. Tiny bones called ossicles (ah' sik uhlz) transfer those oscillations to the cochlea (koh' klee uh), which converts them into electrical signals that are sent to the brain and interpreted as sound.

Think for a moment about the results of the first experiment. Can you now see that sound is a longitudinal wave? After all, the sound traveled from one end of the bottle to the other, and then straight to the candle. Thus, you know the direction of its motion. What about the oscillation of the wave? Do you think the air was oscillating parallel or perpendicular to the motion of the wave? If you think about how the flame blew out, you should realize that the air must have been oscillating parallel to the motion. Had the air been oscillating perpendicular to the motion, the flame might have flickered, but it probably would not have gone out. The experiment, therefore, gives us this important fact to remember:

Sound is a longitudinal wave.

In other words, sound causes the air itself to oscillate, and it oscillates parallel to the motion of the wave. Without air (or some other medium), there can be no sound because there would be nothing for the wave to oscillate.

 The multimedia companion CD has a video that demonstrates the fact that without air, there can be no sound.

The Speed of Sound

Now that you know a little bit about the nature of sound, I want you to understand how the properties of a sound wave affect the way you hear that sound. Equation (14.1) and Figure 14.2 tell us there are basically four characteristics that describe a wave: speed, wavelength, frequency, and amplitude. Perform the following experiment to learn about the first characteristic of sound waves: their speed.

EXPERIMENT 14.2
The Speed of Sound

Supplies:
♦ Two medium-sized rocks
♦ A person to help you
♦ A stopwatch
♦ A 250-meter stretch of sidewalk, pavement, gravel road, or lawn that is relatively straight
♦ A tape measure, meterstick, or yardstick

Introduction: Sound waves travel through air with a certain speed. This experiment will allow you to estimate that speed.

Procedure:

1. Have your helper hold the meterstick and stand right next to you.
2. Walk 10 paces down the sidewalk. Try to make each step cover the same distance as the previous ones.
3. When you are done, have your helper measure the distance between where you started and where you ended up 10 paces later.
4. Repeat steps 2 and 3 twice more.
5. Average the three distances, then divide that average by 10. The result is the average distance in one pace.

6. Give your helper the two rocks and keep the stopwatch for yourself. Start at one end of the sidewalk and, once again, have your helper stand right next to you.
7. Walk the same kind of paces that you walked before until you have counted off enough paces to equal 250 meters. This tells you that you and your helper are roughly 250 meters apart.
8. Have your friend bang the two rocks together. He should hold the rocks so that it is easy for you to see when they hit each other. Notice that you hear the sound of them hitting each other a moment *after* you see them touch. That's because you are using light to see the rocks. Light travels so quickly that, at these kinds of distances, you can assume you see the rocks touch at the very instant they actually touch. Sound, however, travels much more slowly than light. As a result, you do not hear them bang together until a moment after you actually see them bang together.
9. Now that you have seen the effect, it is time to measure how long it takes for the sound to travel from your helper to you. Once again, have your helper bang the rocks together. This time, however, start the stopwatch the moment you SEE the rocks touch each other, and stop the watch the moment you HEAR the bang. The stopwatch should indicate that less than a second has passed.
10. Repeat the previous step nine times and average the result.
11. Divide 250 meters by the average of the times you measured. The result is the speed of sound.
12. Put everything away.

What speed did you measure in the experiment? It may not be very accurate. After all, the distance you measured was not very precise. Also, there is a lot of experimental error involved in starting and stopping a stopwatch over such a short time interval. Even though you tried to average out that error by making the measurement 10 times and averaging the result, you can't get rid of the error completely. Nevertheless, you might have come close to the correct answer.

What is the correct answer? Well, it depends on the temperature. The speed of sound in air is given by the following equation:

$$v = (331.5 + 0.6 \cdot T)\frac{m}{sec} \tag{14.2}$$

In this equation, "v" stands for the speed of sound, while "T" stands for the temperature. In order for this equation to work, the temperature used must be in units of Celsius. To determine the correct measurement for Experiment 14.2, then, you would need to know the outside temperature in degrees Celsius. Then you could plug the temperature into the equation (the way I do it in the example below) and determine what the correct answer should be.

EXAMPLE 14.2

If the temperature is 68 °F (20 °C), what is the speed of sound?

In order for Equation (14.2) to work, the temperature must be in Celsius. That's what's given in parentheses:

$$v = (331.5 + 0.6 \cdot 20)\frac{m}{sec}$$

How do you work this equation? Remember that in equations like this, you must do the multiplication first. Then you add the result of that multiplication to 331.5:

$$v = (331.5 + 12) \, \frac{m}{sec}$$

$$v = 343.5 \, \frac{m}{sec}$$

Notice that I did not put the units for "T" into the equation. I am supposed to do that with *most* equations. With this equation, however, it is *set up* assuming that the temperature will be in Celsius. As a result, there is no need to include the unit in the equation, because the units have been worked out already. This is one of the *few* equations in which you need not carry the units through. You must remember, however, that the equation *requires* the temperature to be in Celsius. The answer, then, is 343.5 m/sec.

In your experiment, you probably got an answer between 290 and 400 m/sec. The experiment you performed was not all that accurate, however, so do not be concerned about the actual answer you got. One of the more important things to draw from the experiment is the experience of seeing the *cause* of a sound before hearing the *sound itself*.

The technique you used in Experiment 14.2 can also be used when watching a thunderstorm. If you've ever watched lightning before, you probably have experienced seeing a flash of lightning and then hearing the thunderclap a few moments later. Remember from our discussion of lightning back in Module #8 that thunder and lightning are actually formed at the same time. When the return stroke of charge from the ground leaps to the cumulonimbus cloud in the storm, the air is heated very quickly. That causes the air to expand quickly. This causes a wave which, when it hits your ear, gets translated into the "boom" of thunder.

If lightning and thunder are created at the same time, the delay you experience between seeing a lightning flash and hearing the thunder is due to the time it takes sound to travel to your ears. Remember, light travels very quickly. The speed of light is so great that the time it takes for light to travel even several miles is simply too small for you to measure. Thus, as far as you are concerned, you see a lightning bolt essentially the same instant it is formed. Sound travels much more slowly, however. As a result, you often do not hear the thunder until much later. Study the following example to see what I mean.

EXAMPLE 14.3

A physicist is watching a thunderstorm. She sees a flash of lightning and then hears a thunderclap 2 seconds later. If the air temperature is a cool 15° C, how far away from the physicist was the lightning formed?

Because light travels so quickly, we can assume that the lightning was formed at the instant in which the physicist sees it. The time delay that the physicist observes, then, is simply the time it took for the sound to travel from the point at which the lightning was created to the physicist. First, we need to know the speed of sound. This can be determined by Equation (14.2):

$$v = (331.5 + 0.6 \cdot T)\frac{m}{sec}$$

$$v = (331.5 + 0.6 \cdot 15)\frac{m}{sec}$$

$$v = (331.5 + 9)\frac{m}{sec}$$

$$v = 340.5\frac{m}{sec}$$

Now that we know the speed, we can determine the distance the sound traveled. Remember from Module #9 that speed is defined by Equation (9.1):

$$speed = \frac{distance\ traveled}{time\ traveled} \qquad (9.1)$$

We can use algebra to rearrange this equation:

$$distance\ traveled = (speed) \times (time\ traveled) \qquad (14.3)$$

If you don't know algebra yet, don't worry. Just treat this as a new equation: Equation (14.3). This is an equation with which, given the speed and time, we can calculate the distance. That's what we have in this problem. We know the speed of sound, and we know the time it took for the sound to travel to the physicist. Thus, we can calculate the distance it traveled:

$$distance\ traveled = (speed) \times (time\ traveled)$$

$$distance\ traveled = (340.5\ \frac{m}{sec}) \times (2\ \cancel{sec}) = 681\ m$$

The lightning, therefore, was formed <u>681 m</u> from the position of the physicist.

Although the way I solved the example is the most accurate way to determine how far away a lightning strike is, there is an easy method that gives relatively good results as well. As you learned in Module #8, thunderstorms usually are the result of cold fronts moving in under warm fronts. Thunderstorms, therefore, usually result in cooler temperatures. A "good guess" for the temperature in a thunderstorm is about 16 °C. At that temperature, sound travels at about 341 meters per second. Well, 341 meters is about 1/5 of a mile. In other words, during a thunderstorm, you can estimate the speed of sound to be 1/5 of a mile per second. As a result, for every second of delay between the lightning strike and the thunder, the lightning strike was about 1/5 of a mile away. If you count 2 seconds between a lightning flash and the resulting thunder, then, the lightning struck about 2/5 of a mile away. Although I will *not* allow you to use this rule of thumb to answer problems, you can use it when you are watching lightning strikes!

ON YOUR OWN

14.3 What is the speed of sound in air when the temperature is 28 °C?

14.4 During a thunderstorm, the temperature is 18 °C. If you see a lightning flash and hear the thunder 1.5 seconds later, how far away did the lightning actually strike?

The Speed of Sound in Other Substances

Although we usually think of sound traveling through air, it is important to realize that sound can travel through any substance it can oscillate in order to make waves. When we hear a sound, it is usually the result of waves traveling through the air. That's not always the case, however. Do you remember Experiment 6.1? In that experiment, you listened to sound that traveled through a string. You did that experiment to illustrate the fact that the way in which sound waves travel through a substance can be used to determine the properties of that substance. I used that experiment to discuss how scientists have learned a great deal about the interior structure of the earth just by observing how waves travel through the earth.

Since Experiment 6.1 demonstrated to you that sound travels differently in different substances, it shouldn't surprise you that the speed of sound varies from substance to substance. Table 14.1 lists a few substances and the approximate speed of sound in each.

TABLE 14.1
The Speed of Sound in Certain Substances

Substance	Speed of Sound	Substance	Speed of Sound
Air (25 °C)	346 m/sec	Steel	5029 m/sec
Alcohol	1186 m/sec	Aluminum	5093 m/sec
Fresh Water	1435 m/sec	Iron	5128 m/sec
Wood (oak)	3848 m/sec	Glass	5503 m/sec

Do you notice a trend in the data? Air is a gas, while alcohol and fresh water are liquids. The rest of the substances in the table are solids. Notice that the speed of sound in the liquids is about three times the speed of sound in air. In addition, the speed of sound in the solids is somewhere between two and five times higher than the speed of sound in the liquids. Thus, sound travels faster in liquids than it does in gases, and it travels faster in solids than it does in liquids.

If an object travels in a medium faster than the speed of sound in that medium, we say that the object is traveling at **supersonic** speeds.

Supersonic speed – Any speed that is faster than the speed of sound in the substance of interest

Some jets routinely travel through the air faster than sound. In aviation, the speed of these jets is often measured in terms of the speed of sound. This speed unit is known as the **Mach** (mahk) number. When a jet travels at the speed of sound in air, it is said to be traveling at Mach 1. If a jet is traveling at twice the speed of sound, it is said to be traveling at Mach 2. The F-35 Lightning II jet, for example, is a military strike fighter with a maximum speed of Mach 1.8. This means it can travel 1.8 times faster than the speed of sound. The NASA space shuttle exceeds Mach 10 after dropping out of orbit and coming in for a landing!

An interesting phenomenon known as a **sonic boom** is generated when an object travels through air faster than the speed of sound in air.

Sonic boom – The sound produced as a result of an object traveling at or above Mach 1

This phenomenon is illustrated in Figure 14.5.

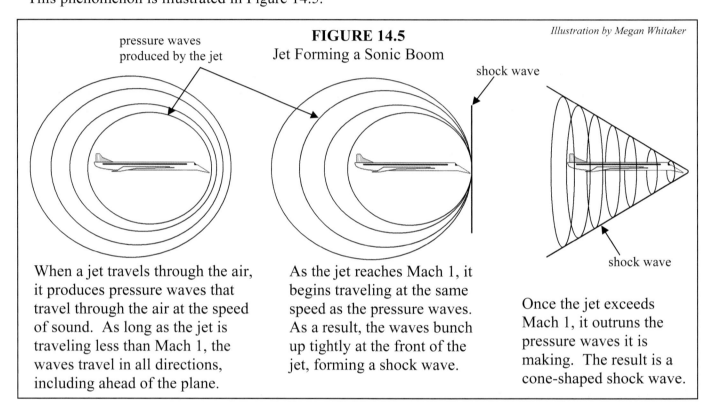

FIGURE 14.5
Jet Forming a Sonic Boom

Illustration by Megan Whitaker

pressure waves produced by the jet

shock wave

shock wave

When a jet travels through the air, it produces pressure waves that travel through the air at the speed of sound. As long as the jet is traveling less than Mach 1, the waves travel in all directions, including ahead of the plane.

As the jet reaches Mach 1, it begins traveling at the same speed as the pressure waves. As a result, the waves bunch up tightly at the front of the jet, forming a shock wave.

Once the jet exceeds Mach 1, it outruns the pressure waves it is making. The result is a cone-shaped shock wave.

As a jet travels, it produces pressure waves that travel away from the plane in all directions, at the speed of sound. As long as the jet travels slower than the pressure waves it produces (in other words, less than Mach 1), the waves travel in all directions, including ahead of the jet. Now, of course, because of the jet's motion, the wave compressions in front of the jet are closer together than the wave compressions behind the jet. When the jet reaches Mach 1, however, it moves right along with the pressure waves it produces. This causes the compressions of the waves to "pile up," making a huge wave called a shock wave. Like a thunderclap, this wave of air creates a very loud boom – a sonic boom. When the jet exceeds Mach 1, it actually outruns the sound waves it produces. This causes the waves to pile up at the edge of a cone. When that cone reaches your ears, you hear the sonic boom.

Sonic booms can be destructive to human ears, but they can also be destructive to buildings, etc. After all, remember that sound is a wave that travels through the air. When the huge wave associated with a sonic boom hits a building, it can shake the building rather dramatically, causing damage. As a result, jets try to travel at or above Mach 1 only in areas of little or no population. The Concorde, for example, was a commercial airliner (it is no longer in service) that could travel faster than sound. It usually did not reach speeds of Mach 1 or higher until it was over an ocean.

ON YOUR OWN

14.5 Remember from Module #9 that the outer core of the earth is liquid but the inner core is solid. If a geophysicist is studying how sound waves travel through the core, would he expect the sound waves to travel faster in the inner core or the outer core?

14.6 A jet is traveling at Mach 1.8 when the temperature of the surrounding air is 0 °C. What is its speed in m/sec?

Sound Wavelength and Frequency

You now know a lot about the speed of sound, so it is time to move on to the other characteristics of a wave. In this section, I want to concentrate on how the wavelength and frequency of a sound wave affect what we hear as sound. As you learned already, wavelength and frequency are inversely proportional to each other. When wavelength is large, frequency is small, and vice-versa. Thus, we often think of wavelength and frequency together. Perform the following experiment to see how the wavelength of a sound wave affects how you hear the sound.

EXPERIMENT 14.3
Wavelength and Sound

Supplies:

♦ Water
♦ Glass or plastic bottle (A glass bottle is best, and 2-liter is the ideal size. It must have a narrow neck. A jar will not work well.)
♦ Eye protection such as goggles or safety glasses

Introduction: The wavelength of sound waves has a dramatic effect on how we hear the sound. This experiment demonstrates the effect.

Procedure:

1. Empty the bottle and rinse it out with water.
2. Hold the bottle up to your mouth so that the top edge of the bottle opening just touches your bottom lip.
3. Pursing your lips, blow across the top of the bottle. It may take some practice, but you will eventually produce a sound that sounds like it is coming from a horn. Blow a few times to get an idea of what that sound sounds like.
4. Fill the bottle ¾ full of water and repeat steps 2 and 3. Blow a few times to get a good idea of what the sound sounds like.
5. Write in your laboratory notebook how this sound differed from the first one you made.
6. Empty some of the water out of the bottle so that the bottle is now only half full. Repeat steps 2 and 3 again.
7. Write in your laboratory notebook how this sound differed from the previous one you made.

8. Empty some of the water out of the bottle so that the bottle is now only ¼ full. Repeat steps 2 and 3 again.
9. Write in your laboratory notebook how this sound differed from the previous one you made.
10. Empty the rest of the water out and repeat steps 2 and 3 one more time. The sound you get now should be essentially the same as what you started with.
11. Clean up your mess.

What was the difference in the sounds you produced with the bottle? The sound should have had essentially the same volume in each case. The difference should have been in the **pitch** of the sound you heard.

Pitch – An indication of how high or low a sound is, which is primarily determined by the frequency of the sound wave

The terms "high" and "low" in this definition do not refer to volume. Instead, they refer to a musical scale. When the bottle was empty, the sound produced should have been deep and low, much like the low notes a singer would sing. When the bottle was nearly full, the sound produced should have been higher and more shrill, like the high notes a singer would sing. The less water the bottle had in it, the lower the sound should have become.

Why was there a difference in pitch? Well, when you blew across the top of the bottle, you moved air around inside the bottle. The air began traveling up and down in the bottle in response to how you were blowing. Since you blew at a reasonably constant rate, air began traveling up and down in the bottle, forming a wave. The wavelength of the wave produced was determined by how far the air could travel up and down the bottle. When the bottle was empty, air could travel all the way to the bottom of the bottle. Thus, you produced sound waves with a *long* wavelength. When the bottle had a lot of water in it, there wasn't much distance over which air could travel. As a result, the waves produced had a *short* wavelength.

The experiment, then, demonstrates that sound waves with a long wavelength have a low pitch, while sounds with a short wavelength have a high pitch. Remember, wavelength and frequency are inversely proportional to one another. Thus, long wavelengths make low (small) frequencies and small wavelengths make high (large) frequencies. This tells us that when the frequency of a sound wave is low, pitch is low. When frequency is high, pitch is high. This is something you need to remember.

Sound waves with low pitch have low frequency.
Sound waves with high pitch have high frequency.

As long as you are dealing with sound traveling through air, the pitch of a sound is determined by either wavelength or frequency. Just remember that wavelength and frequency are inversely proportional. Thus, sound waves with long wavelength have low frequencies and low pitch. Sound waves with short wavelengths have high frequencies and high pitch. We usually think of pitch in terms of frequency, however, since it is actually the frequency of the waves that your ear detects.

Have you ever seen a person playing a flute? The flautist (that's the term for someone who plays the flute) blows in one side of the flute and then raises or lowers caps that cover holes in the flute. Based on what holes the flautist uncovers, you hear different sounds with different pitches. How does that work? It works much the same as your experiment did. When the flautist uncovers certain holes in the flute, he or she is changing the wavelength of the waves produced. This, in turn, changes the frequency of the sound waves, which changes the pitch of the sound that you hear.

Nearly all instruments utilize some method to change the wavelength of sound waves in order to change the pitch of the sounds being generated. Instruments that you blow into in order to create the sound have some means of changing the distance over which the air travels in the instrument. This changes the wavelength of the sound, which changes the frequency and, therefore, the pitch. Even stringed instruments do this, just in a slightly different way.

A stringed instrument (like a guitar) has a series of strings. When the string is plucked, it begins to vibrate. This causes the string to push air back and forth, making a sound wave. If you watch a guitar player, he or she will change the length of the string that is plucked by holding the string down at different positions along the neck of the guitar. Since the length of the string that vibrates changes, the wavelength of the sound wave produced changes. This changes the pitch of the sound.

Now it is important to realize that what scientists call "sound" is not necessarily what people think of when they hear the word "sound." Most people think of sound as what people hear. Scientists, however, think of sound simply as waves in the air. As a result, there are plenty of "sounds" we do not hear. Remember, what we hear as sound is actually a result of the signals sent from the cochlea to the brain. We do not hear the waves themselves. The signals made by the cochlea transmit the frequency of the wave to the brain, and the brain interprets this as pitch.

The human ear, though elegantly designed, cannot detect all frequencies of waves in the air. In general, human ears are sensitive to waves with frequencies between 20 Hz and 20,000 Hz. Longitudinal waves with these frequencies are called **sonic** waves. The musical notes with which we are most familiar have frequencies in the range of several hundred Hz. Middle "C," for example, has a frequency of 264 Hz. Waves with frequencies higher than 20,000 Hz are called **ultrasonic** waves, and waves with frequencies below 20 Hz are called **infrasonic** waves. The only difference between these waves is their frequencies. Nevertheless, only sonic waves produce what most people call sound. Some animals, however, can hear waves that are not sonic. Bats, for example, can hear sounds with frequencies up to 100,000 Hz, while cats can hear sounds with frequencies up to 40,000 Hz. Whales and elephants, on the other hand, can hear infrasonic waves.

ON YOUR OWN

14.7 Many flautists also play the piccolo, an instrument that looks like a very small, short flute. Which instrument (the flute or the piccolo) can produce notes with the highest pitch?

14.8 Are the wavelengths of ultrasonic waves shorter or longer than the wavelengths of sonic waves?

The Doppler Effect

The fact that the pitch of the sound you hear is related to the frequency of the sound wave leads to an interesting effect known as the **Doppler Effect**. This effect, named after Austrian physicist Christian Doppler, is best demonstrated by experiment.

EXPERIMENT 14.4
The Doppler Effect

Supplies:

♦ A car with a horn and a parent to drive the car
♦ A straight street (It could be the one you live on, but it might work better to find one away from peoples' homes.)
♦ Eye protection such as goggles or safety glasses

Introduction: Since the pitch of a sound depends on the frequency of the sound waves produced, the pitch of a sound is affected by the motion of the object making the sound. This experiment will demonstrate that effect.

Procedure

1. Have your parent drive the car to one end of the street.
2. Stand at the other end of the street, off to one side. **Be careful!!!! Do not get too close to the street!**
3. Have your parent drive down the street toward you with a speed of at least 20 miles per hour. A few seconds before the car reaches you, have your parent blow the horn in a single blast until he has completely passed you.
4. Note how the horn sounds before the car passes you and after the car passes you. Note the difference in your lab notebook.
5. As long as the people who live on the street (if there are any) are not too irritable, have your parent repeat the procedure, this time from the other direction.
6. Have your parent stop the car and blow the horn. Note the pitch and compare it to what you heard in the other parts of the experiment.

What did you hear in the experiment? When the car was traveling toward you, the pitch of the horn should have been higher than when the car passed you and started traveling away from you. This tells you that the frequency of the sound waves reaching your ears changed. After all, if the pitch of a sound changes, you know that the frequency of the sound wave changes. Does that mean the horn was emitting one sound as the car traveled toward you and a different sound as the car began traveling away from you? No, of course not. The horn emitted the same sound the whole time. The pitch of that sound was the same as the pitch you heard in step 6 of the experiment.

Why did the pitch change when the car passed you? The horn continued to emit sound waves with the same frequency, but you heard the pitch of the horn change when the car passed you. Why? It is a result of the fact that sound is a wave. When a sound-emitting object is stationary and you are also stationary, the waves it produces hit your ear at the same frequency as when they left the sound-producing object. Thus, you hear the true frequency of the sound.

However, when a sound-producing object is moving, the compressions and rarefactions of the sound waves get bunched up in front of the object and stretched out behind the object (see Figure 14.6 on the next page). This decreases the wavelength of the waves in front of the object, which increases their frequency. If you are standing in front of the object as it is moving, then, you will hear a pitch that is higher than the pitch the object actually produces. Once the object begins moving away from you, the waves that hit your ears are the ones that are stretched out behind the object. As a result, the compressions and rarefactions are farther away from one another. This increases the wavelength and, therefore, decreases the frequency of the sound that hits your ears. As a result, the pitch is lower than the pitch the object actually produces. Since this might be a bit difficult to understand, study the following figure.

FIGURE 14.6

Illustrations from the MasterClips collection

The Doppler Effect

The horn from a car produces sound waves at a constant frequency. When the car moves, the horn emits those waves as the car travels. Thus, after it has emitted one wave, it moves forwards to emit the next. This causes the waves to be bunched up in front of the car and stretched out behind the car.

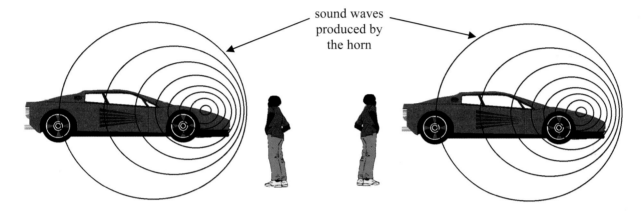

sound waves produced by the horn

Since the sound waves get bunched up in front of the car, the wavelength is shorter, so the frequency is higher. If the car is heading toward you, then, you will hear a pitch that is higher than the pitch the horn produces.

When the car passes you, the sound waves that reach your ear are the ones traveling behind the car. They are stretched out, which gives them a larger wavelength and thus a lower frequency. This results in a pitch that is suddenly lower than the pitch the horn produces.

ON YOUR OWN

14.9 Suppose Experiment 14.4 were reversed. In this version of the experiment, the car sits still while your parent sounds the horn, and you run as fast as you can toward the car. Would the horn sound like it had a higher pitch, lower pitch, or the same pitch as it had when both you and the car are standing still?

The Volume of Sound

So far, I have discussed the speed, wavelength, and frequency of sound. It is now time to discuss the last aspect of a wave and see how it affects sound. In Figure 14.2, I noted that all waves have amplitude. Does this affect what you hear when the sound wave hits your ear? If so, how? After all, the frequency (or wavelength) affects the pitch you hear. How does the amplitude of a sound wave affect the sound you hear? Once again, this is best demonstrated by experiment.

EXPERIMENT 14.5
The Amplitude of a Sound Wave

Supplies:

♦ Eye protection such as goggles or safety glasses
♦ If you have access to a stringed instrument such as a violin, guitar, cello, or banjo, use it for this experiment. If you do not have access to such an instrument, you will need:

  ♦ Rubber band
  ♦ Plastic tub (like the kind that margarine or whipped cream comes in)

Introduction: The amplitude of a wave tells you how big the wave is. For sound waves, the amplitude has a very easy-to-detect effect on the nature of the sound produced.

Procedure:

1. If you do not have a stringed instrument, make a simple one by stretching the rubber band all the way around the plastic tub. Do this so that the rubber band stretches tightly across the open end of the tub as well as across the bottom of the tub.
2. Hold the instrument so that you can watch a string (or the rubber band) when you pluck it.
3. Pluck a string only slightly. Watch how the string vibrates and listen to the sound it produces.
4. Using the same string each time, pluck the string harder and harder. Do not pluck the string so hard that it will break, however! Each time you pluck harder, listen to how the sound changes and observe how the string vibrates.
5. Put everything away.

What did you see and hear in the experiment? When you plucked the string only slightly, the string vibrated only slightly and the sound produced was not very loud. As you plucked the string harder, however, the string vibrated a lot more. In addition, the sound was louder. You should not have noticed any change in pitch between when the string was plucked hard or softly. You should only have noticed a change in volume. What does this tell you? When the string vibrates more vigorously, it pushes more air than when it vibrates only slightly. Thus, the sound waves produced by a vigorously vibrating string have larger amplitude than the sound waves produced by a string that vibrates only slightly. This tells us:

The amplitude of a sound wave governs how loud the sound is.

Large-amplitude sound waves are loud; small-amplitude sound waves are relatively quiet. Now, of course, if you are far from the source of a sound, the sound is not as loud as if you are close. Why? Because as a sound wave travels through air, its amplitude decreases. In an open space, then, the volume you hear can be reduced by simply moving away from the source of the sound. In closed spaces like auditoriums, however, moving further from the source will reduce the direct volume of the sound, but sometimes reflections off walls or in corners can actually increase the volume.

Remember when I discussed sonic booms earlier? A sonic boom is loud because when the sound waves produced by a supersonic jet begin to bunch up, their amplitudes add together. As a result, the amplitude of the sound wave that comes from a supersonic jet is huge. The same can be said for a thunderclap. The reason a thunderclap is so loud stems from the fact that the heat produced in a lightning strike is so large that it bunches up a lot of air in the compressions (crests) of the sound wave.

When you turn the volume up on your television, radio, or stereo, you are simply causing the device to produce sound waves of larger and larger amplitude. The larger the amplitude of the sound waves, the louder the sound is. Extremely loud sounds can damage your hearing because of the amplitude of the waves. Remember, your ear detects sound waves with the tympanic membrane. The larger the amplitude of the wave, the more violently the tympanic membrane vibrates. Extremely loud sounds such as explosions can cause the membrane to tear painfully due to the sudden increase in the violence of its vibrations. Worse, however, the constant onslaught of loud sounds such as power tools and loud stereo systems can destroy the delicate cells in the cochlea (see Fig. 14.4) that are responsible for turning those vibrations into signals the brain can understand. If those cells die, they can never be replaced, and that will result in severe hearing loss and continual ringing in your ears. Ringing in your ears, then, is a sign that you have been exposed to sounds loud enough to damage your hearing.

Now although it is possible to harm or destroy your hearing, your ears have a remarkable range when it comes to the loudness they can withstand. They have a remarkable range because the cells in the cochlea do not respond linearly with increasing sound wave amplitude. In other words, when the amplitude of a sound wave doubles, the response of the cells does not double. They are designed to reduce the sensitivity of their response as the amplitude of the sound waves that hit the ear increase. As a result, a sound wave with ten times more amplitude does not sound ten times louder.

The excellent design of the human ear requires scientists to use a special scale to measure the loudness of a sound. We call this scale the **bel** scale, and it is named in honor of Alexander Graham Bell, the inventor of the telephone. The bel scale measures the **intensity** of a sound wave, which is determined by the amplitude. Thus, intensity is really just another way of expressing wave amplitude. In the bel scale, an increase in one bel corresponds to a 10-fold increase in sound wave intensity. The threshold of human hearing is defined as 0 bels, and physical damage can occur in the ear when sounds reach the level of 13 bels.

You may have never heard of bels, but you have probably heard of **decibels**. As you learned in Module #1, the prefix "deci" means one tenth. Thus, a decibel is simply one tenth of a bel. Since the bel is a relatively large unit for sound, physicists tend to talk about decibels rather than bels. That's what I will do from now on. In terms of decibels, then, the threshold of human hearing is 0 decibels, and physical damage to the ears is caused when sound reaches a loudness of 130 decibels. Table 14.2 lists some common sounds and their loudness in decibels.

TABLE 14.2
The Loudness of Some Common Sounds

Sound	Decibels	Sound	Decibels
Soft Whisper	20	Gasoline-Powered Mower	95
Normal Conversation	40	Typical Rock Concert	115
Busy Traffic	70	Possible Pain To Ears	120
Pneumatic Drill	80	Possible Damage to Ears	130

If you look at the inside back cover of the book, you will find a **noise thermometer** developed by the Baccou-Dalloz hearing safety group. It tells you how long you can listen to sounds of a given loudness before risking damage to your ears.

Now remember, an increase of 1 bel (10 decibels) results in a sound wave intensity increase of a factor of 10. Thus, the sound waves that come from a soft whisper have 100 times (10 x 10) the intensity of the sound waves at the threshold of human hearing.

If you think about that for a moment, you should get a really good appreciation for how well our ears are designed! Since the threshold of human hearing is 0 decibels, and since physical damage can occur at 130 decibels, that tells us the human ear has a range of 13 bels. Each increase of one bel (10 decibels) is a factor of ten increase in the intensity of the sound waves. Thus, the human ear can detect sound waves as much as 10,000,000,000,000 times its threshold before it might be damaged. That is an *incredible* range. Isn't that amazing? What does that tell you about the human ear? It tells you there is no way such a marvelous wave detector could exist by chance! The range of sounds over which the human ear can hear is just one of the many examples that tell us this world and the life that inhabits it were *created*.

Make sure you understand the bel scale by studying the example below and solving the "On Your Own" problem that follows.

EXAMPLE 14.4

The sound from a typical vacuum cleaner is about 60 decibels, while the sound of a rifle firing is about 140 decibels. How many times larger is the intensity of the waves coming from the rifle as compared to those coming from the vacuum cleaner?

Remember, the bel scale is set up so that every increase in 1 bel is the same as a tenfold increase in the intensity of the sound wave. The first thing we have to do, then, is convert decibels back into bels. That's easy, because we know that "deci" means 0.1. Thus 1 decibel = 0.1 bel:

$$\frac{60 \text{ decibels}}{1} \times \frac{0.1 \text{ bel}}{1 \text{ decibel}} = 6 \text{ bels}$$

$$\frac{140 \text{ decibels}}{1} \times \frac{0.1 \text{ bel}}{1 \text{ decibel}} = 14 \text{ bels}$$

The rifle, then, is 8 bels louder than the vacuum cleaner. Since each bel unit represents a 10-fold increase in sound wave intensity, the total increase is calculated by taking 10 and multiplying it by itself eight times. This means the intensity of the rifle's sound wave is 10 x 10 x 10 x 10 x 10 x 10 x 10 x 10 = <u>100,000,000 times larger</u> than the intensity of the vacuum cleaner's sound wave.

ON YOUR OWN

14.10 The sound from a typical power saw has a loudness of 110 decibels. How many times larger is the intensity of the sound waves from a power saw as compared to those of normal conversation (40 decibels)?

Uses of Sound Waves

Sound waves are useful to us in ways other than hearing. Remember, we can't hear ultrasonic or infrasonic sound waves, but they are sound waves nevertheless. Because of the way sound waves travel, we can use them to "see" things we otherwise could not see. As you already have learned, we can use sound waves to understand what the inside of the earth looks like, even though we have never seen it. Typically, the sound waves used for this purpose are infrasonic, so they have frequencies lower than 20 Hz.

When sound waves encounter an obstacle, a portion of the wave travels through the obstacle, but another portion is reflected backward. The fraction of the wave reflected depends on the type of obstacle encountered. One way you can experience the phenomenon of reflected waves is to stand at the edge of a canyon and yell. You will hear an echo that results from the sound waves you produced reflecting off the canyon walls and coming back to your ears again.

It turns out that when you talk in your house, a portion of the sound waves you form is reflected off the walls and back into your ears. You do not hear an echo, however. Why? Well, the walls in your home are simply too close. Since sound travels relatively quickly, it hits the walls and bounces back to your ears so fast that your brain cannot tell the sound wave leaving your mouth from the one reflected off the walls. If you go to a canyon, however, the sound waves bounce back to your ears from a much greater distance. As a result, your brain can distinguish between the original wave and the reflected one.

In general, a sonic wave must take about 0.1 seconds to reflect off an obstacle and travel back to your ears for your brain to perceive it as an echo. Based on the average speed of sound in air, then, you need to be about 34 meters away from an obstacle in order for you to hear an echo as a result of sound waves bouncing off the obstacle. That's why you only hear echoes in settings like canyons or long, empty hallways.

One application that uses reflected sound waves is the ultrasonic ruler. This device is a small box that emits ultrasonic waves. The circuitry in the device measures the temperature of the air and determines the speed of sound for that temperature. When the wave hits a wall or other obstruction, part of the wave is transmitted through the obstruction, and part of the wave is reflected back. That part that is reflected back is detected by the ultrasonic ruler, and the time it took to travel to the obstruction and back is measured by the circuitry. The ultrasonic ruler then uses the speed of sound and the time it measured to calculate the distance from the device to the obstruction. Thus, a person simply holds the device and points it to a wall, and the device determines the distance to that wall with a precision of better than 0.5 cm.

Ultrasonic waves can also be used as a medical imaging tool. When a sound wave hits an obstruction, part of the wave is reflected, and part is transmitted. If the obstruction is stationary, the reflected and transmitted waves are the same frequency, but they each have lower amplitudes than the original wave. If ultrasonic waves are directed at a person, a portion of the waves gets transmitted into the person's body. As those waves travel through the body, they will continue to travel until they hit another obstruction. At that point, a portion of the waves will be reflected, and a portion will be transmitted. If wave sensors are tuned to detect that portion of the waves that were transmitted through the body but reflected back by an obstruction encountered in the body, the detectors can use the same principles the ultrasonic ruler uses to determine the distance to the obstruction within the body.

If several such waves are directed across a large area in the human body, this procedure can determine the general shape of the obstruction within the body. The most popular application of this is used for pregnant mothers. Using this technique, an ultrasonic imager can produce the general shape of a fetus in the mother's body. An example of such an image is shown in Figure 14.7.

FIGURE 14.7
Image Courtesy of Strong Memorial Hospital
An Ultrasonic Image of a Human Fetus

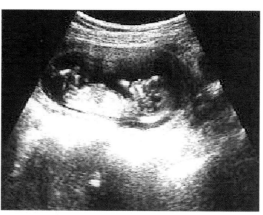

Another well-known application of this same basic technique is **sonar**. In sonar, ultrasonic waves are emitted, and sensors detect the reflected portions of those waves. The sensors end up creating an image of any obstruction in their path, much like the image shown in Figure 14.7. Although sonar is best known as the way a submarine tracks ships and other submarines, the most efficient sonar known to humankind exists in the bat.

Since bats tend to feed at night, they need to be able to "see" things in the dark. The way they do it is through a sonar system that produces images like that of the sonar in a submarine. The differences between a submarine's sonar and a bat's sonar, however, are substantial. For example, the bat's sonar provides significantly more information than a submarine's sonar and is *significantly* more efficient. First of all, rather than just emitting one or a few frequencies of ultrasonic waves, bat sonar produces a wide range of ultrasonic frequencies. Because materials react differently to different frequencies of sound waves, this allows the bat to use the amplitude of the reflected waves to determine the nature of the obstacle from which the ultrasonic waves were reflected. A bat's sonar is so precise in this regard that it can distinguish an insect from a stick or leaf by simply analyzing the amplitudes of the reflected sound waves for each frequency!

In addition, the bat can process the information given by its sonar system much more quickly than the fastest computer man can create. This allows it to identify obstacles and insects so quickly that it can fly around without running into anything and still detect, target, and eat up to five insects each second! All this is done in a sonar system that has a mass of less than 1 gram! This makes the bat's sonar system significantly more efficient than the best sonar human science can produce, and at the same time, it gives the bat a *lot* more information!

Although the bat's sonar system is the most efficient known to humankind, it is not the only natural sonar system. Porpoises use sonar to navigate as well, because eyesight is limited underwater. Such technological marvels sprinkled throughout nature scream loudly and clearly that nature is not the result of chance; it is the result of design!

ANSWERS TO THE "ON YOUR OWN" PROBLEMS

14.1 Wavelength and frequency are inversely proportional to one another. Thus, if wavelength is increased, <u>frequency is decreased</u>.

14.2 When the question asks how many waves will hit you every second, it is asking for the frequency of the waves. We have speed (0.5 m/sec) and wavelength (0.25 m), so we just need to use Equation (14.1):

$$f = \frac{v}{\lambda}$$

$$f = \frac{0.5 \, \frac{\cancel{m}}{sec}}{0.25 \, \cancel{m}} = 2 \, \frac{1}{sec}$$

This tells us that <u>2 waves will hit you every second</u>.

14.3 This is a simple application of Equation (14.2). The temperature is already in degrees Celsius, so we are ready:

$$v = (331.5 + 0.6 \cdot T) \, \frac{m}{sec}$$

$$v = (331.5 + 0.6 \cdot 28) \, \frac{m}{sec}$$

$$v = (331.5 + 16.8) \, \frac{m}{sec} = \underline{348.3 \, \frac{m}{sec}}$$

14.4 To determine how far away the lightning struck, we will assume that the light from the lightning bolt reaches the physicist's eyes pretty much instantaneously. Thus, the time delay between seeing the lightning and hearing the thunder tells us the distance. First, however, we need to determine how quickly the sound travels:

$$v = (331.5 + 0.6 \cdot T) \, \frac{m}{sec}$$

$$v = (331.5 + 0.6 \cdot 18) \, \frac{m}{sec}$$

$$v = (331.5 + 10.8) \, \frac{m}{sec} = 342.3 \frac{m}{sec}$$

Now that we know the speed of sound in this thunderstorm, we can determine the distance the sound traveled:

distance traveled = (speed) x (time traveled)

$$\text{distance traveled} = (342.3 \; \frac{m}{sec}) \times (1.5 \; sec) = \underline{513.45 \; m}$$

14.5 Sound waves travel faster in solids than they do in liquids. Thus, <u>the sound waves will travel faster in the inner core than the outer core.</u>

14.6 To determine the speed of the jet, we first have to determine the speed of sound. After all, Mach 1.8 means 1.8 times the speed of sound. Thus, we need to know the speed of sound in order to determine the speed of the jet.

$$v = (331.5 + 0.6 \cdot T) \; \frac{m}{sec}$$

$$v = (331.5 + 0.6 \cdot 0) \; \frac{m}{sec} = 331.5 \frac{m}{sec}$$

Since sound travels at 331.5 m/sec in this situation, Mach 1.8 is 1.8 x (331.5 m/sec) = <u>596.7 m/sec</u>.

14.7 A high pitch means a high frequency. Waves with high frequency have short wavelengths. In general, then, the shorter the wind instrument, the higher the pitch. Therefore, <u>the piccolo produces the notes with the highest pitches.</u>

14.8 Ultrasonic waves have *higher (larger) frequencies* than sonic waves. This means they have <u>shorter (smaller) wavelengths.</u>

14.9 As you run toward the car, you will encounter the crests of the waves faster than if you were standing still. This means that the waves will seem to have a higher frequency when you run toward the car. Thus, <u>the horn's pitch will sound higher than the pitch it actually produces</u>. There is another way to think about this question. Remember from Module #9 that velocity is relative. Whether you approach the car or the car approaches you, you are both approaching each other. Thus, the physics is similar either way.

14.10 The bel scale states that every bel unit corresponds to a factor of 10 in the intensity of the sound wave. Thus, we need to determine how many bel units the sound of a power saw is, as compared to the sound of normal conversation:

$$\frac{40 \; \text{decibels}}{1} \times \frac{0.1 \; \text{bel}}{1 \; \text{decibel}} = 4 \; \text{bels}$$

$$\frac{110 \; \text{decibels}}{1} \times \frac{0.1 \; \text{bel}}{1 \; \text{decibel}} = 11 \; \text{bels}$$

Since the power saw is 7 bels louder than normal conversation, the increase in sound-wave intensity is 7 factors of ten higher. Thus, the power saw has sound waves with intensities that are 10 x 10 x 10 x 10 x 10 x 10 x 10 = <u>10,000,000 times larger than the intensities of sound waves from normal conversation.</u>

STUDY GUIDE FOR MODULE #14

1. Define the following terms:

a. Transverse wave
b. Longitudinal wave
c. Supersonic speed
d. Sonic boom
e. Pitch

2. In designing a car's horn, the engineers test the sound of the horn and decide that its pitch is too low. To adjust the horn, should the engineers change the electronics so as to produce sound waves with longer or shorter wavelengths?

3. A sound wave is traveling through air with a temperature of 30 °C. What is the speed of the sound wave?

4. If the sound wave in problem #3 has a wavelength of 0.5 meters, what is its frequency?

5. A sound wave has a speed of 345 m/sec and a wavelength of 500 meters. Is this wave infrasonic, sonic, or ultrasonic?

6. A physicist takes an alarm clock and puts it in an airtight chamber. When the chamber is sealed but still full of air, the physicist is able to hear the alarm despite the fact that he is outside of the chamber. If the physicist then uses a vacuum pump to evacuate essentially all the air out of the chamber, will the physicist still be able to hear the alarm? Why or why not?

7. Are sound waves transverse waves or longitudinal waves?

8. You are watching the lightning from a thunderstorm. You suddenly see a flash of lightning, and 2.3 seconds later, you hear the thunder. How far away from you did the lightning strike? (The temperature at the time is 13 °C).

9. Sound waves are traveling through the air and suddenly run into a wall. As the sound waves travel through the wall, do they travel faster, slower, or at the same speed as when they were traveling in the air?

10. In the situation described above, what happens to the amplitude of the wave? Is the amplitude of the wave smaller, larger, or the same as the amplitude before the wave hit the wall?

11. A jet aircraft is traveling at Mach 2.5 through air at 1 °C. What is the jet's speed in m/sec?

12. A jet travels through air at 464.1 m/sec. If the air has a temperature of 0 °C, at what Mach number is the jet flying?

13. Why do jets travel at speeds of Mach 1 or higher only in sparsely populated regions?

14. A guitar player is plucking on a string. If he takes his finger and pinches the string to the neck of the guitar so as to shorten the length of the string, will the pitch of the sound emitted increase, decrease, or stay the same?

15. You hear two musical notes. They both have the same pitch, but the first is louder than the second. If you compare the sound waves of each sound, what aspect(s) of the wave (wavelength, frequency, speed, and amplitude) would be the same? What aspect(s) would be different?

16. The horn on your neighbor's car is stuck, so it is constantly blaring. You watch your neighbor get into the car and drive away from you, heading toward the nearest place for automobile service. Compare the pitch of the horn before he starts to drive away to the pitch you hear as he is driving away from you.

17. You are riding your bicycle toward a stationary police car with a siren that is blaring away. Will the pitch of the siren sound lower, higher, or the same as it will sound when you actually stop your bicycle? (Assume the actual pitch of the siren stays constant.)

18. You are standing near an interstate highway trying to talk on a pay phone. You have raised your voice because of the noise, so the loudness of your voice is about 80 decibels. The sound of the traffic on the highway is about 100 decibels. How many times larger is the intensity of the traffic's sound waves as compared to those of your voice?

19. An amplifier can magnify the intensity of sound waves by a factor of 1,000. If a 30-decibel sound is fed into the amplifier, how many decibels will come out?

MODULE #15: Light

Introduction

In this module, you are going to learn some details about the nature of light. This is obviously an important subject to study. Light is such a fundamental part of creation that it is one of the first things mentioned in the Bible:

> In the beginning God created the heavens and the earth. The earth was formless and void, and darkness was over the surface of the deep, and the Spirit of God was moving over the surface of the waters. Then God said, "Let there be light;" and there was light. God saw that the light was good…" (Genesis 1:1-4a)

Without light, life could not exist. The most common waves in creation are electromagnetic waves, which include light. Obviously, then, anyone who wants to learn about science needs to know something about the nature of light.

The Dual Nature of Light

While the general nature of sound is fairly easy to understand, the general nature of light is not. The first serious scientific investigations of light were done by none other than Sir Isaac Newton. In 1704, Newton published a book called *Optiks* in which he reported the conclusions of his research on light. In this book, Newton concluded that a beam of light behaved the same as a stream of particles that all moved in the same direction. This came to be known as the **particle theory** of light. According to this theory, light comes in little packets. We cannot see the individual packets of light, because they are simply too small to distinguish. Thus, just like a stream of water is really composed of individual water molecules, a beam of light is really composed of individual light particles.

The Dutch mathematician and physicist Christian Huygens, who lived at the same time as Newton, disagreed with Newton's conclusions. He considered light to be a wave. He published his own work in which he could explain all of Newton's experiments assuming that light was a wave and not a particle. This was called the **wave theory** of light, and it was largely ignored at the time. In a few years, however, scientists began to do experiments that indicated light does, indeed, behave as a wave. As a result, by the early 1800s, most scientists believed in the wave theory of light.

Although most scientists were convinced of the fact that light is a wave, there was one fundamentally nagging question that scientists could not understand: What is the medium of a light wave? Remember, sound travels through air because it causes oscillations in the air. It travels through solids by causing oscillations in the atoms or molecules that make up the solid. What, then, do light waves oscillate? Scientists knew that light does not cause air to oscillate, because light can travel through a vacuum (an area with no air in it). With nothing to oscillate, waves cannot travel. In the absence of air, then, sound does not exist. Thus, if you put an alarm clock in a vacuum, you will hear no sound coming from it. However, light travels through a vacuum with ease. What, then, does a light wave oscillate?

It took the brilliance of James Clerk Maxwell to answer this question. Hopefully, his answer will finally help you understand why electricity and magnetism are, in fact, one and the same thing.

The experiments and conclusions of Maxwell have led to the following generally accepted view of a light wave:

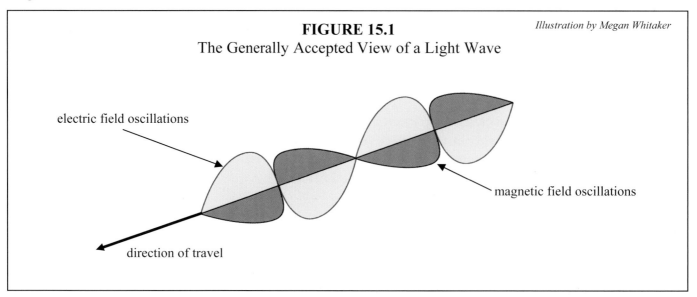

FIGURE 15.1   *Illustration by Megan Whitaker*
The Generally Accepted View of a Light Wave

electric field oscillations

magnetic field oscillations

direction of travel

In this figure, you can see that a light wave is actually made up of two perpendicular waves. The first is an oscillating electric field, and the second is an oscillating magnetic field. Both the magnetic field and the electric field oscillate perpendicular to each other, as well as perpendicular to the direction the light travels.

Now do you see why electricity and magnetism are really the same thing? Both electricity and magnetism work together to produce light! A beam of light is actually a transverse wave in an electric field and a transverse wave in a magnetic field. In order to make light, you must have both waves, and they must be perpendicular to one another. So wherever there is a magnetic field, there must be an accompanying electric field. One cannot exist without the other. As a result, they are really different aspects of the same thing!

Notice that Maxwell's view of light allows us to understand why light can travel through a vacuum. The "stuff" that light causes to heave up and down is composed of an electric field and a magnetic field. Thus, whether or not there are atoms or molecules around will not affect the ability of light to travel. The wave is simply composed of electrical and magnetic energy that oscillates back and forth. As a result, light waves are typically referred to as **electromagnetic waves**.

Electromagnetic wave – A transverse wave composed of an oscillating electric field and a
                magnetic field that oscillates perpendicular to the electric field

Because light is a wave, Equation (14.1) applies just as well to light as it does to sound.

There should be something bothering you at this point. When I discussed the electromagnetic force, I said that it is governed by the exchange of small *particles* of light called photons. If scientists think of light as a wave, how can I say that particles of light exist? The answer to that question is that scientists today believe light has a **dual nature**. Light definitely has wavelike characteristics; thus, it can be thought of as a wave. However, light also has certain particlelike characteristics that *cannot* be explained if light is *only* a wave.

Because light has some properties that indicate it is a wave and other properties that indicate it is a particle, scientists have come up with the **quantum-mechanical theory of light**. In this theory, light is basically viewed as tiny packets of waves. Thus, unlike the wave we normally think of, light waves are not continuous. They are broken up in little packets, each of which is called a photon. Because of this dual nature, light can act as either a stream of photons (and be thought of as a particle) or a bunch of electromagnetic waves (and be thought of as a wave). Although this is a very confusing view of light, it is the best that scientists can do for right now.

To sum this all up, then, light is composed of little packets of waves. Each individual packet can be thought of as a particle, called a photon. At the same time, however, since each packet is composed of electromagnetic waves, light can also be thought of as a wave. Thus, light will sometimes behave as if it is a particle, and at other times it will behave as if it is a wave. Since the waves within a photon are electromagnetic, there is no need for atoms or molecules in order for light to travel. As a result, light can travel through any region of space, regardless of what occupies that portion of space.

How quickly do these wave packets travel? Well, in a vacuum, they move at a stunning 300,000,000 meters per second (about 670,000,000 miles per hour)! Sound travels through air at about 340 meters per second (about 760 miles per hour). Obviously, then, light travels *a lot* faster than does sound. Also, whereas the speed of sound is dependent on the temperature, the speed of light is not.

Although the speed of light does not depend on temperature, it does depend on *the substance* through which the light passes, just as the speed of sound depends on the substance through which sound passes. Unlike sound, however, the speed of light is fastest in gases, slower in liquids, and even slower in solids. Examine Table 15.1 to see what I mean:

TABLE 15.1
The Speed of Light in Certain Substances

Substance	Speed of Light	Substance	Speed of Light
Air (25 °C)	300,000,000 m/sec	**Plastic**	189,000,000 m/sec
Alcohol	225,000,000 m/sec	**Crown Glass**	185,000,000 m/sec
Fresh Water	220,000,000 m/sec	**Flint Glass**	175,000,000 m/sec
Acrylic	200,000,000 m/sec	**Diamond**	125,000,000 m/sec

Notice that the speed of light in air is essentially the same as the speed of light in a vacuum. In liquids (alcohol and fresh water), light travels more slowly. In solids (acrylic, plastic, glass, and diamond), light travels even more slowly.

Do you remember Einstein's Theory of General Relativity? You learned a little bit about it when you learned about gravity. Well, Albert Einstein also developed a theory now known as the Special Theory of Relativity. One of the fundamental assumptions of this theory is that the speed of light in a vacuum represents the *maximum speed* that can *ever* be attained by any object that has mass. Thus, the Special Theory of Relativity states that *nothing with mass* can travel faster than 300,000,000 meters per second. In essence, then, the Special Theory of Relativity says that the speed of light is the ultimate speed limit, because no object with mass can travel faster than light.

The details of this incredible theory are beyond the scope of this course, but it is important for you to realize that its fundamental assumption does, indeed, seem to be true. Many experiments confirm the predictions of special relativity, and no data contradicting the theory can be found. Therefore, most scientists consider it to be a valid scientific theory. As a result, the general view of science is that no matter how much energy you expend, you can never travel faster than the speed that light travels in a vacuum.

ON YOUR OWN

15.1 Which of the pictures below is the best illustration of the quantum-mechanical theory of light?

a.   b.   c.

15.2 Suppose a photon is traveling through air. If the particle suddenly hits a lake, what will happen to its speed?

Wavelength and Frequency of Light

The frequency (and therefore the wavelength) of a sound wave determines the pitch of the sound you hear. What does the frequency (and therefore the wavelength) of a light wave determine about the light? Perform the following experiment to find out.

EXPERIMENT 15.1
Seeing Different Wavelengths of Light
Supplies:

- A flat pan, like the kind you use to bake a cake
- A medium-sized mirror (4 inches by 6 inches is a good size)
- A sunny window (A flashlight will work, but it will not be as dramatic.)
- A plain white sheet of paper
- Water
- Eye protection such as goggles or safety glasses

Introduction: In this experiment, you will see what the wavelength of light waves determines about the property of light. **NOTE**: This experiment is difficult to perform near noon.

Procedure:

1. Fill the pan with water. The water level should be high enough so that a significant portion of the mirror can be submerged.
2. Place the pan of water in direct sunlight from the window.
3. Immerse at least a portion of the mirror in the water and tilt it so that it reflects the light from under the water up and back toward the window.

4. Use one hand to hold the plain white paper above the pan of water, between the pan and the window. Use the other hand to hold the mirror in the water so that it stays tilted.

5. Play with the tilt of the mirror and the position of the white sheet, trying to reflect sunlight with the mirror and land it on the white sheet of paper.

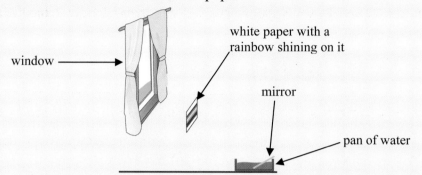

6. If you play with the position of the paper and the tilt of the mirror enough, you should eventually see a rainbow, as shown in the figure above. This may take a little work.

7. Clean up your mess and put everything away.

What did you see in the experiment? If everything went well, you should have seen a rainbow, which is actually the result of separating light according to its wavelengths.

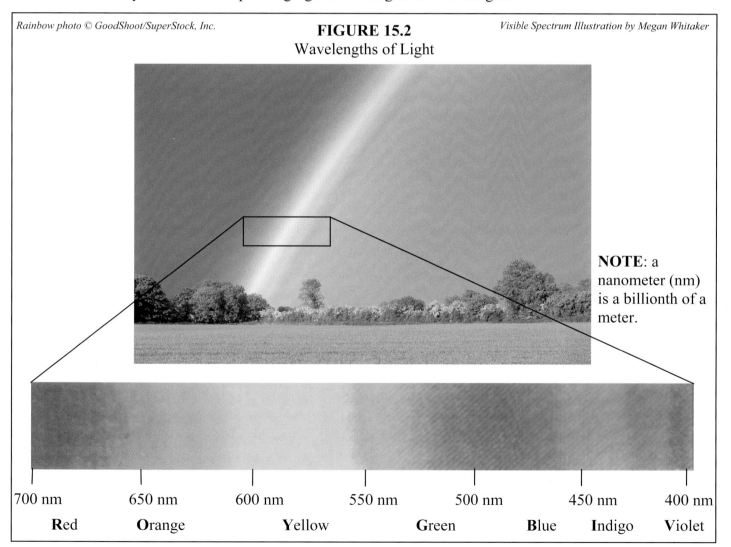

Rainbow photo © GoodShoot/SuperStock, Inc.

FIGURE 15.2
Wavelengths of Light

Visible Spectrum Illustration by Megan Whitaker

NOTE: a nanometer (nm) is a billionth of a meter.

700 nm	650 nm	600 nm	550 nm	500 nm	450 nm	400 nm
Red	**Orange**	**Yellow**	**Green**	**Blue**	**Indigo**	**Violet**

What made the rainbow you saw in the experiment? When light travels through different substances, it tends to bend. I will discuss this in much greater detail later on in this module. The amount that the light bends depends, in part, on the wavelength of the light. Thus, when the sunlight hit the water, it bent. Certain wavelengths bent farther than others. The mirror then reflected the light and it traveled back out of the water. When that happened, the light bent again. Once again, the amount the light bent depended on the wavelength. That was enough to partially separate one wavelength of light from another. As a result, the reflected light was split into different wavelengths. When it shined on the paper, then, it appeared to you as a rainbow.

What we see as white light, then, is really light that is made up of many colors. If we separate the wavelengths, we get different colors. The longest wavelengths of light we see are made up of various shades of red, while the shortest wavelengths of light we see are made up of various shades of violet. The other colors (orange, yellow, green, blue, and indigo) have wavelengths in between.

Although you needn't memorize the wavelength of each color, you *do* need to memorize the *relative* size of the wavelengths in question. In other words, you need to know that red light has the longest wavelength, orange light has shorter wavelength, and so on. This is easy to do if you think about the colors as a single name. If you start with the color that corresponds to the longest wavelength (red) and you put the first letter of each color together, you come up with a man's name: ROY G. BIV. So if you think of ROY G. BIV every time you think of the colors of visible light, you will always know that red light has the longest wavelength, violet light has the shortest, and you will also know the order of all colors in between.

I am going to talk about color more in the last section of this module. For right now, however, I need to point out something very important. Just as there are plenty of sound waves we cannot hear, there are plenty of electromagnetic waves we cannot see. The light we see with our eyes is called the **visible spectrum** of light, and it is only a small part of the electromagnetic waves coming to us from the sun. It turns out that our planet is bathed with electromagnetic waves of many different wavelengths. Our eyes only perceive a small fraction of them. Figure 15.3 is a more complete representation of all electromagnetic waves in creation, which we call the **electromagnetic spectrum**.

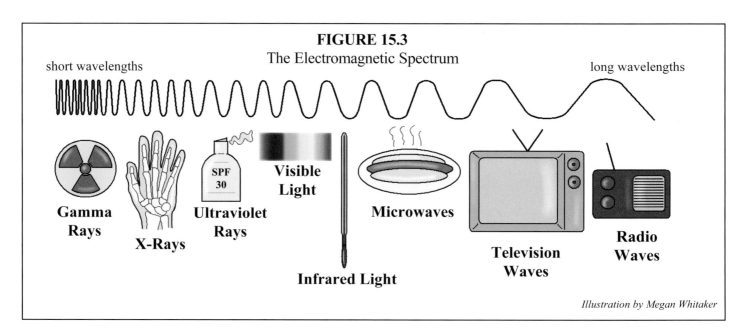

FIGURE 15.3
The Electromagnetic Spectrum

short wavelengths   long wavelengths

Gamma Rays   X-Rays   Ultraviolet Rays   Visible Light   Infrared Light   Microwaves   Television Waves   Radio Waves

Illustration by Megan Whitaker

Since visible light is what we are used to, we usually look at the other parts of the electromagnetic spectrum in terms of where they fall relative to visible light. Electromagnetic waves with wavelengths shorter than visible light are called **ultraviolet light**, **X-rays**, and **gamma rays**. Ultraviolet light has enough energy to kill living tissue. Medical professionals often use ultraviolet lamps to sterilize things. If you put something under an ultraviolet lamp, the ultraviolet light will kill most of the germs (bacteria, etc.) that live on it. As you learned in Modules #2 and #3, the ozone layer protects life on earth from the ultraviolet light that comes from the sun. X-rays, used in medicine so that doctors can see your bones (and other internal structures) without actually opening up your body, have wavelengths even shorter than ultraviolet light. Finally, gamma rays, a form of radiation you learned about in Module #13, have even shorter wavelengths.

Ultraviolet light has enough energy to kill living tissue. It turns out that the shorter the wavelength, the more energy a wave has. Thus, X-rays have even more energy than do ultraviolet rays. In other words, X-rays have *more than enough energy to kill living tissue*. Despite this fact, doctors shine X-rays right on an injured person in order to be able to make a diagnosis. This kills some cells in the patient's body. Why does a doctor take someone who is injured and then shine X-rays on the person so that some of the patient's cells are killed? The answer to that can be found in a cost/benefit analysis, which you learned about in Module #2.

When you are given an X-ray, some of your cells do die. The cells also run the risk of being mutated. That is the "cost" of the X-ray to your body. It sounds bad, but if you remember my discussion of radioactivity from Module #13, it's really not all that bad, as long as it happens in small doses. As long as a person doesn't get *too many* X-rays, the body can replace the lost cells and eliminate any mutated cells. Thus, the cost to the body is not great. The benefits of an X-ray are large. It allows the doctor to make a good diagnosis of the patient without operating. In this case, then, as long as the patient does not have too many X-rays, the benefits far outweigh the cost.

For the technician who performs X-rays all day long at the hospital, however, there is great cost. If that person were exposed to X-rays each time a patient got an X-ray, far too many of his or her cells would die or mutate. In addition, there are no benefits to this exposure, as the technician is not being diagnosed for anything. As a result, the technician giving the patient an X-ray stands behind a shield to avoid the X-rays. If you have ever been given an X-ray before, you might have found it odd that the person giving you the X-ray stood behind shielding, but you did not. Now you should understand why it must be done that way.

Electromagnetic waves with wavelengths just longer than visible light are called **infrared** (in' fruh red) **light**. When a hot object gives off heat, most of the energy is in the form of infrared light. A space heater, for example, gives off a lot of heat. You can see the wires of the space heater glow red, but that is only a small portion of the energy it is emitting. Much of the energy the space heater emits is in the form of infrared light, which you cannot see. If you remember the greenhouse effect discussion in Module #2, the earth gives up most of its energy in the form of infrared light. That's the light that greenhouse gases absorb to keep the atmosphere warm.

Electromagnetic waves with wavelengths slightly longer than infrared light make up the portion of the electromagnetic spectrum called **microwaves**. These are the waves a microwave oven uses to heat food quickly. Believe it or not, when you turn on your microwave oven, you are simply exposing your food to long-wavelength electromagnetic waves.

How do long-wavelength electromagnetic waves heat up your food quickly? It turns out that the particular wavelengths used in microwave ovens are absorbed by water molecules in food. When the waves are absorbed, the water molecules spin due to the energy absorbed with the waves. When they start spinning, there is a lot of friction between them and the other molecules in the food, and that generates heat. That heat cooks your food. A microwave oven heats food quickly compared to a conventional oven because, in a conventional oven, the heat must travel into the food being cooked. As a result, the food must get hot on the outside before it can get hot on the inside. In a microwave oven, the microwaves are causing the water molecules *throughout* the food to spin. Thus, the food is exposed to heat all over right away. That makes the food cook a *lot* more quickly.

Electromagnetic waves with wavelengths longer than microwaves are used to transmit radio and television signals. It might surprise you that the radio and television signals you capture with an antenna are just electromagnetic waves. You can't see these waves, of course, but without them, you would never hear a radio or television program! When you tune a radio or change the channel on a television, you are telling the electronics in the device to look for a particular frequency (thus, a particular wavelength). Electromagnetic waves of that frequency that strike the antenna are then picked up by the electronic circuitry in the device. The information in that signal is decoded, and the result is the radio or TV program you wanted to hear or watch. Television signals have shorter wavelengths than radio signals, and FM radio signals have shorter wavelengths than AM radio signals.

ON YOUR OWN

15.3 Without looking at Figure 15.2 or Figure 15.3, order the following colors in terms of *increasing frequency*: yellow, indigo, red, green.

15.4 If radio signals are really made up of electromagnetic waves, why doesn't a radio station's antenna glow when it transmits its signals?

Reflection

When you were studying sound waves in the previous module, I told you that when sound waves encounter an obstacle, a portion of the sound waves bounces off the obstacle and starts traveling in another direction. That's how we hear echoes. Another portion of the sound waves begins traveling through the obstacle. Well, under the right conditions, the same thing happens to light waves. When light (or sound) waves bounce off an obstacle, we call it **reflection**. Perform the following experiment to learn more about reflection.

EXPERIMENT 15.2
The Law of Reflection

Supplies:

- Eye protection such as goggles or safety glasses
- A flat mirror. The mirror can be very small, but it needs to be flat. You can always tell if a mirror is flat by looking at your reflection in it. If the image you see in the mirror is neither magnified nor reduced, the mirror is flat.
- A white sheet of paper
- A pen

♦ A protractor
♦ A ruler
♦ A flashlight
♦ Black construction paper or thin cardboard
♦ Tape
♦ A dark room

Introduction: When light or sound waves reflect off an obstacle, the law of reflection allows us to determine where the reflected waves will go. This experiment helps you determine that law.

1. Cut the construction paper into a circle that fits the face of the flashlight. Make it so that when the circle is taped to the face of the flashlight, little or no light will be able to escape.
2. At the edge of the circle, cut a small, thin slot. The circle of paper should look something like the drawing below:

3. Now tape the circle to the face of the flashlight, so that light escapes only through the slot.
4. Lay the white piece of paper on a rectangular table or desktop so that its edge is even with the straight edge of the table.
5. Tape the paper down so that it does not move from this position. **NOTE:** Check with your parents before doing this. Tape can harm some tabletops.
6. Use the protractor to make a line that is perpendicular to the edge of the table and centered on the paper. In the end, your setup should look like this:

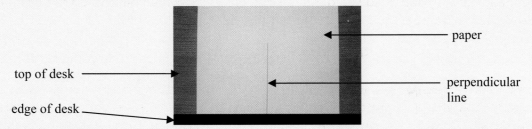

7. Push the mirror up against the edge of the table so that the line you just drew is centered on the mirror and perpendicular to it. Tape the mirror to the edge of the table so it stays there.
8. Turn on the flashlight and turn out the lights.
9. Hold your flashlight so that the slot is on the bottom of the face, touching the paper. Play with the tilt of the flashlight until the light coming from the slot causes a beam on the paper that hits the mirror at the same point where the line touches the mirror. You should then see the beam reflect off the mirror back onto the paper, as show in the photograph below:

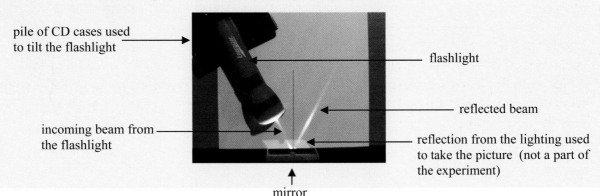

10. Use your pen to carefully trace the path of the beam as it travels from the flashlight and reflects off the mirror.
11. Turn on the lights.
12. Use your protractor to measure the angle of the line representing the path of the incoming beam relative to the perpendicular line you originally drew.
13. Use your protractor to measure the angle of the line representing the reflected beam relative to the same perpendicular line.
14. Do the experiment twice more, changing the position of the flashlight so that the angle the incoming beam makes with the perpendicular line is different each time. In each case, compare the angle made by the incoming beam to that of the reflected beam.
15. Clean up your mess.

Within experimental error, the angles you measured in each trial of the experiment should have equaled each other. Scientists call the angle the light ray from the flashlight made with the perpendicular line the **angle of incidence**. The angle the reflected light ray made with the perpendicular line is called the **angle of reflection**. With that terminology, I can say your experiment should have indicated that the angle of reflection equals the angle of incidence. That's the **Law of Reflection**.

The Law of Reflection – The angle of reflection equals the angle of incidence.

Believe it or not, this simple law is responsible for how mirrors work.

To understand why, you first need to understand why we see things in the first place. As you look at the words on this page, light reflects off the page and up toward your eye. The pattern of reflected light is read by your eye and is converted to electrical impulses sent to your brain. I will discuss this process a bit more in a later section of this module. Your brain then converts these electrical impulses into an image. That's how you see. That's also why you cannot see things without the aid of light. Your eyes cannot send any signals to your brain unless light reflects off the thing you are observing and enters your eyes. Only then can a message be sent to your brain so that it can form an image.

With this in mind, consider a woman looking at herself in a mirror. Why does she see her foot, for example? Well, light reflects off of her foot, hits the mirror, reflects off of the mirror, and enters her eyes:

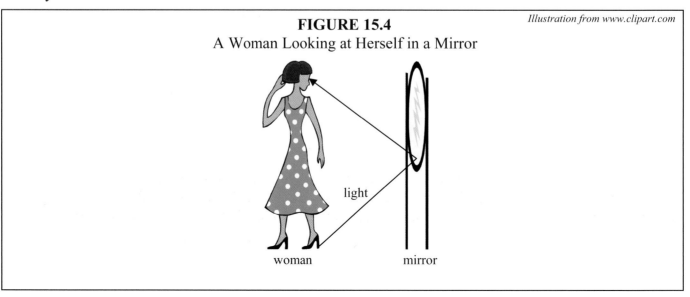

FIGURE 15.4
A Woman Looking at Herself in a Mirror

Illustration from www.clipart.com

light

woman   mirror

The thing to realize about this is that the woman's brain will think that the light travels in a straight line. As a result, her brain extends the light backward, as illustrated by the dashed line in the figure below.

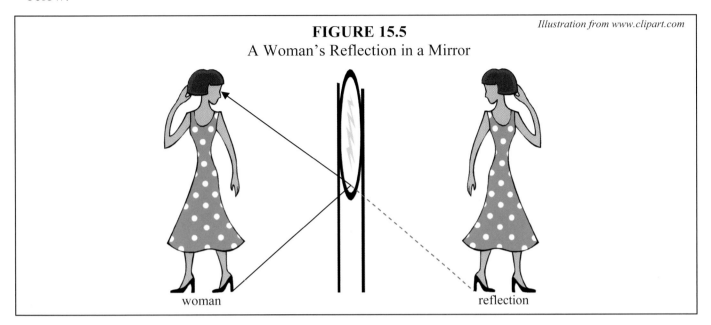

FIGURE 15.5
A Woman's Reflection in a Mirror

Illustration from www.clipart.com

woman   reflection

This makes the woman's brain think that the image of her foot is actually behind the mirror because it thinks that the light hitting her eyes is coming from the start of the dotted line.

That's how images are formed in a mirror. The light that reflects off a mirror is detected by an eye, and the brain that receives the eye's electrical impulses extends the light backward to form an image behind the mirror. The image is, of course, fake. It is simply a result of the fact that the brain interprets light as traveling in a straight line.

ON YOUR OWN

15.5 Draw the path of the light ray in the diagram below to show where the light eventually hits the screen:

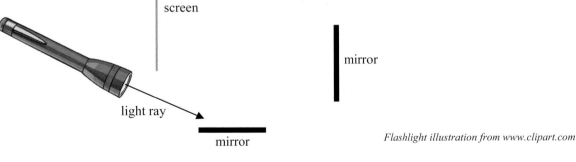

screen

mirror

light ray

mirror

Flashlight illustration from www.clipart.com

Refraction

As I mentioned before, when light or sound waves encounter an obstacle, reflection is not the only thing that can happen. In addition to bouncing off an obstacle, light and sound waves can begin to travel through the obstacle, provided certain conditions are met. When a wave enters an obstacle, it usually bends in response to its change in speed. When this happens, we say the wave has been **refracted**. Perform the following experiment to understand what happens in the process of refraction.

EXPERIMENT 15.3
Refraction of Light

Supplies:

♦ A square or rectangular glass or clear plastic pan (If you have a flat bottle, it will work as well. It just needs to be something with clear, flat sides that can hold water.)
♦ Water
♦ Milk
♦ Spoon
♦ Flashlight with the same cover you used in Experiment 15.2
♦ A sheet of plain white paper
♦ Pen
♦ Protractor
♦ Ruler
♦ Eye protection such as goggles or safety glasses

Introduction: When light encounters a transparent obstacle, some of the light will pass through the obstacle. This experiment will show you how that happens.

Procedure:

1. Draw a line lengthwise down the middle of the plain white sheet of paper.
2. Use your protractor to draw another line perpendicular to the line you just drew. This line should be about 3 inches from one of the edges of the paper, and it should span the entire width of the paper.
3. Use your protractor and ruler to draw a third line that starts at the edge of the paper nearest the line you just drew and travels through the intersection of the lines you drew in steps 1 and 2. This new line should make a 45-degree angle with each of the other lines. In the end, your paper should look something like this:

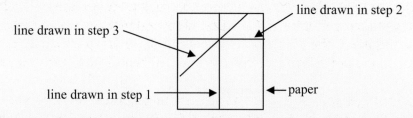

line drawn in step 3
line drawn in step 2
line drawn in step 1
paper

4. Fill the pan half full of water and add ½ teaspoon of milk. Stir it so the water is a little cloudy. This will allow you to see the beam of light as it travels through the water.
5. Set the pan on the paper so one of its flat edges is sitting right on the line you drew in step 2.
6. Fix up your flashlight again so that it is just like what you used in Experiment 15.2.
7. Lay the flashlight on the table with its slot down and then turn off the lights.
8. Position the flashlight so that the light beam shines on the paper and follows the line you drew in step 3 from where it leaves the flashlight until it hits the pan.

9. Look down into the water from directly above the pan. You should see that when the beam hits the pan, two things happen. First, part of the beam is reflected off the pan. The other part of the beam is refracted into the water.
10. Look at the refracted beam relative to the line you drew in step 3. Does the light beam follow that line?
11. Follow the light beam until it hits another one of the pan's sides. What happens there?
12. Clean up your mess.

What did you see in the experiment? First, you should have seen that when the light beam hit the pan, part of it was reflected and part was refracted. This is what happens most of the time when a light wave hits a transparent obstacle. Part of the wave will be reflected and part of it will be refracted. There are certain circumstances where this does not happen, but they are rare. Had you measured the angle of the reflected ray, you would have determined, as you did in the previous experiment, that the angle of reflection equaled the angle of incidence.

Have you ever looked through a window and seen your own reflection? The reason you can look through the window into the outside world is because the window is transparent and light can pass through it. That's also why you can see the lights of a house through its windows.   However, not all the light from the house makes it through the window. When a wave encounters an obstacle, a portion of the wave is always reflected. The reflection you see in a window is a result of the portion of light waves that is reflected off the glass instead of transmitted through it.

What did you notice about the light ray that entered the water in the experiment? The fact that the water was cloudy allowed you to see the ray as it traveled through the water. You should have noticed that the light beam coming from the flashlight did not follow the line you had aimed it along once it entered the water. Instead, the light beam followed a path that was somewhere between the line you had aimed it along and the line that was perpendicular to the edge of the pan. In other words, when the light ray entered the water, it was bent *toward* the line that was perpendicular to the surface the light ray hit. What happened when the light ray hit another side of the pan? You should have once again seen that part of the light was reflected back into the water, and part of the light refracted as it entered the air.

The fact that light rays bend when they are refracted is a general rule of physics. In fact, the rule is even a bit more detailed than that. In general, we can say that if you draw a line perpendicular to the surface the light ray strikes, refracted light will bend toward that perpendicular line if light travels slower in the new substance than in the old substance. If, on the other hand, light travels faster in the new substance than in the old substance, the light ray will bend away from the perpendicular line.

**When light refracts into a substance in which it must slow down,
the light ray will bend toward a line perpendicular to the surface it strikes.**

**When light refracts into a substance in which it speeds up,
the light ray will bend away from a line perpendicular to the surface it strikes.**

These two general rules can be summed up by Figure 15.6 on the next page.

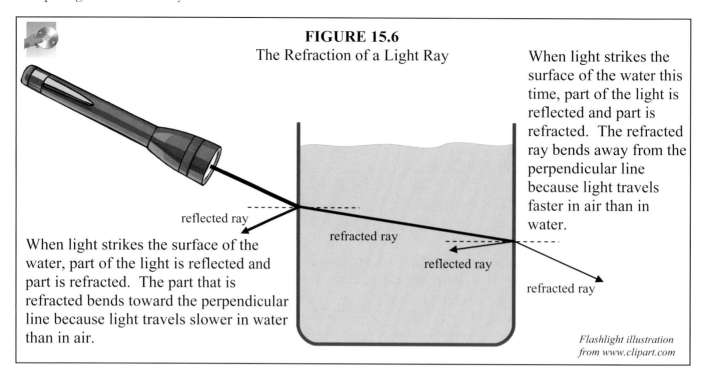

FIGURE 15.6
The Refraction of a Light Ray

When light strikes the surface of the water this time, part of the light is reflected and part is refracted. The refracted ray bends away from the perpendicular line because light travels faster in air than in water.

reflected ray

refracted ray

reflected ray

refracted ray

When light strikes the surface of the water, part of the light is reflected and part is refracted. The part that is refracted bends toward the perpendicular line because light travels slower in water than in air.

Flashlight illustration from www.clipart.com

The refraction of light through different substances is responsible for all sorts of optical illusions. Have you ever been traveling along a road on a hot summer day and noticed what appears to be a puddle of water in the middle of the road in front of you? When you got nearer to where you saw the puddle, it vanished. That "puddle of water" is an optical illusion that is the result of the refraction of light rays. When a road gets hot, a layer of warm air rests right above the road. When light from the sky encounters this layer of hot air, a portion of the light refracts. Rather than striking the road, it is bent into your eyes. Thus, you see a fuzzy image of the sky. Since the sky is blue, you think you are seeing a puddle of water. Instead, you are simply seeing light that comes from the sky and is refracted through the warm air to your eye. This kind of optical illusion is often called a mirage. People traveling through hot deserts are prone to seeing such illusions.

Perform the following quick experiment to see another typical optical illusion that is the result of light refraction.

EXPERIMENT 15.4
The "Magical" Quarter

Supplies:

♦ Quarter
♦ Bowl that is reasonably deep and not transparent
♦ Water
♦ Pitcher or very large glass to hold the water
♦ Eye protection such as goggles or safety glasses

Introduction: Light that travels from one substance to another is bent according to the relative speed of light in each substance. This experiment demonstrates a common illusion that results from this effect.

Procedure:

1. Place the quarter in the bowl.
2. Sit in a chair and position yourself so that you can see the quarter in the bowl.
3. Now slowly scoot your chair back until you can no longer see the quarter, despite the fact that you are looking into the bowl.
4. Once you are at the point where you can no longer see the quarter, do not move your head. Slowly begin to fill the bowl with water from the pitcher. Continue to look at the bowl but do not move your head. Eventually, you should see the quarter re-appear.
5. Clean up your mess.

Why did the quarter re-appear? The reason you see the quarter is that light is reflected off the quarter and hits your eyes. When you moved backward so that you could no longer see the quarter, light was still reflecting off it. Because of the way you positioned your head, however, the light rays that reflected off the quarter ran into the side of the bowl before they reached your eyes. Since the bowl was not transparent, the light could not travel through it. Many other light rays were reflecting off the quarter and leaving the bowl, but those light rays were traveling so steeply that they ended up traveling above your eyes. As a result, no light rays from the quarter hit your eyes, so you did not see the quarter.

When you filled the bowl with water, the light rays were refracted as they left the water. Since light travels faster in air than in water, the light rays were bent away from a line perpendicular to the surface of the water. Thus, light rays were bent *toward* you. As a result, some of the light rays that traveled above your eyes when there was no water in the bowl were suddenly bent into your eyes by refraction, and you saw the quarter again. Figure 15.7 illustrates this effect.

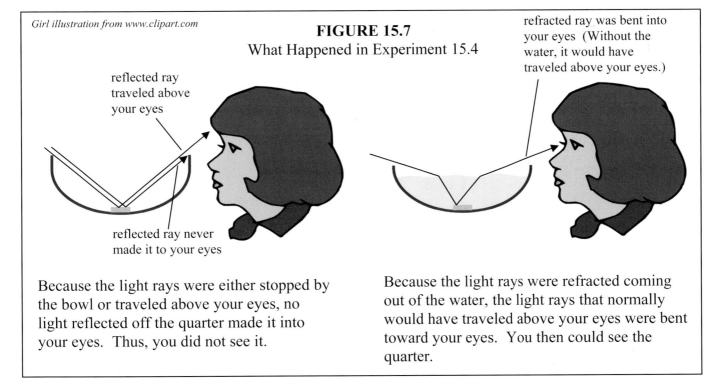

Girl illustration from www.clipart.com

FIGURE 15.7
What Happened in Experiment 15.4

reflected ray traveled above your eyes

reflected ray never made it to your eyes

refracted ray was bent into your eyes (Without the water, it would have traveled above your eyes.)

Because the light rays were either stopped by the bowl or traveled above your eyes, no light reflected off the quarter made it into your eyes. Thus, you did not see it.

Because the light rays were refracted coming out of the water, the light rays that normally would have traveled above your eyes were bent toward your eyes. You then could see the quarter.

Because of this effect, objects under water appear to be at a different place than they really are.

ON YOUR OWN

15.6 The following is a diagram of how a light ray travels from substance A through substance B:

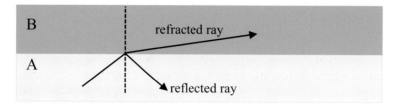

Does light travel more quickly in substance A or substance B?

15.7 A man is spear fishing. He looks into the water and sees a fish in front of him. When he aims his spear, should he aim it at the fish, in front of the fish, or behind the fish?

Before I leave this section, I need to point out two things. First, when light encounters an obstacle, refraction does not always occur. Depending on the substance, there are certain angles of incidence that lead only to reflection, not refraction. Although this situation is rare, it can be useful. **Fiber optic** cables, for example, transport light over great distances because when light enters the cable, it cannot escape. When it hits the edges of the cable, there is little or no refraction; there is only reflection. As a result, even a tiny amount of light can travel a great distance down such a cable.

The second thing I want to point out is that refraction depends, in part, on the wavelength of the light involved. That's why you were able to separate light into its different colors in Experiment 15.1. That's also why we see rainbows. When there are many water droplets in the air, and when the sun shines on those water droplets, the refraction of light through those water droplets forms the beautiful arc of a rainbow.

FIGURE 15.8

Illustration by Megan Whitaker

Making a Rainbow

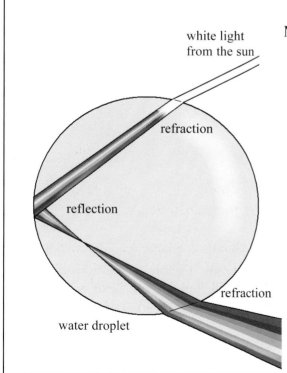

When white light hits a water droplet in the air, some reflects and some refracts into the water droplet. Since the amount of refraction depends partially on the wavelength of the light involved, this separates the white light into its colors. As the refracted light travels through the water droplet, it eventually hits the other side of the water droplet. A portion of the light refracts out of the water droplet, but a portion reflects. The reflected light travels to the other side of the droplet, where a portion is reflected and a portion is refracted. The portion that is refracted has its wavelengths separated even more, because the amount of refraction depends in part on the wavelength of light. With this second refraction, the light has been separated enough for us to distinguish the colors.

You need to notice a couple of things from the figure. First of all, notice where the light enters the droplet of water and where it leaves. This should tell you something. In order to see a rainbow well, there must be water droplets in the air, and the sun must be shining on them from *behind you.* Since the light must be refracted, reflected, and refracted again to make the color separation really strong, the way you best see a rainbow is when you are positioned so that the light shines on the water droplet and the color-separated light leaves the water droplet on the same side. This will only happen when the sun shines on the water droplets from behind you. Not only does the sun have to be behind you, it needs to be at a certain angle. After all, in order to see the rainbow, you must see light that refracts, reflects, and then refracts again. That can only happen when the light shines on the water droplet at certain angles. This is why you do not see a rainbow after every rain shower. It depends on how high the sun is in the sky and where that position is relative to your position.

Second, you need to realize that you do not see all the colors of the rainbow from one water droplet. Of all the rays drawn on the left-hand side of the figure, only one reaches your eyes. There are, however, many water droplets in the air. Thus, you see the different colors from different water droplets. Look at the figure again. Which light is bent the lowest when it leaves the water droplet? The red light is bent the lowest. What water droplets will you see the red light from, then? If the red light is bent low, then in order for it to reach your eyes, the red light will have to come from the *highest* water droplets in the sky. Since the violet light is bent the least, you will see that light coming from the *lowest* water droplets in the sky. Now go back and look at the rainbow in Figure 15.2. A rainbow will always appear with the red light on the top and the violet light on the bottom, because you will see the red light coming from the highest water droplets and the violet light coming from the lowest water droplets.

Lenses

The fact that light rays tend to bend when they travel through transparent objects can be quite useful. For example, consider a light ray traveling through the following object, which is made of glass:

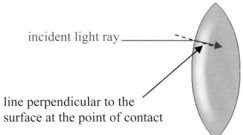

incident light ray

line perpendicular to the surface at the point of contact

Illustration by Megan Whitaker

When the ray strikes the transparent object, it will be refracted. This means the light will bend toward a line perpendicular to the surface at the point of contact. This situation is pictured above.

Now, the light ray will travel through the glass along the path indicated above. At some point, however, the light ray will reach the edge of the glass object and exit. At that point, however, the substance through which the light is traveling will change. Thus, the light will be refracted again. Since light travels faster in air than it does in glass, the refracted light ray is bent away from the perpendicular. This will result in the following picture:

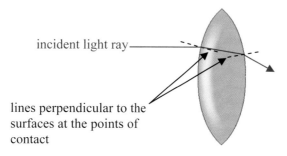

incident light ray————

lines perpendicular to the
surfaces at the points of
contact

Illustration by Megan Whitaker

If you were to do this for several light rays traveling horizontally toward the object, you would get the following picture:

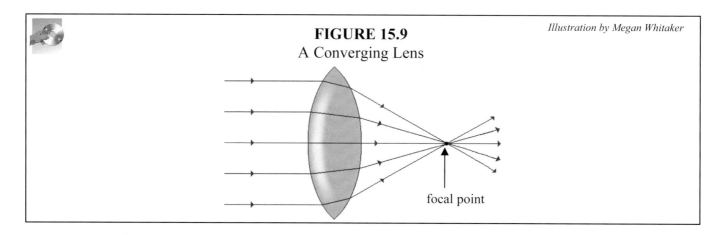

FIGURE 15.9
A Converging Lens

Illustration by Megan Whitaker

focal point

It turns out that a transparent object shaped like the one above will always focus horizontally traveling light rays through a single point, called (of course) the focal point. We call such an object a **converging lens**, because it makes all horizontal light rays converge to a single point. You need to realize that the object above was drawn very wide to easily illustrate how the light ray refracts twice as it travels through the lens. Generally, converging lenses are much thinner than what is drawn in the diagrams above.

If I change the situation a little bit, I get a completely different result. Suppose I have a glass object shaped as follows:

When light rays hit this object, refraction causes a completely different situation from what I got with the converging lens.

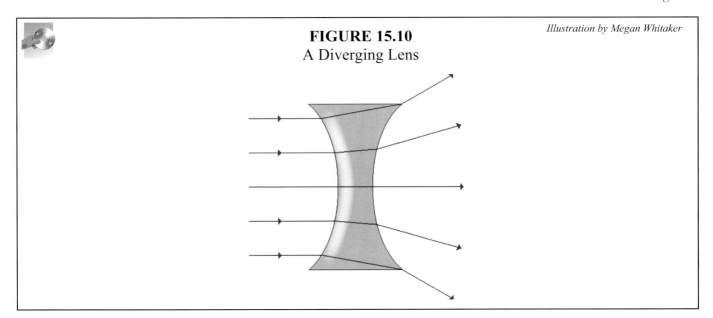

FIGURE 15.10
A Diverging Lens

Illustration by Megan Whitaker

This kind of lens, called a **diverging lens**, bends light rays outward, causing them to diverge away from one another. Once again, please realize that most diverging lenses are much thinner than what I have pictured here. Converging lenses and diverging lenses each have their applications. You will learn one application of each type of lens in the next section.

Notice the difference between converging and diverging lenses. The sides of a converging lens are curved outward. As a result, we say converging lenses have a **convex** shape. The sides of a diverging lens are curved inward. We call this a **concave** shape. This should tell you something: Lenses work because of their curvature. If the curvature changes, the way the lens works changes. In fact, the *type* of curvature (concave or convex) is not the only thing that affects the way a lens works. The *amount* of curvature also plays a role. Try to figure out how the amount of curvature plays a role by answering the following "On Your Own" problem.

ON YOUR OWN

15.8 Consider the two lenses pictured below. Which one focuses light rays closest to the lens?

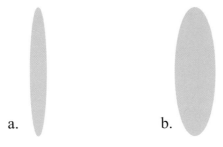

a.   b.

The Human Eye

The most elegant application of a converging lens in all of God's creation can be seen in the eye. Now, there are many, many marvelous facets of the eye, but I just want to concentrate on one: the way it focuses light. As I have said before, the reason we see things is that light reflects off them and enters our eyes. Our eyes then detect the light and send signals to the brain, which forms an image in our mind. I want to study how the eye handles light. First, Figure 15.11 shows a simplified drawing of the human eye:

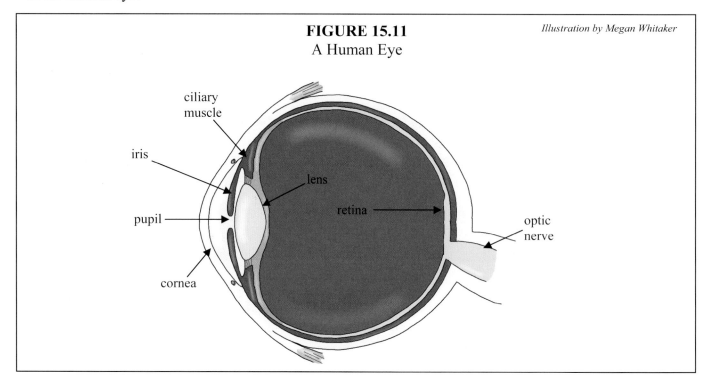

FIGURE 15.11
A Human Eye

Illustration by Megan Whitaker

In simple terms, the eye contains several different optical elements that all work together to produce vision. The eye is covered by a thin, transparent substance called the cornea. It protects the eye from abrasions and the like. It also participates in the focusing of light by refracting light that enters the eye. The iris is a cover that can open up wide or close down to just a small hole. This regulates how much light gets into the eye. The opening left by the iris is called the pupil. When you are in the presence of bright light, the iris closes down to allow only a small amount of light into the eye. This makes your pupil small. When there is little light, the iris opens wide, allowing a larger percentage of the light in. This makes your pupil look large. Once light enters the pupil, it is focused by a converging lens. The light is focused on the retina, which is made up of light-sensitive cells called **rods** and **cones**. When these cells sense light hitting them, they send electrical messages down the optic nerve to the brain, which decodes the messages and forms them into images.

Now here's the really neat thing about the way the eye handles light. Have you ever watched a photographer focus his or her camera? The focus works by moving a converging lens back and forth inside a tube. As the converging lens moves, the point at which the light rays converge moves. A photographer moves the lens of his or her camera back and forth until the light rays converge so as to put the image right on the film of the camera. That results in a sharp, in-focus image on the film. If the object moves in relation to the lens, the image will form someplace else. As a result, the lens must be moved again, in order to get the light rays to converge at the right place.

Just as a camera must focus images on its film in order to take a picture, your eye must focus images on its retina in order for you to see the image clearly. The retina has light-sensitive cells that receive light and send signals to the brain based on the nature of that light. This allows your brain to form the image you see. If you are to see an image clearly, then, it must be focused on your eye's retina.   How does your eye focus the light to your retina?

Believe it or not, the eye *can actually change the shape of the lens* in order to keep the image in the same place, regardless of where the object is! This is accomplished with the ciliary muscle. It squeezes or expands the lens, which changes the lens' focal point. When the lens is expanded so that it is tall and thin, the focal point is far from the lens. When the lens is squeezed down so that it is small and fat, the focal point is close to the lens.

Thus, when an object moves in relation to the eye, the ciliary (sil' ee air ee) muscle changes the shape of the lens, which in turn changes the focal point of the lens to compensate. This keeps the image focused on the retina! This is an amazing feat of physics. To give you some idea of just how amazing this is, think about modern-day cameras. Technology has given us very sophisticated cameras. In fact, most cameras are sophisticated enough to have autofocus. The camera can automatically adjust the position of the lens so that the image stays in focus on the film. Even the most sophisticated camera on earth, however, is still significantly slower in its autofocus capability as compared to the eye, and the image's focus is significantly less resolved!!

Part of the reason for this is the difference between the way a camera focuses and the way your eye focuses. Remember, a camera focuses by moving the lens. The eye, on the other hand, changes the very shape of the lens in order to change how the light rays focus. Moving a lens in order to change where the light converges is not nearly as fast or as accurate as changing the shape of the lens. Unfortunately, cameras cannot use the faster, more accurate technique because *human science cannot make a lens as sophisticated as that which you find in the eye*! Thus, even the best that today's science has to offer cannot come close to mimicking the marvelous design of the eye.

Even Charles Darwin admitted that the eye is such a sophisticated work of engineering that the very idea of an eye forming by chance is preposterous. In his book, *The Origin of Species*, Darwin himself said:

> To suppose that the eye, with all its inimitable contrivances for adjusting the focus to different distances, for admitting different amounts of light, and for the correction of spherical and chromatic aberration, could have been formed by natural selection, seems, I freely confess, absurd in the highest degree. (Charles Darwin, *The Origin of Species* [London: Penguin Classics, 1985], 217)

Of course, even though Darwin admits that the whole idea of the eye forming as a result of evolution is "absurd," he still chose to believe that it did. In fact, he spends many pages trying to convince his reader that this "absurd" idea can actually work. In other words, Darwin had an enormous amount of faith in his hypothesis! When you see incredible engineering like that of the eye, it seems much more reasonable to assume that such a marvel was designed by a very intelligent Designer!

Even the best of designs, however, can be ruined. Sometimes, due to flaws in genetics or due to overuse under the wrong types of circumstances, an eye can develop nearsightedness or farsightedness. These conditions develop when the eye's lens cannot be adjusted enough to make sure the image stays focused on the retina. For example, if you are nearsighted, your eye can use its ciliary muscle to change the lens enough to keep the image of objects close to you focused on the retina. However, as the object moves farther and farther away, the lens's focal point cannot be changed enough to keep the image there. As a result, the image gets blurry because the light is focused *in front of* the retina, *not on* the retina.

To compensate for this, corrective lenses are put in front of the eye. Because light is being refracted too strongly and thus focuses in front of the retina, diverging lenses are used. A diverging lens, such as the one shown in Figure 15.10, refracts light rays so that they diverge from one another. This compensates for the fact that the eye refracts light too strongly, and the result is an image that can be focused on the retina.

A similar situation happens when a person is farsighted. In this case, the eye's lens can adjust to objects far away, but it cannot focus on objects that are close. As a result, corrective lenses are made to refract the light rays entering the eye. In this case, however, converging lenses are used. As you might imagine, since nearsightedness is caused by the eye refracting light too strongly, farsightedness is caused by the eye refracting light too weakly. As a result, a converging lens must be used to correct farsightedness, as it helps refract the light in the right direction before the light hits the eye. This makes up for the fact that the eye cannot refract light strongly enough on its own.

How We Perceive Color

Another remarkable aspect of the eye is how it perceives color. To get an idea of how this marvelous process works, perform the following experiment.

EXPERIMENT 15.5
How the Eye Detects Color

Supplies:

♦ Two plain white sheets of paper (there shouldn't be lines on them)
♦ A bright red marker (A crayon will also work, but a marker is better.)

Introduction: Our eyes are marvelously designed to perceive color. In this experiment, you will use an optical illusion to learn how the eye does this.

Procedure:

1. Use the marker to draw a thick cross on one of the plain sheets of paper. The cross should be about 6 inches long, and the two legs that make it up should be about 3/4 of an inch thick. Color the entire cross so that you have a large, solid bright red cross in the middle of a white sheet of paper.
2. Put the clean sheet of white paper underneath the sheet with the cross on it. Make sure the cross faces you so that you can see it.
3. Stare at the cross for a full 60 seconds. You can blink if you need to, but do not take your eyes off of the cross.
4. After a full 60 seconds of staring at the cross, quickly pull the top sheet of paper out of the way so that you can only see the clean sheet of paper on the bottom.
5. Note what happened in your lab notebook. There is a chance that you will see nothing. Most people, however, will see something rather dramatic.
6. Put everything away.

What happened in the experiment? Most people will have seen a blue-green cross appear for a few moments on the blank sheet of paper. After a while, it should have vanished, however. This optical illusion will not work for some people, especially if they have a tendency toward color blindness. Now let's discuss *why* this illusion occurred.

In order to see light, the retina of each eye is equipped with cells called rods and cones. The cone cells are sensitive to color, while the rod cells are not. The cone cells transmit electrical signals to the brain when they are hit by certain frequencies of light. The brain receives the electrical transmissions and uses them to form an image in your mind. It turns out that some cone cells are sensitive only to low-frequency visible light (red light) while others are sensitive to medium-frequency visible light (green light) while still others are sensitive to higher frequency light (blue light). When colored light hits these cells, they will only send signals to the brain if the light that they are sensitive to is hitting them. Thus, if a mixture of blue and yellow light hits your eyes, the medium- and high-frequency cone cells transmit signals to your brain, but the low-frequency cone cells do not. This is how your brain knows to construct an image in your mind that contains yellow and blue.

In the experiment, while you were looking at the red cross, all of your low-frequency cone cells sensing light from the cross were sending signals to the brain, but the other cone cells receiving light from the cross weren't doing anything. It turns out that cone cells get tired pretty quickly, and when they have sent the same signal to the brain for a period of several seconds, they eventually just shut off. The brain, sensing that no more signals are coming from the cone cells, assumes that they have shut off simply because they are tired, and it holds the same image in your mind until new signals come along. Thus, as you were staring at the cross, the low-frequency cone cells receiving light from the cross eventually shut off. Since no more signals were coming from those low-frequency cone cells, and since no signals had come from the corresponding medium- and high-frequency cone cells, the brain was receiving no more signals. It therefore assumed you were still looking at the cross and continued to hold the image in your mind.

When you yanked the top sheet away, white light began to hit your cone cells where only red light had hit them before. Since white light contains all frequencies, your medium- and high-frequency cone cells began to receive light and transmit signals to your brain. Your low-frequency cone cells, however, were still shut off, so they didn't send any signals, even though they should have. The brain started receiving new signals, but only from the medium- and high- frequency cone cells. So it constructed an image of green (medium frequency) and blue (high frequency) light. Eventually, however, your low-frequency cone cells recuperated from their fatigue and began transmitting again, and, once they did, the brain realized that the eyes were seeing all frequencies of light and thus formed a white image in your mind.

Therefore, the way we perceive color is based on the frequency of the light that hits our eyes. Isn't it marvelous how well designed the eye is to handle such a complex operation? That should tell you something about how marvelous its Designer is!

Adding and Subtracting Colors

Your eyes can discern more than 16 million different colors; however, they need only three types of cone cells to do so. With cone cells that are sensitive to only three basic colors (red, green, and blue), your mind can construct a myriad of colors. Why? Well, these three colors are called

additive primary colors because they can be added together in different proportions to produce virtually any color. Examine the next figure to see what I mean.

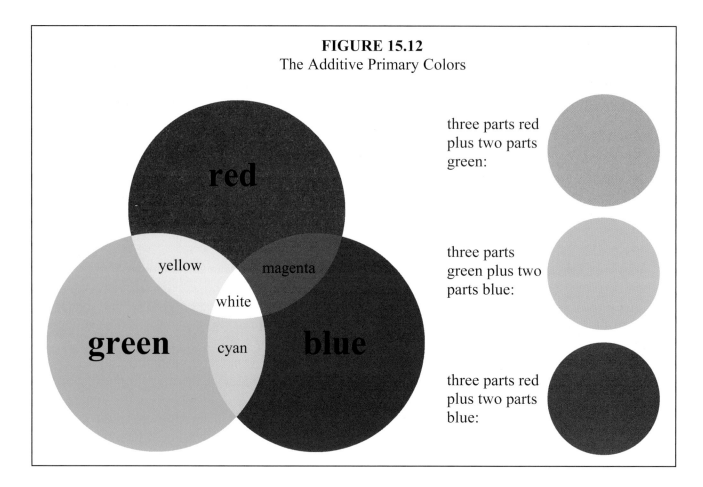

FIGURE 15.12
The Additive Primary Colors

three parts red plus two parts green:

three parts green plus two parts blue:

three parts red plus two parts blue:

On the left-hand side of the figure, you see what happens when the three additive primary colors of light are mixed. Equal parts of red and green, for example, make yellow. Equal parts of blue and green make the color cyan, and equal parts of blue and red make the color magenta. Finally, equal amounts of all three colors of light results in white light. If we vary the amounts of the primary colors, the colors change. The right side of the figure, for example, shows you a few of the colors you can get when you add primary colors in unequal amounts. This is how a color television or a computer screen makes colors. These screens produce only the three additive primary colors. By adding those three colors in varying amounts, however, they can produce more than 16 million different colors!

Although all this makes sense, have you ever tried actually mixing red and green paints or food colorings? If you have, the result was NOT yellow, was it? It was probably mostly black. If red light and green light add to make yellow light, why don't red paint and green paint add to make yellow paint? The reason is that paints and dyes produce color in a *different* way from how color television sets and computer monitors produce it. Remember, computer monitors and color televisions shine light in your eyes. That's why you can see these devices even when the lights are not on in the room. If you were to paint a picture and turn off the lights, however, you would no longer see the picture. That's because the picture does not shine light in your eyes. Instead, white light from the sun or from a light bulb reflects off the picture and hits your eyes. Thus, while televisions and computer monitors *generate* light that shines into your eyes, paints and dyes *reflect* light into your eyes. This makes a dramatic difference in how colors are generated.

Red paint, for example, is red because when light strikes it, the chemical in the paint absorbs all wavelengths of light except those which correspond to the color red. White light hits the paint, but the only light we see reflected off the paint is red light. Thus, we see the color as red. Green paint, on the other hand, absorbs all visible wavelengths except those that correspond to the color green. Thus, when white light hits green paint, only green light wavelengths reflect off it. As a result, we see the color as green because only green light reaches our eyes.

What happens, then, when you mix green paint and red paint? Well, the red paint absorbs all colors of light except red, and the green paint absorbs all colors except green. Between the two paints, then, *all visible wavelengths are absorbed.* As a result, virtually no light gets reflected, and the apparent color is black, which is the absence of light.

Is there a way of mixing paints and dyes in order to come up with different colors? Of course. After all, there are color pictures in this book. These colors are the results of color mixing as well. We do not use red, green, and blue, however. When mixing colors for dyes, inks, and paints, we mix the **subtractive primary colors**, which are **cyan**, **magenta**, and **yellow**. These colors mix so as not to absorb all wavelengths of light. Cyan, for example, absorbs all visible wavelengths except those that correspond to blue and green. Yellow, on the other hand, absorbs all visible wavelengths except those that correspond to red and green. When yellow and cyan mix, then, all visible wavelengths are absorbed except green. Thus, a mixture of yellow and cyan produces green.

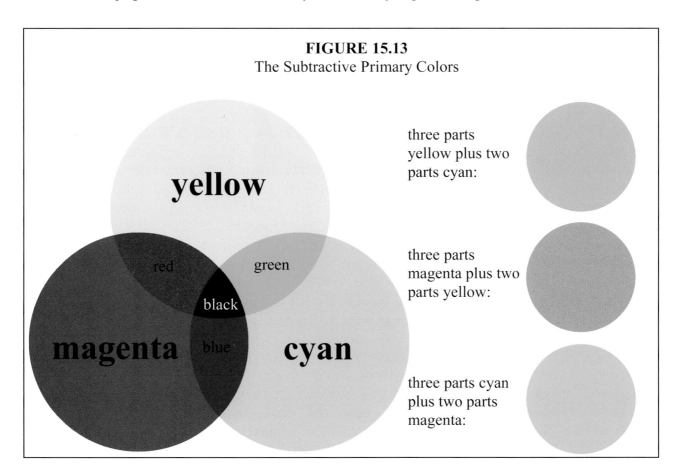

FIGURE 15.13
The Subtractive Primary Colors

three parts yellow plus two parts cyan:

three parts magenta plus two parts yellow:

three parts cyan plus two parts magenta:

If you were to look at any of the pictures in this book under a good microscope, you would actually see dots of cyan, magenta, yellow, and black. When this book was printed, only those four inks were used. Depending on how those inks were placed on the paper, however, different colors of light get reflected off the page, resulting in all the colors you see in the book.

ON YOUR OWN

15.9 Suppose you have two flashlights. You cover the first with green cellophane and shine it on a mirror. When you look at the mirror, you see a green spot of light. If you were to then take the second flashlight, cover it with red cellophane, and shine it on the same part of the mirror on which the green spot is still shining, what color would you see?

15.10 Suppose you took a red shirt and put it in a dark room. Then, suppose you took a flashlight and covered it with green cellophane as described above. If you were to go into the dark room and shine the green cellophane-covered flashlight on the red shirt, what color would you see? Assume the dye on the shirt uses the subtractive primary colors to make its light.

Cartoon by Speartoons

ANSWERS TO THE "ON YOUR OWN" PROBLEMS

15.1 Remember, in the quantum-mechanical view (the currently accepted theory on the nature of light), light is made up of little packets of waves. Thus, (b) is the best illustration of the current view of light. The picture in (a) would be true if light were a pure wave, and the picture in (c) would be true if light were made up of a stream of pure particles.

15.2 According to Table 15.1, light has a speed of 220,000,000 m/sec in fresh water. Thus, when the photon hits the lake, it must slow down.

15.3 You can remember the relative wavelengths of light with the acronym ROY G. BIV. Red has the longest wavelength, and violet has the shortest. With that knowledge then, we can say that for the colors given, red has the longest wavelength, yellow is next, followed by green. Indigo has the shortest wavelength. However, the question asked about frequency. The longer the wavelength, the lower the frequency. Thus, in terms of *increasing* frequency it is, red, yellow, green, indigo.

15.4 A radio station's antenna does not glow because the light it emits is not visible. Radio waves have wavelengths longer than visible light.

15.5 Each time the light is reflected, the angle it makes with the perpendicular must be the same before and after reflection.

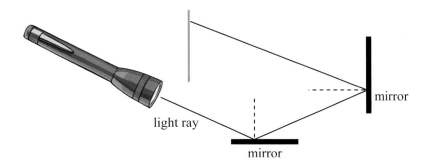

15.6 The refracted light ray bends away from the perpendicular when traveling from substance A to substance B. When light travels into a substance in which it moves more slowly, the light bends *toward* the perpendicular. When light travels into a substance in which it moves more quickly, the light bends *away from* the perpendicular. Thus, light travels more quickly in substance B than in substance A.

15.7 Consider the following diagram:

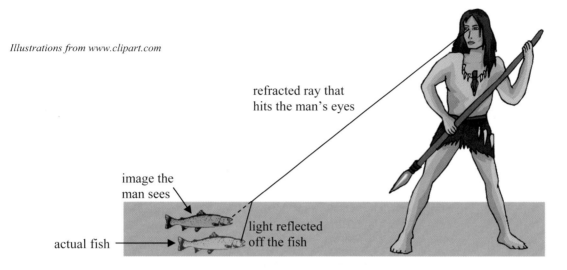

Illustrations from www.clipart.com

refracted ray that
hits the man's eyes

image the
man sees

actual fish

light reflected
off the fish

Because light rays will be refracted away from the perpendicular when they leave the water, the light will bend. However, the man's brain will interpret the light as if it has been traveling straight (remember the reflection discussion). Thus, his eye will extend the light backwards, making the fish appear farther back (and shallower) than the fish truly is. This is what happened in your experiment. When you added water to the bowl, the quarter appeared. It looked like it was farther away from you than it was in reality. Thus, the man must <u>aim in front of the fish he sees</u>.

15.8 Think about it: Lenses work because of their curvature. The more curvature they have, the more they will do their job. Thus, <u>lens (b) will focus the light rays closest</u>.

15.9 The mirror reflects all wavelengths that hit it. When the green hits it, it will reflect green. When the red hits it, it will reflect red. When both hit it, it will reflect both. When your eyes see both colors, your brain will add them to make <u>yellow</u>.

15.10 The red shirt is red because when light strikes it, it absorbs all wavelengths except red. It does this by mixing yellow and magenta. The yellow absorbs all wavelengths except red and green, and the magenta absorbs all wavelengths except red and blue. Thus, red is the only wavelength reflected from the shirt. When the green light shines on it, the green light will be absorbed by the magenta. Nothing will be reflected back. Thus, <u>the shirt will look black</u>. In fact, it won't even look like a shirt. Without any light reflecting back from it, you will not even see the shirt!

STUDY GUIDE FOR MODULE #15

1. Define the following terms:

    a.   Electromagnetic wave
    b.   The Law of Reflection

2. Explain the wave theory of light, the particle theory of light, and the quantum-mechanical theory of light.

3. Sound waves cause air to oscillate. What do light waves oscillate?

4. What does Einstein's Special Theory of Relativity say about the speed of light?

5. Light is traveling through water and suddenly breaks the surface and travels through air. Did light's speed increase, decrease, or stay the same once it left the water?

6. Order the following colors in terms of increasing wavelength: orange, violet, yellow, green. In other words, list the color corresponding to the smallest wavelength first, and end with the color that corresponds to the longest wavelength.

7. Order the colors in problem #6 in terms of increasing frequency. Once again, start with the lowest frequency and end with the highest frequency.

8. Do radio waves have higher or lower frequencies than visible light? What about X-rays?

9. Infrared light is given off by any object that is losing heat. The human body is almost always losing heat to the environment. Why, then, don't human bodies glow at night, since they are emitting light?

10. Light hits a mirror, making an angle of 15 degrees relative to a line drawn perpendicular to the mirror's surface. What angle does the reflected light make with the same line?

11. In the following diagram, will the man see his foot, despite the fact that the mirror does not reach the ground?

mirror

Illustration from
www.clipart.com

12. When light travels from one substance to another, what two things can happen to the direction of the light ray's travel?

13. In a physics experiment, a light ray is examined as it travels from air into glass. If the angle that the light ray makes with a line perpendicular to the glass surface is measured, will the refracted ray bend toward or away from that line?

14. When you look at objects underwater from above the water, they appear to be at a different position than their actual position. Why?

15. In order for you to see a rainbow, what three conditions must be met?

16. What is the difference between a converging lens and a diverging lens?

17. Which of the following lenses is a converging lens? Which is a diverging lens?

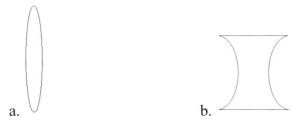

a.   b.

18. What is special about the way the eye focuses light as compared to the way a camera focuses light?

19. Suppose the cone cells on your retina that sense red light no longer work. If you look at a white piece of paper, what color would it appear to be? If you look at a red piece of paper, what color would it appear to be?

20. A shirt is dyed so that it looks violet. What colors of light does the dye absorb?

21. A cyan dye is made of a mixture of substances that absorb all light colors except blue and green. If you took a cyan piece of paper and placed it in a dark room and shined red light on it, what would you see? What would you see if you shined green light on it?

MODULE #16: An Introduction to Astrophysics

Introduction

In the previous module, you learned about light. In this module, then, it only seems natural to talk about the sources of light that exist in creation, as well as the general properties of their environment. In other words, in this module, I will cover stars and the universe. Now, of course, there is no way I can give a complete description of *either* of these interesting topics in just one module. Nevertheless, in this module, I will lay a foundation that will allow you to understand a little bit about the universe that surrounds you. Hopefully, this foundation will give you a reason to go out and learn more on your own.

The Sun

The best place to begin a discussion of astrophysics is with the main source of light for our solar system: the sun. The first thing you need to understand about the sun is that it is just one of billions and billions of light sources that exist throughout the universe: stars. When you look up into the night sky, you see countless points of light. Most of those points of light are stars. The sun that lights our planet is just one of those stars. It is the closest star to us; nevertheless, it is just a star.

Having said that, however, it is important for me to point out that while the sun is "just a star," from a scientific point of view, it seems to be a very special star. For example, the sun exists by itself as an individual star. You might be surprised to learn that this is very rare. The vast majority of stars in the universe have one or more other stars as companions. In these **multiple-star systems**, the stars orbit each other. This would cause severe temperature changes in any planet that orbited such a system, making it extremely difficult for life to exist on that planet.

Another thing that makes the sun special is its size and mass. The sun is huge. It is not the largest star in the universe, but it is *really* big by conventional standards. The sun is essentially spherical (a ball), with a diameter of roughly 865,000 miles. That's big! It is certainly the biggest thing in our solar system. For example, the diameter of the sun is more than *one hundred* times the diameter of the earth. This means that about *one million* planets the size of the earth can fit into the sun. In addition, the sun has a mass of about 2,000,000,000,000,000,000,000,000,000,000 kilograms. That's about 330,000 times the mass of the earth.

As I mentioned before, there are much bigger stars in the universe, but if the sun were as big as they are, it would engulf the earth in its orbit! In addition, there are stars that are smaller than the sun. However, if the earth were to orbit such a star, it would have to be very close in order to get enough energy to support life. If a planet got that close to such a star, the large gravitational forces it would experience would make it far too dangerous to support life. The combination of the sun's mass and size, then, make it the *perfect* star to support life on earth. Of course, if you believe in a Creator, this should come as no surprise. The universe's Creator would certainly choose the perfect star for humankind's home! As this module progresses, I will point out other features that make the sun such a special star in the universe.

So what is this special star made of? Well, it is essentially a big ball of hydrogen and helium gas. Roughly 74% of the sun's mass comes from hydrogen gas, while about 25% comes from helium.

The rest of the sun is made of trace amounts of other elements. This big ball of gas can be split into four distinct regions, as illustrated in Figure 16.1.

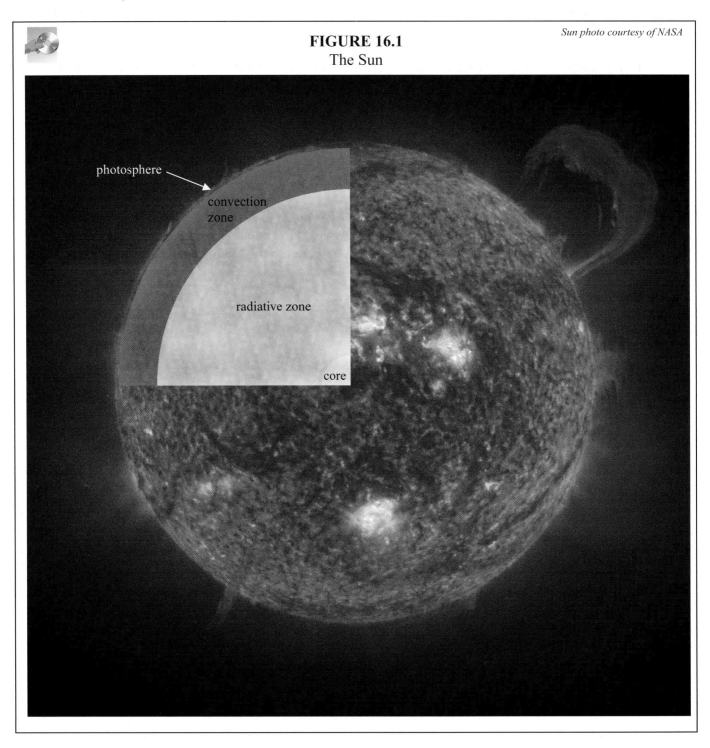

FIGURE 16.1
The Sun

Sun photo courtesy of NASA

photosphere

convection
zone

radiative zone

core

These four regions of the sun (the core, the radiative zone, the convection zone, and the photosphere) all have different properties. The most interesting part of the sun is its **core**, so that's where I'll start.

Now remember, the majority of the sun is hydrogen gas. Despite the fact that we think of hydrogen gas as something that's pretty light (it floats in air, for example), when you get a *lot* of hydrogen gas together (as is the case with the sun), it can be pretty massive. This mass produces a powerful gravitational field that holds the hydrogen gas in the sun and, at the same time, holds the planets in orbit around the sun. The gravitational field of the sun is so powerful that in the core of the sun, the pressure the hydrogen atoms experience is enormous.

This pressure is so enormous that the hydrogen atoms in the sun's core cannot exist in their normal form. Remember, hydrogen atoms have one proton and either zero, one, or two neutrons in the nucleus, depending on the isotope involved. Each of these isotopes has a single electron orbiting the nucleus. In the core of the sun, however, the hydrogen atoms cannot retain their electrons. The enormous pressure in the core creates so much heat that the electrons in the hydrogen atoms escape the attractive force the nucleus exerts on them. As a result, these hydrogen atoms are simply hydrogen nuclei. They are, in essence, "naked" protons, having been stripped of their electrons.

These naked hydrogen nuclei are constantly colliding with one another. These collisions happen frequently and with much violence. When two hydrogen nuclei collide in just the right way, something incredible can happen. The two nuclei can fuse together. The result is a helium nucleus! This process, called **nuclear fusion**, is illustrated below:

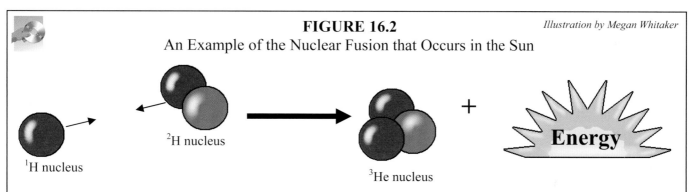

FIGURE 16.2   *Illustration by Megan Whitaker*
An Example of the Nuclear Fusion that Occurs in the Sun

^{2}H nucleus

^{1}H nucleus

^{3}He nucleus

Energy

When two hydrogen nuclei collide just right, the protons and neutrons can stick together, forming a helium nucleus. In this particular drawing, a ^{1}H nucleus collides with a ^{2}H nucleus to produce a ^{3}He nucleus. This results in a lot of released energy, which is why the sun is so hot. Please note that several different nuclear fusion reactions occur in the sun's core. This is just one of them.

Nuclear fusion reactions like this result in the release of an enormous amount of energy. Why? Well, consider the fusion reaction shown above. If you carefully measure the mass of a ^{1}H and a ^{2}H nucleus, you will find that together, they have just slightly more mass than the ^{3}He nucleus that results after fusion. What does that mean? Remember what an object's mass tells us. It tells us how much matter exists in an object. Thus, if the mass of the two hydrogen nuclei that start the process is greater than the mass of helium nucleus produced by nuclear fusion, there is obviously more matter in the two hydrogen nuclei. This tells us that in the process of nuclear fusion, *matter is "lost."*

Think about that for a moment. There is more matter *before* nuclear fusion than there is *after*. What happened? Where did the matter go? Well, do you remember Einstein's Special Theory of Relativity that I mentioned in the previous module? This theory assumes that nothing can travel faster than the speed of light. One of the consequences of this assumption is that matter is really just another form of energy. The reasons for this are far too complicated to explain here. Most scientists don't even understand them. Nevertheless, there is an enormous amount of evidence to support this idea, so most scientists believe it.

In fact, there is even an equation that relates mass and energy. It is a rather famous equation. You have probably seen it.

$$E = mc^2 \tag{16.1}$$

In this equation, "E" is energy, "m" represents mass, and "c" is the speed of light. In other words, if you take mass and multiply it by the speed of light squared, you know how much energy that amount of mass corresponds to.

Equation (16.1) tells us that the matter lost in the process of nuclear fusion is transformed into energy. Since the speed of light is so large, even a tiny amount of mass can be transformed into an enormous amount of energy. For every gram of matter lost as a result of nuclear fusion, enough energy is made to run a 100-Watt light bulb for about 28,500 years! That's pretty amazing, especially in light of the fact that in the core of the sun, 4 *trillion* grams of matter are being lost every second! Obviously, then, the nuclear fusion that takes place at the core of the sun produces *a lot* of energy.

What happens to this energy? Some of it heats up the core, maintaining its temperature of 27,000,000 °F. Most of it, however, is in the form of light. The photons produced make their way out of the core, into the next layer of the sun, the **radiative zone**. In the radiative zone, the gases are still tightly packed, but they are not pressurized enough to cause much nuclear fusion. Nevertheless, because the atoms are so tightly packed, photons keep colliding with them. As a result, it takes a long time for a photon to travel through the radiative zone.

Once out of the radiative zone, the photons are typically absorbed by gases in the **convection zone**. In this region of the sun, the gases are not as tightly packed as they are in the radiative zone. When these gases absorb the photons that come out of the radiative zone, the energy of the photons heats up the gases. As a result, the gases begin to rise. Much like air bubbles that rise through a pot of boiling water, these hot gases rise through the convection zone until they reach the surface, which we call the **photosphere**.

The photosphere is the only part of the sun that we actually see. When gases in the convection zone reach the photosphere, they transfer their extra energy to the gases in the photosphere. This causes the gases from the convection zone to cool down a bit. When they cool down, they sink back to the bottom of the convection zone, where they pick up more photons and start the process all over again.

The gases in the photosphere take the energy from the gases in the convection zone and rise to the top of the photosphere. There the energy is released in the form of electromagnetic waves. These waves have most of the wavelengths of the electromagnetic spectrum; thus, the sun is continually producing radio waves, visible light, ultraviolet light, X-rays, and gamma rays.

Take a look at Figure 16.1 again. Remember, the only part of the sun we see is the photosphere, so everything you see in the photograph portion of the figure is the surface of the photosphere. Notice that there is a lot of activity occurring there. First, the surface of the photosphere is not uniform in its brightness. There are lighter spots and darker spots. In addition, there are "explosions" that result in "spouts" and "arcs" that shoot off the surface of the photosphere. Although scientists still are not sure exactly *what* causes all this activity, they know it has something to do with the sun's magnetic field. The sun has a very strong magnetic field that exerts considerable influence on the state of the photosphere.

Every now and again, sudden and intense variations in the brightness of the photosphere's surface occur. They are called **solar flares**, and they send enormous amounts of energy to the earth in a short amount of time. This energy can cause huge electrical currents in the earth's upper atmosphere, disrupting satellites, radio communications, and even power grids. Although the surface of the sun's photosphere is a place of violent activity, it is rather "tame" compared to other, similar stars in the universe. For example, a group of astronomers studied single stars (remember, most stars have companions) with roughly the same size and composition of the sun. They found that about once every century, these stars have solar flares that are 100 to 100 *million* times more powerful than even the most violent solar flares we have seen coming from the sun. Such solar flares would spell disaster for life on earth. The fact that our sun doesn't have such powerful solar flares is just one more indication of how special a star it is!

ON YOUR OWN

16.1 As I mentioned previously, the sun is mostly hydrogen and helium. As time goes on, will that composition change? If so, will the amount of hydrogen increase or decrease? What about helium?

16.2 Which of the four regions of the sun has the lowest temperature?

Before I leave this section, it is important that I point out to you that the vast majority of the knowledge we have about the sun comes from indirect observation. As a result, we may have a few of these "facts" wrong. For example, the temperature I gave for the core of the sun (27,000,000 °F) has been determined indirectly. It is the result of matching our knowledge of nuclear fusion with our observations of the light coming from the sun. Thus, as long as the nuclear fusion in the sun's core is occurring the way we *think* it is, that is a reasonable temperature. However, if our understanding of how nuclear fusion works in the sun changes, our value for the temperature of the sun's core might change as well. In the same way, many of the "facts" I have told you so far (and many of the "facts" I tell you in the rest of this module) may change as the result of more scientific research.

Nuclear Energy

Since I talked about energy from nuclear fusion in the previous section, it is worthwhile to spend a few moments discussing the nuclear energy we are trying to use here on earth. The sun is powered by nuclear fusion. That's not the kind of nuclear power we currently use to generate electricity. Presently, we use **nuclear fission** to produce some of the electricity that we use. What's the difference between nuclear fusion and nuclear fission? Let's start with the definitions.

Nuclear fusion – The process by which two or more small nuclei fuse to make a bigger nucleus

Nuclear fission – The process by which a large nucleus is split into smaller nuclei

Notice the difference between the two. In nuclear fusion, nuclei join together to make a larger nucleus. In the sun, for example, two hydrogen nuclei fuse to make a larger helium nucleus. In nuclear fission, a large nucleus is split into two smaller nuclei. An example of the nuclear fission process is shown in Figure 16.3.

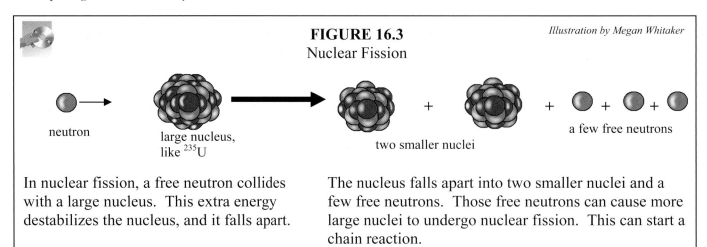

FIGURE 16.3
Nuclear Fission

Illustration by Megan Whitaker

neutron   large nucleus, like ^{235}U   two smaller nuclei   a few free neutrons

In nuclear fission, a free neutron collides with a large nucleus. This extra energy destabilizes the nucleus, and it falls apart.

The nucleus falls apart into two smaller nuclei and a few free neutrons. Those free neutrons can cause more large nuclei to undergo nuclear fission. This can start a chain reaction.

If you were to carefully measure the mass of the neutron and the large nucleus before the nuclear fission took place and then measure the mass of both nuclei and all the neutrons produced at the end of the process, you would find out that, just as in the case of nuclear fusion, some mass is missing. That mass gets converted to energy in the form of heat and light.

Although there are examples of nuclear fission that do not happen as illustrated in Figure 16.3, the process illustrated there is an example of what happens in nuclear bombs and nuclear power plants. Notice that the process requires two things to get it started: a large nucleus (typically ^{235}U or ^{239}Pu) and a free neutron. Notice also what this process produces: two smaller nuclei and a few free neutrons. Thus, the process *produces* one of the things it *needs to get started*: a free neutron.

What does this mean? Well, if you have a bunch of ^{235}U "lying around" somewhere, when a free neutron happens to come along and strike one of the nuclei, nuclear fission can happen. That process will generate a few more free neutrons, which *can each start another fission process*. This can continue so that every single fission process goes out and starts one or more fission processes. This is called a **chain reaction**. For a chain reaction to occur, however, there has to be *enough* of the large nuclei (^{235}U or ^{239}Pu) present. This is called the **critical mass**.

Critical mass – The amount of isotope necessary to sustain a chain reaction

A critical mass of the large nucleus, then, guarantees that the fission process is self-sustaining.

If a chain reaction starts in the presence of more than a critical mass of the large nucleus, each new fission process can start more than one additional fission process, which can each then produce more than one additional fission process, etc. When this happens, the number of fission processes grows so rapidly that energy is created at an enormous rate. The rate becomes so enormous that, eventually, the energy is produced too quickly and the result is a huge explosion. This is the basis of the atomic bomb. In an atomic bomb, significantly more than the critical mass of the large nucleus ^{235}U (or ^{239}Pu) is put in a warhead so that once the chain reaction starts, an explosion is inevitable. If you have significantly more than a critical mass of ^{235}U or ^{239}Pu, then, you can make a bomb. If you do not have that much mass, however, you cannot make a bomb.

With a critical mass (or just a bit more than the critical mass) of the large nucleus, the chain reaction will never grow out of control, so it will never cause a nuclear explosion. However, it will still produce a *lot* of heat. That heat can be harnessed by an electrical generator and can then be used to make electricity. That's the basis of a nuclear power plant. Nuclear fission is run with only a bit more than the critical mass of the large nucleus. As a result, the fission will never lead to a nuclear explosion, but it can be used to make electricity.

The wonderful thing about using nuclear fission to make electricity is that the fuel for nuclear power is reasonably cheap and will last a long, long time. The downside is that nuclear fission can be quite dangerous. Now it is important to realize that the danger of nuclear fission is *not* that a nuclear power plant can create a nuclear explosion. That's physically impossible! In order to make a nuclear explosion, you must have significantly more than the critical mass of the large nucleus you are using. Since nuclear power plants *do not* contain that much mass of the large nucleus, they *cannot* produce a nuclear explosion.

Even though nuclear power plants cannot produce a nuclear explosion, other nasty things can happen. In a normally operating nuclear power plant, the rate at which the fission processes occur is heavily controlled. If the control operations fail, the reaction starts producing too much energy. This will not lead to an explosion, but it can produce so much heat that everything in the vicinity, including the reactor itself, will begin to melt. When this happens, it is called a **meltdown**, and the results can be devastating.

This is what happened at the Chernobyl nuclear power plant in the former Soviet Union in 1986. This particular nuclear power plant did not have many safety protocols, and when the primary controls failed, there was nothing that could keep the reaction from running out of control. As a result, parts of the reactor began to melt. This caused a huge increase in the steam pressure of the plant, causing the system that contains the steam to explode. The result was that many radioactive isotopes were released into the surroundings. More than 30 people were directly killed as a result of the accident, and thousands were exposed to high levels of radiation. To this day, no one can live near where the plant was because the radioactive contamination is so high.

Nuclear power in the form of nuclear fission, then, can be quite dangerous. You have to understand, however, that *all* forms of power production are dangerous. In many power plants, for example, coal is burned to generate electricity. Since 1900, more than 100,000 people have been killed in American coal mines and even more have contracted mining-related diseases such as black lung. Studies indicate that when nuclear power is compared to other forms of power generation, it is responsible for fewer deaths and health maladies than any other form of power production.

Nuclear power in the form of fission also has another serious drawback: The byproducts are radioactive. We have no safe way of disposing this radioactive waste. This can eventually lead to serious environmental problems. Of course, other forms of energy production also lead to serious environmental problems. Coal-burning power plants, for example, dump pollution into the air. The *amount* of pollution they dump into the atmosphere has been reduced considerably (remember the discussion in Module #2). Nevertheless, they still emit pollutants. They are, in fact, the principal contributors to the problem of acid rain.

Although nuclear power in the form of nuclear fission can be dangerous and polluting, it is not clear that it is any more dangerous and polluting than other forms of energy production. There are those who think it is, in fact, one of the safest and cleanest forms of energy production. In France, for example, the scientific community is so convinced that nuclear power is (overall) the safest form of power production that about 80% of the country runs on electricity produced by nuclear power plants.

In order to make energy production safer, better for the environment, and longer-lasting, scientists are trying to use nuclear fusion instead of nuclear fission to produce electricity. Nuclear fusion has few harmful byproducts. Remember, when nuclear fusion occurs in the sun, the product is helium. Helium is not radioactive and has no toxic chemical properties. Thus, using nuclear fusion to produce electricity would almost completely eliminate the radioactivity problem caused by nuclear fission. It is also much safer than nuclear fission. Experiments indicate that nuclear fusion is much easier to halt, allowing for the nuclear fusion process to be stopped quickly. This would avert any meltdown possibilities. Finally, the fuel for nuclear fusion (^{2}H) is virtually unlimited and very inexpensive. Nuclear power from nuclear fusion, then, would be safe, cheap, and almost limitless.

Why don't we use nuclear fusion to make electricity, then? The answer is that from a *technological* viewpoint, we have not mastered the process yet. We *know* that nuclear fusion can be used to make energy. After all, it powers the sun. However, nuclear fusion can happen in the sun because of the intense heat and pressure in the sun's core. In order to get nuclear fusion to work, we have to essentially recreate that environment here on earth. That's a tough job! Right now, nuclear physicists can, indeed, cause nuclear fusion to occur in a variety of different ways. However, in each way used so far, there is an enormous amount of energy wasted in order to create the conditions necessary for the fusion. As a result, the total energy produced is rather small. In other words, right now we have to put an enormous amount of energy into a nuclear fusion reaction, and we don't get enough energy back to make it an economically viable process for the large-scale production of energy.

In the end, then, we know that there are some drawbacks to nuclear fission. Some consider those drawbacks to be quite serious; others consider them to be about the same or even less than the other forms of power production. If scientists and engineers are ever able to overcome the technological problems associated with nuclear fusion, the result would be a much safer, cleaner, and cheaper form of power production. Whether that will ever happen, however, remains to be seen.

ON YOUR OWN

16.3 In a nuclear physics experiment, two ^{7}Li atoms collide to form ^{12}C and two neutrons. Is this nuclear fission or nuclear fusion?

16.4 Suppose nuclear physicists discovered a fission process that always produced two smaller nuclei and *only one* neutron. Would this eliminate the danger of meltdown in a nuclear power plant? Why or why not?

Classifying the Stars in the Universe

The principal tool that scientists use to study the universe is the telescope. Since a telescope collects light, the only structures that can be studied with telescopes are those structures that emit or reflect light. With telescopes, then, scientists have been able to study the planets in our solar system (because they reflect light from the sun), the sun, and the stars outside earth's solar system (because they emit their own light). As a result, the most well-studied structures in the universe are stars.

When scientists study things, they typically like to classify them. Next year, you should start an in-depth study of biology, in which you will learn the classification scheme biologists use to classify all the living organisms on the planet. Scientists like to classify the things they study because classification is a way of taking a large amount of data and ordering it into a manageable system. Thus, when scientists began seriously studying the stars, they searched for ways in which the stars could be classified.

One thing that astronomers noticed early on was that different stars have different colors. When observing our sun, for example, astronomers noted it appears white. You may think it appears yellow, but that's because you usually see it drawn as a yellow orb in the sky. When observing the sun directly, however, you will notice that the light it emits is white. Not all stars emit white light, however. There are stars that predominately emit red/orange light, stars that predominately emit yellow light, and so on.

As astronomers began studying this phenomenon, they began theorizing as to why different stars produced different colors of light. As time went on, evidence began to accumulate that a star's color is actually related to its temperature. It seems that blue stars are the hottest stars in the universe. White stars (like our sun) are a bit cooler than blue stars; yellow stars are cooler yet; and red/orange stars are the coolest of all. The better our technology became, the better we got at determining the temperature of a star. Nowadays, astronomers look at individual wavelengths of light in a process called **spectroscopy** (spek trahs' kuh pee). You will learn more about spectroscopy when you take chemistry. The brightness of certain specific wavelengths of light emitted by a star allows astronomers to measure the approximate temperature of the star.

When an astronomer does such an analysis of a star, he or she places it into one of seven classes. Each class is designated by a letter, called the **spectral letter** of the star. The star's temperature determines which spectral letter is assigned to the star, according to the following table.

TABLE 16.1
Spectral Letters and Star Temperatures

Temperature ($^{\circ}$F)	Spectral Letter
less than 5,500	M
5,500 – 8,000	K
8,001 – 10,300	G
10,301 – 12,500	F
12,501 – 17,000	A
17,001 – 37,000	B
more than 37,000	O

The temperature of the sun (not the core temperature), for example, is 10,000 $^{\circ}$F. This makes it a type G star.

By itself, the classification of stars into spectral groups is not all that useful; however, if you combine this information with one other piece of information, you get a pretty interesting result. Not only do stars vary by color, they also vary by brightness. This is easy to see. If you look up into the night sky, you will find that some stars are bright and others are dim. Why is that?

There are two factors that affect how bright a star is in the night sky. The first is simply how intense the light it emits is. Obviously, the more intense the light a star emits, the brighter it is. The other factor, however, is the star's distance from us. The farther a star is from the earth, the dimmer it appears. When astronomers observe a star, then, they have to consider both factors. In a later section of this module, I will tell you how we measure the distance from us to the stars. For right now, just understand that we can.

When an astronomer observes the brightness of a star and then corrects for the distance from the earth to the star, the result is called the **absolute magnitude** of the star.

Absolute magnitude – The brightness of a star, corrected for distance, on a scale of -8 to +19. The *smaller* the number, the *brighter* the star.

The absolute magnitude of the sun, for example, is +5. This means that it is not a very bright star (a negative absolute magnitude would mean a very bright star).

Now, of course, if you look up in the sky, the sun seems to be the brightest of all stars. It is so bright, in fact, that when the sun is in the sky you are observing (i.e., during the day), its light blocks out the light coming from all the other stars in the universe. Until the earth moves so that the sun is out of the sky you are observing (e.g., at night), you cannot see any other stars. Even though the sun is a relatively dim star, then, it looks bright to us simply because it is close.

Since what we see in the sky is the result of *both* the brightness of the star *and* the distance from the earth to the star, we observe the **apparent magnitude** of the stars.

Apparent magnitude – The brightness of a star as seen in the night sky. The *smaller* the number, the *brighter* the star.

While the sun has an absolute magnitude of about +5, its *apparent* magnitude is about -27! Thus, because it is close to the earth, it *appears* very bright. However, if a star like Arcturus (absolute magnitude of -0.3), were put right next to the sun, it would be *much* brighter than the sun. In the end, then, while we *observe* the *apparent* magnitude of the stars, the absolute magnitude is a much better indicator of the actual properties of the star.

Now we can finally come to the neat part. As early as 1910, two brilliant astronomers, Ejnar Hertzsprung (hurts' sprung) and Henry Russell, began to see that there was a relationship between a star's temperature and its magnitude. They plotted one versus the other and noticed that the stars they put on their chart seemed to fall into groups. When they made their research known, astronomers found their means of classifying stars. The graph that Hertzsprung and Russell developed became known as the **Hertzsprung-Russell Diagram**, which is often abbreviated as the **H-R Diagram**.

In this diagram (shown in Figure 16.4), the temperature of the star is plotted horizontally, and the absolute magnitude is plotted vertically. The hotter the star, the farther to the left it is plotted, and the brighter the star, the higher it is plotted. The background of the graph tells you the color of the star. Remember, the color of a star depends primarily on its temperature. Thus, as one travels from the right side of the graph to the left side, the color goes from red (cooler stars) to blue (hotter stars). Instead of using the temperature on the diagram, I have just put the spectral letters for stars on top of the graph. Once again, a star's spectral letter depends only on its temperature. Thus, the spectral letter is just another indication of the star's horizontal position on this graph.

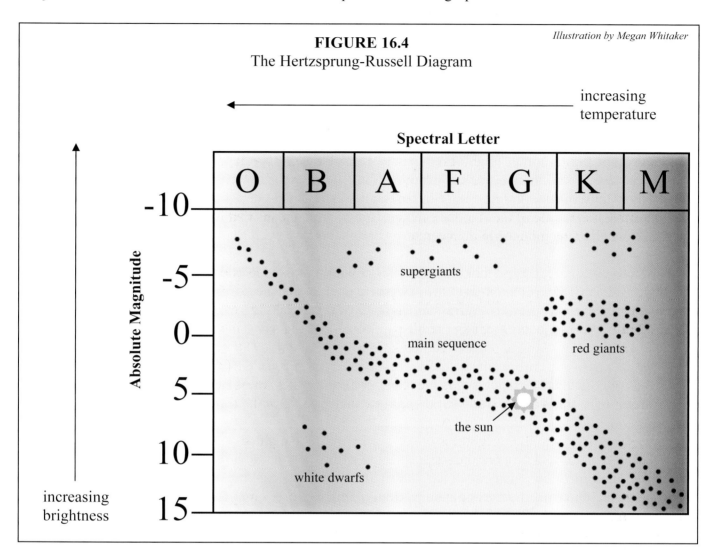

FIGURE 16.4

The Hertzsprung-Russell Diagram

Illustration by Megan Whitaker

increasing temperature

Spectral Letter

O B A F G K M

Absolute Magnitude

-10

-5

0

5

10

15

increasing brightness

supergiants

main sequence

red giants

the sun

white dwarfs

    Each of the dots in the diagram represents a star. These are only a few of the many stars that have been analyzed, but they show a distinct pattern. There is a broad band of stars that fall along a roughly diagonal path from the upper left-hand side of the graph to the lower right-hand side. We call these the **main sequence** stars. Notice that our sun is in this band. Thus, the sun is a main sequence star. Below the band of main sequence stars is a small group of stars called the **white dwarfs**. Directly above the main sequence stars is another group called the **red giants**, and above the red giants is a group of stars called the **supergiants**. In order to determine what basic kind of star an astronomer is studying, then, he or she looks at the position of the star on this chart. The group the star falls into on this chart is the first step in the classification of the star.

    What does this classification tell us about a star? Well, it turns out that the stars in each of these groups have their own, unique properties. About 90% of the stars that astronomers have studied are main sequence stars. These stars, as you might expect, are similar to the sun. They all produce a large amount of their energy from the nuclear fusion of hydrogen into helium. The more massive a main sequence star, the stronger its gravitational field. This means the core temperature and pressure is high, and the rate of nuclear fusion is high. As a result, the more massive the main sequence star, the brighter it is.

In fact, it seems that one of the most important differences between all main sequence stars is their individual mass. When a main sequence star is more massive, it is brighter and warmer. When it is less massive, it is fainter and cooler. Thus, if you look at the H-R Diagram above, you can conclude that the main sequence stars that are basically blue in color are significantly more massive than the main sequence stars that are red in color.

Although there is a strict relationship between mass, brightness, and temperature for main sequence stars, that is not the case for red giants. Red giants, as their name implies, are huge stars. In the core of a red giant, there is nuclear fusion, but it is not the same kind of fusion as that which takes place in a main sequence star. A red giant has a core made mostly of helium. The core of a red giant is significantly hotter than that of a main sequence star, which results in a much brighter star. That's why red giants are high on the H-R Diagram.

In this hot core, three helium atoms undergo nuclear fusion to make carbon atoms. That's the nuclear fusion that powers a red giant. Now despite the fact that a red giant's core is much hotter than that of a main sequence star, the overall temperature of a red giant is lower than most main sequence stars. That's why red giants are red or reddish-yellow.

Supergiant stars are, as the name implies, the largest stars in the universe. Astronomers have observed supergiants that, if put at the center of our solar system, would extend all the way out to the orbit of Saturn! That's a BIG star! These stars are very rare. Despite their brightness, very few have been observed in the universe.

Based on current observations, it seems that white dwarfs are the second most common stars in the universe. Remember, main sequence stars are by far the most common. However, a large number of white dwarfs have been observed as well. If you look again at the H-R Diagram, you will see that the absolute magnitude of white dwarfs is pretty high compared to most of the other stars on the diagram. This means they are not very bright. Since we see a lot of white dwarfs despite the fact that they are not very bright, we must assume they are relatively common in the universe.

As their name implies, white dwarfs are quite small. Many in the universe seem to be about the size of the earth. That's quite small for a star! Despite the fact that white dwarfs are small, they are incredibly massive. Even a teaspoon full of the "stuff" that makes up a white dwarf would weigh several tons here on earth. The matter in a white dwarf, then, is *very* tightly-packed.

As you look at the H-R Diagram in Figure 16.4, you will get some idea of how very special the sun really is. The sun is a main sequence star, which is the most common kind of star in the universe. This leads some astronomers to say that the sun is an "unremarkable" star. These astronomers, however, are not telling the complete story. Not only is the sun special in the ways I have already discussed, it is special when compared to the other main sequence stars in the universe.

Main sequence stars vary in mass from about one-tenth the mass of the sun to about 20 times the mass of the sun. Now remember, the mass of a main sequence star is a major factor in determining how bright it is. If the sun were too bright or not bright enough, it could not support life on earth. Thus, of all the possible values for the mass of a main sequence star, the sun has just the right amount of mass to support life on earth! In fact, as astronomers have catalogued more and more main sequence stars, they have found that nearly 70% of them have such a low mass that they could not safely provide the energy needed for a life-supporting planet. In addition, of the stars in this general region of the universe, the sun is in the top 10% in terms of its mass. Thus, even though it is "just a main sequence star," the sun is clearly very special. Of course, this shouldn't be surprising to you. After all, the earth is a very special place in the eyes of God. Thus, it only makes sense that He would design a very special star to give it the energy it needs to support life!

ON YOUR OWN
Use the H-R Diagram in Figure 16.4 to solve these problems.

16.5 A star has a magnitude of 5, and its temperature indicates it has a spectral letter of "F." What kind of star is it?

16.6 Is the star in the problem above more or less massive than a star with a magnitude of 10 and a spectral letter of K?

16.7 Are red giants cooler or warmer than most white dwarfs?

Variable Stars

In the previous section, I talked about stars that could be easily placed on the H-R Diagram. Not all stars can be easily placed on such a diagram, however, because some stars do not have a constant magnitude. It turns out that the brightness of some stars varies, and as a result, their vertical position on the H-R Diagram would continually change. These are called **variable stars**, and there are two main kinds: **pulsating variables** and **novas**.

The novas are the most spectacular variable stars in the universe. The term "nova" comes from Latin, and it means "new." Thus, a nova is a "new star." This is not a good description for what a nova *is*, but it is a great description for what a nova *appears to be*. Early astronomers noticed that every once in a while, a star would seem to appear at a point in the sky where there was no star before. Thus, it looked like a new star had been born, so it was called a nova. Modern astronomers now know that a nova is the result of an explosion within a star. When a star explodes, it emits a fraction of its mass as a shell of gas. That causes a temporary surge in its brightness, which causes the star to be more visible for a short time.

Although you might think of an explosion as something that would destroy a star, novas can explode many, many times. After all, each explosion might result in only a small fraction of the nova's mass being expelled. As a result, these explosions can occur over and over again. It has also been theorized that some novas actually replenish their mass by attracting debris from other nearby stars, allowing a nova to explode even more often. Many novas explode in regular intervals, some every few days, some every few years.

The extreme example of a nova is a **supernova**. A supernova is a true explosion of a star. When a supernova occurs, the star expands rapidly and brightens enormously, and then fades away permanently. The debris left over from such an explosion is a cloud of bright gases called a **nebula**.

In 1054 A.D., early astronomers recorded observing a flash of light in the sky that seems to be what we would expect of a supernova. If we look at that same position in the sky today, we see the **crab nebula**. Astronomers assume, therefore, that the crab nebula is the debris formed in the supernova explosion.

FIGURE 16.5

The Crab Nebula

Image courtesy of NASA

A much more common type of variable star is the pulsating variable. These stars expand and contract, much like a balloon that is constantly being inflated and deflated. The brightness of the star changes as it expands and contracts. Thus, a pulsating variable's brightness increases and decreases time and time again. Unlike a nova, the star does not eject a fraction of its mass as a result of the expanding and contracting it does. Thus, a pulsating star has a long lifetime. Many pulsating stars have very regular periods of pulsation, which means that the rate at which they expand and contract is quite constant. As a result, the variation in brightness is constant as well.

A very well-studied class of pulsating stars is the **Cepheid** (sef' eyed) **variable** class. These pulsating stars are usually between five and 20 times as massive as the sun. The rate at which they expand and contract is very constant. As a result, the time it takes for them to go from bright to dim is easily measured and does not change. Some Cepheid variables take as little as a day to go from bright to dim, while some take up to a year. These particular variable stars are instrumental in astronomers' attempts to measure long distances in the universe. I will talk about them again in a later section of this module.

For a while, astronomers thought that there was a third kind of variable star, because stars that seemed to be neither novas nor pulsating variables did appear to vary in brightness with time. As more study was done, however, astronomers found that it is possible for two stars to be close enough to each other to actually orbit one another. These are called **binary stars** because they are actually composed of two stars that are quite close to one another. If a binary star system is oriented properly relative to earth, the stars will pass in front of one another as they orbit. This results in one star obstructing our view of the second star. These systems, called **eclipsing binary stars**, vary in apparent brightness not because their absolute magnitude changes but because one of the two stars can block our view of the other. Thus, although these stars appear to be variable stars, they really are not. A binary star is an example of the multiple-star systems I mentioned previously. As I already pointed out, the vast majority of stars are a part of multiple-star systems.

ON YOUR OWN

16.8 Which kind of variable star would tend to exist for the longest time: supernovas, novas, or pulsating variables?

Measuring the Distance to Stars

When I was discussing the classification of stars, I mentioned that in order to measure the absolute magnitude of a star, one must take into account the distance between the earth and the star. How in the world can an astronomer measure something like that? Only now is the unmanned spacecraft Voyager 1 near the edge of our *solar system*, and it was launched in 1977. Other than the sun, the nearest star (Proxima Centauri) is a long way past the confines of our solar system. How, then, can we measure the distance to even the nearest star, since we have never traveled there?

Well, there are two main ways that astronomers measure the distance from the earth to a star: the **parallax method** and the **apparent magnitude method**. The first method, the parallax method, is illustrated below.

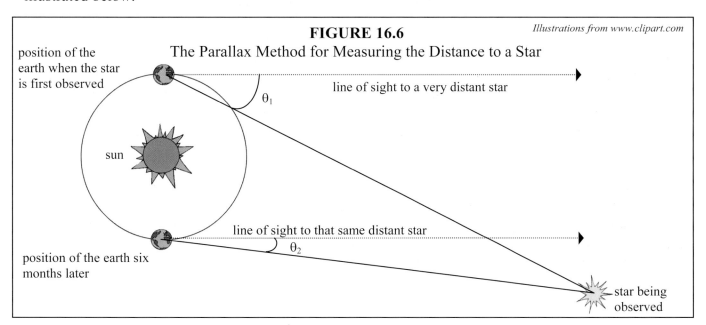

FIGURE 16.6

Illustrations from www.clipart.com

The Parallax Method for Measuring the Distance to a Star

position of the earth when the star is first observed

line of sight to a very distant star

θ_1

sun

line of sight to that same distant star

θ_2

position of the earth six months later

star being observed

When using the parallax method, an astronomer observes a very distant star and then observes the star to which he wants to determine the distance. The astronomer then measures the angle between the lines of sight for those two stars. In the figure, that angle is denoted as θ_1. If the astronomer then waits for six months, the earth will have traveled halfway around the sun. As a result, it will be in a different position in the solar system. If the astronomer then observes the same two stars again and measures the new angle between their lines of sight, he will have a different angle, θ_2. For nearby stars, θ_1 will not be equal to θ_2, because of the change in the earth's position. It turns out that some rather straightforward geometry can be used to develop an exact relationship between the difference in those two angles and the distance to the star.

This method for judging distance can also be used to measure long distances on earth. Airplane navigational systems use it all of the time. It is called "triangulation." The nice thing about this method is that it is exact. It is a result of geometry. Thus, when astronomers use the parallax method to determine the distance to a star, the result is just as accurate as if the astronomer had used a long ruler and measured the distance directly. The bad thing about this method is that it can only be used to measure the distance to *nearby* stars. The farther away the star is, the less the difference between θ_1 and θ_2. For stars that are very far away, we cannot detect a difference in the angles and, as a result, we can no longer use the parallax method.

How far away can astronomers measure using the parallax method? Well, the first thing you have to know to answer that question is the unit that astronomers use to measure distance in space. Most astronomers use the **light year** as a distance unit.

Light year – The distance light could travel along a straight line in one year

Now if you think about it, that's a *long* distance unit. After all, light travels 300,000,000 meters every second. In a year, then, it travels approximately 9,500,000,000,000,000 meters, which is about the same as 6 trillion miles! That's a long way! Using that unit, the parallax method can be used to reliably measure the distance to stars that are a few hundred light years away. If a star is farther away than that, the difference in the line of sight angles is generally too small for astronomers to measure. Proxima Centauri, for example, is the closest star to us (next to the sun, of course). The parallax method tells us that it is 4.3 light years away from us.

If you've read much about astronomy, you know that scientists talk about distances in the universe that are *much* longer than a few hundred light years. For example, astronomers tell us that Deneb, the brightest star in the constellation Cygnus, is about 3,000 light years from us. They also tell us that the Milky Way galaxy has a diameter of about 100,000 light years. How do they get those numbers?

In order to measure distances beyond the limits of the parallax method, astronomers use the apparent magnitude method. The idea behind this method was discovered by American astronomer Henrietta Leavitt. She studied an enormous number of Cepheid variable stars that are fairly near the earth. She noticed that there seemed to be a direct relationship between their pulsation period and their magnitude. When a Cepheid variable star takes a long time to go from bright to dark, the star's average brightness is quite large; thus its magnitude is small. When the star takes a short time to go from bright to dark, the star's average brightness is low; so its magnitude is high. Astrophysicists had already predicted this relationship with a mathematical theory, and Leavitt's data provided evidence for that theory.

Armed with this information, astronomers can measure the distance to any observable Cepheid variable star, regardless of how far away it is. After all, if you have a way of calculating the absolute magnitude of a star, and you then measure the amount of light that makes it to the earth from that star, it is very easy to determine how far away the star is. The trick, of course, is knowing the absolute magnitude of the star to begin with. The relationship that Leavitt demonstrated for Cepheid variable stars gave astronomers that ability. Thus, as long as there is a Cepheid star nearby, the distance to any structure in the universe can be measured using the apparent magnitude method.

Since Leavitt's discovery, other variable stars have been shown to exhibit a relationship between period and magnitude. As a result, astronomers have even more structures in the universe they can use to measure distances. This has allowed astronomers to "map out" a significant fraction of the visible universe.

ON YOUR OWN

16.9 Which distance-measuring method is the most reliable: the parallax method or the apparent magnitude method?

<u>Galaxies</u>

Stars do not exist alone in space. They are generally grouped together in large ensembles known as **galaxies**.

<u>Galaxy</u> – A large ensemble of stars, all interacting through the gravitational force and orbiting around a common center

All the stars that can be seen from earth with the naked eye (including the sun) belong to the same galaxy: the **Milky Way**. Galaxies can be grouped according to their appearance. There are **spiral galaxies**, **elliptical galaxies**, and **lenticular galaxies**. The center of the galaxy, called the **nucleus**, is visible in many of them.

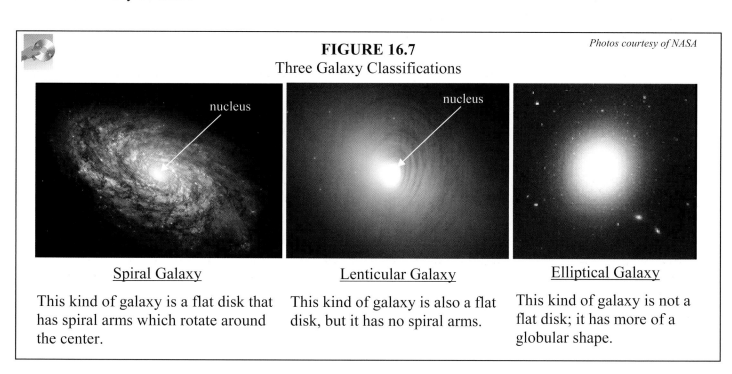

FIGURE 16.7
Three Galaxy Classifications

Photos courtesy of NASA

<u>Spiral Galaxy</u>	<u>Lenticular Galaxy</u>	<u>Elliptical Galaxy</u>
This kind of galaxy is a flat disk that has spiral arms which rotate around the center.	This kind of galaxy is also a flat disk, but it has no spiral arms.	This kind of galaxy is not a flat disk; it has more of a globular shape.

If a galaxy cannot be classified as spiral, lenticular, or elliptical, it is called an **irregular galaxy**.

The Milky Way, the galaxy to which our solar system belongs, is a spiral galaxy. It is about 100,000 light years across, but no more than 2,000 light years thick. That's what I mean when I say that spiral galaxies are flat disks. Compared to the distance across such a galaxy, the thickness of the galaxy is quite small. Our sun is on the inner edge of one of the spiral arms, called the **Orion arm**.

The sun's position in the Milky Way and its behavior in the galaxy make it a very special star. First, its position on the Orion arm is such that its speed as it orbits the galaxy's nucleus matches the speed at which the arms of the galaxy rotate. As a result, it is always in the Orion arm. That is very good. Many stars in the Milky Way orbit the galaxy's center faster or slower than the arms rotate. As a result, they move across the arms of the spiral. This is a very dangerous situation that would preclude the ability of the star to support a planet habitable for life. Second, the orbit of the sun around the nucleus is circular. Many stars have elliptical orbits that bring them close to the galactic center. Once again, this is dangerous, because there are many energetic events that happen near the nucleus. The sun, however, is at the perfect position in the Orion arm and has the perfect orbit to keep life on earth safe!

Lenticular galaxies look a lot like spiral galaxies. They are disk-shaped and also have a prominent nucleus. Lenticular galaxies, however, do not have discernible arms. Instead, the stars rotate around the nucleus in a reasonably even distribution. Elliptical galaxies, on the other hand, are not at all disk-shaped. They have a more globular shape, and the distribution of light in the "glob" is rather uniform, except for the nucleus, which is very bright.

The interesting thing about galaxies is that they rarely exist by themselves. Most galaxies are part of a bigger group of galaxies. The Milky Way, for example, is part of a small group of about 30 galaxies, which is known as the **Local Group**. The two largest galaxies in the Local Group are the Milky Way galaxy and the Andromeda galaxy. These groups of galaxies, in turn, form large **clusters**. The Local Group is on the outer edge of a cluster of galaxies known as the **Virgo Cluster**. Galaxy clusters often group together as well into giant groups known as **superclusters**.

The distribution of these clusters and superclusters in the portion of the universe we are able to observe is not uniform. Instead, they tend to form long, stringy, almost lacelike filaments that arranged around large voids where few or no stars exist. One of these filaments, called the **Great Wall**, stretches across more than half a billion light years in space!

An Expanding Universe

In the early 1900s, astronomers began to notice that the light coming from stars in galaxies other than the Milky Way is a bit different from what was expected. You see, there are certain wavelengths of light emitted by elements when they are excited. These wavelengths of light are called **spectral lines**, and each element has its own, unique pattern of spectral lines it emits when excited. These spectral lines are well known and well understood for most elements. However, when astronomers looked at the spectral lines that come from certain excited elements in the star of another galaxy, the spectral lines were different from what they are when the excited element is on earth. For each element, the spectral lines had longer wavelengths when the light came from other galaxies as compared to those same spectral lines on earth!

Now remember, the wavelength of visible light determines the color of the light. Visible light with the shortest wavelengths is blue, while visible light with long wavelengths is red. Astronomers found that the light coming from other galaxies had longer wavelengths than one would predict. In other words, the wavelengths seemed to be "shifted" to the "red" (long wavelength) end of the spectrum. This phenomenon became known as the **red shift**.

What causes the red shift? Astronomers were not sure, but they had a theory. Do you remember the Doppler effect we studied in Module #14? The Doppler effect tells us that when moving objects emit waves, the frequency (and wavelength) of the waves we observe is different from what we would observe when the object is stationary. If the object moves toward us, the waves get bunched up, and the observed wavelength is smaller than the actual wavelength. If the object moves away from us, the waves get stretched out, and the observed wavelength *is larger than the actual wavelength.*

That's what astronomers saw! They saw that the light coming from most of the other galaxies had wavelengths that were longer than they should have been. Thus, astronomers theorized that the red shift was actually the Doppler effect for light. If that was the case, the conclusion was obvious: Most galaxies in the universe are actually traveling away from the earth. As time went on, astronomers became more and more convinced of the theory that the red shift was, indeed, a Doppler effect, and therefore, most of the galaxies in the universe are moving away from us. There are a few notable exceptions to this general rule. The Andromeda galaxy, for example, seems to be moving toward us because the light that comes from it is bluer than it should be. For the vast majority of galaxies, however, the light they emit does experience a red shift, so the conclusion most astronomers made was that the vast majority of galaxies are moving away from the earth.

In 1929, the American astronomer Edwin Hubble noticed something rather interesting about the red shift. He noticed that the farther the galaxy is away from earth, the larger its red shift. Thus, light that comes from nearby galaxies has slightly larger wavelengths than expected, but the light that comes from very distant galaxies has *significantly* larger wavelengths than expected. As time has gone on, this result has been confirmed by many other observations. What does it mean? Well, astronomers interpret this to mean that the universe is actually expanding. Light that travels through the universe as it expands would get stretched, because it would have to expand with the universe. Thus, if light has been traveling through the universe for a long time (from more distant objects) it would be stretched more than light that had been traveling through the universe for a short time. According to this interpretation, then, the red shift is not the result of the Doppler effect. Instead, it is the result of the fact that the universe is expanding. Thus, most astronomers think the universe is expanding.

Now if the universe is expanding, it could be doing so in many different ways. It could, for example, be expanding the way a balloon expands when it is blown up – it could be expanding away from a central point. If this is the case, then, the universe could be an ever-expanding sphere. However, that is not the way most astronomers think the universe is expanding. Most astronomers think the universe is expanding, but they do not think there is a fixed center. They think the universe is expanding without any specific geometry at all. To contrast these two views, perform the following experiment.

EXPERIMENT 16.1
An Expanding Universe

Supplies:

♦ Balloon
♦ A marker (You need to be able to write on the balloon with the marker.)

Introduction: There are many possible ways the universe could be expanding. This experiment contrasts two of them.

Procedure:

1. Lay the balloon flat on a table. Use the marker to put several dots all over the balloon, on both sides.
2. Bring the balloon to your mouth so that you can blow it up.
3. Hold the balloon so that you can see many of the dots.
4. Blow up the balloon. While you are doing that, notice how the dots move in relation to one another.

What did you see in the experiment? You should have seen that all the dots moved away from each other, regardless of where the dots were. In the minds of many astronomers, this experiment is actually an illustration of how the universe is expanding, but probably not in the way you think it is. According to most astronomers, the *surface* of the balloon (and *only* the surface) represents *all* of space. When you blow up the balloon, space (the surface of the balloon) begins to expand. Because space expands, all the galaxies move away from each other. However, there is no place on the balloon's surface you can point to and say, "Here is the point the surface of the balloon expands away from." Instead, the entire surface of the balloon expands, with no specific geometry. Believe it or not, this is how most astronomers think the universe is expanding.

Please realize that if the universe is expanding in this way, it means the universe *has no center*. Think about the surface of the balloon. If you put your finger on any of the dots and then begin to move your finger away from the dot while still touching the surface of the balloon, what would happen? You would eventually go all the way around the balloon, and your finger would reach the same dot at which you started. If you believe that the universe is expanding in this way, that has to be your view of space. In this view, space has no center. It is continuous, but like the surface of a balloon, continues to curve on itself so that it has no real beginning or end.

Of course, another way to envision the expansion of the universe is to think of the *air inside the balloon* as representing all of space. If you think of the universe expanding in that way, all the galaxies still move away from each other, but you can easily point to the very center of the balloon and say, "This is the point away from which the expansion is taking place." Although this is probably the *easiest* way to picture the expansion of the universe, it is not the way most astronomers think the expansion is actually happening.

In the end, then, there are two views of how the universe is expanding. On one hand, it might be expanding with a defined center and all the galaxies rushing away from the center. That is perfectly consistent with almost all the data we have. On the other hand, it might be expanding because, as space expands, it carries *all structures away from each other*, like the dots on the surface of your balloon. Once again, this is perfectly consistent with all the data we have. Finally, it might not be expanding at all. Remember, the expansion of the universe is the result of an *interpretation* of the red shift. It is possible that the interpretation is wrong!

Which of these three options is right? We don't really know. The vast majority of astronomers believe the universe is, indeed, expanding. I also think it is. Although there are other explanations for the red shift, the expansion of the universe seems to be the best one. The majority of astronomers not only believe the universe is expanding, but they also believe it is expanding without a center, like the surface of the balloon in the experiment. The problem is there is no *scientific* reason to choose that means of expansion over the other one I presented.

Why, then, do most astronomers believe in the former rather than the latter? The answer is *philosophical*, not scientific. Most astronomers do not want to believe there is anything special about any particular point in the universe. If the universe really is expanding around a central point, that central point would be very special from a universal point of view. Since most astronomers do not want to believe there is any special place in the universe, they will only consider the mode of expansion illustrated by the surface of the balloon in Experiment 16.1.

Astronomers who believe in God, however, can be a bit more open-minded. Since God created the universe, He might want it to have a special place. In fact, we know that the earth is special to God. Just as it needs a special sun, the earth might need a special position in the universe as a whole. If earth's solar system is the central point around which the universe expands, that would, indeed, be a special place.

Does it really matter which way the universe is expanding? Actually, it does. A creation scientist by the name of Russell Humphreys wrote a book entitled *Starlight and Time*. The details of this book are well beyond the scope of this course, but you might consider reading it at some point. In this book, he develops an entire theory for the formation of the universe predicated on the assumption that the earth's solar system is at the center of the universe, and the universe is expanding around that point.

One of the really neat things about Dr. Humphreys' theory is that it uses Einstein's General Theory of Relativity to explain an age-old mystery that has puzzled creation scientists for years. A large number of creation scientists (myself included) think that the earth is only a few thousand years old. The vast majority of data in science, in our opinion, is consistent with such an assumption. At the same time, the vast majority of data is inconsistent with the idea that the earth is billions of years old. Thus, a large number of creation scientists believe that God formed the universe and the earth only a few thousand years ago.

If that is the case, however, there seems to be a problem. We can observe stars that are billions of light years away from us. If creation happened only a few thousand years ago, how can we be seeing light from those stars? It would take billions of years for the light to get here. Well, Dr. Humphreys' theory explains this "problem." Using the standard theories and tools that all other astrophysicists use, Dr. Humphreys shows that if the universe is expanding with the earth's solar system as its center, creation could have happened only a few thousand years ago, and we would still be able to see light that took billions of years to travel here!

As I said before, the details of Dr. Humphreys' theory are beyond the scope of this course. However, the point I want to make is rather simple. The majority of scientists believe in a theory called the "big bang." This theory assumes that the universe is expanding, but it assumes that the expansion takes place without a center. This theory concludes that the universe is the result of random chance and is billions of years old. Dr. Humphreys' theory tells us that if we assume the universe is expanding with earth's solar system as its center, the universe need not be the result of random chance, and it need not be billions of years old.

Which theory is right? We do not know. For all we know, they are both wrong! However, we do know that the only real difference between them is a *philosophical* assumption. If you assume one way, you get one theory. If you assume another way, you get another theory. From a scientific point of view, both assumptions are absolutely equal.

Now whether the universe is expanding around a fixed center, with no center at all, or in some other way I did not discuss, the vast majority of astronomers think that it is, indeed, expanding. This is interesting, because although *science* has only been seriously considering such an idea for a hundred years or so, *The Bible* has always indicated that the universe is expanding. For example, Job 9:5-8 says, "It is God who removes the mountains, they know not how…Who alone stretches out the heavens…" In addition, Psalm 104:1-2 says, "Bless the LORD, O my soul! O LORD my God, You are very great; You are clothed with splendor and majesty, covering Yourself with light as with a cloak, stretching out heaven like a tent curtain." In both of these verses, the Bible mentions that God is *stretching* out the heavens. In other words, it has taken human science a couple of thousand years to conclude what the Bible has always said – the universe is expanding!

ON YOUR OWN

16.10 Assume that the universe is expanding, with earth's solar system as its center. Suppose you were in a galaxy other than that of earth. Would you still see a red shift from all the other galaxies in the universe? Why or why not?

Summing It All Up

Well, you have come to the end of your physical science course. I hope you have enjoyed it. More importantly, however, I hope that you have learned something. I hope that you have come to a deeper appreciation for the ingenuity and creative genius of God. Over and over again in this course, you learned about processes in creation that are simply too complex and too well designed to have occured by chance. I hope that, in some cases, you have been filled with awe. The Bible says, "The heavens are telling of the glory of God; and their expanse is declaring the work of His hands" (Psalm 19:1). Anyone who studies science honestly and in a reasonably unbiased manner should easily come to that same conclusion!

ANSWERS TO THE "ON YOUR OWN" PROBLEMS

16.1 <u>As time goes on, the composition will change. The amount of hydrogen will decrease and the amount of helium will increase.</u> Remember, nuclear fusion gives the sun its power. That very process takes hydrogen and converts it to helium. As time goes on, then, hydrogen will be used up and helium will be produced.

16.2 <u>The photosphere has the lowest temperature.</u> The core is the hottest because that's where all the energy is being produced. As the energy travels into the outer regions of the sun, it gets more spread out. Thus, each layer of the sun is cooler than the layer underneath. Since the photosphere is at the top, it is the coolest, because the energy is least concentrated there.

16.3 <u>This is nuclear fusion.</u> Two small nuclei (^{7}Li has three protons and four neutrons) join to make a big nucleus (^{12}C has six neutrons and six protons). If it were fission, a large nucleus would be broken down into smaller nuclei.

16.4 <u>This would eliminate the worry of meltdown in a nuclear power plant, because there could be no chain reaction.</u> Remember, the nuclear fission process can go out of control because *one* fission process can start *several* other fission processes. This can cause the reaction to grow and grow until it is out of control. If *one* fission process can start *only one additional* fission process, the fission process would be sustained, but it could never grow. Based on our understanding of nuclear fission at this time, however, such a fission process is thought to be impossible.

16.5 If the magnitude is 5 and the spectral letter is "F," it falls somewhere on the thick bar in the H-R Diagram below:

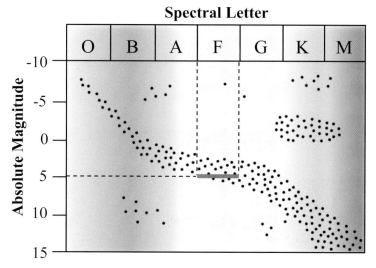

Any point on that bar is clearly in the main sequence portion of the H-R Diagram, so this is a <u>main sequence</u> star.

16.6 With a magnitude of 10 and a spectral letter of "K," this star falls somewhere on the thick line shown in the H-R Diagram:

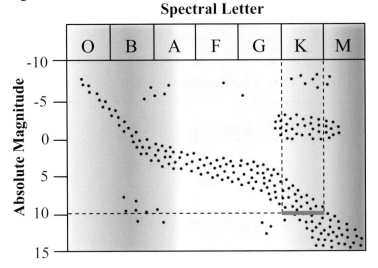

Thus, this is a main-sequence star. Both stars, then, are main sequence stars. For main sequence stars, there is a direct dependence between mass and magnitude. The brighter the star, the more massive. Since a smaller magnitude means a large brightness, the star in 16.5 is more massive than the star in this problem.

16.7 If you look on the H-R Diagram, the white dwarf group is farther to the left than the red giant group. Since temperature increases as you move to the left on an H-R Diagram, red giants are cooler than most white dwarfs.

16.8 Pulsating variables last the longest. Supernovas brighten just once and then disappear forever. Novas can brighten several times, but they lose mass each time. Thus, they eventually go away as well. Pulsating variables do not lose mass when they brighten. Thus, they can exist for a long time.

16.9 The parallax method is the most reliable. It is the direct result of geometry. The apparent magnitude method makes an assumption. It assumes that the magnitude/period relationship that exists for Cepheid variables near the earth is correct for *all* such stars. That's *probably* a good assumption, but there is no way to check it!

16.10 You would still see a red shift from the other galaxies. Think about it. If the universe is expanding outward, then all objects are moving away from each other.   Consider the following picture:

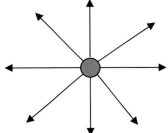

If the circle is the earth's solar system, all galaxies would be moving away from the earth along the arrows. Notice that the arrows get farther and farther from each other. Thus, the space between the galaxies would be expanding, which would still cause a red shift.

STUDY GUIDE FOR MODULE #16

1. Define the following terms:

a. Nuclear fusion
b. Nuclear fission
c. Critical mass

d. Absolute magnitude
e. Apparent magnitude
f. Light year

g. Galaxy

2. From the inside to the outside, name the four regions of the sun.

3. How does the sun get its power? In which region of the sun does this process occur?

4. What part of the sun do we see?

5. A ^{251}Cf nucleus is bombarded with a neutron. It breaks down into a ^{124}Sn nucleus, a ^{120}Cd nucleus and seven neutrons. Is this nuclear fission or nuclear fusion?

6. Two ^{4}He nuclei collide and turn into a ^{7}Be nucleus and one neutron. Is this nuclear fusion or nuclear fission?

7. For both the nuclear fusion that occurs in the sun and the nuclear fission that occurs in a nuclear power plant, what can we say about the mass of the starting materials compared to the mass of what's made in the end?

8. Why is it impossible for a nuclear power plant to have a nuclear explosion?

9. Why is nuclear fusion considered a better option for energy production than nuclear fission?

10. If nuclear fusion is a better option, why don't we use it?

11. Using the H-R Diagram below, classify the following stars:

a. Magnitude -1, Spectral Letter K
b. Magnitude 0, Spectral Letter B

c. Magnitude -7, Spectral Letter F
d. Magnitude 11, Spectral Letter B

Spectral Letter

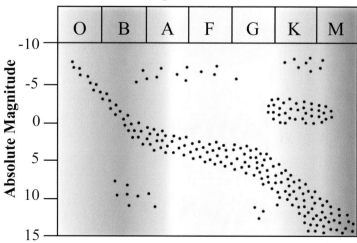

12. Which of the stars in #11 is most like our sun?

13. Order the four stars in #11 in terms of increasing size.

14. Order the four stars in #11 in terms of increasing brightness.

15. Which of the stars in #11 is the coolest?

16. What similarity exists between novas, supernovas, and pulsating variables?

17. What is the big difference between novas, supernovas, and pulsating variables?

18. What most likely formed the crab nebula?

19. What are the two methods for measuring the distance from earth to a star? Which of the two is the most accurate? Which can be used to measure long distances?

20. Why are Cepheid variables so important for measuring long distances in the universe?

21. What are the four basic types of galaxies? To which type does the Milky Way belong?

22. Fill in the blanks: Stars group together to form _____, which group together to form _____, which group together to form _____, some of which group together to form _____.

23. For the first three answers you gave in #22, give the names that apply to those in which earth's solar system belongs.

24. Why do most astronomers believe the universe is expanding?

25. If the universe is expanding, does the geometry of the expansion matter? If so, why?

My Favorite Astronomy Joke

Sherlock Holmes and his faithful companion Dr. Watson go on a camping trip. They find a beautiful spot and set up their tent. After a full day of enjoying nature, they go into their tent and fall asleep. Some hours later, Holmes wakes Dr. Watson and says, "Look up at the sky and tell me what you see." Watson is awestruck. After a moment, he says, "I see countless stars." Mr. Holmes replies, "What does that tell you?" Watson considers for a moment and says, "It tells me that the universe is vast, and it will probably take us several lifetimes to gain even a small amount of understanding as to how it functions and what our place is in it." Mr. Holmes asks, "Anything else?" Mr. Watson thinks for a moment and says, "Based on the position of the stars, I would say it is approximately two o'clock in the morning." Once again, Mr. Holmes asks, "Anything else?" Desperate now, Watson replies, "Because the sky is so clear, we will probably have a beautiful day tomorrow." Once again, Mr. Holmes asks, "Anything else?" Frustrated, Mr. Watson says, "I can't think of anything else. What does it tell you?" Holmes is silent for a moment and then says, "Elementary, my dear Watson. Someone has stolen our tent."

GLOSSARY

The numbers in parentheses indicate the page number where the term was first discussed.

Absolute humidity: The mass of water vapor contained in a certain volume of air (27)

Absolute magnitude: The brightness of a star, corrected for distance, on a scale of -8 to +19. The *smaller* the number, the *brighter* the star. (406)

Acceleration: The time rate of change of an object's velocity (214)

Additive primary colors: The colors red, green, and blue, which can be added in different proportions to form any other color (390)

Adiabatic cooling: The cooling of a gas that happens when the gas expands with no way of getting more energy (124)

Air mass: A large body of air with relatively uniform pressure, temperature, and humidity (172)

Air Resistance: Friction between an object and the molecules of air through which it moves (64)

Alpha decay: The process by which a radioactive isotope changes by emitting a ^{4}He nucleus (328)

Aphelion: The point at which the earth is farthest from the sun (163)

Apparent magnitude: The brightness of a star as seen in the night sky. The *smaller* the number, the *brighter* the star. (406)

Asteroid belt: A band of asteroids that orbit the sun between the orbits of Mars and Jupiter (266)

Asthenosphere: A layer of plastic rock just below the lithosphere (136)

Atmosphere: The mass of air surrounding a planet (55)

Atmospheric pressure: The pressure exerted by the atmosphere on all objects within it (55)

Atom: The smallest chemical unit of matter (3)

Atomic number: The number of protons in an atom (317)

Aurora: An atmospheric phenomenon that appears as glowing regions of brilliant colors that move in the sky (74)

Barometer: An instrument used to measure atmospheric pressure (59)

Bel scale: A scale that measures the volume of a sound. Each bel represents a ten-fold increase in the sound's intensity (359)

Beta decay: The process by which a radioactive isotope changes by allowing a neutron to decay into a proton, beta particle, and an antineutrino (327)

Bohr Model: A model of the atom in which the protons and neutrons are in the center of the atom (the nucleus), and the electrons orbit the nucleus in fixed, circular paths (314)

Brine: A concentrated solution of saltwater (118)

CAFE standards: Government standards that regulate the average number of miles an automobile can travel on a single gallon of gasoline (48)

Calving: The process by which a portion of a glacier breaks off and begins floating in the sea as an iceberg (119)

Catalytic converter: A term commonly used to refer to the device that converts carbon monoxide in the exhaust of an automobile into carbon dioxide (48)

Celsius temperature scale: The temperature scale in which water boils at 100 degrees and freezes at 0 degrees (17)

Centrifugal force: A fictional force that is actually the result of an object's inertia when the object is forced to move in a curve. (263)

Centripetal force: The force necessary to make an object move in a circle. It is directed perpendicular to the velocity of the object, which means it points towards the center of the circle (361)

Chain reaction: A self-sustaining set of nuclear reactions in which neutrons produced by nuclear fission cause more nuclear fission (402)

Charging by conduction: Charging an object by allowing it to come into contact with an object that already has an electrical charge (294)

Charging by induction: Charging an object without direct contact between the object and a charge (294)

Chemical formula: A representation of a molecule that shows the number and type of atoms that make up the molecule (85)

Climate: A steady condition that prevails day in and day out in a particular region of the earth (157)

Cloud condensation nuclei: Small airborne particles upon which water vapor condenses to form clouds (124)

Cohesion: The phenomenon that occurs when individual molecules are so strongly attracted to each other that they tend to stay together, even when exposed to tension (97)

Combustion: A chemical process by which oxygen reacts with a fuel to release energy (29)

Comet: A relatively small, frozen body that travels around the sun, typically in a highly elliptical orbit (269)

Compound: A substance composed of only one type of molecule (5)

Concentration: The quantity of a substance within a certain volume (17)

Condensation: The process by which a gas turns into a liquid (109)

Conventional current: Current that flows from the positive side of the battery to the negative side. This is the way current is drawn in circuit diagrams, even though it is wrong. (298)

Converging lens: A lens that bends light so that horizontally traveling rays are focused to a single point (384)

Coriolis effect: The way in which the rotation of the earth bends the path of winds, sea currents, and objects that fly through different latitudes (169)

Cosmic rays: High-energy radiation originating outside earth's atmosphere (144)

Cost/benefit analysis: An analysis by which the potential benefits of a proposed action are weighed against the potential costs. Typically, an action is desirable if the benefits are higher than the costs. (49)

Critical mass: The amount of isotope necessary to sustain a chain reaction (402)

Dew point: The temperature at which dew forms (183)

Distillation: Evaporation and condensation of a mixture to separate out the mixture's individual components (111)

Diverging lens: A lens that bends light so that horizontally traveling rays are focused away from a single point (385)

Doppler Effect: A motion-induced change in the observed frequency of a wave (355)

Earth's crust: Earth's outermost layer of rock (132)

Earthquake: Vibration of the earth that results either from volcanic activity or rock masses suddenly moving along a fault (148)

Ecosystem: A community of organisms, along with their environment, functioning as a unit (39)

Electrical current: The amount of charge that travels past a fixed point in an electric circuit each second (296)

Electrolysis: The use of electricity to break a molecule down into smaller units (81)

Electromagnetic force: The attraction or repulsion between charged particles or magnetic poles (255)

Electromagnetic wave: A transverse wave composed of an oscillating electric field and a magnetic field that oscillates perpendicular to the electric field (368)

Element: A collection of atoms that all have the same number of protons (5)

Epicenter: The point on the surface of the earth directly above an earthquake's focus (150)

Equator: An imaginary circle around the earth halfway between the north and south poles (163)

Evaporation: The process by which a liquid turns into a gas (25)

Exosphere: The region of the atmosphere above an altitude of roughly 460 kilometers (73)

Experimental error: Experimental difficulties that can cause the results to be incorrect (83)

Factor-label method: A method for converting from one unit or system to another unit or system that involves multiplying fractions (12)

Fahrenheit temperature scale: The temperature scale in which water boils at 212 degrees and freezes at 32 degrees (17)

Fault: The boundary between two sections of rock that can move relative to one another (148)

Firn: A dense, icy pack of old snow (118)

Focus: The point where an earthquake begins (150)

Fog: Condensed water in cloudlike masses near the surface of the earth (124)

Force: A push or pull exerted on an object in an effort to change that object's velocity (241)

Free fall: The motion of an object when it is falling solely under the influence of gravity (218)

Friction: A force that opposes motion, resulting from the contact of two surfaces (240)

Frost point: The temperature at which frost forms (183)

Galaxy: A large ensemble of stars, all interacting through the gravitational force and orbiting around a common center (413)

Gamma decay: The process by which an isotope loses energy by emitting a gamma ray (329)

Geocentric solar system: The view that the planets in the solar system orbit the earth, which is at the center (278)

Glacier: A huge mass of ice formed by compacted snow that slowly flows over land (116)

Global warming: The fear that the greenhouse effect might run out of control, heating the entire earth (35)

Gradient: A gradual change (63)

Gravitational force: The attraction between objects due to their mass (255)

Greenhouse effect: The process by which certain gases (principally water vapor, carbon dioxide, and methane) trap heat that radiates from earth (33)

Greenhouse gas: A gas that traps infrared light as it leaves earth's surface, warming the atmosphere (33)

Groundwater: Water that is held in the soil and rocks (107)

Half-life: The time it takes for half of the original sample of a radioactive isotope to decay (332)

Hard water - Water that has certain dissolved ions in it – predominately calcium and magnesium ions (101)

Heat index: A measurement of the air temperature in relation to the relative humidity, used as an indicator of the perceived temperature (26)

Heat: Energy that is transferred as a consequence of temperature differences (67)

Heliocentric solar system: The view that the planets in the solar system orbit the sun, which is at the center (279)

Heterosphere: The upper layer of earth's atmosphere, which exists higher than roughly 80 kilometers (50 miles) above sea level (60)

Homosphere: The lower layer of earth's atmosphere, which exists from ground level to roughly 80 kilometers (50 miles) above sea level (60)

Humidity: The moisture content of air (25)

Hydrogen Bond: A weak bond between a hydrogen atom in one molecule and another atom (principally oxygen, nitrogen, or fluorine) in another molecule (93)

Hydrologic cycle: The process by which water is continuously exchanged between earth's various water sources (107)

Hydrosphere: The sum of all water on a planet (106)

Ice shelf: A mass of ice that is attached to land and projects out onto the sea (119)

Iceberg: A floating mass of ice broken from a glacier (116)

Igneous rock: Rock that forms from molten rock (133)

Incomplete combustion: Combustion in which not enough oxygen is supplied to completely burn the fuel. Carbon monoxide is a common product. (48)

Inertia: The tendency of an object to resist changes in its velocity (232)

Infrared light: Electromagnetic radiation with energy lower than visible light but higher than microwaves (42)

Infrasonic waves: Waves with frequencies lower than can be detected by the typical human ear (below 20 Hz) (355)

Insulator: A substance that does not conduct electricity very well (187)

Ion: An atom that has lost or gained electrons so it has a net electrical charge (74)

Ionosphere: The region of the atmosphere between the altitudes of roughly 65 kilometers and 330 kilometers, where the gases are ionized (74)

Isobar: A line representing equal atmospheric pressure on a weather map (196)

Isotherm: A line representing equal temperature on a weather map (197)

Isotopes: Atoms with the same number of protons but different numbers of neutrons (319)

Jet streams: Narrow bands of high-speed winds that circle the earth, blowing from west to east (64)

Kinetic friction: Friction that opposes motion once the motion has already started (244)

Lava: Magma that flows out of a volcano (133)

Law of Reflection: The angle of reflection equals the angle of incidence (376)

Light year: The distance light could travel along a straight line in one year (412)

Lines of latitude: Imaginary lines that run east and west across the earth (165)

Lines of longitude: Imaginary lines that run north and south across the earth (165)

Lithosphere: The combination of earth's crust and the region of the mantle above the asthenosphere (136)

Longitudinal wave: A wave with a direction of propagation that is parallel to its direction of oscillation (343)

Magma: Hot, liquid rock (133)

Mass number: The sum of the numbers of neutrons and protons in the nucleus of an atom (318)

Mesopause: The boundary between the mesosphere and the heterosphere (62)

Mesosphere: The region of the atmosphere that spans altitudes of roughly 48 kilometers to 80 kilometers (50 miles) (62)

Metamorphic rock: Igneous or sedimentary rock that has been changed into a new kind of rock as a result of great pressure and temperature (133)

Meteor: A bright trail appearing in the sky when a meteoroid enters earth's atmosphere and is heated by friction (64)

Meteorite: Any part of a meteoroid that lands on the surface of Earth (268)

Meteoroid: An interplanetary piece of matter that has intersected earth's orbit (268)

Mixture: A substance that contains different compounds and/or elements (6)

Model: A schematic description of a system that accounts for its known properties (314)

Molecule: Two or more atoms linked together to make a substance with unique properties (4)

Newton's First Law: An object in motion (or at rest) will tend to stay in motion (or at rest) until it is acted upon by an outside force (230)

Newton's Second Law: When an object is acted on by one or more outside forces, the total force is equal to the mass of the object times the resulting acceleration (241)

Newton's Third Law: For every action, there is an equal and opposite reaction. (246)

Nonpolar molecule: A molecule in which electrons are shared evenly enough so that there are no appreciable electrical charges in the molecule (89)

Nuclear fission: The process by which a large nucleus is split into smaller nuclei (401)

Nuclear force: The force that holds protons and neutrons together in the nucleus. It is a manifestation of the strong force. (325)

Nuclear fusion: The process by which two or more small nuclei fuse to make a bigger nucleus (401)

Nucleus: The center of an atom, containing the protons and neutrons (315)

Open circuit: A circuit that does not have a complete connection between the two sides of the power source. As a result, current does not flow. (302)

Ozone layer: The portion of the stratosphere (20 to 30 kilometers above sea level) containing sufficient ozone to block most of the ultraviolet light from the sun (44)

Ozone: A poisonous gas composed of three oxygen atoms bonded together (42)

Parts per million: The number of molecules (or atoms) of a substance in a mixture for every 1 million molecules (or atoms) in that mixture (41)

Peer review: The process through which scientists review the work of other scientists in an attempt to spot experimental error (84)

Percolation: The process by which water moves downward in the soil, toward the water table (121)

Perihelion: The point at which the earth is closest to the sun (163)

Photon: A small "package" of light that acts like a particle (290)

Pitch: An indication of how high or low a sound is, which is primarily determined by the frequency of the sound wave (354)

Plastic rock: Rock that behaves like something between a liquid and a solid (136)

Plate Tectonics: The theory that earth's lithosphere is divided into large plates that move on the asthenosphere (144)

Polar molecule: A molecule that has slight positive and negative charges due to an imbalance in the way electrons are shared (88)

Polar vortex: Cyclonic circulation in the troposphere centered in the polar regions. (71)

Precipitation: Water falling from the atmosphere as rain, snow, sleet, or hail (109)

Pressure freezing: The phenomenon by which a liquid turns into a solid due to high pressure (138)

Prime Meridian: An imaginary line used as a reference in longitude that runs north to south through Greenwich, England (166)

Radar: Short for "radio detection and ranging," it sends out microwave signals and records the returned signals' strength and time of arrival (194)

Radioactive isotope: An atom with a nucleus that is not stable (327)

Reference point: A point against which position is measured (205)

Refraction: The bending of light as it passes from one medium to another (377)

Relative humidity: The ratio of the mass of water vapor in the air at a given temperature to the maximum mass of water vapor the air could hold at that temperature, expressed as a percentage. (27)

Residence time: The average time a given particle will stay in a given system (112)

Resistance: The ability of a material to impede the flow of charge (300)

Return stroke: An electric current of positive charges that flows up from the ground to a cloud during a lightning flash (189)

Richter scale: Scale that measures the energy of an earthquake. Each step on the Richter scale represents a factor of 32 increase in the earthquake's energy (150)

Salinity: A measure of the mass of dissolved salt in a given mass of water (114)

Scalar quantity: A physical measurement that does not contain directional information (209)

Sediment: Small, solid fragments of rock and other materials that are carried and deposited by wind, water, or ice. Examples would be sand, mud, or gravel (132)

Sedimentary rock: Rock formed when chemical reactions cement sediments together, hardening them (133)

Seismic wave: A wave that travels through the earth, often as the result of an earthquake (135)

Seismograph: An instrument that measures and records seismic waves (135)

Seismology: The study of earthquakes and their effects (150)

Solar system: The sun and the all bodies that orbit it. (260)

Solute: A substance that is dissolved in a solvent (90)

Solvent: A liquid substance capable of dissolving other substances (90)

Sonar: Short for sound navigation and ranging, it is the process of using sound waves to determining the distance and nature of objects (362)

Sonic boom: The sound produced as a result of an object traveling at or above Mach 1 (352)

Sonic waves: Waves with frequencies that can be detected by the typical human ear (20 Hz to 20,000 Hz) (355)

Speed: The rate at which an object travels over a distance (206)

Static friction: Friction that opposes the initiation of motion (244)

Stepped leader: A faint stream of negative charges that emerges from the base of a thundercloud and moves toward the ground (189)

Stratopause: The boundary between the stratosphere and the mesosphere (62)

Stratosphere: The region of the atmosphere that spans altitudes of roughly 11 kilometers to 48 kilometers (30 miles) (62)

Strong force: The attraction that operates at very short range, binding together the constituents of nuclei, as well as neutrons and protons (255)

Subtractive primary colors: The colors cyan, magenta, and yellow, which are used in inks and dyes to form any other color (391)

Supersonic speed: Any speed that is faster than the speed of sound in the substance of interest (351)

Temperature: A measure of the energy of random motion in a substance's molecules (68)

Thermosphere: The region of the atmosphere between altitudes of roughly 80 kilometers and 460 kilometers (73)

Transpiration: Evaporation of water from plants (108)

Transverse wave: A wave with a direction of propagation that is perpendicular to its direction of oscillation (343)

Tropopause: The boundary between the troposphere and the stratosphere (62)

Troposphere: The region of the atmosphere that extends from ground level to roughly 11 kilometers (7 miles) above sea level (62)

Tsunami: An ocean wave caused by violent activity (150)

Ultrasonic waves: Waves with frequencies higher than can be detected by the typical human ear (above 20,000 Hz) (355)

Ultraviolet light: Electromagnetic radiation with energy higher than visible light but lower than X-rays (43)

Updraft: A current of rising air (184)

Vector quantity: A physical measurement that contains directional information (209)

Velocity: The rate at which an object's positive relative to a reference point changes (208)

Visible spectrum: The collection of electromagnetic waves with wavelengths that can be detected by the typical human eye (372)

Water table: The line between the water-saturated soil and the soil that is not saturated with water (121)

Weak force: The force that causes unstable subatomic particles (like neutrons) to decay (255)

Weather front: A boundary between two air masses (173)

APPENDIX A

Seasons in the Southern Hemisphere

If you live in the Southern Hemisphere, the seasons are opposite those in the Northern Hemisphere. As a result, some of the terminology used in my discussions of seasons is slightly different. First, I want to show you Figure 7.3 using Southern Hemisphere terminology:

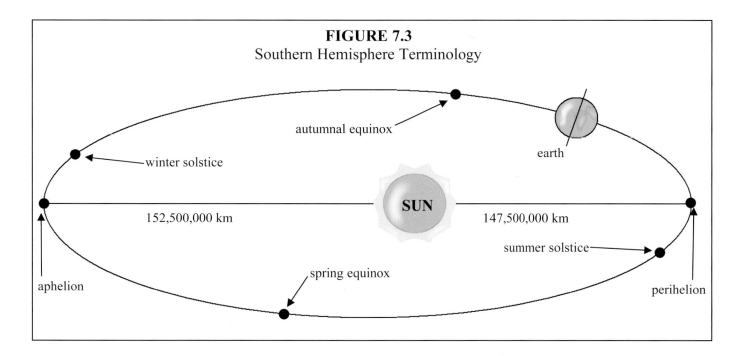

FIGURE 7.3
Southern Hemisphere Terminology

So what's different from the original figure? Notice the names of the equinoxes and solstices. They have changed relative to the original figure. Since it is summer in the Southern Hemisphere during December, it makes no sense to call the solstice that happens on December 21 or 22 the "winter solstice." Thus, that solstice is called the **summer solstice** in the Southern Hemisphere. In the same way, the solstice that occurs on June 21 or 22 is called the **winter solstice**, because it is winter in the Southern Hemisphere at that time. Of course, this means the equinoxes must be reversed as well. Thus, the **spring equinox** occurs on September 22 or 23 in the Southern Hemisphere, because spring falls between winter and summer. Similarly, the **autumnal equinox** occurs on March 20 or 21 in the Southern Hemisphere, because autumn comes between summer and winter.

Because the names of the solstices and equinoxes are different between the hemispheres, many scientists use for their names the month in which they occur. Thus, the summer solstice in the Southern Hemisphere is just called the "December solstice." That way, its name is the same regardless of the hemisphere in which you live. In the same way, the winter solstice would be called the "June solstice," the spring equinox would be called the "September equinox," and the autumnal equinox would be called the "March equinox." Although it makes perfect sense, you rarely see this terminology in high school textbooks.

TABLE 1.1
Physical Quantities and Their Base Units

Physical Quantity	Base Metric Unit	Base English Unit
Mass	gram (g)	slug (sl)
Distance	meter (m)	foot (ft)
Volume	liter (L)	gallon (gal)
Time	second (s)	second (s)

TABLE 1.2
Common Prefixes Used in the Metric System

PREFIX	NUMERICAL MEANING
micro (μ)	0.000001
milli (m)	**0.001**
centi (c)	**0.01**
deci (d)	0.1
deca (D)	10
hecta (H)	100
kilo (k)	**1,000**
Mega (M)	1,000,000

TABLE 1.3
Relationships Between English and Metric Units

Measurement	English/Metric Relationship
Distance	1 inch = 2.54 cm
Mass	1 slug = 14.59 kg
Volume	1 gallon = 3.78 L

Inhaled Air Compared to Exhaled Air

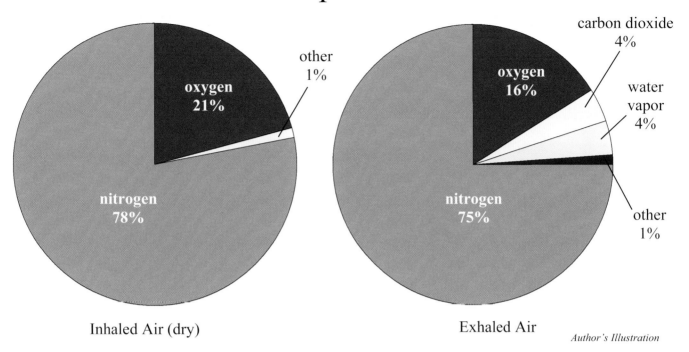

Inhaled Air (dry)   Exhaled Air

Author's Illustration

Carbon Dioxide Levels and Average Global Temperatures

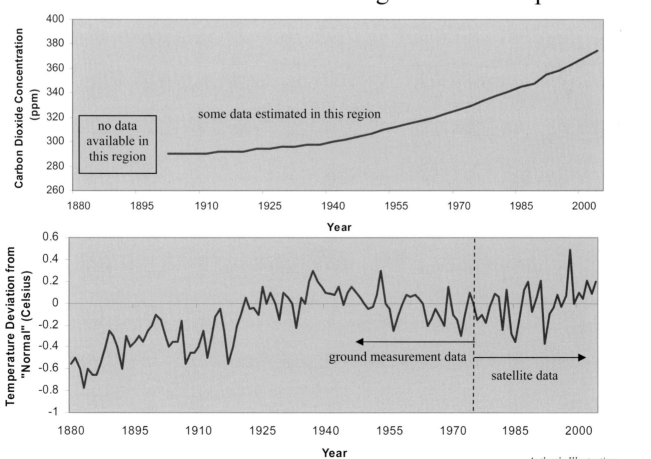

Author's Illustration

Air Pollution Levels in 1975 and 2002

Year	Airborne Lead (μg per cubic meter)	Sulfur Oxides (ppm)	Carbon Monoxide (ppm)	Ground-Level Ozone (ppm)	Nitrogen Oxides (ppm)
1975	0.68	0.0132	10	0.147	0.021
2002	0.02	0.0040	3	0.110	0.018

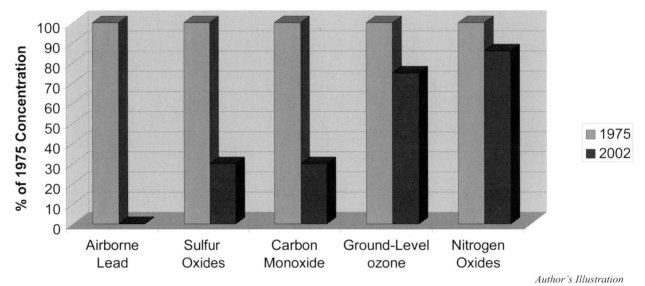

Author's Illustration

The Homosphere and the Heterosphere

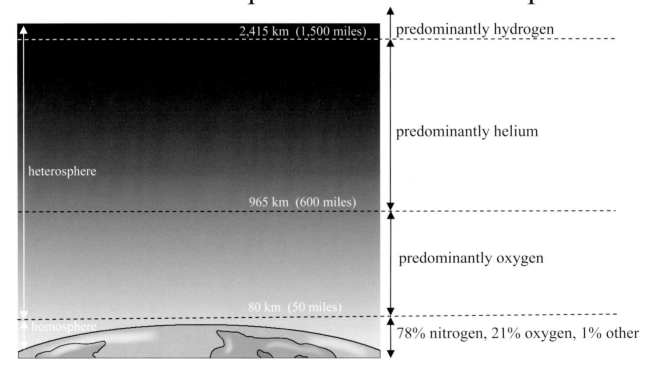

The Homosphere

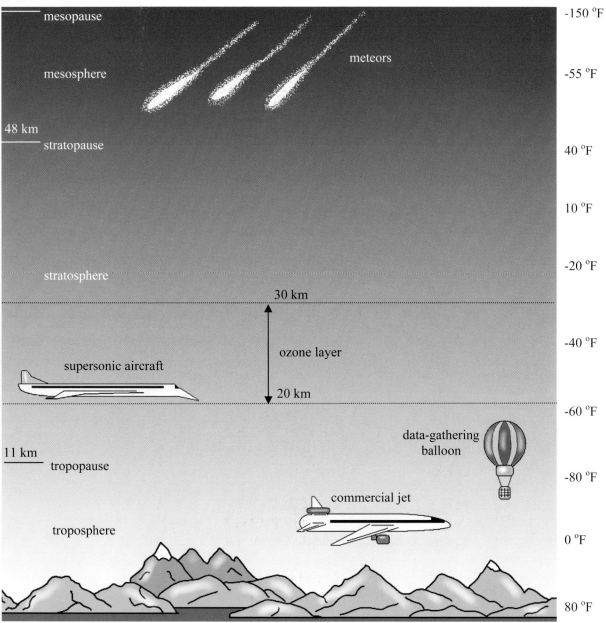

Earth's Atmosphere

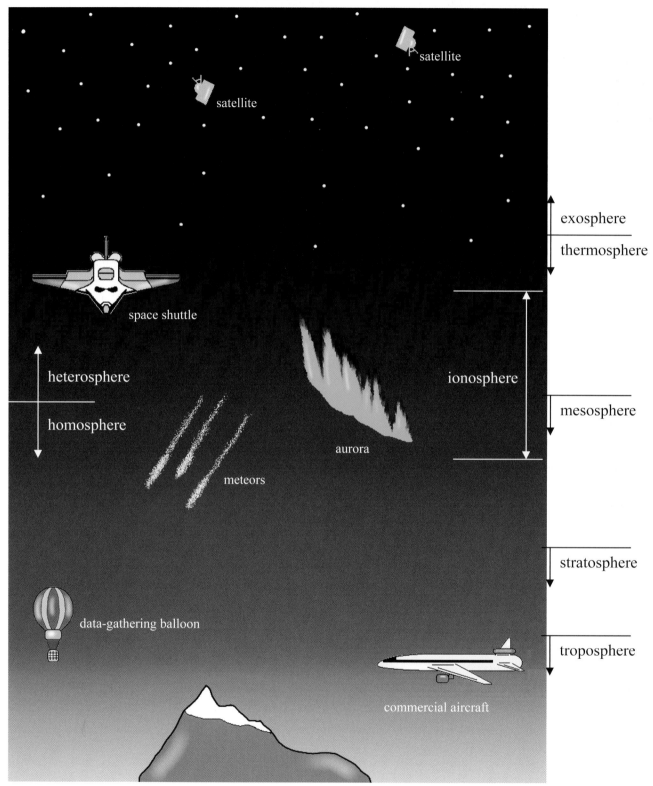

NOTE: In order to show all parts of the atmosphere, this drawing is not to scale.

TABLE 5.1
Water Sources in the Hydrosphere

Water Source	Type of Water	Percent of Hydrosphere
Oceans	saltwater	97.250%
Glaciers and Icebergs	freshwater	2.050%
Groundwater	freshwater	0.685%
Surface Water (not oceans)	mostly freshwater	0.009%
Soil Moisture	freshwater	0.005%
Atmospheric Moisture	freshwater	0.001%

The Hydrologic Cycle

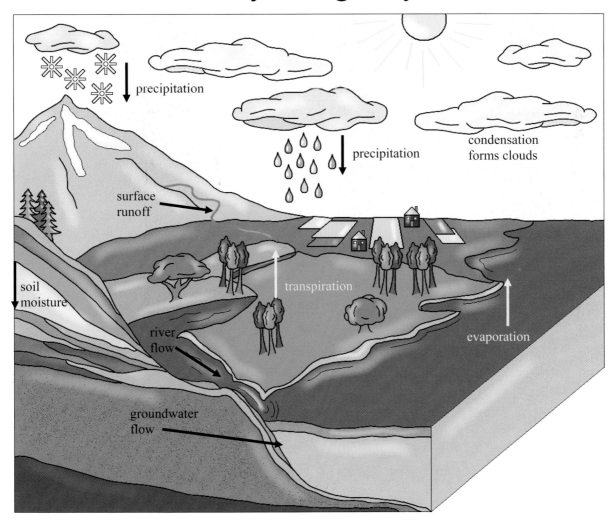

TABLE 5.2
Residence Times for Different Water Sources

Water Source	Residence Time		Water Source	Residence Time
Ocean	4,000 years		Atmosphere	10 days
Glaciers and Icebergs	1,000 years		Lakes	10 years
Groundwater	2 weeks - 1,000 years		Rivers	2 weeks
Soil moisture	2 weeks - 1 year		Swamps	1 - 10 years

The Crust, Mantle, and Core of the Earth

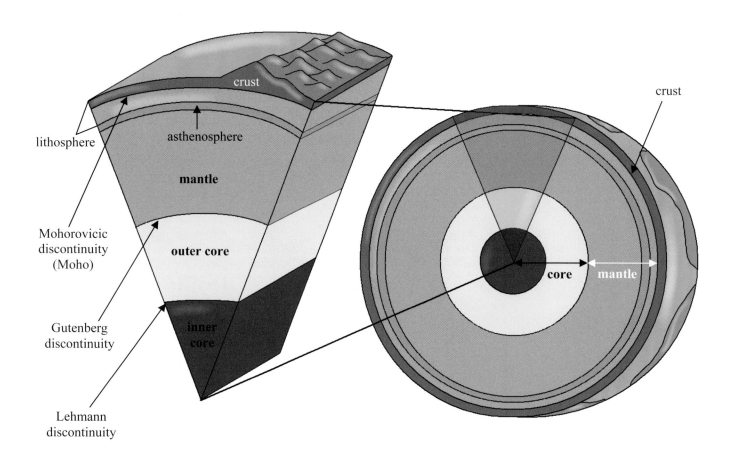

A Summary of Cloud Types

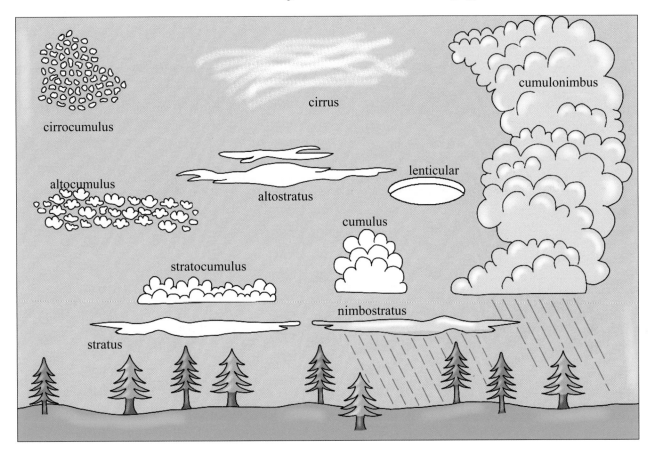

Seasons in the Northern Hemisphere

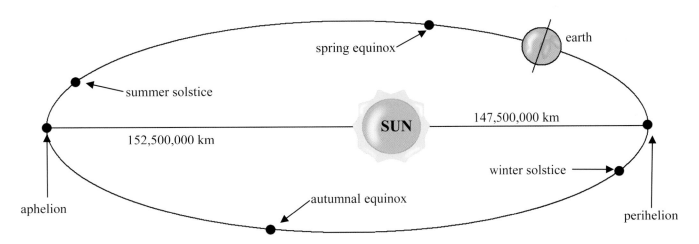

Lines of Latitude and Longitude

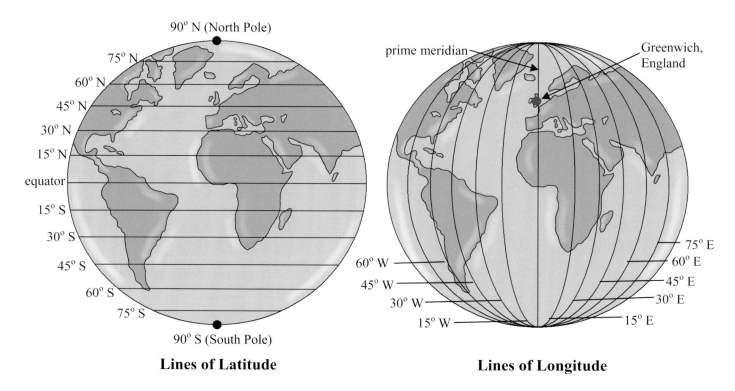

Lines of Latitude   **Lines of Longitude**

Winds in the Earth's Lower Troposphere

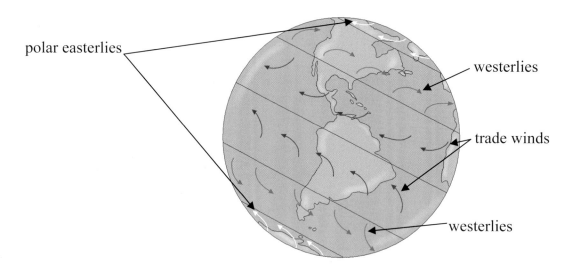

Equations Used in This Course

9.1: $\text{speed} = \dfrac{\text{distance traveled}}{\text{time traveled}}$

9.2: $\text{acceleration} = \dfrac{\text{final velocity} - \text{initial velocity}}{\text{time}}$

9.3: $\text{distance} = \dfrac{1}{2} \times (\text{acceleration}) \times (\text{time})^2$

10.1: $\text{total force} = (\text{mass}) \cdot (\text{acceleration})$

14.1: $f = \dfrac{v}{\lambda}$

14.2: $v = (331.5 + 0.6 \cdot T)\dfrac{m}{\text{sec}}$

Newton's Three Laws of Motion

Newton's First Law – An object in motion (or at rest) will tend to stay in motion (or at rest) until it is acted upon by an outside force.

Newton's Second Law – When an object is acted on by one or more outside forces, the total force is equal to the mass of the object times the resulting acceleration.

Newton's Third Law – For every action, there is an equal and opposite reaction.

Newton's Universal Law of Gravitation

1. All objects with mass are attracted to one another by the gravitational force.

2. The gravitational force between two masses is directly proportional to the mass of each object.

3. The gravitational force between two masses is inversely proportional to the square of the distance between those two objects.

Properties of Centripetal Force

1. Circular motion requires centripetal force.

2. The larger the centripetal force, the faster an object travels in a circle of a given size.

3. At a given speed, the larger the centripetal force, the smaller the circle.

Properties of the Electromagnetic Force

1. All electrical charges attract or repel one another: like charges repel, while opposite charges attract.

2. The force between charged objects is directly proportional to the amount of electrical charge on each object.

3. The force between charged objects is inversely proportional to the square of the distance between the two objects.

TABLE 13.1
Maximum Number of Electrons in Each Bohr Orbit

Bohr Orbit	Electron Capacity
1	2
2	8
3	18
4	32
5	50

TABLE 14.1
The Speed of Sound in Certain Substances

Substance	Speed of Sound	Substance	Speed of Sound
Air (25 °C)	346 m/sec	Steel	5029 m/sec
Alcohol	1186 m/sec	Aluminum	5093 m/sec
Fresh Water	1435 m/sec	Iron	5128 m/sec
Wood (oak)	3848 m/sec	Glass	5503 m/sec

TABLE 14.2
The Loudness of Some Common Sounds

Sound	Decibels	Sound	Decibels
Soft Whisper	20	Gasoline-Powered Mower	95
Normal Conversation	40	Typical Rock Concert	115
Busy Traffic	70	Possible Pain To Ears	120
Pneumatic Drill	80	Possible Damage to Ears	130

THE PERIODIC TABLE OF ELEMENTS

1A	2A	3B	4B	5B	6B	7B		8B		1B	2B	3A	4A	5A	6A	7A	8A
1 **H** 1.01																	2 **He** 4.0
3 **Li** 6.94	4 **Be** 9.01											5 **B** 10.8	6 **C** 12.0	7 **N** 14.0	8 **O** 16.0	9 **F** 19.0	10 **Ne** 20.2
11 **Na** 23.0	12 **Mg** 24.3											13 **Al** 27.0	14 **Si** 28.1	15 **P** 31.0	16 **S** 32.1	17 **Cl** 35.5	18 **Ar** 39.9
19 **K** 39.1	20 **Ca** 40.1	21 **Sc** 45.0	22 **Ti** 47.9	23 **V** 50.9	24 **Cr** 52.0	25 **Mn** 54.9	26 **Fe** 55.8	27 **Co** 58.9	28 **Ni** 58.7	29 **Cu** 63.5	30 **Zn** 65.4	31 **Ga** 69.7	32 **Ge** 72.6	33 **As** 74.9	34 **Se** 79.0	35 **Br** 79.9	36 **Kr** 83.8
37 **Rb** 85.5	38 **Sr** 87.6	39 **Y** 88.9	40 **Zr** 91.2	41 **Nb** 92.9	42 **Mo** 95.9	43 **Tc** (98)	44 **Ru** 101.1	45 **Rh** 102.9	46 **Pd** 106.4	47 **Ag** 107.9	48 **Cd** 112.4	49 **In** 114.8	50 **Sn** 118.7	51 **Sb** 121.8	52 **Te** 127.6	53 **I** 126.9	54 **Xe** 131.3
55 **Cs** 132.9	56 **Ba** 137.3	57 **La** 138.9	72 **Hf** 178.5	73 **Ta** 180.9	74 **W** 183.9	75 **Re** 186.2	76 **Os** 190.2	77 **Ir** 192.2	78 **Pt** 195.1	79 **Au** 197.0	80 **Hg** 200.6	81 **Tl** 204.4	82 **Pb** 207.2	83 **Bi** 209.0	84 **Po** (209)	85 **At** (210)	86 **Rn** (222)
87 **Fr** (223)	88 **Ra** 226.0	89 **Ac** (227)	104 **Rf** (261)	105 **Db** (262)	106 **Sg** (266)	107 **Bh** (264)	108 **Hs** (269)	109 **Mt** (268)	110 **Ds** (281)	111 **Rg** (272)	112 **Uub** (285)	113 **Uut** (284)	114 **Uuq** (289)	115 **Uup** (288)	116 **Uuh** (292)		118 **Uuo** (222)

58 **Ce** 140.1	59 **Pr** 140.9	60 **Nd** 144.2	61 **Pm** (145)	62 **Sm** 150.4	63 **Eu** 152.0	64 **Gd** 157.3	65 **Tb** 158.9	66 **Dy** 162.5	67 **Ho** 164.9	68 **Er** 167.3	69 **Tm** 168.9	70 **Yb** 173.0	71 **Lu** 175.0
90 **Th** 232.0	91 **Pa** 231.0	92 **U** 238.0	93 **Np** (237)	94 **Pu** (244)	95 **Am** (243)	96 **Cm** (247)	97 **Bk** (247)	98 **Cf** (251)	99 **Es** (252)	100 **Fm** (257)	101 **Md** (258)	102 **No** (259)	103 **Lr** (262)

Nonmetals

Standard metals

Transition metals

Inner transition metals

TABLE 15.1
The Speed of Light in Certain Substances

Substance	Speed of Light	Substance	Speed of Light
Air (25 °C)	300,000,000 m/sec	Plastic	189,000,000 m/sec
Alcohol	225,000,000 m/sec	Crown Glass	185,000,000 m/sec
Fresh Water	220,000,000 m/sec	Flint Glass	175,000,000 m/sec
Acrylic	200,000,000 m/sec	Diamond	125,000,000 m/sec

The Visible Spectrum

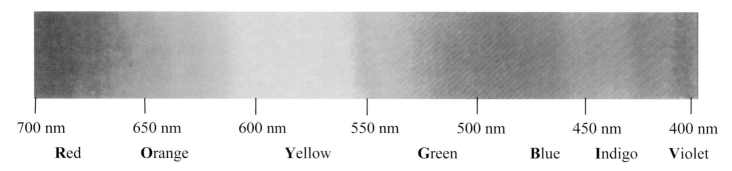

700 nm	650 nm	600 nm	550 nm	500 nm	450 nm	400 nm
Red	Orange	Yellow	Green	Blue	Indigo	Violet

The Electromagnetic Spectrum

short wavelengths   long wavelengths

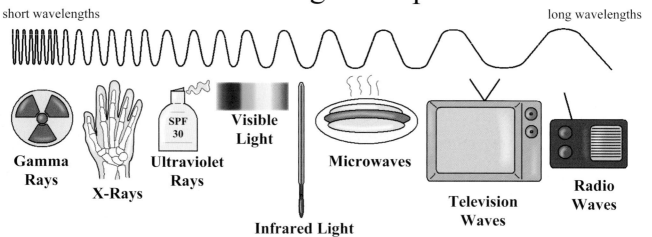

Gamma Rays   X-Rays   Ultraviolet Rays   Visible Light   Infrared Light   Microwaves   Television Waves   Radio Waves

Illustration by Megan Whitaker

The Sun

Sun photo courtesy of NASA

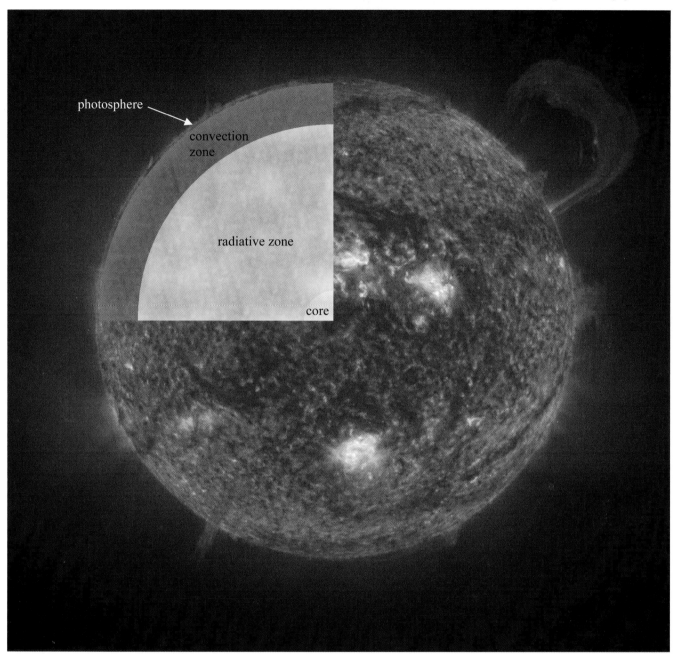

TABLE 16.1
Spectral Letters and Star Temperatures

Temperature (°F)	Spectral Letter
less than 5,500	M
5,500 – 8,000	K
8,001 – 10,300	G
10,301 – 12,500	F
12,501 – 17,000	A
17,001 – 37,000	B
more than 37,000	O

The Hertzsprung-Russell Diagram

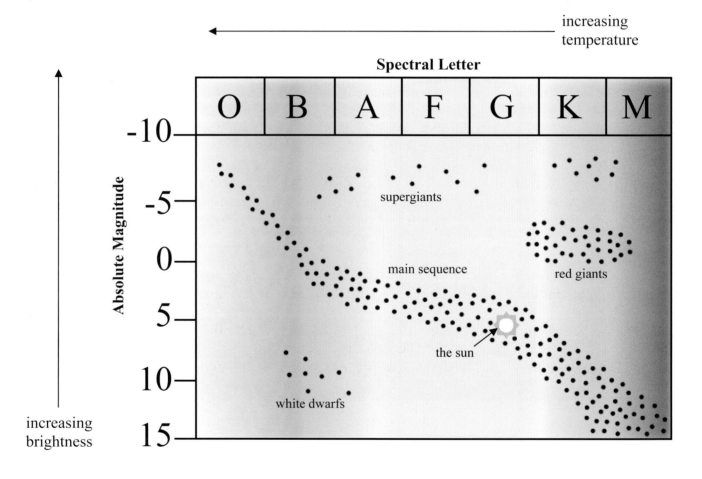

APPENDIX B
MODULE SUMMARIES

Summary of Module #1
Review the vocabulary words listed in Question #1 of the study guide

<u>Fill in the blanks. Many blanks contain more than one word.</u>
Please note: We suggest that you actually write these paragraphs out rather than just filling in the blanks in the book. The act of writing these things out is a form of studying.

1. Atoms are the _____ unit of matter. They are so _____ that you cannot see them. Images of atoms produced by scanning tunneling electron microscopes are not pictures, but are the result of computer _____. Such images are part of the large amount of _____ evidence that indicates atoms exist. When two or more atoms link together, they form a _____, which has its own unique properties.

2. When a substance is made of billions and billions of the same atom, it is called an _____, while substances made up of billions and billions of the same molecule are called _____. Some substances, called _____, are made of more than one kind of atom or molecule. In Experiment 1.1, you watched the molecule known as _____ break down into two elements: _____ and _____. In addition, you saw the _____ in the wire (an element) react with _____ molecules to make copper hydroxycarbonate.

3. When making measurements, the _____ we report are just as important as the numbers. The base metric unit for mass is the _____, while the base English unit for mass is the _____. The base metric unit for weight is the _____, while the base English unit for weight is the _____. Although the weight of an object varies depending on gravity, the _____ does not.

4. The base metric unit for length is the _____, and the base English unit for length is the _____. The base metric unit for volume is the _____, and the base English unit for volume is the _____.

5. In the metric system, prefixes govern the _____ of a unit. The "milli" prefix means _____, while the _____ prefix means 0.01. The "kilo" prefix means _____. Thus, an object with a mass of 1 centigram has _____ mass than an object with a mass of 1 kilogram.

6. The metric unit for temperature is degrees _____. This unit uses no prefixes. In this system, water freezes at _____ and boils at _____.

7. In the Old Testament, a measurement unit for length called the _____ was used.

8. Concentration is the _____ of a substance within a certain _____. At certain concentrations, chemicals behave _____. At other concentrations, those same chemicals can behave _____. Vitamins, for example, are _____ for your body at low concentrations, but they become _____ at high concentrations. In Experiment 1.3, the more concentrated the vinegar, the _____ the antacid tablet disappeared.

9. In this course, we do conversions using the _____ method, in which the measurement you want to convert is multiplied by a fraction that contains both the original unit and the unit you want to convert to.

Solve the Following Problems

10. Convert 34.5 kL into L.

11. Convert 0.00045 g to mg.

12. Which takes up more volume: 45 mL or 0.6 L?

13. How many centigrams are in 13.1 g?

14. If an object has a volume of 45.1 mL, what is its volume in liters?

15. If a road is 13.1 miles long, how many feet long is it? (1 mile = 5,280 feet)

16. How many cm are in 16.2 m?

17. If an object has a mass of 345.6 mg, what is its mass in grams?

18. If a football field is 100.0 yards long, how many feet long is it? (1 yard = 3 feet)

19. Convert 451 grams into kg.

Summary of Module #2
Review the vocabulary words listed in Question #1 of the study guide

1. The moisture content of air is called _____. God has designed you to _____ when you are too warm. This releases water onto your skin, which then evaporates. The process of evaporation requires _____, which is supplied by your skin. As a result, when your sweat evaporates, the net effect is that your skin _____. When the humidity is high, your sweat does not _____ as quickly, and as a result, you do not cool down as well. For this reason, many weather reports include a _____, which is a combination of temperature and humidity.

2. There are two ways of reporting humidity: _____ and _____. If you report the mass of water vapor contained in a certain volume of air, you are reporting the _____. If you report the ratio of the mass of water vapor in the air at a given temperature to the maximum mass of water vapor the air could hold at that temperature, you are reporting the _____.

3. On a day when the relative humidity is high, water evaporates _____. On a day when the relative humidity is low, water evaporates more _____. If the relative humidity is _____, we say that the air is saturated with water.

4. Dry air (air that has all of the _____ removed) is 78% _____, _____ oxygen, and 1% _____. This is an _____ mixture of gases to support life. The oxygen is necessary in order to allow our bodies to run _____ reactions. Without enough oxygen, our bodies would run out of the _____ necessary for life. Too much oxygen in the atmosphere, however can cause _____ problems in people and significantly increase the number of natural _____.

5. The majority of the air we breathe in is nitrogen, and the majority of the air that we breathe out is _____. In addition to nitrogen, the other major gases we exhale are _____, _____, and _____. Of those three gases, we exhale significantly more _____ than the other two. _____ _____ enters the atmosphere as a result of organisms breathing and as the result of fires.

6. Through a process called photosynthesis, plants convert _____ and water into glucose, which they use for food. A byproduct of this process is _____. In addition to allowing plants to manufacture their own food, _____ helps regulate the temperature of the earth. Through a process referred to as the _____, this gas traps heat that radiates from the earth. Without such gases, the average temperature of the earth would be far too _____ to support life.

7. If the greenhouse effect ran out of control, we would have _____, a situation in which the average temperature of the earth increased over time. Although this would be bad, the greenhouse effect is _____, as it makes life on earth possible. Since carbon dioxide is a gas that participates in the greenhouse effect, the fact that the concentration of carbon dioxide in the atmosphere is _____ makes some people fear that _____ may already be happening.

8. The average temperature of the earth has changed _____ in the past 100 years. There was a small _____ in the average global temperature from the late 1800s to the early 1900s, but that was before carbon dioxide levels in the atmosphere _____ significantly. Thus, there is _____ evidence that increasing carbon dioxide concentration causes _____. In addition, the earth was significantly _____ between the ninth and fourteenth centuries than it is today.

9. Ultraviolet light is _____ to living organisms, because it has enough energy to ____ living tissue. Although the sun produces a significant amount of ultraviolet light, most of it is blocked by _____ in the _____ layer. This gas is _____, but the _____ layer is high above sea level, where no one is breathing. Even though most ultraviolet light from the sun is blocked, some gets through, and if your skin is exposed to too much of it, you can get a _____.

10. When we report concentration in parts per million, we are reporting the number of molecules (or atoms) of a substance in a mixture for every 1 _____ molecules (or atoms) in that mixture. The concentration of many pollutants is often expressed in parts per million, as their concentrations are very _____. Despite what many people think, the concentrations of pollutants in earth's atmosphere have been _____ for some time. Thus, the air we are breathing today is _____ than it was 30 years ago.

11. Sulfur oxides are put in the atmosphere when sulfur _____. Sulfur is a _____ in all _____ we burn. The sulfur content of coal can be _____ in a process called "cleaning." Many industries have devices in their _____ that help clean the sulfur oxides out of the mixture of gases that result from burning fuel. These devices are commonly called _____. Although human activity puts sulfur oxides in the atmosphere, there are natural sources as well, one of the most important being _____.

12. Nitrogen oxides are formed when _____ burns. This happens at very high _____, so engines and power plants are major human-made sources of nitrogen oxides. There are, however, many natural sources of nitrogen oxides as well, such as _____, _____, and _____.

13. While ozone in the ozone layer protects living organisms, ozone is a _____. Thus, _____-level ozone is a pollutant, because people breathe it.

14. _____ is a toxic byproduct of incomplete combustion. Unlike carbon dioxide, this gas can be _____, even at concentrations as low as a few hundred parts per million. Automobiles used to be a major source of this gas, but the introduction of _____ significantly reduced the amount produced in automobiles by converting the gas into _____.

15. The U.S. government began issuing standards called _____, which regulate the average number of miles an automobile can travel on a single gallon of gasoline. Although these standards do _____ automobile-related pollution, they also _____ the number of traffic fatalities.

16. When one compares the positive result of an action to the negative result and decides whether or not the positive result was worth the accompanying negative result, we say that the person has done a _____. Any reasonable discussion of air pollution _____ must include such an analysis in order to ensure that the reduced pollution is worth whatever accompanying costs exist.

Solve the Following Problems

17. The concentration of a pollutant in a sample of air is about 0.03%. What is this in ppm?

18. Convert 151 ppm into percent.

19. The current concentration of a gas in an air sample is 0.091 ppm. What is that in percent?

20. Suppose you had a sample of air in which the sulfur oxides concentration is 0.011%. What would the concentration of sulfur oxides be if you expressed it in ppm?

Summary of Module #3
Review the vocabulary words listed in Question #1 of the study guide

1. The mass of air surrounding a planet is called its _____. Everything that comes into contact with the mass of air surrounding the earth is subjected to _____, which is, on average, 14.7 pounds per square inch at sea level. Even though this is a lot of pressure, we don't feel it, because _____ pressure pushes on you from all sides, even from within.

2. In Experiment 3.1, the cans were filled with steam that turned into _____ when the cans were put in ice water. The upright can did not crumple, however, because the steam was replaced with ___ that continued to exert _____ on the inside of the can. The can placed _____ in the water did crumple, however, because ____ could not replace the steam, so very little _____ was being exerted inside the can.

3. A *barometer* measures atmospheric pressure. It is composed of a tube with no *air* inside that is inverted over a pool of _____, which is usually mercury. Since the _____ is pressing down on the pool, and since there is no air exerting _____ inside the tube, _____ is forced up the tube. The _____ of the liquid in the tube is a measure of the _____.

4. When measuring atmospheric pressure, several units can be used. _____ tells you how many pounds are exerted on an 1-inch by 1-inch square. When reported in _____, it tells you the height of a column of mercury in a barometer, in English units. When reported in _____, it tells you the height of the column of mercury in metric units. Finally, pressure can also be reported in _____, which tells you the pressure relative to earth's average atmospheric pressure at sea level.

5. The atmosphere can be divided into two general layers. The _____ is the lower layer, and it contains air that has the same _____ as the air at sea level. The upper layer is called the _____, and the mixture of gases in this layer is not _____. Throughout both layers, however, the total amount of air _____ with increasing altitude.

6. The homosphere is generally divided into three regions. From lowest to highest, they are the _____, the _____, and the _____. The first two layers are separated by the _____; the second two are separated by the _____, and the last layer is separated from the heterosphere by the _____. Throughout all of these regions, as well as the heterosphere, the atmospheric pressure continually _____ with increasing altitude.

7. In the troposphere, the temperature steadily _____ with increasing altitude. This is called the temperature _____ of the troposphere. The troposphere is often called earth's _____ layer, because it contains almost all of earth's clouds, rain, snow, storms, etc

8. Narrow bands of high-speed winds that circle the earth, blowing from west to east are called _____. They are found in the _____ portions of the stratosphere and the _____ portions of the troposphere. They tend to _____ storms and affect which parts of the earth experience high _____ or low _____.

9. In the stratosphere, the temperature _____ with increasing altitude. This is mostly due to the _____, which is found there. In the mesosphere, the temperature _____ with increasing altitude. When rocks from outer space fall into the mesosphere and burn up, they are called _____.

10. When energy is transferred as a consequence of temperature differences, we call it _____. When an object gains energy, the _____ that make it up move faster. A _____ really measures the average speed at which the _____ of a substance are moving. As a result, temperature is a measure of the _____ of _____ in a substance's _____ _____.

11. The "hole" in the ozone layer is actually a seasonal _____ in the concentration of ozone in the ozone layer. It is centered over _____. Human-made substances called _____ are at least partially to blame. Unlike many chemicals, they are so _____ that they can survive the trip up to the ozone layer, where they can destroy ozone. Interestingly enough, this same property makes them _____ to human beings. They are very efficient chemicals that can be used for _____, _____, and _____. Despite their usefulness, their elimination has been called for by the _____. This will, mostly likely, cause an _____ in the number of people who die each year.

12. The "hole" in the ozone layer was discovered _____ CFCs were widely used. However, since the production of CFCs, the "hole" has gotten "_____." Although CFCs are heavy, they are lifted up to the ozone layer by the _____. This is why the ozone "hole" is a _____ phenomenon and why it is centered over _____. While the elimination of CFCs will _____ the depth of the ozone "hole," it will most likely _____ more lives than it will save. The ozone "hole" does *not* contribute to _____. In fact, a reduction in the amount of ozone in the ozone layer will _____ the average temperature of the earth.

13. The heterosphere is generally divided into two layers: the _____ and the _____. While the _____ is lower than the _____, they can both be considered a part of outer space. The number of molecules in the _____ is so small that a thermometer would read incredibly low temperatures. However, the average _____ of the few molecules that are there is very _____. The _____ is composed of those atoms and molecules actually in orbit around the _____. It is difficult to say where the _____ ends and interplanetary space begins.

14. Between the upper portions of the _____ and the lower portions of the _____, there is a region where the atmosphere's gases are ionized. It is called the _____. Atoms are composed of _____ (which have positive electrical charge), _____ (which have negative electrical charge), and _____ (which have no electrical charge). Atoms always have the same number of _____ and _____. This means that overall, atoms have no net _____. When an atom loses (or gains) electrons, there is an _____ of positive and negative charges, and the atom becomes _____. When this happens, it is no longer an atom, but is instead an ____.

15. The Northern Lights and Southern Lights are examples of _____. They appear in the night sky as glowing regions of brilliant _____ that tend to move over the sky in interesting ways. They are the result of high-energy _____ between ionized particles in the _____.

Summary of Module #4

Review the vocabulary words listed in Question #1 of the study guide

1. We can live for as many as two weeks without food, but if we were to go even a few days without _____, we would surely die. Indeed, without water, _____ as we know it simply cannot exist.

2. The use of electricity to break a molecule down into smaller units is called _____. When you use this procedure on water, you produce _____ and _____. If you measure the volumes of each, you will find twice as much _____ as _____.

3. Often, experiments produce incorrect results due to _____. A good scientist tries to _____ the amount of it in an experiment and does not _____ experiments that have a lot of it. When a scientist performs an experiment that seems to lead to a new, interesting conclusion, other _____ in the field look closely at the experiment in an effort to spot _____ that the original scientist did not recognize. This process is called _____. An example of the importance of this process is seen in Drs. Martin Fleischmann and Stanley Pons, who claimed to have discovered _____, a potential source of cheap, unlimited power. They did not submit their experiments to _____ before publicizing their results. As a result, they were embarrassed because other scientists had to publicly announce the _____ in their experiments.

4. The chemical symbol of an atom contains either _____ or _____ letters. If there are _____ letters, only the _____ is capitalized. The letters often come from either the _____ or _____ name of the atom. A _____ tells you the composition of a molecule because the _____ in the chemical formula tell you how many of each atom is present. If there is no subscript next to an atom's symbol, there is _____ of those atoms in the molecule. Thus, the molecule $CaCO_3$ has _____ calcium (Ca) atom, _____ carbon (C) atom, and _____ oxygen (O) atoms.

5. Magnesium hydroxide is a chemical often used in antacid tablets. It has one Magnesium (Mg) atom, two oxygen (O) atoms, and two hydrogen (H) atoms. Thus, its chemical formula is _____. The chemical formula of sodium nitrate is $NaNO_3$. This molecule has a total of __ atoms: __ sodium (Na) atom, __ nitrogen (N) atom, and __ oxygen (O) atoms.

6. Atoms in molecules are linked together with _____, which are made up of _____ electrons. If the atoms in a molecule do not _____ electrons equally, small _____ result within the molecule, and it is called a _____ molecule. In Experiment 4.2, the small _____ charges on the _____ atoms of the water molecules were attracted to the _____ charge on the comb. That's what made the stream of water bend _____ the comb.

7. When you dissolve a substance in a liquid, we say you have made a _____. When making a solution, you use a _____ to dissolve a _____. When you dissolve sugar in water, for example, water is the _____, sugar is the _____, and sugar water is the _____.

8. In general, a polar or ionic solute can only dissolve in a _____ solvent. A nonpolar solute can only dissolve in a _____ solvent. A solute dissolves in a solvent because the molecules of the solvent are _____ to the molecules (or ions) of the solute.

9. In a water molecule, the positive charge on one molecule is attracted to any other _____ charge. In a sample of water, there are many other molecules, so they will tend to align themselves so that the positive charge on the _____ of one molecule will be as close as possible to the negative

charge on the _____ of another molecule. This results in _____, which causes water molecules to be very close to one another. In fact, most molecules that are chemically similar to water are _____ at room temperature. Water, however, is a _____ at room temperature because of _____.

10. While the solid phase of most substances _____ in the liquid phase of that same substance, solid water (ice) _____ in liquid water. This is because the molecules of liquid water are _____ than the molecules in solid water. This convenient fact allows lakes to _____ from the top down. As a result, a reasonably deep body of water will never _____ freeze, because the _____ at the surface insulates the water below. This allows fish (and other aquatic animals) to _____ the winter.

11. Because of hydrogen bonding, individual water molecules are so strongly _____ to one another that they tend to stay together, even when subjected to an outside force. This gives water its _____, which, in turn, causes _____, the phenomenon that caused the needle to float in Experiment 4.5. This same phenomenon is exploited by water striders, allowing them to _____ on water. The _____ of water is also what makes it possible for water to travel up through the zylem of a tall plant.

12. Although water's _____ is strong, it can be overcome. In Experiment 4.6, for example, water "beaded up" on the _____ surface of the glass, because water molecules are attracted to _____ more _____ than they are to the molecules that make up wax. However, the water did not "bead up" on the unwaxed glass, because water molecules are attracted to _____ more _____ than they are to each other.

13. When water has ions like calcium and magnesium dissolved in it, we call it _____ water. It is _____ the result of treatment done to make the water safe to drink. Instead, it is the result of the _____ from which the water is taken. In a _____, calcium and magnesium ions are "exchanged" with either _____ or _____ ions so that the calcium and magnesium ions are not in the water we drink and use. People who are on strict _____ diets should either not soften their water or use more expensive, sodium-free water-softener salts, like _____.

Summary of Module #5
Review the vocabulary words listed in Question #1 of the study guide

1. Water is such a large part of the earth that astronomers often call it the _____ planet. The sum of all water on a planet is called its _____. Of all the planets in our solar system, earth is the _____ that has a large quantity of water in its liquid form. This is because the earth has _____ in its atmosphere and is _____ from the sun.

2. The vast majority of earth's water supply is contained in the _____ as _____. The vast majority of earth's freshwater supply is stored in _____ and _____. The largest source of liquid freshwater is _____. Aside from the sources just mentioned, the other major sources of water in the hydrosphere are _____ (not oceans), _____, and _____.

3. The process by which water is continuously exchanged between earth's various water sources is called the _____. In this process, water gets into the atmosphere predominantly by _____ and _____. Soil moisture is usually depleted by either _____ or _____. Water vapor in the atmosphere can form a cloud through a process called _____. Once water is in a cloud, it can fall back to earth as _____. When this water falls on land and then runs along the surface into a lake, river, or stream, we call it _____.

4. Evaporation and condensation of a mixture to separate out the mixture's individual components is called _____. This process is why water from the ocean can eventually end up in a _____ source, like a lake, river, or stream.

5. The average time a given particle will stay in a given system is called its _____, and in the hydrologic cycle, it varies considerably from source to source. The average time a molecule of water stays in a swiftly flowing river, for example, is _____ than that of a water molecule in a lake. The average time a molecule of water stays in the atmosphere is much _____ than that of a water molecule in the ocean. The _____ was the first work to mention the hydrologic cycle.

6. The chemical name of the salt you put on your food is _____. Although this is the majority of salt in the ocean, chemists use the tem "salt" more _____, and as a result, there are other salts in the ocean. A measure of the mass of dissolved salt in a given mass of water is called _____.

7. Salt is found in the ocean because the only way water can escape the ocean is through _____. As Experiment 5.1 shows, when this happens, the _____ is left behind. Thus, the ocean's average salinity _____ over time. Nevertheless, the salinity of the ocean does vary. Where rivers dump water into the ocean, for example, the salinity is _____ than the average salinity. The average salinity of the ocean indicates it is _____ than even a few million years old.

8. Saltwater freezes at a _____ temperature than does freshwater. In fact, putting salt on ice will often _____ the ice, because the salt molecules _____ water molecules so that they move away from the other water molecules. When the temperature gets low enough, however, even saltwater will freeze, but the salt and water _____ as the solution freezes, usually forming solid water that surround little pockets of concentrated saltwater called _____.

9. Icebergs are composed of _____. They *do not* form as a result of _____ water freezing. In certain polar regions, the water in the ocean does freeze to form _____, but that is not an iceberg. In fact, icebergs come from _____, which are the result of snowfall. When a region is cold enough, the _____ does not melt away during the summer. When new snow falls, the old snow gets packed down into what is called _____. As the mass of snow accumulates, it begins to slide to lower elevations, forming a _____.

10. As glaciers move, they might encounter warmer temperatures, where they begin to _____, feeding various _____ sources of the hydrosphere. Glaciers in the polar regions often do not encounter warmer temperatures, however, and move all the way to the ocean, where they form ____ _____. When the edge of a glacier advances into the ocean, the ice _____ at some points, and large chunks of ice break off the glacier, floating away in the water. This process, called _____, is what makes an _____, approximately 90% of which is _____.

11. Soil moisture can flow down through the soil in a process called _____. If it travels down far enough, it will reach soil that is completely saturated with water. The line between the saturated and unsaturated soil is called the _____. The depth of this line _____ over time. For example, when there is a period of very heavy rains, the depth _____, and when there are periods of little or no rain, the depth _____.

12. If a lake has a high enough salinity to consider it a saltwater lake, there are __ rivers taking water away from the lake. As a result, the only way water can leave is through _____. The _____ is one such lake, and it has a much higher salinity than that of the ocean.

13. Water in the atmosphere exists as either _____ or _____. In order for clouds to form, there must be _____ upon which water can condense. This condensation occurs because as air expands, it gets _____. The scientific name for this process is _____ _____. Water in clouds can be either _____ or _____, depending on the temperature.

14. Adiabatic cooling should not be confused with the fact that most things _____ when they are heated. When you heat something, you are giving it _____. In adiabatic cooling, air is expanding *without* being given _____.

15. A refrigerator uses a substance that is a ____ at room temperature. A compressor in the refrigerator compresses the gas, which _____ it up and forms a lot of _____. Once compressed, the gas is released into a _____ portion of the system, which allows it to _____. This _____ down the contents of the refrigerator. In addition, the gas that had condensed _____, which further cools the system. The pipes that carry the expanded gas are on the _____ of the refrigerator, and the pipes that carry the compressed gas are on the _____ of the refrigerator.

16. _____ is the result of a cloud forming on the ground. Although this used to be called _____, that term is now generally used to refer to a brownish haze that results from pollution. However, that brownish haze is more properly referred to as _____.

17. One of the real environmental problems that exists today is water _____, especially what is occurring to the groundwater supply. Since nearly 50% of the United States gets its _____ from groundwater sources, it has a direct effect on human health.

Summary of Module #6
Review the vocabulary words listed in Question #1 of the study guide

1. The earth is typically divided into five regions: the atmosphere, the hydrosphere, the _____, the _____, and the _____. The deepest region is further subdivided into the _____ and _____. We have learned about the lowest regions with _____, such as observing how sound waves pass through the earth.

2. The earth's crust is its _____ layer of _____. It is separated from the mantle by the _____ _____, which is typically called the _____ for short. We have never been able to drill _____ the crust. The crust also contains _____ and small, solid fragments of rock and other materials called _____. Many of the rocks of the earth's crust are _____, which are formed when chemical reactions cement sediments together. Other rock types found in the crust are _____ (rock that forms from molten rock) and _____ (rock that has been changed as a result of great pressure and temperature).

3. The mantle is _____ the crust, and it is separated from the outer core by the _____ _____. Its principal ingredient is _____. Deeper portions of the mantle have a _____ temperature than shallower portions of the mantle. The crust and the upper layers of the mantle form the _____, and directly below that is the _____, where the rock is called _____ because it behaves like something between a liquid and a solid.

4. When earthquakes occur, they emit vibrations called _____, which travel through the earth, eventually reaching the surface. They can be detected with _____, which can be used to tell how the waves traveled through the inner parts of the earth. This allows scientists to develop _____ of the earth's mantle and core, which allow us to understand their makeup.

5. The core's principal ingredient is _____. In the outer core, the iron is _____, but in the inner core, it is _____. Nevertheless, the inner core has a _____ temperature than the outer core. The reason the inner core is solid is because of _____. The boundary between the inner and outer cores is the _____.

6. Electrical currents in the earth's core are responsible for the earth's _____, the strength of which has been _____ for the past 170 years. In addition, its direction has _____ a few times in the past. The data indicate that at least some of these reversals have happened over a _____ time period.

7. The earth's magnetic field deflects the vast majority of _____ that come from the sun. Without such protection, _____ would cease to exist as a result of the _____ of these particles. If the earth's magnetic field were too small, _____ of them would be deflected. If it were too strong, it would cause deadly _____ that would make life impossible. Thus, the earth has a magnetic field that is _____.

8. There are basically two views of how the electrical currents in the core originated, and they are called the _____ and the _____. The _____ assumes that the earth is billions of years old and is _____ when compared to the data. The _____ assumes that they earth is only thousands of years old and is _____ when compared to the data. The fact that most scientists believe in the _____ in spite of the data indicates that there is no such thing as an _____ scientist. The _____ says that all planets initially had a magnetic field, but

some planet's fields have decayed away to nothing by now. The _____ says that once a planet has a magnetic field, its strength might change, but it will never be completely gone.

9. The theory of _____ views the earth's lithosphere as composed of several "_____" that all move about on the plastic rock of the _____. When they move away from each other, _____ leaks up from the mantle, creating new _____. When they collide, one can slide under the other, generally forming a _____ with mountains on one side. When this happens, _____ is destroyed as it melts into the mantle. When they collide and neither slides under the other, they _____, forming mountains. When they _____ (or shear) against each other, their edges scrape against each other. This motion can result in severe _____.

10. Many of our observations of _____, _____, and volcanoes seem to support the theory of plate tectonics. There are deep trenches at the bottom of the oceans, the characteristics of which are well described by the theory that the plates in that region of the earth are moving _____ _____. In the end, then, most geologists believe that the plate tectonics theory is _____.

11. The fact that the continents appear as if they fit together like a jigsaw puzzle has led some scientists to speculate that years ago, all the continents were connected in a giant supercontinent, which has been called _____. Evidence to support this idea includes the fact that sections of rock from different continents are _____, and they "_____" when you put the continents together the way they are assumed to have existed in _____. Although most scientists believe that the plates have always moved _____, a theory called "catastrophic plate tectonics" uses _____ plate movement as a result of a global catastrophe to explain how the supercontinent split in a short amount of time.

12. Vibration of the earth that results either from volcanic activity or rock masses suddenly moving along a fault is called an _____. A fault is the _____ between two sections of rock that can _____ relative to one another. Wherever a fault exists, there is the possibility of an _____.

13. The most successful theory regarding fault-related earthquakes is the _____. In this theory, as rock masses on a fault try to move relative to each other, they get _____ on one another. As a result, they _____. Eventually, the rock masses _____ of each other, and they "_____" to their normal shape.

14. The point where an earthquake begins is called the earthquake's _____. The _____ is the point on the surface of the earth directly above an earthquake's focus. The study of earthquakes is called _____, and it uses delicate instruments called _____ that can measure vibrations that are too small for us to notice. This has led to a scale that classifies earthquakes based on their strength, called the _____. This scale runs from 0 to 10, and each step along this scale is an increase of approximately ____ in the energy of an earthquake. A earthquake that measures 5 on the Richter scale is ____ times more energetic than one that measures 4 and _____ less energetic than one that measures 8.

15. If a fault exists in which one rock mass is moving up and the other is stationary or moving down, the upward-moving mass of rock will form a _____. When two moving rock masses push against each other with extreme force, the crust can bend in an up-and-down, rolling pattern, forming _____. A mountain formed by lava leaking up through the crust from the mantle is a _____, while one formed by magma that does not leave the mantle is called a _____.

Summary of Module #7

Review the vocabulary words listed in Question #1 of the study guide

1. The term "_____" refers to the condition of the earth's atmosphere (mostly the troposphere) at any particular time. _____, on the other hand, is a steady condition that prevails day in and day out in a particular region of creation.

2. The principal factors affecting the weather are _____, _____ _____, and _____.

3. Meteorologists separate clouds into four basic groups: _____ (fluffy piles of clouds), _____ (layers of clouds), _____ (high altitude, wispy clouds), and _____ (lens-shaped clouds). You generally find each type of cloud at a _____ altitude, but a prefix of "_____" is used to indicate that a cloud type is higher than expected. In general, _____ clouds form at the highest altitudes, while _____ clouds form at the lower altitudes. A prefix of "_____" or a suffix of "_____" is also added if the cloud is dark. Dark clouds are the ones that typically bring _____.

4. Unusually large, upward-moving wind currents can produce huge, towering _____ that most people call "thunderclouds." Cirrus clouds are composed of ____ instead of liquid water. Precipitation-producing stratus clouds are typically called _____. Clouds that look like part cirrus/part cumulus clouds are called _____, while clouds that look a bit like cumulus clouds but are formed where stratus clouds normally formed are called _____. Finally, some clouds have the feathery appearance of cirrus clouds, but they form flat layers like that of stratus clouds and are called _____.

5. Light that comes to the earth from the sun is called _____, which abbreviates "incoming solar radiation." The earth's _____ and its _____ affect how much a region of the earth gets. In addition, cloud cover can _____ the amount of incoming solar radiation. The earth orbits the sun in an oval pattern that mathematicians call an _____. When the earth is at its aphelion, it is the _____ it will ever be from the sun. When it is at its perihelion, it is _____ to the sun.

6. Because of earth's axial tilt, sunlight shines more directly on the _____ when the earth is at aphelion. Thus, it is _____ in the Northern Hemisphere and _____ in the Southern Hemisphere at that time. At perihelion, sunlight shines more directly on the _____. At that time, then, it is _____ in the Northern Hemisphere and _____ in the Southern Hemisphere.

7. At the two _____, the days are _____ long in both hemispheres. As the earth moves from the autumnal equinox (spring equinox in the Southern hemisphere) to the winter solstice (summer solstice in the Southern hemisphere), the days in the Northern Hemisphere are _____ than 12 hours and are getting _____. In the Southern Hemisphere, the days are _____ than 12 hours and are getting _____. From the winter solstice (summer solstice in the Southern hemisphere) to the spring equinox (autumnal equinox in the Southern hemisphere), the days in the Northern Hemisphere are _____ than 12 hours and are getting _____. In the Southern Hemisphere, the days are _____ than 12 hours and are getting _____.

8. Most likely, Christ was born in _____, not December. However, December 25th is celebrated as Christ's birthday because missionaries tried to link it to a pagan holiday that was called the _____ _____.

9. Imaginary lines that run north and south across the earth are called _____, while imaginary lines that run east and west across the earth are called _____. The latitude is ___ at the equator and increases the _____ you move away from it. The longitude is ___ at the prime meridian, which runs through _____. It increases the _____ you move away from the prime meridian.

10. Hot air ____. As this happens it creates a region of ___ pressure. Cold air ____. As this happens, it creates a region of ____ pressure. These effects cause loops of winds to develop as air tries to move from ___ regions of the earth (like the poles) to _____ regions of earth (like the equator). These winds are then bent by the _____, which stems from the fact that different parts of the earth move at different speeds. The result is prevailing winds in the polar regions called _____, prevailing winds in the mid latitudes called _____, and prevailing winds near the equator called _____.

11. Because of the Coriolis effect, a missile fired due north from the equator will end up hitting a target _____ of its launch site, while a missile fired due south from near the North Pole will end up hitting a target _____ of its launch site. The Coriolis effect, however, is _____ to significantly affect how water drains in a basin.

12. Prevailing wind patterns can be easily disrupted by _____. Examples of such winds would be a _____ near the ocean shore, which tends to blow during the day, and a _____, which tends to blow near the ocean shore during the night.

13. An air mass is a large body of air with relatively uniform _____, _____, and _____. The three basic types of air masses are _____, _____, and _____. _____ air masses are very cold and dry. _____ air masses are warm and moist, while _____ air masses are cold and moist. _____ air masses are warm and dry, while _____ air masses are cold (but not as cold as artic air masses) and dry.

14. A weather front is a _____ between two air masses. The four basic types are _____, _____ _____, _____, and _____.

15. When a cold front moves in, _____ clouds are usually formed by the warm air _____ in response to the cold air mass. The temperature in the region tends to _____. Cold fronts generally carry the most _____ weather system, including thunderstorms.

16. When a warm front moves in, the warm air tends to _____ above the cooler air that was in the region. This usually causes a progression of clouds from cirrus to _____ to stratus to _____, which generally heralds a _____ and _____ rain as well as _____ temperatures.

17. Occluded fronts occur when a _____ meets up with a slower-moving _____. They usually result in slow, steady rains followed by _____.

18. A stationary front generally results in weather that doesn't _____ much for a long period of time.

Summary of Module #8
Review the vocabulary words listed in Question #1 of the study guide

1. Eventually, all the water that evaporates into the atmosphere falls back to earth, mostly in the form of _____ . However, water can also leave the atmosphere and return to earth as _____ or _____ .

2. By far, the most common form of precipitation is _____ . There are two theories about how it forms in clouds. The _____ process deals with how rain is formed in cold clouds. The ice crystals in these clouds grow _____ until they can no longer remain _____ in the air. As they fall, they typically pick up more ____ , growing even heavier. Eventually, these ice crystals become so big that they _____ , which results in several ice crystals falling through the cloud. Each of these fragments, until there are billions of _____ falling from the cloud. As they descend, they melt and form ___ .

3. In warm clouds, meteorologists think that rain forms according to the _____ . In this theory, each cloud contains many water droplets. As _____ in the cloud move these droplets around, they _____ with other water droplets. Sometimes the droplets stick together, forming a _____ water droplet. Eventually, a water droplet gets big enough to start _____ through the cloud.

4. Drizzle usually forms in _____ clouds. Sleet is different from freezing rain because sleet is frozen _____ it hits the ground, while freezing rain is not. _____ is formed when an ice crystal or raindrop is blown back into the cloud by an upward gust of wind. If blown high enough, the raindrop will _____ , or the ice crystal will get _____ . Depending on the wind conditions, the ice crystal might be blown back up into the clouds _____ times. Eventually, it gets so big that the upward gusts of wind are _____ strong enough to push it back up into the clouds, and it falls to the earth. Snow starts out as precipitation from a _____ cloud. As the ice crystals fall from the clouds, they _____ , freezing and growing into bigger ice crystals.

5. A thunderstorm begins with a current of rising air, called an _____ . As the air rises, water condenses onto cloud condensation nuclei, which actually ____ the cloud condensation nuclei, making the current of rising air stronger. This is the _____ stage of the thunderstorm. Eventually, the water droplets and/or ice crystals in the cloud become too _____ , and it begins to rain. This marks the _____ stage of the thunderstorm. As the rain falls, it causes winds that blow downward, which are called _____ . These winds eventually overpower the rising currents of air that started the storm, and the entire area is full of only _____ . This marks the _____ stage of the thunderstorm. A single thunderstorm cell typically lasts for less than __ minutes, but a thunderstorm might be composed of _____ cells so that the storm lasts longer.

6. Lightning forms because a charge _____ in a cloud causes charge to build up on the _____ . The positive charges on the ground attract some negative charges from the cloud, forming a _____ _____ . The closeness of the negative charges forces the positive charges up, making the _____ _____ , which is the most powerful part of the lightning strike. The _____ that you hear is the result of air that has been superheated by the return stroke. Although this kind of lightning (called _____ _____ lightning) forms lightning bolts, _____ lightning lights up the sky in big sheets.

7.   Tornadoes start as the result of updrafts that form _____ . In the first stage of their development, known as the _____ stage, the updraft of air forming a cumulonimbus cloud begins being hit by winds blowing in a different direction at higher altitudes. Combined with the updraft, this causes a funnel of air to form, with air whirling both around and up. This is often called a _____ . The funnel of air then touches the ground, starting the _____ stage of the tornado. Once the funnel

touches the ground, it sucks debris up into the funnel, which darkens the tornado. This marks the _____ stage. It is in this stage that the tornado is most destructive. Eventually, the forces that hold the vortex together dissipate, and the tornado gets smaller, entering its _____ stage. Finally, the tornado weakens to the point that it is no longer visible, and it slowly dies out in the _____ stage. When tornadoes form over the water, the result is a _____, which is _____ than a tornado that forms over land. A _____ is even weaker, forming as a result of temperature differences between the ground and the air above it.

8. Hurricanes are more properly called _____, because they always start in the tropics. They begin as a _____ that is fed by the warm, moist air of the tropical sea. If the rotating winds reach a sustained speed of 23 miles per hour, it is "upgraded" to a _____ _____. If the winds reach a sustained speed of 39 miles per hour, the depression is "upgraded" again to a _____ _____. Finally, if the winds reach 74 miles per hour, it becomes a full-fledged hurricane. There are _____ categories of hurricanes, which are based on the wind speeds in the storm. The most pronounced feature of a hurricane is its _____, and the clouds spin around the eye _____ in the Northern Hemisphere and _____ in the Southern Hemisphere. The eye is actually a place of _____ in the midst of the storm.

9. _____ (which stands for "radio detection and ranging"), emits _____ waves at a rate of several hundred per second. As those waves encounter objects, they _____ off the objects and head back toward the radar unit. The time it takes for the waves to travel to an object and then bounce back indicates the _____ to the object. In addition, differences between the outgoing and returning waves provide information that can determine whether a cloud is made up of _____ (a cold cloud) or _____ (a warm cloud). _____ is a well-known tool in both weather and law enforcement. Traffic police use it to determine the _____ of automobiles, while meteorologists use it to measure the _____ of winds and air masses.

10. Weather _____ take data continuously all over the world and give us an accurate, _____ picture of the weather fronts and patterns that exist on a day-to-day basis. They also provide strong evidence that global warming is _____ happening.

11. Weather data is often summarized on a _____ map that allows meteorologists to track fronts and atmospheric pressure. The thin black lines on such a map are called _____, and they represent regions of equal _____ pressure. An "H" on such a map indicates an area of _____ pressure, while an "L" represents _____ pressure. Isobars represent _____ pressure the farther they are from an "L" and _____ pressure the farther they are from an "H."

12. If a thick line on a weather map has only triangles on it, it represents a _____ front, and the way the triangles point tell you the _____ in which the front travels. If it has only ovals on it, the line represents a _____ front, and the side the ovals are on tells you the _____ in which the front travels. If the line has both ovals and circles on the same side, it represents an _____ front, and once again, the side that the symbols are on tells you the _____ in which the front travels. Finally, if the line has ovals on one side and triangles on another, it represents a _____ front.

Summary of Module #9

Review the vocabulary words listed in Question #1 of the study guide

1. Every science relies on the science of *physichs* . As a result, we call it the most *fundimental* of all the sciences. The science of *mechanichs* is the branch of physics that deals with analyzing and understanding objects in motion, the *forces* that are applied to those objects, and the *energy* that exists in them.

2. When studying motion, one must define a *refrence point* , which is a point against which position is measured. If an object's position relative to this point is *changing* , the object is in motion relative to that point. Because motion depends on the reference point, all motion is *relative* .

3. The units for speed and velocity are composed of a *distance* unit divided by a *time* unit. In base metric units, speed is given in *meters/sec* . While *speed* simply tells you how quickly an object is moving, *velocity* tells you how quickly an object is moving *and* the direction in which it moves. Thus, speed is a *scalar* quantity, while velocity is a *vector* quantity. Speed can be calculated with the equation:

$$s = \frac{d}{t}$$

4. When objects travel in the same direction, their relative speed is the _____ between their individual speeds. When they travel in opposite directions, their relative speed is the _____ of their individual speeds.

5. The time rate of change of an object's velocity is its _____. The units for this quantity are composed of a _____ unit divided by a _____ unit _____. In base metric units, it is given in _____. It is a _____ quantity, because it contains directional information. It can be calculated with the equation:

_____

6. An object with an unchanging speed can still have acceleration, provided that its _____ is changing. In physics, the term "acceleration" can also mean that an object is _____, because acceleration is simply the change in velocity, and a decrease in velocity is still a change. If an object is speeding up, its acceleration is in the _____ as its velocity. If it is slowing down, its acceleration is in the _____ as compared to its velocity.

7. When an object falls solely under the influence of gravity, we say that it is in _____. In such a situation, the acceleration is equal to _____ in metric units and _____ in English units. This acceleration is _____ of the characteristics of the object. Thus, in true free fall, a feather and a bowling ball will fall with the _____ acceleration.

8. When an object is in free fall, the distance it drops can be calculated with the equation:

_____

9. Although we generally treat objects falling near the surface of the earth as if they were in free fall, _____ impedes the fall of all objects. Thus, things don't truly free fall unless there is no ___.

However, for most objects, the effect of _____ can be ignored. Thus, when most objects fall near the surface of the earth, we can assume they are in _____.

10. When doing an experiment in which error is a known problem, you can reduce the effects of error by making _several_ measurements and _averaging_ the results.

Solve the Following Problems

11. What is the speed of a boat that travels 20 miles in 45 minutes? Please answer in miles per hour.

12. Label each quantity as a vector or scalar quantity. Also, identify it as speed, distance, velocity, acceleration, or none of these.

    a. 10 meters/second^2 north
    b. 1.2 meters/second
    c. 3.4 feet/hour and slowing
    d. 2.3 miles/minute west

13. A sportscar goes from a velocity zero to a velocity of 15 meters per second east in 2.1 seconds. What is the car's acceleration?

14. What is the height of a building (in meters) if it takes a rock 3.8 seconds to drop from its roof?

15. A car and a truck are traveling north on a highway. The truck has a speed of 42 miles per hour, and the car has a speed of 37 miles per hour. If the truck is ahead of the car, what is the relative velocity?

42 miles per hour north

37 miles per hour north

Illustrations from www.clipart.com

16. If an object travels for 10 minutes with a constant velocity of 11 miles per hour north, what is the acceleration?

17. A car that is traveling at 55 miles per hour south brakes suddenly. It takes 3.5 seconds for the car to come to a full stop. What is the acceleration, in miles per hour^2? (1 hour = 3600 seconds)

18. How far (in feet) did a dropped rock fall if it took 2.3 seconds to reach the ground?

Summary of Module #10
Review the vocabulary words listed in Question #1 of the study guide

1. Sir Isaac Newton discovered _____ laws of motion, developed a theory describing _____, did the famous prism experiment that showed white light is composed of many _____, and in order to help his scientific investigations, he developed a new kind of mathematics that we now call "_____." He was also was a devoutly _____ man who spent as much time studying the _____ as he did studying science.

2. Newton's three laws of motion are:

I. _____

II. _____

III. _____

3. The tendency of an object to resist changes in its velocity is referred to as _____. When a bomb is dropped from an airplane, the bomb _____ hit the ground directly below where the airplane dropped it. Instead, it continues to move in the _____ that the plane was moving when the bomb was dropped, because of Newton's _____ Law of Motion. Thus, a bomber must drop the bomb _____ it is above the target.

4. The reason Aristotle made so many mistakes when describing motion is that he did not know about the existence of _____, a force that opposes motion and results from the contact of two _____. This force exists because on the atomic scale, all surfaces are _____. This affects how close the molecules can get to one another, which affects how much they are _____ to each other. The more they are _____ to one another, the stronger the frictional force. When this force opposes motion once the motion has already started, we call it _____. When it opposes the initiation of motion, we call it _____. Between these two forces, _____ is greater than _____.

5. A force is essentially a push or a pull exerted on an object in an effort to change that object's _____. You can calculate force with the equation:

_____

The units on force are composed of a _____ unit times a _____ unit divided by a _____ unit squared. The standard unit for force is _____, which is also called the "Newton."

6. When multiple forces act on an object, forces in the same direction are _____, and forces in opposite directions are _____. Since friction always opposes motion, the frictional force will always be _____ from the force that is being used to cause motion.

7. When you fire a gun, it "kicks" back towards you. That "kick" is the result of Newton's _____ Law of Motion. When you pull the trigger, you cause a _____ to take place in the chamber. That reaction produces a lot of _____ and _____. The gas is under pressure, so it exerts a force on the _____, pushing the bullet out at an amazing speed. In response, the _____ pushes back against the gas in the gun.

Solve the Following Problems

8. Ignoring friction, what force is necessary to move a 25.0 kg object with an acceleration of 34.5 m/sec^2 to the west?

9. Ignoring friction, what force is necessary to move a 125.0 kg object with a constant velocity of 3.4 m/sec?

10. An object moves with a constant velocity to the north. If the static friction between the object and the floor is 25 Newtons, while the kinetic friction is 15 Newtons, what force is being applied to the object?

11. In order to move a 65-kilogram object, a force of more than 40 Newtons must be exerted. Once it is moving, a force of only 30 Newtons accelerates the object at 0.1 meters per second^2 to the west. What is the force of static friction between the object and the surface upon which it sits? What is the force of kinetic friction?

12. The static frictional force between a 95-kilogram object and the floor is 45 Newtons. The kinetic frictional force is only 22 Newtons. How many Newtons of force must be exerted to get the object moving? What force must be exerted to accelerate the box at 0.5 meters per second^2 to the south?

13. Three forces (besides friction) act on a 50-kg object: 35 Newtons east, 45 Newtons east, and 10 Newtons west. The object accelerates at 0.10 meters per second^2 to the east. What is the kinetic frictional force between the object and the floor?

14. In order to move a box, a worker gets it moving by exerting just slightly more than 75 Newtons of force. To keep it moving at a constant velocity west, however, he exerts 45 Newtons force to the west. What are the static and kinetic frictional forces between the box and the floor?

15. Two men are trying to push an 800-kg rock. The first exerts a force of 200 Newtons north, and the second exerts a force of 150 Newtons north. The rock accelerates at 0.10 meters per second^2 to the north. What is the kinetic frictional force?

Summary of Module #11

1. The weakest of the four fundamental forces in creation is the _____ force, and it is always attractive. The _____ force exists between charged particles. The _____ force governs certain radioactive processes in atoms. Physicists have actually shown that _____ force and the weak force are different facets of the same force. Thus, scientists call this force the _____ force. The _____ force is responsible for holding the center of the atom (called the _____) together. Although this force is strong, its range is very, very _____.

2. The three general principles contains in Newton's Universal Law of Gravitation are:

   I. _____

   II. _____

   III. _____

3. Although the gravitational force is _____, it can be substantial when at least one of the objects involved has a large ____. In addition, the gravitational forces exerted by two objects on one another are _____. Thus, a ball is attracted to the earth because _____ applies a gravitational force on the ball. At the same time, the ____ applies an _____ but _____ force on the _____.

4. _____ force is the force necessary to make an object move in a circle, and it is always directed _____ to the velocity of the object, which means it points to the _____ of the circle. Since the direction of the object moving in a circle is continually _____, it experiences _____ regardless of whether or not its speed stays constant. Centrifugal force is ____ a real force. It is simply a consequence of _____.

5. If the centripetal force operating on an object moving in a circle suddenly disappears, the object begins traveling _____, in the direction it was moving the instant the force disappeared. Centripetal force can be summed up with three basic principles:

   I. _____

   II. _____

   III. _____

6. The gravitational force acts to hold the planets and their moons in an orderly arrangement which we call the _____. The sun's _____ applies a centripetal force to the planets, allowing them to travel around the sun in roughly _____ orbits. The closest planet to the sun is _____, and continuing out from there, you find _____, _____, and ____. Next you find the solar system's highest concentration of _____. As a result, this region is often called the _____. Beyond that you find _____, _____, _____, and _____. Typically, the planets of the solar system are placed into one of two groups: the _____ (Mercury, Venus, earth, and Mars) and the _____ (Jupiter, Saturn, Uranus, and Neptune). Of all the planets, _____ is the hottest because of its _____. _____ was once called a planet, but it is now called a _____. It was demoted when a larger _____ (KBO) named Eris was found.

7. When an object orbits around a planet, we call that object a _____ of the planet. All planets except Mercury and Venus have at least one natural _____, but most have more than one. Saturn, Uranus, Jupiter, and Neptune also have _____, the most pronounced of which are around Saturn. They are actually composed of _____ of rock, ice, and frozen gases.

8. Variations in a body's motion are called _____, and a careful study of them led to the discovery of the planet _____. When they happen to an asteroid, it can be thrown out of its standard orbit and towards earth. When it intersects earth's orbit, it is called a _____. When it actually hits earth's atmosphere, it becomes white-hot, making brilliant streaks of light in the sky. At that point, scientists call it a _____. The intense heat usually breaks it up, except for a few small pieces that fall to the ground and are called _____.

9. Comets are called "dirty _____" because they are mostly composed of dust grains, chunks of dirt, and ____. When a comet passes close to the sun, the solid part of the comet is called the _____, and the "fuzzy" atmosphere around it is called the _____, which can form a long, glowing tail in the night sky. _____ comets typically don't go farther from the sun than the planet _____ and take less than 200 years to make an orbit. _____ comets typically have orbits that extend to the planet _____ or beyond and take more than 200 years to orbit the sun. The _____ contains many bodies that have some characteristics of comets and is thought by many to be a source of _____ comets. There are, however, problems with that view. Scientists forced to believe that the solar system is billions of years old must also believe in the _____ as a source for _____ comets, although there is no evidence for its existence.

10. There are essentially two theories on what causes the gravitational force: the _____ _____ and the _____. The _____ says that gravity is a consequence of how mass bends both space and time, while the _____ states that gravity is a result of the fact that objects with mass exchange particles called _____. Most physicists would say that the _____ is better, since it has some direct evidence supporting it.

11. The Greeks thought all planets (and the sun) orbited the _____. This is called the _____ view of the solar system. As time went on, observations just couldn't be made consistent with this view, so scientists (like Copernicus) suggested the _____ view that the plants orbit the sun.

Solve the Following Problems

12. The gravitational force between two objects ($mass_1$ = 5 kg, $mass_2$ = 2 kg) is measured when the objects are 5 centimeters apart. If the distance between them is increased to 10 centimeters, how does the new gravitational attraction compare to the first one that was measured?

13. The gravitational force between two objects ($mass_1$ = 5 kg, $mass_2$ = 2 kg) is measured when the objects are 5 centimeters apart. If $mass_1$ is changed to 10 kg and $mass_2$ is changed to 6 kg, how does the new gravitational attraction compare to the first one that was measured?

14. The gravitational force between two objects ($mass_1$ = 5 kg, $mass_2$ = 2 kg) is measured when the objects are 5 centimeters apart. The masses are then changed to $mass_1$ = 10 kg, $mass_2$ = 16 kg, and the distance between them is increased to 20 cm. How does the new gravitational attraction compare to the first one that was measured?

Summary of Module #12
Review the vocabulary words listed in Question #1 of the study guide

1. Because of the genius of _____, we now know that the force between charged particles and the force between magnets are both facets of the same force, called the _____. As was the case with Newton, Maxwell studied science as a means of serving _____.

2. The three principles of the electromagnetic force are:

    I. _____

    II. _____

    III. _____

3. The electromagnetic force is significantly _____ than the gravitational force. It is produced by the _____ of small "packages" of light called _____. The more charge a particle has, the more _____ it can exchange. This tells you why the electromagnetic force between charged particles is directly proportional to the charge of the particle. When you randomly throw a ball at a person, the chance of you hitting that person is _____ proportional to the _____ of the distance between you. Thus, the ability for _____ to exchange photons also is inversely proportional to the square of the distance between them.

4. In an atom, there are as many _____ (positive charges) as there are _____ (negative charges). As a result, atoms are electrically _____. When an atom loses _____, it ends up with a net positive charge and is called a positive ____. When an atom picks up extra _____, it ends up with a net negative charge and is called a negative ____.

5. When you charge an object by allowing it to come into contact with an object that already has an electric charge, you are charging by _____. This gives the newly charged object the _____ type of charge (positive or negative) as the original object. When you charge an object without direct contact between the object and a charge, you are charging by _____, and the newly charged object typically has a charge _____ that of the original charge.

6. A battery _____ electrical charge. One side of the battery is a source of electrons, so it is considered _____. The other is the place where the electrons want to go, so it is considered _____. When the two sides of a battery are hooked together with a metal, _____ will flow through the metal from the _____ side of the battery to the _____ side. A battery's _____ tells you how hard the battery "pushes" _____ from one side to the other.

7. The amount of charge that travels past a fixed point in an electric circuit each second is called the _____ in the circuit. It is usually measured in _____, which are abbreviated as "____" or "__." Both the _____ (amps) and the _____ (volts) of a circuit are needed to know how powerful the circuit is.

8. Current that flows from the positive side of the battery to the negative side is called _____ _____. This is the way current is drawn in circuit diagrams, even though it is _____. The ability of a material to impede the flow of charge is called that material's _____, and it converts the energy of the charge flowing through the circuit into _____ and sometimes _____. The _____ of metal,

the _____ of the metal, and the _____ of the metal all affect its resistance. The longer the metal, the _____ the resistance, and the wider the metal, the _____ the resistance.

9. The same number of _____ flow out of a toaster as the number that flow into it. The toaster does use up something, however. It uses _____. As electrons flow through a circuit, the collisions they experience convert the _____ produced by the electromagnetic force into _____.

10. A circuit that does not have a complete connection between the two sides of the power source is called an _____. Current _____ flow through an open circuit. This how a switch works. When the switch is "off," the circuit is _____, and no current can flow. When the switch is "on," a _____ is made, and current begins to flow.

11. When light bulbs are hooked in a circuit in _____, one broken light bulb will cause them all to go out. When light bulbs are hooked in _____, the other light bulbs will still work even if one or more break.

12. All magnetic force results from the movement of _____ particles. The atoms of most materials are not _____, so the electrons in the material have random motion. This causes the individual magnetic fields that result from that motion to _____. The result, then, is __ magnetic behavior. However, certain materials under certain conditions can have their atoms arranged so that the electrons have the _____ general motion. When that happens, the result is a _____.

13. All magnets have two poles: the _____ and the _____. Opposite poles _____ one another, and like poles _____ one another. Because all magnets have two poles, they are sometimes called _____. The strength of a magnet depends on what _____ of the atoms in the material are _____. The larger the percentage, the _____ the pole of a magnet.

Solve the Following Problems

14. The force between two charges is measured when the objects are 5 centimeters apart. The charges on each are then doubled, and the distance between them is increased to 20 cm. How does the new force compare to the first one that was measured?

15. The force between two charges is measured when the objects are 5 centimeters apart. The charges are cut in half, and the distance between them is decreased to 2.5 cm. How does the new force compare to the first one that was measured?

16. Draw the conventional current and the flow of actual electrons in the following circuit:

17. Draw the conventional current in the following circuits:

a.   b.   c.

Summary of Module #13
Review the vocabulary words listed in Question #1 of the study guide

1. Atoms are made up of _____, _____, and _____. The _____ is the smallest and least massive of the three. It also has a _____ electrical charge. The _____ is next in terms of mass. It is about 2,000 times more massive than the _____ and has a _____ electrical charge. The _____ is the heaviest of the three, being just a bit more massive than the _____. It has ___ electrical charge. By itself, the _____ is not stable. If it is not in the nucleus of an atom, it will decay into a _____, an _____, and an antineutrino in a matter of minutes.

2. A _____ is a schematic description of a system that accounts for its known properties. The _____ model of the atom has the _____ and _____ packed together in the center of the atom, which is called the _____. The _____ orbit the _____, much like the planets in the solar system orbit the sun. Although this model is partially _____, it is still the first model students learn when it comes to the atom. The more correct model is called the _____ model, but it is a bit too complex to learn right away. Regardless of the model, we know that atoms (and therefore all of matter) are mostly empty _____.

3. One of the most important characteristics of an atom is its number of protons, which is also called its _____. This tells you what kind of atom it is. Atoms have equal numbers of protons and _____, so the atomic number also tells you how many _____ an atom has. The _____ is the sum of the numbers of neutrons and protons in the nucleus, so once you know the number of protons and the _____, you can figure out how many _____ are in the nucleus.

4. A collection of atoms that all have the same _____ of protons is called an "element." On the periodic chart, the chemical symbol for an element is usually the first ____ or ___ letters from the _____ or _____ name of the element. Looking at the periodic chart, you can see that oxygen (O) has an atomic number of ___. This means it has ___ electrons and ___ protons. An ^{18}O atom, then, has ___ neutrons, while ^{16}O has ___ neutrons. Since ^{16}O and ^{18}O all have the same number of protons but different numbers of neutrons, they are _____. In the same way, of the following list of atoms: ^{40}Ar, ^{40}Ca, ^{41}K, ^{41}Ca, ^{45}Sc, and ^{42}Ca, the isotopes are _____.

5. If you were to draw an atom of ^{31}P according to the Bohr model, you would start by drawing a nucleus that had _____ and _____. It would also have ___ electrons orbiting the nucleus in the nearest orbit, ___ electrons orbiting the nucleus in the next orbit out, and ___ electrons orbiting the nucleus in a third orbit that was farther from the nucleus. In the same way, the Bohr model of ^{84}Sr would have _____ and _____ in the nucleus. There would be ___ electrons in the first Bohr orbit, ___ electrons in the next, ___ electrons in the third Bohr orbit, and ___ electrons in the fourth Bohr orbit.

6. Although protons are positively charged and thus should _____ one another, experiments have shown that they exist packed together inside the _____. This led scientists to speculate that there is a _____ force that is attractive at very short distances and is strong enough to overcome the repulsive electromagnetic force between protons. Hideki Yukawa showed that the exchange of tiny particles called _____ could account for such a force, and he gave a rough prediction of their mass. The detection of _____-lived particles with just that mass confirmed the existence of the force.

7. The nuclear force is a short-range force because pions exist for only a ____ time. Thus, if two protons (or a proton and a neutron) want to exchange a pion, they must do it _____. The nuclear force is

actually a manifestation of the _____ force, which is also manifested in the exchange of _____ between quarks. This allows _____ and _____ to exist.

8. The weak force governs _____. An atom with a nucleus that is not stable is called a _____ isotope. The three main ways unstable nuclei can decay is through _____ decay (where a neutron turns into a proton, _____, and antineutrino), _____ decay (where the nucleus emits a ^{4}He nucleus), and _____ decay (where energy is released in the form of a high-energy photon).

9. The hydrogen isotope known as "tritium" (^{3}H) undergoes beta decay. The daughter product is ____. When the isotope _____ undergoes beta decay, the daughter product is ^{32}S. When ^{133}Xe undergoes beta decay, the daughter product is _____. In each case, a _____ (electron) and an antineutrino are also produced.

10. When ^{238}U undergoes alpha decay, the daughter product is _____. When _____ undergoes alpha decay, ^{218}Po is produced. When ^{210}Po undergoes alpha decay, the daughter product is _____. In each case, a _____ nucleus is also produced.

11. When ^{60}Ni is produced by the beta decay of _____, it has excess energy. The ^{60}Ni gets rid of that excess energy by radioactive decay, but it stays ^{60}Ni. Thus, it decays by _____ decay.

12. The _____ of a radioactive isotope is the time it takes for half of the original sample to decay. Consider, for example, ^{239}Np, which has a half-life of 2 days. If you start with 1,000 grams of ^{239}Np, you will have ____ grams left after 2 days and _____ grams left after 4 days. In 10 days, you would have _____ grams left. In ____ days, you would have only about 0.977 grams left.

13. Even though a sample of radioactive isotope never really goes away completely, at some point, the amount of radioactive isotope left is so small that it can be _____. If we keep a radioactive sample around long enough, then, it will _____ to be radioactive, for all practical purposes.

14. Radioactive dating is the process by which scientists use the _____ of certain substances to determine how old an object is. For example, in carbon dating, scientists use the fact that ___ decays with a half-life of 5,700 years. Because living organisms continually exchange _____ with their surroundings, while an organism is alive, it contains the same amount of _____ as does the _____ around it. When the organism dies, however, that exchange _____, and the amount of ____ begins to decrease as a result of radioactive decay. Thus, if you know how much ____ was in the _____ when an organism died, you can determine how long ago death occurred by looking at the difference between the ____ in the dead organism and the amount that was in the atmosphere when it died. The difference is assumed to be the result of _____, and using the known half-life, you can determine the _____ that elapsed since the organism died.

15. The main problem with carbon dating is determining the _____ of ^{14}C in the organism when it died. Scientists can use _____ to measure the amount of ^{14}C in the atmosphere at a given year, and that gives them the ability to make a good assumption about the _____ of ^{14}C in the organism when it died. However, the oldest tree ring analyzed in this way is _____ years old, so carbon dating is really only reliable for things that are _____ years old or younger.

16. Other radioactive dating methods use similar _____, and the fact that many radioactive dates are in conflict with each other or with generally accepted dates indicates the _____ are poor.

Summary of Module #14
Review the vocabulary words listed in Question #1 of the study guide

1. In a wave, there are both _____ (the highest points on the wave) and _____ (the lowest points on the wave). The distance between the crests (or the distance between the troughs) is called the _____, and it is symbolized with the Greek letter __. The height of the wave is the called the _____. The _____ of a wave indicates how many waves hit a certain point every second.

2. Frequency and wavelength can be related to one another through the equation:

_____

In this equation, "f" is the _____ of the wave, "v" is the _____ of the wave, and λ is the _____. The units for _____ are 1/sec, which are typically abbreviated as ___.

3. There are two basic forms that waves can take. A _____ is a wave with a direction of propagation that is perpendicular to its direction of oscillation. A _____ is a wave with a direction of propagation that is parallel to its direction of oscillation. In a _____, the places where the medium "bunches up" are called _____, while the "spread out" sections are called _____.

4. _____ are longitudinal waves that generally oscillate ___. When those waves reach the _____ membrane of the ear, the membrane vibrates. Those vibrations are then transmitted to your _____, which interprets them as _____.

5. The speed of sound in air is dependent on the air's _____, and it can be found using the equation:

_____

Since the speed of light is significantly _____ than the speed of sound, you can see a faraway event _____ you hear any sound associated with it. Sound travels _____ in liquids than it does in gases, and it travels _____ in solids than it does in liquids.

6. If an object travels in a medium faster than the speed of sound in that medium, we say that the object is traveling at a _____ speed. Typically, we use the _____ number to denote such speeds. A rocket traveling at _____ 3, for example, is traveling at three times the speed of sound. The sound produced as a result of an object traveling faster than sound is called a _____.

7. The _____ of a sound wave is governed primarily by its frequency, while the volume is determined mostly by its _____. When a singer sings low notes, for example, the sounds waves she produces have ____ frequency. When she sings high notes, the sound waves she makes have a _____ frequency. When the singer is singing softly, the sound waves she produces have a ____ amplitude, and when she sings loudly, the sound waves she makes have a _____ amplitude.

8. Longitudinal waves with frequencies that can be detected by the human ear are called _____ waves. Waves with frequencies higher than what the human ear can sense are called _____ waves, and waves with frequencies lower than what the human ear can detect are called _____ waves.

9. The fact that the pitch of a car's horn changes as the car passes by you is a result of the _____ _____. This effect exists because as a sound source moves, the waves in front of the source _____ together, producing a wave with a _____ frequency than what you would hear if the source were stationary. The waves behind a moving source are _____ out, resulting in a frequency _____ than what you would hear if the source were stationary.

10. The bel scale measures the _____ of a sound wave, which is determined by the _____. In this scale, each unit corresponds to a factor of ____ increase in the intensity of the sound wave. Thus, a sound wave that measures 7 bels is _____ times more intense than a sound wave that measures 4 bels. The more common measurement associated with this scale is the decibel. It takes _____ decibels to make a bel. As a result, a sound measuring 80 decibels has an intensity of __ bels.

11. Sound waves used to probe the inside of the earth are typically _____ waves, while sound waves used to measure distances and image things inside the human body are typically _____ waves. Another use of such waves is _____, a technique used both by the military and by animals such as bats. Despite our best efforts, however, the bat's _____ is significantly more _____ than anything made as a result of human science and technology.

Solve the Following Problems

12. What is the frequency of a wave that travels at a speed of 5 meters per second and has a wavelength of 1.5 meters?

13. A wave whose wavelength is 0.15 m travels with a speed of 150 meters per second. What is its frequency?

14. What is the speed of sound in air that has a temperature of 22 $^{\circ}$C?

15. You hear the thunder from a lightning flash 2.3 seconds after you see the flash. If the air has a temperature of 11 $^{\circ}$C, how far away did the lightning strike occur?

16. You see lightning, and then hear the thunder 1.3 seconds later. If the air has a temperature of 18 $^{\circ}$C, how far away did the lightning strike?

17. One sound has a level of 20 decibels. The other has a level of 60 decibels. How many times more intense is the second sound?

18. An amplifier can multiply the intensity of a sound by 1,000. If a 30 decibel sound goes in, how many decibels will the sound be after the amplifier has amplified it?

Summary of Module #15
Review the vocabulary words listed in Question #1 of the study guide

1. In the _____ theory of light, a beam of light behaves the same as a stream of particles that all move in the same direction. In the _____ theory, light is considered a wave. Modern scientists believe that light has a ____ nature, acting both like a _____ and a _____. In the _____ theory, light is basically viewed as tiny packets of waves.

2. Because of the work of James Clerk Maxwell, a light wave is considered a _____ wave composed of an oscillating _____ field and a _____ field that oscillates perpendicular to the _____ field. As a result, light waves are typically called _____.

3. Although the speed of light does ____ depend on temperature, it does depend on _____ through which the light passes. In liquids light travels _____ than it does in air, and in solids light travels _____ than it does in liquids. Einstein's Special Theory of Relativity says that the speed of light in a vacuum represents the _____ speed that can ever be attained by any object that has mass.

4. The wavelength of visible light determines its _____. The 7 basic colors in the rainbow, in order of *increasing* wavelength, are: _____, _____, _____, _____, _____, _____, and ___. While the light we can see with our eyes is part of the _____ spectrum of light, the collection of all electromagnetic waves in creation is called the _____ spectrum.

5. Ultraviolet light, X-rays, and gamma rays have wavelengths _____ than visible light. Although they have so much energy that they can ___ living tissue, there are some uses for them. Infrared light, microwaves, television waves, and radio waves have wavelengths _____ than visible light.

6. When light bounces off an obstacle, we call it _____. When this happens, the angle of incidence will _____ the angle of _____. Images form in a mirror because light that _____ off a mirror is detected by an eye, and the _____ that receives the eye's electrical impulses extends the light _____ to form an image behind the mirror. The image is, of course, _____. It is simply a result of the fact that the brain interprets light as traveling in a _____ line.

7. When a wave enters an obstacle, it usually _____ in response to its change in speed. When this happens, we say that the wave has been _____. When light enters a substance in which it must slow down, the light ray will bend _____ a line perpendicular to the surface it strikes. When light enters a substance in which it speeds up, the light ray will bend _____ a line perpendicular to the surface it strikes. When you are looking at an object underwater, it will appear to be in a location that is _____ from its actual location, because the light rays _____ when they leave the water to hit your eyes.

8. When white light hits a water droplet in the air, some _____ and some _____ into the water droplet. Since the amount of _____ depends partially on the _____ of the light involved, this separates the white light into its colors. As the light travels through the water droplet, it eventually hits the other side. A portion of the light _____ out of the water droplet, but a portion _____. The _____ light travels to the other side of the droplet, where a portion is _____ and a portion is _____. The portion that is _____ has its wavelengths separated even more, because the amount of _____ depends in part on the wavelength of light. With this second _____, the light has been separated enough for us to distinguish the colors. As a result, the best way to see a rainbow is for the sun to be _____ you.

9. When a lens focuses horizontally traveling light rays through a single point (called the _____ point), we call it a _____ lens. The sides of such a lens have a _____ shape. When a lens bends horizontally traveling light rays so that they begin traveling away from each other, we call it a _____ lens. The sides of such a lens have a _____ shape.

10. The most elegant application of a converging lens in all of God's creation can be seen in the _____. The eye is covered by a thin, transparent substance called the _____. Light enters the eye through the _____, which is essentially an opening left by the _____. When you are in the presence of _____ light, the _____ closes down to allow only a small amount of light into the eye. When there is _____ light, the _____ opens wide, allowing a larger percentage of the light in. Once light enters the _____, it is focused by a _____ lens. The light is focused onto the _____, which is made up of light-sensitive cells called _____ and _____. When these cells sense light hitting them, they send electrical messages down the _____ nerve to the _____, which decodes the messages and forms them into images.

11. In order to focus light onto the retina, the eye's lens actually _____. This is done through the action of the _____, which squeezes or expands the lens. Human science cannot make a lens as _____ as that which you find in the eye.

12. If you are _____, your eye can use its ciliary muscle to change the lens enough to keep the image of objects close to you focused on the retina. However, as the object moves _____ away, the lens's _____ point cannot be changed enough to keep the image there. As a result, the image gets blurry because the light is focused _____ of the retina. Because light is being refracted too strongly, a _____ lens can be used to correct this problem. When you are _____, your eye's lens can adjust to objects far away, but it cannot focus on objects that are close. This is because the eye refracts light too _____. A _____ lens must be used to correct this problem.

13. The cones in your retina are used to detect the _____ of the light you are seeing. Some cone cells are sensitive only to _____-frequency visible light (red light), while others are sensitive to _____-frequency visible light (green light), while still others are sensitive to _____-frequency visible light (blue light).

14. The additive primary colors are ____, _____, and ____. Television screens and computer monitors _____ these colors to make all the colors you see. Red and green, for example, add in equal parts to make _____, while _____ and red add in equal parts to make magenta.

15. While the additive primary colors can add to make all the colors you see, the _____ primary colors are used for inks and paints. These three colors are _____, _____, and _____. When equal amounts of yellow and magenta inks are mixed, for example, the result is _____ ink. When equal amounts of cyan and _____ inks are mixed, the result is _____ ink.

16. The colors we see from objects are a result of the wavelength of light that _____ off them and hits our eyes. The dye that colors a shirt, for example, uses the _____ primary colors to determine what wavelengths _____ off the shirt and hit our eyes. As a result, if a blue shirt is put in a dark room and magenta light is shined on it, the shirt will appear to be _____, since the magenta light is made with the additive primary colors red and blue. The cyan in the blue dye of the shirt will absorb the red that is in the magenta light, leaving only blue to be reflected. If a yellow light were shined on the blue shirt in a dark room, it would appear _____.

Summary of Module #16
Review the vocabulary words listed in Question #1 of the study guide

1. Although the sun is a _____ sequence star, there are several things that make it very _____ when compared to other stars in the universe. The vast majority of stars in the universe exist in _____ systems, where stars orbit each other. This would cause severe _____ changes in any planet that orbited such a system, making it extremely difficult for _____ to exist on any such planet. There are much bigger stars in the universe, but if the sun were as big as they are, it would _____ the earth in its orbit! In addition, there are stars that are smaller than the sun. However, if the earth were to orbit such a star, it would have to be _____ in order to get enough energy to support life. If a planet got that close to such a star, the large _____ forces it would experience would make it far too dangerous to support life. Of the stars in this general region of the universe, the sun is in the top 10% in terms of its _____. The combination of the sun's mass and size, then, make it the _____ star to support life on earth.

2. The sun is essentially a big ball of _____ and _____ gas. The part of the sun that we can see is called the _____. Underneath that you find the _____, and underneath that, the _____. The deepest part of the sun, however, is its _____, where nuclear _____ reactions turn _____ into _____. Those reactions produce _____, which is what makes the heat and light that the sun emits.

3. Every now and again, sudden and intense variations in the brightness of the _____ occur. These variations are called _____, and they send enormous amounts of energy to the earth in a short amount of time, which can _____ satellites, radio communications, and even power grids. Although the surface of the sun's photosphere is a place of violent activity, it is "_____" compared to other, similar stars in the universe. Single stars with roughly the same size and composition of the sun release solar flares that are 100 to 100 million times more _____ than even the most violent solar flares that we have seen coming from the sun.

4. When a large nucleus is split into smaller nuclei, it is called _____. This process can result in a large amount of _____, and it is the basis of how nuclear _____ plants make electricity. When two or more small nuclei fuse to make a bigger nucleus, it is called _____, and that is what powers the sun.

5. Nuclear fission reactions require a _____ and a large nucleus, and they produce two or more smaller nuclei and several _____. Because of this situation, one nuclear reaction can start _____ _____ nuclear reactions. If there is a _____ mass of the large nucleus, this can lead to a _____ _____. If there is a lot more than a _____ mass of the large nucleus, the _____ can get out of control, resulting in a nuclear explosion.

6. While nuclear power is reasonably cheap and will last a long, long time, it can be _____. A nuclear power plant _____ explode, because there isn't enough of the large nucleus to allow the chain reaction to get that out-of-control. However, if the control systems fail, a _____ can occur, which is what happened to the _____ nuclear power plant in the Soviet Union in 1986. Nuclear fission also produces _____ byproducts, and there is no clean way to dispose of them. Although nuclear fission can be dangerous and polluting, it is not clear that it is any more dangerous and polluting than other forms of energy production. Coal-burning power plants, for example, dump pollution into the _____, and coal mining has resulted in more than 100,000 _____ in the U.S. since 1900.

7. The _____ of a star is determined by the star's temperature. The _____ of a star as it appears in the night sky is called the star's apparent magnitude, while its _____ after being corrected for the _____ from the earth to the star is its absolute magnitude. Plotting the absolute magnitude of stars versus their temperature makes a _____, which is used by astronomers to classify stars.

8. On the Hertzsprung-Russell Diagram, the _____ stars form a roughly diagonal band that goes from the upper left of the graph to the lower right of the graph. _____ stars form a diffuse band at low absolute magnitudes and various temperatures. _____ stars are found at low temperatures and absolute magnitudes of about zero to -5. _____ stars are found at high temperatures and high absolute magnitudes.

9. Main sequence stars are the most _____ in the universe. The more massive a main sequence star is, the _____ its absolute magnitude. White dwarves seem to be the next most _____. They are _____ and not very _____. They are, however, very _____. Supergiants are the _____ stars in the universe. They are very bright and seem to be _____ in the universe. Red giants are _____ stars that are very bright. They produce their energy by nuclear _____, but it is different from the kind that takes place in main sequence stars.

10. Stars with absolute magnitudes that change are called _____, and there are two main kinds: _____ and _____. _____ are exploding stars, the most extreme being _____, which expand rapidly and brighten enormously and then fade away _____. The debris left over from such an explosion is a cloud of bright gases called a _____. A _____, on the other hand, regularly expands and contracts without losing _____. This changes its _____ on a regular basis. One particular type of pulsating variable, the _____, is important, as it is used to measure universal distances that are too long to be measured with the more precise method known as _____. _____ binary stars vary in apparent brightness not because their absolute magnitude changes but because one of the two stars can _____ our view of the other.

11. A light year is defined as the _____. Since light travels quickly, this is a very _____ distance.

12. A large ensemble of stars, all interacting through the gravitational force and orbiting around a common center is called a _____. There are four main types: _____, _____ _____, _____, and _____.

13. Our galaxy, the _____, is a _____. Our sun is on the inner edge of the _____ arm of that galaxy. Our galaxy is part of a small group of about 30 galaxies, which is known as the _____ _____. This group of galaxies is on the outer edge of a cluster of galaxies known as the _____.

14. The fact that light coming from distant galaxies has longer wavelengths than expected is referred to the _____ shift. Although it was once thought that this was a _____ shift, it is now considered evidence that the universe is _____. Most astronomers think the universe is _____ without a _____. However, some think that there is a _____ which is roughly marked by earth's solar system. If this is true, light from galaxies that are billions of light years away could have traveled to earth while just a few _____ years passed on earth.

APPENDIX C
A COMPLETE LIST OF LAB SUPPLIES

Module #1

- Eye protection such as goggles or safety glasses
- A small, clear glass (like a juice glass)
- Baking soda
- Tap water
- A 9-volt battery (the kind that goes in a radio, smoke detector, or toy. DO NOT use an electrical outlet, as that would be quite dangerous! A 1.5-volt flashlight battery will *not* work.)
- Two 9-inch pieces of insulated wire. The wire itself must be copper.
- Scissors
- Some tape (preferably electrical tape, but cellophane or masking tape will work.)
- A spoon for stirring
- A long piece of string
- A large tabletop (like the top of a kitchen table or a big desk)
- A person to help you
- Some cellophane tape
- A pencil
- Vinegar
- 6 Tums® tablets (You can use another antacid tablet, but it must have calcium carbonate as its active ingredient.)
- Measuring cups
- 3 large glasses (They each must be able to hold at least 2 cups of liquid.)

Module #2

- Eye protection such as goggles or safety glasses
- A small glass, like a juice glass
- Two cotton balls
- Tap water
- A bulb thermometer (It must be able to read room temperature and slightly higher, and it must have a bulb at the end.)
- A small piece of plastic such as a Ziploc® bag or a square cut from a trash bag.
- A reasonably large glass or jar
- A candle (**DO NOT** use a lighter or any other gas or alcohol burner. You must use a candle in order to keep the experiment safe.)
- Matches
- 2 cups of hydrogen peroxide (sold at any drugstore)
- Baker's yeast
- A bottle (A plastic, 1-liter soda pop bottle, for example)
- A balloon
- A teaspoon

- A large, clear Ziploc® freezer bag (It needs to be large enough so that the thermometer can be "zipped" inside it.)
- Sunny windowsill (If it's not sunny today, just wait until it is.)
- Vinegar
- Baking soda

Module #3

- Eye protection such as goggles or safety glasses
- Stove
- Frying pan
- Two empty, 12-ounce aluminum cans (like soda pop cans)
- Two bowls
- Water
- Ice cubes
- Tongs
- Plastic bottle (The best volume would be 1 quart or 1 liter, but any size will work.)
- Balloon

Module #4

- Eye protection such as goggles or safety glasses
- Water
- 9-volt battery (A new one works best.)
- Two test tubes (You can purchase these at a hobby store. If you cannot get them, skip the experiment or use the tubes that florists put on the stems of cut flowers.)
- Juice glass (It must be deep enough so that when it is nearly full of water, the battery can stand vertically in the glass and still be fully submerged in the water.)
- Epsom salts (You can get these at any drugstore or large supermarket.)
- Tablespoon
- Vegetable oil
- A Styrofoam® or paper cup
- A comb
- A pen
- Five glasses
- Two stirring spoons
- Paper towel
- A measuring spoon that measures ½ teaspoon
- Sugar
- Table salt
- Canola oil (or some kind of cooking oil other than olive oil)
- Olive oil
- Stick of butter or margarine (It must be fresh from the refrigerator so that it is solid.)
- Ice cube
- Stove
- Saucepan

- Knife (A serrated one works best. You will use it to cut the butter.)
- Bowl
- Metal paper clip (Use a standard-sized paper clip. A big one will probably not work.)
- Toilet paper
- Dish soap
- Scissors
- A smooth glass surface (The underside of a drinking glass works well.)
- Wax (A candle will work.)
- Sink

Module #5

- Eye protection such as goggles or safety glasses
- Water
- Salt
- Ice
- Tablespoon
- Teaspoon
- Small saucepan
- Saucepan lid or frying pan lid larger than the saucepan used
- Large bowl (It should not be plastic, as it will get hot.)
- Potholders
- Zippered plastic sandwich bag
- Stove
- Measuring cup
- Plastic bowl that holds more than 2 cups of water
- Freezer
- Small plate
- Strainer
- Small glass or cup
- A clear, plastic 2-liter bottle (the kind that soda pop comes in) with the lid
- A match

Module #6

- Eye protection such as goggles or safety glasses
- Two metal spoons
- About 3 feet of string (Nylon kite string is ideal, but any reasonably strong string will work. Thread and yarn do not work well.)
- Large sink with a plug
- Water
- A shallow pan (a pie pan, for example)
- Cornstarch
- Measuring cups
- A 1.5-volt battery (Any size cell [AA, A, C, or D] will do; just make sure it is nothing other than one of those. A battery of higher voltage could be dangerous.)

- Tape (Electrical tape works best, but cellophane tape will do.)
- Large iron nail (at least 3 inches long)
- Metal paper clip
- 2 feet of insulated wire (24-gauge wire works best. It should not be thicker than 18-gauge.)
- A hard-boiled egg (You might want a second in case you mess up the first time.)
- A dull knife, like a butter knife
- A marker or something else that will make a mark on the egg shell

Module #7

- Daily local weather information source that contains:
    1. High and low temperatures for yesterday
    2. High and low atmospheric (sometimes called "barometric") pressure for yesterday.
    3. Amount of precipitation for yesterday
    If you have a hard time finding this information, check the course website I described in the "Student Notes" at the beginning of the book. You will find links to websites that contain it.

Module #8

- Eye protection such as goggles or safety glasses
- Balloon
- Dark room
- A source that gives you the weather forecast for tomorrow

Module #9

- Eye protection such as goggles or safety glasses
- At least four eggs
- Two pieces of reasonably strong cardboard (like the cardboard found on the back of writing tablets)
- Several books
- A pair of scissors
- A large tray or cooking sheet
- Newspapers or paper towels
- Kitchen table
- A large (at least 21 cm by 27 cm), heavy book
- A small (about 3 cm by 3 cm) piece of paper
- A stopwatch (must read hundredths of a second)
- A chair or small stepladder
- A ball or rock (something heavy so that air resistance won't be a factor)
- A tape measure (A meterstick or yardstick will work, if you do not have a tape measure.)

Module #10

- Eye protection such as goggles or safety glasses
- A coin

- A 3-inch by 5-inch index card (note that I listed the units)
- A small glass (like a juice glass)
- A raw egg
- A hard-boiled egg
- Aluminum pie pan
- A pair of scissors
- A marble or other small ball
- An unfinished board that is at least 2 feet long
- A block eraser
- An ice cube
- A small block of wood
- A relatively flat rock
- Sandpaper
- Several books
- A ruler
- A plastic, 2-liter bottle (like the kind soda pop comes in)
- A stopper that fits the bottle (It could be rubber or cork, but you cannot use the screw-on cap. It has to be something that plugs up the opening of the bottle but can be pushed out by a pressure buildup inside the bottle. Modeling clay can work as well. You could also try a large wad of gum, as long as the gum has dried out and has the texture of firm rubber.)
- A cup of vinegar
- Two teaspoons of baking soda
- Aluminum foil
- Four pencils

Module #11

- Eye protection such as goggles or safety glasses
- A mechanical pen
- A black marker
- Thin string or thread (preferably white)
- Five metal washers, all the same size
- Stopwatch
- Scissors
- A soft seat cushion from a couch (A soft bed will work as well.)
- A bowling ball (A heavy rock will work as well.)
- A marble
- Two balls (Baseball-sized balls are best, but any will do.)
- Two people to help you
- A large, open space

Module #12

- Eye protection such as goggles or safety glasses
- Three balloons (Round balloons work best, but any kind will do.)
- Thread

- Cellophane tape
- A clear glass
- A plastic lid that fits over the glass. This lid can be larger than the mouth of the glass, but it cannot be smaller. The top of a margarine tub or something similar works quite well.
- A paper clip
- Aluminum foil
- A pair of pliers
- A 1.5-volt battery (Any AA-, C-, or D-cell battery will work. Do not use any battery other than one of those, though, because a higher voltage can make the experiment dangerous.)
- Scissors

Module #13

There are no experiments in Module #13.

Module #14

- Eye protection such as goggles or safety glasses
- Plastic wrap
- Scissors
- Tape
- Candle (It needs to be either in a candle holder or able to stand up securely on its own.)
- Match
- Plastic 1-liter or 2-liter bottle (the kind soda pop comes in)
- Large pot
- Wooden spoon
- Large bowl
- Rice
- Two medium-sized rocks
- A person to help you
- A stopwatch
- A 250-meter stretch of sidewalk, pavement, gravel road, or lawn that is relatively straight
- A tape measure, meterstick, or yardstick
- Water
- Glass or plastic bottle (A glass bottle is best, and 2-liter is the ideal size. It must have a narrow neck. A jar will not work well.)
- A car with a horn and a parent to drive the car
- A straight street (It could be the one you live on, but it might work better to find one away from peoples' homes.)
- If you have access to a stringed instrument such as a violin, guitar, cello, or banjo, use it for this experiment. If you do not have access to such an instrument, you will need:

    - Rubber band
    - Plastic tub (like the kind that margarine or whipped cream comes in)

Module #15

- ♦ Eye protection such as goggles or safety glasses
- ♦ A flat pan, like the kind you use to bake a cake
- ♦ A flat mirror. The mirror can be very small, but it needs to be flat. You can always tell if a mirror is flat by looking at your reflection in it. If the image you see in the mirror is neither magnified nor reduced, the mirror is flat.
- ♦ A sunny window (A flashlight will work, but it will not be as dramatic.)
- ♦ Five plain white sheets of paper
- ♦ Water
- ♦ A pen
- ♦ A protractor
- ♦ A ruler
- ♦ A flashlight
- ♦ Black construction paper or thin cardboard
- ♦ Tape
- ♦ A dark room
- ♦ A square or rectangular glass or clear plastic pan (If you have a flat bottle, it will work as well. It just needs to be something with clear, flat sides that can hold water.)
- ♦ Milk
- ♦ Spoon
- ♦ Quarter
- ♦ Bowl that is reasonably deep and not transparent
- ♦ Pitcher or very large glass to hold the water
- ♦ A bright red marker (A crayon will also work, but a marker is better.)

Module #16

- ♦ Balloon
- ♦ A marker (You need to be able to write on the balloon with the marker.)

INDEX

-D-

-X, Y, Z-

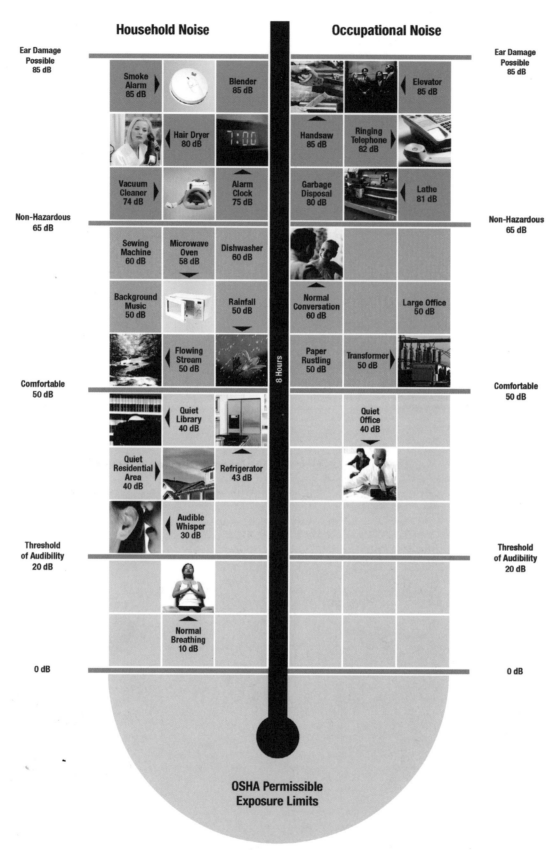

Household Noise

Occupational Noise

Ear Damage Possible 85 dB

Ear Damage Possible 85 dB

Smoke Alarm 85 dB

Blender 85 dB

Elevator 85 dB

Hair Dryer 80 dB

7:00

Handsaw 85 dB

Ringing Telephone 82 dB

Vacuum Cleaner 74 dB

Alarm Clock 75 dB

Garbage Disposal 80 dB

Lathe 81 dB

Non-Hazardous 65 dB

Non-Hazardous 65 dB

Sewing Machine 60 dB

Microwave Oven 58 dB

Dishwasher 60 dB

Background Music 50 dB

Rainfall 50 dB

Normal Conversation 60 dB

Large Office 50 dB

Flowing Stream 50 dB

Paper Rustling 50 dB

Transformer 50 dB

Comfortable 50 dB

Comfortable 50 dB

Quiet Library 40 dB

Quiet Office 40 dB

Quiet Residential Area 40 dB

Refrigerator 43 dB

Audible Whisper 30 dB

Threshold of Audibility 20 dB

Threshold of Audibility 20 dB

Normal Breathing 10 dB

0 dB

0 dB

8 Hours

OSHA Permissible Exposure Limits

This "noise thermometer" lists several noises you may encounter, as well as their loudness as measured in decibels (dB). As you go up the thermometer, noises get louder and, when they reach a certain loudness, hearing damage is possible. The middle line shows you the time that OSHA (the Occupational Safety and Health Administration in the United States) allows workers to be exposed to such noises. The thermometer is continued on the next page.